Managing with Microsoft Project 2000

Send Us Your Comments

To comment on this book or any other PRIMA TECH title, visit our reader response page on the Web at www.prima-tech.com/comments.

How to Order

For information on quantity discounts, contact the publisher: Prima Publishing, P.O. Box 1260BK, Rocklin, CA 95677-1260; (916) 787-7000. On your letterhead include information concerning the intended use of the books and the number of books you wish to purchase.

Managing with Microsoft Project 2000

Lisa A. Bucki

PRIMA TECH

A DIVISION OF PRIMA PUBLISHING

A Division of Prima Publishing

Prima Publishing and colophon are registered trademarks of Prima Communications, Inc. PRIMA TECH is a trademark of Prima Communications, Inc., Roseville, California 95661.

Publisher: Stacy L. Hiquet
Marketing Manager: Judi Taylor
Associate Marketing Manager: Jody Kennen
Managing Editor: Sandy Doell
Acquisitions Editor: Stephen Graham
Project Editor: Estelle Manticas
Editorial Assistant: Cathleen D. Snyder
Technical Reviewer: Ray Coker
Copy Editor: Hilary Powers
Interior Layout: Marian Hartsough
Cover Design: Prima Design Team
Indexer: Sharon Hilgenberg

Microsoft is a registered trademark of the Microsoft Corporation.

Important: Prima Publishing cannot provide software support. Please contact the appropriate software manufacturer's technical support line or Web site for assistance.

Prima Publishing and the author have attempted throughout this book to distinguish proprietary trademarks from descriptive terms by following the capitalization style used by the manufacturer.

ISBN: 0-7615-1986-6
Library of Congress Catalog Card Number: 9965574
Printed in the United States of America

00 01 02 03 04 II 10 9 8 7 6 5 4 3 2 1

About the Author

Lisa A. Bucki has over ten years' experience in computer training and computer book publishing. She was Associate Publisher of Alpha Books, an imprint founded to address the needs of beginning users. Bucki has authored or co-authored nearly 40 books and multimedia products, including the previous two editions of *Managing with Microsoft Project* and Prima's *Get Your Family on AOL 5 In a Weekend*. Bucki leads beginning-to-intermediate Microsoft Project training classes for North Carolina-based SofTrain, Inc. (www.SofTrainInc.com).

Contributing author Jack Dahlgren has been engaged in project planning and scheduling in the construction and high tech industries for seven years, and has used a wide variety of tools and techniques.

Contents at a Glance

Introduction

Over time, managers have tried any number of techniques for running projects and teams: to-do lists, meetings with lists on white boards, copious e-mail messages, or even clumsy spreadsheets and homegrown databases. None of these approaches cut it today. Anyone leading a project in today's lean and mean business environment shoulders heavy responsibility and pressure, and must make the project happen on time and on budget, often with a minimum of resources. Thus, project managers need tools that lend speed and precision to both the project planning process and each project's execution.

In the last few years, the developers of the leading project management program, Microsoft Project, have taken great steps in honing this software tool into an effective management weapon. The new release, Project 2000, covers all the bases, enabling you to review and control many facets of a project from start to finish.

With Project, there's a significant payoff for your time investment in learning how to use the software. Not only will you be more organized, but you'll be able to help your team be more effective as well. You'll be able to anticipate problems and your ability to make resource estimates will improve, so that over time you'll become a stronger manager.

This book is designed to help you make the most of your company's financial investment in Project, as well as your professional investment—the time you'll spend learning to work with Project, and the impact Project will have on your performance.

Who Should Read This Book

This book assumes that you or your company have already purchased and installed the Project software. This book is for anyone who needs to be able to work with Project on short notice, such as:

- Managers and assistants whose company has adopted Project

- Managers beginning to use Project as a method to standardize the planning process
- Project or team leaders who need to use Project to create graphical printouts of task assignments, or to allocate resources between several projects
- Leaders who need to coordinate a diverse set of resources that may include colleagues from many departments, outside consultants, or even cross-company teams
- Project or team leaders who want to take advantage of the company network, a company intranet, or the Internet to communicate about tasks, progress, and completion
- Professional, certified project managers who have purchased Project to implement an organized planning system for their companies or clients

How This Book Is Organized

Whether you review the chapters from start to finish or browse around to review specific subjects, *Managing with Microsoft Project 2000* is structured for easy use. Here's a brief review of what you'll find in each part of the book:

Part I, "Easy Introduction to Project," gives you background information on project management and the Microsoft Project software. Here you will learn how to get the most out of Project, and you'll get a jump-start on your Project skills with a hands-on tutorial session that leads you through some of the key Project operations.

Part II, "Project Management Basics," focuses on the minimum you need to know to set up a project. You'll learn how to create a file in Project, set the overall project parameters, define the tasks that must be completed, and indicate the resources that will be used to complete each task.

Part III, "Making Adjustments to Projects," teaches you how to work out project kinks. You'll learn how to identify and resolve resource overcommitments, adjust tasks, and track a project's progress.

Part IV, "Viewing, Formatting, and Printing Projects," discusses using the information you so diligently captured in Project. You'll choose different display formats for a project, print, work with forms and reports, review costs, and use outlining features.

Part V, "Handling Multiple Projects," builds on the skills you mastered previously, showing you how to move and copy information between projects, create and use project templates, combine projects and resources, and use master projects and subprojects.

Part VI, "Sharing and Publishing Project Information," covers using information from Project in other Microsoft Office applications, exporting project information, and setting reminders in Microsoft Outlook. It also provides information on online features for sending assignments or updates to team members, publishing project information on the Web, and more.

Part VII, "Working with Advanced Features," shows you how to customize the way you work with Project and create macros to make your work in Project even more efficient.

Conventions Used in This Book

To make it easier for you to use this book, the following "shorthand," or conventions, are used to present different kinds of information. You should review these conventions before moving on:

- **Key combinations.** Pressing and holding one key while pressing another key is called a key combination. In this book, key combinations are indicated by a plus sign (+) separating the keys you have to press. For example, Ctrl+O is a key combination that requires you to press and hold the Ctrl key while pressing the O key.

- **Menu commands.** A phrase like "Choose File, Open" means to open the File menu and click on the Open command.

- **Text you type.** When you need to type some text to complete a procedure, the text appears in bold, as in the following:

  Type the name for the task, such as **Request Price Quotes**.

Special Features of This Book

At times, I'll provide you with information that supplements the discussion at hand. This special information is set off in easy-to-identify sidebars, so you can review or skip these extras as you see fit. You'll find the following features in this book:

Tips and more tips. Tips provide shortcuts or alternatives for using features, as well as ideas for using a particular feature on the job.

Note

Notes provide supplemental information that either clarifies an operation, provides greater technical detail, or gives you background information about the subject at hand.

Caution

Cautions protect you from what can be your worst computing enemy—yourself. When particular operations are risky and might cause you to lose some of your work, I'll forewarn you.

ON THE
CD

This book includes a CD-ROM of resources, including practice files, to help you get more from Project. (See Appendix B, "What on the CD?," to learn more about what it offers.) When I want to advise you of a practice file on the CD-ROM that you can use to try out particular skills, I'll use a box like this.

PART I
Easy Introduction to Project

The Project Management Process and Project

IN THIS CHAPTER

- The benefits of project management
- Key tools provided in Project
- Overview of planning a project
- What you need to be successful with Microsoft Project

The students I've taught have shared an almost universal feeling about Microsoft Project and project management: both are difficult and time-consuming. Students who have invested the time to learn more about what Project and project management have to offer, however, have come to see that a disciplined approach offers real advantages over scribbled notes and hope—namely, you can get a job done smoothly, impressing your bosses, clients, vendors, and coworkers in the process. As you pick up this book and start up Microsoft Project 2000 for the first time, keep in mind that you must build a foundation before you can put up a building.

The information in this chapter provides the foundation for your knowledge of Microsoft Project. Although the chapter (and the book) can't teach you the broad discipline of project management, I'll try to outline for you some of the basic project management principles that should guide how you'll use Microsoft Project. The chapter also covers some of the realities and benefits of using Project to plan and manage your endeavors.

Understanding Why You Should Manage Projects

"Project management" used to be primarily a catchphrase used to flesh out a résumé. At best, in many cases, it meant keeping a long to-do list and dealing with problems after someone else had pointed them out. In its broadest sense, the label "project manager" could describe any individual who could complete most of his or her own work assignments.

In today's business climate, project management has emerged as a serious discipline, one that is being incorporated into programs at technical schools and universities worldwide. For example, certain MBA programs include project management courses. You can earn undergraduate and graduate degrees in project management. Some international organizations, such as the Project Management Institute, at http://www.pmi.org, train project management professionals, certify them with designations such as Project Management Professional, and provide accreditation for project management courses. Finally, some consulting firms now specialize in providing project management services, and some businesses have developed formalized project manager positions.

Even if you don't have specific training in project management, you—like millions of others—might discover that project management skills are essential to career success. You need to have a precise handle on the steps involved in a project, the resources you'll need, the time each portion of the project will take, and how much the whole thing will cost.

Business trends from the past decade are making those with project management skills increasingly valuable as managers or team leaders. Following are just a few examples:

- The continuing market pressure to run lean, efficient companies compels us to accomplish more with fewer resources. As resources become more scarce, one must plan further in advance and become more skilled at identifying and eliminating conflicts.

- Increasing adoption of technology facilitates management reliance on more precise, accurate, and quickly generated information. You need the skills to plan more accurately, respond immediately to information requests, and support your requests for additional resources. You'll have greater credibility and effectiveness when you're more disciplined in your approach.

- In today's smaller workgroup or team environment, each team member's role has become less specialized. Thus you must carefully define each person's role within the context of a particular project.

- The efficiency of online communication has led to virtual teams — geographically dispersed individuals who must work together as a cohesive unit. The fact that a team member is halfway across the country makes that person no less important to your overall mission. With virtual teams, you need to communicate frequently about deadlines and progress and make sure you're getting feedback about issues and problems so that you can resolve them before they sidetrack your schedule or budget.

- To bring products to market more quickly, most companies distribute tasks across several departments; by doing so, different project phases can be handled concurrently. In such cross-departmental situations, tracking performance and communicating expectations has become more challenging and necessary.

- Companies that are under headcount restrictions, or that are unwilling to invest in specialized technology, increasingly rely on outside contractors for a variety of functions. Project management techniques and tools can help in keeping these outside resources on track.

Management Techniques Offered in Project

You'll be surprised at how just a little time spent with Microsoft Project's features can make you look organized and impress your colleagues. Consider this true story: My husband took a job as a project manager with a large international manufacturer of audiocassettes and CDs. A month or so later, his primary client placed an order for several million units of product—one of the largest orders that the plant had ever handled. The pressure was on my husband, both from the head honchos at the plant and from the client. So, to prepare, he launched Microsoft Project (which few of his colleagues ever bothered to start, let alone use). He typed in the list of tasks, start dates, and the approximate length of time each task could take. He added a few summary tasks to make the list a little clearer. Then, he printed only the list of tasks, called the Task Sheet. At the meeting to kick off the project, he handed out the task list and his other materials, and the clients and his bosses loved it. His company's president even said, "This is exactly what we should be doing for every job." The order went off like clockwork, and all my husband did to become the hero was type in some information. He didn't even use many of Project's most powerful features!

Keeping your arms around far-flung details and resources for big projects used to require several tools. You outlined the project with a word processor, budgeted with a spreadsheet, plotted progress on paper timelines, and so on. Microsoft Project 2000 handles all of the key facets of project planning by blending traditional project management models such as Gantt charts and critical path analysis with more contemporary techniques—printing custom calendars, importing information from other programs, and quickly e-mailing assignments. With Project, you can track the completion of various tasks, manage costs, reassign resources, and more.

Overall, the process you follow when using Project is to create a schedule by defining the tasks that need to be completed, determining the probable cost for each task, and determining what employees, supplies, contractors, and other resources are needed to complete the task. After you establish the schedule, you can fine-tune it to decrease the total time frame, deal with resource conflicts, and so on. Finally, you can track the team's progress and communicate the schedule to others from start to finish by printing an overall chart, printing charts about individual resources, generating reports for your manager, and e-mailing information to other team members.

Thus Project offers a variety of techniques for establishing, modifying, and managing the parameters for each project plan you pull together.

Key Benefits of Using Project

New users often wonder whether it's worth the time investment to learn the Project program and enter all the necessary information about a project. Why not simply stick with a word processor and spreadsheet to get the job done? Well, because you don't want to use a regular hammer when the job calls for a sledge-hammer or jackhammer. Project not only makes the basic job of managing projects easier, it also offers features and capabilities that give you more control over the scope of the project.

You'll realize the following benefits if you use Project as a planning and management tool:

- **Manage more information.** Project can track thousands of tasks and resources per project, and many pieces of information about each task and resource. Only your computer's memory and other resources limit the amount of information you can enter in a Project file.

- **Gain accuracy.** Because Project can calculate the task and project schedules based on other information you provide, it helps you create a project plan that's more realistic. Project also performs dozens of calculations that would be difficult or time-consuming for you to perform manually, increasing the number of data points that you can consider when you develop your project plan or need to make schedule and budget decisions.

- **Automatically create project diagrams.** Project automatically generates Gantt charts (Figure 1.1), calendars, and other graphs and views to provide a look at how project tasks relate and a method to relay information to others.

Figure 1.1
A graphical schedule for the project helps you see the timing for individual tasks.

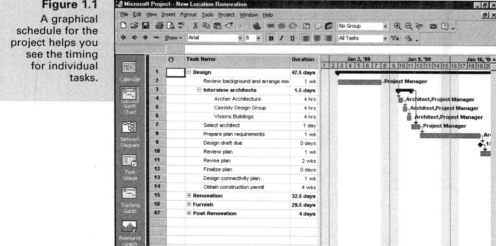

- **Track specific aspects of the project and anticipate problems.** You can take a look at the costs, commitments, or available starting date of a particular resource.

- **Track overall progress.** As you enter task completion information, you can compare progress with the original plan. In addition, you can add a status date to help you update progress more quickly and to clarify when you last updated the project.

- **Generate forms and reports to share information.** You can choose from a variety of predefined forms and reports, or create custom forms for particular situations. Figure 1.2 shows an example of a report.

- **Communicate via e-mail and the Web.** Project is optimized to enable you to share project information via existing e-mail tools, such as Microsoft Outlook. You can publish Project information as a Web page or develop a Web site to manage team messages, to give everyone involved in the project a central location to go for more information.

- **Capture historical data.** As you use Project, you gather information to build a history of how tasks and the whole project actually progressed. For example, you can see how long a particular type of task took, whether a particular resource has a tendency to be on time or run late, and how much the overall plan cost your company. Then, when you move on to later projects, you can refer to the data you've accumulated in past Project files to refine your latest plan.

Figure 1.2
Generate reports like this to-do list to communicate more effectively.

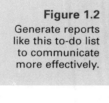

Getting the Most out of Project

All the benefits I've laid out so far sound great, and they are. But, as I've found when using Project and through speaking with students and consultants, the "no free lunch" rule of thumb applies. You need to be prepared to make a few investments when it comes to shifting from a casual model of project management to the more formal approach demanded by Project. If you try to hang onto your old approach, you may not experience the benefits you expect.

So, as you work through this book and begin to implement Project, you should be prepared to take some concrete steps:

- **Invest time in training.** Project is fairly complex as applications go. You can use multiple methods to perform many operations, and there are dozens of views and tables and hundreds of fields of information that you can view.

- **Develop a plan for implementing Project.** You should not plan to run all your mission-critical projects using the software from Day 1. Instead, start using Project to track one or two of your smaller assignments. As your proficiency builds, ramp up to using Project across the board.

- **Make sure the resources are in place to maintain the Project information.** The program delivers a host of calculations to help you drive a project forward, but those calculations depend on the quality and timeliness of the information that you provide. You (or your organization) must make decisions about who will be responsible for maintaining information in Project, how often that information should be updated, and how updates will be gathered—via regular status meetings or another means. Your company needs to dedicate the person-hours to maintain the Project information, and you as the project manager need to ensure you have the discipline to maintain an orderly process.

- **Retool your planning style, to some degree.** I often alert students that Project forces you to do what you should be doing already. That is, if you aren't accustomed to making a realistic estimate of the time that every task in a project takes, and you don't typically have a formal schedule for following up with resources about the progress of tasks, and so on, you'll find that you won't get what you need from Project. You have to change your style.

Don't let any of this dissuade you from using Project. You can compare using Project to maintaining a huge customer database. Updating dozens or hundreds of customer records is decidedly tedious. However, it's a worthwhile investment because of the value that the database yields to the organization. Similarly, your investment in learning Microsoft Project and building and maintaining project files will be rewarded many times over through the leaps in effectiveness that you'll make.

Caution

> Microsoft followed the lead of the Project Management Institute in considering a *project* an endeavor that has a set starting point (start date) and ending point (finish date), with a specific goal to accomplish in that time. The project will have an overall goal or goals, which can be broken down into groups of specific tasks. Each project file you create should pertain to a specific project, not a specific time period or group of resources. For example, you shouldn't use Project to track all the ongoing assignments for a department or team, especially when those assignments relate to different projects.

The Planning Process

As mentioned earlier, you need do little more than enter a list of tasks and schedule them to get a great deal of benefit from Microsoft Project. Then, if you later want to start making resource assignments and using other features, you're free to do so.

That being said, if you do plan to take advantage of all that Project offers, you should expect to use the following overall process in building and exploiting a project file:

1. Establish the initial parameters for the project, including when the project starts and what calendar the work follows—that is, whether work will proceed round the clock, one shift a day, or on some other basis.

2. Create the list of tasks. This part of the process includes estimating how long each task will last and when each will begin. You'll establish relationships between tasks, where you identify whether a particular task must finish before another can begin. You can use constraints to give Project less flexibility in rescheduling tasks. This process may also involve grouping the tasks in a logical order, if applicable, using outlining features.

3. Add resources and costs. You will enter the list of people, equipment, and other resources that will complete the tasks in the project, and enter the costs, usually in terms of hourly rates, for using each resource. (In some cases, you may have to assign a particular cost to a task rather than a resource.)

4. Make assignments. This part of the process is where you identify which resource or resources will be working on each particular task in your list.

5. Fine-tune your schedule. After you have the basic plan in place, it's time to reexamine it to eliminate instances where you've overbooked resources and to look for opportunities to improve the schedule. Project provides you tools for adjusting your schedule. For example, the Resource Graph view shown in Figure 1.3 helps you identify instances when a resource has too much work assigned on a given day.

6. Save a snapshot of your plan. Once you have the plan in place to the best of your ability, you can save that information as the *baseline*. Later, Project can compare actual project progress to the baseline.

7. Enter actual information. As your project gets under way, you can enter information about the amount of work completed, actual start and finish dates, and actual costs.

8. Communicate with the team. You can use team and Internet features to make assignments and request updates.

9. Review information and generate reports. Project provides a variety of views so that you can find and print the information that's pertinent. It also offers predefined reports that you can use to communicate about project progress, upcoming tasks, the budget, and more.

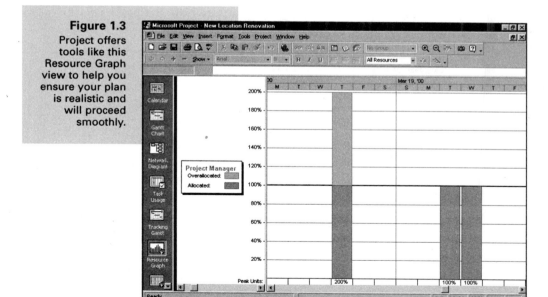

Figure 1.3
Project offers tools like this Resource Graph view to help you ensure your plan is realistic and will proceed smoothly.

This book covers each part of the just-outlined process, as well as other topics such as customizing Project.

Learning More about Project Management

A book covering every feature of the Microsoft Project program alone would be well over a thousand pages, so I've had to make choices about what Microsoft Project and project management information to include for you here. If you're interested in learning more about the discipline of project management or perhaps even pursuing further education in that area, the best site to consult is the Project Management Institute (PMI) at http://www.pmi.org.

PMI offers a variety of publications and education opportunities, as well as its certification program. Its site offers valuable links to the following types of information:

- **The PMI Bookstore.** This area of the site offers more than 1,000 project management books for sale.
- **Links to Registered Education Providers.** These consultants, universities, and educational sites have been approved by PMI to provide project management educational opportunities and degree or certification programs.
- **Coverage of upcoming events.** PMI keeps a calendar of seminars, expos, and other events sponsored by itself and related organizations.

Project Basic Training

IN THIS CHAPTER

- Specifying basic project information
- Viewing information in your project plan
- Establishing the overall order for tasks
- Adding resources and making assignments
- Saving the project starting point
- Telling Project about completed work
- Generating reports

To satisfy those of you who like to jump in headfirst, this chapter presents the opportunity to try out key Project features using sample files from the CD-ROM for this book.

I still recommend you use the rest of this book to learn the theory behind the skills presented here and to develop a more fully rounded understanding of Project 2000. But, by working through the examples in this chapter, you'll at least get a firsthand look at how powerful Project's features are, and how easy the system can be to get started with.

Changing Project Information and Calendar

Every project plan starts with two vital pieces of information. The project *start date* tells Project when work is to begin on the project. By default, Project schedules all tasks from the project start date. The project calendar (or *base calendar*) you choose clarifies how Project should schedule tasks—whether a one-day task takes place over a standard 8-hour workday or over a 24-hour workday that's common in three-shift manufacturing facilities.

ON THE

CD

The first step in each exercise in this chapter explains what CD-ROM file to open to perform the exercise. Please note that these files aren't intended to form a series. Each exercise stands alone, and a particular file may have more or less information in it than the file you used in an earlier exercise, or different settings and options applied. This is to help ensure that each sample file does the best possible job of demonstrating the applicable features.

This first exercise shows you how to specify the project start date and the base calendar for a project file. Keep in mind that the sample file you'll use already includes some information in it, so you can see the impact of your choices. In the real world, Project will prompt you to specify the project start date, base calendar, and other information each time you start a new file, so that those settings will be in place before you enter any task information. Start the exercise now:

1. Open the *Seminar Plan Chapter 2.1* file you copied or installed from the book CD-ROM.

Note

To start Project first, choose Start, Programs, Microsoft Project. If you just installed Project 2000, you may see a message prompting you to register Project. Click Yes to complete the registration process.

Note

You can copy or install the files from the CD to the folder of your choice on your hard disk, as described in Appendix C. Open the files from the folder to which you copied them.

2. Use the scroll bar at the bottom of the left pane of the window (which holds the Task Sheet) to scroll the Start and Finish columns into view, as in Figure 2.1. Observe the entries in the Start column. Notice that the first task starts on 1/8/99 in this file, and that other tasks have been scheduled from that date.

3. Scroll the Task Sheet to bring the Task Name and Duration columns back into view, then scroll down the list of tasks and click on task 21 (the task in row 21). Notice that this task is scheduled to have a 4-hour duration. Also notice that the total Duration entry that appears for task 18, a task that summarizes and totals the amount of work for tasks 19 through 23, lists 196 hours.

4. Press Ctrl+Home to return to the first task in the project file.

5. Choose Project, Project Information. The Project Information dialog box appears.

Figure 2.1
Observe the entries in the Start column.

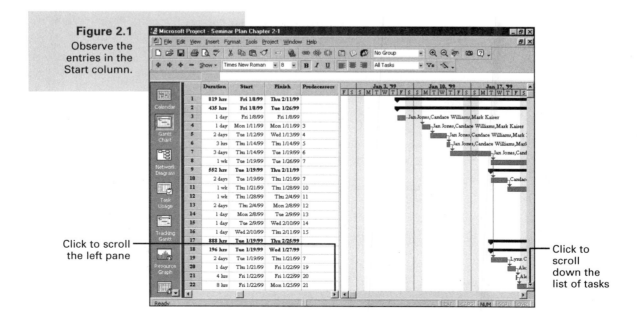

Click to scroll the left pane

Click to scroll down the list of tasks

6. Open the Start Date drop-down list in the dialog box. In the pop-up calendar that appears, click on the year at the top of the calendar. Click on the up spinner button beside the year twice to change the year to 2001, then click on an empty spot in the top of the calendar. Leave the 8 date selected on the calendar and press Enter. The Start Date should now have *Mon 1/8/01* as its entry.

7. The Calendar drop-down list displays the currently selected base calendar for the project file. In this case, the file uses the 24 Hours calendar. Open the Calendar drop-down list and click on the Standard choice. At this point, the Project Information dialog box entries should look like Figure 2.2.

8. Click on OK to close the dialog box and apply your settings.

9. Scroll the Start and Finish columns of the Task Sheet into view, as in Figure 2.3. Now, the first task starts on 1/8/01 in this file, and other tasks have been rescheduled from that date.

Caution

If you had manually entered dates in the Start column of the Task Sheet for some tasks (as opposed to allowing Project to help with the scheduling, as I did when I built the sample file), Project would not reschedule those tasks if you changed the Project start date. (Starting with Chapter 4, you'll learn how to let Project handle the scheduling for you.) Similarly, it would not reschedule the tasks if you had already marked them as completed. If you tried to set a start date that's in the past, Project would display a message telling you that you can't make such a change.

Figure 2.2
Use the Project Information dialog box to specify the project start date and base calendar.

Project Information for 'Sem...'	? X
Start date:	Mon 1/8/01
Finish date:	Thu 3/11/99
Schedule from:	Project Start Date
	All tasks begin as soon as possible.
Current date:	Tue 5/2/00
Status date:	NA
Calendar:	Standard
Priority:	500
Help	Statistics...	OK	Cancel

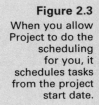

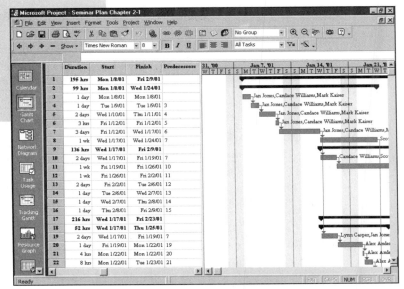

10. Scroll the Task Sheet to bring the Task Name and Duration columns back into view, then select (click on) task 21 again. This task still has a 4-hour duration. But look up at the Duration column entry for task 18. It now displays 52 hours in total for tasks 19 through 23. This is because the Standard calendar that you chose in Step 7, along with the task settings for the individual tasks, have forced Project to recalculate the total duration. In this instance, a 1-day task is 24 hours under the 24 Hours calendar, but only 8 hours under the Standard calendar. While this is a simplistic example, it gives you an idea of the impact of your project calendar choice.

11. Choose File, Save to save the file.

12. If the Planning Wizard dialog box appears, leave the top option button, for saving the file without a baseline, selected. Then click on OK to finish saving the file.

13. Choose File, Close to close the file.

14. Click on the New button at the far left end of the Standard toolbar. This button enables you to create a new blank Project file. The Project Information dialog box appears automatically. As in this exercise, you could use this dialog box to choose the start date, calendar, and other information for your new project file.

15. Instead, click on Cancel to finish this exercise.

Change Project Views

If you've used other Microsoft programs, particularly those in the Office Suite, you know that each program offers a few different views or ways of presenting information onscreen. Project offers many more views than the typical Microsoft application, and gives you more options for adjusting the view.

For example, the default view in Project is called the *Gantt Chart view*. It features the spreadsheet-like Task Sheet in its left pane and the Gantt bars in the right pane. You can adjust the Task Sheet in the left pane to display a different *table*, or collection of columns (fields). The default table is the Entry table (for entering new tasks), but you also can display a Cost table (for entering and viewing cost information), a Summary table, and others. Other views contain a *form* resembling a dialog box in a bottom pane of the window, and you can similarly display different fields of information in the form portion of the view.

Project also provides a couple of different ways to move between views and tables. You need to learn how to move around to find the right location to enter information. Project performs dozens of calculations behind the scenes for your project, so learning to navigate gives the added benefit of enabling you to view information of value. Begin the next exercise:

1. Open the *Seminar Plan Chapter 2.2* file you copied or installed from the book CD-ROM.

2. Look at the icons in the vertical bar along the left side of your screen. The bar is called the View Bar, and you can use its icons to display different views. Click on the Calendar icon at the top of the View Bar. The Calendar view (Figure 2.4) appears immediately.

If the View Bar ever disappears on you, choose View, View Bar to redisplay it.

3. Click on the Gantt Chart button in the View Bar to return to the Gantt Chart view.

4. Click on the small down arrow button in the lower-right corner of the View Bar until you see the More Views icon, then click on it. The More Views dialog box appears.

5. Click on the Cancel button.

6. Choose View, More Views. The More Views dialog box appears again.

7. Scroll down the Views list in the dialog box, click on Task Entry (Figure 2.5), and click on Apply. The Task Entry view appears, with a form pane at the bottom.

Figure 2.4
You can use the
View Bar to
change to other
Project views,
such as the
Calendar view
shown here.

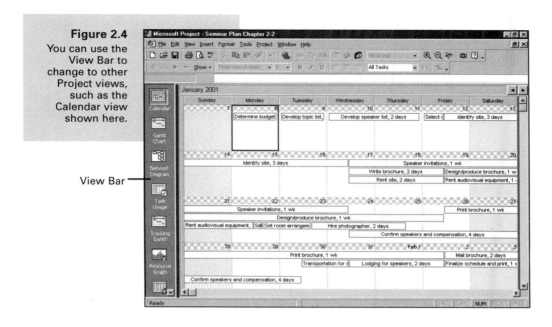

View Bar

Figure 2.5
The More Views
dialog box lists
all of the
available views.

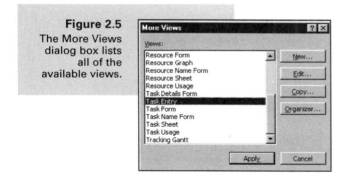

8. Click on task 3 in the Task Sheet in the top pane of the view.

9. Right-click on the form pane in the bottom of the window, then click on Resource Work in the shortcut menu. Note the changes in the bottom pane.

10. Choose View, Gantt Chart (the equivalent of clicking on the Gantt Chart icon on the View Bar). Project doesn't do what you'd expect—it displays something similar to the Gantt Chart view in the bottom pane rather than closing the pane.

11. Choose Window, Remove Split. The bottom pane closes, and the default Gantt Chart view appears.

12. Scroll the Task Sheet to the right and note its column (field) names: Task Name, Duration, Start, Finish, Predecessors, Resource Names.

13. Right-click on the gray Select All button in the upper-left corner of the Task Sheet, where the column headings and row headings intersect. Click on Cost in the shortcut menu that appears, as in Figure 2.6.

14. Scroll the Task Sheet to the right again, and notice the new collection of columns (fields).

15. Choose View, Table: (table name), Entry. This returns to the default table for the Task Sheet in the Gantt Chart view.

16. Choose Edit, Go To or press F5. The Go To dialog box appears. Type 35 in the ID field and click on OK. The Task Sheet scrolls down.

17. Press Ctrl+Home. Project redisplays task 1 in the Task Sheet, but you can't see its corresponding Gantt bar in the right pane.

18. Click on the Go To Selected Task button, third from the right on the Standard (top) toolbar. The Gantt bar for task 1 scrolls back into view.

19. Choose File, Close to close the file, and click on No if Project asks whether you want to save changes to the file.

Figure 2.6
Use the shortcut menu for the Select All button to display a new table.

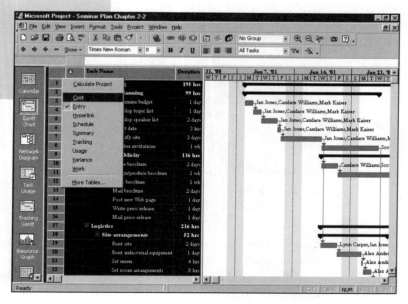

Add, Outline, and Link Tasks

If you've worked with a spreadsheet or table in a database or word processor, you'll have no problem entering new tasks in Project. You enter new tasks in the Task Sheet portion of the Gantt Chart view (or any other view that includes the Task sheet). Each row in the sheet holds a single task. You click on a cell in the row, enter the pertinent information, and press Tab to move along to the next cell.

I recommend that you limit yourself to making only the Task Name and Duration field entries for new tasks. Then you can use the outlining and linking features in Project to have Project calculate actual task schedules for you. (If you manually enter Start and Finish dates, Project might apply what's called a *constraint*, which gives it less flexibility in recalculating a task's schedule.)

Outlining helps you group related tasks, so that Project can summarize information about that task group for you. Linking establishes relationships between tasks. The default link type, a Finish-to-Start link, tells Project, "Start the second linked task after the first one finishes." Start the exercise now to see how linking can work for you when you add tasks into your schedule:

1. Open the *Seminar Plan Chapter 2.3* file you copied or installed from the book CD-ROM.

2. Press Ctrl+Down Arrow to scroll the Task Sheet down to row 32, which holds the last task in the list, *Purchase signage.*

3. Click in the Task Name cell of row 33. This is where you'll start entering new tasks.

4. Enter the new task information listed in Table 2.1. Press Tab to move to the next column to the right, and use the arrow keys to move around, too. Notice that by default, Project schedules each new task from the project start date, 1/8/01. Also notice that when you don't include an abbreviation (such as h for hours) with an entry in the Duration column, Project assumes you're entering the duration in days, so an entry of 1 becomes **1 day**.

5. Press Ctrl+Home to return to the top of the Task Sheet.

6. Choose Tools, Options, then click on the View tab if needed. Click to check the Project Summary Task check box near the bottom of the dialog box, then click on OK. This inserts a summary task, task 0, which summarizes the entire schedule for the project.

7. Drag over the Task Names for tasks 2 through 16, and then click on the Indent button on the Formatting (bottom) toolbar. As shown in Figure 2.7, Project indents those tasks below task 1.

Table 2.1 New Task Entries for Seminar Plan Chapter 2.3

Task (Row) #	Task Name	Duration
33	Special event	1
34	Verify room/catering arrangements	1h
35	Greet speakers	.5h
36	Registration	1h
37	Event	8h
38	Event wrap-up	1
39	Pay bills	4
40	Write thank you letters	2
41	Write event summary	1
42	Write/send follow-up press release	2

Indent button
Outdent button
Show Subtasks button
Hide Subtasks button
Show button

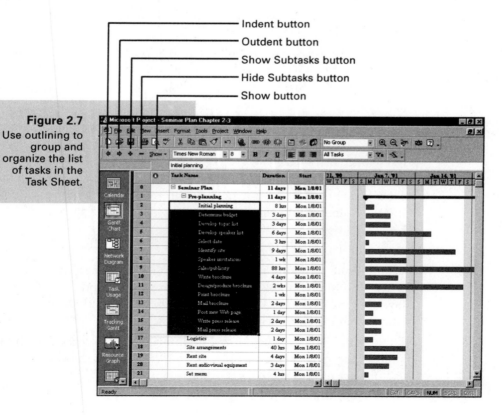

Figure 2.7
Use outlining to group and organize the list of tasks in the Task Sheet.

Note

> The indented tasks are *subtasks* or *detail tasks*. (In fact, all tasks are detail tasks or subtasks until you start indenting some and outdenting or promoting others.)
>
> The task at the level above the subtasks in the outline is called the *summary task*. You will create multiple summary and subtask levels in this exercise. You'll learn more detail about task levels in Chapter 15, "Working with Outlining."

8. Drag over the Task Names for tasks 18–32, and then click on the Indent button once.

9. Drag over the Task Names for tasks 19–23, and then click on the Indent button once. Also indent these groups of tasks once more: 25–27 and 29–32.

10. Drag over the Task Names for tasks 34–37, and then click on the Indent button once. To finish outlining, drag over the Task Names for tasks 40–42, and then click on the Indent button once.

11. Press Ctrl+Home to move back to the top of the Task Sheet.

12. Drag over the Task Names for tasks 3 through 8, and then click on the Link Tasks button on the Standard toolbar. As you can see in Figure 2.8,

Figure 2.8
Linking establishes the sequence of tasks and enables Project to help calculate the task schedule for you.

Link Tasks button

Unlink Tasks button

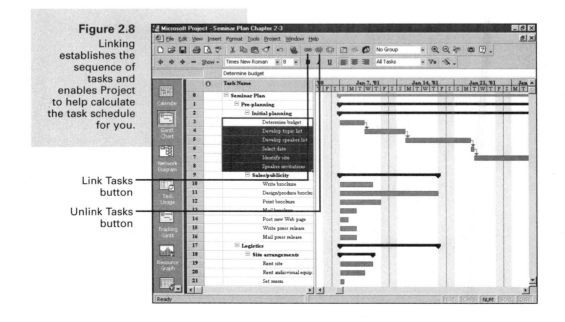

Project applies the default link type to the selected tasks, and recalculates schedules for the linked tasks so that each one follows the preceding one chronologically. (Note that I've made the Task Sheet display smaller for some of the figures here so you can better see the linking.)

13. Also link these groups of tasks: 10–16, 19–23, 25–27, 29–32, 34–37, and 39–42.

14. Now it's necessary to link tasks between the outline groups, because too many tasks are still scheduled concurrently in the schedule. Scroll up the Task Sheet and click on the Task Name cell for task 7. Press and hold the Ctrl key, and click on the Task Name for task 10. Release the Ctrl key, then click on the Link Tasks button. This links tasks between the two summary groups in the outline, and reschedules the tasks in the lower (later) summary group. Click on another task to remove the selection from tasks 7 and 10.

15. Using the Ctrl+click method, select and link the following pairs of tasks: 7 and 19, 8 and 25, 27 and 29, 32 and 34, and 37 and 39. You can scroll around the Gantt chart at the right side of the Gantt Chart view to see the quite extensive links that you've created.

16. Press Ctrl+Home. Move the mouse pointer over the Gantt bar for the project summary task. As shown in Figure 2.9, a pop-up tip shows the new project finish date that Project calculated after you linked tasks.

Figure 2.9
Pointing to a Gantt bar shows the task schedule. In this case, you see the project schedule that Project has calculated based on the links you've added.

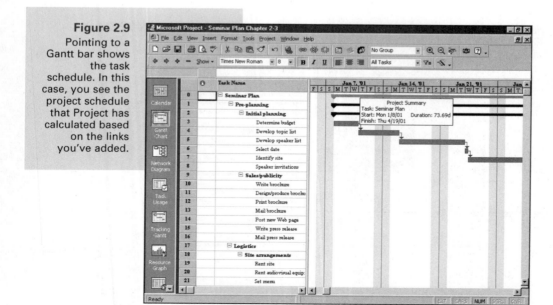

17. Choose Edit, Go To. Enter 37 in the ID text box, then click on OK. Scroll the Gantt bar for task 37 into view, if needed. If you compare its Start date (4/5/01) and Finish Date (4/6/01) and look at its Gantt chart bar, you'll notice that the task starts on Thursday but ends on Friday. This is a problem, because you want your seminar to occur on a single day. To fix this, you need to enter the duration for task 37 in elapsed hours, which tells Project to schedule the time continuously, despite the project base calendar and other linked tasks.

18. Click in the Duration cell for task 37, enter **8eh**, and press Enter. If you check the task Start and Finish dates and Gantt bar again, you'll now see that it starts and ends on the same day.

19. Save your changes to the Seminar Plan Chapter 2.3 file without saving a baseline, then close the file.

Add and Assign Resources

Resources comprise the people, equipment, and materials that perform the project tasks. Project 2000 actually offers two different types of resources. *Work resources* are people or equipment who finish a task over time by expending hours of work. You typically pay an hourly fee for using work resources. *Material resources* represent goods consumed by a task. For example, pouring a building foundation might consume 10 cubic yards of concrete. You typically pay by the quantity (cubic yard, dozen, ream) for material resources.

You add resources in to the Resource Sheet for your project to make them available to the project plan, and then you use another view to assign those resources to particular tasks. This exercise gives you practice with adding resources and making task assignments.

One last note before getting started. By default, Project uses what's called *effort-driven scheduling*, meaning that adding more resources to a task causes Project to decrease the task duration. It makes sense for certain types of tasks and when you are in the early stages of planning. If you think a task will take three weeks' work for one person, two people can probably get it done in a week and a half. On the other hand, in some instances, you don't want Project to use effort-driven scheduling; you want the duration to remain fixed. For example, if your company is hosting a one-day seminar, that seminar will last all day no matter how many employees (resources) you assign to the seminar task. If you assigned four employees (resources) to the task representing the seminar, you wouldn't want Project to decrease its duration to .25 days. You'll also see how to turn off effort-driven scheduling and fix the task duration in this exercise, which you should do before you add the resources.

1. Open the *Seminar Plan Chapter 2.4* file you copied or installed from the book CD-ROM. If you look at the Gantt chart, you can see resource names beside the Gantt bars. That's because this file already holds some resource information and resource assignments.

2. Double-click on the Task Name for task 6 to display the Task Information dialog box. Because this *Select date* task represents a three-hour meeting, you don't want the duration to change when you assign multiple resources to it. So you need to turn off effort-driven scheduling and fix the duration for the task. To do so, click on the Advanced tab in the dialog box, clear the check beside the Effort Driven check box, and then open the Task Type drop-down list and choose Fixed Duration (see Figure 2.10). Click on OK to close the dialog box.

3. Also turn off effort-driven scheduling and fix the duration for tasks 21, 22, 36, and 37.

4. Scroll down the View Bar and click on the Resource Sheet icon. The Resource Sheet view appears. This is where you enter new resources in Project.

5. Enter the new resource information shown in rows 14 and 15 of Figure 2.11 into the exercise file. Row 14 holds a work resource and row 15 holds a material resource. Notice that you use a drop-down list to specify the entry for the Type column. You only need to enter a *material label* for material resources to specify the pricing unit you'll use for the resource,

Figure 2.10
Turn off effort-driven scheduling on the Advanced tab of the Task Information dialog box.

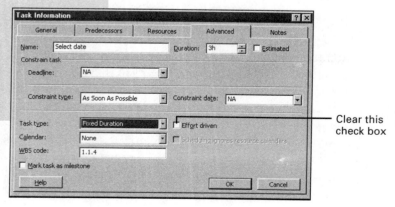

Clear this check box

Figure 2.11
Enter the new resource information shown in rows 14 and 15.

	ⓘ	Resource Name	Type	Material Label	Initials	Group	Max. Units	Std. Rate	Ovt. Rate	Cost/Use	Ac ▲
1		Jan Jones	Work		JanJ	Marketing	100%	$45.00/hr	$0.00/hr	$0.00	Pro
2		Alex Anderson	Work		AlexA	Marketing	100%	$20.00/hr	$0.00/hr	$0.00	Pro
3		Candace Williams	Work		CandaceW	Communicat	100%	$30.00/hr	$0.00/hr	$0.00	Pro
4	◈	Scott Paul	Work		ScottP	Communic	100%	$25.00/hr	$8.00/hr	$8.00	Pr-
5		Phil Stevens	Work		PhilS	IT	100%	$35.00/hr	$0.00/hr	$0.00	Pro
6		Lynn Casper	Work		LynnC	Sales	100%	$25.00/hr	$0.00/hr	$0.00	Pro
7		Mark Kaiser	Work		MarkK	Sales	100%	$20.00/hr	$0.00/hr	$0.00	Pro
8		Atherton Printing	Work		Atherton	External	100%	$0.00/hr	$0.00/hr	$0.00	Pro
9		Reliable Mailing Servic	Work		Reliable	External	100%	$0.00/hr	$0.00/hr	$0.00	Pro
10		Quickie Couriers	Work		Quickie	External	100%	$0.00/hr	$0.00/hr	$20.00	Pro
11		Letterhead	Material	Ream	LH			$25.00		$0.00	Pro
12		Envelopes	Material	Box	EN			$20.00		$0.00	Pro
13		Bulk Postage	Material	Piece	BP			$0.22		$0.00	Pro
14		Lydia Scott	Work		LydiaS	Sales	100%	$20.00/hr	$0.00/hr	$0.00	Pro
15		Standard Postage	Material	Piece	SP			$0.33		$0.00	Pro

such as cubic yard, dozen, ream, and so on; leave the column blank for work resources. The Std. Rate column holds the cost per hour for work resources, and the cost per unit (material label) for material resources.

Note

Look at the Quickie Couriers Resource in row 10—it doesn't have a Std. Rate entry. This resource uses the Cost/Use column, instead, because it charges a set fee every time you use it for the task in a schedule rather than computing an hourly fee for each specific delivery. You can use a cost per use in conjunction with a standard hourly rate, if that's how a resource bills your company.

6. Use the method of your choice to return to the Gantt Chart view. Time to assign some resources to some tasks.

7. Click on the Assign Resources button on the Standard (top) toolbar. It's the button that has two faces on it. The Assign Resources dialog box opens.

8. Click on the Task Name cell for task 6. You can see if you check its Gantt bar that it currently has no resources assigned. This is one of the tasks for which you turned off effort-driven scheduling, so assigning resources will not change the task's duration. In the Assign Resources dialog box, click on Jan Jones, and then click on Assign. A check appears beside her name in the dialog box, telling you that she's been assigned to the task. Leave task 6 selected, click on Candace Williams in the Assign Resources dialog box, then click on Assign. Click on Mark Kaiser, then click on Assign. As shown in Figure 2.12, Project assigns all three resources to the task.

9. Scroll down the Task Sheet if needed (the Assign Resources dialog box stays open), and click on the Task Name for task 20. Notice its Duration

Assign Resources button

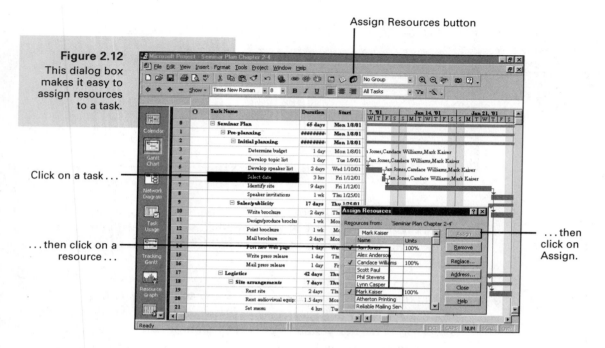

Figure 2.12
This dialog box makes it easy to assign resources to a task.

Click on a task . . .

. . . then click on a resource . . .

. . . then click on Assign.

is 1.5 days. In the Assign Resources dialog box, scroll down the list of resources, click on Lydia Scott (the new work resource you entered), then click on Assign. Project assigns Lydia and adjusts the task duration, because you left effort-driven scheduling enabled for the task.

10. Next, you'll see how to make a material resource assignment. Click on the Task Name cell for task 16. Scroll up the list of resources in the Assign Resources dialog box to check which resources have been assigned to the task. You have the needed work resources for this mailing task, along with the Letterhead and Envelopes material resources. However, you need some Standard Postage. Because you know that half a ream of letterhead and half a box of envelopes is 250 pieces, you know you need to pay for postage for 250 releases. Click in the Units column beside the Standard Postage resource. Type **250** as shown in Figure 2.13, and then click on Assign.

11. Make the additional resource assignments outlined in Table 2.2. (Some of the listed tasks may already have other resources assigned; in such a case, just add the listed resources.) Keep your eye on whether or not durations change as you make resource assignments.

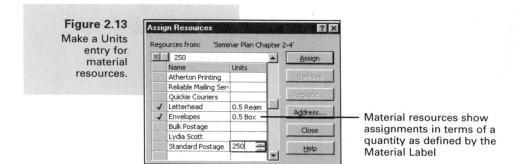

Figure 2.13
Make a Units
entry for
material
resources.

Material resources show
assignments in terms of a
quantity as defined by the
Material Label

Table 2.2 New Task Entries for Seminar Plan Chapter 2.4

Task (Row) #	Resource(s) to Assign	Task (Row) #	Resource(s) to Assign
21	Alex Anderson	36	Alex Anderson
	Mark Kaiser		Scott Paul
	Lydia Scott		Mark Kaiser
22	Alex Anderson		Lydia Scott
	Mark Kaiser	37	Jan Jones
	Quickie Couriers		Alex Anderson
	Lydia Scott		Candace Williams
29	Lydia Scott		Scott Paul
30	Lydia Scott		Phil Stevens
31	Lydia Scott		Lynn Casper
	Letterhead [2]		Mark Kaiser
	Envelopes [1]		Lydia Scott
	Standard Postage [500]	42	Standard Postage [500]
32	Lydia Scott		

12. Click on the Close button to close the Assign Resources dialog box.

13. You've seen how to enter costs that accumulate based on resource assignments. However, some costs relate to the task. For example, you'll typically pay a lump sum fee to rent a location for a seminar rather than an hourly rate. Project calls these costs *fixed costs*. Use the Cost table of the

Figure 2.14

The Fixed Cost column in the Cost table holds a one-time cost associated with a particular task.

16	Mail press release	$0.00	Prorated
17	⊟ **Logistics**	**$0.00**	**Prorated**
18	⊟ **Site arrangements**	**$0.00**	**Prorated**
19	Rent site	$2,500.00	Prorated
20	Rent audiovisual equipme	$1,500.00	Prorated
21	Set menu	$10,000.00	Prorated
22	Set room arrangements	$0.00	Prorated
23	Hire photographer	$1,000.00	Prorated
24	⊟ **Speaker arrangements**	**$0.00**	**Prorated**
25	Confirm speakers and co:	$5,000.00	Prorated
26	Transportation for speak	$250.00	Prorated
27	Lodging for speakers	$1,750.00	Prorated

Task Sheet to enter fixed costs. Choose View, Table: (table name), Cost. The Cost table appears. Note that its Total Cost column holds entries. Project calculated these costs based on the hours of work required by each task, multiplied by the standard rate you entered for all resources assigned to the task, plus any per-use costs.

14. For tasks 19–21, 23, and 25–27, make the Fixed Cost column entries shown in Figure 2.14. (I've adjusted the column widths so you can better see the task names in the Figure.)

15. Choose View, Table: (table name), Entry to return to the default table for the Task Sheet in the Gantt Chart view.

16. Save your changes to the Seminar Plan Chapter 2.4 file without saving a baseline, then close the file.

Saving the Baseline

Saving a *baseline* stores all the information for your original project plan within the project file: original task start and finish dates, amount of work assigned via various resources, the original cost information Project calculated based on your entries, and so on. After you save the baseline and start marking work completed or entering actual costs, you can go back and compare your progress versus the original (baseline) plan. Use this exercise to see how to view and store the baseline information:

1. Open the *Seminar Plan Chapter 2.5* file you copied or installed from the book CD-ROM.

2. Choose View, Table: (table name), Variance to display the Variance table. Scroll the Task Sheet (table) pane of the view to the right so you can see the Baseline Start and Baseline Finish fields, which presently have no information because you haven't saved the baseline. When you save the

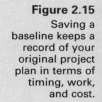

Figure 2.15
Saving a baseline keeps a record of your original project plan in terms of timing, work, and cost.

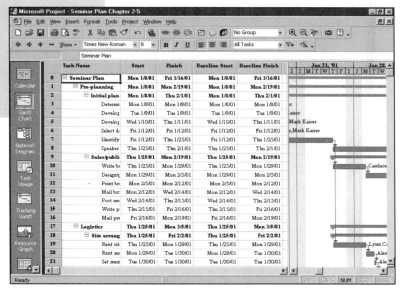

baseline, Project copies the dates from the Start field into the Baseline Start field, and the dates from the Finish field into the Baseline Finish field.

3. Choose Tools, Tracking, Save Baseline. The Save Baseline dialog box appears.

4. Leave the Save Baseline option button selected, then click on OK. As shown in Figure 2.15, the baseline columns now hold the copied baseline information.

5. Choose View, Table: (table name), Entry to display the default Entry table.

6. Save and close the file.

Tracking and Rescheduling Work

As time passes, you need to tell Project how much work has been completed on the tasks in the Task Sheet, enter any actual cost information that applies (if it differs from the baseline cost information that Project calculated), and also reschedule tasks as needed. There are many ins and outs to this process, so consult Chapter 9, "Comparing Progress versus Your Baseline Plan," to learn more. Use these exercise steps, on the other hand, to get started:

1. Open the *Seminar Plan Chapter 2.6* file you copied or installed from the book CD-ROM.

2. Right-click on any toolbar, then click on Tracking to display the Tracking toolbar.

3. Select tasks 3–6 by dragging over their Task Name entries, then click on the 100% button on the Tracking toolbar. As shown in Figure 2.16, a check mark indicator appears for completed tasks. A small black line also appears in the center of the Gantt bars to mark the task as complete.

4. Select task 7 and click on the 75% button on the Tracking toolbar.

5. Select task 8 and click on the 25% button on the Tracking toolbar.

6. Click on the Start cell for task 10, *Write Brochure.* Type a new start date of **1/26/01**, and then press Enter. In the Planning Wizard dialog box that appears, click on the second option button, Move The Task...And Keep The Link, then click on OK.

7. Choose View, Table: (table name), Variance to display the Variance table. Compare the Start and Baseline Start fields for task 10. The Baseline Start field holds the original start date saved in the baseline plan, and the Start field holds the new start date you entered in Step 6. Also check the Start Variance field. Because you delayed a task, there is now a start variance.

8. Choose View, Table: (table name), Cost to display the Cost table.

Figure 2.16
When work finishes on a task, use the Tracking toolbar's 100% button to mark it as complete.

Tracking toolbar

Indicator for completed tasks

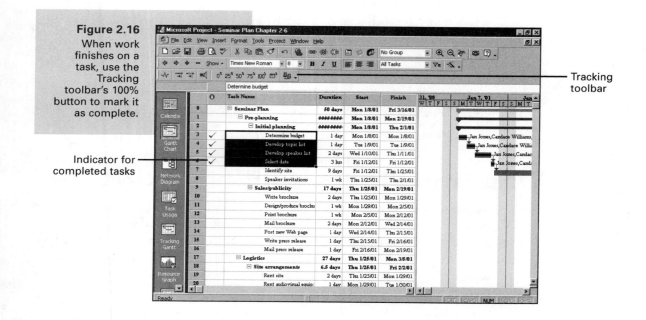

Note

Don't let the casual meanings of "positive" and "negative" throw you off! A positive start or finish variance indicates that a task or project is *behind schedule,* and a negative start or finish variance means that the task or project is *ahead of schedule.* Positive cost variance numbers mean a task or project is over budget, and negative cost variance numbers mean a task or project is under budget.

9. For task 3, *Determine Budget,* click on the Total Cost cell. Type **800** (to reflect the fact that someone bought pizzas for the work session), and press Enter.

10. Scroll to review the Baseline field, which holds the original cost, and the Variance field, which reflects the difference between the Baseline value and the new total cost you entered.

11. Choose View, Table: (table name), Entry to display the default Entry table.

12. Choose Project, Project Information. Click on the Statistics button in the Project Information dialog box. A dialog box presenting statistics about the amount of work completed and cost expended versus the baseline appears. (See Figure 2.17.)

13. Click on Close to close the dialog box.

14. Save and close the file.

Figure 2.17
After you enter tracking and cost information, Project can calculate any variances.

Project Statistics for 'Seminar Plan Chapter 2-6'

	Start		Finish	
Current	Mon 1/8/01			Fri 3/16/01
Baseline	Mon 1/8/01			Fri 3/16/01
Actual	Mon 1/8/01			NA
Variance	0d			0d

	Duration	Work	Cost
Current	50d	906.5h	$44,330.00
Baseline	50d	906.5h	$44,290.00
Actual	8.34d	115h	$3,615.00
Remaining	41.66d	791.5h	$40,715.00

Percent complete:
Duration: 17%   Work: 13%

Close

Reporting Project Information

Project contains a number of built-in report formats to make communicating with your team members as effortless as possible. You can generate reports about overall project information, assignments, upcoming tasks, or costs, or even create your own specialized reports. Follow this exercise to run through displaying and printing a report:

1. Open the *Seminar Plan Chapter 2.7* file you copied or installed from the book CD-ROM.

2. Choose View, Reports. The Reports dialog box appears, displaying the available report categories.

3. Double-click on Costs. The Cost Reports dialog box appears (Figure 2.18).

4. Double-click on Budget. The Budget report appears onscreen.

5. Click on the Print button at the top of the report preview window.

6. Change any needed settings in the Print dialog box, then click on OK to print.

7. Click on the Close button to close the report preview.

8. Save and close the file.

Caution

It's inconvenient, but you can't use Project to keep track of the report data you display and print on any given day. If you need an electronic snapshot of the data from your project, you'll have to export the data to a file. Chapter 20, "Using Project with Other Applications," covers the export process.

Figure 2.18
Here are Project's cost reports. Project offers other types of reports, and you can create custom reports.

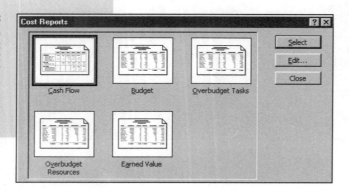

PART II
Project Management Basics

Working with Files and Help

In This Chapter

- How to start Project
- Help resources in Project
- Going online for more help
- Managing files
- How to exit Project

So you've broken Microsoft Project 2000 out of the box and installed it. You're all set up, but where do you go? With many applications, how to get started is obvious. To begin working in Word, for example, you just start typing. In Excel, you just click on cells and type numbers and formulas. With Project, the starting point is not so obvious, but don't worry. This chapter and the next introduce the steps you need to take to begin your work and set up a project.

Starting Project

As with most other Windows applications, the easiest way to start Project is via the Windows taskbar:

1. Click on the Start menu button; then point to Programs.
2. Click on Microsoft Project.

If Project doesn't appear as a choice on the Start menu, follow these steps to add a shortcut icon to your desktop for starting the program:

1. Double-click on the My Computer icon on your desktop to open the My Computer window.
2. Double-click on the icon for the drive where Project 2000 is installed, usually the C drive.
3. By default, Project installs to a subfolder in the Program Files folder along with other Microsoft Office applications. Thus to get to it, first double-click on the icon for the Program Files folder to open it, and then double-click on the icon for the Microsoft Office subfolder. Then double-click on the icon for the Office subfolder. If you chose to install Project in a different folder, you should open that folder instead.
4. In the Office folder, point to the Microsoft Project program file icon, labeled Winproj, press and hold the right mouse button, and drag the icon over the desktop. When you release the mouse button, a shortcut menu appears. Click on Create Shortcut(s) Here, as shown in Figure 3.1.

After you add a Project shortcut to the desktop, you can double-click on it at any time to start Project.

No matter what method you use to start Project, by default you'll see the Welcome! Help window shown in Figure 3.2 the first time you start the program. This screen offers several choices for how to proceed, as well as a check box:

- **What's New.** Follow this link if you've upgraded from Project 98 and want to learn about new features and how they might affect your existing Project files.

Figure 3.1
After you release the right mouse button, click on Copy Here to create a shortcut icon for Project on the desktop.

Project program file

Figure 3.2
Click on one of the links in the Project Help window to get overview help about Project.

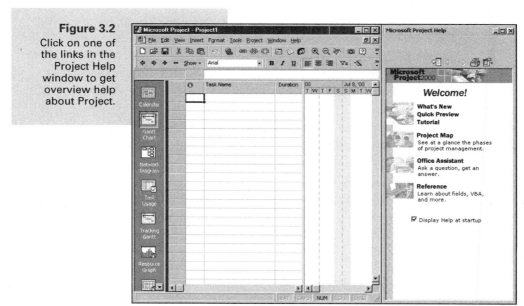

- **Preview.** Click on this link and then on the Next link to view on-screen information about Project and its benefits.

- **Tutorial.** Click on this link to use the tutorial, which offers background information about the project planning process and brief lessons that walk you through the process of creating a project schedule.

Figure 3.3
The Map in Help outlines the project planning process.

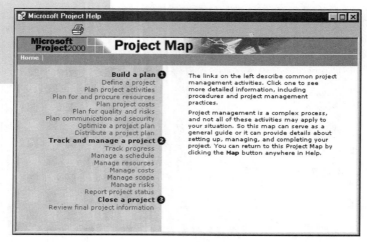

- **Project Map.** Click on this link to view a list or map (see Figure 3.3) that outlines the process of creating and monitoring a project schedule. Follow links to find out about topics of interest.

- **Office Assistant.** Click on this link to open the Office Assistant, which you can use to search Help for answers to your specific questions. You'll learn more about using the Office Assistant shortly.

- **Reference.** Use this link to access Help listings that describe the various Project fields, troubleshooting help, and more.

- **Display Help at Startup.** Click on this check box to clear it—before clicking any of the other help links—to have Project open a blank project file during subsequent startups without opening the Project Help window.

After you follow one of the links, click on the Home link near the top of subsequent Help windows to return to the Welcome! window.

If you prefer not to work with help right off the bat, click on the Close button in the upper-right corner of the Welcome! Help screen. Doing so hides the Help window so you can see more of the Project application window and the new blank project file. You can display interactive help after you begin working (see "Accessing Interactive Help Features" later in this chapter).

Understanding the Project Screen

When Project displays a new blank project, the screen looks like Figure 3.4. By default, you'll see the Gantt Chart view for the new project. This screen enables you to enter tasks for your project. At the far-left side of the screen is the View Bar, which you can use to change the way information is displayed in Project. In addition to the View Bar, the Project window features two gridlike panes. In the left pane, you enter the name of the task, its duration, and other columns of task information. (Chapter 4, "Setting Up a Project," covers creating tasks in more detail.) The right pane displays each task you create as a graphical bar in a weekly schedule, so you can see at a glance how long a task lasts, or where tasks overlap in time.

Project 2000 looks like the other Microsoft Office applications (Word, Excel, PowerPoint, Access, and Outlook), so the Project application feels familiar and you learn quickly to find and use Project features. The top of the screen displays a title bar and menu bar with commands, as in other Windows applications. Below the menu bar, two toolbars appear by default; each toolbar button is a

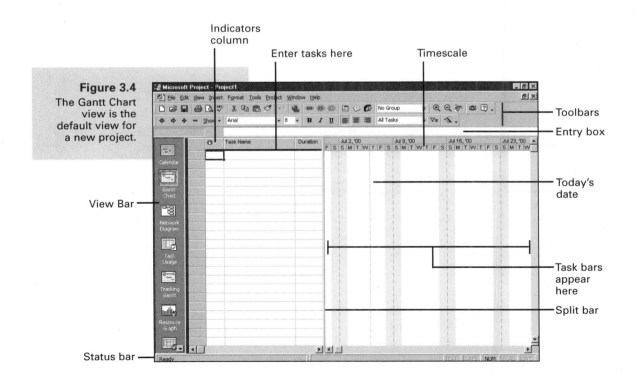

Figure 3.4
The Gantt Chart view is the default view for a new project.

shortcut for executing a particular command. A text entry box appears between the toolbars and the panes that show the data you've entered; you can use this box to enter and edit task entries. The box changes in appearance when you use it, as you learn in the next chapter.

Looking at the View Bar

Project 2000 includes an on-screen feature called the View Bar. As its name suggests, the View Bar allows you to select a different screen layout or view for the various types of information stored in a Project file. For example, a particular view might show a graph you're looking for, and another view might make it easier to enter a certain type of information, such as information about a resource (a person who will be working on a project). Some views are graphical, some provide information about tasks, and so on. Don't worry about what each view looks like for now. You learn more about the various views in chapters where they apply and in Chapter 11, "Working with the Different Project Views."

Each icon in the View Bar represents a particular view in Project. Click on the icon for the view you want in order to switch to that view. To scroll the View Bar and see additional view icons, click on the down-arrow button at the bottom-right corner of the View Bar. After you click on the down-arrow button once, an up-arrow button appears in the upper-right corner of the View Bar, as shown in Figure 3.5.

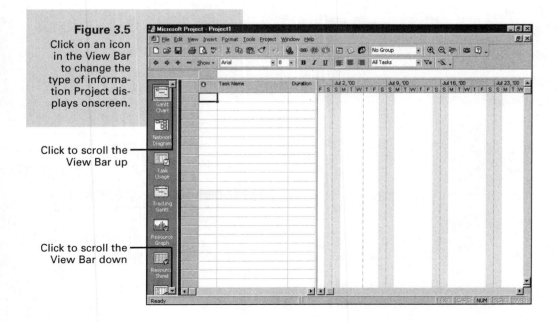

Figure 3.5
Click on an icon in the View Bar to change the type of information Project displays onscreen.

Click to scroll the View Bar up

Click to scroll the View Bar down

When you move the mouse pointer over the icon for a particular view, the icon takes on a 3-D appearance. Then you can click on the icon to change to the view.

Note

You can use the View, View Bar command to hide and display the View Bar. When you hide the View Bar, the view name appears along the left side of the screen.

Looking at the Toolbars

Project by default displays two toolbars, Standard (top) and Formatting. To discover what a particular toolbar button does, simply place the mouse pointer on it to display a yellow ScreenTip describing the button (see Figure 3.6).

Project enables you to control the toolbar display, to select the shortcuts you prefer to work with, and to control how much of your screen the toolbars use. As shown in Figure 3.7, you can drag a toolbar to another location onscreen, which automatically places the toolbar in a floating window that you can resize by dragging any of its borders. To return the toolbar to its original location, double-click on the toolbar window title bar.

The fastest way to choose which toolbars appear onscreen is to right-click on a toolbar to display the shortcut menu. A check beside a toolbar name in the list indicates that the toolbar is presently displayed (toggled on). To select or deselect a toolbar, click on its name on this shortcut menu. To close the shortcut menu without changing a toolbar selection, click outside the menu (or press Esc).

Tip

Chapter 24, "Customizing Microsoft Project," shows you how to customize your toolbars by adding new buttons. It also explains how to create your own toolbar to make Project as easy as possible for you to use.

Figure 3.6
Point to a toolbar button to learn what it does.

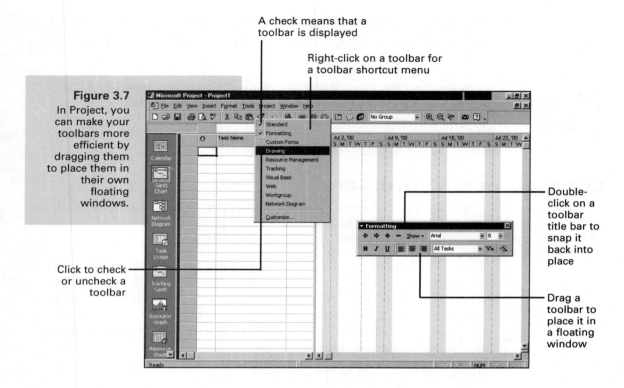

Figure 3.7
In Project, you can make your toolbars more efficient by dragging them to place them in their own floating windows.

A check means that a toolbar is displayed

Right-click on a toolbar for a toolbar shortcut menu

Double-click on a toolbar title bar to snap it back into place

Drag a toolbar to place it in a floating window

Click to check or uncheck a toolbar

Getting Help When You Need It

Project offers several different "flavors" of help, via the Help menu. The most common way to start working with the Help system is to access the list of available Help topics. To do so, choose Help, Contents and Index.

Displaying the Microsoft Project Help window (see Figure 3.8) enables you to choose from among three tabs, each offering a different kind of help:

- **Contents.** The Contents tab lists several folders or topic areas within the Help system. To view the topics within a folder, double-click on the folder or click on the plus sign beside it so that its icon changes to an open folder and its contents (additional folders and topics) are displayed. A question page icon indicates specific topics. Click on any topic to view it in the pane at the right or in its own window. To close a folder, if needed, also double-click on it or click on the minus sign that appears beside it.

Figure 3.8
After you access the Help Topics: Microsoft Project window, you can click on a tab to select the kind of help you need.

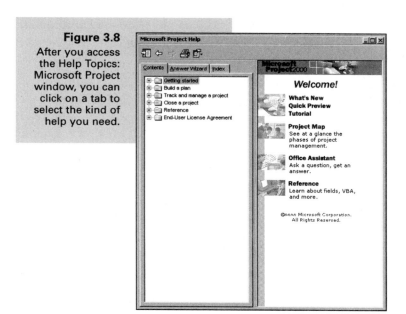

- **Answer Wizard.** The Answer Wizard tab lets you type a question in and search for matching topics. Type your question or the activity you want to find out about into the What Would You Like To Do? text box on the Answer Wizard tab, and then click on Search. The Select Topic To Display list box displays a list of potentially matching topics. Click on a topic in that list box to see help about it in the pane at the right side of the Microsoft Project Help window.

- **Index.** If you have a rough idea of the topic you're searching for and how it might be referenced in Help, click on the Index tab. The 1. Type Keywords text box prompts you to type all or part of the topic you want information about. The 2. Or Choose Keywords list scrolls to display the terms and phrases that most closely match your entry. Whenever you see an entry you want to view in the 2. Or Choose Keywords list, double-click on it. The 3. Choose A Topic list displays help topics relating to the term you selected. Click on a term in this bottom list to see help about it in the right pane.

After you display a Help topic in the right pane of the Microsoft Project Help window, follow links (or hyperlinks, which are blue and underlined by default) to browse through all the help about that topic. Also use the Back and Forward buttons on the Help window toolbar to browse, much as you would in Web browser software like Internet Explorer.

You can click on the Options button on the Help window toolbar to open a menu with options for working with the help topic information. Choosing Print from the menu, for example, enables you to print the Help topic. Drag over text in the right pane of the Help window to select it, then right-click with the mouse. Choose Copy in the shortcut menu that appears to copy the Help topic contents to the Windows Clipboard, so you can paste that information into another document— say, an e-mail message to a colleague who needs help with a Project feature. The Hide button on the toolbar hides the right pane of the Help window, at which point the button turns into the Show button. Click on the Help window Close button to close the Microsoft Project Help window altogether.

Another Help menu choice can provide instant help for the task at hand. Click on the Help menu to open it, and then click on What's This? to get information about what you're doing; alternately, press Shift+F1. The mouse pointer turns into a question mark pointer. Click on the on-screen item that you're curious about, and Project displays a pop-up description of it. Click outside the description to close it.

The new Project version also offers a few more forms of help, which you can review next in this chapter.

Note

If you see a Question Mark button at the right end of a dialog box title bar, you can click on it and then click an item in the dialog box for pop-up help about the item. If the dialog box doesn't offer a Question Mark button, right-click on the dialog box option you want help with, then click on What's This? in the shortcut menu.

Checking ScreenTips

Project 2000 features expanded ScreenTip help. In addition to displaying Screen Tips about toolbar buttons, you can display ScreenTips about other on-screen features. For example, you can point to part of the timescale to see the precise calendar date or dates that the specified portion of the timescale represents. You also can point to any column header in the Task Sheet portion of the left side of the default Gantt Chart view. As shown in the example in Figure 3.9, the ScreenTip that appears includes a link to a help description of the field contents. Click on the link in the ScreenTip to see that help.

Figure 3.9
Project offers
ScreenTips
about column
headings and the
timescale.

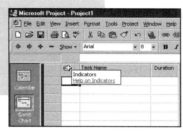

Using the Office Assistant

The Office Assistant allows you to ask for help in plain English, similar to the Answer Wizard. You type in a question, and the Office Assistant searches the Help system and displays a list of topics that may answer your question. Follow these steps to display and work with the Office Assistant:

1. You can launch the Office Assistant in a few ways: by choosing Help, Microsoft Project Help, by pressing F1, or by clicking on the Microsoft Project Help button on the Standard toolbar. No matter which method you use, the Office Assistant opens onscreen, and its yellow question bubble opens. The bubble prompts you to type a question.

2. Type your question; it replaces the prompt in the bubble. Figure 3.10 shows an example question typed into the Assistant: "How do I save a project file?"

3. Click on the Search button, located beneath the area where your question appeared when you typed. The Office Assistant searches all the Help topics, and lists topics that might answer your question in the yellow bubble. If there are more topics than can appear in the bubble at one time, a See More choice with a down-pointing triangle button appears at the bottom of the topic list; click on it to review the additional topics. After you do so, a See Previous choice appears at the top of the list so you can redisplay the initial list of topics.

4. When you see the Help topic you want, click on the round button beside it. A Help window appears onscreen to give you steps, information, or links to more specific topics. Review the Help and follow links as needed, and then click on the Help window Close button to close the window.

5. When you finish working with the Office Assistant, you can right-click on the Assistant and choose Hide to remove the Office Assistant from your screen.

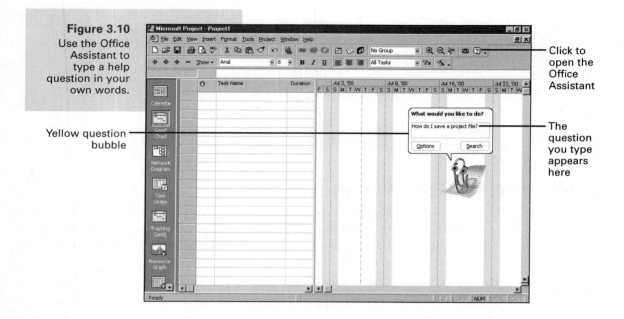

Figure 3.10
Use the Office Assistant to type a help question in your own words.

Yellow question bubble

Click to open the Office Assistant

The question you type appears here

Or, rather than closing the Office Assistant after getting Help about a question, you can leave the Assistant onscreen as long as you need to by simply clicking outside the yellow question bubble. To redisplay the yellow question bubble at any time, click on the Office Assistant character.

Accessing Interactive Help Features

Earlier in this chapter, you learned that Project's Welcome! window offers you the option of reviewing a few different types of interactive onscreen Help. If you choose not to view that interactive help and not to display the Welcome! screen each time you start Project, you can redisplay the interactive Help using the Help menu. If you click on the Help menu and point to Getting Started, Project displays a submenu with three choices that lead you back to interactive Help:

- **Quick Preview.** Click on this command, which displays the same Help as the Watch A Preview choice in the Welcome! window, to view an onscreen review of Project's key features and how they can help you. The Quick Preview window appears in Figure 3.11. To navigate in the Quick Preview window, click on the Next and Back buttons to move through the screens consecutively. Click on the window Close button to close the Quick Preview.

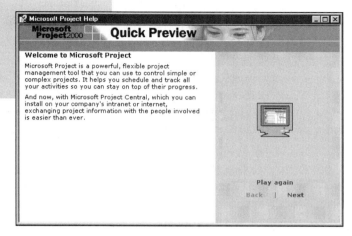

■ **Tutorial.** This submenu choice displays the same tutorial you get from the Tutorial choice in the Welcome! window. This help offers lessons that walk you through the process of creating a project schedule. The initial window for this type of help lists tasks along the left. Click on one of these topics to display help or a lesson about the topic in the right pane of the Help window. When you enter a lesson, you can use the next (>>) and back (<<) buttons near the top of the right pane of the Help window to navigate through the contents in the lesson. Again, use the window Close button to conclude using this type of help.

■ **Project Map.** Click on this choice to view the Project Map Help window with links to the operations that fall under three broad project planning areas: 1. Build A Plan, 2. Track And Manage A Project, and 3. Close A Project. Clicking on an operation under a planning area displays help with a more detailed breakdown of the steps the operation entails. You can read the help, and click on additional links in the Help to drill down to subsequent levels of detail. Click on the window Close button to finish working with this type of help.

Getting Help on the Web

Although software publishers do provide manuals and online help along with their products, the help that comes with the software itself has become slimmer. To supplement the help that ships with products such as Project, Microsoft maintains a Web site providing additional help. To go online (assuming you have a

Web browser installed and your Internet connection set up) choose Help, Office On The Web.

Your Web browser program (such as Internet Explorer or Netscape Navigator) launches. Depending on how your system is configured to connect to the Internet, you may see the same Dial-Up Connection dialog box you use to connect with dial-up connections with Internet Service Providers (ISPs); this dialog box prompts you to connect to the Internet. Click on the Connect button (or the correct button for your configuration) to connect and display the page in your Web browser.

After it makes the connection, your Web browser displays a Microsoft Office Update Web page like the one shown in Figure 3.12. (The contents of the page change over time.) You can click on various links on the page to chase down the help you need, such as downloading or ordering updates and repair patches for Project. You can print a Project Web page after it's fully displayed. Or you can save a copy of many Web pages to your hard disk, so you can open those pages at a later time (without connecting to the Internet), and read or print them. Use the Browser's File, Save As command to save Web help for later reference. When you finish checking out the Project Web information, you can close your browser and disconnect or surf on to another Web location.

Figure 3.12
Microsoft's
Project Web
coverage can
help you answer
your questions
or find support
products and
consultants
for Project.

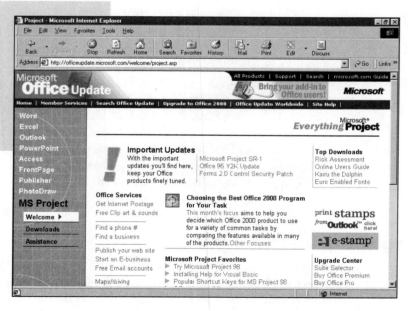

Tip   If you don't find the help you need on the Project Web site or would have to pay for technical support, you can try visiting the Project newsgroup, *microsoft.public. project*. (On Internet newsgroups like this, users of all levels post questions or offer help to other users.) Questions posted to this very active newsgroup often garner a response in a matter of hours.

Working with Files

As in all other applications, in Project you must store your work by saving it to a file on your computer's hard disk. You won't be able to track your project's progress if you can't use your file repeatedly, so it's essential to be careful when saving your files and to choose file names that are specific and descriptive. This makes it easy to find the file you need. This section looks at preserving and organizing your work.

Starting a New File

As you learned earlier in this chapter, you can open a new blank file when you launch the Project 2000 application. There might be occasions, however, when you finish working with one file and then want to create a new file without exiting Project. Doing so is easy. Either click on the New button on the Standard toolbar (it's at the far left and looks like a piece of paper), or choose File, New and then double-click on the Blank Project icon. Project opens the Project Information dialog box for the new file, and gives the file the temporary name ProjectX, where X is a number sequentially assigned to each new file you open in a Project work session. The Project Information dialog box enables you to enter facts such as the starting and ending dates for the project. (You'll learn in detail how to work with this dialog box in Chapter 4, "Setting Up a Project.")

After you click on OK to accept the information you entered for the new file, Project displays the empty file onscreen. It puts the file's temporary name in the title bar until you save the file and assign a unique name to it. (See the section titled "Saving a File," later in this chapter.)

Opening an Existing File

If you've ever opened files that have been previously created and saved in other Windows applications, you'll be relatively comfortable with Project's Open dialog box. This dialog box enables you to open Project files you previously saved, so you can enter new information, change the view, print the file, and more.

To open a file, follow these steps:

1. Choose File, Open. Alternately, you can press Ctrl+O, or click on the Open button on the Standard toolbar. (It's second from the left, and looks like an open file folder.) The Open dialog box appears (see Figure 3.13).

Note

> In Windows 95 (or later) systems, the folder that appears by default in the Look In list is usually My Documents, which is located on the C drive. However, if you're running Project with Windows NT or NT Workstation, the default folder is usually Personal, which is a subfolder of the folder that holds your Windows NT Workstation files.

2. Click on the down arrow beside the Look In list, and click on the disk drive where your Project file is stored to select that drive and display its list of folders in the dialog box.

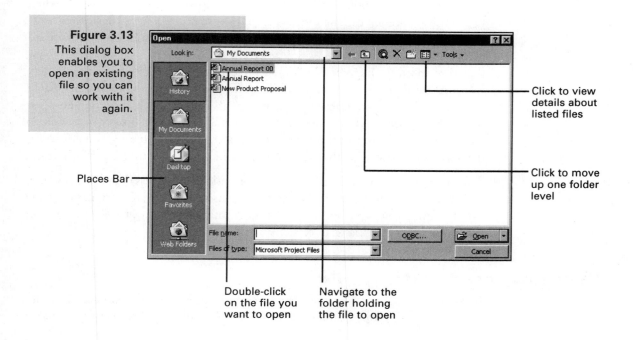

Figure 3.13
This dialog box enables you to open an existing file so you can work with it again.

Places Bar

Click to view details about listed files

Click to move up one folder level

Double-click on the file you want to open

Navigate to the folder holding the file to open

Note

The Project Open and Save dialog boxes now feature the Places Bar at the left side. To find a particular file more quickly, click on the History button there to see files and folders you've used recently. The My Documents button takes you back to your default My Documents folder. The Desktop choice lists folders and files stored on the Windows desktop. You can use the Favorites and Web Folders choices to find files stored in a subfolder of the Windows\Favorites folder or from a folder on a corporate Web site, respectively. Click on the Tools button in the Open dialog box and then on the Add To Favorites command in the menu that appears to add a selected file or folder to your list of Favorites.

If you're using a Windows 98 machine that's set up for multiple user logon, you *must* use the My Documents folder icon to return to *your* My Documents folder.

3. Double-click on a folder in the list of folders that appears; this displays the contents of that folder in the dialog box list. You might need to double-click on one or more subfolder icons to reach the file you want to open.

Note

You also can open a Project 98 file in Project 2000. However, if you try to open a file from an older version of Project and it doesn't work, that file may need to be saved in the .mpx format in the older Project version. Then, choose MPX from the Files of Type drop-down list of the Project 2000 Open dialog box to find and open the file.

4. When the file you want to open appears in the list, double-click on its name (or click on its name, and then click on Open) to load the file into Project. If you want to view or print the file but don't want to edit it, click on the down list arrow for the Open button and select the Open Read-Only choice. This option prevents you from making unwanted changes to the file.

After you select the file to open, Project displays it onscreen, ready for you to alter it, print, or whatever. If you are opening a file created in Project 98, Project may display a message telling you that some tasks might be scheduled a bit differently under Project 2000. Click on OK to close this dialog box. In addition, if a file contains macros and Project's virus protection features are enabled, you may see a dialog box asking whether you want to enable or disable the macros. Refer to Chapters 24 and 25 for more on working with macros and macro protection.

If you recently worked with a file and want to open it again, there's a shortcut; check the bottom of the File menu to see if the file name is listed there. By default, Project displays the names of the files you most recently worked on. If you see the name you want, click on it to open the file.

Finding a File with the Open Dialog Box

As the sizes of hard disks on individual computer systems—and the sizes of networked drives—increase to several gigabytes each, it becomes harder for users to keep track of files. The best human memory can be challenged by hard disks with dozens of folders and thousands of files, even if you're diligent in organizing your folders and files. Or you might have many files that are similar and you need to use a Find feature to distinguish among them. To facilitate this, Microsoft has built file-finding help into the Open dialog box in most of its applications.

When you perform a find, you can use wild-card characters if you remember part of a file name. Project will list files with names similar to the name you specified using wild cards. The asterisk (*) wild card stands in for any group of characters in the location where you use it within a file name. For example, entering **a*** in the File name text box results in a list of all file names that begin with the letter a, such as Annual Report and Accidents. The question mark (?) wild card stands in for any single character in the location where you use it. For example, entering **anders?n** in the File name text box finds files named Anderson and Andersen.

If you're working in the Open dialog box and can't remember the exact location of the file you want to open, follow these steps to perform a basic find:

1. Click on the Tools button in the Open dialog box, then choose Find in the menu that appears. The Find dialog box opens. If you want to remove one of the criteria you defined, click on it in the list of criteria, and then click on Delete. To remove all the criteria, click on New Search.

2. To add a new criterion to the list, start by selecting either the And or Or option button. And means that Find must match the original criteria (if any) and the new criterion you're specifying. In contrast, Or means that the file can match any one (or more) of the criteria you specified.

3. For the criterion you're creating, use the Property drop-down list to select the file property that will be used in the Find operation, and use the Condition list to indicate how the Property and Value entries should correspond.

4. Finally, enter the Value that the Find operation should look for in that criterion. For example, if you have selected *Property* from the Keywords list, you might enter **report** in the Value text box. If the Value entry contains more than one word, surround the entry with quotation marks, as in **"1999 report."**

5. Click on the Add To List button to finish defining the criterion. Figure 3.14 shows an example.

6. Repeat Steps 2 through 5 to add more criteria based on file properties.

7. To fine-tune a single text criterion further, select it by clicking on it in the list of criteria. Then select either the Match All Word Forms check box (when you want to match multiple tenses such as "run" and "ran") or the Match Exactly check box (when you want to match the exact capitalization you used).

8. Use the Look In drop-down list to specify a disk or folder to be searched. If you want to search all folders on the current drive, make sure that the root folder (C:\, for example) for the drive is specified in the Look In list. Then select the Search Subfolders check box.

9. (Optional) To save the search (that is, all the criteria you specified), click on the Save Search button, enter a name for this search in the Name text box, and then click on OK.

Figure 3.14
You can create a list of criteria to increase the power of a Find operation.

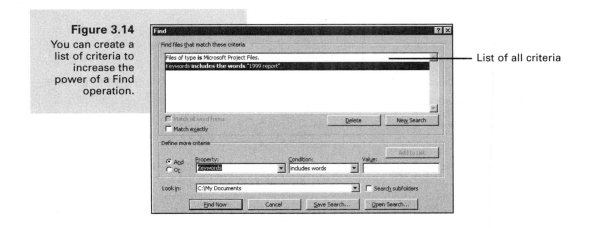

Note

> To reuse a search you saved, click on the Open Search button in the Find dialog box, select the named search in the Open Search dialog box, and click on Open. You also can use Delete or Rename in the Open Search dialog box to delete or rename saved searches.

10. Click on the Find Now button to execute the search. (At this point, you may be prompted to install the Office Find Fast feature.) Follow the prompts to do so to provide Project the means to search the specified folders for the files. When the search is finished, Project displays a message in the lower-left portion of the Open File dialog box telling you how many files match the search criteria you specified. If only one file matches the specification, that file is highlighted in the dialog box.

11. Double-click on the name of the file you want to open (or click to select its name, and then click on Open).

Saving a File

Saving a file on disk preserves it (as permanently as possible, given the imperfections of electronic storage media) so that you can work with it again. The first time you save a file, you also have the opportunity to give the file a unique name. Project 2000 enables you to take advantage of Windows 95 and 98 long file names. You can enter up to 255 characters, including spaces; however, keep in mind that the 255 characters must include the path, slashes, and so on. Therefore, the real limitation for the file name is closer to 230 characters. This enables you to create file names that are substantially more descriptive and useful than the old DOS 8-character names.

To save a file for the first time and give it the name of your choice, perform the following steps:

1. Choose File, Save. Alternately, you can press Ctrl+S, or click on the Save button on the Standard toolbar. (It's the third button from the left and looks like a floppy disk.) The Save As dialog box appears (see Figure 3.15).

2. Navigate to the drive and folder where you want to save the file, using the Save In drop-down list and the folders that appear below it. (Double-clicking on a folder icon opens that folder so you can store the file there.)

3. Type a name for the file in the File Name text box. Try to use something descriptive, even if it's lengthy, such as **Rider Bike Product Introduction**.

4. Click on the Save button to save the file.

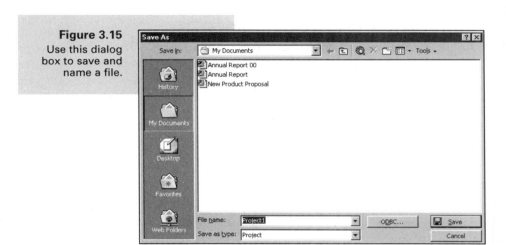

Figure 3.15
Use this dialog box to save and name a file.

After you save a file for the first time, you can save changes you make to it in the future by pressing Ctrl+S (or clicking on the Save button on the Standard toolbar).

There might be occasions, however, when you want to save a file with a new name. For example, if you have a lengthy project, you might want to save a version of the main project file at the end of each month, to keep a record of your progress and create a series of progressive backup copies of your file. In such a case, you must first save your file to ensure that the existing version reflects your most current changes. Next, reopen the Save As dialog box by choosing File, Save As. In the Save As dialog box, you can (but don't have to) change the selected folder to specify a new location for the renamed file. Then type the new name, such as **March 01 Rider Bike Product Introduction**, and click on Save to finish creating the new version of the file.

Tip

Each time you use Save As, you create a new copy of your file and leave the older version intact on disk. You might use Save As daily to copy a file, use it monthly to ensure you have a relatively up-to-date spare copy of the file, or even make copies to test the impact of changes you make to your schedule. I recommend you include the date in the file name (as in "My Project 5-1-00," "My Project 5-8-00," and so on). To create extra copies of your Project files, you also can use My Computer or Windows Explorer to copy and rename the file. Microsoft Project files with larger amounts of task and resource information might tend to become corrupted when you use Save As, so use My Computer or Windows Explorer to copy those files, instead.

File Protection and Backup Options

Part of the beauty of Project is that its files can be used easily in a networked environment. At any time, other team members can open the master plan for a project and review where things stand or update information about tasks as they are completed. The downside to this, of course, is that it is difficult to control who can view the file and how changes are made.

The Save As dialog box provides a method for applying some protection to files; you can protect files the first time you save them or after the fact. Open the Save As dialog box by choosing File, Save the first time you save the file, or by choosing File, Save As for existing files. If necessary, specify the folder where the file should be saved, and then enter the file name. Next, click on the Tools button, and then choose General Options in the menu that appears to open the Save Options dialog box (see Figure 3.16).

If you want Project to automatically create a backup copy of the file each time you save it, click on the Always Create Backup check box to check it.

Create a Protection Password if you want users to enter a password to be able to open the file. Enter a Write Reservation Password if you want to allow users to view a read-only version of the file without a password but want to require a password for a user to be able to edit the file and save the edited version.

Caution

Passwords in Project are case-sensitive. Be careful to record the correct password and its capitalization in a secure location.

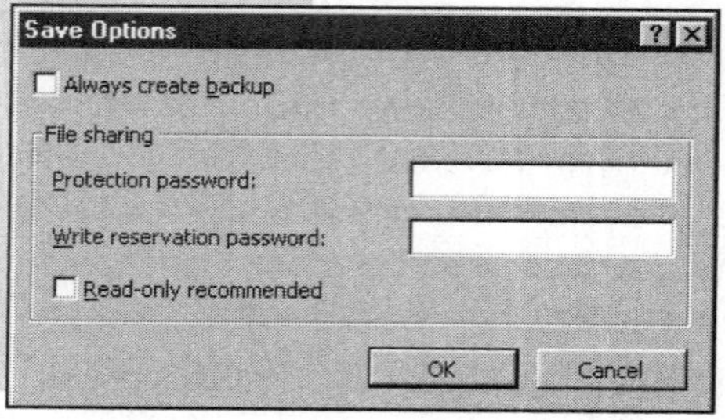

Figure 3.16
Protect your files, especially when they are on a network, by specifying a password protection and backup option.

Save Options

☐ Always create backup

File sharing

Protection password: [   ]

Write reservation password: [   ]

☐ Read-only recommended

[OK]   [Cancel]

Click on the Read-Only Recommended check box if you want Project to display a dialog box giving the user the option of opening a read-only version of the file each time it is opened.

After you specify any desired save options, click on OK. If you specify a new password (or change a password), Project asks you to enter the password again to verify it. Do so, and then click on OK. Click on Save to close the Save As dialog box and put your protection options in place.

If you ever want to make changes to the specified protection options—for example, change a password—just open the file, reopen the Save Options dialog box, and make whatever changes you want. To remove a password, double-click it to select the whole password, and then press Backspace or Delete. Click on OK and then on Save to finalize the changes and return to your project file.

Saving and Opening a Workspace

You might encounter situations where you regularly need to work with several Project files at once. For example, if you frequently copy information between two project files (such as one for all tasks in your group and one for a specific project), it might be more convenient to have them open automatically and appear side by side onscreen. You might even want to have each file appear in a particular view.

Project allows you to save such an onscreen configuration of multiple files and settings as a *workspace*. To reopen multiple files, position them precisely onscreen, and specify the appropriate views and settings, all you have to do is open a single workspace file.

Note

Workspace files have a different file name extension to help the Open dialog box distinguish them from regular Project files.

To create a workspace file:

1. Open all the project files that you want to include in the workspace.
2. Arrange the files onscreen (as covered in the next section), and specify the appropriate view for each file. (Views are covered where they apply throughout the book. They are also covered in detail in Chapter 11, "Working with the Different Project Views.")

Figure 3.17
Create a workspace so you can easily open multiple files.

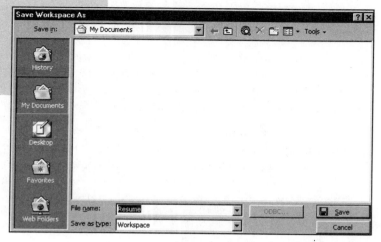

3. Choose File, Save Workspace. The Save Workspace As dialog box appears, with Workspace automatically selects as the Save As Type choice (see Figure 3.17).

4. Select the folder where you want to save the workspace file by using the Save In list and double-clicking on folders as needed below the list.

5. Type a name for the workspace in the File Name text box. (By default, Project suggests the name "Resume," but you can enter any name you want.)

6. Click on Save to finish saving the workspace.

Opening a workspace is virtually identical to opening a file. Use any of three methods: choose File, Open; press Ctrl+O; or click on the Open button on the Standard toolbar. In the Open dialog box, navigate to the folder where the workspace file is saved. Click on the down arrow to open the Files Of Type drop-down list, and select Workspaces from the list. When you see the name of the workspace file you want opened, double-click on the name.

Selecting, Arranging, and Closing Files

Each time you open a file in Project, it remains open until you specifically close it after you finish working with it (and presumably after you save it). If you're viewing each open file at full-screen size (maximized), the easiest way to switch

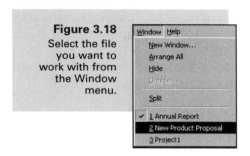

Figure 3.18
Select the file you want to work with from the Window menu.

between open files is to use the Window menu. To choose which file to display, open the Window menu and click on the name of the file you want to select (see Figure 3.18). (You can also click on the button for the file on the Windows taskbar.)

Notice that the Window menu offers some other useful options:

- **New Window** opens a new window of an open file. This option enables you, for example, to show two different views of the same file onscreen.
- **Arrange All** arranges all the open files and windows so that they fill the screen, with each file at least partially visible.
- **Hide** hides the currently selected file or window; this is handy if you want a file out of view during your lunch break, for example.
- **Unhide** displays a list of hidden windows so that you can redisplay one.
- **Split** breaks the current file into two panes so that you can display different areas of a file simultaneously.

After you finish working with a particular file and save it, you should close the file so that it is no longer consuming system memory. To close the current file, choose File, Close.

Turning on Auto Save

The Microsoft folks have added a long-overdue feature in Project 2000: Auto Save. When you turn on Auto Save, Project will save your file at an interval you designate, whether it's every 5 minutes or every 20 minutes. This protects your files against losses that might be caused by power fluctuations or system crashes.

To turn on Auto Save, choose Tools, Options. Click on the Save tab in the Options dialog box that appears. Click on the Save Every check box to check it, and then enter an interval in the Minutes text box. Choose either the Save Active Project Only or Save All Open Project Files button. I also recommend that you click on the Prompt Before Saving check box to clear the check in it. Otherwise, you'll have to confirm every Auto Save operation. Click on OK to close the Options dialog box and apply your Auto Save settings.

Exiting Project

When you finish with your work in Project, you can close the program in any of several ways:

- Press Alt+F4.
- Click on the Close box in the upper-right corner of the Project application window.
- Choose File, Exit.

If you haven't saved your work before you try to close Project, Project asks whether or not you want to save your changes. Click on Yes to do so, or on No to exit without saving.

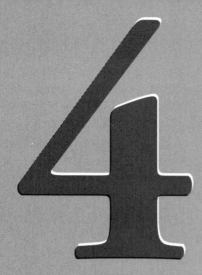

Setting Up a Project

IN THIS CHAPTER

- Establishing an overall schedule for your project
- Controlling the base calendar schedule for the project
- Defining each task in the schedule
- Working with the order of the tasks
- Setting up milestones
- Understanding file properties

Traditionally, when you were assigned a new activity on the job, one of the first things you did.was sit down with a yellow notepad and compile a to-do list. You made notes about steps you needed to take to complete the whole project and perhaps sketched out schedules for individual assignments. As you completed each step, you simply scratched the item off your list and adjusted subsequent deadlines as needed.

The first step of the planning process in Project 2000 resembles the yellow pad method. You begin by mapping out your time frame and the tasks to be completed.

Managing Project Start and End Dates

As discussed in Chapter 3, "Working with Files and Help," the Project Information dialog box appears (see Figure 4.1) each time you start a new project file by choosing File, New. You use this dialog box to work with the overall time schedule for your project.

The first two text boxes in the dialog box are Start Date and Finish Date. Initially, the Start Date entry displays the system date for your computer, and the Finish Date entry is grayed out (disabled). That's because you enter only one of these dates; Project calculates the other one for you based on the tasks you enter for the project and how long each task lasts. So to determine how the duration of your schedule is calculated, you can use one of the following two methods:

- **Have Project calculate the Finish Date.** Leave Project Start Date as the Schedule From selection, and change the Start Date entry, if needed.

- **Have Project calculate the Start Date.** Click on the arrow beside the Schedule From drop-down list, and select Project Finish Date. Then, edit

Figure 4.1
Use the Project Information dialog box to establish overall timing for your project.

Project Information for 'Project1'		
Start date:	Thu 6/1/00	
Finish date:	Thu 6/1/00	
Schedule from:	Project Start Date	
	All tasks begin as soon as possible.	
Current date:	Thu 6/1/00	
Status date:	NA	
Calendar:	Standard	
Priority:	500	
Help	Statistics...	OK Cancel

the Finish Date entry. However, you should note that with this method, Project schedules all tasks to occur as late as possible, which may not be the scheduling method you prefer.

When you enter or edit either Start Date or Finish Date, you can type the date in m/dd/yy or mm/dd/yy format in the appropriate text box. You don't need to enter the abbreviation for the day of the week; Project specifies it after you finish making changes to the Project Info settings.

If you type the date, however, you need to have a calendar at hand to ensure you type the correct date—for a Monday rather than a Sunday, for example. Project provides a method for entering dates more easily, though. When you see a down arrow at the right end of any text box that holds a date (in the Project Information dialog box and others throughout Project), click on the arrow to display a calendar you can use to select a date. For example, Figure 4.2 shows the calendar that opens when you click on the down arrow beside the Start Date text box. Click on one of the arrows near the top of the calendar to display an earlier or later month. You also can click on the month or year at the top of the calendar to change it. If you click on the month name, a drop-down list of months appears, in which you can click on the desired month. If you click on the year, spinner buttons appear; click on one of them to change the year, then click elsewhere on the calendar. After you display the correct calendar for the month and year, click on a date to choose it and close the calendar.

The Current Date text box allows you to calibrate your project schedule with the actual calendar. Each time you open the Project Information dialog box, Project uses the system date from your computer as the current date. By default, however, the dates used to schedule all new tasks you add to the project will be the Start Date or Finish Date you specified (depending on which of those entries Project

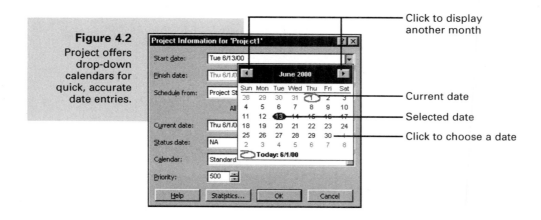

Figure 4.2
Project offers drop-down calendars for quick, accurate date entries.

is calculating for you). For example, if you chose Project Finish Date for the Schedule From entry and entered 6/9/00 as the Finish Date, the tasks you entered will be scheduled with a finish date of 6/9/00, regardless of the Current Date entry. Conversely, if you're scheduling the project from the Start Date and enter 6/1/00 as the Start Date entry, Project schedules all new tasks you enter with a start date of 6/1/00. You can instead use the Current Date entry to schedule the start date for new tasks you enter into the project plan. See the later section called "Scheduling Tasks from the Current Date" to learn how this works.

The last two settings that you really need to adjust when you set up your new project are the Calendar and Priority settings. (For information on setting and working with a Status Date, see Chapter 9, "Comparing Progress versus Your Baseline Plan.") The Calendar setting determines the base calendar, or the working hours and days for the project. This calendar determines the number of hours per week available in the project schedule. (You also need to specify the working schedule for each resource as explained in Chapter 6, "Managing Resources.") You can select one of the following choices from the Calendar drop-down list:

- **Standard.** This choice, the default, assigns corporate America's standard work week to the project. The project schedule is based on a Monday through Friday work week, with daily working hours of 8 A.M. to noon and 1 P.M. to 5 P.M.—thus, each workday is eight hours and each work week is 40 hours.

- **24 Hours.** If you make this selection, the schedule is continuous. Each workday is 24 hours long, and work is scheduled seven days a week.

- **Night Shift.** This option provides a schedule based on a 40-hour night shift week as scheduled in many companies, from Monday evening through Saturday morning:

Days	Scheduled working hours
Mondays	11 P.M. to 12 A.M.
Tuesday through Friday	12 A.M. to 3 A.M.
	4 A.M. to 8 A.M.
	11 P.M. to 12 A.M.
Saturdays	12 A.M. to 3 A.M.
	4 A.M. to 8 A.M.

Project uses the Priority setting in the Project Information dialog box in instances where you share resources between project files and use Project's automated features for adjusting assignments so particular resources aren't overbooked. (I'll get into those features more in later chapters, because they're intermediate-to-advanced in

Note

The number of working hours per day is important because it affects how Project calculates the schedule for a task. For example, if you estimate that a certain task will take 24 hours under the Standard calendar, Project assigns that task three workdays. Under a 24-hour calendar, the task gets a single day. Unless your resources truly will be working 24 hours a day, selecting 24 Hours as the Calendar setting can cause Project to underestimate the schedule drastically. The section titled "Adjusting the Project Base Calendar" in this chapter explains how you can customize a calendar in Project.

nature.) You can specify a Priority setting of between 1 and 1000 by typing the setting you want into the dialog box. Or, you can click on the spinner buttons beside the text box to change the setting. A higher Priority setting means that the project file will have more importance when it shares resources with other project files. If you tell Project to find and fix overbooked resources in the files sharing those resources, Project will tend not to remove resources from or change task scheduling in the files with the highest Priority settings.

After you make your final choices, click on OK to close the Project Information dialog box.

Changing Project Information

After you create project information, it's by no means set in stone. You can reopen the Project Information dialog box at any time to make changes to the options there. In addition, you might want to check the calculated Start Date or Finish Date for the schedule after you specify actual start and finish dates for particular tasks. To view or change schedule information, choose Project, Project Information. When the Project Information dialog box appears, make any changes that you want, and then click on OK to close the dialog box.

Be careful when making changes to the settings in the Project Information dialog box after you add tasks to the schedule. For example, selecting a different Calendar can have a drastic effect on your project's timeline. Also, if you make a change to the project Start Date or Finish Date and have tasks that you marked as finished or that you set up to start or end on a specific date that falls outside the new overall schedule (see Chapters 9 and 5, respectively), Project will warn you after you click on OK in the Project Information dialog box (see Figure 4.3). You can click on OK and then reschedule individual tasks to fit within the new schedule, or click Cancel and choose a new start or finish date.

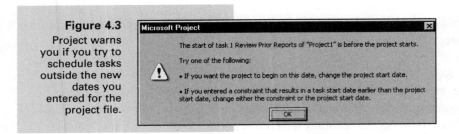

Figure 4.3
Project warns you if you try to schedule tasks outside the new dates you entered for the project file.

Viewing Project Statistics

Project provides numerous ways to review the information you entered for a project. In fact, it automatically tracks particular project statistics for you, so you can review the overall status at a glance in the Project Statistics dialog box (see Figure 4.4).

Project Statistics button on the Tracking toolbar

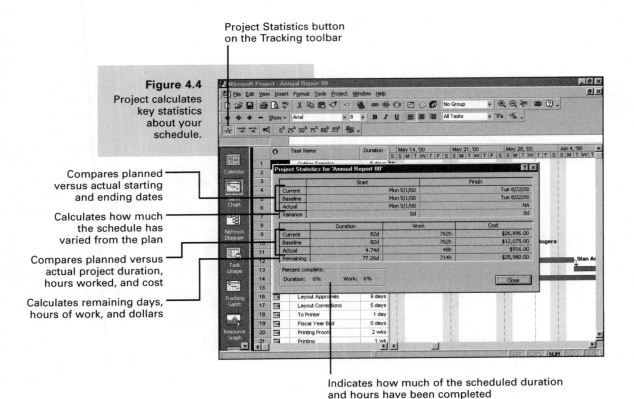

Figure 4.4
Project calculates key statistics about your schedule.

Compares planned versus actual starting and ending dates

Calculates how much the schedule has varied from the plan

Compares planned versus actual project duration, hours worked, and cost

Calculates remaining days, hours of work, and dollars

Indicates how much of the scheduled duration and hours have been completed

You can open the Project Statistics dialog box using either of two methods:

- Display the Tracking toolbar by right-clicking on any onscreen toolbar and then clicking on Tracking. Click on the Project Statistics button at the far left on the Tracking toolbar.
- Choose Project, Project Information. Click on the Statistics button in the Project Information dialog box.

Project does not allow you to edit or print the information in the Project Statistics dialog box. When you finish viewing the information, click on the Close button to exit the dialog box.

Tip

Although Project won't print the Project Statistics dialog box information directly, you can print a report that does include the information—the Project Summary report in the Overview category of reports. After you've built your project file, see Chapter 14, "Creating and Printing a Report," to learn how to print reports.

Adjusting the Project Base Calendar

As you just learned, when you create a new project file, you assign a base calendar for the schedule using the Calendar drop-down list in the Project Information dialog box. Thus, unless you select the 24 Hours base calendar, each workday in the schedule is eight hours long, and it takes three working days to complete a 24-hour task.

There might be instances, however, when you want to change the working calendar slightly. For example, if the project you are tracking is a plan for some kind of special event that takes place on a Saturday, you need to make that Saturday a working day. If you want certain workdays to be 10 hours long, you can make that change. Or you can mark company holidays as nonworking days if you need to do so. This section explains how to alter the base calendar for your project schedule.

Caution

Make sure that you specify base calendar changes before you begin building your project schedule to ensure that a calendar change doesn't cause unpredictable results. In addition, under the default method of resource-driven scheduling, if you assigned a special calendar to a resource, that calendar overrides your base calendar. Be sure that you make the same changes to custom resource calendars, when needed, to keep them in sync with the base calendar.

Note

You can use Project's options to change the default workday and work week schedule no matter what base calendar you assign to each file. For example, you can specify a different day as the start of the work week, or specify that the Default Start Time for each working day is 7 A.M. Of course, you should edit the project base calendar or the custom calendar you're using for the project to match, because the default Options settings will override the calendar if you don't. To access these settings (described in Chapter 24, "Customizing Microsoft Project"), click on the Options button in the Change Working Time dialog box or choose Tools, Options, and then click on the Calendar tab. Just make sure that you change the Calendar options and the base calendar *before* you enter task information. Changing either after the fact can unexpectedly change task durations and ruin your careful scheduling.

Changing Working Hours or Adding a Day Off

Project gives you the flexibility to change the working hours for any day in any base calendar, or to specify any day as a nonworking day. (I do, however, recommend that you instead create your own custom base calendar as described under "Creating a Custom Calendar," to leave the original calendars intact and to skip the step of having to add vacation and holiday information in every Project file, because the following steps apply the calendar changes to the current file only.) To do so, follow these steps:

1. In Gantt Chart view, choose Tools, Change Working Time. The Change Working Time dialog box appears, as shown in Figure 4.5.

Figure 4.5
Use this dialog box to make changes to a calendar schedule.

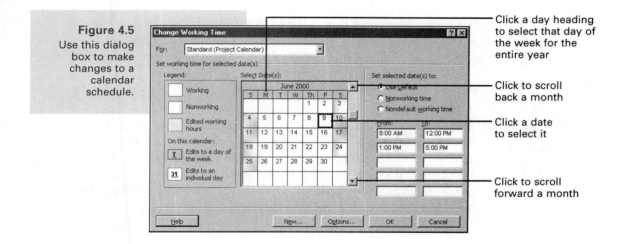

Click a day heading to select that day of the week for the entire year

Click to scroll back a month

Click a date to select it

Click to scroll forward a month

2. Open the For drop-down list to select the calendar you'd like to edit, if needed.

3. To select a date on the calendar, use the scroll bar beside the calendar to display the month containing the date you want to adjust, and then click on the date. Or, if you want to select a particular day of the week for the entire year, click on the day column heading. For example, click on F to choose every Friday for the entire year. You also can drag across the day headings to select more than one day, or Monday through Friday, for example.

4. To specify the selected date or dates as nonworking, click on Nonworking Time in the Set Selected Date(s) To area of the dialog box. Dates you specify as Nonworking should include holidays, vacation days, and other times when no work can be scheduled on the project.

The Use Default choice returns selected dates to the default working hours or non-working time specified in the Calendar tab of the Options dialog box (not the default for the base calendar). So here's the best sequence to follow. First set the Calendar tab settings in the Options dialog box. Then copy one of the base calendars that Project provides to create a custom calendar, using the Use Default button to set selected dates to match the Calendar options. Then, if you really flub the calendar or mistakenly click on the Use Default button, you always can go back to the original base calendar and start anew.

5. To change the Working Time (daily working hours) for the selected date or dates, click on the Nondefault Working Time choice under Set Selected Date(s) To. Then edit or delete the desired From and To entries.

6. Continue editing the calendar as needed, repeating Steps 3 through 5 to change the schedule for additional dates. As you change the schedule for each date, Project marks the edited date in the calendar with bold and underlined lettering and light-gray shading. (When you edit a day of the week for the whole calendar, an underline appears under the day abbreviation in the day column head.)

7. Click on OK to close the Change Working Time dialog box and implement the scheduling changes you made.

Creating a Custom Calendar

It's a good idea not to make your changes to the actual base calendar you selected for a project file—keep it as a neutral starting form, so you can use it again. Instead, save your changes in a custom calendar, then select that calendar for the project. (The resources you assign to the project can also use the custom calendar.) To create a custom calendar, follow these steps:

1. In Gantt Chart view, choose Tools, Change Working Time. The Change Working Time dialog box appears.

2. Click on the New button. The Create New Base Calendar dialog box appears, as shown in Figure 4.6.

3. Because the Name text is highlighted, you can simply type a new name for the custom schedule.

4. Below the Name text box, click an option button to select whether you want to create a new base calendar or make a copy of an existing base calendar. If you opt to copy a calendar, which is the default setting, select the desired base calendar from the Calendar drop-down list.

5. Click on OK. Project returns to the Change Working Time dialog box, where the custom calendar you created appears as the For drop-down list selection.

6. Make any schedule changes you want for your custom calendar, as described in the preceding set of steps.

7. Click on OK to close the Change Working Time dialog box.

8. Choose Project, Project Information to display the Project Information dialog box.

9. Open the Calendar drop-down list, and choose the newly-created calendar.

10. Click OK to close the dialog box and apply the new calendar.

Figure 4.6
Copy an existing calendar or create a custom calendar so that you leave Project's original calendars intact.

Adding and Deleting Tasks

After you set up the overall parameters for the schedule, you're ready to begin entering the individual "jobs" that need to be done. This phase of building the project blueprint is most analogous to jotting down a to-do list, with each task roughly equating to a to-do item.

Note

Technically, Project considers your list of tasks the *Work Breakdown Structure*. As you become more comfortable with Project, you can use its outlining features to outline the list of tasks, grouping tasks in more logical stages of work. See Chapter 15, "Working with Outlining," to learn more about organizing the WBS.

Generally, you add tasks to the schedule in the default Gantt Chart view. In this view, enter basic information about each task in the Task Sheet, located just to the right of the View Bar.

As shown in Figure 4.7, the Task Sheet resembles a spreadsheet grid. You enter information about each task in a single row in the Task Sheet. You can use the scroll bar at the bottom of the Task Sheet to display more columns; each column, also called a *field,* holds a particular type of information.

By default the Task Sheet displays the Entry table. Each table is a particular set of the available fields in Project; the section called "Choosing a Table" in Chapter 11, "Working with the Different Project Views," gives you more information about

Figure 4.7
Enter tasks in the Task Sheet.

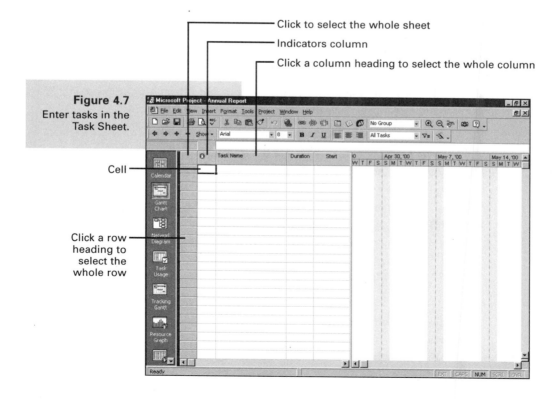

the available tables and how to display one in the Task Sheet. But the default Task Sheet (with the Entry table displayed) includes these fields:

- **Indicators (i).** This column holds small icons called *indicators* that provide information about the current task. For example, if you add a note to a task, as described later in this section, a note indicator appears in the indicators field for the task. (You'll learn more about the various indicators later in this section and in later chapters where they apply.) You can't enter information in this column; Project automatically displays and removes applicable indicators as needed.

- **Task Name.** This column holds the descriptive label you assign to identify each task. Use names that are recognizable enough to differentiate individual tasks. The name can include spaces as well as upper- and lowercase characters. And, although the name can include more than 100 characters, as a rule you should stick with names that are as brief and descriptive as possible.

- **Duration.** This column holds the time you're allowing for the completion of each task. If you enter no duration, Project assumes a default duration of one day (1d). Project assumes other durations to be in days unless you specify otherwise (see "Using Differing Durations" later in this chapter).

- **Start.** This column holds the date that work is scheduled to begin on for a particular task. Unless you specify otherwise, Project assumes this date is the project Start Date (or it's calculated from the Finish Date if you opted to schedule the project from its finish date) specified in the Project Information dialog box. So, unless you want Project to use a default or calculated date, you need to enter a specific date in the Start field for a task.

When you change the date that Project is calculating (the date in either the Start or Finish column for the task in the Task Sheet, depending on whether the project is set up to calculate from the project start or finish date, as specified in the Project Information dialog box), Project automatically changes the Task Sheet Duration field for the task to reflect your change. For example, say that you enter a Duration of one day (1d) for a task that's being calculated from a Start of 2/9/00. If you change the date in the Finish column from 2/9/00 to 2/11/00, Project changes the duration to 3d.

Caution

In general, you don't want to make entries in the Start or Finish column for any task. Let Project calculate these entries for you as you link tasks and otherwise build the schedule.

- **Finish.** This column holds the date when work on each task is to be completed. If you specified that Project should schedule tasks from the starting date in the Project Information dialog box, then the date in this column is automatically calculated based on the entries in the Duration and Start columns. In other words, you don't have to make an entry in this field when you're building the schedule. Project will calculate it for you. (On the other hand, if Project is scheduling tasks from the ending date, then the date in the Start column is calculated and you should make entries in the Duration and Finish Date columns.) If you will be using linking to establish task relationships as described in "Linking and Unlinking Tasks" in Chapter 5, "Fine-Tuning Tasks," Project will even calculate the Start Date for some tasks for you.

- **Predecessors.** This column indicates when a task is linked to one or more preceding tasks. Project can fill in this column for you, or you can use this column to establish links.

- **Resource Names.** This column enables you to enter one or more resources (team member, outside contractor, and so on) responsible for completing a task. Chapter 6, "Managing Resources," explains how to create resources for use in your schedule.

Entering tasks in the Task Sheet works much like making spreadsheet entries. Although later chapters cover some of the entries for a task in more detail, here's an overview of the steps for creating a task:

1. Click on the cell in the Task Name column of the first available row in the Task Sheet. Clicking selects the cell and prepares it for your entry. Alternately, you can press Tab to move from the Indicators column to the Task Name column.

2. Type the name of the task. For example, you might type a name such as **Develop Theme Proposal.** As you type, the text appears in the entry box above the Task Sheet, as shown in Figure 4.8. To complete the entry, press Tab, or click on the Enter button with the green check mark (beside the Entry box above the Task Sheet); then click on the next cell to the right in the Duration column. Clicking on the Cancel button instead of the Enter button stops the entry altogether.

Tip

To quickly enter a list of tasks, press Enter after each task name you create. Project assigns each task a 1 day duration and the default Start Date, although the Duration column displays 1 day?, with the question mark reminding you to adjust the default duration, if needed, at a later time. You also can adjust the other entries.

Figure 4.8
You can accept
or cancel the
entry you make
in any cell.

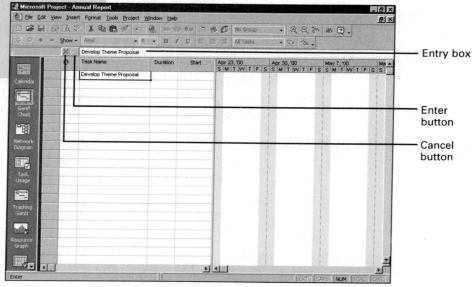

3. Type a number, such as 3, for the new duration entry. Alternately, click one of the spinner buttons that appear at the right side of the Duration cell to increase or decrease the value. The new entry appears in the Entry box as you type. Unless you include more duration information, as described later in the section "Using Differing Durations," Project assumes the duration to be in days. To finish the entry, press Tab; alternately, you can click on the Enter button, scroll to the right, and then click on the Start cell for the task. (If you're working on a task that you later plan to link to other tasks, allowing Project to calculate the Start Date, you can enter the Duration and stop right here or go on to Step 6.)

4. The Start cell is selected. To let Project schedule everything for you, press Tab twice to skip this cell and the Finish cell, then skip to Step 6. However, if a task must or can't start until a particular date, type the desired starting date in mm/dd/yy format and click on the Enter button. Alternately, click on the down arrow that appears beside the Start cell to display a calendar, and use the calendar as needed to choose a month and day. This finishes the basic task creation and creates a bar for the task in the Gantt Chart pane on the right side of the screen (see Figure 4.9). If Project is set to automatically calculate backward (based on the ending date, which by default is the Project Finish Date in the Project Info dialog box), do not change the Start column entry; go to Step 5.

Figure 4.9
Project creates a
Gantt Chart bar
to represent your
task graphically
on the schedule.

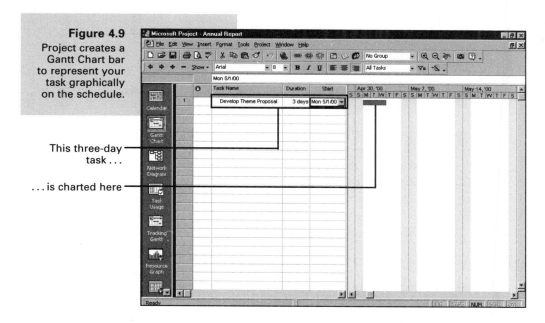

This three-day
task . . .

. . . is charted here

Note

When you enter a task's specific Start Date as described in Step 4, Project
assigns the *Start No Earlier Than* constraint to the task, meaning that
Project will not reschedule the task for you based on calculations or links
you create. You can either manually remove the constraint (see "Setting
Task Constraints" in Chapter 5), or opt not to enter a Start Date for each
task and then use linking to schedule tasks (see "Linking and Unlinking
Tasks" in Chapter 5).

5. Press Tab (or scroll, and then click on the Finish cell for that task). Type
   the desired ending date in mm/dd/yy format and click on the Enter
   button to complete it. Alternately, click on the down arrow that appears
   on the Finish cell to display a calendar, and then click on the calendar to
   choose the month and day.

6. (Optional) Make entries in the Predecessors and Resources cells, as
   described in Chapters 5 and 6. Press Tab or click on the Resources cell after
   your Predecessors entry. Note that when you select a cell in the Resources
   column, a down arrow appears. After you add resources to the project, as
   described in Chapter 6, you can simply click this down arrow and click
   one of the available resources in the list to select that resource for the task.
   Go to Step 7 after you make the Resources entry.

7. To create the next task, you need to move to the next row of the Task Sheet. To do so, scroll and click to select the first cell (the Task Name cell) in the next row; alternately, you can press Enter, and then press Ctrl+Left Arrow (or the Home key) to select that cell.

8. Repeat Steps 2 through 7 as many times as needed to enter all the tasks for your project.

As you enter tasks, Project numbers them in the row heading area, starting with task 1. Based on all the tasks you create and the durations you enter for them, Project calculates the total schedule for the project. To check the total schedule, choose Project, Project Information. The Project Information dialog box will then include the calculated Start Date or Finish Date, which will be grayed out to tell you it's a calculated value.

Scheduling Tasks from the Current Date

Most project schedules occur in stages or evolve over time. For example, you may have a lengthy group of tasks that begin a few weeks after the Start Date. Or you may want to add tasks that start on the Current Date rather than the Start Date if the Start Date was a week or two ago. If you tell Project to schedule new tasks from the Current Date rather than the Project Start Date, it saves you the step of editing Start Date entries when you create tasks.

By default, Project takes the Current Date setting from the system date kept by your computer's system clock. You can, however, change the Current Date to any date that you want: a month ago or a month forward, for example. Then you change an option for the current project file to specify that Project should schedule new tasks from the Current Date. After you take both those actions, Project will schedule each new task you add into the Task Sheet from the Current Date that you set up, assuming that date isn't earlier than the project Start Date.

Follow these steps to set up Project to schedule new tasks from the Current Date:

1. Choose Project, Project Information.

2. Change the Current Date entry to the desired date.

3. Click on OK to close the dialog box.

4. Choose Tools, Options.

5. Click on the Schedule tab.

6. Open the New Tasks drop-down list in the Scheduling Options For area of the dialog box and choose Start on Current Date. (You would choose Start on Project Start Date to return to the default scheduling method.)

7. Click on OK. At this point, Project will schedule all new tasks you add in the Task Sheet with a Start Date of the Current Date you specified in Steps 1 through 3.

Displaying a Project Summary Task

As you'll learn in Chapter 15, "Working with Outlining," you can organize the tasks in the Task Sheet using outlining tools like those found in Microsoft Word. Ideally, you would think about outlining as you build the task list and outline before you link tasks, but I can't cram each and every task entry feature into this one chapter. So, the outlining discussion will have to wait a bit.

But, you may want to turn on one special outline feature right from the beginning of the project—the *project summary task.* The project summary task appears as task 0 in the list of tasks, so you won't confuse it with other tasks in the list. The project summary task summarizes the overall length of the project; its Start Date is the Start Date for the earliest task, and its Finish Date is the Finish Date for the latest task. So the project summary task provides you with another means of viewing the overall project schedule.

To display the project summary task, choose Tools, Options. The Options dialog box appears. Click on the View tab, if needed. In the Outline Options For area near the bottom of the dialog box, click on the Project Summary Task choice to check it. Click on OK to close the Options dialog box. As Figure 4.10 illustrates,

Figure 4.10
The project summary task appears as task 0 and shows you the overall project schedule at a glance.

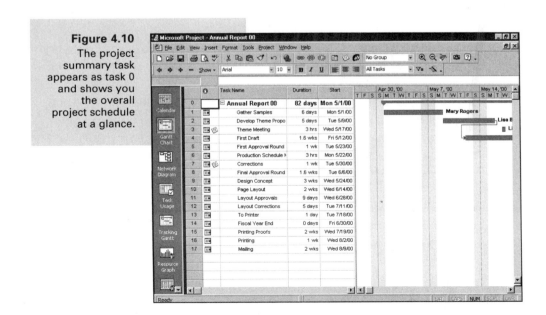

the project summary task appears as task 0 and displays information about the overall project Duration, Start Date, and so on. Also notice that the project summary task uses a special type of bar on the Gantt Chart at the right side of the view. You'll learn more about summary Gantt bars like this in Chapter 15.

The project summary task initially uses the project file name as its Task Name. You can edit the project summary task Task Name to make it more descriptive, if you wish. Continue to the next subsection to learn how to edit tasks.

Editing a Task

No matter how well-formulated a business plan is, you can count on it to change. For example, you might start out using somewhat generic names for your tasks— or even code names. Later, after the project is announced, you might want to replace the temporary names with the real project names. Or, after consulting a particular resource, you might discover that you overestimated the time required to complete a particular task, so you might want to change the duration you specified for that task.

To edit any of the cell entries for a task, click to select the cell you want to edit. Use one of the following methods to make your changes:

- To replace the cell entry completely, start typing. Whatever you type completely replaces the previous entry. Click on the Enter button when you finish making the replacement entry.

- If spinner buttons or a down arrow appear, use them to change the entry as described earlier in the steps at the beginning of this section, "Adding and Deleting Tasks."

- To make changes to only part of an entry, click to position the insertion point in the entry box, or drag to highlight the text you want to replace. Type your changes. After you place the insertion point in the entry box, you can edit text as you would in most word processors, using the arrow keys, Backspace, and more. When you finish making your changes, click on the Enter button.

- To edit the entry directly in the cell, press the F2 key or double-click on the cell to enter an Edit Mode (as with other Microsoft products), so you can type your changes. Press Enter when you finish making the changes.

Using Differing Durations

As you've seen, when you assign a duration for a particular task, Project by default interprets that duration in terms of days. Each day consists of a full day's worth of working hours, depending on the base calendar you set for the schedule using the Calendar drop-down list in the Project Information dialog box. So, if your project is based on the 24 Hours calendar, each day of duration consists of 24 working hours; on the Standard calendar, each day of duration consists of 8 working hours.

For the Night Shift base calendar, each "day" of duration is eight hours—but each working day spans two calendar days. For example, a task that begins on a Friday and is scheduled to last 1d starts Friday at 11 P.M., when the working day starts, and spans to 3 A.M. on Saturday. After a one-hour lunch break, the workday and task continue from 4 A.M. to 8 A.M., which is the end of the shift.

Note

Under the Night Shift Calendar, keep in mind that when you enter a start date for a task, Project schedules the task for the workday that begins at 11 P.M. of that start date and runs over to the next day. Thus, if you want work to be completed on a task during the early morning hours of a given day (12 A.M. to 3 A.M. and 4 A.M. to 8 A.M.), specify the preceding date as the start date for the task.

Obviously, not every task requires 8 to 24 hours. Likewise, not every task is completed within the bounds of the workday hours (as much as we wish they all would be). For example, if you want to include a key meeting on your schedule, it's likely you only need to block out a few hours for it, not an entire day. On the other hand, if you expect a supplier to work during the weekend to deliver a product, or you know something will be shipped to you during a weekend, you need to schedule a task outside normal working hours.

Project enables you to control the exact amount of time a task will take to finish, based on the abbreviation, or *duration label,* you include with the entry in the Duration column of the Task Sheet. Some duration abbreviations are for *elapsed durations,* where you specify work according to a 24-hour, seven-day-per-week calendar even though that isn't the base calendar for the project. To specify the new duration, enter the correct abbreviation along with your numeric entry. Table 4.1 lists the basic abbreviations or duration labels.

Table 4.1 Duration Labels (Abbreviations)

Time Unit	Abbreviations	Example
Minutes	M	30m means 30 working minutes
	Min	
	Mins	
Hours	H	30h means 30 working hours
	Hr	
	Hrs	
	Hour	
Days	D	30d means 30 working days
	Dy	
	Day	
Weeks	W	30w means 30 working weeks
	Wk	
	Week	
Months	Mo	2mo means 2 working months
	Mons	
	Months	
Elapsed minutes	Em	30em means 30 consecutive elapsed minutes
	Emin	
	Emins	
Elapsed hours	Eh	30eh means 30 consecutive elapsed hours
	Ehr	
	Ehrs	
	Ehour	
Elapsed days	Ed	30ed means 30 consecutive elapsed days
	Edy	
	Eday	
Elapsed weeks	Ew	30ew means 30 consecutive elapsed weeks
	Ewk	
	Eweek	
Elapsed months	Emo	2emo means 40 consecutive elapsed days*
	Emons	
	Emonths	

*Assumes that you've specified each month to be 20 working days using the Calendar tab of the Options dialog box in Project.

Project also offers smart duration labels, making it even easier for you to enter durations. Basically, this feature enables you to make slight "mistakes" when you enter duration labels. For example, if you inadvertently include a space and enter 5 h instead of 5h, Project can still correctly interpret your entry as 5 hrs (five hours).

● ●

Tip

Project 2000 also enables you to indicate when you've estimated a Duration entry. If you include a question mark at the end of your entry, as in **2w?**, Project displays the Duration as **2 wks?**, reminding you that the actual duration might vary dramatically and affect your schedule. You can *filter* the task list so that it shows all tasks with estimated durations, giving you a way to focus in on potential trouble spots in the schedule. Chapter 11, "Working with the Different Project Views," explains how to filter the Task and Resource Sheets.

● ●

When you enter an elapsed time, the Gantt Chart bars at the right reflect how the task falls in terms of real time. For example, Figure 4.11 compares the actual scheduled time for a task entered as three working days (3d) and a task entered as 24 elapsed hours (24eh). When scheduled as standard workdays, a 24-hour period covers three days; as elapsed hours, however, a 24-hour period occupies a single day on the Gantt Chart.

Figure 4.11
Elapsed times are scheduled consecutively.

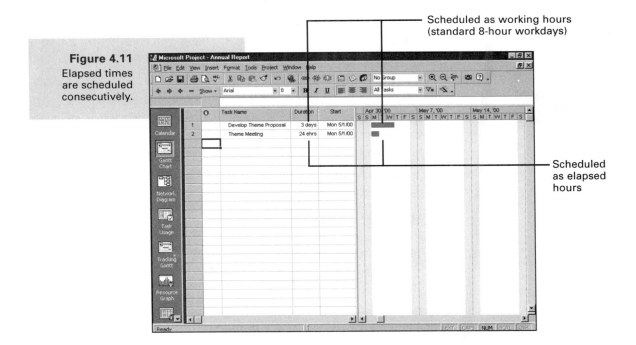

Selecting, Inserting, and Deleting Tasks

When you're creating any kind of business plan, you start with the overall framework and refine it as you go along, adding details as you flesh out some ideas and discard others. You might discover the need to adjust the framework for your project by adding new tasks to the Task Sheet as you discover that they're necessary, or dropping them as you determine that they're extraneous or already included within the scope of other items. Project gives you total flexibility in determining which tasks appear on the Task Sheet.

Use the following steps to add a task to your Task Sheet:

1. Select any cell in the row above which you want to insert a new task. To select the cell, use the scroll bars at the far right and bottom of the screen to display the cell, and then click in it. Alternatively, you can use the arrow keys to reach a cell in the appropriate row.

2. Press the Insert key (or choose Insert, New Task) to insert a new blank row.

3. Enter information for the new task, as discussed earlier in this section.

Use the following steps to delete a particular task:

1. Select a cell in the row in the Task Sheet that holds the task. To select additional consecutive tasks after you select a cell in the first one, drag with the mouse or press Shift and an arrow key to extend the selection through all the tasks you want to delete. To select additional tasks that are noncontiguous, press and hold down Ctrl while you click in cells in additional rows.

• •

Tip You can click on the Select All button in the upper-left corner of the Task Sheet to select the entire Task Sheet. To select an entire task row, click on the task number in the row heading at the left side of the Task Sheet.

• •

2. Use one of the following methods to remove selected tasks:
   - Press the Delete key.
   - Choose Edit, Delete Task.
   - If you've selected the entire task row, right-click on the selected task to display a shortcut menu; then click on Delete Task (see Figure 4.12).

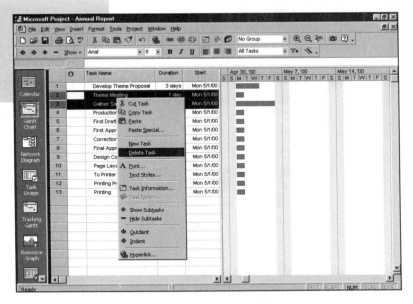

Figure 4.12
The shortcut menu speeds up the job of deleting or inserting tasks.

Caution

Project doesn't warn you about lost information when you choose to delete a task, even if other tasks are linked to the task you're deleting. If you mistakenly delete a task, immediately do any of the following: choose Edit, Undo; press Ctrl+Z; or click on the Undo button on the Standard toolbar. Be aware that deleting a task that's linked to other tasks can dramatically affect your schedule, causing Project to move tasks that followed the deleted task to a much earlier date, for example.

Note

Notice that the task shortcut menu also offers an Insert Task command. You can choose that command to insert a new task row above the currently selected task row.

Filling Table Entries

Project 2000 offers a great new feature that works just like a popular feature in Excel: the *fill* feature. You can use the fill feature to copy a cell entry in the Task

Sheet (or Resource Sheet) to cells below or to the right. For example, if you have a number of tasks that you expect to last two days apiece, you can fill that duration rather than typing it multiple times. You can fill either contiguous cells or cells scattered throughout the sheet, as described here:

- **Contiguous cells.** Make the entry to fill in the desired cell. With the cell selected, point to the black fill handle at the lower-right corner of the cell border until the mouse pointer changes to crosshairs. Drag the mouse in the direction to fill, such as down (see Figure 4.13), and release the mouse button when you've filled all the cells as needed.

- **Noncontiguous cells.** Again make the entry to fill in the desired cell and be sure to leave the cell selected. Press and hold the Ctrl key, and click on the other cells to which you want to fill the first entry. Then open the Edit menu, point to the Fill command, and click on the Down choice (or press Ctrl+D).

Note

You can create a series of entries and drag to fill (repeat) it. For example, you can enter **1d**, **2d**, and **3d** in three consecutive cells in the Duration column. Select all three cells by dragging over them, and *then* drag the fill handle to repeat all three entries.

ON THE

CD

I've included the **Annual Report Chapter 4** file on the CD-ROM for this book. After you install or copy it to your system's hard disk, you can use it to practice techniques such as filling task information, changing durations, moving and copying tasks, or even changing the calendar for the project.

Figure 4.13
Drag the fill handle to copy cell entries on the Task Sheet (or Resource Sheet).

	ⓘ	Task Name	Duration	Start
1		Develop Theme Proposal	3 days	Mon 5/1/00
2		Theme Meeting	1 day	Mon 5/1/00
3		Gather Samples	5 days	Mon 5/1/00
4		Production Schedule Meeti	1 day	Mon 5/1/00
5		First Draft	2 days	Mon 5/1/00
6		First Approval Round	1 day	Mon 5/1/00
7		Corrections	1 day	Mon 5/1/00
8		Final Approval Round	1 day	Mon 5/1/00
9		Design Concept	1 day	Mon 5/1/00
10		Page Layout	1 day	Mon 5/1/00
11		To Printer	1 day	Mon 5/1/00
12		Printing Proofs	1 day	Mon 5/1/00
13		Printing	1 day	Mon 5/1/00

— Fill handle

— Crosshair pointer

Moving and Copying Tasks

One of the many features that makes Project more efficient than a yellow pad for process planning is that you can easily change the order of the tasks on your list. There's no more endless renumbering or trying to figure out which arrow points where to indicate the final order of tasks.

The easiest way to move a task on the Task Sheet is by dragging the task information (see Figure 4.14). Click on the row number for the task you want to move; this selects the whole task. Point to one of the selection borders until the mouse pointer turns into an arrow; then click and drag the row into its new position. As you drag, a gray insertion bar indicates exactly where the task row will be inserted if you release the mouse button.

You can also drag and drop cells to move their contents. Point to the cell border until you see the white arrow mouse pointer, click and drag, and then release the mouse button to drop the cell into place. However, be sure you're doing what you want to do—if you drop the cell onto a cell that already holds an entry, the dropped cell contents overwrite the old cell contents.

Cut button

Copy button

Paste button

Figure 4.14
Dragging a task to a new location enables you to rearrange tasks quickly.

Gray insertion bar

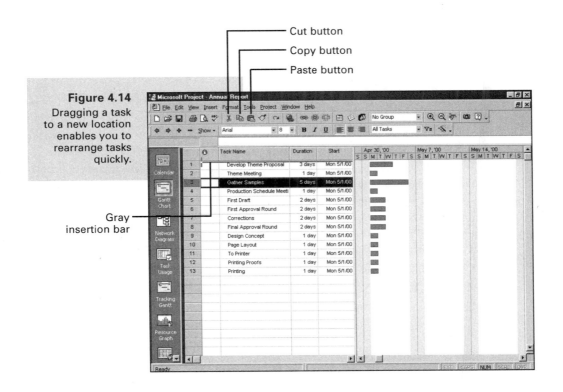

Dragging is convenient when the task you want to move is relatively close to the new location. It's a bit more difficult to drag a task into place, however, if you have to scroll other tasks to do so. Likewise, when you want to copy a task from one location to another, you need a different process to do the job. For example, if you have two tasks that will run on the same schedule and be completed by the same resource, it's much easier to copy the original task and then edit the task name on the copy. In such cases, use the following steps to move or copy the task:

1. Click on the row number for the task you want to move or copy to select the whole row.

2. If you want to move the task, choose Edit, Cut Task. Alternatively, you can press Ctrl+X, click on the Cut button on the Standard toolbar, or right-click on the selection to display a shortcut menu, and then select Cut Task.

   If you want to copy the task, choose Edit, Copy Task. Alternatively, you can press Ctrl+C, click on the Copy button on the Standard toolbar, or right-click on the selection to display a shortcut menu and then select Copy Task.

3. Click in any cell in the row above where you want to insert the task you cut or copied.

4. Choose Edit, Paste. Alternatively, you can press Ctrl+V, click on the Paste button on the Standard toolbar, or right-click to display a shortcut menu, and then select Paste. Project pastes the task as a new row.

Cut-and-paste (or copy-and-paste) operations can also be used to move or copy information in individual cells. When you select a cell, the Edit and shortcut menu commands change to Cut Cell and Copy Cell. After copying or cutting the selected cell, as just described for rows, select a destination cell and then paste the cut or copied information. When you paste a cut or copied cell, the pasted information replaces any existing information in the selected destination cell. (It's not inserted above the cell you selected.)

• •

You can select more than one row or cell to cut or copy by clicking and dragging over multiple row numbers or multiple cells.

• •

Clearing Task Information

Cutting or deleting a task removes the task altogether from the Task Sheet. The remaining rows close the space vacated by the cut task. There might be instances, however, when you want to remove the information from a task while keeping the row that was occupied by that task in place. For example, you might know that you want to replace the old task with information about a new task. If you simply change the entries for the old task, however, you might neglect to edit one, resulting in a schedule error.

An alternative to cutting information in a task or cell is to *clear* the information. Clearing removes cell contents but leaves all cells in place. Unlike cut information, however, cleared information can't be pasted, so you should clear material only when you're sure it's no longer needed.

Use these steps to clear information from your Task Sheet:

1. Select the task row or cell you want to clear.
2. Choose Edit, Clear. A submenu appears, offering you a choice of the kind of information to clear.
3. Choose the kind of information to clear by clicking on the appropriate submenu item, as follows:

   - **All.** Choosing this item removes the task contents, formatting, and any note you added for the task (the next section explains how to add a note).
   - **Formats.** Choosing this item returns the selected task or cell contents to the default formatting, removing any formatting you added (such as a new font or color).
   - **Contents.** Choosing this item is equivalent to pressing Ctrl+Delete. It removes the contents of the selected task or cell.
   - **Notes.** Choosing this item clears any note you added for the task (as described in the next section).
   - **Hyperlinks.** Choosing this item removes any hyperlinks you created in a task to enable the user to jump to a Web page on the Internet or a company intranet. Chapter 22, "Using Project with the Web," explains how to create hyperlinks.
   - **Entire Task.** Choosing this item clears the contents of the entire task when you haven't selected the entire task row.

Adding a Task Note

A *task note* enables you to capture information that doesn't need to appear within the Task Sheet but does need to be recorded with the schedule. For example, you might create notes in situations like these:

- If you have a task that is a reminder of a meeting, you can create a note listing materials you need to bring to the meeting.
- If a task relates to research gathering that will be completed by a resource other than yourself, you can include a note mentioning information sources that the designated researcher should check.
- If a task deals with proofreading or fact-checking, you can use a note to list the details that need to be reviewed.

Adding a note to a task is a straightforward process. Select the task row—or a cell in the task—for which you want to create a note. Right-click on the selected area, or open the Project menu. Choose Task Notes. Alternately, click on the Task Notes button on the Standard toolbar. The Task Information dialog box appears with the Notes tab selected. Click on the Notes text entry area, if necessary, and then type your note (see Figure 4.15). Press Enter to start each new line in the note. You can add special formatting to notes by using the buttons at the top of the Notes text area. The first button enables you to change the font for any text you select by dragging over it in the note; it opens the Font dialog box, which Chapter 16, "Other Formatting," covers. The next three buttons align the current note line (which holds the blinking insertion point) left, center, and right, respectively. The fifth button adds or removes a bullet to the beginning of the current line of the note. The last button enables you to insert an embedded object into the note, such as information from Excel or a bitmap image; Chapter 20, "Using Project with Other Applications," provides more information on working with embedded objects.

When you finish typing the note, click on OK to close the Task Information dialog box. Project inserts an icon in the Indicators column for the task to remind you that you added a note for that task.

Understanding Indicators

As you saw earlier in this chapter, an Indicators column appears at the far-left side of the Task Sheet in the default Gantt Chart view. The Indicators column remains blank until you begin entering information in other columns and changing the options for tasks. Then, depending on the settings you choose, indicator icons may appear in the Indicators column. Each indicator icon reminds you of a particular piece of information about a task. For example, the indicator icon in Figure 4.16 shows that a note has been added to task 3 in the Task Sheet.

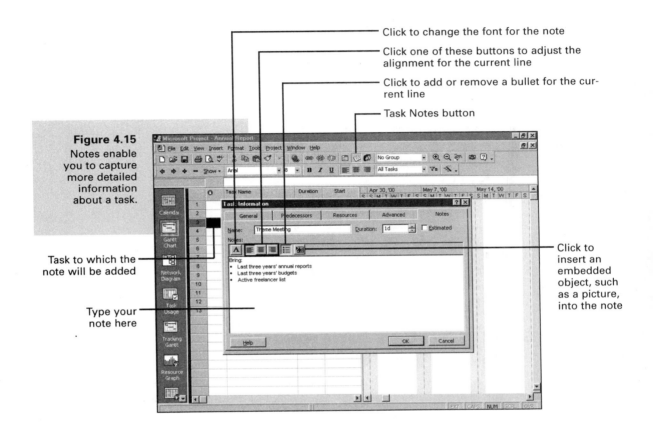

Click to change the font for the note

Click one of these buttons to adjust the alignment for the current line

Click to add or remove a bullet for the current line

Task Notes button

Figure 4.15
Notes enable you to capture more detailed information about a task.

Task to which the note will be added

Type your note here

Click to insert an embedded object, such as a picture, into the note

Figure 4.16
Indicator icons appear in the Indicators column to tell you that you specified particular task options or added information such as a note to a task.

Note indicator

	ⓘ	Task Name	Duration	Start
1		~~Gather Samples~~	~~5 days~~	~~Mon 5/1/00~~
2		Develop Theme Proposal	3 days	Mon 5/1/00
3	📝	Theme Meeting	1 day	Mon 5/1/00
4		Production Schedule Meeti	1 day	Mon 5/1/00
5		First Draft	2 days	Mon 5/1/00
6		First Approval Round	2 days	Mon 5/1/00
7		Corrections	2 days	Mon 5/1/00
8		Final Approval Round	2 days	Mon 5/1/00
9		Design Concept	1 day	Mon 5/1/00
10		Page Layout	1 day	Mon 5/1/00
11		To Printer	1 day	Mon 5/1/00
12		Printing Proofs	1 day	Mon 5/1/00
13		Printing	1 day	Mon 5/1/00

Other indicator icons tell you whether a task has been completed, whether a task has been completed by a date you specified, whether you need to e-mail task information to the resource who will be completing the work, and so on. When you begin entering resource information as described in Chapter 6, you'll see that indicators can also give you more information about a particular resource's status. I'll identify particular indicators throughout the book as I describe settings that cause an indicator to appear. If you can't recall what a particular indicator beside a task means, move the mouse pointer over the indicator cell to display pop-up messages like the ones shown in Figure 4.17.

Figure 4.17
Point to the indicators for a task or resource to see a pop-up description of what each indicator represents.

	ⓘ	Task Name	Duration	Start
1		Gather Samples	5 days	Mon 5/1/00
2		Develop Theme Proposal	3 days	Mon 5/1/00
3		Theme Meeting	1 day	Mon 5/1/00
4		This task has a 'Finish No Later Than' constraint on Tue 5/9/00.		Mon 5/1/00
5				Mon 5/1/00
6		Notes: 'Bring: Last three years' annual reports		Mon 5/1/00
7		Last three years' budgets Active freelancer list'		Mon 5/1/00
8		Final Approval Round	2 days	Mon 5/1/00
9		Design Concept	1 day	Mon 5/1/00
10		Page Layout	1 day	Mon 5/1/00
11		To Printer	1 day	Mon 5/1/00
12		Printing Proofs	1 day	Mon 5/1/00
13		Printing	1 day	Mon 5/1/00

Adjusting the Task Sheet

By default, the Task Sheet occupies roughly the left third of the screen in Gantt Chart view, and offers six columns with preset names and sizes. The narrow screen area allocated for the Task Sheet means that you might spend more time than you prefer scrolling or tabbing back and forth to display particular cells or columns (fields). Or, if you have a column where the entries become rather lengthy, the column might be too narrow to display the column contents. Finally, the columns provided by default might not capture all the information you want to have available on the Task Sheet. As you'll see next, Project allows you to control the appearance of the Task Sheet (and the Resource Sheet, which you'll see in Chapter 6) to customize it for your project creation needs.

Sizing the Sheet and Columns

One of the first changes you might want to make is to display more of the Task Sheet to make editing easier. This change isn't permanent, so while you're entering information about various tasks in your schedule, for example, you can fill most of the Project application window with the Task Sheet. After you enter the task information, you can return the Task Sheet to its previous size so that the Gantt Chart pane of the window becomes visible again.

You can resize the screen area occupied by the Task Sheet by dragging. A split bar separates the Task Sheet pane from the Gantt Chart pane on the right. Move the mouse pointer onto that split bar, and the pointer changes to a split pointer with a double-vertical line and left and right arrows. Press and hold the mouse button, and then drag the split bar to move it. A gray, shaded line (see Figure 4.18) indicates where the bar will be repositioned; when this line reaches the location you want, release the mouse button.

Just as you can drag to resize the whole Task Sheet area, you can drag to resize the width of any column or the height of any row. To change a column width, point to the right border of the column heading, beside the column name. To change a row height, point to the bottom border of the row, below the row number. The mouse pointer changes to a resizing pointer with a line and a double-headed arrow. Press and hold the mouse button, and then drag the border to change the size of the column or row. A dotted line indicates what the new size of the column or row will be; when the column or row reaches the new width or height you want, release the mouse button.

Figure 4.18
With a single drag operation, you can view more of the Task Sheet for easier task entry.

Gray line indicates the new pane size

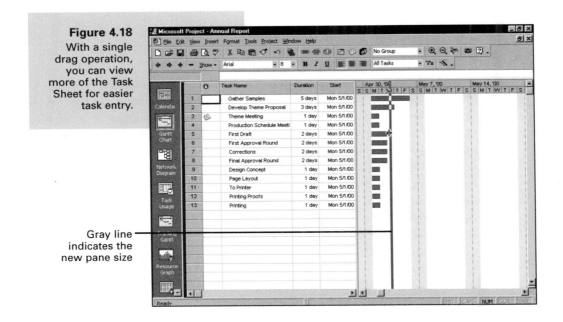

Tip

To resize a column to the optimum width for all its entries, double-click on the right border of the column heading.

Adding Columns (Fields)

When there are many pieces of data to capture about a particular process, six or seven measly columns cannot do the job effectively. Furthermore, you might want to display some information that Project normally calculates behind the scenes for you. For example, if a given task is being completed by a particular resource at a certain hourly rate, and you entered the actual hours the resource spent to complete the task, you might want to see the resulting cost onscreen. You might even want the Task Sheet to display certain information that you can print and distribute to others. Table 4.2 lists several predefined *columns* (also called *fields*), many of which are self-calculating, that you can add to the Task Sheet. Project offers more than 100 fields that you can use for tasks, so Table 4.2 describes only the most significant ones. If you choose to display a *table* other than the default Entry table in the Task Sheet, you see a whole new collection of fields. Rather than adding a column into the default Entry table on the Task Sheet, you may want to create your own custom table to leave the original intact. Chapter 11, "Working with the Different Project Views," explains how to display different tables in the Task or Resource Sheet, and how to create custom tables.

Note

Project's online help system contains a listing of all the Task Sheet field types, including a detailed description of each one. To view the list, choose Help, Contents and Index. Click on the Index tab, and then type field in the 1. Type Keywords text box and then click on the Search button. Scroll down the 3. Choose a Topic list box until you start seeing the different field names. The field type appears in parentheses after the field name. For more information on a particular field, click on it in the list to display help about it in the pane at the right. Notice that Project considers certain fields to be *assignment* fields. (Chapter 7, "Resolving Overallocations and Overbooked Resources," explains what assignments are.) You can display assignment fields in the Task Sheet, as well.

Table 4.2 Other Fields You Can Display in the Task Sheet

Field Name	Description
Actual Cost	Calculates the actual cost for the hours or material units required to complete a project, or lets you enter an actual cost if the project was completed for a fee.
Actual Duration	Calculates the actual time that has elapsed since the scheduled start of the task, based on your entry in a Remaining Duration or Percent Complete field if displayed.
Actual Finish	Lets you enter the actual task completion date if it differs from the scheduled date.
Actual Overtime Cost and Actual Overtime Work	Calculates the actual overtime expenses or actual overtime work incurred to date for all resources.
Actual Start	Lets you enter the actual task starting date if it differs from the scheduled date.
Actual Work	Calculates or lets you enter the work completed for the task.
Baseline (various fields)	Displays the total planned cost, duration, finish, start, and work for the task.
BCWP	Baseline Cost of Work Performed: Displays the projected actual cost, calculated from the budgeted baseline cost and the percentage of work actually completed.
BCWS	Budgeted Cost of Work Scheduled: Lets you compare the cost of what has actually been accomplished (BCWP) versus the cost of what you planned to accomplish by a particular date.
Contact	Enables you to enter a contact name for the resource assigned to complete the task, if that contact person's name is different from the resource name. For example, you may list a consulting company as the overall resource, but your contact person in the contact column.
Cost Variance	Calculates the difference between the baseline cost and scheduled work cost for tasks in progress, and between the baseline and actual cost for finished tasks—negative values indicate that a cost came in under budget.
Critical	Indicates whether a task is critical or noncritical, via calculations based on the Total Slack field entry and some other dialog box entries for the task.
Duration Variance	Displays the difference between the baseline duration for the task and the currently scheduled duration.

Table 4.2 Other Fields You Can Display in the Task Sheet *(continued)*

Field Name	Description
Finish Variance	Calculates the difference between the planned (baseline) finishing date for the task and the currently scheduled finishing date—negative values indicate that the task is now scheduled to finish earlier than initially planned.
Hyperlink	Contains the name for a hyperlink you can click to open a document on your hard disk, a network, or the World Wide Web. For example, you can edit the entry in this column so that it gives only the file name rather than the full path to the file.
Hyperlink Address	Contains the actual address for a hyperlink, no matter what name you assign in the hyperlink column; clicking the address in this column opens the hyperlinked document.
ID	Calculates a task's current position in the schedule, even if two tasks have the same name.
Overtime Cost and Overtime Work	Adds the actually incurred and remaining overtime costs or work for all resources assigned to the task.
Percent (%) Complete	Calculates or lets you enter the percentage of a task's duration that has passed.
Percent (%) Work Complete	Calculates or lets you enter the percentage of a task's work that has been completed.
Remaining (various fields)	Calculates or lets you enter the cost, duration, or work still available to complete a task.
Resource (various fields)	Displays the group, initials, or names for the resources assigned to the task.
Start Variance	Calculates the difference between the scheduled (baseline) starting date and the actual starting date.
Successors	Lists later tasks that depend on (are linked to) the current task.
Total Slack	Indicates, when the value is positive, that there is time in the schedule to delay the task.
Update Needed	Specifies when schedule changes need to be communicated to a resource via the TeamUpdate command.
Work	Calculates the total work that all resources are scheduled to dedicate to the task.
Work Variance	Calculates the difference between the baseline amount of work scheduled for the task and the work currently scheduled.

The process for adding a new column resembles adding a new task to the schedule. Here are the steps:

1. Click in any cell in the column next to the location where you want to insert the new column. The inserted column will appear to the left of the column where you selected a cell.

2. Choose Insert, Column. (As an alternative to Steps 1 and 2, you can click on the column heading to select the entire column, right-click on it, and then click on Insert Column.) The Column Definition dialog box appears (see Figure 4.19).

3. Click on the down arrow to display the Field Name drop-down list. Use the scroll bar to display the name of the field you want to add, and then click on the name to select it.

4. (Optional) If you want the inserted column to be identified with a name other than the built-in field name (say, "Actual $" rather than "Actual Cost"), click to place the insertion point in the Title text box, and then type the name you want.

5. (Optional) If you want the title for the new column to be left- or right-aligned, rather than centered, click to open the Align Title drop-down list, and then select an alignment choice from the list that appears.

6. (Optional) If you want the entries that Project displays or that you make in the new column to be left-aligned or centered automatically, rather than right-aligned, click on the down arrow to display the Align Data drop-down list, and then select the alignment you want.

7. (Optional) If you know that the contents in the new column will require many characters (for example, a long hyperlink address) or very few characters (for example, a one- or two-character ID number), double-click on the value shown in the Width text box, then type the new number of characters you want the column to display. Alternately, you can click on the spinner buttons at the right side of the Width text box to use the mouse to increase or decrease the value.

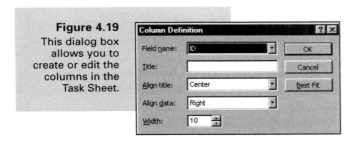

Figure 4.19
This dialog box allows you to create or edit the columns in the Task Sheet.

Figure 4.20
I've inserted a new column, % Complete, before the Duration column.

	ⓘ	Task Name	% Complete	Duration	Start
1		Gather Samples	0%	5 days	Mon 5/1 /00
2		Develop Theme Proposal	0%	3 days	Mon 5/1 /00
3	🗎	Theme Meeting	0%	1 day	Mon 5/1 /00
4		Production Schedule Meeti	0%	1 day	Mon 5/1 /00
5		First Draft	0%	2 days	Mon 5/1 /00
6		First Approval Round	0%	2 days	Mon 5/1 /00
7		Corrections	0%	2 days	Mon 5/1 /00
8		Final Approval Round	0%	2 days	Mon 5/1 /00
9		Design Concept	0%	1 day	Mon 5/1 /00
10		Page Layout	0%	1 day	Mon 5/1 /00
11		To Printer	0%	1 day	Mon 5/1 /00
12		Printing Proofs	0%	1 day	Mon 5/1 /00
13		Printing	0%	1 day	Mon 5/1 /00

8. Click on OK to finish creating the column. The column you specified appears in the Task Sheet, as shown in the example in Figure 4.20.

Caution

You need to be somewhat careful about which fields you add and how to use them. If you add a calculated field (one for which Project calculates the entry) into the Task Sheet, such as BCWP, you don't want to make your own entries into that new field—or Project won't let you, depending on the field. You also don't want to add the Baseline fields and enter your own information into them, because Project copies information into those fields when you save your baseline plan. The most safe fields to add and use for your own purposes are the Text fields (Text1 through Text30), which Project offers for custom uses.

Hiding, Deleting, and Editing Columns

In some instances, you might realize that you don't want to see a Task Sheet column, no longer need it, or need to make changes to it so that it's more useful and relevant to everyone using the project schedule you created.

Hiding a column removes it from the display but leaves its information intact. Therefore, you may want to hide a column after you have entered all the information for it, or when you'd prefer to focus on other columns. For example, you may decide that you really don't need to see the Indicators column when you're entering basic task information, so you can hide that column. To hide a column, first click on the column heading to select the entire column. Right-click on the selected column or choose Edit, Hide Column. Alternately, you can drag the right border of the column heading all the way to the left, so that the column disappears.

To redisplay the column and its contents, use the Insert, Column command as just described to add the column to the Task Sheet.

Caution

> If you hid the Task Name field column, you can redisplay it by inserting the Name column into the Task Sheet. When you do so, enter Task Name in the Title text box of the Column Definition dialog box, and choose Left as the Align Data choice. Again, however, I suggest that you make a copy of the default Entry table for the Task Sheet and then make changes to it, so you can always redisplay the default Entry table. Refer to Chapter 11, "Working with the Different Project Views," for more on displaying and customizing tables.

In cases where a column is no longer needed, you can delete it, but Project hides this capability so you won't accidentally delete vital project information. To delete a column, click on the column heading to select the column, and then press Delete.

To edit an existing column, you need to display the Column Definition dialog box containing information about that particular column. To do so, double-click on the column name in the column heading. Make the changes you want in the Column Definition dialog box, and then click on OK to accept them. When you edit a column (as opposed to when you first create it), you might find it useful to click on the Best Fit button in the Column Definition dialog box. Clicking this button resizes the column so that it's wide enough to fully display every entry already made in that column.

Dealing with the Planning Wizard

As you start entering information about tasks, you might discover that a Planning Wizard dialog box appears from time to time. The Planning wizard pops up to point out situations where you might need to make a decision about the information you're entering; the dialog box prompts you with specific, easy choices (see Figure 4.21). For example, the Planning wizard might ask whether you want to establish a link between tasks, or it might point out that you're about to create an error in your schedule.

To continue working after the Planning Wizard dialog box appears, click to select an option button to respond to the Planning wizard's question. If the Planning wizard has asked you this particular question previously and you no longer want to be reminded of the issue, click to select the Don't Tell Me About This Again check box. Click on OK to finish working in the Planning Wizard dialog box.

Figure 4.21
The Planning wizard helps you make decisions about the task information you are entering.

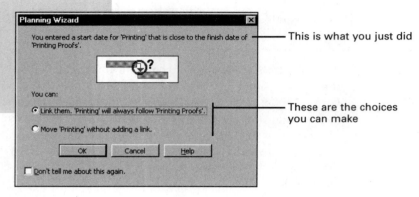

This is what you just did

These are the choices you can make

Clicking Cancel closes the Planning Wizard dialog box and also cancels the task entry or edit you were making.

You can turn off all the Planning wizard suggestions. Chapter 24, "Customizing Microsoft Project," explains how to use the Options dialog box to control certain Project features, including the Project wizard.

Creating Milestones

Milestones were once stone markers used to identify one's relative position along a road—the particular distance to a certain city on that road. Figurative milestones enable you to gauge your progress through life, through a particular phase of your career, or through a particular process. Milestones in your Project files let you mark a particular point of progress or a particular event during the course of a project.

For example, suppose that the project you're managing is the creation and production of your company's annual report, and the company's fiscal year ends June 30. Producing the annual report is tricky, because you want to release it as soon as possible after the close of the fiscal year. Yet you have to wait for the final, audited financial information for the year in order to compile the report. In this case, you might mark the end of the fiscal year with a milestone, to help you keep that key, approaching date in mind. In other cases, you might want to mark particular dates, such as the date when you're 25 percent or 50 percent through your total allotted schedule.

Figure 4.22
This Gantt Chart
view shows a
sample
milestone.

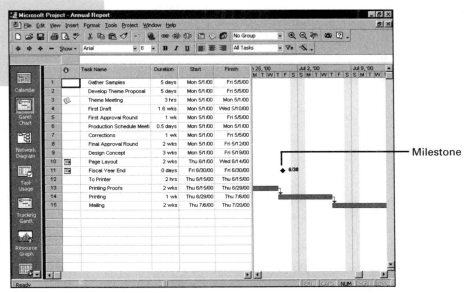

Figure 4.22
This Gantt Chart view shows a sample milestone.

Creating a milestone isn't very different from creating a task. You insert a task into the Task Sheet, if needed, and then enter information about the task. To specify the task as a milestone, give it a duration of 0 days by entering **0** in the Duration column. Project then identifies the new task as a milestone, and displays a milestone marker for it in your schedule's Gantt Chart (see Figure 4.22).

Looking at Project Properties

As with the files you create in other Microsoft applications, Project tracks certain properties, or details, to search for files more efficiently, and more. Some of the properties tracked for your Project files include statistics about the task scheduling and tracking information you enter in the file.

You can review the properties for a particular file by opening the Properties dialog box. To do so, choose File, Properties. This dialog box offers five tabs, some that calculate and display information and others that enable you to add details about the file:

- **General.** This tab displays the file type, creation date, date the file was last modified, DOS file name, and more.

- **Summary.** This tab is selected by default. It allows you to enter or edit information about your name, your company, your manager, a title for the file or project, a category to identify the file, keywords to uniquely identify the file if you're trying to find it using Windows search capabilities, and more.

- **Statistics.** This tab indicates when the file was created and last modified, and also when the file was last printed, who last saved it, how many times it has been revised, and how many total minutes have been spent editing the file.

- **Contents.** This tab displays some key facts about the scheduling information you entered, including the scheduled dates and total projected cost. Figure 4.23 illustrates what this tab looks like.

- **Custom.** This tab enables you to create a custom property to facilitate finding the file from Windows. For example, you can create a custom property to assign a unique number—such as the job number for the project—to the file. If you create a custom job number field for all your Project files, you can search for any project file by its job number. To create a custom property, specify values for the Name, Type, and Value text boxes, and then click on the Add button.

Figure 4.23
You can view schedule information via the Properties dialog box.

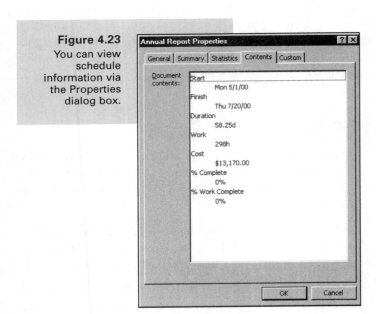

Fine-Tuning Tasks

In This Chapter

- Graphically managing task schedules
- Identifying and creating tasks that you know will repeat
- Working with links that show relationships between tasks
- Understanding how lead times and lag times affect your schedule
- Applying constraints that further specify when the task should be performed
- Reviewing and changing other information stored about a task

Most designers and artists who create masterpieces don't start by creating subtle shading and fine lines, just as architects don't start a building design by selecting a brick color. In putting the whole picture together, most people—professionals and amateurs alike—start by sketching out a rough idea of what they want. Then they go back and draw in the details.

In Chapter 4, "Setting Up a Project," you learned how to sketch out the schedule for your project in the default Gantt Chart view. This chapter helps you to continue working in the Gantt Chart view to begin the refinement process, making changes here and there, and starting to draw in some details to make your plan clear.

Creating and Editing Tasks with the Mouse

The last chapter focused on working in the Task Sheet to create and edit task information. You learned to change the schedule for a task by editing the duration, start date, and finish date. In many cases, to change the schedule for a task, you simply have to change an entry in one of the columns in the Task Sheet.

There are, however, a few limitations when you use the Task Sheet to schedule your tasks. By default, Project schedules each task's start or finish date on the same date as the project's Start Date or Finish Date, depending on the settings you selected in the Project Information dialog box. Thus you have to change the start or finish date for virtually every task you enter (or use linking to have Project calculate approximate start dates for you, as described later in this chapter).

Another limitation when using the Task Sheet is that if you're not an ace typist, entering information cell by cell can be quite tedious. Also, you might not be comfortable with counting dates in your mind and visualizing where weekends fall; you may prefer to work on an actual calendar instead.

If any of the preceding points applies to you, then you might prefer to create and edit tasks on the Gantt Chart pane of the Gantt Chart view. Project allows you to define the schedule for a new task—or change the schedule for an existing task—by using the mouse directly on the Gantt Chart.

You should make all of these changes before you save your baseline plan. (Chapter 9, "Comparing Progress versus Your Baseline Plan," covers saving a baseline.) You want your final plan to be as accurate as possible. Then, when you later start entering information about actual work completed and task schedule changes, you'll be able to compare your progress and changes with a clearly defined starting point.

ON THE

CD

If you want to practice the skills presented in this chapter, such as dragging to make tasks and linking tasks, use the *Annual Report Chapter 5* file you copied or installed from the CD-ROM for this book.

Dragging to Create a New Task

When you create a new task by dragging, you place it on the schedule exactly where you want it to appear. Creating tasks in this way is akin to using a marker to draw a line through successive dates on a calendar to block them out for a particular purpose. To use the mouse to add a task to your schedule, do the following:

1. Scroll the Gantt Chart pane to the approximate dates where you want to schedule the new task. (Use the scroll bar at the bottom of the pane.)

2. If needed, scroll down to the task row where you want to place the new task.

3. Point to the location that is roughly where the row for the task and your desired start date for the task intersect.

4. Press and hold down the mouse button—the mouse pointer changes to a crosshair. Drag to the right to begin defining the task. As you drag (see Figure 5.1), the outline for the Gantt Chart bar appears, and an informational Create Task pop-up box shows you the dates you are establishing for the task.

5. When the bar for the task is the length you want it, and the Create Task pop-up box displays the dates you want to schedule for the task, release the mouse button. Depending on where you draw the new task in relation to other tasks, the Planning wizard might appear to ask you whether to link the task with another (more on linking later in this chapter). Click on the appropriate option, and then click on OK to finish creating the task. The new task bar appears on the Gantt Chart, and the new start date, finish date, and duration appear in the appropriate columns in the corresponding row of the Task Sheet.

6. Click to select the Task Name cell for the new task, and enter a name (see Figure 5.2).

7. Enter any other information that's needed for the task on the Task Sheet. If you want to remove the question mark in the Duration field for the new task (which means the Duration entry is considered an estimated duration), edit the Duration cell.

This box shows the schedule
you're creating for the task

Figure 5.1
Dragging directly
on the Gantt
Chart is an easy
way to add a
new task to your
schedule.

The gray shaded
outline indicates
where the task bar
will appear

Crosshair
pointer

Figure 5.2
After you add
the new task,
give it a
meaningful
name.

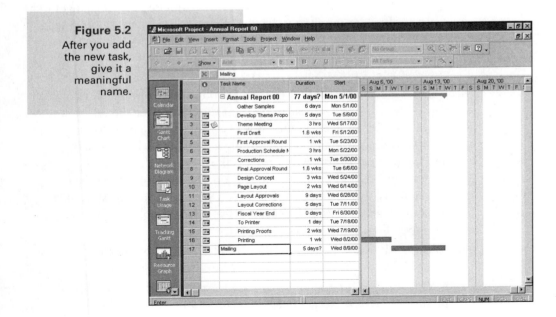

Note

Notice that when you create a task by dragging, an icon appears in the Indicators column for the task. This indicator appears because Project automatically assigns a Start No Earlier Than constraint to the start date for the task.

You can drag from left to right (start to finish) or from right to left (finish to start) when you're creating a task.

Dragging to Move or Reschedule a Task

If you're inclined to work with the schedule via the Gantt Chart, you'll be happy to know that you also can use the mouse to move and change the schedule for a task.

When you move a task with the mouse, the duration for the task never changes; in effect, dragging the task simply changes the Start Date and Finish Date entries. To move a task on the Gantt Chart, point to the task bar until the mouse pointer changes to a four-headed arrow. Press and hold down the mouse button; Project displays a Task pop-up box containing information about the task (see Figure 5.3). Drag the task to its new location; when you drag, the mouse pointer changes to a two-headed arrow, a gray outline appears to indicate the bar's position, and the changing task dates are reflected in the Task box. You can drag the task to the left to schedule it earlier, or to the right to schedule it later. Release the mouse button when the dates you want appear in the Task box. Again, if the Planning wizard appears to ask whether you want to link the moved task, select the option you prefer and click on OK to finish moving the task.

As with using the mouse to add a new task, when you use the mouse to reschedule a task, Project assigns the Start No Earlier Than constraint to the Start Date for the task. For accuracy in scheduling, you may want to move this constraint, as described later under "Setting Task Constraints."

When you're using the mouse to move or otherwise work with a task, you might notice that at times the text in the Task pop-up box or other pop-up box becomes bold. This means that releasing the mouse button would return the task to its dates, with no changes.

Figure 5.3
While you're moving a task bar, information about the task appears onscreen.

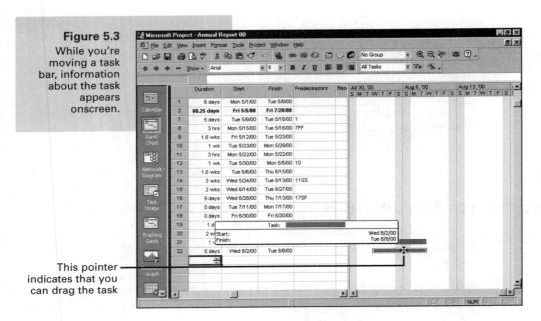

This pointer indicates that you can drag the task

Caution

If you selected Project Start Date for the Schedule From option in the Project Information dialog box, you need to reset the Start Date in that dialog box if you drag a task before the present start date. If you're scheduling the project from the Finish Date, you need to reset that date if you drag a task past the present finish date.

You can change the finish date, and thus alter the task's duration, by dragging the right end of the task bar. (You can't resize the task bar from its left end.) Simply point to the right end of the bar on the Gantt Chart so that the mouse pointer changes to a right-pointing arrow. Press and hold down the mouse button; the Task box appears as shown in Figure 5.4. Drag to the left to make the task shorter or to the right to make the task longer. When the Duration value in the Task pop-up box is what you want, release the mouse button to complete the change. When you drag to change the duration, the control you have might not be as precise as it would be if you made the change in the Duration column of the Task Sheet. For example, in the Task Sheet you can enter small increments of duration, such as **7.25d.** When you drag, however, you can only reset the duration in increments of .5d, so you can choose 7.0d or 7.5d, but not 7.1d or 7.25d.

Figure 5.4
Dragging on the Gantt Chart is a quick way to change the task's scheduled completion date.

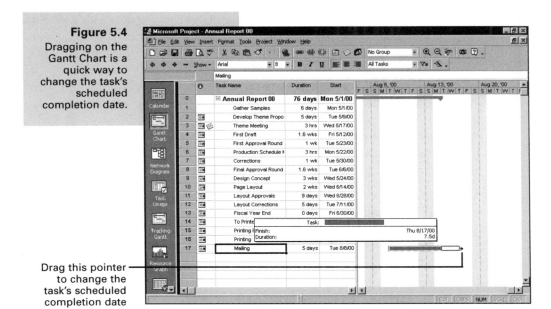

Drag this pointer to change the task's scheduled completion date

Caution

If you try to drag the completion date to a time that's before the starting date, Project resets the task duration to 0 days and converts the task to a milestone. See Chapter 4, "Setting Up a Project," to learn more about milestones.

If you use the mouse to change the finish date for a task with no constraint applied, Project in this instance leaves that situation as is and does not add a constraint. When the task already has a Start No Earlier Than constraint, Project leaves that constraint intact.

It's possible to use the mouse to change both the start date and duration for a task, but it requires two separate operations. First, drag the task's Gantt Chart bar to reposition it at the correct start date. Second, resize the duration by clicking and dragging the right end of the bar.

Splitting a Task

Chapter 4 discussed how Project works with durations you enter. For example, if you enter a duration of one week (1 wk) for a task, Project assumes the task will take 40 hours of work to complete, assuming the project calendar uses a 40-hour workweek. However, there are instances where you might know that a task won't take 40 hours, even when the start and finish dates need to be a week apart. For example, if a resource spends all day Monday on the task, waits a few days for information to arrive from a supplier, and then spends Friday afternoon finishing the task, the resource worked only 1.5 days (12 hours) on the project. If the resource is from an outside supplier or another department in your company that charges your department for time, it is in your best interest to home in on the actual time spent on the task to accurately account for project costs, while keeping the true schedule dates intact.

Project 2000 offers a feature called task splitting to help you create an accurate picture of when tasks start and finish (the duration), while also tracking how much work (in person hours) occurs and when it occurs. When Project tracks working time accurately, it can then calculate costs accurately rather than overstating them. So, returning to the example, say you know a task will take about 1.5 days of work hours, and you want it to start on the morning of 5/8/00. Because of the delay while the resource is waiting to receive information, the finish date will be a week later, on 5/15/00. Therefore, you should enter the task with a 1.5 day duration and a start date of 5/8/00. Then, you can split the task and drag the last .5 day of the task to the true finish date, 5/15/00. Then the duration appears as 1 full week, while Project uses 1.5 days of work to calculate the resource's commitment and costs for the work.

Follow these steps to use your mouse to split a task:

1. Scroll the Gantt Chart pane to the task bar for the task that you want to split. Double-check to ensure the task start date is the date when all work will begin. This ensures that you have a more accurate picture of how long the split between tasks can be when you create the split, avoiding the need to repeatedly move the split task around or adjust the split.

2. Click on the Split Task button on the Standard toolbar. Alternately, choose Edit, Split Task. The Split Task pop-up box appears, and the mouse pointer changes to a split pointer, with two vertical lines to the left and a right-pointing arrow.

3. Point to the Gantt bar for the task you want to split. Move the pointer left or right until the date listed as the starting date in the Split Task pop-up box is the date when you want the split (the nonworking period between the split portions of the task) to begin. Figure 5.5 shows the Split Task pop-up box.

4. When you see the correct starting date for the split in the Split Task pop-up box, press and hold the left mouse button, and then drag the split

Split Task button

Figure 5.5
You can click on the Split Task button, and then drag with the split pointer to move a portion of a task to a later time.

Shows the Start date for the period between the split portions of the task

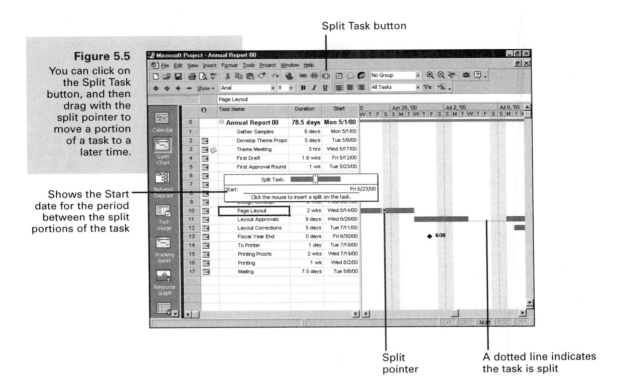

Split pointer

A dotted line indicates the task is split

portion of the task to the right. When you start dragging, the Split Task pop-up box changes to the Task pop-up box, which also appears when you drag to create a new task, and includes start and finish dates for the portion of the task you're moving.

5. When the Task pop-up box displays the correct starting date—the date you want work to resume on the task—release the mouse button to drop the split portion of the task into place.

Tip

If you click on the Split Task button, and then decide that you don't want to split a task, click on the Split Task button again or press Esc.

You can split as many tasks as you want in a schedule, or even place multiple splits in the same task bar. In fact, if you double-click on the Split Task button on the Standard toolbar, it remains turned on so that you can make as many splits as you want in the project. Click on the Split Task button again to turn it off.

As you fine-tune your schedule, you may find a split task that no longer needs to be split. To remove the split in the task, point to the right-hand portion of the split task bar (that is, the Gantt bar for the split task). Press and hold the left mouse button, and drag the bar to the left; when it touches the left-hand portion of the split task bar, release the mouse button. The portions of the split task will merge back into a single task.

Similarly, if you want to adjust the length of the split, drag the right-hand portion of the split task and release the mouse button when it reaches the starting date you want. Dragging the leftmost portion of a split task bar reschedules the entire task, leaving the split intact.

Creating Recurring Tasks

Splitting tasks is a great solution for breaking up work over a span of time. However, there's an even better technique for brief tasks that occur regularly over a particular period of time, such as weekly team meetings, monthly reports to a client, and so on. Rather than entering a separate task for each one-hour meeting or each half-day of report preparation, you can automatically schedule tasks that will occur at set intervals; these are called *recurring tasks*.

You can schedule monthly team meetings, a weekly conference call, or a daily status report. You can even set tasks to occur more than once each week—for example, every Monday and Wednesday.

Although you can create recurring tasks from a few different views in Project, adding these tasks from the Gantt Chart view often works best, because there you get a clear picture of where the recurring tasks fit in.

To add a recurring task to your schedule, perform the following steps:

1. In the Task Sheet, click to select the row or a cell in the row that the first instance of the recurring task should precede. You do this because the recurring task will be inserted as a summary task on a single row of the Task Sheet, with the subtasks representing each recurrence hidden from view. (See Chapter 15, "Working with Outlining," to learn more about viewing subtasks.) Because the recurring tasks aren't dispersed throughout the task list by default, you need to place the summary recurring task early in the schedule, where users of the file will notice it.

2. Choose Insert, Recurring Task. The Recurring Task Information dialog box appears, as shown in Figure 5.6.

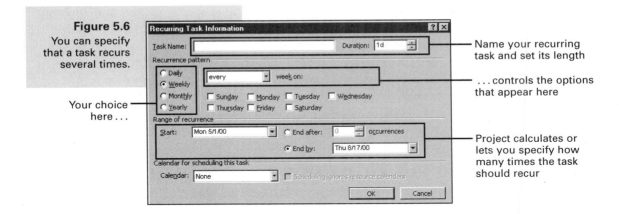

Figure 5.6
You can specify that a task recurs several times.

Name your recurring task and set its length

...controls the options that appear here

Your choice here...

Project calculates or lets you specify how many times the task should recur

3. Enter the desired Name and Duration for the task by clicking in each text box and typing the values you want. Remember that you can use abbreviations to specify the exact timing you want to assign, such as **2h** for a two-hour task.

4. Click to select one of the choices in the Recurrence Pattern area of the dialog box: Daily, Weekly, Monthly, or Yearly.

5. Specify the interval between recurrences. The available choices vary depending on the option you selected in Step 4. Basically, you can choose from the following:

   ■ **Daily.** Use the drop-down list to specify whether the task appears every day, every second day, every third day, and so on, up to every twelfth day. The Day choice includes all days in the schedule, and the Workday choice only schedules the recurring task on days included in the calendar for the project.

   ■ **Weekly.** Use the Week On drop-down list to specify whether the task appears every week, every second week, and so on, up to every twelfth week. Next, select each day of the week on which you want the task to recur. Change the entry in the From text box (in the Length area of the dialog box) only if you want to schedule recurrences starting before— or a specified interval after—the project start date. Use the To option to specify an ending date for the recurrence; otherwise, click on the For Occurrences option and specify the number of times that the task should be scheduled after the start date. Note that if you click on the down arrow beside either the From or the To choices, a pop-up calendar palette appears so you can make sure you're selecting a working day (rather than a weekend or other nonworking date).

- **Monthly.** Use the Day option button to specify the day of the month (by date number, such as the 25th of every month). Then use the corresponding drop-down list to specify whether to schedule the task in every month of the project time frame. If you want to schedule the recurring task by a day of the week rather than a date within each month, click on the The option button. Then use its drop-down lists to specify particular weekdays when the task should be scheduled, and whether to schedule the task every month. The Length options work exactly like the ones described under Weekly.

Whenever possible, schedule tasks by selecting a day of the week rather than entering a date. This helps you avoid scheduling any instances of the recurring task on a nonworking date.

- **Yearly.** Click on the option button beside the upper text box, and enter a single schedule date for the recurring task. Or click on the The button and use the drop-down lists to choose a month, weekday, and particular weekday in that month (first, second, and so on) for the task. Again, the Length options work as described under Weekly.

6. If you want the recurring task to use a particular calendar, choose the proper calendar from the Calendar drop-down list. This will help ensure that Project doesn't schedule a recurrence of the task on dates designated as holidays, for example. Also, if you want Project to ignore calendars you set up for your resources (more on that in the next chapter), click on the Scheduling Ignores Resource Calendars check box to check it.

7. Click on OK to accept your choices. If, by chance, one or more of the recurrences you scheduled appears on a day that's not a working day according to the project calendar, Project asks if you want to reschedule the task (see Figure 5.7). To reschedule the task and continue, click on Yes.

The recurring task appears in the Task Sheet in boldface, with a plus (+) outlining symbol to indicate that it's a summary task (see Figure 5.8). If you look at the row numbers to the left, you'll notice that some numbers no longer appear. For example, if the summary task appears in row 2 but the next row in the sheet is row 7, it's because rows 3–6 are hidden rows that each contain an individual recurrence. The duration, start date, and finish date for this summary task will span all the recurrences of the task, although you might not be able to see the Duration field entry at first. If you see a series of pound (#) signs filling the Duration column, double-click on the right border of the Duration column heading to increase the column's size.

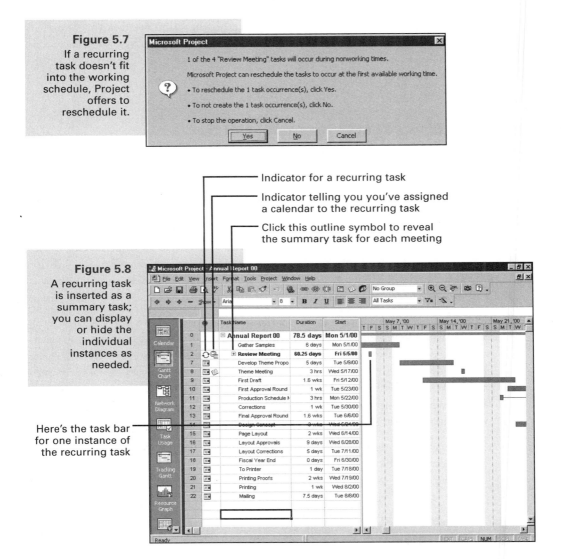

Figure 5.7
If a recurring task doesn't fit into the working schedule, Project offers to reschedule it.

Figure 5.8
A recurring task is inserted as a summary task; you can display or hide the individual instances as needed.

Indicator for a recurring task

Indicator telling you you've assigned a calendar to the recurring task

Click this outline symbol to reveal the summary task for each meeting

Here's the task bar for one instance of the recurring task

To adjust the schedule for the recurring task, click in any cell in the summary task row. Press Shift+F2; alternately, choose Project, Recurring Task Information. (You also could double-click in a cell in the task, or right-click in a cell in the task, and then click Recurring Task Information.) Make the changes you want, and then click on OK to complete your changes.

To delete the recurring task, select the summary task by clicking on its row number; then pressing Delete (or by opening the Edit menu and clicking on Delete

Task). Alternately, right-click on the heading for the summary task row and click on Delete Task. If the Planning Wizard dialog box appears, click on OK to confirm the deletion. This deletes the summary line and all the hidden rows that represent recurrences of the task.

Linking and Unlinking Tasks

One major drawback to the yellow pad method of project planning is that it forces you into a simplistic thinking. Because each task is on a separate line, it is separate and distinct from all other tasks on the list. That's perception, not reality.

Most projects don't progress in so neat a fashion. Many tasks are completely independent of one another, but sometimes tasks need to occur simultaneously. Other times, one task cannot start until another finishes. Some tasks need to start or finish simultaneously. Such a connection between the "destinies" of two tasks is called a *task relationship*. In Project, you define task relationships by creating *links*.

Links in your schedule define how tasks should proceed. The first task in a link, which usually must be completed before the other linked tasks can start, is called the *predecessor*. Tasks that follow and depend on predecessors are called *successors*. A predecessor can have more than one successor, and successors can serve as predecessors for other tasks, creating a chain of linked events. A successor task can even have multiple predecessors—for example, in a situation where three tasks must finish before one successor task can start.

One detail that might be difficult to get your arms around is that a predecessor task is identified by its ID number in the Predecessors field of the Task Sheet. The task ID is based on the task's current position (which row it's in) on the Task Sheet, not its individual schedule. It's perfectly okay to specify the task in row 20 as the predecessor to the task in row 12 in a Finish-to-Start link (described next), as long as the finish date for the row 20 task precedes the start date for the row 12 task. Task ID numbers change automatically if you move tasks to a new row or sort the tasks in the Task Sheet.

ON THE

CD

The *Annual Report Chapter 5.2* file on the CD-ROM (copy or install the file to your hard disk) for this book contains a list of tasks with no special start dates or constraints added. All the tasks start from the project file start date. Use that file to practice linking and to see how Project schedules tasks when you link them.

Link Types

Project offers four types of links. Links are visually represented by lines and arrows between tasks in Gantt charts, calendars, and PERT charts that are based on your schedule. Each link is identified with a particular abbreviation:

- The most common kind of link is a *Finish-to-Start (FS) relationship*, where the first task must be finished before the next task can begin (see Figure 5.9). For example, a product prototype might need to be approved before prototype testing can begin. An FS relationship is the simplest type of link to create. It's the default link type, and Project creates an FS relationship if you don't specify a different link type.

- A *Start-to-Start (SS) relationship* specifies that the predecessor task must start so that the successor task can start (see Figure 5.10). Use this type of relationship in situations where you want resources to work closely together, such as when an internal engineering department is working in concert with freelance resources. In this case, you're specifying that the successor task can't start before the predecessor; if your engineering department's kicked off its task, then the freelancer can start.

- A *Finish-to-Finish (FF) relationship* means that the predecessor task must finish before the successor can finish (see Figure 5.11). Such a situation might arise when multiple tasks must be completed simultaneously, but the predecessor task is more lengthy or resource intensive than any

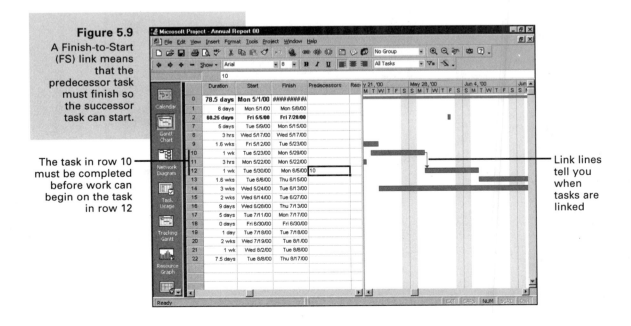

Figure 5.9
A Finish-to-Start (FS) link means that the predecessor task must finish so the successor task can start.

The task in row 10 must be completed before work can begin on the task in row 12

Link lines tell you when tasks are linked

Figure 5.10
A Start-to-Start (SS) link indicates when the predecessor task must be underway so that its successor can start.

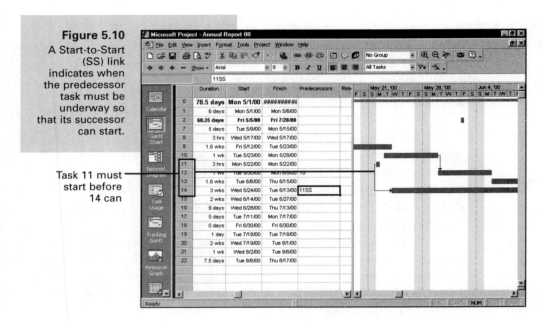

Task 11 must start before 14 can

Figure 5.11
A Finish-to-Finish (FF) relationship identifies when the predecessor task must finish before the successor can.

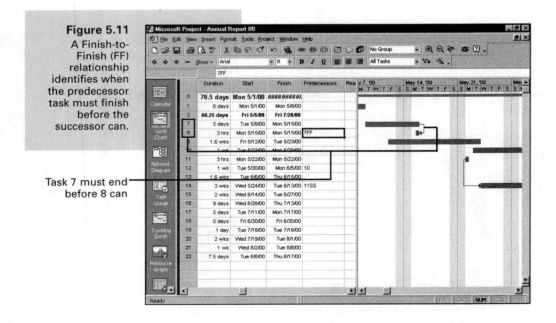

Task 7 must end before 8 can

successor task. For example, say that you're creating the first issue of a new magazine. When the page layout task (the predecessor) ends, the proofreading task (the successor) can end, because pages must be completed before they can be proofread.

■ A *Start-to-Finish (SF) relationship* is a bit more complex than the other relationships, and therefore is used less often. In such a relationship, the predecessor task cannot finish until the successor task begins (see Figure 5.12). Consider this accounting example: A company's quarterly or annual books have to remain "open" until the period-end closing procedures begin, no matter when that actually occurs.

Caution

At times, when you create a particular relationship that requires it and when the successor task has no constraints applied to its schedule, Project might change the schedule for a successor task so that its schedule is consistent with the linked task. For example, if you create an FF relationship and the successor task's finish date is earlier than the predecessor's finish date, Project shifts the successor task's schedule so that it has the correct finish date, yet retains its original duration. Project might also shift successor tasks that are attached to any predecessor task you move, so don't be too surprised.

Figure 5.12
A Start-to-Finish (SF) relationship identifies when the successor task must start before the predecessor can end, such as when corrections must begin before approvals can be finalized.

Task 17 must get underway before Task 16 can end

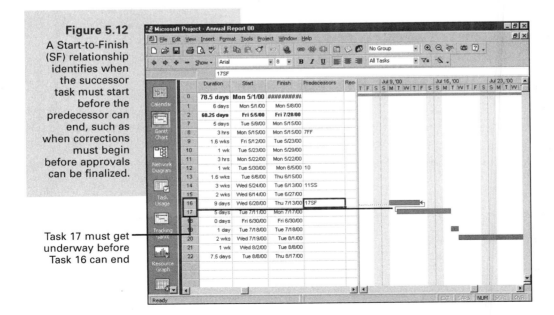

Linking Tasks on the Task Sheet

Recall from the description of the Task Sheet in Chapter 4, "Setting Up a Project," that one of the columns in the default Task Sheet is the Predecessors column. You can use this column to create links simply by typing; to do so, follow these steps:

1. Click to select the cell in the Predecessors column in the row holding the task that will be the successor task. For example, if you want the task in row 12 to start when the task in row 10 finishes, click on the Predecessors cell in row 12.

2. Type the row number for the predecessor task.

3. If you want to designate a Start-to-Start, Finish-to-Finish, or Start-to-Finish link rather than the default Finish-to-Start link type, type its abbreviation using upper- or lowercase characters (for example, **10ff**). You don't need a space between the predecessor's row number and the abbreviation. Your entry might resemble any of the ones shown in Figures 5.10, 5.11, and 5.12.

4. (Optional) To specify an additional predecessor, continue the entry by typing a comma followed by the task number and link type abbreviation (without any spaces).

5. (Optional) Repeat Step 4 if you want to add other predecessors.

6. After you create all the links you want in the successor task's Predecessors cell, press Enter to finalize the setup.

If you decide to make a change to a link, simply edit the link information by clicking in the appropriate Predecessors cell and making your changes.

Linking Tasks with the Mouse

To create a default Finish-to-Start (FS) link, you can drag between task bars on the Gantt Chart to create the link. Point to either of the task bars until you see the four-headed arrow pointer. Press and hold the mouse button, and drag to the other task bar. As you drag, a Finish-to-Start Link pop-up box appears as in Figure 5.13. Release the mouse button to finish creating the link.

You also can create links between tasks shown in Calendar view by dragging between the tasks. You learn more about these views in Chapter 11, "Working with the Different Project Views."

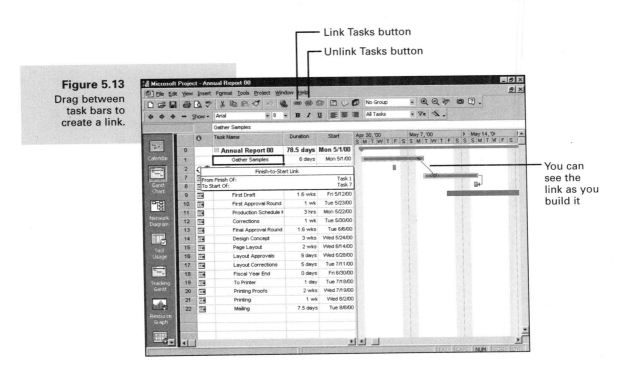

Figure 5.13
Drag between
task bars to
create a link.

Linking Tasks with the Toolbar

Using a toolbar button along with the Task Sheet can make even faster work of creating links between tasks—but only if you want to create the default type of link, an FS relationship. Also, links created with the method described next always assume that the task that's lower in the task list (with the higher row number) is the successor task; therefore, Project adjusts that successor task's schedule, if needed, to ensure that it follows the predecessor.

One of the advantages to using the mouse to create your links is that you don't have to scroll right to the Predecessors column (which, at the default Task Sheet pane size, scrolls the Task Name column out of view), so you can see the task's name as well as the Gantt bar representing its schedule. The following steps also make it easy to link several tasks in a single operation:

1. Drag to select cells in two or more adjacent tasks. If you want to select noncontiguous tasks, click a cell in the predecessor task row, press and hold down Ctrl, and click a cell in the successor task row—both cells will be selected. If you want to select additional noncontiguous tasks, continue to hold down Ctrl and click cells in other rows.

2. Click on the Link Tasks button on the Standard toolbar. Alternately, press Ctrl+F2, or choose Edit, Link Tasks. Project creates the links between the tasks in the rows you selected.

ON THE

CD

Try this technique in particular in the *Annual Report Chapter 5.2* file on the CD-ROM for this book. Select some tasks, click on the Link Tasks button, and observe how Project reschedules the tasks.

Linking via Task Information

The Task Information dialog box lets you view and alter numerous crucial details about a task. This dialog box offers five tabs of information, including the Notes tab that you learned about when creating task notes in Chapter 4, "Setting Up a Project," and the Predecessors tab, which enables you to create and edit links to predecessors for the selected task. The obvious disadvantage to this method is that you have to be familiar with details about the predecessor task you want to choose, or the schedule for the predecessor, because you might not be able to view that information while the dialog box is open.

To open the Predecessors tab in the Task Information dialog box, click in a cell in the task for which you want to create or work with predecessors (that is, a cell in the successor task row). Press Shift+F2; alternately, click on the Task Information button on the Standard toolbar; or if you prefer, choose Project, Task Information (or right-click on the task and then click on Task Information). As another method, you can simply double-click on a cell in the successor task row in the Task Sheet. When the Task Information dialog box appears, click on the Predecessors tab.

To add a predecessor, type the ID (row) number for the predecessor task in the first cell of the ID column below the Predecessors choice. Press Enter or Tab, or click on the Enter button (it looks like a check mark) beside the Predecessors text box above the column heads. (The text entry area here operates just like the one above the Task Sheet.) Project enters the predecessor's task name.

Project offers a second, easier method of specifying a predecessor task in the Task Information dialog box. Click on the Task Name cell in the first empty row of the Task Name column of the Predecessors tab in the Task Information dialog box. A down arrow appears at the right side of the cell. Click on the arrow to open a drop-down list giving the Task Name for each task in the schedule. Click on the name of the predecessor task, as shown in Figure 5.14. Click on the Enter button to finish choosing the predecessor.

Whether you specify the predecessor by ID or Task Name, by default Project enters Finish-to-Start (FS) in the Type column as the link type. To specify a different type, click on the Type cell for a predecessor, and do one of the following:

- Select the type that currently appears in the text entry box, type the abbreviation for the preferred type of link, and click on the Enter button (which looks like a check mark).
- Click on the down arrow at the right end of the text entry box to display a drop-down list of link types, and then click on the preferred type of link.

You can add additional predecessor tasks in lower rows of the tab. To edit any link, click on the appropriate cell in the predecessor row, and then edit it in the text entry box or use a drop-down list for the cell, if available, to make another choice. To remove a predecessor, click on the ID cell for it; then drag over the ID number that appears in the text entry box, press Backspace to remove it, and click on the Enter button. When you finish using the tab to add or edit predecessors, click on OK to close the Task Information dialog box.

Note

For information about the Lag column for predecessor tasks, see the "Working with Lead Times and Lag Times" section later in this chapter.

Figure 5.14

Open the drop-down list for the selected Task Name cell; then click on the name of the predecessor task.

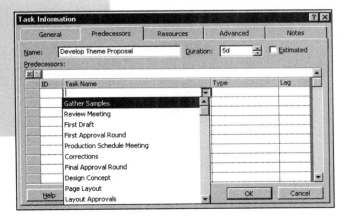

Unlinking Tasks or Changing the Link Type

To remove a link between tasks or change the type of link, you have to work from the successor task, not the predecessor task. Removing a link does not change the schedule for the successor task, unless that schedule was changed by Project when the link was created. If Project did automatically adjust the successor task schedule based on a link you added, then when you remove the link, Project returns the successor task to its original schedule.

Use any of the following methods to break a link or change the link type:

- Click on any cell in the successor task row to select it; then click on the Unlink Tasks button on the Standard toolbar. (This technique applies to breaking the link only.)

- Click to select the Predecessors cell in the successor task row of the Task Sheet. To remove the link, right-click on the cell, then choose Clear Contents. Otherwise, click in the Entry box above the Task Sheet, edit the link type abbreviation, and click on Enter to finish changing the link.

Caution

> **Do not press Delete to clear the contents of the Predecessors cell. Doing so deletes the entire task rather than the task link. Click on the Undo button on the Standard toolbar immediately if you mistakenly delete a task.**

- Click on the Task Information button on the Standard toolbar (or use the method of your choice) to open the Task Information dialog box, then click on the Predecessors tab. Delete the ID number for the predecessor to remove the link; change the Type column entry for a predecessor to change the link type.

- Double-click on the appropriate link line between two tasks in the Gantt Chart. Choose Delete in the Task Dependency dialog box that appears to remove the link. Or open the Type drop-down list, click on a different link type, and then click on OK. Note that the (None) choice in the Type drop-down list removes the link, too.

Working with Lead Times and Lag Times

Reality dictates the way your schedule must progress, and how Project enables you to define task relationships. Time is *analog*, or continuous. Although it can be expressed in discrete units, such as minutes and seconds, it flows and blends together. Moreover, events blend together in time; even though tasks might seem to follow one after another, they probably flow together more loosely, overlapping or occurring after a delay.

Project accounts for this flexibility of time by enabling you to schedule *lead time* and *lag time* for linked tasks. Adding lead time causes the successor task to overlap with the predecessor task; this means that even though the task link is, for example, Finish-to-Start, the successor task can start before the predecessor task is finished.

Adding lag time on a Finish-to-Start relationship allows you to insert a delay between the finish of the predecessor task and the start of the successor task. For example, if a predecessor task is scheduled to end on a Wednesday, you can schedule the successor task to begin the following Wednesday without breaking the link between the two tasks.

You can schedule lead or lag time by entering the proper code for it in the Predecessor column entry (by appending it to the predecessor task number and task type specification), or by entering the code in the Lag column of the Predecessors tab of the Task Information dialog box, or in the Lag text box of the Task Dependency dialog box. You specify lead time using a minus sign (–) and lag time using a plus sign (+). You can specify the timing in terms of duration intervals (2h for two hours, 2d for two days, and so on) or as a percentage of the predecessor task's duration.

For example, if you want to create a Finish-to-Start link to task 7 with a two-day lead time, enter **7FS–2d** on the Task Sheet in the Predecessors cell for the successor task. If you're entering the lead time in the Lag column (Task Information dialog box) or Lag text box (Task Dependency dialog box), you only have to enter **–2d**. A Lag entry using percentages might be **7FS–50%** (on the Task Sheet) or **–25%** (in either of the dialog boxes), which respectively would insert lead time equivalent to 50 percent or 25 percent of the predecessor task's duration before the start date of the successor task. To specify lag time (a pause) rather than lead time, you simply use a plus sign rather than a minus sign in your entries. Figure 5.15 shows lead time and lag time added to tasks in an example schedule.

Caution

Even though by default the abbreviation for a Finish-to-Start (FS) relationship doesn't appear in the Predecessors column of the Task Sheet, you must type that abbreviation when specifying lead time or lag time.

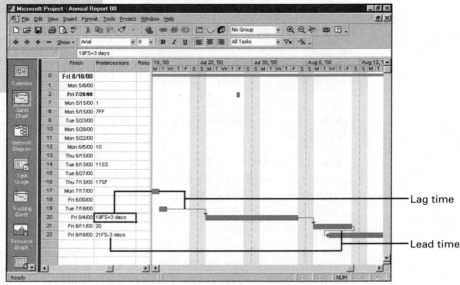

However, there's a glitch when you're creating lead time. Project might not automatically reschedule the successor task to an earlier start date when you create lead time. In such a case, which occurs when Project is not set to automatically recalculate schedule changes, you have to adjust the start date for the successor task in the Start column of the Task Sheet, or press F9 if you see Calculate in the status bar. This tells Project to move the successor task's Gantt Chart bar to the left to show the lead time. You can reduce lead time by dragging the successor task bar rightward, but you can't increase lead time by dragging it to the left. In general, dragging the Predecessor task bar moves both tasks.

By contrast, you can create lag time by dragging the Gantt Chart bar for an existing successor task to the right. As soon as you release the mouse button, Project displays (by default) the Planning wizard. Choose the Move The Task (Task Name And New Start Date) And Keep The Link option button, then click on OK to add the lag time. (This also adds a Start No Earlier Than constraint to the successor task.) Likewise, you can reduce the amount of lag time between tasks by dragging the Predecessor task bar to the right or increasing its duration by dragging its right end to the right. You can increase the lag time in either direction by dragging the successor task bar in either direction.

Note

> Project offers you two ways to build cushion time into your project schedule. The first is to schedule extra time for some tasks, and the second is to assign the anticipated duration for a task, but to build in some lag time after the task. I prefer the latter method, especially when I'm dealing with a resource outside my company. I give the outside resource a task deadline that is at least a couple of days before the real (internal) date. I recommend this technique because it not only provides cushion time but also allows you some time to review the work from the outside resource—prudent if you haven't previously dealt with that resource.

Setting Task Constraints

As you learned elsewhere in this book, Project calculates a project finish date or start date for you depending on the duration and nature of the tasks you create. This book has focused quite a bit already on the flexibility you have in moving or rescheduling parts of tasks.

That flexibility is great if you're the only person able to edit the schedule. If, however, you want to make the schedule a bit more solid in most cases, you can establish constraints for tasks, just to make tasks a bit more difficult to move and to control how the schedule progresses. Table 5.1 reviews the constraints.

To create constraints for a task, perform the following steps:

1. Click on a cell in the Task Sheet row of the task you want to create constraints for.

2. Right-click on the task or choose Project, Task Information. Alternately, press Shift+F2, or click on the Task Information button on the Standard toolbar, or double-click on the Task. The Task Information dialog box appears.

3. Click on the Advanced tab to see the advanced options (see Figure 5.16).

4. Click on the Constraint Type down arrow to see a list of constraint types. Select the type of constraint you want for the selected task.

5. Click on the Constraint Date text box down arrow, and use the pop-up calendar to specify the new date to define the constraint.

6. Click on OK to close the dialog box and finalize the constraint.

Table 5.1 Constraints for Controlling Individual Task Scheduling

Constraint	Abbrev.	Description	Flexible/Inflexible
As Soon As Possible	ASAP	Ensures that the task starts as soon as possible, based on the completion of any predecessors, and is the default constraint if you enter only the duration for the task.	Flexible
As Late As Possible	ALAP	Ensures that the task starts as late as possible when the project is being scheduled from its finish date, and is the default constraint if you enter only the duration for the task in this type of schedule.	Flexible
Finish No Earlier Than	FNET	Prevents a task from finishing when premature, and is the default if you edit or enter the task's finish date.	Inflexible when tasks are scheduled from the project finish date; flexible when tasks are scheduled from the project start date.
Start No Earlier Than	SNET	Prevents a task from starting before the specified date, and is the default if you edit or enter the task's start date.	Inflexible when tasks are scheduled from the project finish date; flexible when tasks are scheduled from the project start date.
Finish No Later Than	FNLT	Sets the drop-dead deadline for the task, but enables the task to start earlier if needed.	Inflexible when tasks are scheduled from the project start date; flexible when tasks are scheduled from the project finish date.
Start No Later Than	SNLT	Sets the absolute latest date when the task can commence, but enables the task to start earlier if needed.	Inflexible when tasks are scheduled from the project start date; flexible when tasks are scheduled from the project finish date.
Must Finish On	MFO	Specifies that a task must finish no sooner or later than a specified date.	Inflexible
Must Start On	MSO	Specifies that a task must start no sooner or later than a specified date.	Inflexible

Figure 5.16
Use this tab of the Task Information dialog box to create constraints.

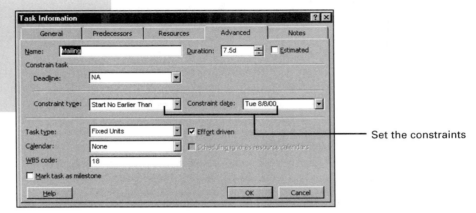

Set the constraints

You may have noticed that as you moved tasks away from the date from which the project is being scheduled (the start date by default), a small, square, grid-like icon appeared in the Indicators column. This icon represents a particular type of constraint. By default, where you're moving a task from the beginning of the project to a later date (that is, moving the start date for the task), the task has a Start No Earlier Than (SNET) constraint. You also may have noticed that this constraint isn't always "enforced" by Project as you build links; successor tasks move as needed to honor the links. That's because SNET constraints are flexible in projects scheduled from the Start Date (chosen from the Schedule From drop-down list in the Project Information dialog box).

Flexible constraints aren't anchored or restricted to a particular date; they can move as needed as you create links or add resources. In contrast, an inflexible constraint prevents a task from being rescheduled unless you change the constraint. Some constraints can be flexible or inflexible, depending on the Schedule From choice for the project. Table 5.1 also clarifies when particular constraints are flexible or inflexible. The indicator for an inflexible restraint is slightly different from that for a flexible constraint, as shown in Figure 5.17.

Figure 5.17
The top indicator represents a flexible constraint, and the bottom one represents an inflexible constraint.

Adding a Task Deadline

Project 2000 offers a new deadline setting on the Advanced tab of the Task Information dialog box. When you're tracking the project and a task finishes later than the deadline you specified, an Indicator appears in the indicators column to alert you of that fact. This feature might be useful, for example, if a contract with an outside resource calls for financial penalties for missed deadlines.

To specify a deadline, double-click on the desired task to display the Task Information dialog box. Click on the Advanced tab. Enter the deadline date in the Deadline text box or use its drop-down calendar to choose the deadline date, then click OK to apply the deadline.

Using Go To to Find a Task

Scroll bars enable you to scroll through the various parts of each view. For example, you can scroll up and down to see different rows of the Task Sheet, and can scroll left and right to see other columns. Pressing Page Down and Page Up moves the display by one screenful of information. Likewise, you can scroll up, down, left, and right to display different areas of the Gantt Chart. Moving around the Task Sheet and clicking a task certainly changes the part of the Task Sheet that you see, but selecting a Task in the Task Sheet doesn't automatically scroll the Gantt Chart to the task bar for the selected task. Additionally, scrolling to the correct task bar on the Gantt Chart could be slow. Instead, you can use the Go To feature to jump directly to both the Task Sheet task and task bar you want, or just to the task bar.

To use Go To, choose Edit, Go To (Ctrl+G). The Go To dialog box appears (Figure 5.18). Enter the ID number (row number) of the task you want to jump to in the Task Sheet and scroll the Gantt Chart to display the task bar for the selected task. To simply scroll the Gantt Chart to a particular date, click on the Date text box down arrow and select the date you want to see in the Gantt Chart. Click on OK to finish your Go To selection and adjust the display.

If you already clicked on a cell in a task in the Task Sheet and want to quickly display the task bar for that task on the Gantt Chart pane at the right side of the Gantt Chart view, click on the Go To Selected Task button on the Standard toolbar.

Figure 5.18
Use the Go To dialog box to jump to a particular task in the Task Sheet and Gantt Chart, or just to the Gantt Chart.

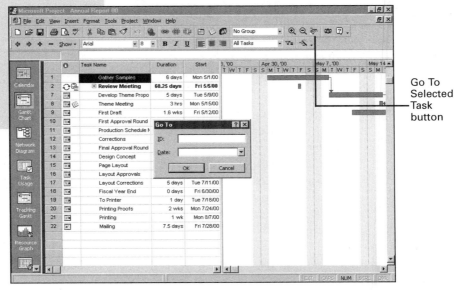

Go To Selected Task button

Editing Other Task Information in the Task Information Dialog Box

So far, you worked in the Predecessors, Advanced, and Notes tabs of the Task Information dialog box. The fastest way to display this dialog box is to click in a cell in the task that you want to learn more about or change information for, and then click on the Task Information button on the Standard toolbar. You can click on any tab in the Task Information dialog box to display its options, edit them as needed, and then click on OK to close the dialog box. This section takes a brief look at the options not examined thus far.

You can select multiple tasks by dragging across cells or holding down the Ctrl key while you click on noncontiguous tasks. Then, click on the Task Information button. This displays the Multiple Task Information dialog box so that you can change a task setting for all the selected tasks. For example, you could apply a constraint for all the tasks or change the duration for all the tasks.

Changing the Task Calendar

You learned in Chapter 4 how to select a base calendar for a project file, as well as how to create and apply a custom calendar that takes into account holidays, nonstandard working hours, and so on. In Project 2000, you can also specify a calendar for a task, if it varies from the base calendar you've established for the project.

For example, assume you work in a manufacturing plant and are managing the design and first run production of a new product. Tasks early in the project might involve primarily the design and front-office staff for the company—engineers, designers, financial analysts, and so on. As these tasks normally occur during a standard workday, you would assign the Standard calendar (or your custom calendar that approximates the Standard calendar). However, when the manufacturing lines start setting up for and running the first order, those lines typically run on three shifts, so you might want to assign the 24 Hours calendar.

To change the base calendar for a task, display the Task Information dialog box for the task. (The fastest way to do so is to double-click on any cell in the task.) Click on the Advanced tab in the dialog box, then click on the Calendar down arrow to display the calendars (Figure 5.19). Click on the calendar to use in the drop-down list. If you want the specified task calendar to override any calendars specified for the resources assigned to the task, click on the Scheduling Ignores Resource Calendars check box to check it. Click on OK to close the dialog box. An indicator in the Indicators column specifies that you've assigned a calendar other than the project base calendar to the task.

Figure 5.19
To ensure proper scheduling for a task, apply a calendar to the task.

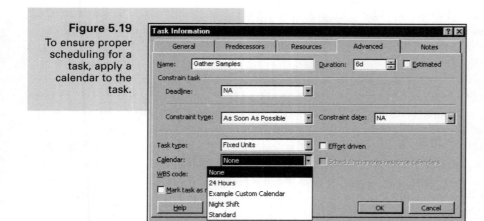

Changing Other Task Information

The first tab in the Task Information dialog box is the General tab (see Figure 5.20). It lets you work with general parameters for the task, like its start and finish date, which you learned to adjust via other methods.

The Predecessors tab was described earlier in this chapter. It enables you to alter the task name and duration, as well as specify predecessors for the selected task to create links. The Resources tab is covered in Chapter 6, "Managing Resources." This tab enables you to assign one or more resources (coworkers, vendors, and so on) to complete the specified task.

In addition to the Constrain Task options you learned about in the preceding section, the Advanced tab (refer to Figure 5.16) offers a few more options of interest. The Mark Task As Milestone check box converts the task bar to a milestone marker without changing the duration.

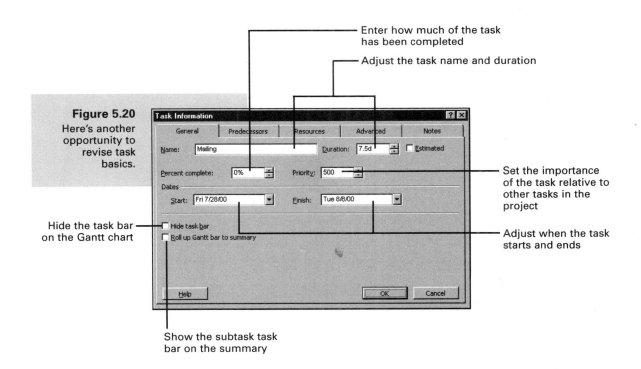

Enter how much of the task has been completed

Adjust the task name and duration

Figure 5.20
Here's another opportunity to revise task basics.

Set the importance of the task relative to other tasks in the project

Hide the task bar on the Gantt chart

Adjust when the task starts and ends

Show the subtask task bar on the summary

If you want to use a specialized coding system, enter the code to use for the task in the WBS Code text box. If you want the number of resources you add to a task to influence task durations, make sure the Effort Driven text box remains checked. The final tab, Notes, is where you enter and edit notes about the selected task, as described in Chapter 4.

Note

As an example, you might want to use WBS codes starting with 9000 (9001, 9002, and so on), or you might want to use the year as a code prefix (0001, 0002, and so on). This latter method can be useful if your project schedule falls into more than one calendar year. See Chapter 15, "Working with Outlining," for more about creating and using WBS codes.

Managing Resources

IN THIS CHAPTER

- What resources are in Project
- How the resources you select affect the schedule
- Adding work and material resources for your project
- Determining how much each resource will cost
- Controlling how a resource's time is scheduled
- Removing a resource
- Viewing and editing assignments

If you're a person who lives by your lists, then the first several chapters of this book might already have introduced you to the key concepts you need to be familiar with when using Project.

In those chapters, you learned the steps for building and scheduling the tasks associated with your plan. All the information you've compiled so far, however, doesn't answer the most critical question of all: How in the world is everything on the list going to get done?

What Is Effort-Driven (Resource-Driven) Scheduling?

Resources complete the tasks you specified in a plan or schedule. Coworkers or team members may come to mind first, but *resources* can refer to the whole range of essentials. For example, a resource can be an outside freelancer or consulting firm; it can be a vendor that provides printing or manufacturing; it can be raw materials or supplies needed for a project, such as paper that needs to be purchased for a printing job; it can even be a piece of equipment you might need to use during a project, whether that equipment exists in your company and is shared by others, or is leased from an outside firm. In a nutshell, *resources* include all the people, supplies, and equipment used to complete tasks in a project.

You face several challenges when you try to assign resources to a project:

- You're generally limited in the number of resources available to you. That is, you can't ask just anyone in your company to handle a task for you. You have to work with the resources made available to you and figure out how to maximize the contribution each one makes.

- You're generally competing with others for each resource's time. For example, a resource from your company's marketing department might be handling items for you and five other colleagues in a given week.

- Even if money is no object, you generally can't just hand an entire project off to outside resources. It takes an insider—you or someone else—to coordinate and manage contracted outside resources and ensure that your tasks don't suffer because of an external resource's commitments to other clients.

- Even in the most extreme circumstances, certain tasks require at least a minimal amount of a resource's time. For example, if a task requires that a resource fly from a faraway city to your city with an approval mock-up of a new product, and you know the flight plus the commute from the airport always requires eight hours, you simply can't ask the resource to do it in six. People like to deliver excellent, timely work, but most haven't perfected the ability to warp time.

If you had any education in economics, you'll recognize that the preceding points sound a lot like the concept of *scarcity*. When resources in a marketplace are scarce, competition for the resources increases, so that people pay more for them and have to use them more wisely.

With scarcity of resources or anything else, what you can accomplish is limited by your access to the resources to do it. You can't make steel, for example, if scarcity makes coal so expensive that you can't afford to buy it for the furnace.

Project takes resource scarcity into account by using effort-driven scheduling (also called resource-driven scheduling) by default. Under effort-driven scheduling, Project may adjust a task's duration to take into account both the amount of work the task requires and the amount of resources assigned to it. For example, suppose that you have a task with a duration of four days, and the default calendar for the project calls for 8-hour workdays. This means that the task's work in hours is 32. Suppose, however, that you assign two full-time resources to the task, each of whom works the full hours per day. Under effort-driven scheduling, Project correctly adjusts the task's duration to two days, because each resource will apply 16 hours of work to the task over two days, completing the full 32 hours. So Project adjusts the finish date for the task accordingly. In contrast, if you assigned only one resource and that resource works less than full time, Project would extend the task's schedule.

Note

You can override the effort-driven duration for any task. To learn how to do so, see the "Overriding an Effort-Driven Duration" section later in this chapter.

Effort-driven scheduling results in the resources you select having a critical impact on your plan. As you create resources and make the related choices described in the remainder of this chapter, keep in mind how those choices might affect the overall schedule. If you encounter difficulties or conflicts as you create and work with resources, read Chapter 7, "Resolving Overallocations and Overbooked Resources," and Chapter 8, "Optimizing the Schedule," which provide techniques for addressing those difficulties.

Viewing and Using the Project Resource Sheet

The Task Sheet, which you learned to work with in earlier chapters, specifies what needs to happen in a project and when it needs to happen. (I'll assume that someone in your company knows why it needs to happen.) The Resource Sheet for your schedule allows you to specify who will make it happen, and how.

Use the Resource Sheet to build the list of resources you'll need to complete all the tasks you listed on the Task Sheet for the schedule. To view the Resource Sheet, shown in Figure 6.1, choose View, Resource Sheet. Or scroll down the View Bar, and click on the Resource Sheet icon. Just as each row in the Task Sheet holds information about a single task, each row in the Resource Sheet holds details about a single resource. Each column represents a particular field, or type of information. You can add columns that show information Project calculates, such as cost variances.

To select a cell in the Resource Sheet, click on it, or drag to select (highlight) groups of cells. Alternatively, use the arrow keys to move the cell selector around. To select an entire column or row, click on the column name or row number.

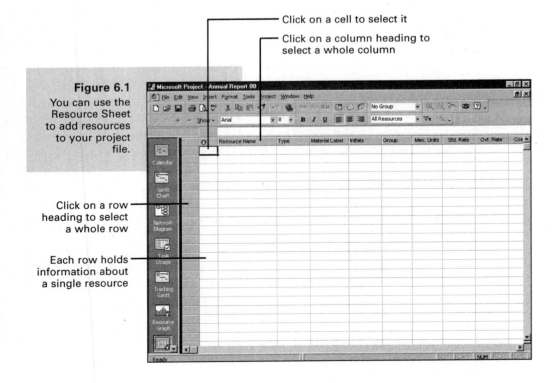

Figure 6.1
You can use the Resource Sheet to add resources to your project file.

Click on a cell to select it

Click on a column heading to select a whole column

Click on a row heading to select a whole row

Each row holds information about a single resource

Right-clicking on any selection opens a shortcut menu with commands that you can perform on the selection. For example, you can select a row, right-click, and then click on New Resource on the shortcut menu to insert a new blank resource at the selected location in the Resource Sheet.

Note

You can make adjustments to the size and position of columns or add columns in the Resource Sheet just as you did in the Task Sheet. The steps are virtually the same in the Resource Sheet as they were in the Task Sheet. To learn more, see the section "Adjusting the Task Sheet" in Chapter 4, "Setting Up a Project." One important column you might want to add is for resources' e-mail addresses. Project 2000 offers dozens of new fields for both the Task Sheet and Resource Sheet.

Setting Up a New Resource

Project 2000 now offers two different types of resources: work resources and material resources. When you add resources to your plan, you need to specify their type. *Work resources* consist of people or entities that perform hours of work for you, like employees and consultants. *Material resources* represent things a task consumes, like reams of paper, expensive color copies or proofs, blueprint reproduction, overheads and slides for meetings, promotional kits, or storage disks. You track material usage to increase the accuracy with which Project can calculate project costs. Not surprisingly, these consumables can add up quickly—with a dramatic impact on your project's bottom line.

By default, the Resource Sheet has 12 columns that enable you to enter information that might be crucial to your plan, plus a column where indicators appear. This section takes a look at the basic method for making entries in these columns, as well as the columns that are most essential to use in defining the resource. Because the remaining columns deal with resource calendars and costs, both of which require a detailed discussion, I'll cover those columns later in this chapter, after you get your feet wet here.

ON THE

CD

The *Annual Report Chapter 6* file you copied or installed from the CD-ROM for this book contains task information, but no resources. At the very least, you can use the file to practice adding resources and making assignments to existing tasks. If you open the file and see a message that the last task in the file can't be completed on time, simply click OK to bypass the message.

Work Resources

To start a new work resource, click on the Resource Name cell of a new blank row in the Resource Sheet and type the resource name. As you type, the Enter button and Cancel button appear beside the text entry box above the column headings (see Figure 6.2). To finish entering the name, click on Enter. Project fills in some default information about the resource, such as entering *Work* as the resource Type and entering *100%* in the Max. Units column. After you enter the resource name, you can press the Tab key to move to any column to the right, or press Enter to move down to the next row and list all resources by name only.

Caution

To remove the contents of a cell in the Resource Sheet, do not simply click on the cell and press Delete. Doing so removes the entire resource, not just the contents of the selected cell. Instead, right-click on the cell, and then click on Clear Contents to empty the cell while keeping the resource in place.

Cancel button

Enter button

Entry box

Figure 6.2
Navigate in the
Resource Sheet
as you do in the
Task Sheet.

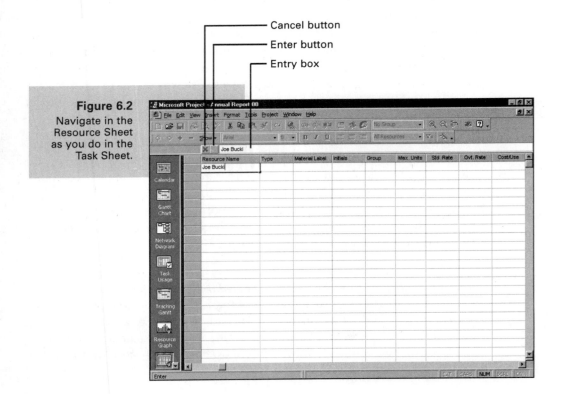

The style you use to create resources is up to you. You can use the Tab key after each entry to move across the row and complete each field entry for that resource. Or you can simply enter all the resource names, and then come back to each row and fill in the details. As noted at the start of this section, several of the columns or fields are basic, yet essential in identifying each resource as you assign it to tasks in your plan:

- **Resource Name.** Enter the full name for the resource, such as the name of a team member, supply vendor, or independent contractor.

- **Initials.** Don't be afraid to use long resource names. Project also enables you to identify a resource by its initials, entered in this column. By default, Project uses the first initial of the first name of the Resource Name entry in the Initials column. You should, however, select the Initials entry and type another entry that's more specific. I recommend that you make them more specific than a person's first and last initials, because it's pretty common to encounter people with the same initials. One approach is to use all or part of the first name, along with the last initial, as in JoeB, short for Joe Bucki.

- **Group.** When your resource belongs to a group and it might be significant to identify that group for the purposes of your project, enter the group name in the Group column. For example, if your team members come from several departments in your company, and you want to track each department's contribution, enter the department name or tracking number. Or, if you're working with several different contractors for a project, each of whom needs to be entered as a separate resource, you can enter Contract in the Group column for each of them to be able to track their collective performance.

• •

You can fill entries down a column in the Resource Sheet, just as you can fill entries in the Task Sheet. Select the cell holding the entry to fill (copy), then drag the fill handle in the lower-right corner of the cell.

• •

- **Max. Units.** The default entry for this column, 100%, means that for each scheduled workday, the resource offers one person (or machine, or so on) for the full duration of the workday; this is known as a single *assignment unit*. Entries of less than 100% indicate part-time work (more on that in Chapter 7), but entries of more than 100% don't assign overtime (more on overtime in Chapter 8). Entries of more than 100% mean that the resource might be offering additional people (or machines) for assignments. So, for example, if a resource offers four people to handle each task, you would change the Max. Units entry for the resource to 400%.

When you select the Max. Units field in a row, spinner buttons appear at the right side of the cell, so you can use the mouse to increase or decrease the entry rather than typing. (Alternately, you can specify assignment units in the Max. Units column in decimal values, with 1 in decimal terms being equivalent to 100% in percentage terms. Use the Show Assignment Units As A drop-down list on the Schedule tab of the Options dialog box, described in Chapter 24, "Customizing Microsoft Project," to change this setting.)

- **Code.** This column at the far right side of the Resource Sheet enables you to enter an alphanumeric code to identify the resource. This code might be a department number that corresponds to your entry in the Group column, or a unique number such as a Purchase Order number that you obtained for payment of the resource.

After you enter this basic information about several resources, your Resource Sheet might resemble the one shown in Figure 6.3.

Material Resources

You use the same process to enter material resources—make field entries and press Tab to move between fields—but you need to be sure to choose Material from the Type drop-down list and to fill in the Material Label column. The

Figure 6.3
Here's what the Resource Sheet looks like after you sketch out resources.

		Resource Name	Type	Material Label	Initials	Group	Max. Units	Std. Rate	Ovt. Rate	Cos
1		Joe Bucki	Work		JoeB	Design	100%	$0.00/hr	$0.00/hr	
2		Steve Poland	Work		SteveP	Contract	100%	$0.00/hr	$0.00/hr	
3		Mary Rogers	Work		MaryR	Comm	100%	$0.00/hr	$0.00/hr	
4		Stan Axel	Work		StanA	Acct	100%	$0.00/hr	$0.00/hr	
5		Lisa Gray	Work		LisaG	Comm	100%	$0.00/hr	$0.00/hr	
6		Ryan Printing	Work		Ryan	Contract	100%	$0.00/hr	$0.00/hr	
7		Stamps Mailing	Work		Stamps	Contract	100%	$0.00/hr	$0.00/hr	

material label represents the quantities you're using to measure the amount of material purchased and consumed. For example, if you're buying sets of color proofs, you could enter **set**. If you'll be paying for slides by the page, enter **page**. If your project will consume other materials by the gross, dozen, or thousand, enter the appropriate material label.

Optionally, you can include an entry in the Initials, Group columns, and Code columns, but note that you cannot make an entry in the Max. Units column. Project assumes a 1 for this column, which can stand for a single item, a ream, a gross, or any other measure you need to use. (Just add a note to the resource entry to clarify what measure you're using.) When you assign the resource to the task, you can increase the units setting to reflect how much of the material is actually consumed. Figure 6.4 shows some material resources added in to a Resource Sheet.

Displaying Resource Information

If you're not comfortable working in the spreadsheet-like cells of the Resource Sheet and would prefer a more convenient format in which to enter and edit the information about a resource, you can use the Resource Information dialog box shown in Figure 6.5. The General tab of the Resource Information dialog box enables you to enter basic task information, as well as other schedule-related

Figure 6.4
Material resources require the Material choice in the Type column.

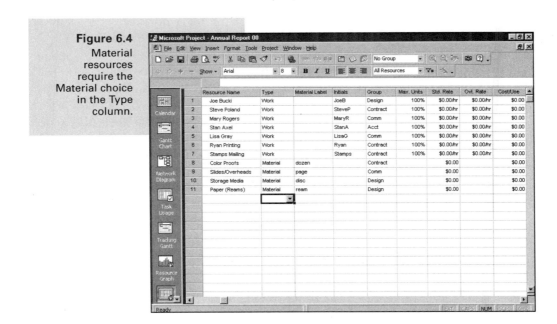

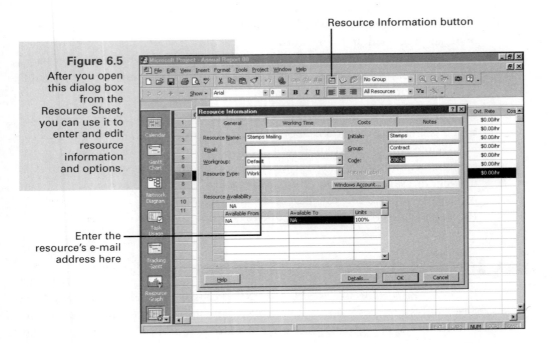

Resource Information button

Figure 6.5
After you open this dialog box from the Resource Sheet, you can use it to enter and edit resource information and options.

Enter the resource's e-mail address here

information. The dialog box also offers three other tabs, which are described where they apply in this chapter and the next.

To open the Resource Information dialog box for a resource in any view in Project that shows all or part of the Resource Sheet, start by clicking in a cell in the row for the desired resource. Then choose Project, Resource Information (or right-click, and then click on Resource Information). Alternately, press Shift+F2 or click on the Resource Information button on the Standard toolbar. Enter or edit information about the resource in the dialog box, and then click on OK to close the dialog box and accept the entries you made. Your changes appear in the appropriate columns for the selected task in the Resource Sheet.

When you open the Resource Information dialog box for a material resource, the dialog box Working Time tab, as well as some of the choices on the General tab, are grayed out or disabled. Logically, the tab and fields in question don't really apply to material resources, so Project makes them unavailable.

Tip

You also can display information about a resource by double-clicking in any cell in that resource's row in the Resource Sheet.

You can create a new resource by clicking on a blank row of the Resource Sheet, opening the Resource Information dialog box, entering information about the new resource, and clicking on OK.

Assigning Resource Costs

There's a cost associated with every resource, even when the resource is seemingly free because it comes from within your company. In fact, tracking your use of internal resources throughout the year can be useful during year-end budgeting, when your company determines how costs from administrative or service departments are allocated to (charged to) departments that are profit centers. For example, you don't want your department to be charged for a third of the marketing department's time if your department only used about 10 percent of that time (based on the hours tracked in your project), while two other profit centers each used 45 percent.

Similarly, you want to be smart about using resources with the correct responsibility level for projects, and resource cost can help you make such decisions. For example, say that one task in a project involves calling various companies for examples of annual reports to use as idea-starters for the project. A designer in your company is paid about $20 per hour, and an administrative assistant is paid $15 per hour, and both resources have the ability and the time to make the calls. In this case, it's much more efficient to have the less expensive resource, the administrative assistant, handle the calls. Such a strategy frees up more of the designer's time for true creative work, yielding better financial and design results on your project and more time for other projects.

Caution

If your company doesn't require you to track internal resource costs, you still should enter a standard rate (Std. Rate) of some type (even a dummy rate) for the resource. Project needs a standard rate for some of its calculations.

Three columns on the Resource Sheet let you assign default costs to the work performed by a resource. For most of these entries, you can simply select the cell and make your entry. Here are the fields that control costs on the Resource Sheet:

- **Std. Rate.** Enter the cost for work performed by a work resource during normal working hours. To indicate an hourly rate, simply enter the hourly cost, such as 20 for $20 per hour. However, if the resource charges or will be paid by the minute (m), day (d), or week (w), enter the appropriate abbreviation along with your cost, such as 2000/w for $2,000 per week. You also can enter yearly salary amounts using the y abbreviation, and Project calculates the appropriate compensation for the actual length of the task. For material resources, enter the cost per unit—material label—for the resource. Make sure you choose a cost that's consistent with the measure you entered in the Material Label column. For example, if one unit of the resource equals one set of color proofs, then enter the cost for the entire set of color proofs as the Std. Rate, not the cost per proof page. If each resource unit equals a single ream of paper, enter the cost per ream as the Std. Rate, not the cost per 10-ream box. If you specified thousand as the material label, enter the cost per thousand.

- **Ovt. Rate.** If there's a possibility the resource will be working overtime on your project and your company is willing (or required by law, as for hourly, nonexempt workers) to pay a premium for the overtime, enter the overtime rate for the resource in this column, using the same method and abbreviations described above for the Std. Rate column. This helps Project calculate the additional cost of overtime work assigned in the project during estimating and tracking.

  You cannot enter an Ovt. Rate for material resources. However, if the material resource cost will vary, you can set up different cost rate tables for it as described later in this chapter, in the section called "Creating Variable Pay Rates with Cost Rate Tables."

- **Cost/Use.** A work or material resource might have a set cost every time you use it; this cost might be the total cost for using the resource, or might supplement the hourly rate. For example, a courier service might charge you a set fee per delivery rather than an hourly rate. Or a resource might charge you a set travel fee for visits to your office in addition to an hourly rate. Or you might incur a delivery cost for each shipment of a material resource. Enter an amount in the Cost/Use column (such as 15 for $15) to charge that fee to your project each time you assign the resource to a task and the task is completed.

If you're a consultant and need to provide both schedules and cost estimates for clients, assigning costs to every resource can help you build a reasonably accurate cost estimate. Build some cushion into the cost estimate you provide to your client (especially if the client's requirements are ill-defined), unless the client is willing to pay for budget overruns.

Setting How Costs Are Calculated

As you just learned, the costs for a resource can be calculated based on units of work completed, a per use fee, or both. Most people, however, aren't foolish enough to pay for work before it's completed — and doing so isn't typically a standard accounting practice. On the other hand, it's not reasonable to expect that all task costs for any given task will hit your project's bottom line after the work on the task is completed, especially if the task lasts more than a week or so.

To have a realistic picture of the costs incurred for your project at any given date, you need to specify the correct option for the resource's costs using the Accrue At column in the Resource Sheet or the Cost Accrual down on the Costs tab of the Resource Information dialog box. After you click on a cell in the Accrue At column on the Resource Sheet, a down arrow appears at the right end of the cell. Click on this arrow to display the Accrue At choices (see Figure 6.6), which are identical to the Cost Accrual drop-down list choices on the Costs tab of the Resource Information dialog box, and then click on the method you want to select for the current resource:

- **Start.** Specifies that a resource's total cost for a task is expended as soon as work on the task starts. Use this method if you need to pay for contract work when the work begins. This choice also applies when a resource has only a per use cost that's due in advance, such as having to pay for a supply item when you order it.

Figure 6.6
Use the drop-down list to select an Accrue At method.

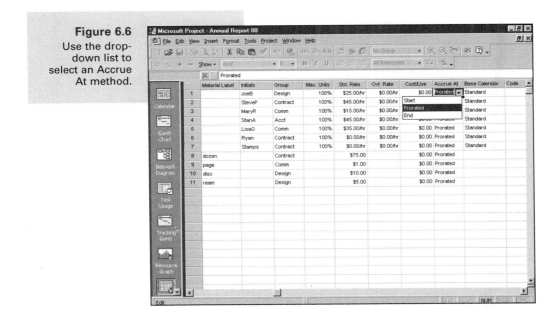

- **Prorated.** Under this method (the default), costs hit your project's bottom line as the work progresses. For example, if a resource charges $10 per hour and you've told Project that the resource has completed 10 hours of work on a task, under this Accrue At method, the project shows $100 in expenses to date for the task. Use this method when tracking expenses for resources within your company, or for resources that you need to pay on a regular monthly basis.

Caution

> Using the Prorated Accrue At method for resources that you work with only on a Per Use fee structure can lead to inaccurate reporting, because you might owe the full fee even if you need the resource for less time. For example, if you rent certain equipment, there might be a per use minimum fee, due in advance. Make sure that you change the Accrue At method to Start or End for such resources.

- **End.** This method specifies that the expense will officially be charged to the project when the task is completed. Use this choice when you need to approve work before payment or when payment isn't due until work on a task is completed.

Creating Variable Pay Rates with Cost Rate Tables

Businesses' ongoing efforts to trim and accurately predict costs dictated that Project offer precise, flexible methods of tracking costs. In Project 2000, you can set up cost rate tables to help you account for moving targets such as the following:

- **Scheduled pay rate or material cost increases or volume purchase decreases.** If an internal resource's pay will increase on a particular date during the schedule, Project can automatically increase the Std. Rate (standard rate) and Ovt. Rate (overtime rate) for the resource on the date you specify in the default cost rate table for the resource. If cost for a material resource will increase starting on a particular date, you can indicate when the standard rate will change. Similarly, if an external resource's rates will increase or decrease (due to surpassing a minimum volume breakpoint) on a particular date (typically the start of a new calendar year or the effective date for a new contract), you can have Project automatically apply the rate increase when it kicks in by specifying the rate change on the resource's default cost rate table.

- **One resource, many rates.** For some resources, you might pay different rates depending on the nature of the work needed to complete different tasks. You'll typically encounter such a cost structure when you're working with an outside resource such as a consulting company. Such companies usually charge one rate for work by a partner or account manager, and another rate for work performed by assistants. Or, for example, the firm might charge one rate for research, another for designing a campaign or publication, and another for account administration. When a resource charges different rates for different tasks, you need to create a separate cost rate table for each rate, and then assign the appropriate cost table for each task you assign to the resource, as described later in this chapter under "Changing the Cost Table for an Assignment."

> *Tip* If a consulting firm doesn't provide a rate reduction for work handled by assistant-level folks, ask for such a reduction to reduce your costs.

- **Mixing hourly with per use costs.** A resource might charge a per use fee or other type of fee for some types of tasks, but not others. For example, if an outside consulting firm charges a fixed fee for preparing your monthly company newsletter but charges you an hourly fee for all other work, you'll need separate cost rate tables for the resource. One cost rate table would hold the per use fee, and the other would hold the hourly rate. Then you could assign the rate table that applies to each task assignment.

- **Periods with special rates.** If you have to convince a resource to work at a time when that resource wouldn't typically be working, that resource might charge a premium rate. For example, a resource might charge double the hourly rate for work during the week between Christmas and New Year's Day. In such a case, you would enter the increase starting date and rate on a row of the resource's default cost rate table, and then on the next row enter the date when the rate would return to normal, along with the normal rate.

You use the Resource Information dialog box to create cost rate tables for a resource. Follow these steps to edit or adjust a cost rate table:

1. In the Resource Sheet, click in a cell in the row for the resource for which you want to create a cost rate table; then click on the Resource Information button on the Standard toolbar. Or, double-click in a cell in the resource row. The Resource Information dialog box appears.

2. Click on the Costs tab to display its options. The Cost Rate Tables area of the dialog box offers five tabs, each of which represents a separate cost rate table. The A (Default) tab's rates will be used for the resource unless you create entries on another cost rate table tab (B through E) and specify that tab for an assignment as described later in the chapter.

3. To specify a rate change for the resource, enter an Effective Date on the next empty row of the tab—in this case, the A (Default) tab. Then, enter the new Standard Rate or Overtime Rate in the appropriate cell on that row, or a new Per Use Cost on that row. You have to change each rate; Project does not calculate a new Overtime Rate if you change the Standard Rate. You can enter positive or negative percentages to have Project calculate each rate increase or decrease respectively. For example, if you know an internal resource will receive a 4 percent pay increase on a particular date, you can enter that increase percentage (as shown in Figure 6.7) rather than calculate dollars and cents.

4. Repeat Step 3 as many times as needed to build the A (Default) cost rate table. Each cost rate table can hold up to 25 rate changes.

5. To create a new cost rate table, click on another tab under Cost Rate Tables.

6. If you're working with the first row on another Cost Rate Table tab, don't edit its Effective Date entry; this will designate the rate entries on that row

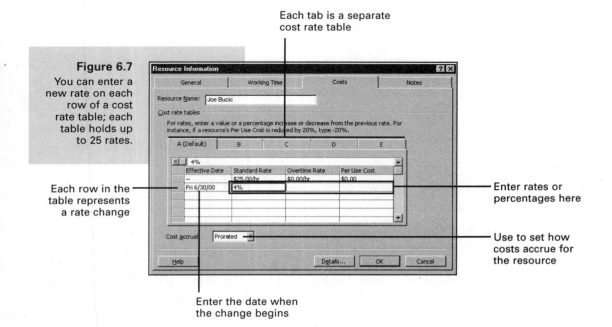

Figure 6.7
You can enter a new rate on each row of a cost rate table; each table holds up to 25 rates.

as the "base" or "default" rates for the new cost table. Otherwise, create the rates on the table as described in Steps 3 and 4.

7. Repeat Steps 5 and 6 to specify additional cost rate tables. You can create up to five for each project file.

8. When you finish making cost rate table changes for the resource, click on OK to close the Resource Information dialog box.

Once you've established an effective date and rate change, Project automatically applies the new rate to work completed and materials consumed starting on that effective date.

Working with Fixed Costs

Some tasks have a particular cost no matter which resource handles the work. For example, you might know from experience that the freight for a particular shipment of products costs approximately $1,000 if you use either of two shippers. Or you might know what a particular type of material costs, or have an accurate estimate of what it costs to complete the task.

In such a case, if the cost won't vary and you don't plan to assign a specific resource to the task, assign a fixed cost for the task rather than creating a resource entry with a per use or other cost assignment. You have to go back to Gantt Chart view to start this process, as indicated in the following steps:

1. Choose View, Gantt Chart, if you're not already at the Gantt Chart view. Or click on the Gantt Chart icon in the View Bar.

2. Open the View menu, point to Table, and click on Cost. (You also could right-click on the Select All button where the sheet row and column headings intersect, then choose Cost from the shortcut menu that appears.) The Task Sheet pane at the left side of the view changes to display columns specific to tracking costs for the tasks, as shown in Figure 6.8.

3. Click to select the Fixed Cost cell for the task for which you want to assign a fixed cost.

4. Type the amount (in dollars) of the fixed cost; for example, type 500 for $500. Press Enter or click on the Enter button next to the text entry box to complete entering the fixed cost.

5. (Optional) Return to the view in which you were working by using a choice on the View menu; for example, open the View menu and click on Resource Sheet or click on the Resource Sheet icon in the View Bar. To simply change the Task Sheet pane of your Gantt Chart view back to its normal entry mode, open the View menu, point to Table, and click on Entry.

Figure 6.8
You enter a fixed cost in this table of the Task Sheet rather than on the Resource Sheet.

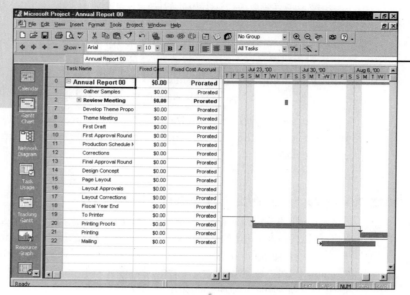

Enter fixed costs in this column

Working with Resource Calendars (Work Schedules)

By default, when you assign a work resource to a task, Project assumes that the resource will follow the Standard base calendar.

Thus, if the normal workday is 8 hours, the resource's typical workday is 8 hours. Under this scenario, it takes the resource three working days to complete a task that's 24 hours (three days) in duration. Sometimes, however, a resource's real working schedule differs from that of the project.

Under Project's effort-driven default scheduling method, you need to ensure that you specify the real working schedule for each resource to develop an accurate schedule. For example, if the base calendar for the project is set to 24 Hours, but the resource works only 8 hours per day, the durations for the tasks you assign to that resource need to be three times longer than the base calendar would cause Project to assign.

You don't have to—and in fact, can't—specify a specific calendar for a material resource. Material resources don't have working time or a calendar associated with them.

Choosing a Calendar

Use the Base Calendar column of the Resource Sheet to select the appropriate working schedule for a resource. The base calendars available for resources are the same as those available for projects. The 24 Hours calendar runs round the clock, seven days a week. The Standard calendar provides 40 hours per week, scheduled 8 A.M. to noon and 1 P.M. to 5 P.M., Monday through Friday. The Night Shift schedule also offers 40 hours per week, scheduled from Monday evening through early Saturday morning. If you created a custom calendar as described in Chapter 4, it appears on the list, as well.

To change the Base Calendar entry for a resource, click on the Base Calendar cell for the resource. When you do so, a down arrow appears at the right end of the text entry box. Click this arrow to display the three choices, click on the calendar you want, and then press Enter or click on the Enter button next to the text entry box.

Setting Work Resource Availability

You may find yourself competing for a highly desirable work resource. For example, a resource may be tied up with other projects until three weeks after your project starts. In such a case, rather than tediously marking nonworking days in the resource's base calendar (see the final part of this section, next), you should instead specify availability dates for the resource. Similarly, if you're sharing a resource with another department, Project offers an easy availability setting to account for that without adjusting the resource's working calendar. Project uses availability settings and the resource's base calendar together to determine whether a resource can take on a task and to calculate how long it will take the resource to complete the task.

When you're working in the Gantt Chart view, Project will let you assign a resource to a task that occurs during a period when you indicated that a resource isn't available. If you check the Resource Usage view (described later in this chapter) or other views that highlight when you assign too much work to a resource (see Chapter 7, "Resolving Overallocations and Overbooked Resources"), you'll clearly see that you assigned a task to a resource that's not available.

Follow these steps to change a resource's availability:

1. In the Resource Sheet, click on a cell in the row for the resource for which you want to set availability; then click on the Resource Information button on the Standard toolbar. Or double-click on a cell in the resource row. The Resource Information dialog box appears, with the General tab selected.

2. To specify the first date on which the resource becomes available, click on the first line in the Available From column under Resource Availability, then enter a date or choose it from the drop-down calendar.

3. If the resource will become unavailable again after a certain date, specify that date in the Available To column on the same row. However, leave the Available To cell set to "NA" if the resource will remain available.

• •

If you're removing availability dates you entered for a resource, click on the Available For Entire Project option button, which removes the From and To settings.

• •

4. Use the Units text box or spinner buttons to specify how many work units the resource will provide during the period of availability. Figure 6.9 shows an availability period designated for a resource.

Note

As your project progresses and you view the Resource Sheet, a resource's Max. Units column entry will vary according to the current system date and the periods of availability you indicated. In other words, if you view the Resource Sheet on a date during which you indicated the resource would not be available, the Max. Units entry for that resource will be 0%. Don't change the entry in the Resource Sheet at this point, because it will create an unwanted availability entry, and potentially throw off Project's calculations.

Figure 6.9
If the work resource will only be available between certain dates, you can specify them on the General tab of the Resource Information dialog box.

Resource Information	? ✕

General	Working Time	Costs	Notes

Resource Name: Steve Poland   Initials: SteveP

Email: Group: Contract

Workgroup: Default   Code:

Resource Type: Work   Material Label:

Windows Account...

Resource Availability

Available From	Available To	Units
5/1/2000	6/30/2000	100%

Help   Details...   OK   Cancel

5. If the resource will be unavailable for additional periods during the span of your project schedule, indicate the dates and units of availability on subsequent rows under Resource Availability.

6. Click on OK to finish changing the resource's availability settings.

Customizing a Resource Calendar

Sometimes you need to adjust the base calendar for a resource. For example, a resource might work two shifts per day, four days per week. Or a resource might be unavailable on Wednesdays, or only available to work half-time for a few days during the schedule. To ensure that the effort-driven scheduling properly adjusts the durations of tasks to which you assign this resource, and to prevent you from scheduling the resource for times when it is unavailable, make sure that you adjust the selected base calendar for any resource that has special scheduling requirements.

To do so, follow these steps:

1. In the Resource Sheet, use the Base Calendar column to select the working schedule that most closely approximates the actual availability of the resource.

2. In the Resource Sheet, click in a cell in the row for the resource for which you want to set availability; then click on the Resource Information button on the Standard toolbar. Or double-click in a cell in the resource row. When the Resource Information dialog box appears, click on the Working Time tab to display it, as shown in Figure 6.10. Alternately, after you click in a cell in the resource's row, choose Tools, Change Working Time.

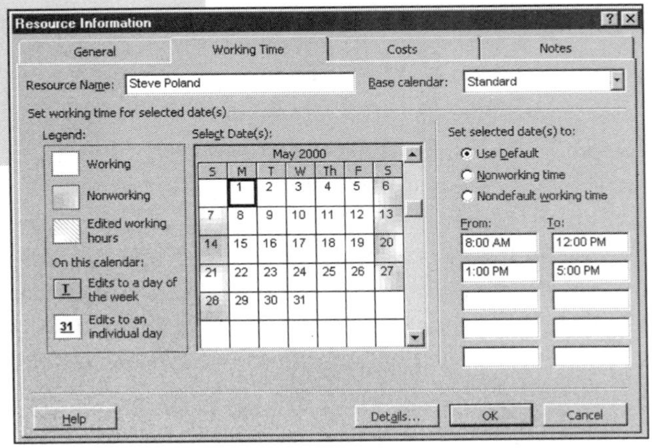

Figure 6.10
You can customize the base calendar for a resource.

3. To specify whether the resource works on a particular day, click on the date you want to change on the calendar. (Click on a day column head to change that day for the whole year.) Then, in the Set Working Time For Selected Date(s) area of the dialog box, click on Working Time or Nonworking Time as needed. Dates to specify as nonworking include holidays and vacation days.

● ●

The Use Default selection returns a date to its default scheduling according to the selected base calendar. This includes both rescheduling the task as a working or nonworking day and returning the Working Time entries to the defaults for the selected date.

Unlike a project schedule, a resource doesn't need its own custom calendar. Project already tracks individual base calendar changes you make by resource name.

● ●

4. To change the Working Time (daily working hours) for a date, select the date, and then make sure either the Working Time or the Use Default option button is selected for it under For Selected Dates. In the Working Time area, edit or delete the desired From and To entries.

5. Continue scrolling the Calendar view as needed, repeating Steps 3 and 4 to change the schedule for additional dates. As you change the schedule for each date, Project indicates the edited date in the calendar by marking the date with bold and underlining and filling the date box with light-gray shading.

6. Click on OK to close the dialog box and implement the scheduling changes you specified.

Adding a Resource Note

Just as you can add more detailed notes about a particular task you created, you can use a note to capture information about a specific resource. This feature can be particularly important when you're working with outside resources, or when a resource is handling especially complex tasks. For example, you can use a note to record detailed contact information for the person you're working with at an external vendor. Or you can add a note to a resource explaining why the resource has a per use fee in addition to an hourly rate. You can remind yourself of the names of key clients the resource has served in the past, in case someone working with your project file is interested in knowing more about the project resources.

To enter or edit note information about a resource in the Resource Sheet, do the following:

1. Click in a cell in the row holding the resource for which you want to create a note.

2. Open the Project menu or right-click to open the resource shortcut menu. Click on Resource Notes. Alternately, click on the Resource Notes button on the Standard toolbar. The Resource Information dialog box appears, with the Notes tab selected. (If you double-click on the resource entry instead, you can then click on the Notes tab in the Resource Information dialog box.)

3. Click in the Notes text box, and then type or edit the text of your note (see Figure 6.11). Press Enter to start each new line in the note. You can add special formatting to notes using the buttons at the top of the Notes text area. The first button enables you to change the font for any text you select by dragging over it in the note; it opens the Font dialog box, which Chapter 16, "Other Formatting," covers. The next three buttons align the current note line (which holds the blinking insertion point) left, center, and right, respectively. The fifth button adds or removes a bullet at the beginning of the current line of the note. The last button enables you to insert an embedded object into the note, such as information from Excel

Resource Notes button

Figure 6.11
Use the Notes tab in the Resource Information dialog box to enter and format your notes about a resource.

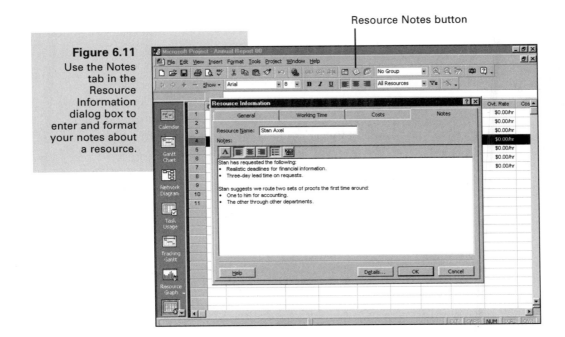

or a bitmap image; Chapter 20 provides more information on working with embedded objects. If you highlight and delete all of this text, Project removes the note altogether from the resource.

4. Click on OK to close the Resource Information dialog box.

After you add a note to a resource, you can point to the note indicator on the Resource Sheet to display the note in a pop-up box.

Assigning a Resource to a Task

Until now, this book has described tasks and resources as somewhat separate, discrete entities. You enter information about tasks in one part of Project and information about resources in another. In this section, you learn to mesh these two forms of information in your schedule. Keep in mind that the resources you assign to a particular task might cause Project to adjust the task's start or finish date depending on the availability of the resource. If a resource assignment causes a schedule change you don't want, use one of the methods described later in this section to choose a different resource for the task.

To assign resources to a particular task, you need to return to the location where you list the tasks for your schedule, the Task Sheet in the Gantt Chart view, or (in most cases) another view, the Task Entry view. To speed your work with resources, you might also want to display the Resource Management toolbar. To do so, right-click on any toolbar onscreen and choose Resource Management.

Note

You also can work with task and resource information in other views. Chapter 11, "Working with the Different Project Views," introduces more of the available views and helps you work with task and resource information. Most of the options in other views, however, work like the ones described here. Therefore, after you learn to display the views discussed in Chapter 11, you can apply the techniques you learn here to working in those views, as well.

If you're most comfortable working in the Task Sheet, you might prefer to assign resources there by using the Resource Names column, which provides a drop-down list of available resources. Switch to the Gantt Chart view, if necessary, by choosing View, Gantt Chart; or click on the Gantt Chart icon in the View Bar. Scroll the Task Sheet pane so that it shows the Resource Names column. Click in the cell for the task to which you want to assign a resource. If you remember the

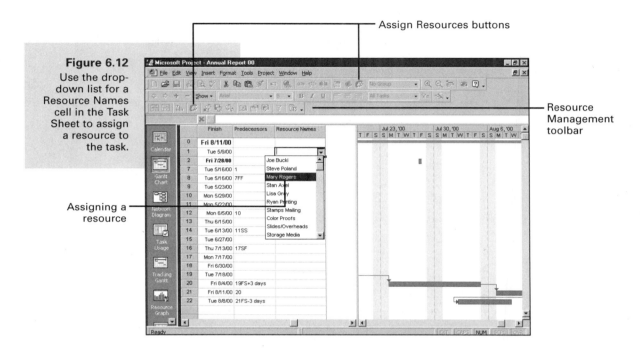

Assign Resources buttons

Figure 6.12
Use the drop-down list for a Resource Names cell in the Task Sheet to assign a resource to the task.

Resource Management toolbar

Assigning a resource

full resource name, type it in the selected cell and press Enter. Otherwise, click on the down arrow that appears at the right end of the cell; click on the name of the resource you want (see Figure 6.12), and then press Enter or click on the Enter button.

If you type the name of a brand-new resource in the Resource Names column of the Task Sheet in Gantt Chart view, Project adds a new row for that resource in the Resource Sheet. You then can choose View, Resource Sheet or click on the Resource Sheet icon in the View Bar to switch to the Resource Sheet, where you can enter the remaining information about the resource.

If you're not comfortable with a lot of typing, or plan to enter multiple resources and want a faster method, you can use the Assign Resources dialog box.

To open this dialog box, click in a cell in the task for which you want to add resources. Open the Tools menu, point to Resources, and click on Assign Resources. Alternately, click on the Assign Resources button on the Standard or Resource Management toolbar, or press Alt+F10. The Assign Resources dialog box appears, as shown in Figure 6.13.

Figure 6.13
The Assign
Resources dialog
box might be
faster when you
need to work
with many
resource
assignments.

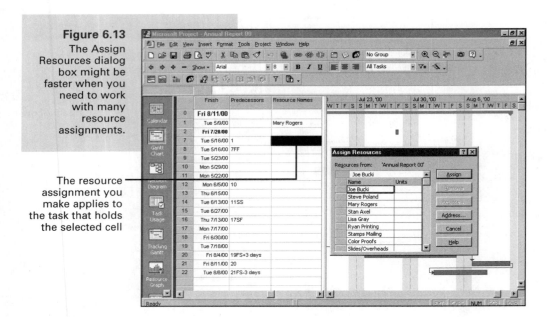

The resource
assignment you
make applies to
the task that holds
the selected cell

To assign a resource to the cell you selected, click on the desired resource name in the Resources From list. Adjust the Units entry as needed. For example, you can change a work resource to 50% Units for the task, or assign more than one unit of a material resource (such as 5 if the resource is reams of paper). Click the Assign button to finish assigning the resource.

Or point to the gray box at the left end of the row holding the desired resource in the Assign Resources dialog box, drag the resource, and drop it into place on a task. You can continue using this dialog box to assign resources to other tasks. Simply select the Resource Names cell for another task, and then use the Assign Resources dialog box to select and assign the resource. When you finish assigning resources, click on Close to close the Assign Resources dialog box.

Note

If you have information about a resource entered in your Windows Address Book, you can click the Address button in the Assign Resources dialog box to display the Select Resources dialog box, which lists your Address Book entries. Click the contact in the list at the left, then click the Add button. Clicking OK closes the dialog box and adds the contact information from the Address Book to your list of resources. This saves you some typing and ensures that correct e-mail address information for the resource is entered into Project.

A final way to assign a resource to a single task from the Task Sheet is to right-click on the task, and then click on the Task Information command (or click on the Task Information button on the Standard toolbar). In the Task Information dialog box, click on the Resources tab. Click on the first blank Resource Name row, click on the down arrow that appears beside the cell, click on a resource name, and then click on the Enter button. Click on OK to close the Task Information dialog box.

The biggest drawback to a couple of the resource assignment techniques just described is that unless your screen is big enough to display the whole Task Sheet, you might not be able to see the name of the task to which you're assigning a resource. You can use another view, Task Entry view, to enable you to be clear about which task you're entering a resource for. This view is sometimes referred to as the Task Form. To use this view to assign resources to tasks, do the following:

1. To switch to Task Entry view, click on the Task Entry View button on the Resource Management toolbar. Alternately, choose View, More Views or click on the More Views icon in the View Bar; then, in the Views list, scroll down to Task Entry, click on it, and click on Apply. The Task Entry view appears, as shown in Figure 6.14.

Task Sheet

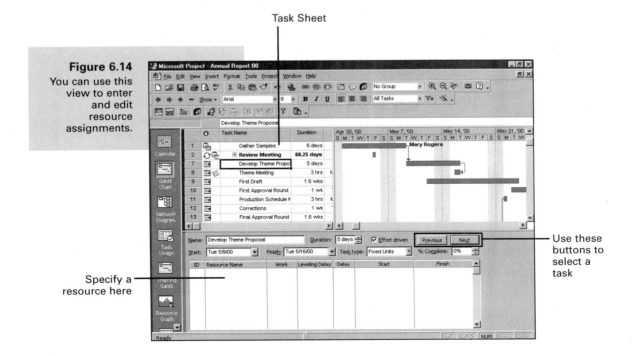

Figure 6.14
You can use this view to enter and edit resource assignments.

Specify a resource here

Use these buttons to select a task

2. Select a task by choosing it from the Task Name column of the visible portion of the Task Sheet, or by using the Previous and Next buttons in the lower pane of the view.

3. Click on the first blank row of the Resource Name column of the lower portion of the view. A highlight appears on the name of the selected task in the Task Sheet.

4. Click on the down arrow that appears at the right end of the selected cell under Resource Name, and then click on the name of the resource you want to select. Click on OK (which appears in place of the Previous button) to complete your entry. After you do so, information about the selected resource appears in the lower pane of the display, as shown in Figure 6.15.

5. Repeat Steps 2 through 4 to assign resources to other tasks.

When you finish working in Task Entry view, open the View menu and click on the appropriate menu command to return to another view, such as Gantt Chart. If the window remains divided into upper and lower panes, remove the split by choosing Window, Remove Split.

Figure 6.15
Here's how a resource assigned to a task appears when displayed in the Task Entry view (Task Form).

Resource assigned to the task

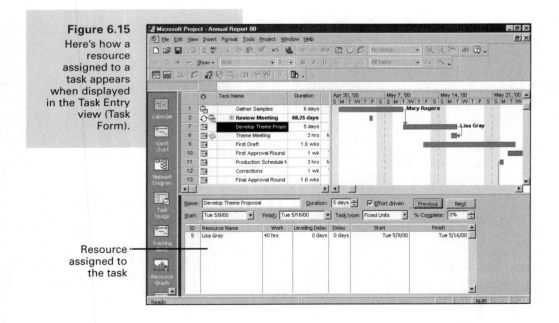

Start Dates and Delays

As you can see in the lower pane of the Task Entry view in Figure 6.15, the view shows the task and resource names, task duration, number of work hours the resource will require to finish the project, and Start and Finish dates. Beside the Start column, however, you'll find the Delay column. You can use this column to specify that you don't want a resource to begin exactly when the start of the working day begins, or that you have more than one resource assigned to the task (see the next two chapters for more details) and want one to start a certain length of time after the others, perhaps to check their work.

To enter a delay for a resource, switch to Task Entry view and display the task information by clicking on the task in the Task Name column of the Task Sheet (or by using the Previous and Next buttons). Click in the Delay column and enter the delay time period, along with a time unit specification such as **h** for hours or **d** for days. Figure 6.16 shows an example.

Click on OK in the lower pane of the view to complete specifying the delay. If necessary—for example when you're creating a delay for the sole resource assigned to the task—Project adjusts the start and finish dates for the task. Keep in mind that such changes can introduce scheduling conflicts, particularly if other linked tasks depend on the scheduled completion of the task you're working with.

Figure 6.16
You can create a delay to adjust the start of a resource's work.

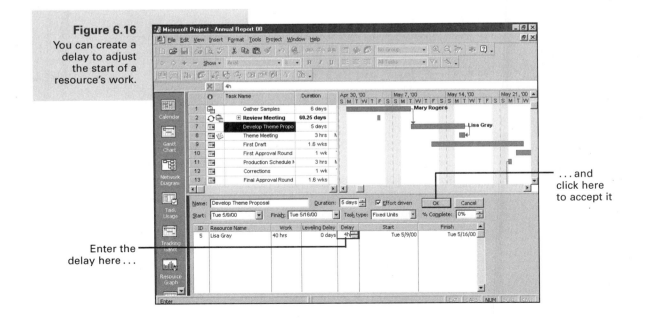

Enter the delay here . . .

. . . and click here to accept it

Overriding an Effort-Driven Duration

This chapter has noted repeatedly that under Project's default effort-driven method of scheduling tasks, the work resources you assign to a task might cause Project to adjust the schedule for the task depending on the resource's availability (Max Units on the resource sheet or the Units specified for a particular period of availability on the General tab of the Resource Information dialog box), where each unit represents one person working full time on the task, as determined by the resource's base calendar, compared with the calendar for the task. By default, the total number of hours allocated to the task (called the work) remains constant as you add more resources (units), with Project adjusting the duration accordingly. For example, if a four-day task has the Standard eight-hour calendar, and a resource also uses the Standard eight-hour calendar as its working calendar but has 200% Max Units Available (two people working full-time on the task), applying that resource to the task reduces its duration to two days.

Note

The equation Duration*Units = Work establishes the relationship between the duration, units, and work for a task. So Project does a little algebra to arrive at the equation that keeps work constant and adjusts the duration under the default effort-driven scheduling settings: Duration = Work/Units.

You can stop Project from making duration, work, or units changes for selected tasks, if you want, by changing the Task Type setting:

- **Fixed Units.** This is the default when effort-driven scheduling is enabled. Adding more resources makes the duration shorter, and removing resources increases the duration.

- **Fixed Work.** This setting disables effort-driven scheduling, and in most cases has the same effect as changing a task type to fixed units: Adding resources shortens the duration, and removing resources increases the duration. There's an exception, though. Each resource can't provide more work (hours) per day than the task's schedule allows. For example, if you create a four-day task and select Fixed Work as the Task Type, then you assign a resource with 200% set as its Max. Units Available setting on the General tab of the Resource Information dialog box. For a Fixed Unit task, Project would decrease the task duration to two days, but for a Fixed Work task the duration remains at four days, because a single resource can't work more than the allotted number of working hours per day on the task. Project halves the available units so that the work setting and duration can remain constant.

- **Fixed Duration.** This setting keeps the duration constant when you apply resources to the task. For example, if your project requires filing accounting information by a particular federal filing deadline, you'll want the duration and schedule for the task to remain fixed. Adding resources to this task decreases the amount of work each resource contributes on each day. For example, if you apply two full-time resources to a four-day task, Project doesn't cut the duration in half; it cuts the number of hours (work) each resource supplies each day in half.

You can specify the task type for a task in the Task Entry view by selecting the task in the visible portion of the Task Sheet. Then click on the Task Type drop-down list in the bottom area of the view, and click on the desired task type. You can also specify a task type for a task from any view that shows the Task Sheet. Right-click on the task you want to fix, and then click on Task Information; alternately, click on the task, and then click on the Task Information button on the Standard toolbar. The Task Information dialog box appears. Click on the Advanced tab. Open the Task Type drop-down list (see Figure 6.17), and then click on the task type you want. Click on OK to close the dialog box.

Note

If you want all new tasks to be scheduled with the task type you select, use the Default Task Type drop-down list on the Schedule tab of the Options dialog box. Chapter 24, "Customizing Microsoft Project," explains how to change this and other default settings.

Figure 6.17
Use the drop-down list shown in this dialog box to control whether Project adjusts the task's schedule.

Task Information	? X

| General | Predecessors | Resources | Advanced | Notes |

Name: Gather Samples   Duration: 6 days   ☐ Estimated

Constrain task

Deadline: NA

Constraint type: As Soon As Possible   Constraint date: NA

Task type: Fixed Units   ☑ Effort driven
  Fixed Duration
Calendar: Fixed Units
  Fixed Work   ☐ Scheduling ignores resource calendars
WBS code:

☐ Mark task as milestone

Help   OK   Cancel

Turning Off Effort-Driven Scheduling

You also can turn off the effort-driven scheduling feature for a task to disable the Duration*Units = Work equation, so that adding more resources doesn't automatically decrease the duration, but instead adds more units and work. On the Advanced tab of the Task Information dialog box, clear the check mark beside Effort Driven. Then, to fix the task duration, choose Fixed Duration as the task type using the Task Type drop-down list.

Deleting Resources

There are instances when a resource is no longer needed, either within a task assignment or within the Resource Sheet. At that point, you'll want to delete it.

From a Task

To delete a resource from a task, you can use any of a number of methods, depending on the current view. From the Task Sheet view, click in any cell in the task for which you want to remove the resource. Open the Assign Resources dialog box by clicking on the Assign Resources button on the Standard or Resource Management toolbar (or pressing Alt+F10). In the Assign Resources dialog box, click on the resource to delete, which has a check mark beside it to indicate that it's assigned to the current task. Click Remove to remove the resource. From here, you can use the dialog box to add and remove resources for other tasks, or can simply click on Close to close the dialog box.

You can use Task Entry view to make removing a resource from a task even easier. Simply click on the name of the resource to delete in the Resource Name column of the bottom pane, then press Delete, and then click on OK.

Selecting a cell in the Resource Names column and pressing Delete deletes the whole task entry, not just the resource. To delete the Resource Names entry only, right-click on the appropriate cell and click on Clear Contents.

From the Project

Just as you can use the Resource Sheet to add new resources to a project, you can use the Resource Sheet to remove entries for resources you no longer use. For example, say that you added the name of a person from another department to the resource list, but that person has been transferred to another city and is no longer available to work on the project. After you open the View menu and click

Resource Sheet or click on the Resource Sheet icon in the View Bar, use either of the following methods to remove the resource:

- Select any cell in the resource you want deleted, then press Delete.
- Click on the row number for the resource you want deleted; this selects the whole row. Choose Edit, Delete Resource (or right-click on the selected row to access the shortcut menu, and then click on Delete Resource).

Working with Assignments

Project provides a way of looking at the interplay between tasks and the resources assigned to complete them. A view that shows assignments lists each task in the Task Sheet as a summary task, with each resource assigned to the task listed in a subtask row below the task. Each resource listing under the task is an assignment—a specific task assigned to a specific resource. So if you have a task to which you assigned three resources, that task has three assignments—one for each resource.

Assignments not only enable you to reexamine which resources will be handling which tasks, they also provide an additional level of detail for adjusting your schedule. For example, you can adjust start and finish dates for one assignment (one resource working on a particular task) without adjusting the start and finish dates for the task as a whole or the other resources assigned to the same task.

Viewing Assignments

The Task Usage view offers a Task Sheet that includes both tasks and assignments. To switch to Task Usage view, choose View, Task Usage. Or, click on the Task Usage icon on the View Bar. The view—complete with tasks and assignments—appears onscreen, as shown in Figure 6.18. Click the Go To Selected Task button, if needed, to scroll the actual task schedule for the selected task into view in the right pane.

Note

You can also view assignments in the Resource Usage view, covered in the next chapter. The Resource Usage view lists each resource as a summary task, with individual assignments for that resource listed as subtasks.

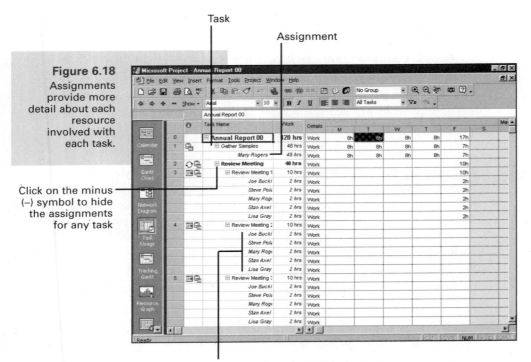

Task

Assignment

Figure 6.18
Assignments provide more detail about each resource involved with each task.

Click on the minus (–) symbol to hide the assignments for any task

Multiple assignments for one task

In the Task Usage view, each task has a symbol that you can use to display or hide the assignments for that task. Click on the minus (–) symbol to hide the assignments and the plus (+) symbol to redisplay them. Or you can use the outlining buttons on the Formatting toolbar (see Chapter 15, "Working with Outlining") to hide and display assignments for a task.

Displaying Assignment Information

The Assignment Information dialog box offers the settings for fine-tuning a selected assignment. To display the Assignment Information dialog box for an assignment, click in a cell in the assignment row, and then click to open the Project menu or right-click in the selected cell. In the menu or shortcut menu that appears, choose Assignment Information. After you click in a cell in an assignment row, you also can click on the Assignment Information button on the Standard toolbar. Finally, you can simply double-click on a cell in the assignment row. No matter which method you choose, the Assignment Information dialog box appears (see Figure 6.19).

Assignment Information button

Assignment Notes button

Figure 6.19
The Assignment
Information
dialog box offers
settings not
found elsewhere.

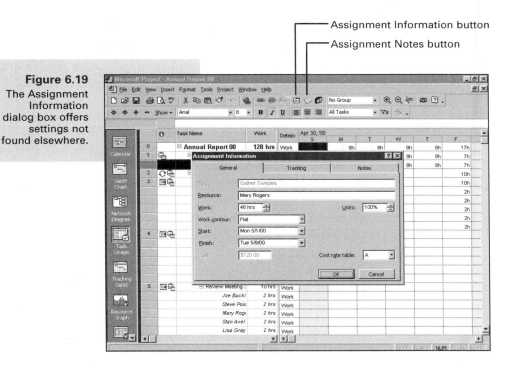

Figure 6.19
The Assignment Information dialog box offers settings not found elsewhere.

I'll discuss specific settings in this dialog box where they apply later in the book, and simply touch on its three tabs here. After you make your changes in the Assignment Information dialog box, click on OK to close it and make your changes take effect. Here's what you'll find on the three tabs:

- **General.** This tab allows you to adjust how much time the resource can spend on the assignment, such as when the resource can start work, how many units the resource can allocate to the assignment, and more.

- **Tracking.** Use this tab to enter actual work the resource has completed on the assignment and the actual timing of that work.

- **Notes.** Use this tab to add a note for the assignment, using the same process described earlier under "Adding a Resource Note." You can display this tab directly for an assignment by clicking on the Assignment Notes button on the Standard toolbar.

Changing the Cost Table for an Assignment

The section earlier in this chapter called "Creating Variable Pay Rates with Cost Rate Tables" explained how to create different cost rate tables for a resource, which you can use when a resource charges a different rate or fee for different types of work. Although rate changes within the A (Default) rate table apply automatically to all tasks on the dates that you specify, you must manually apply a different rate table to any assignment to which it applies. You do so by using the Assignment Information dialog box in the Task Usage view. Click in a cell in assignment's row to specify the assignment; then click on the Assignment Information button on the Standard toolbar or use one of the other methods described earlier for displaying the Assignment Information dialog box. On the General tab, click to open the Cost Rate Table drop-down list, and then click on the cost rate table to use it. Click on OK to close the dialog box and accept your change.

PART III
Making Adjustments to Projects

Resolving Overallocations and Overbooked Resources

IN THIS CHAPTER

- What it means to overallocate a resource
- Finding overallocation problems in your plan
- Using leveling to eliminate overbooked schedules
- Addressing overallocations on your own

I'm sure you've heard colleagues moan, "I wish there were more than 24 hours in a day, because I can't seem to get enough done." It might be a cliché, but only because it reflects our common tendency to cram too many activities into each and every day. As a leader under pressure, you'll need to fight this natural tendency when creating your project plans.

Project 2000 provides features designed to help you make your schedule realistic and attainable. Some of the best of these features quietly point out to you when you may have created an unrealistic schedule, such as assigning a resource 16 hours' worth of work on an 8-hour workday.

Discovering Overallocation

Early in the book, you learned to sketch out your schedule by simply listing the tasks to accomplish. Chapter 5 helped you make adjustments to the tasks you listed to help them flow together more cohesively. Chapter 6 focused on giving you the information you need to determine who handles what for your project. Now you need to go back and look at whether the resources you assigned to your project make sense.

Because Project uses effort-driven scheduling by default, you generally don't have to worry about having too few or too many resources assigned to a particular task. If the resource's working hours enable the resource to handle the task more quickly, Project shortens the task duration. Conversely, Project automatically lengthens the task if needed. For example, suppose that your schedule is based on a 24 Hours base calendar, but the resource you want to use follows the Standard calendar with 8-hour days. A task scheduled for one 24-hour day will be rescheduled to take three days if you assign the 8-hours-per-day resource to it.

Instead, what you need to be concerned about is assigning a resource to separate tasks that occur simultaneously. If your list includes 25 different tasks, then in theory, any number of them could partially occur during the same week. Say that the task in row 5 (task 5) begins on the Monday of the third week of your project. The task in row 7 (task 7) begins the same week, but on Thursday. You assigned the same resource to both tasks. Each of the tasks needs to be handled as quickly as possible, so it requires that the assigned resource give it full-time attention during the eight-hour workday defined for the project schedule. The problem is obvious; during Thursday and Friday, the resource needs to handle two full-time tasks. Thus, for Thursday and Friday, you've overallocated (overbooked) the selected resource.

You might be able to quickly spot overallocations in Gantt Chart view when tasks are close together in your list. Generally, though, you'll only be able to see 20 or so task rows onscreen at any time (depending on your screen resolution), so you can't visually compare the tasks in, let's say, rows 1 and 25 without scrolling back and forth. For that reason, Project provides a couple of other methods, described next, for quickly finding overallocations.

ON THE

CD

The CD-ROM for this book includes a file named *Annual Report Chapter 7*, which you can use to practice the techniques covered in this chapter. Keep in mind that the example files on the CD aren't intended to form a sequence, so you may see dramatic changes in task schedules, resource assignments, and so on between the various files.

Finding Overallocations with the Resource Management Toolbar

If you need to identify an overallocation in the default Gantt Chart view, use the Resource Management toolbar. To display the Resource Management toolbar, right-click on any toolbar onscreen; then select Resource Management. To go to a task in the Task Sheet that's assigned to an overallocated resource, click on the Go To Next Overallocation button on the Resource Management toolbar. Project selects the indicator cell of the task with the overallocated resource, as shown in Figure 7.1. Clicking on the Go To Next Overallocation button again takes you to

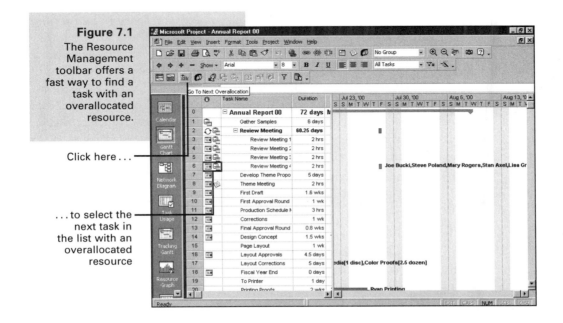

Figure 7.1
The Resource Management toolbar offers a fast way to find a task with an overallocated resource.

Click here . . .

. . . to select the next task in the list with an overallocated resource the next task in the list with an overallocation. If you click on the Go To Next Overallocation button when there are no more overallocated tasks in the list, you see a message telling you that there are no further overallocations. Click on OK to close the message box and continue.

Looking at Resource Usage in Other Views

To make a good decision about how to fix an overallocation, you have to know when the overallocation occurs and how extensive the overallocation is. Have you assigned 24 hours' worth of work for an 8-hour day, or have you assigned only an extra hour or two? For more extensive schedules, you might have multiple over-allocations, and might even have overallocated more than one resource on the same date.

Project offers a couple of options for getting a clearer overall picture of the over-allocations in your schedule. (These are views, which you'll learn more about in Chapter 11, "Working with the Different Project Views.")

First, you can display the resource usage in a tabular format. To do so, choose View, Resource Usage, or click on the Resource Usage icon on the View Bar. The Resource Usage view appears onscreen, as shown in Figure 7.2. The Resource Name column in this view lists each resource you added to the schedule and lists each of the resource's assignments below the resource name. The Work column shows you the total amount of work (in hours) that you scheduled for the resource beside the resource name, as well as the amount of work scheduled for each assignment. The scrolling pane on the right side of the screen shows you the amount of work you assigned to each resource on each date. You can see which resources are overallocated at a glance, because Project displays the Resource Name and Work entries in bold red text and displays an indicator telling you the resource needs leveling. Figure 7.2 shows overallocations for both the Steve Poland and Joe Bucki resources. If you look to the right along the row of an overallocated resource, you'll see that Project also highlights the particular dates on which you overbooked the resource according to the resource's work calendar. For example, on Friday during the week of May 28, both Joe and Steve are scheduled for 10 hours of work, 2 hours more than their calendars (and Max Units settings) allow them to handle.

• •

Click on an assignment for a resource (assignments appear below the resource name) in the left pane of the Resource Usage view, then click on the Go To Selected task button on the standard toolbar to scroll the corresponding portion of the timescale into view.

• •

This indicator means that the resource needs leveling

Overallocated resource appears in bold red text

Total work assigned to the resource

Figure 7.2
The Resource Usage view summarizes how much work you've assigned.

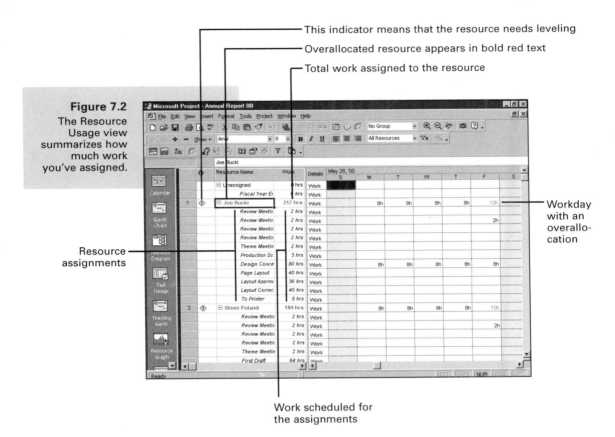

Workday with an overallocation

Resource assignments

Work scheduled for the assignments

The Resource Allocation view combines the tabular layout for the Resource Usage view with a lower pane where you can see the assignments for the selected resource as a Gantt Chart. To display the Resource Allocation view, you can click on the Resource Allocation View button on the Resource Management toolbar. If you haven't displayed that toolbar, choose View, More Views; then double-click on Resource Allocation in the Views list of the More Views dialog box. Project displays your schedule in the Resource Allocation view. When you select a resource from the Resource Usage view in the upper pane, a Gantt chart in the lower pane shows you the tasks for the resource, so you can see which ones overlap (are scheduled for the same dates). Figure 7.3 shows that Steve Poland has overlapping tasks. This view is ideal for changing the schedule for overallocated resources, as you'll see later in the "Manually Cutting Back the Resource's Commitments" section; refer to that section for more information about working in this view. If you switch back to the Resource Sheet (by choosing View, Resource Sheet), overallocated resources are also indicated in bold red text. You won't get any information, however, about where in the schedule the overallocation occurs.

Resource Allocation View button

Overallocated resource has an indicator
and is in bold red text

Selected resource

Figure 7.3
The Resource
Allocation view
shows the work
summary and a
Gantt Chart for
the selected
resource.

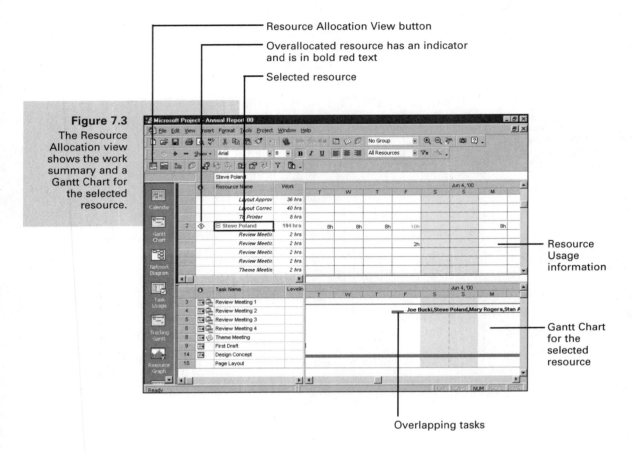

Resource
Usage
information

Gantt Chart
for the
selected
resource

Overlapping tasks

Caution

When you display another view from the Resource Allocation view, the
screen may remain split into upper and lower panes. Choose Window,
Remove Split to restore the view to normal.

Creating and Printing an
Overallocated Resources Report

Project can automatically create and print a report that lists each overallocated
resource and the tasks assigned to that resource. Reports don't let you edit
the information entered in your schedule, but they serve as a convenient tool
for looking at particular types of information when you're making a decision.
Chapter 14, "Creating and Printing a Report," provides more details about

generating and printing the various types of reports in Project, but here's a brief rundown of how to have Project compile an Overallocated Resources report:

1. Choose View, Reports to access the Reports dialog box.

2. Double-click on Assignments, or click on it once, and then click on Select. The Assignment Reports dialog box appears (see Figure 7.4).

3. Double-click on Overallocated Resources, or click on it once, and then click on Select. Project creates a list of overallocated resources for you and displays it onscreen.

4. To take a closer look at the information, as in Figure 7.5, click on the report with the zoom pointer, which looks like a magnifying glass.

Figure 7.4
Project offers reporting about resource assignments.

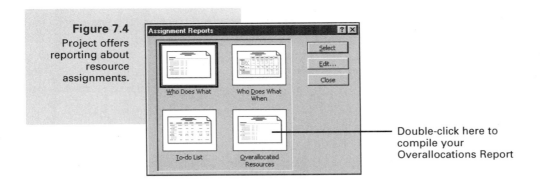

Figure 7.5
You can take a closer look at the reporting about your resource assignments.

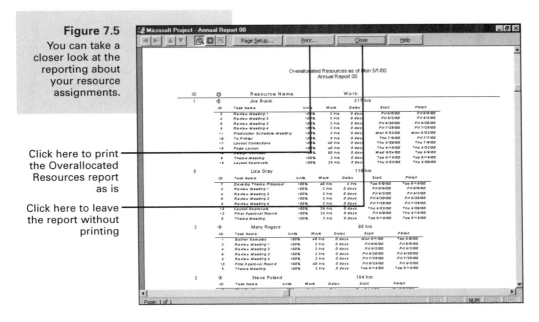

5. Click on the Print button on the toolbar above the report to print the report. Or you can click on the Close button, and then click on Close again in the Reports dialog box.

Using Leveling to Fix Overallocations

When you've overbooked a resource, something has to give. You want to eliminate huge peaks in a resource's workload to achieve an even, realistic flow of work. The process of smoothing out the workloads for resources is called *resource leveling*. Project can level resource schedules automatically, when you specify, for any schedule where Project calculates the finish date automatically.

To level resources, Project basically delays a conflicting task, or splits the task and moves part of it to a later time when the resource has available working hours. (You'll learn how to manually specify delay time later in this chapter, in the "Creating a Delay" section.) Project decides which tasks to delay by examining the information you entered about tasks, in particular looking for *slack*. Slack occurs when a task can be moved to a later date without delaying another task or the end date of the project.

When tasks are linked, Project takes the links into consideration before delaying a particular task. This is important because linked tasks may be handled by different resources, and you don't want to create a problem for another resource as a result of the leveling. For example, if two tasks are linked using the default Finish-to-Start (FS) link type and there's no lag time between the two tasks, the first task can't be moved without moving the second task as well, unless you change the nature of the link.

Note

The next chapter provides more detail about working with slack, but here's a quick example. Suppose that a resource is scheduled to handle a task that begins on Monday, 10/16/00, and has a duration of four days. The next task assigned to the resource begins on Monday, 10/23/00, and has the Start No Later Than (SNLT) constraint, meaning that it cannot move beyond its scheduled start date. Thus, there's one day of slack between the two tasks. The 10/16/00–10/19/00 task can only be delayed one day to a 10/17/00–10/20/00 schedule, because the resource must start working on the second task on the following Monday.

Here are a few more important issues to keep in mind before you level:

- Schedules built backward from the finish date have no slack, so there's nowhere to move any tasks. You have to work manually to level resources for this type of schedule.

- By default, it's conceivable that Project may move a task that's listed earlier in the schedule, say in row 2, rather than the later conflicting one that's, say, in row 5. Project moves whichever task is easier to move based on links and other factors, regardless of its ID number or order in the Task Sheet. For example, compare the tasks for Steve Poland before and after leveling in Figure 7.6. Task 5 has a Must Start On constraint, so Project moved Task 1 and created a problem, because Steve needs to conduct research for the presentation before he can write the presentation. In some cases, such moves do not make sense. Be sure to double-check leveling results carefully.

- Project can't change history. If a task has already started, Project can't move it altogether when leveling a resource schedule.

- Automatic leveling can have a massive impact on the flow of your schedule. If your schedule is very complex, or you want to limit the scope of the changes made but still take advantage of leveling, use leveling for one resource at a time (see the following steps that explain how to use leveling). Check the results after leveling each resource.

Figure 7.6

Leveling decisions aren't based on a task's order in the Task Sheet, as shown in this example of the same set of tasks before and after leveling.

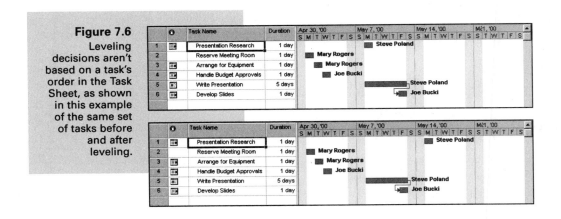

Setting Options and Leveling

Project allows you to level resources with the Resource Leveling command on the Tools menu. As you proceed through the leveling process, Project gives you the opportunity to set numerous leveling options. To use leveling, follow these steps:

1. Open the file with the resources you want to level, and make any desired adjustments to tasks, such as changing link types and priorities (see the "Reprioritizing Tasks before Leveling" section later in this chapter).

Tip

If you want to level a schedule but also be able to see the original dates, create a copy of the schedule file (by choosing File, Save As, and then giving the file a new name). Then apply leveling to the copied file. Reopen the original file if you want to compare.

2. (Optional) If you want to level a single resource, change to Resource Sheet, Resource Usage, or Resource Allocation view; then click on the resource name for the resource you want to level. (Press Ctrl and click on other resource names if you also want to select those resources for leveling.)

3. Choose Tools, Resource Leveling. The Resource Leveling dialog box appears (see Figure 7.7).

Caution

If you don't select a resource from one of the resource views, Project levels the whole schedule, and does not warn you before doing so.

Figure 7.7
Select leveling options in this dialog box.

| Resource Leveling | ? X |

Leveling calculations
- ○ Automatic   ● Manual
- Look for overallocations on a [Day by Day ▼] basis
- ☑ Clear leveling values before leveling

Leveling range for 'Annual Report 00'
- ● Level entire project
- ○ Level From: [Mon 5/1/00 ▼]
-    To: [Tue 8/8/00 ▼]

Resolving overallocations
- Leveling order: [Standard ▼]
- ☐ Level only within available slack
- ☑ Leveling can adjust individual assignments on a task
- ☑ Leveling can create splits in remaining work

[Help] [Clear Leveling...] [Level Now] [OK] [Cancel]

4. If you want Project to automatically level the schedule each time you make a change in a task or resource assignment, select the Automatic option button in the Leveling Calculations area of the dialog box. Otherwise, you have to reopen the Resource Leveling dialog box to level the schedule again after you make any changes. If, however, you want to retain control of when and how leveling occurs, leave the Manual option button selected.

5. The Look For Overallocations On A . . . Basis option specifies how precise leveling is. The default choice, Day By Day, compares the hours of work assigned to a resource on each day with the working hours available in the resource's calendar for that day. For the Standard calendar, then, any day with more than eight hours of work is marked as overallocated and will be leveled. Say, though, that you don't need to be that precise. If you assign a resource 12 hours of work that happens to fall on the same day, but that work really can be completed any time within the week, you can choose Week By Week so the work won't be leveled. The Look For Overallocations On A . . . Basis offers these choices, from most precise to most loose: Minute By Minute, Hour By Hour, Day By Day, Week By Week, and Month By Month.

6. If you previously leveled the schedule and want Project to remove the old leveling as it applies the new leveling, leave the Clear Leveling Values Before Leveling check box checked. If you turn this option off and Project has already delayed a task when you previously applied leveling, then it's possible for Project to delay the task even further if you level again.

7. If you don't want to level the entire project schedule, you can specify a range of dates to level in the Leveling Range For area of the dialog box. To specify the schedule date when you want the leveling to start, click on the Level From option button; then click on the down arrow on the accompanying text box and select a date from the pop-up calendar that appears. Click on the down arrow beside the To text box and use the pop-up calendar to select a date beyond which you don't want to level resources; if you want to level the remainder of the project, select a To date that is later than the project's finish date.

8. Use the Leveling Order drop-down list in the Resolving Overallocations area of the dialog box to tell Project how to choose which tasks to delay or split. This drop-down list offers three choices. The default is Standard, in which Project considers links, slack, dates, and priorities to determine which task to delay. If you select ID Only, Project delays the overlapping task that appears latest in the Task Sheet and thus has the highest ID number. If you select the final choice, Priority, Standard, the priority you

assigned to tasks takes precedence over other factors in determining which tasks to delay.

9. By default, the Level Only Within Available Slack option is not selected, meaning that Project can adjust the finish date of your schedule as needed when it moves tasks. However, this could lead to a delay of weeks or even months in your schedule, depending on the scope of your project. If you don't want the leveling operation to change the finish date, check this option so that Project moves tasks only within available slack time.

10. You may have several resources assigned to a task, and if only one of those resources is overallocated, Project can level only the overallocated resource. To have leveling work on individual resources in this way, leave the check mark beside Leveling Can Adjust Individual Assignments On A Task. Clear the check box if you would prefer that Project reschedule the entire task, even when only one of the resources handling the task is overbooked.

11. If you want Project to delay tasks and not split them, click to clear the check beside Leveling Can Create Splits In Remaining Work.

12. Click on the Level Now button. If you selected a particular resource to level as described in Step 2, or are displaying your schedule in one of the resource views, Project opens the Level Now dialog box (see Figure 7.8).

13. Leave the Entire Pool option selected to level all resources, or click on Selected Resources to tell Project to level only the resources you selected in Step 2.

14. Click on OK to complete the leveling operation. When a resource has been leveled, it no longer appears in bold red type.

15. (Optional) If you're not happy with the leveling changes, immediately click on the Undo button on the Standard toolbar, press Ctrl+Z, or choose Edit, Undo Level.

If you've leveled the resource and then view information about that resource in the Resource Allocation view, the Gantt Chart pane at the bottom of the view clearly shows the effects of leveling. As shown in the example in Figure 7.9, each Gantt bar becomes a double bar, with the top portion showing the original schedule for the task and the bottom portion showing the leveled schedule.

Figure 7.8
Specify whether to level all resources in your project.

Level Now

- Entire pool
- Selected resources

OK

Cancel

Original (preleveled)
schedule for the assignment

Figure 7.9
The Resource
Allocation view
helps you
compare a task
schedule before
and after
leveling.

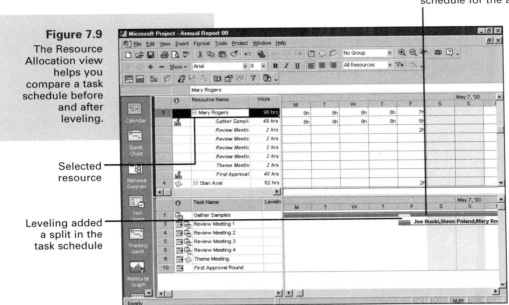

Selected
resource

Leveling added
a split in the
task schedule

Clearing Leveling

As illustrated, you work with resources to add leveling—but when you need to remove leveling, you work with tasks. Thus you need to be in a view where you can select tasks, such as Gantt Chart view, where the Task Sheet appears in the left pane, or Resource Allocation view, where you can select task assignments for a particular resource in the lower pane of the view.

Caution

> You can't select a resource name from any Resource Sheet and clear leveling. You have to be working from a task-oriented view or pane. You'll know you're in an incorrect place if the Clear Leveling button isn't available in the Resource Leveling dialog box.

Removing leveling removes any delay or split that Project inserted for a task or tasks during leveling. To remove leveling, perform the following steps:

1. Select a task-oriented view.

2. (Optional) If you only want to remove leveling from a particular task, click on that task name. (If you select the Resource Allocation view, you'll

also have to select a resource that has been leveled in the upper pane, and then click on the task assignment to level in the lower pane.) To select more than one task, press and hold down the Ctrl key and click on additional task names.

3. Choose Tools, Resource Leveling. The Resource Leveling dialog box appears.

4. Click on the Clear Leveling button. Project opens the Clear Leveling dialog box (see Figure 7.10).

5. If you chose one or more particular tasks to have leveling removed in Step 2, make sure the Selected Tasks option button is selected. Otherwise, click on Entire Project to remove all the leveling.

6. Click on OK to remove the leveling. (Note that even after you clear leveling from a resource or task, the bottom pane of the Resource Allocation view will continue to show split bars for the tasks that were previously leveled.)

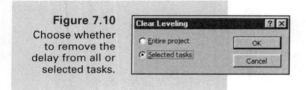

Figure 7.10
Choose whether to remove the delay from all or selected tasks.

Reprioritizing Tasks before Leveling

The last section of Chapter 5 provided an overview of the settings in the Task Information dialog box. To open the Task Information dialog box, double-click on any task in the Task Sheet of the Gantt Chart view. The first tab in that dialog box, the General tab, enables you to enter and edit the basic information that defines the task, such as its name and duration. One of the settings in that dialog box is the Priority text box, shown in Figure 7.11.

By default, all regular tasks are assigned a priority setting of 500, meaning that each task is equally important in the schedule. You can specify which tasks are more important by changing the Priority setting to a value between 1 and 1000, with a higher value symbolizing a greater priority. (You can prevent Project from delaying a task at all during leveling by entering 1000.)

Project uses the priority settings as a factor in automatic leveling, and the priority is given even more precedence if you select the Priority, Standard choice in the Resource Leveling dialog box. Project delays tasks with lower priority settings before moving those with higher priority settings.

Figure 7.11
The Priority text box allows you to define the relative importance of tasks.

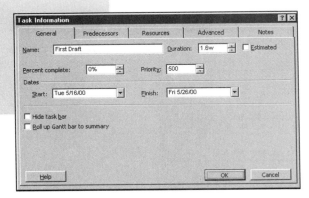

Tip

You can sort your list of tasks by priority. See Chapter 11, "Working with the Different Project Views," for details.

You should change task priorities before leveling, when necessary. Assuming that you'll be doing much of your leveling work in the Resource Allocation view, here's how to change a task's priority from that view:

1. In the upper pane of the Resource Allocation view, select the resource scheduled to handle the task for which you want to set the priority (usually an overallocated resource) by clicking on it.

2. In the lower pane, right-click on the task for which you want to set the priority—this opens the shortcut menu shown in Figure 7.12—and click on Task Information. Alternately, double-click on the Task Name in the lower pane or click on the Task Information button on the Standard toolbar.

3. On the General tab of the Task Information dialog box, drag over the entry in the Priority text box, then type the new Priority value you want.

4. Click on OK to close the Task Information dialog box.

Caution

Recurring tasks are automatically set with a 1000 priority. Changing this setting for a recurring task could have unwanted results, such as having Project delay a recurring task when leveling. Obviously, in the real world, the meeting or other repeating event that the recurring task represents would likely occur as scheduled, so the unwanted delay could create issues with resource schedules.

188 PART III • MAKING ADJUSTMENTS TO PROJECTS

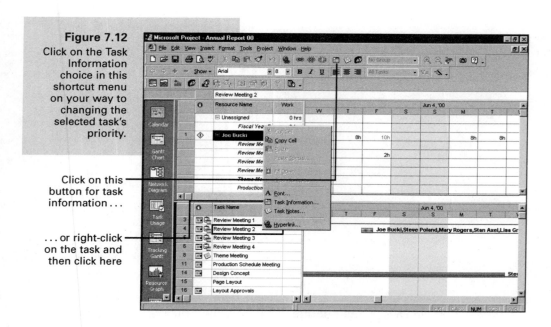

Figure 7.12
Click on the Task Information choice in this shortcut menu on your way to changing the selected task's priority.

Click on this button for task information...

...or right-click on the task and then click here

Use a similar approach to make such changes from other views that show a list of tasks.

Manually Cutting Back the Resource's Commitments

Although Project's automatic leveling offers a no-brain way to ensure that your resources can handle the work you assigned, some resource adjustment chores require thought. For example, as noted earlier in this chapter, if you set up your schedule file to have Project calculate its start date based on a finish date you entered, you can't use automatic leveling to deal with overallocations. Other instances where you might not want to use automatic leveling are if the tasks involved are high in priority, or if you need a solution that is more creative than simply delaying some tasks.

The methods described next allow you to resolve overallocations with precision and flexibility. To perform most of these adjustments, you work in Resource Allocation view. In the next chapter, you learn to adjust the schedule and make some resource adjustments from the Task Entry view.

Creating a Delay

Automatic leveling creates a delay for a task, so that tasks for a resource no longer overlap in the schedule. Without considering task linking, lead time, or lag time, this delay generally means that the second task starts after the first task ends, so the work flows in a continuous stream. If you enter a delay manually, you can create a delay of any length. For example, you might want to do the following:

- Build in extra delay time of a day or two (or more) between the tasks, in case the resource's first task takes longer than planned.

- Enter a smaller delay that still lets the two tasks overlap by, let's say, one day; then you can use another method, such as adding another resource or specifying overtime, to take care of the smaller overallocation.

To enter a delay of the length you prefer, do the following:

1. In Resource Allocation view, click on the resource name for the overallocated resource in the upper pane.

2. In the lower pane, click on the task name for the task you want to delay. Remember that entering the delay will move the task's start date; this technique doesn't work for schedules calculated backward from the project's finish date.

3. Press the right arrow or Tab key to scroll one column to the right (to the Leveling Delay column). You can also use the horizontal scroll bar below the Task Sheet in the lower pane to scroll over; then click on the desired cell in the Leveling Delay column.

4. Enter the delay that you desire (see Figure 7.13) and press Enter.

When you press Enter, Project pushes out the task. It adjusts the task's Start column entry and moves the task to the right on the Gantt chart. For example, compare Figure 7.14 with Figure 7.13.

Caution

Delays are scheduled in elapsed days (edays), meaning that nonworking days for the resource are included in the delay time frame. You cannot schedule a delay in terms of workdays (d). If you enter a delay of 1w (one week), Project converts that entry to 7ed. Thus, after you enter a delay, make sure that Project actually delays the task far enough based on the schedule's working days. Or enter the delay using the appropriate elapsed time abbreviation, such as eweeks or ehours.

Figure 7.13
It's possible to manually enter a delay.

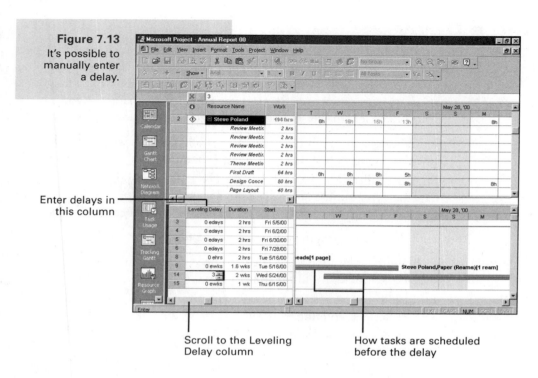

Enter delays in this column

Scroll to the Leveling Delay column

How tasks are scheduled before the delay

Figure 7.14
After you specify a delay value, Project moves the task based on that value.

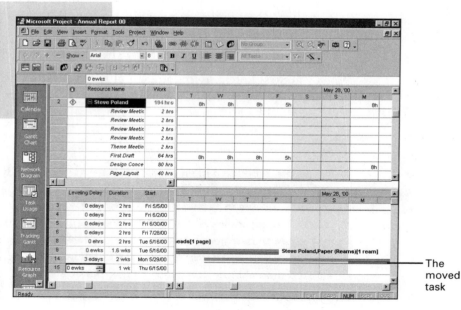

The moved task

Removing or Replacing an Overbooked Resource

There will be times when delaying a task is not an option. For example, you might be required to finish a product by a particular date or else lose a customer's order. Additionally, certain tasks might need to be completed before the end of a financial period. Finally, a task might be so pivotal in your schedule—and linked to so many successor tasks down the line (see the next chapter to learn more)—that delaying it will ruin your entire schedule.

In situations like this, you need to look closely at the resource you've assigned, rather than the schedule. You might be forced to remove a resource from a task (especially if you assigned more than one task to the resource) or to replace the resource with another one that's available to complete the task. Here's how to do so:

1. In Resource Allocation view, click on the resource name for the overallocated resource in the upper pane.
2. In the lower pane, click on the task name for which you want to remove or replace the resource.
3. Choose Tools, Resources, Assign Resources (or press Alt+F10). Alternately, click on the Assign Resources button on the Standard toolbar or the Resource Management toolbar. The Assign Resources dialog box appears.
4. Click to select the assigned resource, which should have a check mark beside it.
5. To take the resource off the task, click on the Replace button. Project immediately removes the resource from the task and changes the name of the Assign Resources dialog box to Replace Resource.
6. Click on a new resource for the task in the With list, and then click on OK. Project reassigns the task, removing it from the task list for the original resource and adding it to the task list for the newly selected resource.

Changing resource assignments in this way can fix one overallocation but create another; if the new Resource Name entry changes to bold red text, you've got a new overallocation to deal with. Pay careful attention to the results of your resource reassignment.

Click on the Close button to put away the Assign Resources dialog box when you finish working with it.

Part-Time Work

There might be times when you're not in a position to delay one task or another altogether, perhaps because a third successor task is unable to start until its predecessor starts, as in an SS relationship. Or there might be an instance where you don't want to remove a resource from a task altogether, but do want to scale back its commitment to the task and add another resource (as described in Chapter 8, "Optimizing the Schedule") to help finish the task in a timely fashion.

In such cases, you have the option of cutting back a resource to a part-time commitment to a task. Here's how:

1. In Resource Allocation view, click on the resource name for the overallocated resource in the upper pane.

2. In the lower pane, click on the name of the task for which you want to reduce the resource assignment.

3. Choose Tools, Resources, Assign Resources (or press Alt+F10). Alternately, click on the Assign Resources button on the Standard toolbar or the Resource Management toolbar. The Assign Resources dialog box appears.

4. Click on the Units cell for the assigned resource, which should have a check mark beside it. Begin typing to replace the existing Units entry, as shown in Figure 7.15. If the original number was 100%, type a number that's less than 100% to indicate how much of each workday you want the resource to spend on the selected task. For example, if you want the resource to work on the task for half the day, type 50. If the original number was 1.00, type a decimal value, such as .5 for half-time work.

5. Press Enter to finish your entry; then click on the Close button to close the Assign Resources dialog box. On the Gantt Chart for the task, an indication beside the Resource label tells you what portion of the workday the resource will spend on the assignment (see Figure 7.16). If the task uses a resource-driven duration type, Project adjusts the task's duration

Figure 7.15
You might want to change the resource's time commitment during the duration of the task.

Assign Resources	? X
Resources from: 'Project1'	

Name	Units	
Joe Bucki		Assign
✓ Steve Poland	50	Remove
Mary Rogers		Replace...
		Address...
		Cancel
		Help

Figure 7.16
Check any Gantt
Chart bar for
part-time
resources.

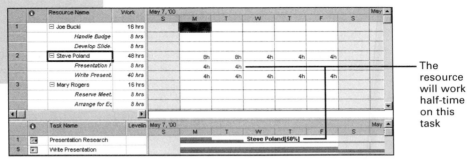

The
resource
will work
half-time
on this
task

(lengthening the Gantt chart bar) so that the resource works the same total hours on the task. For example, if a task originally has a one-week duration and you reduce the resource's commitment to half-time, the duration is extended to two weeks.

Caution

> If you enter a number that's greater than 100%, Project does not assume that you want the resource to work overtime. It instead assumes that the resource has the proportion of extra time available within the bounds of the workday. For example, if the resource is a consulting firm you're working with, and you change the Units entry to 200%, Project assumes that two members of the firm will work on your task each day, or if the resource has a defined 8-hour a day calendar then Project assumes you have just assigned that resource 16 hours that day. To learn how to specify overtime for a task, see "Authorizing Overtime Work for a Task" in Chapter 8, "Optimizing the Schedule."

Avoiding Underallocations

If you remove a resource from a task altogether in Resource Allocation view, that task no longer appears on the assignment list for any resource. Therefore, you should make a note of the task name and ID (row) number before you remove its resource. Make sure that you go back to Gantt Chart view (or any other view where you can assign resources to tasks) and add a resource for the task. Otherwise, the task is completely underallocated and there's no resource scheduled to handle it.

An even trickier situation occurs if you change a resource from a full-time to a part-time commitment to a task. If the task has a fixed duration, Project will not increase the task's duration when you cut back the resource to a part-time commitment. In reality, the task still requires the same number of hours it initially did, but on the schedule there are fewer hours of work scheduled to get the task done. For example, suppose that you have a task with a 3d duration, which equates to 24 hours of work by the project's 8-hours-per-day base calendar. The task type is Fixed Duration, which means that the task's start and finish dates don't change. If you cut back a resource assigned to this task to half-time work for the task, Project assumes that only 12 hours of work are now required on the task. In such a case, you need to add one or more additional part-time resources to the task to replace the 12 hours of work that the first resource no longer provides. (The "Adding Resources for a Task" section in Chapter 8, "Optimizing the Schedule," covers how to do this.)

If you cut back a resource assignment to part time but the task duration doesn't change, you should check the task type. If it's Fixed Duration, make sure that you add more resources for the task as needed.

Note

Remember that you can quickly check a task's duration type by clicking on the task name in any task list, and then clicking on the Task Information button on the Standard toolbar. Click on the Advanced tab; then check the Task Type drop-down list. Click on OK to close the dialog box.

Changing the Resource's Work Schedule

The "Working with Resource Calendars (Work Schedules)" section in Chapter 6, "Managing Resources," explains how to assign a calendar for a resource to determine how many hours per week the resource works and to set days the resource has off. Rather than cutting back a resource's commitment to a project, you can change a resource's schedule, adding more hours or days to remove the overallocations. Although you might not have much leeway to do this for resources within your company (you can't make certain people work extra hours without paying overtime, for example), there are instances when adjusting a resource's calendar or selecting a new calendar can resolve an overallocation. Consider the following examples:

- If a salaried employee is willing to give up a holiday or weekend day to complete a task, you can make that day a working day in the calendar. For example, if an employee has to attend a trade show on a weekend, you can specify those weekend days as working days.

- On a day that requires an evening or morning meeting, you can adjust the working hours for the resource.

■ If you're working with a vendor that normally has a standard eight-hour workday but can work around the clock when you request it, make the request and change that resource's schedule.

Although you can refer to Chapter 6, "Managing Resources," to review the details of making changes to the working days and hours for a resource, here's a quick way to select a different calendar for a resource:

1. Double-click on the resource name in any view or resource list, or in the Resources From list in the Assign Resources dialog box. The Resource Information dialog box appears.

2. Use the Base Calendar drop-down list on the Working Time tab to select another calendar, as shown in Figure 7.17.

3. Click on OK to complete the change.

Figure 7.17
You can quickly change the base calendar for a resource.

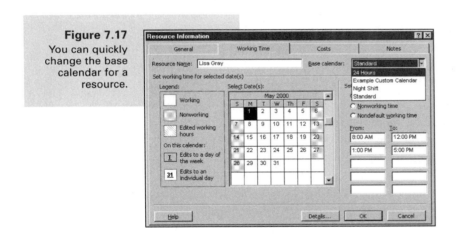

Using Contouring to Vary Workload

Project 2000 offers another feature intended to help you realistically plan workloads—workload contouring. Although contouring doesn't necessarily resolve all overallocations, it can help. Also, it does enable you to adjust how many hours per day a resource is scheduled to work on a task, so you can have more flexibility in working smaller tasks in around other tasks, or helping tasks overlap without creating an overallocation.

Simply put, contouring an assignment adjusts the hours per day that a resource is scheduled to work on the assignment. You can choose one of several contouring patterns to automatically distribute the hours for an assignment. For example, say you have a two-week task, and you assign a single full-time resource to handle it. If you apply a bell curve contour to that assignment, Project extends the task schedule to four working weeks, so it can redistribute the hours per day the resource works on the task in a bell-shaped pattern. The first two days, the resource is scheduled to work .8h on the task, the next two days 1.6 hours, and so on. The resource's work will peak at a full day during the middle of the task schedule, and then gradually drop back to .8h for the last two days. You can set these kinds of contouring for an assignment in the Resource Allocation, Resource Usage, Task Usage, or any other view where you can open the Assignment Information dialog box for an Assignment:

- **Front- or back-loaded.** This contour increases the hours per day from the start to the finish of the task, or decreases the hours per day from the start to the finish.

- **Early-, late-, or double-peak.** The work peaks to a full eight-hour day near the start or finish of the project (but not on the first or last day, as under a front- or back-loaded schedule), or both.

- **Bell.** As described, this contour smoothly allocates the hours per day to peak during the middle of the task. Generally, this contour doubles the task duration.

- **Turtle.** Similar to a bell curve, this schedule peaks in the middle, but allocates more full-time workdays, so the duration isn't extended as far as it would be under a bell contour.

- **Edited.** When you edit the hours for one or more days of the assignment in the Resource Usage or Task Usage view, you've created an edited or custom contour (described later in this section). This is the only type of contour that's not automatic or predefined.

- **Flat.** Choose this contour to return to the default, scheduling the same number of work hours per day through the completion of the task.

To use the Assignment Information dialog box to assign an automatic or predefined contour to an assignment, follow these steps:

1. In the Resource Usage or Task Usage view, double-click on the assignment to which you want to apply an automatic contour. Or click on the assignment, and then click on the Assignment Information button on the Standard toolbar, which is the equivalent of choosing Project, Assignment Information. The Assignment Information dialog box appears.

2. Open the Work Contour drop-down list, as shown in Figure 7.18. Then click on the type of work contour you want to use.

3. Click on OK to finish setting the contour.

Figure 7.18
Set a work contour in the Assignment Information dialog box.

4. If the Planning wizard appears to warn you that the change may cause a scheduling conflict due to constraints, you can click on the Continue option button, and then click on OK. Figure 7.19 shows a contoured work assignment. Applying the contour didn't completely remove the overallocation, but reduced the scheduled work on the overallocated days to a level that's only slightly above the resource's full workday.

As I noted earlier, sometimes a contour doesn't seem to fix an overallocation the way it should. I've run into at least one instance where this is the case. For example, I created a recurring task for a two-hour Review Meeting. The second Review

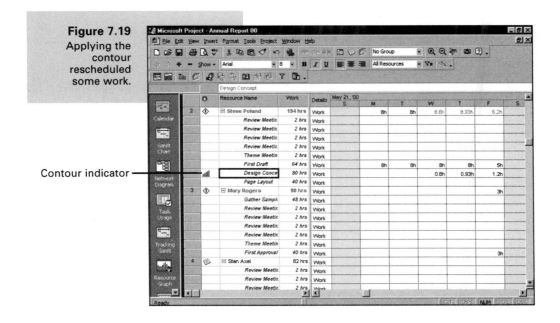

Figure 7.19
Applying the contour rescheduled some work.

Contour indicator

Meeting assignment created an overallocation with another task, which I called Design Concept. I tried applying an automatic contour to the Design Concept task to reduce the hours for it on the day of the second Review Meeting, but found that even when the total hours for the day dropped below eight hours, the task was still overallocated. I did find a workaround, which involved working with the Units assigned to the second Review Meeting and then creating an edited contour for the Design Concept task.

First, for this example, I opened the Assignment Information dialog box for the second Review Meeting assignment for the overallocated resource. Because it was a two-hour meeting, I changed the Units setting on the General tab to clarify for Project that the meeting would use only 25% of the resource's day. (You could skip this first part of the workaround, but be aware that if you do, the date may still show up as a red overallocation, even if the total work hours for the date fall within the bounds of the resource's calendar.)

Then I created the edited contour. To create an edited contour, click on the cell for the day that you need to contour. As shown in Figure 7.20, I clicked on the cell for F (Friday), 6/2/00 for the Design Concept assignment. Type the new value for the cell, including the hours (h) abbreviation if you'd like (Project assumes the value you enter will be in hours), and then press Enter. Project reduces the work scheduled for that date of the assignment and adds an edited contour indicator for the assignment. In my example, it also removed the resource overallocation as a result.

Figure 7.20
Editing the assigned hours for a particular date within a particular assignment creates an edited assignment.

Edited assignment indicator

Click in a cell, then type a new value to change the hours assigned

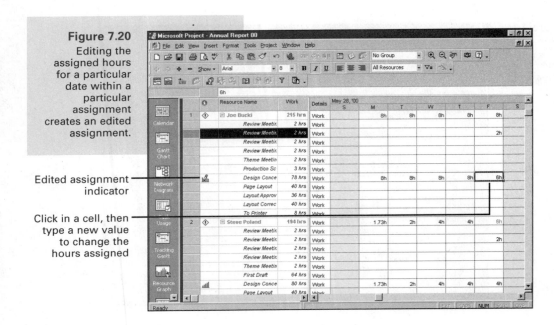

Optimizing the Schedule

IN THIS CHAPTER

- Understanding which tasks are critical and how they affect your schedule

- Looking for ways to finish critical tasks more quickly

- Finding "dead" time in the schedule and taking it out

- Giving yourself more room by adjusting the project base calendar

When you lead a project, you have to use a lot of creativity to bring everything together on time and within budget. You need to look at different ways to apply the resources you have, check for every place where you can trim time, and do everything you can to ensure that as many tasks are moving along simultaneously as possible.

In Chapter 7, you looked at how to make your schedule attainable by ensuring that you didn't assign too much work to any particular resource. Now you can apply your managerial creativity to tighten up your schedule to ensure that it gets the job done as quickly as possible.

Identifying and Tightening the Critical Path

In the Midwest and northern regions of the United States, the building industry is seasonal because some building tasks can't be completed under certain weather conditions. For example, if the weather isn't right, the foundation can't be constructed; if the foundation isn't constructed, the framing for the walls and roof can't be erected; without the framework, other key systems can't be installed. After the most important features of the building are in place, however, the schedules for many tasks are a bit more flexible; for example, work on finishing the exterior can proceed at the same time as work on the interior.

In the building example, the tasks that can't be delayed without drastically affecting the overall schedule—the foundation and framing work, for example—are called critical tasks.

Your schedule will have critical tasks, as well. If any of these tasks slip (either begin late or take more time than you allowed), the finish date for your project will move further out. Together, the critical tasks form the critical path for your schedule, the sequence of tasks that must happen on time for the project to finish on time. Although moving tasks that aren't on the critical path might even out resource assignments or help you improve milestones, such changes won't really affect the full schedule for your project. (If you've set up the Project file so that Project calculates the schedule from a specified Finish Date, the schedule does not have a critical path.)

Thus if you want to reduce the overall timeframe for your project, you need to reduce the length of time it takes to complete the critical path. You need to be able to identify which tasks form the critical path and focus on making adjustments to compress the schedules for those tasks without needlessly inflating costs.

You'll have the greatest impact in reducing a project's overall schedule if you add more resources to critical tasks. Or, you may want to rethink the order flow of tasks—see if more can run simultaneously, for example.

Caution

> **The techniques covered in this chapter can introduce resource overallocations. After you make any of the changes you'll learn about in this chapter, check for resource overallocations as described in Chapter 7, "Resolving Overallocations and Overbooked Resources."**

You can use a formatting technique to identify critical tasks in the Task Sheet in Gantt Chart or Task Entry view (you'll learn about the latter shortly), which is the easiest way to highlight critical tasks. You can also format critical tasks in the lower pane of Resource Allocation view, but that formatting won't appear if you switch back to Gantt Chart or Task Entry view. Further, you can format the color of the Gantt bars for critical tasks in the Gantt Chart view. You can also run the Gantt Chart wizard to format the Gantt bars for critical tasks. The section called "Quick and Dirty Gantt Chart Formatting" in Chapter 11, "Working with the Different Project Views," describes the Gantt Chart wizard.

ON THE

CD

> **Once again, the CD-ROM offers a practice file, *Annual Report Chapter 8*, for your use with this chapter. If you open the file and see a message that the last task in the file can't be completed on time, simply click OK to bypass the message.**

To highlight the critical tasks in your schedule, follow these steps:

1. Click in the visible portion of the Task Sheet in whichever view you're presently using. For example, in Gantt Chart view, click in the left pane of the screen, or in Task Entry View, click in the upper pane.

2. Choose Format, Text Styles. The Text Styles dialog box appears.

3. Click on the drop-down list arrow to display the Item To Change choices, and then click on Critical Tasks (see Figure 8.1). This choice means that the formatting choices you make next will apply to any task that's part of the critical path.

4. In the scrolling Font list, display and click on the name of a font to use for the critical task text.

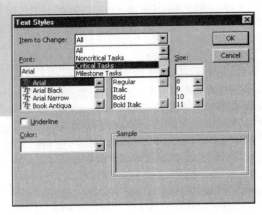

Figure 8.1
Use this dialog box to specify how you'd like to identify critical tasks in the Task Sheet.

5. Use the Font Style list to apply attributes such as bold or italic to the text. Depending on the font, italic is often a better choice than bold because it more clearly differentiates the text when printing.

6. Use the Size list to select a size for the critical task names in the list. Enlarging the type emphasizes the critical task names and makes them easier to read.

7. Click to select the Underline check box if you want to apply underlining to the critical path tasks.

8. Finally, click to open the Color drop-down list (see Figure 8.2), and click on the color you want to apply to the critical task text in the Task Sheet.

9. Click on OK to apply your changes and close the Text Styles dialog box.

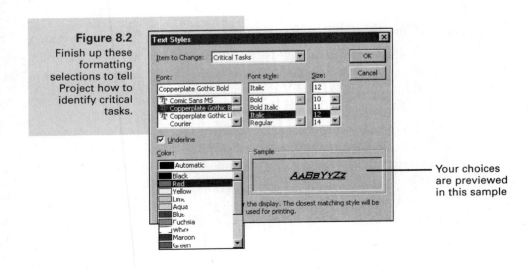

Figure 8.2
Finish up these formatting selections to tell Project how to identify critical tasks.

Your choices are previewed in this sample

The text formatting changes you specified now apply to all the tasks that are critical to your schedule in the Task Sheet.

10. Choose Format, Bar Styles. The Bar Styles dialog box appears.

11. In the list of bar types near the top of the dialog box, click on the cell that holds *Split* in the Name column.

12. Click on the Insert Row button.

13. Type **Critical** as the Name column entry for the new row.

14. Open the Show For . . . Tasks drop-down list for the new row and click on Critical, as shown in Figure 8.3.

15. On the Bars tab at the bottom of the dialog box, choose another color from the Color drop-down list under Middle.

16. Click on OK to finish formatting the Gantt bars for critical tasks.

Figure 8.4 shows an example of how your project might look in Gantt Chart view with special formatting applied to the critical tasks in both the Task Sheet and the Gantt chart.

Caution

> Your changes might cause a column in the Task Sheet to be filled with pound signs so that you can't see the data the column contains. If this happens, try repeating the preceding steps with different settings (especially the font size) until you find settings that work. Or you can autofit the column width by double-clicking on the right border for the header of the column to be widened.

Figure 8.3
You also can use this dialog box to specify a different look for the Gantt bars for critical tasks.

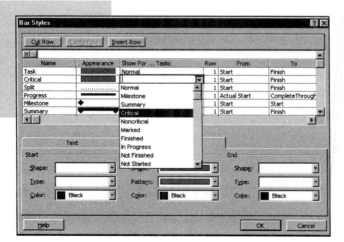

Figure 8.4
Critical path tasks now appear as you specified in the Task Sheet.

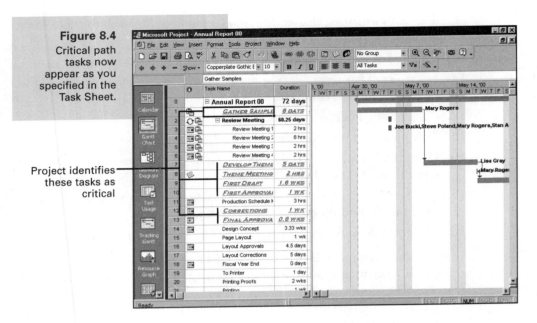

Project identifies these tasks as critical

You can use filtering to limit the displayed lists of tasks to critical tasks only. To learn how to filter the Task Sheet, see "Filtering the Task Sheet or Resource Sheet" in Chapter 11.

If you use the preceding steps and only one task changes (it may typically be the last one), Project isn't making an error. It simply means that your schedule doesn't include a true critical path, perhaps because you don't have many tasks linked, you've included a lot of lag time, or you haven't assigned many constraints.

You can go back, however, and take the time to define task relationships (links) and add constraints to tasks (such as defining that a task should start no later than a particular date) using the Advanced tab of the Task Information dialog box. When you make alterations to task information that identify some tasks as critical, Project applies the critical path formatting.

Note

To tighten up the schedule for critical tasks if you're assigning more resources to them, Project needs tasks that have the effort-driven task type. Double-click on the task in a Task Sheet, click on the Advanced tab, check the Effort Driven check box, and make sure the task is using the default Fixed Units task type.

Using Task Entry View

After you identify which tasks are critical in your schedule, you can begin examining them one by one to look for areas where you can make adjustments to decrease the duration of each critical task. You could simply double-click on each task in the Task Sheet and use the Task Information dialog box to make your changes, but that would be time-consuming—and wouldn't let you immediately see the effects of your changes on other tasks that were linked. It's better to use another view you haven't yet seen, Task Entry view, which displays Gantt Chart view in the upper pane and an area for entering and changing task and resource information in the lower pane. Switch to Task Entry view in one of the following ways:

- Click on the Task Entry View button on the Resource Management toolbar, if that toolbar is displayed.

- Choose View, More Views (or click on the More Views icon in the View Bar). In the Views list of the More Views dialog box, double-click on Task Entry.

No matter which method you use to reach it, Task Entry view appears onscreen, as shown in Figure 8.5.

Task Entry View button

Use these buttons to move between tasks

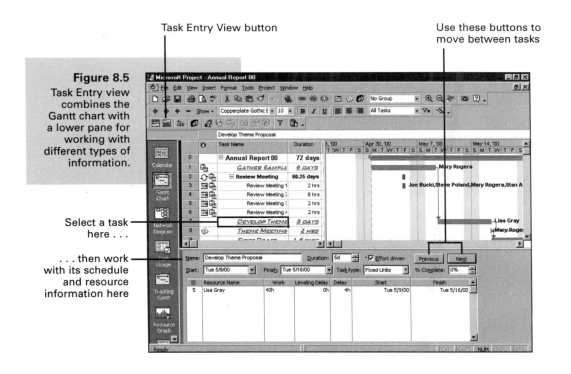

Figure 8.5
Task Entry view combines the Gantt chart with a lower pane for working with different types of information.

Select a task here . . .

. . . then work with its schedule and resource information here

Figure 8.6
It's possible to adjust the lower pane of the Task Entry view.

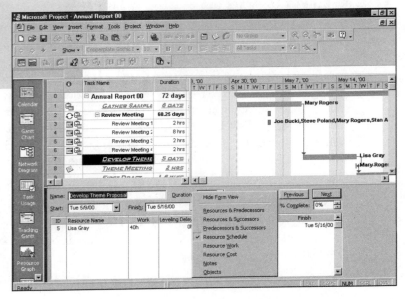

You can vary the details that appear in the lower pane of Task Entry view. In fact, some of the details you can modify here aren't available in other areas such as the Task Information dialog box. To change the information in the lower pane of Task Entry view, right-click on the pane to open its shortcut menu (see Figure 8.6). Then click on one of the choices to change the pane. The top choice on the shortcut menu, Hide Form View, closes the bottom pane of Task Entry view, essentially returning to Gantt Chart view.

When you're working in Task Entry view, you can jump back and forth between panes, selecting a task in the upper pane, making changes in the lower pane, and then selecting a different task in the upper pane, changing its settings in the bottom pane, and so on.

Understanding Driving Resources

So far, for simplicity's sake, you've been looking at tasks with a single resource assigned to them. Imagine how restricted your options would be, though, if each task your team handles could only be assigned to one resource! Teams, by definition, mean that people work together to accomplish a goal. You can think of a goal in terms of the overall project, or in terms of any individual task. This means that you can use more than one resource (a mini-team, if you will) to accomplish each task in your schedule.

Before I explain how to assign additional resources to a task, you need to understand that Project doesn't treat all resources assigned to a task the same. Rather, Project looks at the resource that's assigned to do the most work for the task, called the *driving resource*.

The time that the driving resource has available to work on the task determines the task's duration. If you want to shorten the task's duration, you must do one or more of the following:

- Add more hours to the resource calendar, which you learned to work with in Chapter 6.

- Make more units available for the resource, indicating that the resource is adding more staff members to handle the task.

- Add another resource so that you can reduce the number of hours the driving resource needs to spend working on the task.

The second and third techniques are described next.

Adding Resources for a Task

If a critical task is being handled by a resource outside your company, you can start optimizing your schedule by asking that resource to assign more workers or equipment to the task to finish it more quickly. For example, the resource might be willing to assign three people or three pieces of equipment to your task to get it done in a third of the time originally planned. Keep in mind, though, that adding more resource units to a critical task can be tricky. Project always decreases the task duration directly in proportion to the number of additional resource units. Thus, if you increase the units from 100% or 1 (one full-time person) to 200% or 2 (two full-time people), Project automatically cuts the task duration in half; however, the two resource units might not get the task done in half the time. It might take a little longer, because the resources need to communicate among themselves. To allow for this possibility, consider building a lag time between the critical task and any successor tasks that depend on its completion. Then, when you track the actual finish date, Project will accurately capture the amount of work applied.

To increase the number of units for a resource assigned to a critical task, follow these steps from Task Entry view:

1. Click on the task name of the critical task in the top pane, or use the Previous and Next buttons in the bottom pane to display the information for the critical task.

2. Right-click in the bottom pane of the Task Entry view; then click on Resource Work.

3. Click in the Units column of the bottom pane and type a new value, as shown in Figure 8.7.

4. Click on the OK button in the bottom pane of the Task Entry view to finish the entry. Project adjusts the Duration for the task to reflect that the added resource units will finish the task more quickly.

You can also change the Units setting via the Assign Resources dialog box. To do so, click on the critical task in the Task Sheet of Gantt Chart view or in the upper pane of Task Entry view. Click on the Assign Resources button on the Standard toolbar or Resource Management toolbar. Or choose Tools, Resources, Assign Resources. Click in the Units column for the resource assigned to the task, type a new value (see Figure 8.8), and press Enter or click on the Enter button to finish changing the entry. Then close the Assign Resources dialog box.

If you don't have the option of increasing the number of resource units available to handle the task, you can add more resources to enable you to reduce the number of hours of work the driving resource must allocate to the task, thereby shortening the task's duration. For tasks with the default Fixed Units task type and for the Fixed Work task type, adding another resource automatically reduces the task duration. (Remember, Project uses the equation Duration = Work/Units to adjust the duration.) If you add one more resource, Project automatically gives each resource half of the work; Project assumes the resources will work concurrently, so the task can be completed in half the time.

Figure 8.7
You can add more resource units to shorten the task duration.

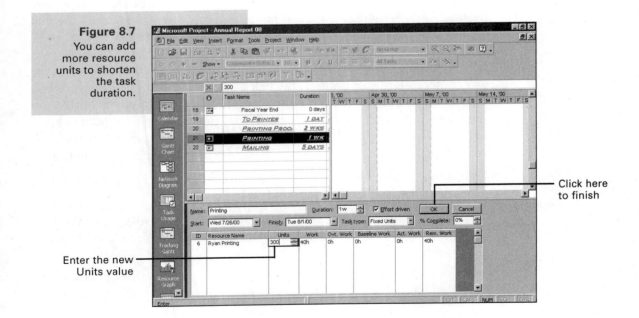

Click here to finish

Enter the new Units value

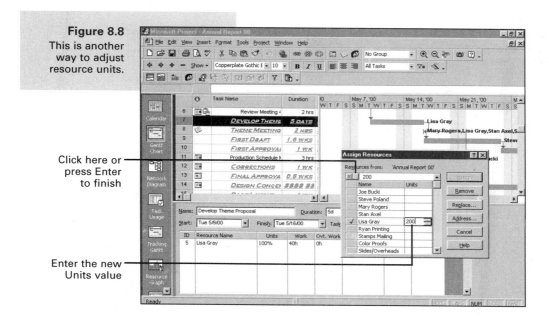

Figure 8.8
This is another way to adjust resource units.

Click here or press Enter to finish

Enter the new Units value

Follow these steps to add more resources to a critical task and decrease the task's duration:

1. Change to Task Entry view.

2. In the upper pane, click on a cell to select the critical task for which you want to add more resources.

3. In the lower pane, click in the first blank row of the Resource Name column. A drop-down list arrow appears at the far-right end of the text entry box.

4. Click to display the drop-down list; then click on a resource in the list to select it (see Figure 8.9).

5. Click on the OK button in the lower pane or the Enter button beside the text entry box to finish your entry. The new resource appears in the lower pane (see Figure 8.10). If you refer to Figure 8.9, you'll notice that the Work column for the original resource held 64h, for the 64 hours of work required to complete the task in the assigned duration. In Figure 8.10, you can see that these working hours have been adjusted in light of the new resource; the new resource offers 32h in the Work column, for a total of 64h between the two resources. The Duration entry drops from 1.6w in Figure 8.9 to .8w in Figure 8.10.

Figure 8.9
Here's how to add another resource to a task.

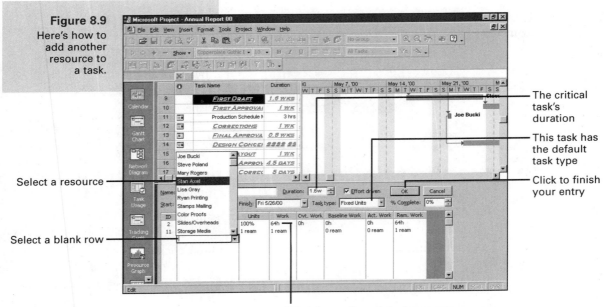

Select a resource

Select a blank row

The critical task's duration

This task has the default task type

Click to finish your entry

Work hours the original resource needs to complete the task

The task is no longer highlighted as critical . . .

. . . because adding the new resource decreased the duration

Figure 8.10
By default, adding a new resource decreases the task duration.

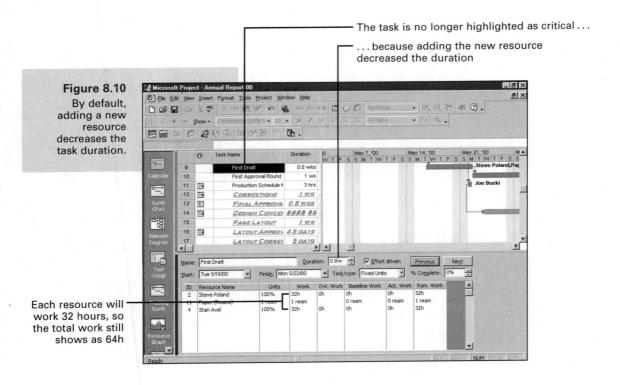

Each resource will work 32 hours, so the total work still shows as 64h

If the task has the Fixed Duration task type, adding an additional resource does not decrease the task duration. Instead, you must manually adjust the work hours for each resource so that their total matches the number of work hours available for only the original resource. You can also control the proportion of work each resource has, no matter what the task type, by splitting the work evenly between the two resources or letting the driving resource retain the bulk of the work. Using the examples in Figures 8.9 and 8.10, you can specify 40 hours of work for the original resource, Steve Poland, and 24 hours of work for the new resource, Stan Axel. The total work given for the two resources then equals the 64 hours originally scheduled for Steve Poland (see Figure 8.11). To change each resource's Work entry, click in the Work column for the resource, type a new value (Project assumes you're specifying hours), and click on the OK button in the lower pane.

As an alternative to using the bottom pane of the Task Entry view to add resources, you can open the Assign Resources dialog box. (Click on the Assign Resources button on the Standard toolbar after clicking on the top pane of Task Entry view.) Then you can drag new resources from the assignment box to the critical task. To do so, click on the resource you want to drag, and then point to the gray box at the left of the resource name until you see the resource pointer (see Figure 8.12). Press and hold down the mouse button, and then drag the resource to the correct task name in the top pane and release the button.

The duration reflects the work hours
scheduled for the driving resource

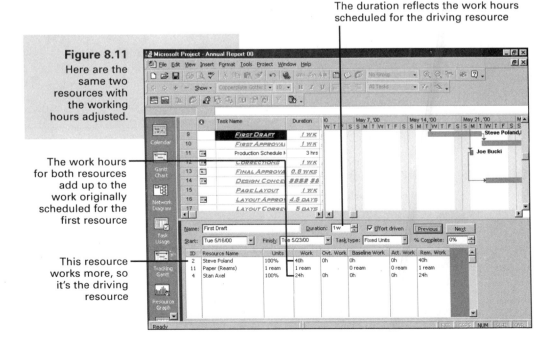

Figure 8.11
Here are the same two resources with the working hours adjusted.

The work hours for both resources add up to the work originally scheduled for the first resource

This resource works more, so it's the driving resource

Figure 8.12
You can drag a
resource from
the Assign
Resources dialog
box to the
correct task
name.

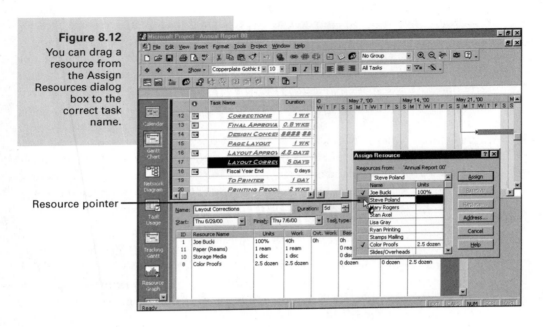

Resource pointer ————

Caution

There are a couple of other ways to add resources, but those methods don't let you adjust the hours each resource will spend on the task to tighten up the task duration. (In case you're curious, you can add resources using the Resource Names columns of the Gantt Chart view by typing in additional resource names and separating the entries with a comma. Or you can use the Resources tab of the Task Information dialog box to add more resources.) Your best bet is to add more resources by using the techniques described in the preceding section.

Authorizing Overtime Work for a Task

Companies, particularly large ones, are obligated to compensate most hourly employees for overtime work. In some cases, you might also need to pay overtime charges for outside resources you bring in for your project. Overtime costs are required especially for any resources that are union workers. To protect the bottom line, Project generally doesn't let you simply add extra shifts (overtime hours) for a resource by changing the Units entry to a value greater than 100% (or 1.00, if you're using decimal values). As you learned earlier, changing the Units entry generally assumes that more than one worker from the resource will work on the task simultaneously or that a salaried employee will devote time outside the normal workday to get the task done.

You also can't specify overtime by simply changing the working calendar so that a resource has more hours in the day. (You can use that technique, however, to resolve overallocations for salaried resources.) Project forces you to enter overtime hours in another way to ensure that overtime costs are calculated correctly, according to the overtime rate you entered when you added the resource to the file (see Chapter 6, "Managing Resources"), and to ensure that you approved the overtime work.

The Task Entry view provides you the means to allocate overtime work for a task. After you add overtime, Project changes the task's duration to reflect the extra working hours per day provided by the overtime. Here's how to authorize overtime hours for a resource assigned to a critical task:

1. Change to Task Entry view.

2. In the upper pane of Task Entry view, click on a cell in the critical task to which you want to assign overtime work. Information about the resources assigned to the task appears in the lower pane.

3. Right-click on the lower pane and click on Resource Work. The pane changes to display more information about the resource's work schedule (see Figure 8.13).

Figure 8.13
You can enter overtime when you view Resource Work information in the lower pane of Task Entry view.

The selected critical task

Enter overtime here

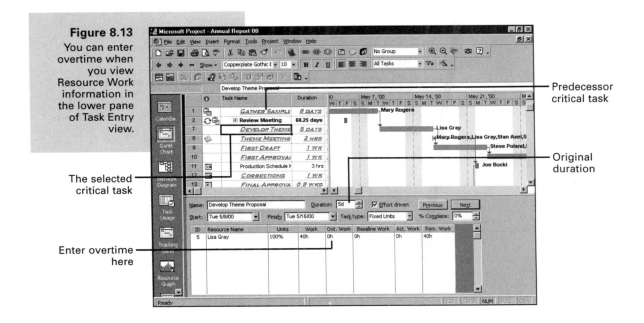

Predecessor critical task

Original duration

Figure 8.14
Here's the revised Resource Work information.

This task and its predecessor are no longer critical

New duration

Authorized overtime work

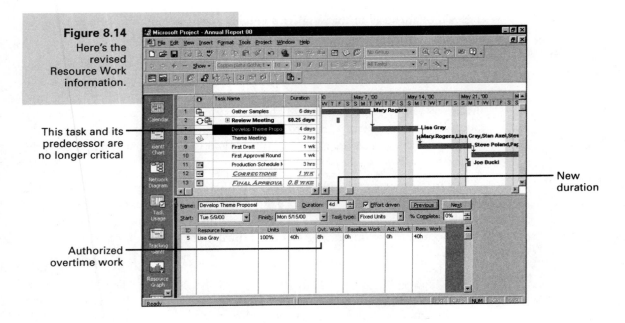

4. Click in the Ovt. Work cell belonging to the resource for which you want to specify overtime hours. Type the number of overtime hours you want to authorize, and then click on the OK button in the lower pane. Project enters the overtime hours and tightens the task's Duration entry accordingly (see Figure 8.14).

Note

Adding overtime introduces slack in the schedule, which in turn might remove the critical designation for the task to which you add overtime or (depending on task links and other task information) for one or more predecessor tasks.

Using Multiple Critical Paths

In most instances, a task needs to have links to successor tasks (other tasks that cannot start or finish until the predecessor task starts or finishes, depending on the nature of the link) or have particular constraints set to be marked as critical and be part of the critical path. But that doesn't mean that tasks without successors or constraints can finish late without affecting the overall schedule. For example, if you set a project finish date of 6/30/00, all tasks must finish by that date for the project to finish on time.

Project 2000 allows you to display *multiple critical paths* to mark more tasks as critical and help you identify potential trouble spots that could bog down your project. When you display multiple critical paths, Project resets certain information for tasks that have no constraints or successors, to make those tasks (and often any predecessors) critical.

Chapter 4 explained that even though a Task Sheet or Resource Sheet typically shows only a half-dozen or so fields (columns) in any given view, there are dozens of other fields you can display if needed. Many of these fields contain information that Project calculates to help it make decisions, such as determining which tasks are critical. Project uses two of these calculated fields to determine whether or not a task has slack and therefore whether or not it's critical: the *late finish date* and the *early finish date*.

A task cannot slip beyond its late finish date without delaying the finish of the whole project. When a task has no constraints or successors, Project sets the task's late finish date as the project finish date. This makes sense, because a task without constraints or links can move around in the schedule without affecting other tasks, but it still must finish by the project completion date. A task cannot finish before its early finish date, which Project calculates based on the task's duration, start date, resources, links, and so on. In other words, Project assumes that a task with a 2w duration requires a minimum of two weeks. Therefore, if a task without successors or constraints falls in the middle of a lengthy project schedule, there could potentially be weeks between the early start date and the late finish date. Project considers this time *total slack*, but you might consider it crucial lead time that you don't want to waste. When you turn on multiple critical paths, Project changes the late finish date for such tasks to the same date as the early finish date, eliminating that slack to make the tasks (and some predecessors) critical. Therefore, turning on multiple critical paths can highlight other groups of related tasks in the schedule to which you might want to add more resources or overtime, to ensure those tasks finish on time. To display multiple critical paths in Project, choose Tools, Options. Click on the Calculation tab, and then click to place a check beside Calculate Multiple Critical Paths, as shown in Figure 8.15.

Working with Slack

Part of what defines a critical task is its impact on other tasks, depending on the relationships you established between tasks. Sometimes, there's room between related tasks, so the task scheduled first can slip (be delayed or take longer to

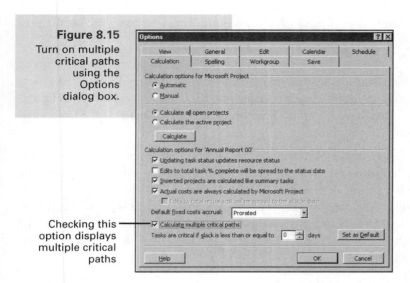

Checking this
option displays
multiple critical
paths

finish than scheduled) without delaying the start or completion of the successor task. That room between tasks is called float time or *slack*. (As noted in the preceding section, if a task doesn't have a successor task, then the task's slack is any time between the task's early start date and late finish date.) Slack between tasks is called *free slack*. Slack between a particular task and the project finish date is called *total slack*, and basically tells you how long the task can slip without affecting the project finish date.

Total slack measurements can be negative. That happens when you have two linked tasks, both of which are constrained to start on particular dates. If you change the duration of the predecessor task to make it longer and don't add any lead time for the successor task (so it can start before the finish of the predecessor), you'll create negative slack. In optimizing your schedule, make sure that you look for negative slack measurements and make changes to eliminate them, to ensure that the critical path is realistic. If the total slack for a task is less than a minimum amount you specified (which you'll learn to change shortly), Project identifies the task as a critical task.

You can display the free slack and total slack for the tasks in a schedule in the Task Sheet portion of Gantt Chart view or Task Entry view. Follow these steps to check the slack measurements for tasks:

1. Display Gantt Chart or Task Entry view.

2. Click anywhere in the Task Sheet portion of the view.

3. Choose View, Table for a submenu of options (see Figure 8.16), and click on Schedule.

4. Use the scroll bar for that portion of the window to scroll right until you see the Free Slack and Total Slack columns (see Figure 8.17).

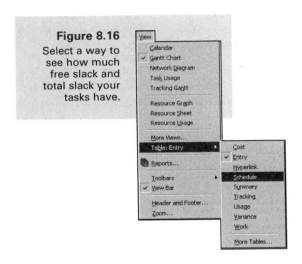

Figure 8.16
Select a way to see how much free slack and total slack your tasks have.

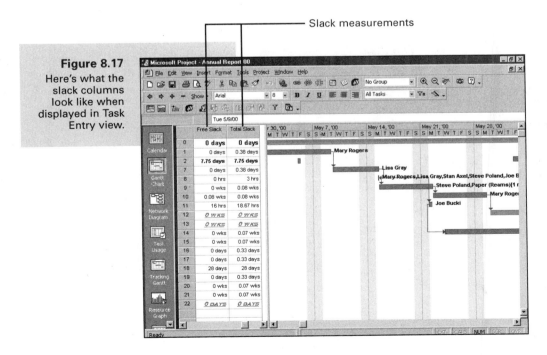

Figure 8.17
Here's what the slack columns look like when displayed in Task Entry view.

Changing How Much Slack Makes a Task Critical

Although Chapter 24, "Customizing Microsoft Project," covers how to adjust many important Project features, one feature relating directly to slack and critical tasks bears mentioning here. You can change the minimum amount of slack that tasks must have to avoid being designated as critical tasks. By default, any task with 0 or fewer days of total slack is designated as a critical task.

Increasing this setting designates more tasks as critical, giving you the opportunity to scrutinize them to look for ways to tighten the schedule. To change the option that controls which tasks are designated as critical, use these steps:

1. Choose Tools, Options. The Options dialog box appears.

2. Click on the Calculation tab to display its settings (see Figure 8.18).

3. Double-click on the entry in the Tasks Are Critical If Slack Is Less Than Or Equal To . . . Days text box, and type a new entry. For example, type **3** to have Project designate any task with less than or equal to three days of total slack as a critical task.

4. Click on OK to close the dialog box. Project updates critical task designations in light of the new setting.

Figure 8.18

Use the Calculations tab in the Options dialog box to control which tasks are critical.

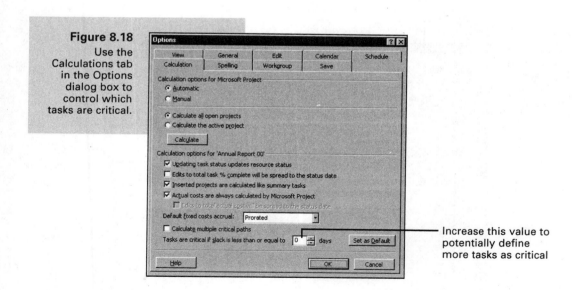

Increase this value to potentially define more tasks as critical

Adjusting Lead and Lag Times

Lead times and lag times can have a great impact on the slack available for a task, as well as the critical path. (The "Working with Lead Times and Lag Times" section in Chapter 5 explains the basics of lead and lag times.) Constraints allowing, you can add slack time by removing lead time or adding lag time. For example, you might change the Lag entry for a successor task from −2d to 0d to remove lead time. Adding slack time generally lengthens the schedule to some degree. Depending how much slack you add, Project might remove a task from the critical path. This can be beneficial in your planning if you're really unsure how well you estimated the schedule for a task.

In contrast, to use lead and lag times to tighten the critical path, here are a few things you can do:

- Add lead time for a successor task where none exists, assuming that you can move up the start date of the successor task. For example, entering **−3d** creates three days' worth of lead time for a successor task.

- Add more lead time for a successor task with an FS link to its predecessor, as long as no constraint prohibits you from moving up the successor task.

- Cut back lag time, or eliminate it altogether, if constraints allow. For example, a 5d lag entry builds in five days of lag time; you might be able to change such an entry to **3d** or **2d**.

You can choose any of a number of techniques to adjust the lead and lag times for a task. For example, you can double-click on a task name, click on the Predecessors tab in the Task Information dialog box, and then edit the Lag column in the Predecessors list. Or you can use the lower pane of Task Entry view to work with lead and lag time, as follows:

1. In the upper pane, click on the name of the critical task for which you want to work with lead and lag times.

2. Right-click on the lower pane; then choose Predecessors & Successors on the shortcut menu that appears. The lower pane changes to show other tasks linked to the selected task, either as predecessors or successors (see Figure 8.19).

3. Click on the cell in the Lag column for the link you want to edit. Type a new lag setting, and then click on OK in the lower pane. Project adjusts any task schedule as needed, according to your change. For example, Figure 8.20 shows the result of adding lead time to task 13's predecessor task, task 12. The task in row 12 is no longer a critical task after the change.

4. To adjust lead and lag times for another task, select the task in the upper pane, and then make changes as needed in the lower pane.

Figure 8.19
The bottom pane has been adjusted to let you work with linked tasks.

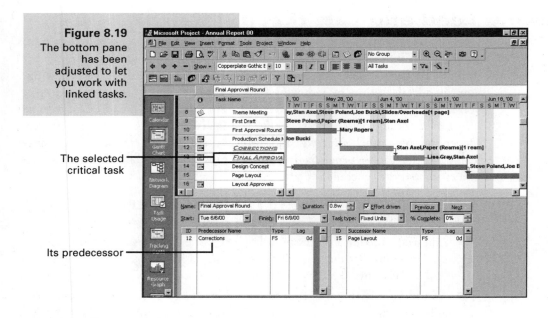

The selected critical task

Its predecessor

Figure 8.20
Here's an example of working with linked tasks.

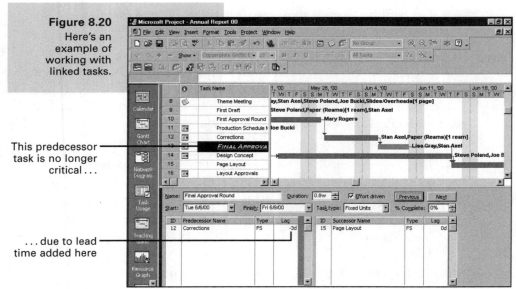

This predecessor task is no longer critical . . .

. . . due to lead time added here

Changing Constraints to Tighten the Schedule

Sometimes, constraints prohibit you from changing lead and lag time, or a schedule conflict arises if you try to do so. If you have the Planning wizard enabled, it warns you if a lead or lag time change will create such a conflict. For example,

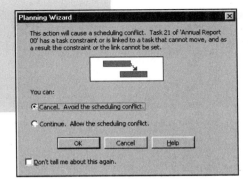

Figure 8.21 shows the message that appears if you try to add lag time before a task that's constrained to finish on (Must Finish On) a particular date.

It is a good idea to review all the constraints you assigned to tasks, looking for constraint changes that will allow you to tighten the schedule. In some cases, you might want to change constraints to ensure that a task stays on the critical path. Here are a few ideas of the types of constraint changes you can make:

- Change more tasks to As Soon As Possible (ASAP) constraints so that you can add lead times.
- Remove Finish No Earlier Than (FNET) constraints for predecessor tasks, especially if they're linked to a successor with an FS link.
- Use more Must Finish On (MFO) constraints to prevent predecessor tasks from slipping further out.

To see a list of the constraints you assigned to tasks so that you can quickly identify which constraints you want to change, do the following:

1. Change to Gantt Chart view or Table Entry view and click on a task name in the list.
2. Choose View, Table, and click on More Tables.
3. In the Tables list (with the Task option button above it selected), double-click on Constraint Dates, or click on it once and then click on Apply. The Task Sheet changes to include Constraint Type and Constraint Date columns. You can drag the split bar from the upper pane and use the scroll bar for the task list to display those columns (see Figure 8.22).

To quickly change constraints while the list of task constraints is onscreen, double-click on the desired task name to display the Task Information dialog box. Click on the Advanced tab. In the Constraint Task area, use the Type drop-down list and Date text box to specify a change to the constraint.

Figure 8.22
Project lists
constraints;
scroll through
the list to check
for constraints
you might want
to change.

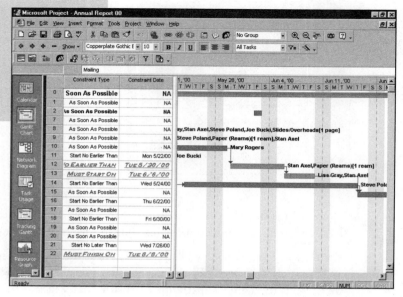

Ignoring Constraints to Remove Negative Slack

If your project has hundreds of tasks, manually reviewing and changing constraint types could take a long time. Although you may want to use the manual route to really fine-tune your schedule, Project offers an alternative for situations where you only want to eliminate negative slack from the schedule. (As an example, negative slack occurs when a successor task can't start until its predecessor finishes, but the predecessor's finish date is after a Start No Later Than or Must Start On constraint date for the successor.)

Basically, negative slack means that accomplishing both tasks within all the constraints is physically impossible, so you need to remove that negative slack. You can tell Project to ignore constraints and move tasks, where needed, to remove every instance of negative slack in the schedule, as follows: Choose Tools, Options. Click on the Schedule tab; then click to clear the check mark beside the Tasks Will Always Honor Their Constraint Dates choice. Click on OK.

It's OK to leave some tasks marked as critical in your schedule. After all, reality can prohibit you from building in lead time, adding resources or overtime, or using the other techniques covered in this chapter. Just remember, if your project schedule starts running behind, you should always look to the critical tasks first for opportunities to apply more resources and improve the schedule.

Comparing Progress versus Your Baseline Plan

IN THIS CHAPTER

- Capturing the original project information and schedule
- Reporting work that has been completed
- Preserving updated information and saving an interim plan
- Determining whether your project is on time, ahead of schedule, or running behind
- Deleting a baseline

Because a project often calls on a varied combination of resources, tasks, and other factors, you need to act as a "deejay" to make sure that the right tune plays at the right time (tasks stay on schedule), that the volume is right (everything's done correctly), and that the floor stays full of dancers (your resources remain available and able to work when you need them).

This chapter shows you how to compare actual progress on a project with the schedule you had planned, so that you can make adjustments, if needed, to meet your project goals.

Final Considerations before Saving the Baseline

By this point, you should have everything in your project plan in place. You should have entered all the tasks, created links between them, and used constraints and other features to control their schedules. You should have entered all your resources in the Resource Sheet, including costs for using each resource. After assigning resources to tasks, you should have adjusted the assignments, costs, and schedules as needed to perfect the plan.

In other words, you should strive to make your plan as accurate as possible before you proceed with the subject of this chapter—saving and using baseline information. In the real world, you should verify the following items to confirm that your plan is realistic before you save the baseline:

- If the plan requires resources outside your department or company (or resources otherwise not under your control), verify each outside resource's availability and willingness to take on the required tasks.

- Make sure you have accurate cost quotes when required, particularly for very expensive tasks or those that require highly specialized or custom work. Being disciplined in this regard may take a bit longer, but it reflects more positively on you in the long run—and ensures that you'll have an adequate budget in place to complete the project.

- If you have to verify the project budget, goals, or time frame with the leadership in your company or with the client, be sure to do so. This gives you the opportunity to make any needed adjustments before you save the baseline.

Creating the Baseline

When you're relatively young and the doctor puts you through your first thorough physical, the doc's not being paranoid and looking for imaginary illnesses.

The physician is gathering your vital statistics while you're in good health, so that there will be a basis for comparison if you ever begin feeling ill. If your blood pressure is very low when you're healthy, a slight climb in the pressure can signal to your doctor that something serious is going on. But a doctor who doesn't have your normal blood pressure reading might not catch the fact that your new reading is higher than normal. Those original health measurements your doctor takes become the baseline, the starting point for future comparison.

Project enables you to take a baseline reading of your schedule, too. Thus you'll have a record of where you started that you can use to diagnose any problems that crop up in the schedule and budget. When you save a baseline for your schedule, Project records all timing, work, and cost details about your plan. Then you can compare information you entered about the actual work performed, actual task duration, start and finish dates, and actual costs with your original plans. (You'll learn how to do so later in this chapter.)

The first time you save any project file after adding information to it, Project opens the dialog box shown in Figure 9.1, which asks whether you want to save the baseline for your new file. To save the baseline information, click on the bottom option button, and then click on OK. If you don't want to save the baseline (because you haven't added all the information for the schedule), leave the top option button selected, and then click on OK.

Caution

Every time you save the baseline, the save process overwrites any baseline information you saved previously. If you want to take a snapshot of your task start and finish dates at any given time and leave the baseline intact, save an interim plan. See the "Saving and Viewing an Interim Plan" section later in this chapter.

Figure 9.1
When you add information to your file and are trying to save it, Project asks if you want to add a baseline.

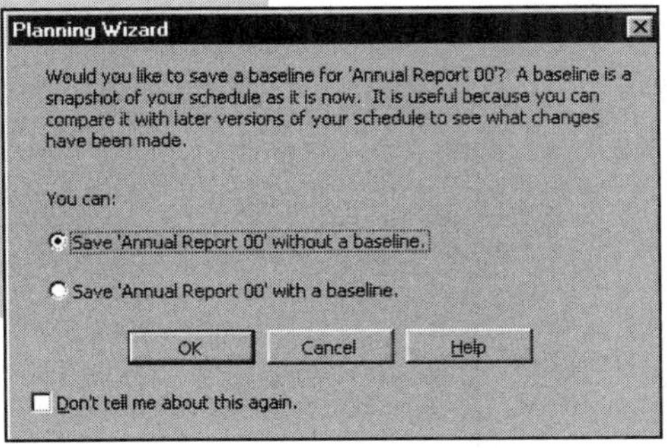

Planning Wizard

Would you like to save a baseline for 'Annual Report 00'? A baseline is a snapshot of your schedule as it is now. It is useful because you can compare it with later versions of your schedule to see what changes have been made.

You can:

○ Save 'Annual Report 00' without a baseline.

○ Save 'Annual Report 00' with a baseline.

[OK] [Cancel] [Help]

☐ Don't tell me about this again.

You shouldn't save a baseline until you enter all your task and resource information, as described in the first section of this chapter. You can also save a baseline for only part of the project, by selecting certain tasks to track in detail.

Here are the steps for creating your schedule baseline:

1. Enter all the task and resource information you want to save as part of the baseline. It doesn't hurt to double-check to make sure that everything's in place, including links and fixed task costs you might have overlooked.

2. (Optional) If you want to save only certain tasks, select the rows you want in the Task Sheet in Gantt Chart view. (Make sure you're in Gantt Chart view by choosing View, Gantt Chart, or by clicking on the Gantt Chart icon on the View Bar.) Select the tasks you want by pointing to the row number for the top row and dragging down to highlight (select) the rows. To select noncontiguous rows, press and hold down Ctrl and then click on each additional row.

3. Choose Tools, Tracking. A submenu of commands appears.

4. Choose Save Baseline. The Save Baseline dialog box appears (see Figure 9.2).

5. If you saved baseline information for all the tasks, leave the Entire Project option button selected and click on OK to continue. If you selected specific tasks for the baseline, click on the Selected Tasks option button; then click on OK. In either case, Project stores the baseline information.

ON THE

CD

> The book's CD-ROM contains the *Annual Report Chapter 9* file that you can use to play around with the features in this chapter. This file has all the resource information in place, and all but a couple of (acceptable) resource overallocations have been removed. Keep in mind that the start date for this project file is 5/1/00, so you may need to change your system date or the Current Date setting in the Project Information dialog box to a date after 5/1/00 for some features to work.

Figure 9.2
Using this dialog box, you can save baseline information easily at any time.

Save Baseline	? X
● Save baseline	
○ Save interim plan	
Copy:	Start/Finish
Into:	Start1/Finish1
For: ● Entire project ○ Selected tasks	
Help	OK	Cancel

Viewing Baseline Information

After you save the baseline information, you might want to look at the baseline values for reference or print them out for others on the team. To view the baseline information, use a variation of the Task Sheet called the Baseline Table. The "Choosing a Table" section in Chapter 11, "Working with the Different Project Views," provides more details, but here are the basic steps for viewing this table of baseline information:

Note

The baseline information also appears in one of Project's reports, the Project Summary report in the Overview category. For more on project reports, see Chapter 14, "Creating and Printing a Report."

1. Make sure that you're in Gantt Chart view by choosing View, Gantt Chart, or by clicking on the Gantt Chart icon in the View Bar. Gantt Chart view appears with a cell selected in the Task Sheet.

2. Choose View, Table: (table name) and click on More Tables. The More Tables dialog box appears (see Figure 9.3).

3. Make sure that you leave the Task option button selected at the top of the dialog box. In the Tables list, select Baseline by double-clicking on it, or by clicking on it once and then clicking on Apply. Project displays the baseline columns in the Task Sheet.

4. Scroll the Task Sheet to the right a bit and drag the vertical split bar to the right to display more of the Task Sheet, so that you can see the baseline columns (see Figure 9.4).

If you want to return to the regular Task Sheet view at any time, choose View, Table: (table name), Entry. You can also display the Variance Task Sheet table, which includes the Baseline Start and Baseline Finish fields, plus variance fields

Figure 9.3

Selecting a table here changes the columns that appear in the Task Sheet.

More Tables	? ☒
Tables: ⦿ Task ○ Resource	
Baseline	New...
Constraint Dates	
Cost	
Delay	Edit...
Earned Value	
Entry	Copy...
Export	
Hyperlink	Organizer...
Rollup Table	
Apply	Cancel

Figure 9.4
You can now view the baseline information you saved.

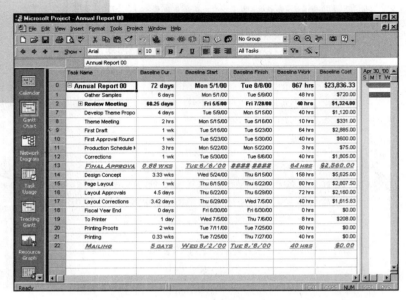

that show the difference between the baseline fields and the information currently in the Start and Finish fields.

Entering Completed Work

Project would be an even better product if you could attach a "work meter" to each and every resource that would automatically capture what the resource does and report that information to Project. Because the world isn't that high-tech yet, you'll have to tell Project what work has been completed on scheduled tasks.

Although Project offers you several means of entering information about actual work completed, one of the most convenient methods is the Tracking toolbar. To display the Tracking toolbar, right-click on any onscreen toolbar, and then choose Tracking. The Tracking toolbar appears, as shown in Figure 9.5. You'll use several of its buttons as you update and view information about completed work in the Gantt Chart view. I'll describe each button when you need it.

Choosing a Status Date

You'll learn in this chapter and the next one that Project automates some features for updating completed work. In addition, Project calculates how much work has

Figure 9.5
The Tracking toolbar offers buttons to speed the process of entering specific information about tasks.

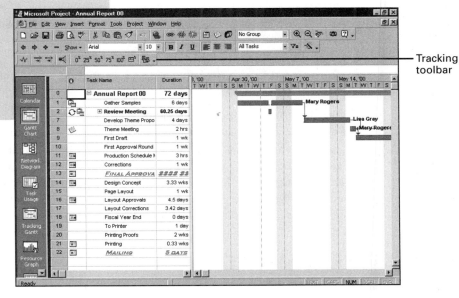

Tracking toolbar

been completed, costs that have accumulated, and whether the project is ahead or behind schedule and budget. Normally, when you're updating the work completed in a schedule, Project assumes that you're marking all the work completed as of the current date (which is determined by your computer's system clock by default). However, there may be instances where you want Project to use a different date when updating work and performing calculations regarding completed work and accumulated costs. For example, say that every Friday at 4 P.M. your group has a status meeting to discuss progress on individual tasks. You check with resources on Wednesday so you can update information about work completed as of the day of the meeting (Friday). The date to which your status information really applies is the following Friday. So, to make it easier to use some methods to enter your updates and to ensure that Project's status calculations are accurate, you should enter that Friday's date as the status date. However, it is important to remember that the Update Project dialog box and the Update As Scheduled button on the Tracking toolbar use the current date for project updates, unless the status date is a later date. In that latter case, work will be marked completed as of the status date.

To change the project status date before you enter completed work information, follow these steps:

1. Choose Project, Project Information. The Project Information dialog box appears.

2. Open the Status Date calendar and use it to specify an alternate date. Alternately, if you want to use the Current Date setting as the status date and remove a Status Date entry you made previously, drag over the entry in the Status Date text box, and then type **NA**.

3. Click on OK to close the Project Information dialog box and finish setting the status date.

If you haven't yet saved your baseline, you can change the Current Date setting in the Project Information dialog box to a much earlier date, then go back and adjust the original task schedules, as long as you haven't marked any work completed on them. You might need to do this, for example, if you're trying to backtrack and enter tasks that you left out of the project plan but now need to include. Changing the Current Date as needed just makes the job a little faster, so you don't have to respond to a number of Planning wizard warnings.

Updating Task by Task

There are at least three ways to tell Project about work that has been completed on a task or a selected set of tasks. The first method, updating completed work information with the mouse, is probably the most time-consuming but it allows you to see an indication of the completed work immediately. With this method, you can update work using the calendar, indicating that, for example, someone has completed three out of five days of work scheduled for a task. Project calculates the percentage of work completed. To update task completion information using your mouse, work with the Gantt bars in Gantt Chart view. Point to the left end of the bar for the task you want to update, so that the mouse pointer changes to a percentage pointer. Press and hold the left mouse button and drag to the right (see Figure 9.6). As you drag, a Task information box appears, telling you how many days will be marked as completed. When you release the mouse button, Project indicates the percentage of the task that has been completed by placing a dark completion bar within the Gantt bar for the task you modified (see Figure 9.7). If a task has not started on time and you need to enter information about the actual starting date, use the method described next to update the task.

The second method also allows you to update tasks one at a time, but gives you some options about how you specify that the work is completed. This method enables you to specify the actual start and finish dates for the task when those dates differ from the dates you scheduled. To use this method, follow these steps:

1. Select the task or tasks you want to update in the Task Sheet. Keep in mind, though, that you can't select a summary task (the "master" task for a set of recurring tasks) to update it; you can only select the subtasks

Figure 9.6
The percentage pointer indicates that you can update your task by dragging.

Task information

Percentage pointer

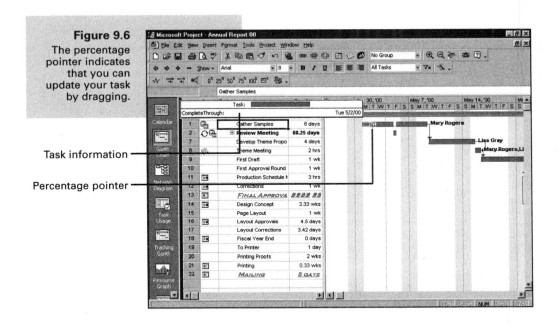

Figure 9.7
The dark bar within the Gantt bar for the first task shows the portion of work completed on the task so far (all of it).

This indicator appears when you mark a task as completed

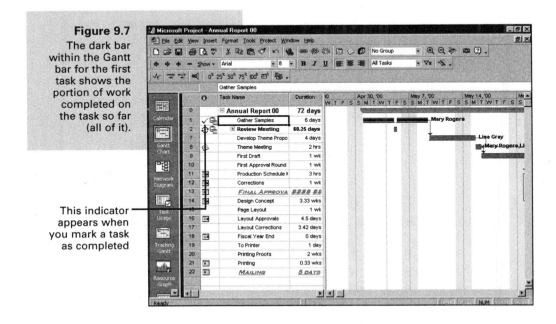

Figure 9.8

Enter actual data about a task's schedule and work completed here.

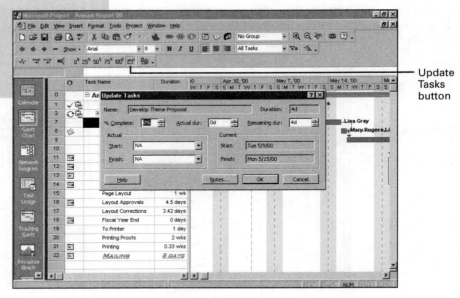

Update Tasks button

within a summary task. For more on working with summary tasks and subtasks, see Chapter 15, "Working with Outlining."

2. Choose Tools, Tracking, Update Tasks. Alternately, click on the Update Tasks button on the Tracking toolbar. The Update Tasks dialog box appears (see Figure 9.8).

3. Enter information about the work that has been completed using one of the following three methods:

■ Enter a percentage value, such as **10** for 10%, in the % Complete text box, which is highlighted by default when you open the Update Tasks dialog box. Project changes the duration settings for you when you finish updating the task.

■ Enter the number of days of work completed in the Actual Dur text box. If you want to use a duration other than the default (days), enter the duration abbreviation with the value you enter, such as **w** for weeks. Project calculates the percentage completed information and the remaining duration information.

■ Enter the number of days of work you estimate are remaining for the task in the Remaining Dur text box. Again, if you want to enter a duration that's not in days, include the appropriate duration abbreviation. When you specify work completed this way, Project calculates the percentage completed and duration.

4. If it looks like the actual starting or finishing date for the task will differ from those dates entered in the Current area of the Update Tasks dialog box, change the Start and Finish text box entries accordingly. Enter the new dates in mm/dd/yy format, or click on the drop-down arrow beside either text box and use the pop-up calendar to specify the date. (By default, these text boxes contain **NA**.) Note that if you make a date entry in the Finish text box in the Actual area of the Update Tasks dialog box, Project will mark the task as 100% complete, because a task can't have an actual finish date if it's not finished.

5. If you want to add notes describing special circumstances about why a task might be ahead of or behind schedule, click on the Notes button, enter the information in the Notes dialog box that appears, and then click on OK.

6. Click on OK in the Update Tasks dialog box. Project updates the tasks, moving and adjusting any tasks as needed to reflect your changes in the Actual Start or Finish dates. It also uses a dark bar to mark the percentage of completed work you indicated for the selected tasks.

The final method for updating tasks is more "quick and dirty," and gives you less flexibility in specifying exact percentages or days of completed work. For this method, select the task or tasks you want to update in the Task Sheet, then click on one of the five percentage buttons (0%, 25%, 50%, 75%, or 100%) on the Tracking toolbar. Project updates the Gantt chart accordingly. Of course, you use the 0% button to remove any completed work that you previously specified. For example, if you thought an external resource had completed half a task, but you discover that no work has actually been completed (maybe your contact person initially fibbed to you), you can select the task and click on the 0% button to show the true percentage measurement.

Caution

If you select multiple tasks in the Task Sheet before opening the Update Tasks dialog box, you can enter actual duration or actual start and finish information. Keep in mind, however, that these changes apply to all of t he selected tasks. An instance in which such a "global" change might be useful is if the project starting date was delayed and a number of tasks started later than planned. Generally, you should select multiple tasks only when you want to enter the same % Complete value for all of them.

The Update As Scheduled button (second from the left on the Tracking toolbar) specifies work completed for the selected tasks based on the scheduled start dates and the status date (or the current date, if the status date is set before the current date). Project assumes that all work scheduled between those dates has been completed, and enters the work update information accordingly, adding dark tracking bars to the Gantt chart.

Updating Tasks by Resource

In some instances, you might not have information to enter about the work completed for all the tasks that were under way recently. For example, say that in the last week, you received a progress report from only one outside contractor; other outside contractors and internal resources assigned to some of the same tasks have not reported. In such a situation, you need to be able to enter work completed on a resource-by-resource basis. You can use either the Task Usage view or Resource Usage view to enter actual work completed by a specific resource.

Using Task Usage View

If you still want to view tasks in order according to their ID or order in the Task Sheet, you can switch to the Task Usage view, which lists the tasks in order and then lists the resource assignments below each task. Then you can find the task you need and enter a value for completed work for the resource assignment. Follow these steps to enter completed work for a resource in Task Usage view:

1. To change to Task Usage view, choose View, Task Usage; or click on the Task Usage icon on the View Bar.

2. Choose View, Table: (table name), Work. This changes the columns that appear in the Task Sheet portion of the view, so that the sheet now displays the column where you enter completed work.

3. Drag the vertical split bar to the right so that you can see the Actual column of the Task Sheet portion of the view. You enter completed work values in this column.

4. Scroll to the task for which you want to update resource work; then click in the Actual column for the resource's assignment under the task.

5. Enter a completed work value in the cell, as shown in Figure 9.9. Project assumes that you're entering a value in hours.

6. Press Enter or click on the green Enter button on the Entry box to complete the entry.

Figure 9.9
In Task usage view, you can enter the work completed on an assignment by a resource.

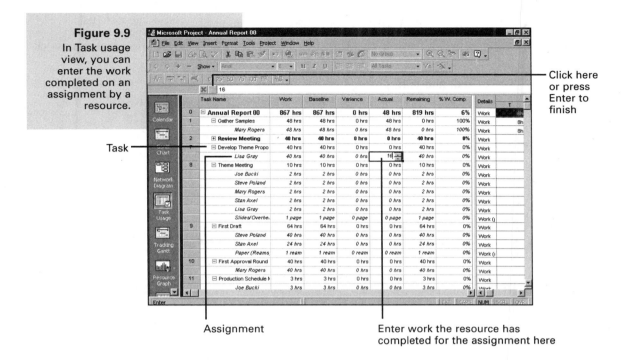

Click here
or press
Enter to
finish

Task

Assignment

Enter work the resource has
completed for the assignment here

Tip

If you want to enter the total work completed on a task in Task Entry view, select the Actual cell for the row that holds the task information (rather than an assignment row below the task), and enter the work value.

Using Resource Usage View

If only one or two resources have reported completed work to you, you don't want to sift through the Task Sheet in Gantt Chart view or Task Usage view and hunt for each task handled by the resource to update it. Instead, you can use the Resource Usage view, which lists assignments by resource. This method works best if your organization uses timesheets where resources identify how many hours per day they spend on each assigned task. At the end of the week, you'll find that it's easiest and fastest to update the work information from the timesheets and track progress on the job if you're in Resource Usage view.

To update completed work in Resource Usage view, follow these steps:

1. To change to Resource Usage view, choose View, Resource Usage, or click on the Resource Usage icon on the View Bar.

2. Choose View, Table: (table name), Work. This adds several more columns to the Resource Sheet portion of the view, including the column where you enter completed work.

3. If necessary, drag the column header for the Resource Name column to the right so that you can clearly see the assignment names indented beneath each resource. Then drag the vertical split bar to the right so you can see the Actual column for the Task Sheet portion of the view. You enter completed work values in this column.

4. Scroll to the resource for which you want to update completed work; then click on the Actual column cell for the appropriate assignment under the task.

5. Enter a completed work value in the cell, as shown in Figure 9.10. Project assumes that you're entering a value in hours.

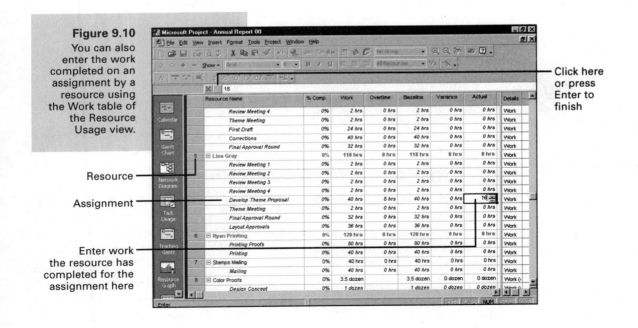

Figure 9.10
You can also enter the work completed on an assignment by a resource using the Work table of the Resource Usage view.

Resource

Assignment

Enter work the resource has completed for the assignment here

Click here or press Enter to finish

6. Press Enter or click on the green Enter button on the Entry box to complete the entry.

Note

> Don't forget that you can hide columns in the Task Sheet portion of the view to make data entry easier. For example, you might want to hide the % Comp., Work, Overtime, Baseline, and Variance columns in Figure 9.10. To hide a column, right-click on the column heading; then click on Hide Column.

Using Assignment Information

In either the Task Usage or Resource Usage view, you can double-click on any assignment to open the Assignment Information dialog box. Click on the Tracking tab to display its entries. Then enter the completed work value (in hours) in the Actual Work text box (see Figure 9.11), or adjust the % Work Complete entry to use a percentage to specify how much work has been completed. If the assignment began early or late, change the Actual Start date, too. Click on OK to finish entering the work.

Figure 9.11
You can enter completed work as well as actual start and finish dates on the Tracking tab of the Assignment Information dialog box.

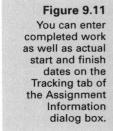

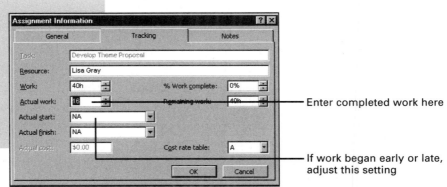

Enter completed work here

If work began early or late, adjust this setting

Entering Daily Values (Custom Time Period Tracking)

Chapter 7, "Resolving Overallocations and Overbooked Resources," explained how to tell Project to distribute hours worked on a task in the pattern of your choice. By default, when you assign a resource to a task, Project uses the flat contour and divides the work evenly over the duration of the project. That is, for a four-day task, the resource will be scheduled to work eight hours per day for four days. If you apply a contour to the assignment, however, Project extends the task duration and reallocates the daily work in a pattern such as a bell curve, in which the resource works fewer hours at the start and finish of the assignment and full time during the middle of the assignment. Chapter 7 also explained how to create an edited contour so that you could control how many hours on a given day the resource is scheduled to work.

Similarly, you may need to have exact control over how you enter completed work for a resource to ensure your project tracking is accurate. For example, say a resource is assigned to work full time on a task for five days, but actually only completes six hours of work per day for the first three days. Here's how to enter such precise settings for work completed:

1. Change to the Task Usage view or Resource Usage view.

2. Right-click on the right pane of the view (the yellow area that displays work per day). Then click on Actual Work. Alternately, choose Format, Details, Actual Work. In the right pane, the schedule for each assignment is split into two rows. The top row, Work, holds scheduled entries. The bottom row, Act. Work (which may appear as "Act. W" unless you increase the width of the Details column), is where you enter work completed for the assignment.

3. Scroll to the resource assignment for which you want to enter daily work values.

4. Click in the cell in the Act. Work row for the appropriate date, and then type the work value. Figure 9.12 shows an example.

5. Press Enter or click on the green Enter button on the Entry box to complete the entry.

Note

When you enter daily Act. Work values that are less than the scheduled values in the Work row, Project automatically extends the assignment duration (unless a constraint prevents it from doing so), adding an hour to the end of the resource assignment for each hour of shortfall.

Figure 9.12
You can use the right pane of either the Task Usage or Resource Usage view to enter daily completed-work values.

Enter an actual work value for a particular day

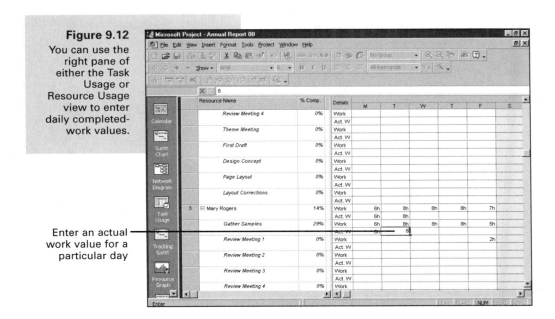

Updating Project Information

Project offers one final path for indicating how much work has been completed for tasks you select, or for all the tasks in the project: the Update Project dialog box. To open and use this dialog box to update completed work information for the tasks in your schedule, follow these steps:

1. (Optional) If you want to update only selected tasks, select the tasks in the Task Sheet in Gantt Chart view by dragging over the task row numbers or dragging to select cells in the rows for the tasks you want.

2. Choose Tools, Tracking, Update Project. The Update Project dialog box appears (see Figure 9.13).

Figure 9.13
This is yet another method for updating information about work completed.

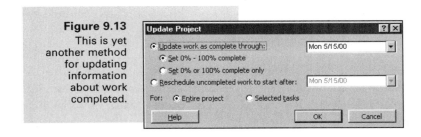

3. Leave the Update Work As Complete Through option button selected. By default, the date that appears here is the status date, described earlier, or the current date, if you haven't specified a status date for your project or if the status date precedes the current date. If you don't have information that's absolutely current, you might want to change the date in the text box beside this option button to reflect the date through which you're certain work has been completed.

4. Choose among the following option buttons:

   ■ The Set 0%–100% Complete option button, which is selected by default and marks the work completed based on the percentage of work between the task's start date and the date specified in Step 3.

   ■ The Set 0% or 100% Complete Only option is an all-or-nothing choice. It marks the task as 0% completed if its finish date is after the date specified in Step 3, or 100% if it was scheduled to finish on or before the date specified in Step 3.

5. If you selected a range of tasks in Step 1, choose the Selected Tasks option button at the bottom of the dialog box.

6. Click on OK. Project closes the dialog box and marks the appropriate tasks with indicators of how much work has been completed.

Rescheduling Work

Work doesn't always start as planned. For example, if you schedule painters to handle some outdoor painting and it rains, there's no choice but to start the painting on a later, drier day. You might also encounter situations in which a resource begins work on a task but can't finish it on the scheduled date due to problems such as scheduling conflicts or unforeseen absences from work. In such instances, you need to reschedule the task to a time frame that's realistic—which means moving all or some of the work after the current date in the schedule. When a task needs to be rescheduled, it has *slipped*.

Of course, you have the option of dragging the Gantt chart bar for the task into a new position, or dragging to reschedule the finish date for a partially completed task. However, Project also offers methods for quickly rescheduling all tasks for which work was to start (or finish) prior to the current date.

When you reschedule a task, if you indicate that no work has been completed on it, Project moves the task so that its start date becomes the status date or the current date. If you mark the task as partially complete, Project leaves the original start date in place but extends the task schedule so that the work yet to be done begins on the status date or current date. This is called *splitting* an in-progress task. The Gantt chart bar for the task displays the split. (Review the topic "Splitting a Task" in Chapter 5 to learn more about split tasks.)

Select the tasks that you want to update in the Task Sheet, and then choose one of the following methods to reschedule the task:

- Display the Update Project dialog box as just described. Click on the Reschedule Uncompleted Work To Start After option button (refer to Figure 9.13). Then enter the date when the rescheduled work should begin in the accompanying text box. Click on the Selected Tasks option button, and then click on OK to let the work slip.

- Click on the Reschedule Work button on the Tracking toolbar (the third button from the left) to move the selected tasks so that uncompleted work begins on the status date or the current date.

Caution

Keep in mind that rescheduling work can have a dramatic impact on your schedule when you're rescheduling linked tasks, especially those that are critical. The Planning wizard may display warnings when you try to reschedule work, as well. Always make sure that you check the impact of rescheduling work on the overall project plan, and then deploy more resources if warranted.

Using Progress Lines

Progress lines on a Gantt chart mark a particular date and compare how in-progress tasks are advancing with relation to that date. They help you see at a glance how drastically a task may be lagging or exceeding its schedule. The mouse provides the fastest way to add a progress line to the schedule. Click on the Add Progress Line button on the Tracking toolbar; then click on the date for the progress line on the Gantt chart. The progress line appears, as shown in Figure 9.14.

If you want to add several progress lines that recur at regular intervals, or to control certain progress line settings, follow these steps:

1. Choose Tools, Tracking, Progress Lines. The Progress Lines dialog box appears.

2. Click on the Dates And Intervals tab, if it isn't selected.

3. To display a *current progress line,* which has special highlighting and is meant to highlight the current date or a status date you set (so you can have a daily look at where you stand), check the Always Display Current

Click this button . . .   . . . then click on a date to add a progress line

Figure 9.14
Progress lines let
you know when
tasks are on
schedule.

Work on this task
is running behind

Work on this task
is ahead of
schedule

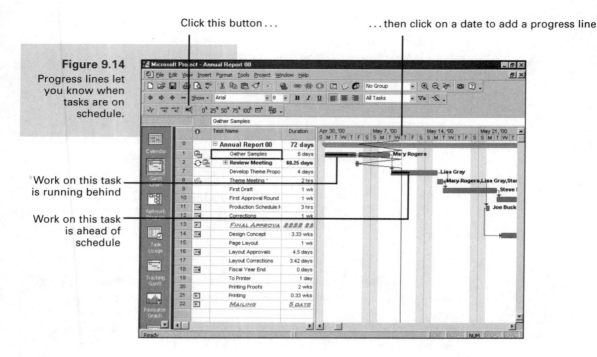

Progress Line check box. Then click on an option button to specify
whether you want that current progress line to appear At Project Status
Date or At Current Date.

4. To add recurring progress lines to the schedule, click on the Display
Progress Lines At Recurring Intervals check box, activating the options
below it, as shown in Figure 9.15. Choose whether to add the lines daily,

Figure 9.15
Use the Progress
Lines dialog box
to manually add
progress lines,
especially
recurring ones.

Click on a progress
line date; then click
on Delete to remove
that progress line

Choose options
here to create
recurring
progress lines

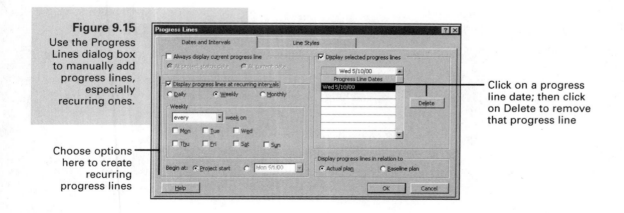

weekly, or monthly by clicking on the appropriate option button. As with setting a recurring task, the choices that coincide with each option button are slightly different, but involve making schedule choices. For example, for the Weekly option, you need to select a day of the week and choose whether the lines should appear every week, every other week, or at intervals up to 12 weeks apart. Finally, beside Begin At, specify whether the progress lines should start appearing from the Project Start or a particular date that you specify.

5. Under Display Progress Lines In Relation To, specify whether the progress lines should compare the progress with the Actual Plan or Baseline Plan.

6. If you want to delete a progress line you added with the mouse, click on the date in the Progress Line Dates list, and then click on the Delete button.

7. Click on OK to finish creating progress lines.

Saving and Viewing an Interim Plan

Baseline plans let you look at where you started with your schedule and resource plans. In contrast, an interim plan serves as a snapshot of changes you've made down the line, and shows how far you've come with a project. For example, you can set a milestone for the date when the project is 25 percent through its total schedule and get a record of how things stand at that point. You may find that your baseline plan has become meaningless because the schedule and assignments have changed so much. In such a case, your interim plan should become your "working baseline." If you save an interim plan, it captures the current information (or information from a previous interim plan). Saving interim plans can also be thought of as saving "multiple baselines." You can save up to 10 interim plans for your project.

Consider this hypothetical situation: Your resource completed task 1 but took twice as long as you had anticipated. You can look at similar tasks later in your schedule, adjust them to reflect the new knowledge, and save an interim plan. Any changes you make after saving that interim plan are not added to the interim plan; they're added to the main scheduling fields for your project. You can save numerous interim plans to keep a record of where significant schedule changes occur. This could be helpful if, for example, your company routinely uses follow-up meetings after the completion of a project to analyze what worked well and troubleshoot things that didn't. You can arm yourself for the discussion by creating interim plans and adding task notes about when and why key tasks slipped.

The initial steps for creating an interim plan resemble the initial steps for saving the baseline. Here are those initial steps and the rest of the steps needed to save your interim plan and view its information:

1. Enter all of the task and resource information you want to save as part of the interim plan. For example, make changes to the Start and Duration fields for tasks, or change resource assignments that were in place when you saved your baseline plan.

2. (Optional) If you want to save selected tasks, select the rows you want in the Task Sheet in Gantt Chart view.

3. Choose Tools, Tracking, Save Baseline. The Save Baseline dialog box appears.

4. Click on the Save Interim Plan option to select it; this enables the Copy and Into drop-down lists.

5. From the Copy drop-down list (see Figure 9.16), select the two fields of information from the Task Sheet you want to save in your interim plan. For the first interim plan, you should always select either Start/Finish (the default) or Baseline Start/Finish. For subsequent interim plans, choose the fields you specified in the Into drop-down list (see the next step) for the last interim plan you saved, so that the new interim plan gives you a record of which tasks have slipped more than once.

6. Use the Into drop-down list to specify what Project will call the fields in which it saves the interim plan dates. For your first interim plan, use Start1/Finish1, for your second interim plan, use Start2/Finish2, and so on.

7. If you want to save interim dates for only the tasks you selected in Step 2, select the Selected Tasks option.

8. Click on OK. Project saves the interim plan dates in new fields; you can add them to the Task Sheet to view their contents by completing the rest of these steps.

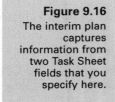

Figure 9.16
The interim plan captures information from two Task Sheet fields that you specify here.

9. In the Task Sheet, click on the column name of the column to the right of where you want to insert an interim plan field.

10. Choose Insert, Column (or right-click and then click on Insert Column on the resulting shortcut menu). The Column Definition dialog box appears.

11. Click on the drop-down list arrow to display the Field Name list; then scroll down and click on the name of the interim plan field to be inserted at that location. For example, you would click on Start1 to display the first field from your first interim plan (see Figure 9.17).

• •

To select a field name faster, open the Field Name drop-down list and then type a letter to scroll the list. For example, typing **S** scrolls quickly to the fields that start with S.

• •

12. If needed, make changes to other fields in the Column Definition dialog box; then click on OK to finish adding the field. It appears in the Task Sheet as shown in Figure 9.18.

13. Repeat Steps 10–12 to add any other interim plan fields you want to view to the Task Sheet.

Caution

Saving an interim plan doesn't automatically save cost information from the Cost field to the Cost1 field, and so on. If you want to use the numbered Cost fields to track interim cost information, you need to add the desired numbered cost field (Cost1, Cost2, and so on) to the Cost table of the Task Sheet, then copy the information from the Cost field using the Copy and Paste buttons on the Standard toolbar.

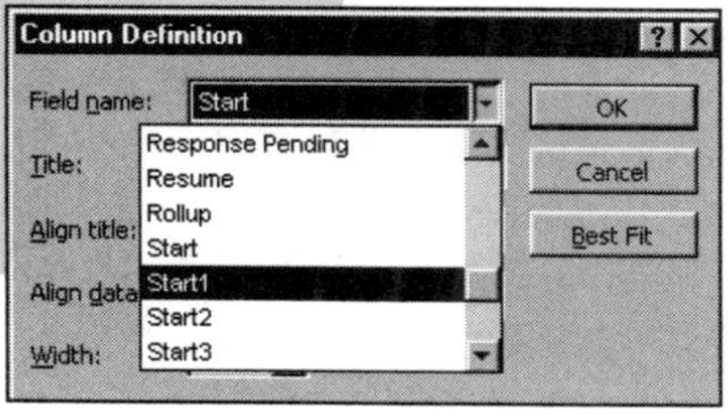

Figure 9.17
You can choose to add an interim plan field to the Task Sheet.

Column Definition

Field name: Start

Response Pending
Resume
Rollup
Start
Start1
Start2
Start3

OK
Cancel
Best Fit

Title:
Align title:
Align data:
Width:

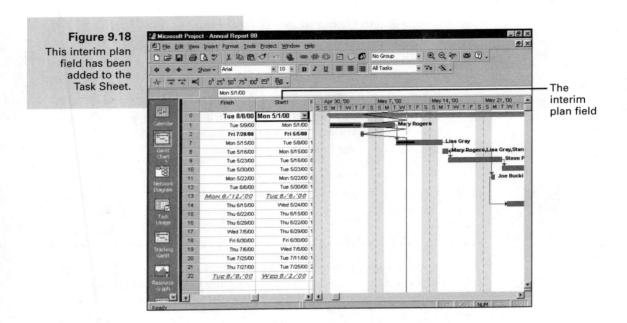

Figure 9.18
This interim plan field has been added to the Task Sheet.

The interim plan field

Viewing Baseline versus Actual Information

Because there are so many different kinds of information captured in your Project file, the baseline information you store and the actual information you enter about work completed doesn't appear automatically. To close this chapter, I'll show you a few different ways to view this information, depending on how much and what kind of detail you want to see.

Using Tracking Gantt View

The Tracking Gantt view in Project lets you do virtually everything you can do in Gantt Chart view, such as dragging and moving tasks, updating links, or entering information about work that has been completed for a project. In addition, though, Tracking Gantt view uses Gantt bars that provide greater detail about work progress on tasks, so you can see at a glance which tasks are on schedule or falling behind. This is much more convenient than scrolling through various columns on the Task Sheet.

In this view, each Gantt bar is really two bars (see Figure 9.19). The bottom portion, usually gray even on a color monitor, shows you the baseline schedule for

Figure 9.19
Tracking Gantt
view works like
regular Gantt
Chart view,
but the bars
provide more
information
about your tasks.

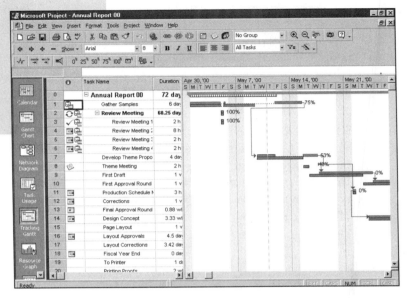

the task, assuming you saved a baseline plan for the project. The top portion
shows the current schedule for the project, in a lightly shaded bar. As you enter
actual work information for the task, the portion of the bar representing the work
completed becomes solid rather than shaded. By default, the top portion of the
bar is blue if the task is on schedule or work has not yet begun on it. If the task
is behind schedule (meaning that its finish date has passed but you haven't yet
marked the task as 100% complete), the top portion of the bar appears in red, a
color commonly used to alert you that it's time to panic.

To display Tracking Gantt view, choose View, More Views or click on the More
Views icon in the View Bar. In the More Views dialog box, scroll down the Views
list to the Tracking Gantt choice. Double-click on this choice (or click on it once
and click on Apply).

Caution

Tracking Gantt view can be a bit unpredictable. If you switch to this view
and don't see anything in the Gantt chart pane at the right, first make
sure that Project hasn't scrolled the displayed dates beyond the schedule
for the project. Press Alt+Home to go to the beginning of the project in
the Gantt Chart view. If that's not the solution, click on the Go To
Selected Task button on the Standard toolbar.

Other Tracking Views

If you want access to the baseline and tracking information in tabular form, you can change the Task Sheet so that it displays the information you want. To do so in any view that contains the Task Sheet, click in a cell in the Task Sheet; then choose View, Table: (table name), Tracking. The Task Sheet now displays tracking information (see Figure 9.20).

In Chapter 4, "Setting Up a Project," you learned how to display the Project Statistics box via the Project Information dialog box. The Project Statistics dialog box offers information about the baseline schedule for the project, including work and cost information, as well as the actual work completed and dollars spent. You can also open this dialog box by clicking on the Project Statistics button (the first button) on the Tracking toolbar. The dialog box appears as shown in Figure 9.21. Click on the Close button when you finish reviewing the information in the dialog box.

Figure 9.20

The Task Sheet now shows tracking information in tabular form. I've expanded the size of the Task Sheet by dragging the vertical split bar to the right.

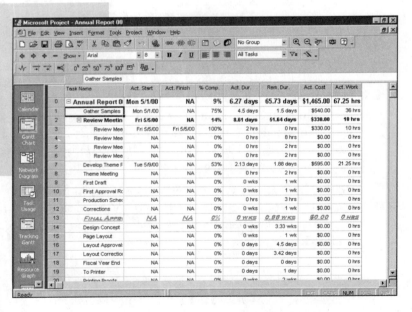

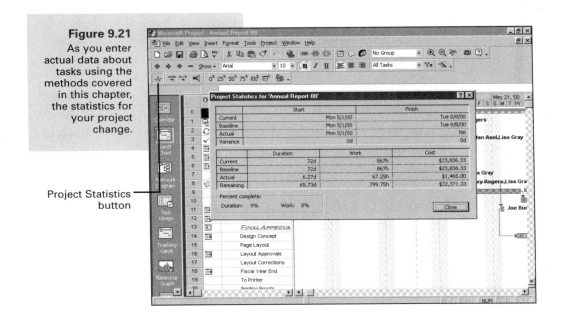

Figure 9.21
As you enter actual data about tasks using the methods covered in this chapter, the statistics for your project change.

Project Statistics button

Clearing a Baseline

Project 2000 now offers the ability to clear any baseline and interim plan information that you've saved. You might want to use this feature to get back to square one with the information in a project file, or to save a project file as a template (both reasons to discard the baseline information). Use these steps to clear a baseline or interim plan from your project file:

1. If you want to clear baseline information for selected tasks only, drag over those tasks in the Task Sheet to select them.

2. Choose Tools, Tracking, Clear Baseline. The Clear Baseline dialog box appears (Figure 9.22).

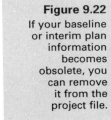
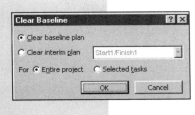

Figure 9.22
If your baseline or interim plan information becomes obsolete, you can remove it from the project file.

3. If you want to clear the baseline plan, leave Clear Baseline Plan selected. To clear an interim plan instead, choose the Clear Interim Plan option button, then use the drop-down list beside the option button to choose the fields that hold the interim plan information to clear.

4. If you selected any tasks in Step 1 and want to clear the plan information for those tasks only, click on the Selected Tasks option button.

5. Click on OK. Project clears the baseline information without warning or alerting you.

PART IV
Viewing, Formatting, and Printing Projects

10

Viewing and Managing Costs

IN THIS CHAPTER

- Viewing and finding task costs
- Looking at resource costs
- Previewing cost reports
- Reporting costs to others
- Managing costs and cash flow

When you're an independent contractor, you have to keep your eye on three key aspects of any project you manage for your client. First, you have to ensure that the work you deliver is of the highest quality. Second, you have get the job done on time—or even earlier. Finally, you have to track costs like a maniac to ensure that you not only charge the client a fair price but also make a fair profit.

A project manager within a company needs to think like an independent contractor. The work your team delivers has to be top quality and on time—and delivered at a cost that helps your company stay profitable.

This chapter shows you how to get crucial mileage from all the resource and task cost information you entered into Project.

Viewing and Finding Task Costs

Chapter 9, "Comparing Progress versus Your Baseline Plan," explains how to tell Project how much work has been completed on a task. In addition, although you might not be able to see it immediately, Project can use the task completion information you entered to calculate the actual cost for that completed work, based on hourly rates for resources and other cost information you entered.

You might not be able to see the costs immediately because Gantt Chart view doesn't display any cost information by default. You have to learn techniques for examining cost information in various ways, depending on what type of information you want to view. Project enables you to view accumulated costs (costs based on actual work completed plus any fixed and per use costs) by task, by the whole project, or by the resources completing the work. The remainder of this section describes how you can access each type of cost information and make sure that task costs are calculated for you.

ON THE

CD

Use the *Annual Report Chapter 10* file from the book's CD-ROM to experiment with cost information. Again, this file has more cost information entered into it than the earlier practice files, so don't be surprised if you see different budget figures than appeared earlier.

Controlling Whether Costs Are Updated Based on Work Completed

By default, Project automatically updates the calculated costs for a task or resource when you update information about how much work has been completed on a task. Project calculates cost values by multiplying the number of hours of work completed for a task by the hourly rate for the resource completing the task.

You can turn calculation off, however, if you need to. The primary reason not to have Project calculate these values as you go is to avoid calculation delays while you're updating information about the work completed on various tasks. You will also want to turn off automatic calculation if you need to enter actual cost information before you indicate that work has been completed on the project. (See the section later in this chapter called "Changing How Costs Add Up" to learn more about entering actual costs.)

To ensure that Project correctly calculates information about actual costs based on the work you mark as completed, or to turn off automatic calculation, follow these steps:

1. Choose Tools, Options. The Options dialog box appears, with many tabs.
2. Click on the Calculation tab to display its options (see Figure 10.1).

Figure 10.1
The Calculation tab offers options for controlling how Project reacts when you enter scheduling information.

When this option is checked, Project automatically calculates actual expenses

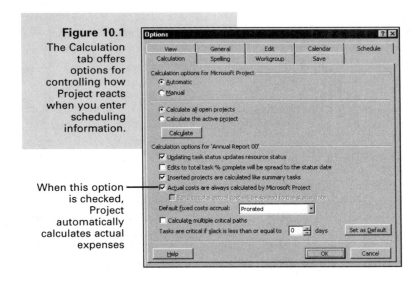

3. Leave the check in the Actual Costs Are Always Calculated By Microsoft Project check box if you want Project to update all calculated cost information whenever you update task completion information. Clear the check box if you prefer to enter actual cost information or calculate actual costs periodically. When this option is turned on, it's enabled for all files you open in Project.

Caution

If you check the Actual Costs Are Always Calculated By Microsoft Project check box after you've already entered actual cost information, the calculated costs will wipe out the actual costs you entered.

4. Click on OK to close the Options dialog box. If you turned on automatic calculation, a message box warns you that actual cost entries will be overridden. Click on OK to close the message box. Your change takes effect immediately.

Viewing Task Costs

One way to look at the expenses associated with your project is task by task. For example, your plan might include particular tasks for which you really need to watch expenses, such as work handled by an outside contractor with a particularly high hourly rate. Or you might need to provide information about the costs you estimated for a particular task to a team member negotiating to have that task completed, so the team member will know the highest price you're willing to pay to have the task completed.

Project offers a couple of methods by which you can take a look at how costs are adding up for a task based on the work completed for that task. Either method enables you to enter or edit cost information when you need to, such as when the actual fixed cost turns out to be less than the fixed cost you initially estimated.

The first method involves adjusting the columns shown in the Task Sheet; do this in any view that displays the Task Sheet, such as Gantt Chart view or Task Entry view. To display actual cost information in the Task Sheet, choose View, Table: (table name), Cost. The Task Sheet changes to include several columns with cost information. Drag the vertical split bar (if there is one) to the right to display additional columns of cost information, as shown in Figure 10.2. (The View Bar is hidden in the figure so that you can see all the columns.) To return the Task Sheet to its regular view, choose View, Table: (table name), Entry.

Figure 10.2
You can adjust the Task Sheet so that it displays cost information.

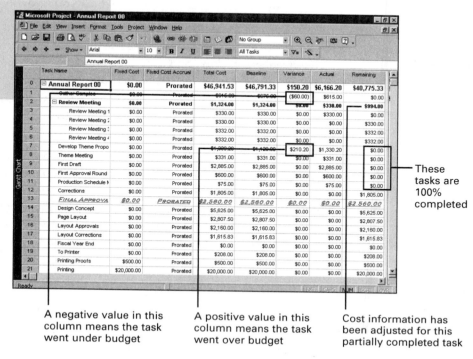

A negative value in this column means the task went under budget

A positive value in this column means the task went over budget

Cost information has been adjusted for this partially completed task

These tasks are 100% completed

Tip

Before you save a project baseline or enter information about work completed, don't forget to use the Task Sheet view shown in Figure 10.2 to enter a fixed cost for any task where it's feasible to do so, such as the ones shown for tasks 20 and 21 in Figure 10.2 in the Fixed Cost column. Even if you have only rough estimates for these costs, you should add them to ensure that you won't see too much of a budget variance after you enter actual costs. Remember, fixed costs apply on a task-by-task basis. Any other hourly or per use costs you enter for resources assigned to the task will be added to the fixed cost to yield the task cost (total cost).

Displaying cost information in the Task Sheet, as just described, is useful when you want to view the costs for many tasks. There might be instances, however, when you don't want to change the Task Sheet's appearance, but you do want to view the cost information for a particular task. You can do so by displaying the Cost Tracking form (you'll learn more detail about forms in Chapter 13, "Working with Forms"). Use one of the following methods to access the Cost

Tracking form after you select a task for which you want to view task information in the Task Sheet:

- Display the Custom Forms toolbar by right-clicking on any toolbar onscreen and clicking on Custom Forms. Click on the Cost Tracking button (second from the left) on this toolbar.

- Choose Tools, Customize, Forms. The Custom Forms dialog box appears (see Figure 10.3). Click on the Task option button if it isn't already selected. In the Forms list, double-click on Cost Tracking (or click on it once, and then click on Apply).

When you use either of the methods just described, the Cost Tracking form appears (see Figure 10.4). As you can see, this form offers several text entry boxes with various bits of task cost information, including the baseline cost (how much you estimated the work on the task would cost), the actual cost of the work performed so far, and any remaining (Rem) budgeted cost. It also calculates the variance between the baseline cost and the current cost.

You can change several of the entries in this dialog box. Note, however, that if Project is calculating the task cost based on hourly cost rates you entered for a resource, any edits you make in the Total text box will revert to the calculated value as soon as you close the dialog box (unless you turn off automatic calculation). To close the dialog box after making the changes you want, click on OK.

Figure 10.3
Use this dialog box to display a form giving you cost information about a single task.

Cost Tracking button on the Custom Forms toolbar

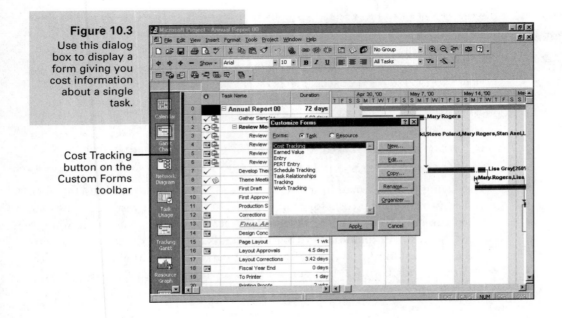

Figure 10.4
This form displays cost information for a single task.

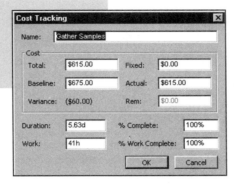

Note

A positive variance means that a task has gone over budget. A negative variance means that the task costs remain under the baseline budget.

Looking at Resource Costs

Chapter 7, "Resolving Overallocations and Overbooked Resources," covers how to identify when you've assigned too much work to a resource. Similarly, there might be situations where you want to review exactly how much each staff member or piece of equipment associated with your project costs. This information can help you make intelligent decisions about cost cutting, or can help tease your memory about invoices that are coming due as the project schedule progresses. As usual, Project gives you several options for precisely how to view resource costs. Each of these is covered next.

Note

If you haven't finished adding all the resources to your schedule, you can change the default standard hourly rate and overtime rate for new resources (so that it's no longer $0 for each). Do so using the General tab in the Options dialog box. Chapter 24, "Customizing Microsoft Project," covers setting this type of option.

Individual Resource Costs

The way you'll typically want to view resource costs is to view the total costs assigned to each resource. You can view this kind of information by adjusting the columns shown in the Resource Sheet, which Chapter 6, "Managing Resources," showed you how to use to add resources to your schedule. Here are the steps for displaying the Resource Sheet and displaying resource cost information in it:

1. If the Resource Sheet isn't currently onscreen, choose View, Resource Sheet, or click on the Resource Sheet icon on the View Bar. The Resource Sheet appears.

2. Choose View, Table, Cost. The Resource Sheet displays columns of cost information, as shown in Figure 10.5.

Note

To return to regular Resource Sheet view, choose View, Table, Entry.

Each column in the Resource Sheet contains a particular type of cost information, and most are self-explanatory. One that isn't so obvious is the Cost column, which contains the current total cost of the work scheduled for the resource, taking into account any task duration changes, as opposed to the baseline amount you initially planned. The cost information in all columns consists solely of calculated information; you can't edit any of these values. In fact, if you click on a cell in one of the cost columns, you'll see that the entry in the text entry box above the Resource Sheet appears "grayed out"—if you try to edit it, you can't.

Figure 10.5
You can adjust the Resource Sheet to display cost information, as shown here.

	Resource Name	Cost	Baseline Cost	Variance	Actual Cost	Remaining
1	Joe Bucki	$4,900.33	$4,900.33	$0.00	$175.00	$4,725.33
2	Steve Poland	$8,550.00	$8,550.00	$0.00	$1,980.00	$6,570.00
3	Mary Rogers	$1,365.00	$1,425.00	($60.00)	$1,275.00	$90.00
4	Stan Axel	$4,770.00	$4,770.00	$0.00	$1,260.00	$3,510.00
5	Lisa Gray	$4,060.20	$3,850.00	$210.20	$1,470.20	$2,590.00
6	Ryan Printing	$0.00	$0.00	$0.00	$0.00	$0.00
7	Stamps Mailing	$0.00	$0.00	$0.00	$0.00	$0.00
8	Color Proofs	$262.50	$262.50	$0.00	$0.00	$262.50
9	Slides/Overheads	$1.00	$1.00	$0.00	$1.00	$0.00
10	Storage Media	$10.00	$10.00	$0.00	$0.00	$10.00
11	Paper (Reams)	$22.50	$22.50	$0.00	$5.00	$17.50

After you change the Task Sheet or Resource Sheet to display cost information, you can print the information. See Chapter 12, "Proofing and Printing a View," for more details.

Resource Group Costs

You might recall that one of the columns in the default version of the Resource Sheet is the Group column. In this column, you enter information to tell Project that a particular resource has something in common with other resources. For example, you might enter Comm in the Group column to identify each resource from the Communications department in your company. Or you might enter Contract to identify each freelance or contract resource on the team. You might enter Equipment to distinguish nonhuman resources with an hourly cost.

After you display resource cost information as just described, you can reduce the list to display only resources that are part of a particular group and associated costs for only those resources. (This is a filtering operation; you learn more about filtering in Chapter 11, "Working with the Different Project Views.") To do so, follow these steps:

1. Display cost information in the Resource Sheet as previously described.

2. On the Formatting toolbar, click on the arrow beside Filter to display a drop-down list (see Figure 10.6).

Figure 10.6
You can use this choice on the Formatting toolbar to limit the resources that Project lists.

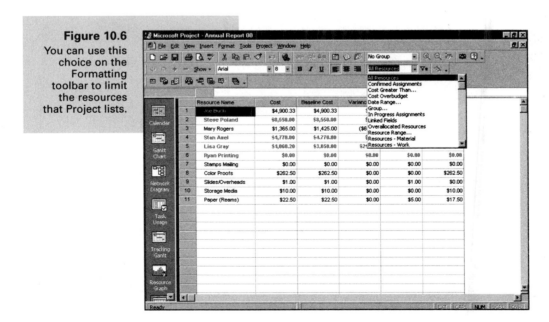

3. Click on Group in the Filter drop-down list. The Group dialog box appears.

4. Enter the name of the group for which you want to view costs in the Group Name text box (see Figure 10.7). You don't have to match the capitalization you used when you identified the resource group in the Group column (Project treats "comm," "Comm," and "COMM" as equivalent), but you do have to use the exact spelling.

5. Click on OK to close the dialog box. The Resource Sheet displays cost information for only those resources that you identified as part of the specified group (see Figure 10.8).

If you want to return to displaying all your resources in the Resource Sheet, choose All Resources from the Filter drop-down list on the Formatting toolbar.

Figure 10.7
Specify a resource group for which you'd like to see cost information.

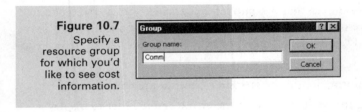

Figure 10.8
Here's the cost information for a group of resources.

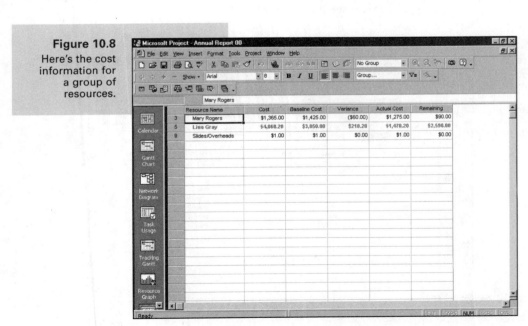

Graphing Individual Resource Work and Costs

In addition to showing task information in graphical form with a Gantt or Network Diagram chart, you can show some resource information in a chart. You'll learn more about adjusting various views in the next chapter, but here's a quick look at how to display graphical information about resource costs:

1. Choose View, Resource Graph, or click on the Resource Graph icon on the View Bar. By default, Project shows a graphical representation of the work scheduled for the resource that you selected in the Resource Sheet.

2. Right-click on the right pane of the view (where the graphical information appears), or choose Format, Details. On the shortcut menu (see Figure 10.9) or submenu that appears, choose Cost or Cumulative Cost. Project adjusts the graph in the right pane to show the exact cost amounts on the dates when they accrue (see Figure 10.10), or a running total of the costs for the selected resource as they will accumulate (see Figure 10.11).

3. If you want to view a cost graph for another resource, use the scroll bar below the left pane where the resource name appears (refer to Figure 10.9) to move between resources. You can also press Page Up to display the graph for the previous resource, or Page Down to display the graph for the next resource. Pressing Alt+F5 displays the graph for the first resource in the Resource Sheet.

Figure 10.9
You're en route to changing the resource information to a cost graph.

Use this scroll bar to display the graph information for other resources

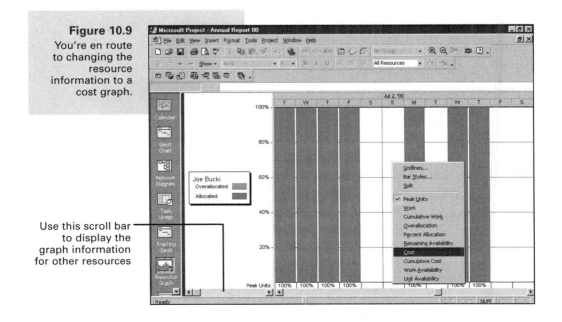

Figure 10.10
Here you're graphing costs for a particular resource on particular dates.

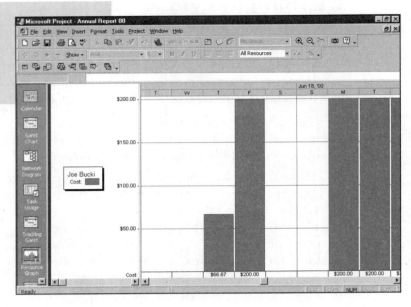

Figure 10.11
Here you're graphing how resource costs accumulate over time.

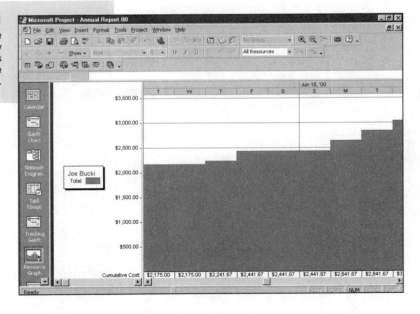

Viewing the Project Cost

In addition to viewing cost information about specific tasks or resources, you can view how costs are adding up for the entire project. Access information about project costs via the Project Information dialog box, which you've seen in a couple of earlier chapters in this book. To display total costs for your project, choose Project, Project Information. In the Project Information dialog box that appears for your project, click on Statistics.

The Project Statistics dialog box appears (see Figure 10.12). After you review the cost information, click on Close to exit the Project Statistics dialog box.

A Word about Earned Values

The term *earned value* measures whether particular tasks are on budget and schedule. In fact, when you view earned value information in either the Task Sheet or the Earned Value dialog box, you actually get to look at several statistics, which are listed in Table 10.1. That's a lot of ways to slice up the information and might be more than you ever want to know about the costs associated with your tasks.

There are two places to view all this cost information: the Task Sheet or the Earned Value dialog box. To display earned value information in the Task Sheet, follow these steps:

1. If you aren't already in Gantt Chart view, switch to it by choosing View, Gantt Chart.

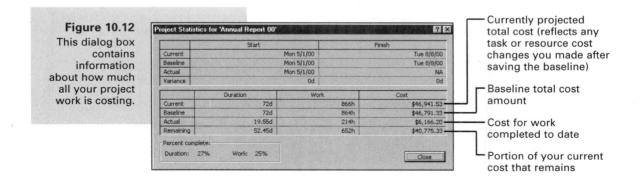

Figure 10.12
This dialog box contains information about how much all your project work is costing.

Currently projected total cost (reflects any task or resource cost changes you made after saving the baseline)

Baseline total cost amount

Cost for work completed to date

Portion of your current cost that remains

Table 10.1 Earned Value Statistics Tracked by Project

Abbreviation	Description
BCWS	Budgeted Cost of Work Scheduled is the cost you budgeted for work scheduled up to the current date in your baseline plan.
BCWP	Budgeted Cost of Work Performed is calculated by multiplying the percentage of work actually completed on a task (as of the current date) by the cost you budgeted for the task in the same time frame.
ACWP	Actual Cost of Work Performed calculates the cost for work performed to date on a task, based on the hourly, per use, and fixed costs you entered.
SV	Schedule Variance is the difference between BCWS and BCWP (BCWS–BCWP). This value compares the money you planned to spend (in your baseline) by the current date to the money you budgeted to spend for work performed by the current date. This figure simply shows how your budgeted costs have changed since you established the baseline. A positive SV value indicates that your current plan calls for spending more than your original plan did.
CV	Cost Variance shows how reality compares with the current budget; it subtracts BCWP from ACWP to tell you whether the work completed is over budget (indicated by a positive value) or under budget (indicated by a negative value).
BAC	Budgeted At Completion is the amount you budgeted for the complete task, including fixed costs and per use costs. This amount is from your baseline plan.
EAC	Estimate At Completion is the amount presently budgeted for the complete task; it reflects any changes you made to the amount of work scheduled, hourly costs, fixed costs, or per use costs since saving the baseline plan.
VAC	Variance At Completion compares the EAC with the BAC to see whether you'll be spending more (indicated by a positive value) or less (indicated by a negative value) than initially planned to complete the task.

2. Choose View, Table, More Tables. The More Tables dialog box appears.

3. Make sure that the Task option is selected, and then double-click on Earned Value in the Tables list (or click on it and then click on Apply). The Task Sheet shows all the earned value amounts.

4. Drag the vertical split bar to the right so that you can review as many earned value amounts as needed (see Figure 10.13).

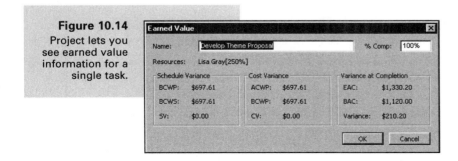

Figure 10.13
You now can view a listing of earned value amounts.

Task Earned Value button

Forms button

If you want to view the earned value information for a single task in a convenient format, click on its task row in any view that includes the Task Sheet. Next, click on the Task Earned Value button on the Custom Forms toolbar, if you've displayed that toolbar as explained earlier in this chapter. Alternatively, choose Tools, Customize, Forms or click on the Forms button on the Custom Forms toolbar. In the Custom Forms dialog box, make sure that the Task option is selected, and double-click on Earned Value in the Forms list. Either way, the Earned Value dialog box appears (see Figure 10.14). When you finish viewing the earned value information, click on OK to close the dialog box.

Figure 10.14
Project lets you see earned value information for a single task.

Earned Value	✕

Name: Develop Theme Proposal   % Comp: 100%

Resources: Lisa Gray[250%]

Schedule Variance
BCWP: $697.61
BCWS: $697.61
SV: $0.00

Cost Variance
ACWP: $697.61
BCWP: $697.61
CV: $0.00

Variance at Completion
EAC: $1,330.20
BAC: $1,120.00
Variance: $210.20

OK   Cancel

Note

> If there's a Per Use cost for a resource in addition to an hourly cost, the Per Use cost always accrues when work begins on the task.

Previewing Cost Reports

Chapter 14, "Creating and Printing a Report," covers how to display, format, and print various reports in Project. These reports gather and calculate myriad types of data for you. Because budget information is so important to any project planning process, Project provides many types of cost and budgeting reports—five, to be exact. To display these cost reports, choose View, Reports. In the Reports dialog box, double-click on the Costs icon. The Cost Reports dialog box appears and offers icons for five different reports; select and compile a report by double-clicking on its icon. Figures 10.15 through 10.19 show examples of the available reports. Click on Print in any report display to print that report, or click on Close to return to the Reports dialog box.

Figure 10.15
The Cash Flow report presents an update of how much you spent per task each week.

Microsoft Project - Annual Report 00							
	4/30/00	5/7/00	5/14/00	5/21/00	5/28/00	6/4/00	6/11/00
Annual Report 00							
Gather Samples	$555.00	$60.00					
Review Meeting							
Review Meeting 1	$330.00						
Review Meeting 2					$330.00		
Review Meeting 3							
Review Meeting 4							
Develop Theme Proposal		$952.16	$378.04				
Theme Meeting			$331.00				
First Draft			$2,601.84	$283.16			
First Approval Round				$505.88	$94.13		
Production Schedule Meeting				$75.00			
Corrections					$1,363.75	$461.25	
Final Approval Round						$2,425.00	$135.0
Design Concept				$754.50	$1,695.50	$1,855.00	$1,320.0
Page Layout							$748.5
Layout Approvals							
Layout Corrections							
Fiscal Year End							
To Printer							
Printing Proofs							
Printing							
Mailing							
Total	$885.00	$1,012.16	$3,310.88	$1,618.53	$3,473.38	$4,731.25	$2,203.5

Cash Flow as of Thu 5/4/00
Annual Report 00

Page: 1 of 2   Size: 1 row by 2 columns

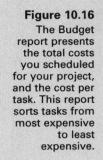

Figure 10.16
The Budget report presents the total costs you scheduled for your project, and the cost per task. This report sorts tasks from most expensive to least expensive.

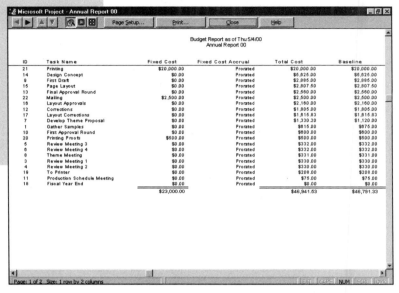

Figure 10.17
The Overbudget Tasks report points out where expenses are going to get out of hand.

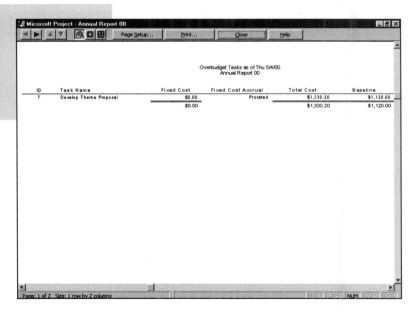

270   PART IV • VIEWING, FORMATTING, AND PRINTING PROJECTS

Figure 10.18
The Overbudget Resources report identifies when a resource has had to work more (and therefore costs more) than you had planned in your baseline.

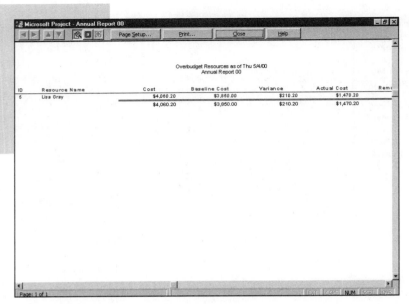

Figure 10.19
The Earned Value report shows earned value calculations for each task, as well as totals for the project.

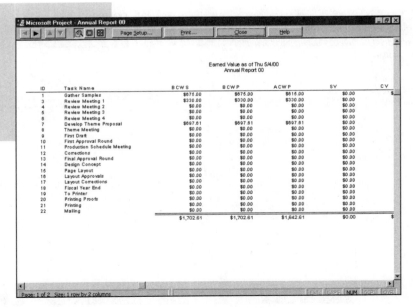

Changing How Costs Add Up

When you added resources to the project file using the default view of the Resource Sheet, you used the Accrue At column to note when costs for work performed should be charged to the project as an actual cost. Most costs accrue in a prorated fashion, meaning that for each percentage point of the task that's marked as completed, a corresponding amount of the budgeted expense is charged as an actual cost. For tasks that have the Start setting in the Accrue At column, the total budgeted cost for the task becomes an actual cost as soon as any work is completed on the task. In contrast, for tasks where Accrue At is set to End, no actual costs accumulate until you mark the task as 100% completed.

In most cases, cash flow is as important to project management as the ultimate bottom line is. One of the biggest scams a consumer can fall prey to occurs when dealing with certain unscrupulous home repair contractors. The contractor gives the best estimate for a repair job but asks for all or a large part of the money up front. You hand over a check, and the contractor disappears into thin air without doing anything. Just as you'd certainly want to delay payments to a home repair contractor, it's in the interest of any business to delay project expenses until the work is completed to your satisfaction.

If you review task costs and it seems that too many have accrued too early in the schedule, look for tasks for which you can postpone accrued costs. (Negotiate with your resources, of course, to ensure that your changes reflect reality.) You want to be able to change as many tasks as possible to accrue at the end of work on the task. (This isn't the realistic choice for most internal resources, of course—they're getting paid all the time, and your company cheerfully assigns you the cost as soon as you use them.) Where you can't have tasks accrue at the end, at least lobby for prorated cost approval and minimize the number of tasks that accrue at the start of work on the task. To review or change Accrue At information, display the Resource Sheet and review or change your choice in the Accrue At field. Alternately, right-click on a resource in the Resource Sheet, and then click on Resource Information to open the Resource Information dialog box for that resource. On the Costs tab, change the entry in the Cost Accrual drop-down list box as needed.

Note

If you changed the Resource Sheet to display earned value or other information instead of the default entry information, you must change it back to adjust how costs accrue. With the Resource Sheet onscreen, open the View menu, point to Table, and click on Entry.

Changing a Fixed Task Cost

After work has been completed on a task, most external resources present you with a bill. Alternately, your company's accounting department might inform you how much of an allocated (shared) cost your group or department has to pay for the completion of a task. Even though you usually aren't dinged for a fixed cost until the work on the task is completed, by default Project prorates fixed costs based on how much of the task work has been completed. If you want Project to add in entire fixed costs at the start or end of the work on the task, follow these steps:

1. Choose Tools, Options. The Options dialog box appears, with many tabs.
2. Click on the Calculation tab to display its options.
3. Open the Default Fixed Costs Accrual drop-down list and choose Start or End.
4. Click on OK to close the Options dialog box. Your change takes effect immediately.

Whether the actual (fixed) cost for a task is higher or lower than what you budgeted in the Task Sheet, when you receive the bill or charge, you need to compare it with the Fixed Cost entry you made for the task and adjust the entry upward or downward. Follow these steps to enter the actual, final fixed cost for a task after work on the task has been completed:

1. If you're not already in Gantt Chart view, change to it by choosing View, Gantt Chart.
2. Choose View, Table, Cost. The Task Sheet adjusts to show columns of cost information.
3. Click on the Fixed Cost cell in the row for the task for which you want to enter actual data.
4. Type the new entry (see Figure 10.20).
5. Click on the Enter button or press Enter to finish your edit.

Note

If you want to change the accrual method for a single fixed cost rather than all of them, change the entry in the Fixed Cost Accrual column, as shown in Figure 10.20.

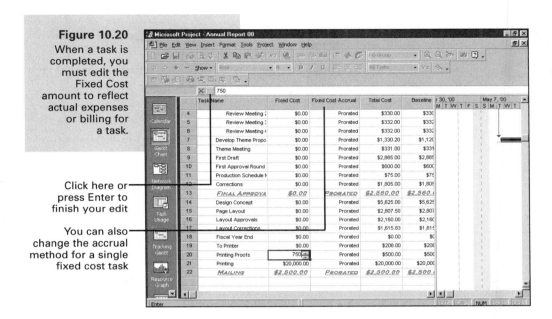

Figure 10.20
When a task is completed, you must edit the Fixed Cost amount to reflect actual expenses or billing for a task.

Click here or press Enter to finish your edit

You can also change the accrual method for a single fixed cost task

Overriding a Calculated Resource Cost

Just as your original Fixed Cost entry might not reflect the final, actual cost, a calculated expense based on the amount of hourly work completed by a resource might not reflect the final charge to you for that work. This might happen when a resource (particularly a freelance resource) has to work more hours or days than you estimated, but because of a contractual obligation, the resource only bills you the original amount; in such a case, entering all the hours the resource worked would make the calculated cost higher than the final bill. Other times, a resource might have reason to bill you more for a task than had been initially agreed upon, even if the days or hours of work completed remained consistent with your estimate.

In either case, you need to adjust the actual costs for the task without changing the number of hours or days worked on the task. There's only one way to do so before a task is 100% completed, and it involves the following steps:

1. Choose Tools, Options. The Options dialog box appears, with many tabs.

2. Click on the Calculation tab to display its options.

3. Click to clear the check beside the Actual Costs Are Always Calculated By Microsoft Project option.

4. By default, actual costs you enter are distributed (accrued) along the full duration of the task. If you want to spread the actual cost only through

Caution

Remember that once you disable automatic calculation, turning it back on will override all the actual costs you entered while it was turned off. Therefore, it's best to follow the steps listed here only after your project is finished. Project offers another approach for entering actual costs that's the best of both worlds. You can override a calculated resource cost after you mark a task as 100% completed and remaining costs (Rem. Cost) for the tasks are calculated as $0, without turning off automatic calculation.

the project status date you entered, click to check the Edits To Total Actual Cost Will Be Spread To The Status Date check box.

5. Click on OK to close the Options dialog box.

6. Switch to Gantt Chart view and click on the task for which you want to enter an actual cost that's different from the cost calculated by Project.

7. Choose View, More Views, or click on the More Views icon on the View Bar. The More Views dialog box appears.

8. Scroll down the Views list and double-click on Task Entry (or click on it and click on Apply). Project displays the Task Entry form in the lower pane.

9. Right-click on the lower pane and click on Resource Cost. The pane changes to display cost information about the resource.

10. Click on the Act. Cost column and edit the entry as needed (see Figure 10.21).

11. Click on the OK in the form pane to finish your entry.

12. (Optional) Use the Previous and Next buttons to display information about the resource work for other tasks, and repeat Steps 9 and 10 to edit the Act. Cost entries.

To remove the lower pane and return to regular Gantt Chart view, choose Window, Remove Split.

Entering Exact Daily Costs

You can use the Task Usage view to see and enter actual costs per day for an assignment. To do so, you must first turn off automatic calculation (refer to "Controlling Whether Costs Are Updated Based On Work Completed"), because you can't edit Act. Cost entries for a particular assignment even when work on a task is 100% complete. Then, follow these steps to see and edit daily costs for an assignment:

1. Switch to the Task Usage view. (The fastest way to do so is to click on the Task Usage icon on the View Bar.)

Figure 10.21
You can edit the actual cost for a resource's work when it's different from the calculated amount. Either turn off automatic calculation or wait until the task is 100% completed.

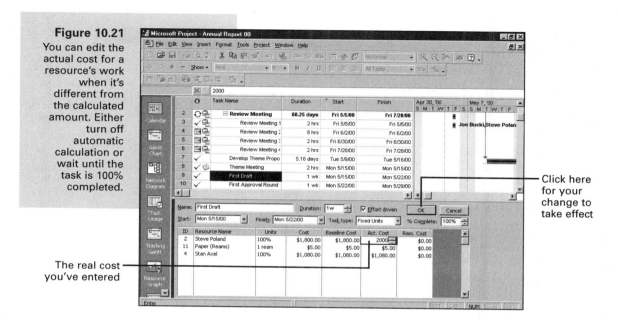

Click here for your change to take effect

The real cost you've entered

2. Right-click on the right pane of the view, or choose Format, Details. In the shortcut menu or submenu that appears, choose Cost. This choice adds a row of Cost cells for each assignment to the right pane, showing the original calculated daily costs for each resource assignment.

3. Right-click on the right pane of the view, or choose Format, Details. In the shortcut menu or submenu that appears, choose Actual Cost. This choice adds a row of Act. Cost cells for each assignment to the right pane, showing the daily actual cost for each resource.

4. Display the assignment for which you want to enter actual cost information, and then click on the Act. Work cell for the date you want in the right pane.

5. Type the new cost figure (see Figure 10.22), and then press Enter or click on the Enter button on the entry box to finish your entry. Project updates the Act. Cost and the cost information for the assignment for that date.

Note

The cells in the grid in the right pane of Task Usage or Resource Usage views are called *timephased fields* or *timephased cells*. That's because they let you focus in on a particular date and enter precise work and cost measurements for that date.

Figure 10.22

For more precise final cost information, enter the actual cost for a particular date of an assignment after displaying Actual Cost information in Task Usage view.

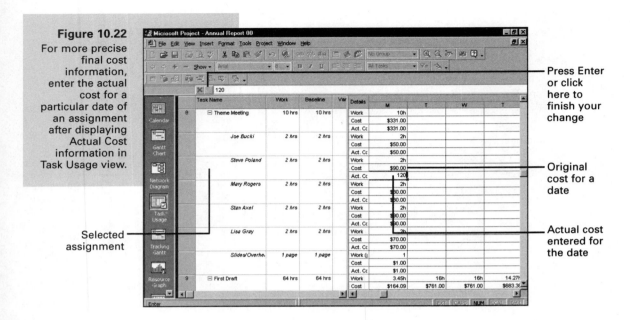

Press Enter or click here to finish your change

Original cost for a date

Actual cost entered for the date

Selected assignment

Cutting Back Costs

When you're developing your overall project schedule, or after work is under way and you're seeing that some of your actual cost amounts are exceeding the amounts you budgeted, you might need to look for ways to cut back costs. Here are just a few ways that you can reduce your overall budget:

- Look at the schedules for more expensive tasks—the Budget report (refer to Figure 10.16) can help you identify these—and see if you can decrease the scheduled work for them or negotiate a more favorable fee or hourly rate.

- Cut back the working time allotted for later tasks.

- Return to your cost estimates and see if you have time to substitute less expensive resources for more expensive ones.

- Cut back the amount of work handled by an expensive resource, perhaps by adding resources with lower hourly rates to share the expensive resource's workload.

Working with the Different Project Views

IN THIS CHAPTER

- Reviewing the views
- Choosing a view
- Working with tables, including how to control table information by sorting and filtering
- Grouping sheet information
- Using GanttChartWizard
- Adjusting whether charted information is displayed on a weekly, monthly, or other timescale
- Creating your own views and organizing views

Project enables you to capture a huge amount of information about the tasks and resources associated with your plan. In theory, you could use a spreadsheet program or word processor to store all these details; to a limited degree, they let you chart or display information in alternative formats. But those kinds of programs do not provide the same flexibility in viewing and presenting your information that Project does.

Project offers this flexibility to allow you to be efficient at entering schedule and resource information, and to be proficient at reviewing the schedule and gleaning key facts. The different ways that Project presents information are called views, and this chapter reviews the views.

Reviewing the Views

Earlier chapters in this book periodically explained how to change the view so that you could work with different kinds of information. The views used in earlier chapters included the Gantt Chart, Resource Graph, Resource Sheet, Task Usage, Resource Usage, and Task Entry views.

Project views can present information in a table or spreadsheet-like grid (as the Task Sheet and Resource Sheet do), in a graphical format (as Gantt bars do), or in a fill-in form format (where you select fields or text boxes and then enter the information you want to view). Some views use a single method to present information, and some present information in various ways by having multiple panes onscreen. When a view uses only one method to organize information, such as a form, it's called a single-pane view.

Note

Project prints information using the currently selected view. However, Project doesn't print forms or the Relationship Diagram view, so a view that includes only a form won't print at all. When printing is unavailable, the Print button on the Standard toolbar is disabled (grayed out).

In addition to thinking about how views appear onscreen, you need to select a view based on the type of information you want to work with. Some views primarily provide information about tasks, and other views primarily provide information about resources. Here are the predefined views you'll find in Project:

- **Bar Rollup, Milestone Date Rollup, and Milestone Rollup.** Use these views after running the Rollup_Formatting macro that comes with Project to roll up the Gantt bars for subtasks onto the summary task Gantt bar.

Each view provides slightly different formatting for the rolled-up tasks. See the section "Using the Rollup Views" near the end of this chapter for a look at how to use these views.

- **Calendar.** This single-pane view (see Figure 11.1) displays tasks on a monthly calendar, using a bar and label to indicate each task's duration.

- **Detail Gantt.** In this variation of Gantt Chart view, the Task Sheet includes Delay information, and the Gantt bars indicate slack time and any task slippage (changes in the task schedule since you saved the baseline). Figure 11.2 shows Detail Gantt view.

- **Gantt Chart.** This is the default view in Project; it includes the Task Sheet in the left pane and Gantt bars showing task durations and relationships in the right pane.

- **Leveling Gantt.** In this variation of Gantt Chart view, the Task Sheet includes a Leveling Delay column to indicate any tasks that Project delayed when you used automatic resource leveling (refer to Chapter 7, "Resolving Overallocations and Overbooked Resources," to learn more about resource leveling). In addition, the Gantt bars are each split into two smaller bars. The upper bar shows the task's original schedule, and the lower bar shows its current schedule, with darker shading indicating the percentage of work completed on the task.

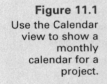

Figure 11.1
Use the Calendar view to show a monthly calendar for a project.

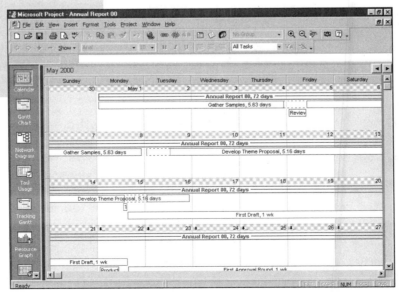

Figure 11.2
Detail Gantt view
presents more
information than
regular Gantt
Chart view.

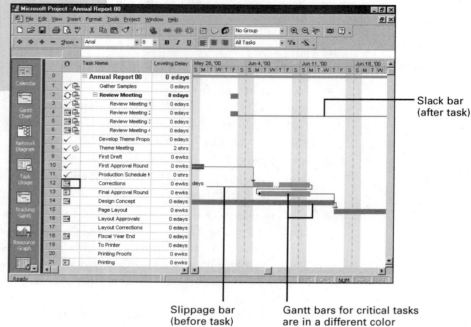

Slack bar
(after task)

Slippage bar
(before task)

Gantt bars for critical tasks
are in a different color

- **Network Diagram and Relationship Diagram.** The Network Diagram view (which is similar to the PERT Chart view in the previous version of Project) displays tasks in a format resembling a flow chart (see Figure 11.3). You can drag to link tasks, or right-click on a task and click on Task Information to adjust the task schedule and resource assignments. The Relationship Diagram shows a more simplified diagram of how tasks flow.

Tip

On the Network Diagram chart, you can also drag to add new tasks to the schedule. Drag diagonally to create a box with the mouse. Right-click on the new task box, and then click on Task Information. Provide the details about the task in the Task Information dialog box, and then click on OK. To delete a task in Network Diagram view, click on the chart box (node) to select it and press Delete. Or, to select multiple boxes, drag over an area that is larger than and surrounds the boxes to be deleted. When you release the mouse button, a gray selector appears around the boxes. Press the Delete key to remove the task boxes from the chart.

- **Resource Allocation.** This view presents the Resource Usage view in the upper pane and the Task Sheet and Gantt chart in the lower pane.

100% completed task

In-progress task

Critical task, which has bold outline

Figure 11.3
If you prefer a flow chart like format, use the Network Diagram view.

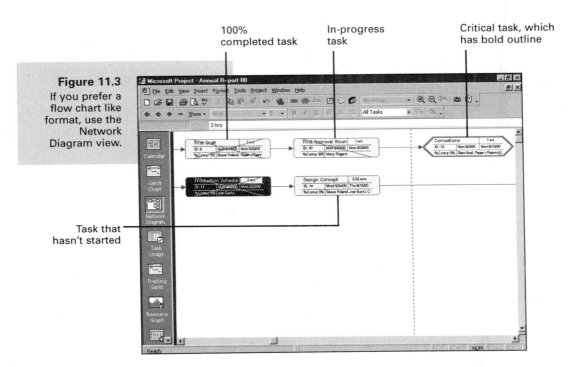

Task that hasn't started

- **Resource Form.** This is a form you use to enter and edit information about a specific resource. It lists all the tasks assigned to that resource, resource cost information, and more (see Figure 11.4).

- **Resource Graph.** This view (examples of which are shown in Chapter 10, "Viewing and Managing Costs") can graph information about a resource's daily and cumulative costs, scheduled work and cumulative work, overal-located times, percentage of work allocated, and availability. To change the type of information on the graph, right-click on the chart area of the view and use the resulting shortcut menu to choose which information is charted.

- **Resource Name Form.** This abbreviated version of the Resource Form lists the resource name and its assigned tasks.

- **Resource Sheet.** This view provides a grid of cells you can use to add resources to your project file. Chapter 6, "Managing Resources," covers the Resource Sheet in detail.

- **Resource Usage.** This view, covered in various earlier chapters, combines the Resource Sheet on the left, which identifies the assignments for each resource, with a timephased grid on the right that you can use to enter daily actual costs, daily scheduled work and completed work, and more.

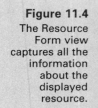

Figure 11.4
The Resource Form view captures all the information about the displayed resource.

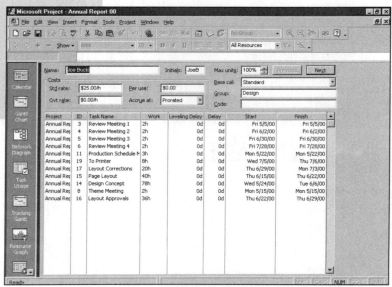

Right-click on the right pane to choose which details you want to view or enter in it.

- **Task Details Form.** Similar to the Resource Form, this full-screen form displays task scheduling information, constraints, assigned resources, and more. You can view or edit information in this form, as you can in others.

Tip

••
You can right-click on a blank area of any form to adjust what it displays.
••

- **Task Entry.** This view displays the Gantt chart in the upper pane and the Task Form in the lower pane. It lets you perform detailed editing of task information in the lower pane, so you can see how your changes affect the Gantt chart. You can right-click on the Task Form to select which information it displays.

- **Task Form.** This form (Figure 11.5) lets you change the task name, schedule, work completion information, and assigned resources.

- **Task Name Form.** This is the simplest variation of the Task Details Form. It enables you to change the task name and assigned resources.

- **Task Sheet.** This view shows the Task Sheet at full-screen size rather than in combination with other view panes.

Figure 11.5
Task Form view lets you focus on task assignments.

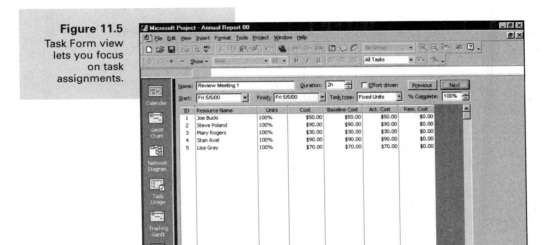

- **Task Usage.** Various chapters have already covered how to display and work with this view, which groups resource assignments by task. Use the timephased grid at the right to view and enter daily work and cost values. Right-click on the right pane to choose what details you want to view or enter in it.

- **Tracking Gantt.** Chapter 9, "Comparing Progress versus Your Baseline Plan," discusses this variation of regular Gantt Chart view. In Tracking Gantt view, the Gantt bars are divided into upper and lower segments. The lower portion of each bar shows the task's original schedule, and the upper portion shows the task's current schedule.

Choosing a View

It's pretty obvious where to begin when you want to select a new view—the View menu. The top eight commands on this menu take you directly to the specified view: Calendar, Gantt Chart, Network Diagram, Task Usage, Tracking Gantt, Resource Graph, Resource Sheet, and Resource Usage. In addition, the View Bar at the left offers an icon for each of those eight views; click on an icon to display the view it represents.

Note

> If you're changing from a combination view that includes more than one pane to a view that includes only a single pane, the extra pane often won't close on its own. To close it, choose Window, Remove Split (or double-click on the dividing line between the panes). If the bottom pane is a form, you can also right-click on it, and then choose Hide Form View. Finally, if you're changing from a split view to a single-pane view, press and hold the Shift key when you select the new view from the View menu to both remove the split and display the selected view.

If you want to display a view that's not listed on the menu or the View Bar, follow these steps:

1. Choose View, More Views, or click on the More Views icon on the View Bar. The More Views dialog box appears (see Figure 11.6).
2. Scroll the Views list, if needed, to the view you want.
3. In the Views list, double-click on the name of the view you want (or click on the name and click on Apply).

In views that include upper and lower panes, click within the pane you want to work in to make that pane the active view, or press F6. The Active View Bar along the edge of the screen darkens to indicate which pane you selected to work in.

If you switch to any view that includes a Gantt chart and you don't see anything in the pane, first make sure that Project hasn't scrolled the chart to dates before or beyond the schedule for the project. Try clicking on the Go To Selected Task button on the Standard toolbar to scroll to the right area. Or press Alt+Home to go to the project start task/milestone or Alt+End to go to the project end task/milestone.

Figure 11.6
The More Views dialog box lets you choose a view that's not on the View menu or View Bar.

More Views	? X
Views:	
Milestone Rollup	New...
Network Diagram	
Relationship Diagram	Edit...
Resource Allocation	
Resource Form	Copy...
Resource Graph	
Resource Name Form	Organizer...
Resource Sheet	
Resource Usage	
Task Details Form	
Task Entry	
Task Form	
	Apply Cancel

Adjusting a Sheet

The Task Sheet and Resource Sheet present information in various columns (fields). Depending on the operation at hand, you may want to view columns that contain different information. For example, Chapter 10, "Viewing and Managing Costs," explains that you can display columns of actual and projected cost information in the Task Sheet. You can also control which rows appear in the current sheet and the order in which those rows appear. This section covers how to adjust the appearance or content of information presented in the Task Sheet or Resource Sheet.

Changing Row Heights

In previous versions of Project, you couldn't wrap text within a column when the column entries were too wide to fit. Your only option was to resize the column to make it wide enough to display the new entries. In Project 2000, you can resize the height of a row that contains a column entry that's too wide. When you do so, Project wraps cell entries to more than one line where needed so they fit within the column width. Since Project prints information as it appears onscreen, resizing the rows will ensure that your printouts are more readable for recipients.

To resize the row height, drag the bottom row border below the row number. As shown by the comparisons in Figure 11.7, Project immediately wraps cell text. To return the row to its original height, drag the bottom row border up until it touches the bottom border for the row above. When you release the mouse button, Project automatically snaps the row back to its original height.

Figure 11.7
Project's new row resizing feature enables you to wrap text in cells.

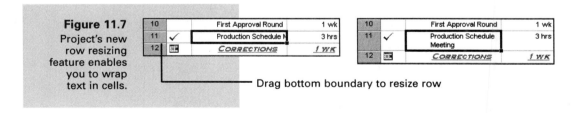

Drag bottom boundary to resize row

Choosing a Table

In Project, each particular group of columns shown in a Task Sheet or Resource Sheet is called a *table*. To display one of the predefined sets of columns, therefore, you choose a different table for the currently displayed sheet. Of course, different tables are provided for the Task Sheet and Resource Sheet, because you track different information for tasks than you do for resources. When you select a particular table for a sheet and then print the view that includes the sheet, Project prints only the columns that are part of the presently selected table. Tables 11.1a and 11.1b list the many table types that are available.

Table 11.1a Tables Available for a Task Sheet

Table	Description
Baseline	Displays the baseline schedule dates, work, and cost for tasks.
Constraint Dates	Lists constraint types and dates you entered for tasks.
Cost	Shows fixed cost information you entered for a task, as well as calculated resource costs.
Delay	Tells you when a task has been delayed as a result of resource leveling.
Earned Value	Includes columns that provide earned value analysis for cost and schedule variance.
Entry	The default; provides columns that enable you to set up new tasks.
Export	When you export task data, Project uses this table, which includes more task fields than many of the others.
Hyperlink	Displays links you created to Web pages or files on a network, such as a link to a memo file with more information about a task.
Rollup Table	When you use the Rollup views, adds columns so you can control Gantt display features such as whether text appears above the rolled-up bars.
Schedule	Presents task start and finish information, as well as information about slack time.
Summary	Presents scheduled task start and finish dates, percent of work completed, and budgeted cost and work hours.
Tracking	Presents information you entered about actual task start and finish dates, remaining duration, and actual costs.
Usage	Shows start, finish, work, and duration for each task.
Variance	Lists baseline start and finish dates along with the current dates, and shows the variance between the two sets of dates.
Work	Allows you to track work statistics, such as the baseline number of hours scheduled for a task, the actual hours worked, variance between the two, and so on.

Table 11.1b Tables Available for a Resource Sheet

Table	Description
Cost	Displays the baseline cost you estimated for resources, the current scheduled cost, the cost actually incurred, and more.
Earned Value	Displays the calculated earned value statistics described in Table 10.1. For example, displays the earned value schedule and cost variance.
Entry	The default; provides columns that enable you to define new resources.
Entry—Material Resources	Displays only the Resource Sheet columns needed for entering material resources; for example, this table doesn't include the Ovt. Rate column.
Entry—Work Resources	Displays only the Resource Sheet columns needed for entering work resources; for example, this table doesn't include the Material Label column.
Export	When you export resource data, Project uses this table, which includes applicable resource fields.
Hyperlink	Displays links you created to Web pages or files on a network, such as a link to a resource's Web page.
Summary	Includes information about hourly rates and work hours scheduled for a resource on a project, and more.
Usage	Displays the resource name and number of hours of work by that resource scheduled for the project.
Work	Lists scheduled and actual work hours by a resource, overtime work authorized, percentage of work completed, and more.

Note

If you try to use a table that's not available for a Resource Sheet, Project displays a message box telling you that you need to choose or create another table.

When you want to establish which table is used by a Task Sheet or Resource Sheet, first select the sheet. Next, choose View, Table, and click on the name of the table you want. If the desired table is not listed, choose More Tables. The More Tables dialog box appears (see Figure 11.8). If needed, select Task or Resource at the top of the dialog box to list the appropriate kinds of tables. Select a table from the Tables list by double-clicking on it (or by clicking on it and clicking on Apply).

Figure 11.8
Here's where
you choose a
table that's not
on the Table
submenu.

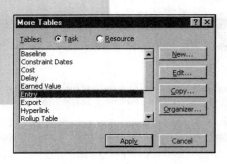

Filtering the Task Sheet or Resource Sheet

By default, each Task Sheet or Resource Sheet displays all of the tasks or resources you entered for the project, no matter which table you've selected. There might be an occasion, though, when you want to see only some of the tasks or resources listed. For example, if you need to provide your client with a list of tasks that have been completed, or a list of all resources from a particular resource group, you can filter the sheet to display only certain rows.

Tip

Filtering a sheet and then printing it is a quick and dirty method of creating a report about key facts from your schedule.

To filter the current sheet, use the Filter drop-down list on the Formatting toolbar (see Figure 11.9). The available Filter choices differ depending on whether a Task Sheet or Resource Sheet is currently displayed. (This figure shows the Task Sheet choices.) Some filter choices are followed by an ellipsis (a set of three dots), which indicates that if you choose that particular filter, Project will ask you to supply more information to help it select the rows to display. For example, if you select Date Range..., Project displays the dialog box shown in Figure 11.10, asking you to enter a date to begin specifying the time frame within which the displayed tasks must fall. In this case, you would enter a starting date, click on OK, enter an ending date, and click on OK again so that Project could filter the list.

To return to the full listing of tasks or resources after you're done with the filtered version, select All Tasks or All Resources from the Filter drop-down list.

If you prefer not to use the Formatting toolbar but still want to filter tasks and resources, choose Project, Filtered For to display a submenu, and click on the name of the filter you want. If the name doesn't appear, choose More Filters to open the More Filters dialog box (see Figure 11.11). Use this dialog box to select the filter you want.

Figure 11.9
Use the Filter drop-down list to control which rows appear in a sheet.

The ellipsis (...) beside a filter means that Project will prompt you for details about which rows to select

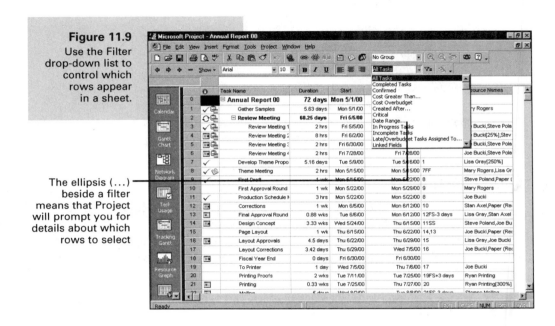

Figure 11.10
A filter might request that you provide more information; in this case, you need to enter the first date for a range.

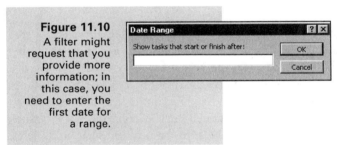

Figure 11.11
Access more filters via this dialog box.

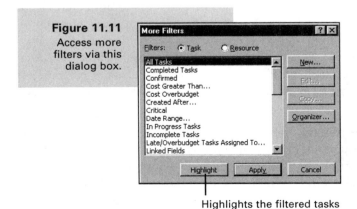

Highlights the filtered tasks

Note

Optionally, you can click on the Highlight button in the More Filters dialog box to apply a highlight color to the filtered tasks or resources, rather than hiding the rows that don't contain the right type of information. If you do this, all rows still appear onscreen, with the filtered tasks in the highlight color. You can also hold the Shift key and select the filter from the Project, Filtered For submenu to apply a highlighted filter.

Using AutoFilter

Project offers yet another type of filtering, AutoFilters. Project AutoFilters work just like those in Microsoft Excel. Basically, you turn on the AutoFilters feature, and then choose an AutoFilter using the filtering arrow that appears on a Task Sheet or Resource Sheet column header. AutoFilters offer two advantages over the filtering just described:

- You can filter by any column, which you can't really do with regular filtering.
- You can choose specific criteria for filtering the list.

To apply AutoFiltering to a Task Sheet or Resource Sheet, choose Project, Filtered For, AutoFilter. Alternately, click on the AutoFilter button on the Formatting toolbar. An AutoFilter button appears on the header for every column in the displayed Task Sheet or Resource Sheet. Click on the AutoFilter button for a column head to display the available AutoFilters for that column; the AutoFilters available depend on the type of information contained in the column. For example, because the AutoFilter list shown in Figure 11.12 is for a column that holds dates, you can choose to filter the Task Sheet to list only tasks that have a Start date that's This Week, This Month, and so on. The Duration column AutoFilters enable you to filter the list to show only tasks with a duration that's more than a week, only tasks with a duration that's less than a week, or other tasks with similar durations. If you want to list only the tasks being handled by a particular resource, choose one of the AutoFilters for the Resource Names column. To remove the AutoFilter from any column, open the AutoFilter drop-down list and click on the (All) choice.

You can create a more complex AutoFilter by specifying your own filter criteria. To do so, open the AutoFilter drop-down list for the column that contains the information you want to use to filter the list. Choose (Custom . . .) to display the Custom AutoFilter dialog box. Open the first drop-down list, as shown in Figure 11.13, and then click on an operator (test) choice. For example, to display all dates later than a particular date (in a date-oriented column), choose the Is

The AutoFilter button on
the Formatting toolbar

Figure 11.12
After you turn on
AutoFiltering,
click to open an
AutoFilter list,
and then click on
an AutoFilter.

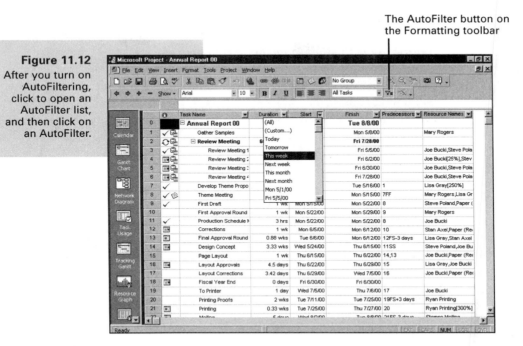

Greater Than operator. Open the drop-down list to the right on the first row and choose the entry representing the value that the operator should use to evaluate the list, such as the particular date the Is Greater Than operator should use. For a date field, for example, if you choose Is Greater Than, and then choose Fri 6/2/00, Project filters the list to display only tasks with an entry after Fri 6/2/00 in the filtered column.

If the field entries must match two criteria, leave the And option button selected. If the field entries can match either of two criteria, click on the Or option button. Choose the operator and value from the bottom two drop-down lists in the dialog box to specify the second criterion. Click on OK to apply the custom AutoFilter for the column.

Figure 11.13
Enter criteria for
your own
AutoFilter in this
dialog box.

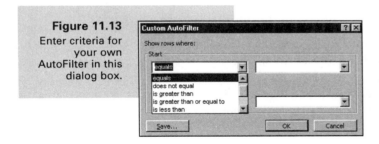

Note

> Instead of clicking on OK to apply a custom AutoFilter, click on the Save button in the Custom AutoFilter dialog box; enter a Name for the AutoFilter in the Filter Definition In '(Current File)' dialog box, and click to enable the Show In Menu check box to have the AutoFilter appear on the Filtered For submenu. Then click on OK to save it. You can also use this dialog box to add even more criteria for a filter, by choosing entries in the And/Or, Field Name, Test (operator), and Value(s) columns.

You can AutoFilter as many columns as you want. For example, you can choose the This Month AutoFilter for the Start column. Then choose the AutoFilter for a particular resource in the Resource Name column to display only tasks that the selected resource is scheduled to begin working on during the current month. This would give you a clear picture of current and upcoming near-term assignments for that resource.

When you finish working with all AutoFilters, turn the AutoFiltering feature off (it toggles on and off). To do so, choose Project, Filtered For, AutoFilter, or click on the AutoFilter button on the Formatting toolbar. Project removes the AutoFilter buttons from the sheet column headers.

Sorting Information

By default, the information in your Task Sheet or Resource Sheet (and any accompanying charts in the view you selected) appears in the order in which you added it to the project. Even if you select a different table or filter, the basic order in which the rows appear remains static unless you adjust that order. For example, you might want to sort the Resource Sheet by the name of the resource.

If you're sorting by name, keep in mind that Project, by default, sorts by the first letter listed, which is generally the first name if the resource is a person. If you want to be able to sort the resource list by last name, I suggest creating a Resource Sheet table (see the later section "Creating a Table or Filter") that includes a new column for last names. You'll need to reenter the last names there, after which you can sort by that column instead of the one that lists the whole name.

To sort a sheet, choose Project, Sort, then click on the name of the field (column) to sort by. The fields listed vary depending on whether you're working in a Task Sheet or a Resource Sheet. For a Task Sheet, you can sort by Start Date, Finish Date, Priority, Cost, or ID. For a Resource Sheet, you can sort by Cost, Name, or ID. If the field you want to sort by does not appear on the Sort submenu, click on Sort By. The Sort dialog box will appear (see Figure 11.14).

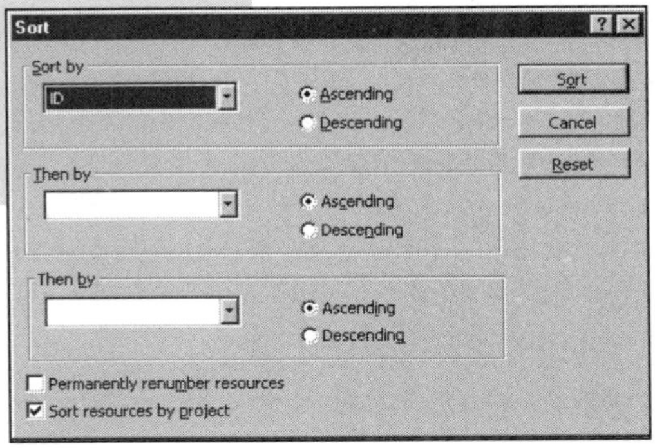

Figure 11.14
Use this dialog box to access more fields to sort by.

Click to open the Sort By drop-down list, and then choose the name of the field that contains the information by which you want to sort. Choose Ascending or Descending to specify whether the information should be sorted in lowest-to-highest order (A–Z) or highest-to-lowest order (Z–A). For example, when you sort tasks by the Cost field, Project by default reorders them from most expensive to least expensive; you might prefer to see the least expensive items first.

To sort by additional fields as well, use the other drop-down lists provided in this dialog box. Click on OK to complete the sort.

Caution

When you select the Permanently Renumber Tasks or Permanently Renumber Resources check box, Project changes the ID numbers for the sorted tasks and resources to reflect their new order. This would prevent you from resorting tasks in the Task Sheet by the ID field to return them to their original order, which can destroy your project plan. Similarly, you wouldn't be able to return your list of resources to its original order. If you've filtered tasks or resources already, or if you deselected the Keep Outline Structure check box in the Task Sheet, the permanent renumbering option is unavailable. If Keep Outline Structure is deselected, subtasks will not remain with their summary tasks after the sort.

Grouping Information in the Task Sheet or Resource Sheet

Project 2000 includes a new feature that's somewhat akin to a multiple sort—the new grouping capability. When you apply a group to the Task Sheet or Resource

Sheet, Project adds a row with the name for each group and places the appropriate task or resource rows within each group. Project also typically arranges the groups in an ascending order, generally from lesser values to higher values. For example, if you group the Resource Sheet by Complete and Incomplete Resources, Project first lists the group of resources with 0% of their work complete, then lists the group of resources with 1–99% of their work complete, and then places resources with 100% of their work complete in the last listed group. The yellow group rows also display value subtotals, where applicable in instances where sheet columns display cost information.

You can group tasks using the Complete and Incomplete Tasks, Constraint Type, Critical, Duration, Duration Then Priority, Milestones, Priority, Priority Keeping Outline Structure, and Team Status Pending groups. You can group resources using the Complete and Incomplete Resources, Resource Group, Response Pending, Standard Rate, and Work vs. Material Resources groups. Project displays the proper grouping choices depending on whether you're working in a view that includes the Task Sheet or Resource Sheet. To apply a group, choose Project, Group By, then click on the name of the group to apply. Or open the Group By drop-down list near the right end of the Standard toolbar, and then click on the group to apply. In Figure 11.15, I displayed the Entry table of the Resource Sheet, and then applied the Resource Group group. So the yellow group rows display the cost subtotals for each group.

Group By drop-down list

Figure 11.15
Yellow bars define groups in the Task or Resource Sheet.

Resource Name	Cost	Baseline Cost	Variance	Actual Cost	Remaining
⊟ **Group: Acct**	**$4,770.00**	**$4,770.00**	**$0.00**	**$1,260.00**	**$3,510.00**
Stan Axel	$4,770.00	$4,770.00	$0.00	$1,260.00	$3,510.00
⊟ **Group: Comm**	**$5,426.20**	**$5,276.00**	**$150.20**	**$2,686.20**	**$2,740.00**
Mary Rogers	$1,365.00	$1,425.00	($60.00)	$1,215.00	$150.00
Lisa Gray	$4,060.20	$3,850.00	$210.20	$1,470.20	$2,590.00
Slides/Overhead	$1.00	$1.00	$0.00	$1.00	$0.00
⊟ **Group: Contract**	**$8,042.50**	**$8,812.50**	**$230.00**	**$2,210.00**	**$6,832.50**
Steve Poland	$8,780.00	$8,550.00	$230.00	$2,210.00	$6,570.00
Ryan Printing	$0.00	$0.00	$0.00	$0.00	$0.00
Stamps Mailing	$0.00	$0.00	$0.00	$0.00	$0.00
Color Proofs	$262.50	$262.50	$0.00	$0.00	$262.50
⊟ **Group: Design**	**$4,932.83**	**$4,932.83**	**$0.00**	**$180.00**	**$4,752.83**
Joe Bucki	$4,900.33	$4,900.33	$0.00	$175.00	$4,725.33
Storage Media	$10.00	$10.00	$0.00	$0.00	$10.00
Paper (Reams)	$22.50	$22.50	$0.00	$5.00	$17.50

You can customize the group display, too. To do so, first apply the group you'd like to use. Then choose Project, Group By, Customize Group By. The Customize Group By dialog box appears. To add another group, choose the first blank cell under Field Name in the Group By The Following Fields area near the top of the dialog box. Click on the down arrow that appears, and then choose the name of the new field to group by. Use the drop-down list for the Order cell beside the new group cell to choose a sort order for the group. You can use the Font, Cell Background, and Pattern choices to change the display settings for the new group or any existing group you choose in the Group By The Following Fields list. Figure 11.16 shows a new group added into the list.

If any group includes numerical data, you can choose an interval for the group by clicking on the Define Group Intervals button. The Define Group Interval dialog box appears. Open the Group On drop-down list and choose Interval. Change the entry in the Start At text box, if you want to set a particular starting value for the first group. Then change the Group Interval text box entry to specify the interval. For example, if you want to display cost information by increments (groups) at $500 intervals, you would change this entry to **500**. If you want to display task or work completion percentage values in increments of 25% (rather than just 0%, 1–99%, or 100% as in the example I cited earlier in this section), you would enter **25**. After you finish making the interval settings, click on OK.

Back in the Customize Group By dialog box, click on the Save button if you want to save the custom group. Enter a name for the group in the Name text box of the Save Group dialog box, check the Show In Menu check box if you want to be able to access the group via the Project, Group By submenu or the Group By drop-down list on the Standard toolbar, and then click on OK. Click on OK in the Customize Group By dialog box to close the dialog box and apply the new group.

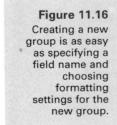

Figure 11.16
Creating a new group is as easy as specifying a field name and choosing formatting settings for the new group.

Note

> You can use the Project, Group By, More Groups command to open the More Groups dialog box to select and work with groups.

To remove a group you've applied, choose Project, Group By, No Group or choose No Group from the Group By drop-down list on the Standard toolbar.

Quick and Dirty Gantt Chart Formatting

Chapter 16, "Other Formatting," details all the options for formatting bars in a Gantt chart, as well as for formatting information in the Task Sheet and elsewhere. Right now, however, you might want a quick way to adjust the Gantt bars appearing in any view that includes a Gantt chart. To avoid the need to master the commands on the Format menu, you can use GanttChartWizard to walk you through the key steps for adjusting how the Gantt chart bars look. To start GanttChartWizard, click on the GanttChartWizard button on the Formatting toolbar (last button on the right), or choose Format, GanttChartWizard. The GanttChartWizard—Step 1 dialog box appears. Click on the Next button to open the GanttChartWizard—Step 2 dialog box (see Figure 11.17). In this

GanttChartWizard button

Figure 11.17
GanttChart-Wizard idiot-proofs the process of changing the appearance of your Gantt bars.

This sample changes to reflect the option button you select

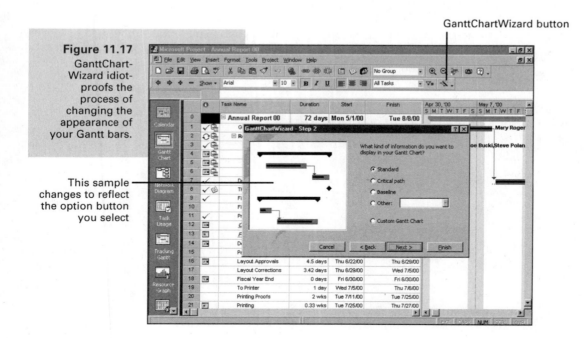

Note

> If you select any custom option (listed last in each GanttChartWizard dialog box), the dialog box that follows enables you to specify details about the option. Obviously, the details you can specify vary depending on the particular option. Additionally, the step number of the subsequent dialog box varies depending on the dialog box from which you selected the custom option.

dialog box, click to select the type of information you want to appear in your Gantt chart.

Make your selection and click on Next to continue. The GanttChartWizard—Step 9 dialog box appears, allowing you to indicate what kinds of labels you want to appear with the Gantt bars. (The step numbers on the dialog boxes are not sequential; they vary depending on the choices you make.) The default is to label the task bars with both the resources and dates assigned to the task, but you can change this. Specify your choice, and then click on Next. The GanttChartWizard—Step 13 dialog box appears. Select whether you want Project to include lines indicating links between tasks in the Gantt chart, and then click on Next. The GanttChartWizard—Step 14 dialog box appears so that you can finish the process. Click on Format It, and Project formats your Gantt chart exactly as you specified. Then click on Exit Wizard to return to your project.

Changing and Zooming the Timescale

The graphical portion of any view usually presents information in terms of a schedule. The schedule units used in that portion of the view, usually shown along the top of the view, are called the *timescale*. By default, Project uses a weekly timescale at the top of the graphical display in most views; this is the *major timescale*. Below each week, the *minor timescale* slices the schedule into days.

Why would you want to change the timescale? Well, you might want to make the schedule more compact for easier printing (select a monthly timescale) or more extended to provide greater detail. To change the timescale, follow these steps:

1. Make sure the pane that includes the graphical display is the active view.
2. Choose Format, Timescale. The Timescale dialog box appears (see Figure 11.18). You can also right-click on the timescale onscreen and then click on Timescale, or double-click on the timescale onscreen.

Zoom In the timescale

Zoom Out the timescale

Figure 11.18
Adjust how your
chart measures
time by
changing the
timescale.

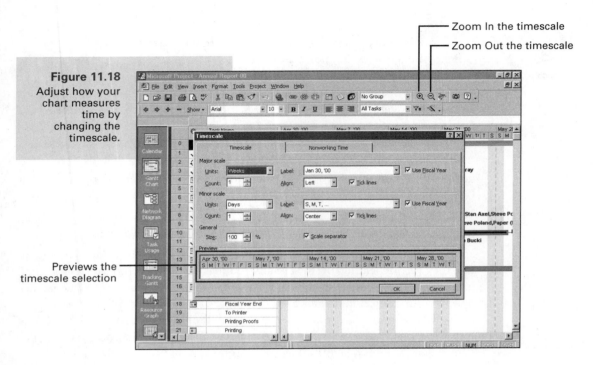

Previews the
timescale selection

3. Set up the major timescale in the Major Scale area. Use the Units drop-down list to adjust the measurement (days or months, for example). In the Count text box, enter a value to control how many of the timescale units are labeled. For example, **3** means that Project labels every third unit on the major timescale (the top row of time units, which shows the larger units of time you're displaying on the timescale). Select a date-numbering style from the Label drop-down list, and use the Align drop-down list to specify how the labels will be aligned. Select the Tick Lines check box if you want vertical dividing lines to appear between timescale units. And leave the Use Fiscal Year check box checked if you want the timescale to adjust the major scale labels according to the current fiscal year; this is crucial when you choose Quarters as the major scale Units setting.

Note

To select the month on which your fiscal year starts (which in turn affects the timescale display), choose Tools, Options. Click on the Calendar tab, and then choose the proper month from the Fiscal Year Starts In drop-down list. Click on OK to finish the fiscal year setting.

4. Set up the minor timescale in the Minor Scale area. (The minor timescale is the bottom row of time units, which shows smaller units of time to subdivide the major timescale. For example, if the major timescale is set to days, the minor timescale might show hours.) These settings work like the ones described in Step 3.

5. If needed, adjust the percentage shown in the Size text box to show more or less of the charted information in the same space.

6. The Scale Separator check box, when selected, adds a horizontal line to separate the major and minor timescales. Select or deselect this option as you prefer.

7. If the Nonworking Time tab is available for the selected Gantt chart, click on that tab to display its options (see Figure 11.19). This tab lets you control how nonworking time (such as holiday and weekend time) is charted. By default, nonworking time appears as gray vertical bars on the timescale.

8. You might want to change how the working time is charted for a calendar other than the Standard calendar. For example, you could specially highlight nonworking time for a particular calendar. In such cases, select the calendar to adjust from the Calendar drop-down list.

9. Use the Color and Pattern drop-down lists to specify the charted appearance of the nonworking time.

10. In the Draw area, select an option button to control how the charted nonworking time interacts with the charted tasks. Behind Task Bars means that Project always draws the task bars over the nonworking time. In Front Of Task Bars means that the nonworking time "bars" appear in front of the charted task bars. Do Not Draw tells Project not to indicate nonworking time at all.

Figure 11.19
You can use these options to specify whether nonworking time is charted.

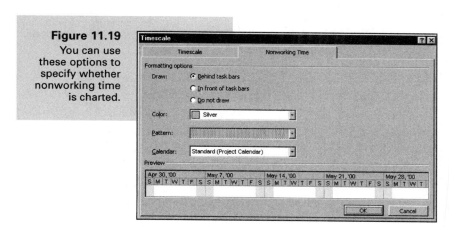

Caution

> If you specify nonworking time in days, you must schedule the minor timescale in days or smaller units. Otherwise, Project is unable to chart the nonworking time.

11. Click on OK to finish making your timescale settings. Your chart adopts a new appearance, as shown in Figure 11.20.

You can change the timescale in the Calendar view by right-clicking on one of the day names, and then clicking Timescale. For the Calendar view, the Timescale dialog box offers three tabs: Week Headings, Date Boxes, and Date Shading. Use the Week Headings tab to specify how the monthly, weekly, and daily headings appear on the calendar. You can specify whether each week displays 7 days or 5 days (the latter means that weekends are hidden). Also, select the Previous/Next Month Calendars check box if you want the calendar to include small thumbnail views of the months before and after the current month. Use the Date Boxes tab to control what appears in the gray shaded area along the top of each date box, or to display another shaded row (and control its contents) at the bottom of each date box. You specify what appears at the left or right side of each shaded area and can control the pattern and color of the shading. Finally, use the Date Shading tab to control the shading for working days, nonworking days, and other types of dates in the base calendar for the schedule or in resource calendars.

Figure 11.20
The Gantt chart reflects the adjusted timescale.

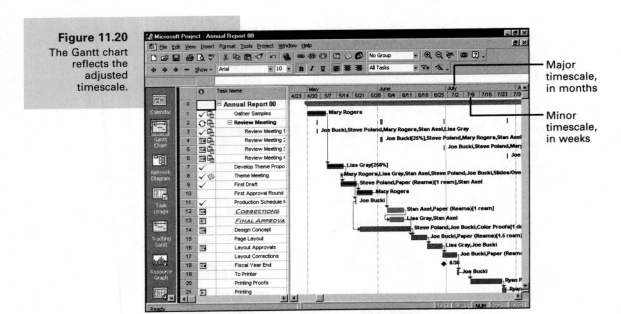

Creating a Table or Filter

The More Tables and More Filters dialog boxes each contain New and Copy buttons at the right. You can use these buttons to create tables and filters from scratch or based on an existing table or filter. For example, you might want to be able to quickly display a few added fields (columns) in a particular sheet. You might also want to create a set of fields completely different from the tables Project provides. (For example, you might want only the task name, resource initials, and remaining work for tasks.)

Creating your own tables or filters is actually a better approach than making a change to one of Project's default offerings. If you create and save your own custom table or filter, you can display it as needed. Then, when you need the default table or filter, it's still available.

Note

> You can use the Edit button in the More Tables, More Filters, or More Views dialog box to edit the selected table, filter, or view. Make changes using the dialog box that appears, and then click on OK to finish. But remember, it is not a good practice to edit a default table, filter, or view; rather, copy and rename it first, and then edit the copy.

To create and save a custom table, follow these steps:

1. Display the More Tables dialog box. To do so, choose View, Table, More Tables.

2. (Optional) If there's an existing table similar to the table you want to create, click on its name in the Tables list to select it.

3. Click on the New or Copy button. No matter which button you choose, the Table Definition dialog box appears (see Figure 11.21).

4. Edit the Name for the table, if needed.

5. If you want the custom table to appear as a choice on the Table submenu, leave the Show In Menu check box selected. Otherwise, clear this check box so that the table is listed only in the More Tables dialog box.

6. To remove a row that appears (if you're working on a copy of an existing table), click on the Field Name cell in that row; then click on the Cut Row button.

7. To add a new field, click on the Field Name cell in the first blank row. Next, click on the field down arrow to display a scrolling list of all available fields. Click on the field you want. If needed, edit the Align Data, Width, Title, and Align Title columns for the new field. If you don't

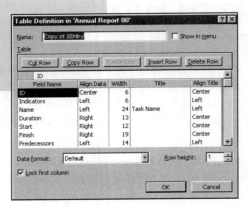

Figure 11.21
You can add and remove fields here to create a custom table.

make an entry in the Title column, Project displays the Field Name in the column header for the field.

8. Continue adding and adjusting field rows. You can use the Copy Row, Paste Row, and Insert Row buttons to move selected rows or to insert a new blank row between existing rows.

9. If your table includes date fields and you want to change how they appear (for example, you want to spell out the month name), use the Date Format drop-down list.

10. If you want each table row to have more height (to make it more attractive or legible), increase the value in the Row Height text box by clicking on the existing entry and editing it.

11. The Lock First Column check box "freezes" the far-left column so that you can't edit it, and it won't scroll out of view. Clear this check box if you don't want either condition to apply.

12. Click on OK. Project saves your table and adds it to the Tables list in the More Tables dialog box.

13. Click on Close to exit the More Tables dialog box without applying the table, or click on Apply to apply the new table to the current sheet.

Just as you can save a custom table, you can save a custom filter using a process very similar to the one just described. Choose Project, Filtered For, More Filters. In the More Filters dialog box, select the filter you want to use to create the custom filter, if any. Click on the New or Copy button. The Filter Definition dialog box appears.

Tip

• •

I strongly recommend creating a custom filter by copying an existing filter because it's easier and faster to edit filtering criteria than to create new ones from scratch.

• •

Edit the filter name and specify whether you want it to appear as a choice on the Filtered For submenu. Each row you edit or create in the Filter list area contains a single filter criterion. The Field Name cell for each row contains the name of the field you want to filter by. To specify a field, click on the Field Name cell; then click on the field's down arrow to display the list of field names. Click on the one you want. Next, click on the Test cell for this criterion. This holds the operator that Project uses to evaluate the selected field. To change the test, click on the arrow to display the field box drop-down list, and then click on the operator you want.

Next, use the Value(s) column to specify which data the test will compare to the field contents. You can type a value or date in this column (see Figure 11.22), or use the field drop-down list to select another field to compare the data with. If you enter a value that involves a work amount or schedule amount, be sure to include a time abbreviation with your entry. For example, you might build a criterion with Remaining Work under Field Name, Does Not Equal under Test, and 0h under Value(s). Finally, if you want to filter by more criteria, use the And/Or column to specify whether the filtered rows must match all entered criteria (And) or just one of the entered criteria (Or).

Click on the Show Related Summary Rows check box to select it if you want the filtered list to display summary tasks that match the filter specifications. Click on OK to finish creating the filter, and then close the More Filters dialog box by clicking on Apply. Project applies your new filter to the current sheet.

You can create a filter that's interactive—meaning it opens a dialog box prompting you to enter the information to filter for—using the Value(s) column in the Filter Definition dialog box. Specify the And/Or, Field Name, and Test choices you want. Then enter the message the dialog box should display, surrounded by quotes, with a question mark following the quotes. For example, you can create an interactive filter that prompts you to specify a percentage of work complete, then filters the list by the percentage you enter. To do so, choose % Complete

Figure 11.22
You can type an entry in the Value(s) column or open its drop-down list and specify a field entry to compare with the Field Name entry.

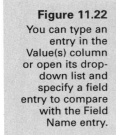

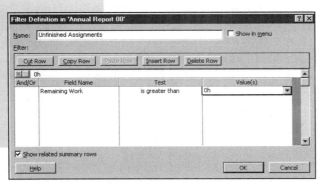

from the Field Name drop-down list in the Filter Definition dialog box, and choose equals from the Test drop-down list. Then, click on the Value(s) cell for that row, type "**Enter percentage:**"?, and press Enter. Click on OK to finish creating the filter. Then, if you choose the filter from the More Filters dialog box, a dialog box appears, using the words you typed in the Value(s) cell to prompt you to enter a percentage. If you want the interactive filter to prompt you for a range of dates or values, choose Is Within or Is Not Within as the Test, and then enter "**From:**"?,"**To:**"? in the Value(s) cell. Using two sets of quotation marks, two question marks, and the comma tells the filter to prompt for two values. Note that you need to make sure that the prompt you enter in the Value(s) column makes it clear whether the reader should enter a value or a date. For example, if the Field Name the filter uses contains dates, prompting the user to enter a number or percentage would cause the filter not to work.

Creating a Custom Field with a Pick List

Project 2000 offers you new flexibility in customizing fields you insert into a table you create. You can create a custom field with a *pick list*—a drop-down list of entries from which the user can select a choice. This speeds up data entry, since the user doesn't have to type a particular entry in that field. Use these steps to customize a field so it includes a pick list:

1. Create and display the new table. In the table you create, add in a "placeholder" column for the custom field. I suggest inserting one of the text fields (Text1, Text2, and so on), with the title you want to use for the custom field. As an example, I'll enter **Location** as the title for a field I've added to a custom resource sheet table. This Location field will offer a list of three locations: New York, Reno, and Denver. This field will be used to specify the city where each resource is located.

2. Right-click on the field header you want to customize, and then choose Customize Fields in the shortcut menu. The Customize Fields dialog box appears (Figure 11.23). Under Field, it should have Task or Resource correctly selected, depending on the nature of the custom table you selected. The Type drop-down list should have the proper field type (in this case, Text) selected. If not, choose the proper field type. Then select another placeholder field, if needed, in the list of fields.

3. To supply a unique field name (not just a field title) to the field you selected, click on the Rename button. Enter the new field name in the text box of the Rename field dialog box, and then click on OK.

4. Under Custom Attributes, click on the option button beside the Value List button to tell Project that you want to create a pick list of potential

Figure 11.23
After you add a field to a custom table, you can automate or customize the field.

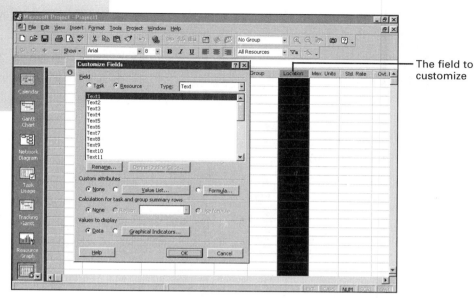

The field to customize

values for the entries in the field. Click on OK to close the warning dialog box that appears—you're working with your own new field, which has no data to overwrite, so you don't have to worry about it.

5. Click on the Value List button. The Value List For "Field Name" dialog box appears.

6. Use each row in the Enter Values To Display In Dropdown List area of the dialog box to enter the Value and Description for each item in the pick list. Figure 11.24 shows the city entries for my example.

7. If you want one of the list values to be the default entry for the field, check the Use A Value From The List As The Default Entry For The Field check box, click on the Value entry to use as the default, then click on the Set Default button.

8. If you want users to have the option to make unique entries in the field (entries other than those on the pick list), choose the Allow Additional Items To Be Entered Into The Field option button. To have Project add any new entries into the value list, check the Append New Entries to the Value List check box. To be prompted to verify such additions, check Prompt Before Adding New Entries.

9. Finally, change the setting under Display Order For Dropdown List if you want to use the Sort Ascending or Sort Descending order for the pick list, instead of the default By Row Number order.

Figure 11.24
Type in the Value (name) and description for each item in your pick list.

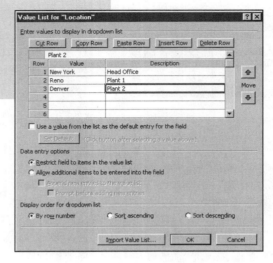

10. Click on OK to close the Value List For "Field Name" dialog box, and click on OK again in the warning dialog box. This takes you back to the Customize Fields dialog box.

11. Click on OK to finish customizing the field. A down arrow should appear immediately beside the first blank cell in the newly customized field. Clicking on this arrow will give you the list you specified, as shown in Figure 11.25.

Note

If your task list has summary rows or you plan to use grouping, you can click on the Rollup option button under Calculation For Task And Group Summary Rows, then choose the calculation type to display in the custom field position from the Rollup drop-down list. Or, if you want to display graphical indicators for the data in the Task or Resource Sheet rather than actual values, click on the Graphical Indicators button under Values To Display. Use the options at the top of the resulting dialog box to specify whether you want to display graphical indicators for summary or nonsummary (subtask) rows. Then use the first Test For drop-down list to specify a comparison operator, enter the comparison value in the Value(s) column, and choose the graphical indicator to display in the field when the data matches the comparison from the Image drop-down list on the same row. Create any other needed tests (comparisons) on subsequent rows, and then click on OK.

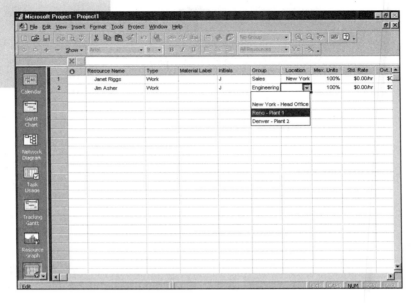

When you go to the length of customizing a field in your custom table, make sure you copy the custom table and custom field into the GLOBAL.MPT file to make it available to all your project plan files. See the later section "Dealing with the Organizer to Work with Views, Macros, Tables, and More" to learn how to copy items into GLOBAL.MPT.

Creating a Custom Field That Calculates

You can also add a custom field that calculates numerical data from existing Project fields that hold data. Or you can have Project perform any custom calculation that you'd like. Using Project's calculation capabilities brings you two benefits: greater accuracy because Project is doing the math, and less work because you don't have to do the calculations.

Follow these steps to create a custom calculated field in a custom table:

1. Create and display the new table. In the table you create, add in a placeholder column for the custom field. In this case, you may want to insert one of the cost (Cost1, Cost2, and so on) or value fields (Value1, Value2, and so on), as applicable, with the title you want to use for the custom field. As an example, I'll enter **Cost Plus Markup** as the title for a Cost1 field I've added to a custom resource sheet table. This field will take the resource Cost (total cost for work assigned to the resource) and mark it up

by 15 percent. Let's say I need to know that value, because that 15 percent represents a markup fee that will be passed along to the client.

2. Right-click on the field header you want to customize, then choose Customize Fields in the shortcut menu. The Customize Fields dialog box appears (refer to Figure 11.23). Under Field, it should have Task or Resource correctly selected, depending on the nature of the custom table you selected. The Type drop-down list should have the proper field type (in this case, Cost) selected. If not, choose the proper field type. Then select another placeholder field, if needed, in the list of fields.

3. To supply a unique field name (not just a field title) to the field you selected, click on the Rename button. Enter the new field name in the text box of the Rename Field dialog box, and then click on OK.

4. Under Custom Attributes, click on the option button beside the Formula button to tell Project that you want to create a calculated field. Click on OK to close the warning dialog box that appears—you're working with your own new field, which has no data to overwrite, so you don't have to worry about it.

5. Click on the Formula button. The Formula For "Field Name" dialog box appears.

6. The insertion point appears in the large Edit Formula text box by default. Build your formula by choosing fields and formulas from the Field and Function drop-down lists, by clicking on the mathematical operator buttons, and by typing in values as needed. For example, Figure 11.26 shows a formula I've created by inserting the Cost field (it's in square brackets), choosing the multiplication operator (*), and entering **1.15**. This formula multiplies the Cost field value for each resource by 1.15 (115 percent), to arrive at the value of the cost plus a 15 percent markup.

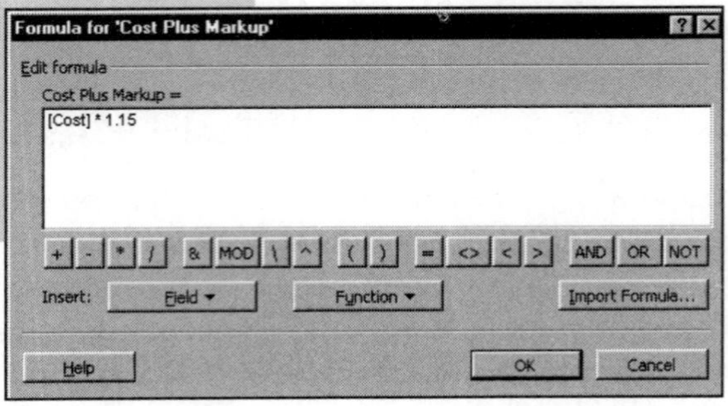

Figure 11.26
You can set up a custom field to calculate information for you.

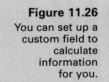

7. Click on OK when you finish creating the formula, then click on OK again to close the Customize Fields dialog box. Project immediately displays the results of the custom calculations if the project file already holds the needed data, as shown in Figure 11.27.

Figure 11.27
The Cost Plus Markup field holds the results of the custom calculation illustrated in Figure 11.26.

	Resource Name	Cost	Cost Plus Markup	Baseline Cost	Variance	Actual Cost	Remaining
1	Janet Riggs	$2,000.00	$2,300.00	$0.00	$2,000.00	$0.00	$2,000.00
2	Jim Asher	$7,800.00	$8,970.00	$0.00	$7,800.00	$0.00	$7,800.00

Creating a View

Unlike a table or filter, a new view is often easier to create from scratch than by editing one that already exists. Project enables you to create and save a single-pane view that combines a specified table and filter. Thus, if you want to create a view that uses a custom table or filter, you need to create the custom table or filter first. To create a new single-pane view, follow these steps:

1. Choose View, More Views, or click on the More Views button on the View Bar. The More Views dialog box appears.

2. Click on the New button. Project uses the Define New View dialog box to ask if you want to create a Single View or Combination View. Leave Single View selected, and then click on OK. The View Definition dialog box appears (see Figure 11.28).

3. Enter a Name for your new view.

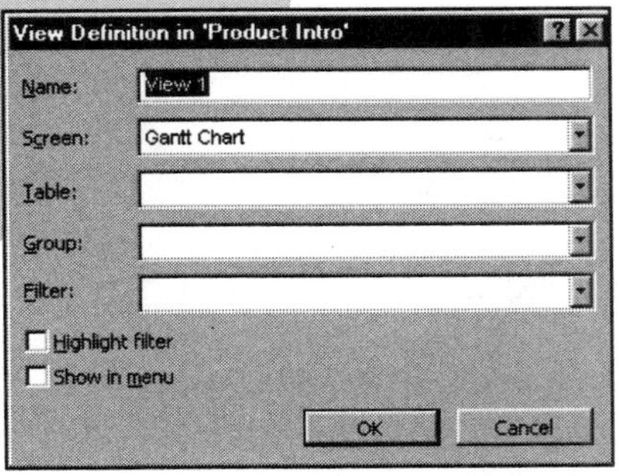

Figure 11.28
Project helps you view your schedule exactly as you want to.

View Definition in 'Product Intro'

Name: View 1
Screen: Gantt Chart
Table:
Group:
Filter:
☐ Highlight filter
☐ Show in menu

OK   Cancel

4. Use the Screen drop-down list to specify whether you want your view to offer a sheet, form, or chart. For example, select Relationship Diagram to display task information in your view using the abbreviated form of the Network Diagram chart.

5. If you selected a sheet style for your screen, use the Table drop-down list to specify a table that controls which columns of information appear in your view.

6. Use the Group drop-down list to apply a predefined group to the sheet portion of the view.

7. Use the Filter drop-down list to control which rows of information appear in your view.

8. If it's available, click on Highlight Filter to highlight data that matches the filter, rather than hiding the data that doesn't match the filter.

9. Click on the Show In Menu check box to select it if you want the new view to appear as a choice on the View menu or an icon on the View Bar.

10. Click on OK to finish creating your view, and then apply the view by clicking on Apply, or simply close the More Views dialog box by clicking on Close.

A combination view displays two single-pane views in upper and lower panes onscreen. If you want a combination view to include a custom single-pane view, you need to create the single-pane view first and then create the combination view.

To create a combination view rather than a single-pane view, select Combination View in the Define New View dialog box (Step 2 in the preceding set of steps). The View Definition dialog box appears again, but this time it resembles Figure 11.29.

Type the Name you want for the view. Use the Top drop-down list to select the view that will appear in the upper pane, and use the Bottom drop-down list to select the single-pane view that will appear in the lower pane. Select the Show In Menu check box if you want the new view to appear as a choice on the View

Figure 11.29
This dialog box is where you specify details of the combination view you're creating.

View Definition in 'Product Intro'	? ×

Name: View 1

Views displayed:

Top:

Bottom:

☐ Show in menu

OK   Cancel

menu or as an icon on the View Bar. Then click on OK to finish making the view and return to the More Views dialog box. Exit this dialog box as described in the preceding set of steps.

Dealing with the Organizer to Work with Views, Macros, Tables, and More

By default, the custom tables, filters, views, reports, and other items that you create are saved with the open, active project file only. This means that you can select one of these custom items only when that particular project file is open and active. If you want a custom view, filter, or other item to be available to other project files, you need to copy the custom item to the GLOBAL.MPT file. To do this, you use the Organizer, which enables you to specify where custom items are stored.

You might have noticed earlier in this chapter that the More Tables, More Filters, and More Views dialog boxes each contain an Organizer button. Clicking on that button in any dialog box opens the Organizer dialog box. You can also display the Organizer by choosing Tools, Organizer. The tab that appears on top in this dialog box varies depending on which dialog box you were in when you clicked on the Organizer button. For example, if you were in the More Views dialog box, the Views tab is selected when the Organizer dialog box opens. To deal with a different type of item, click on the appropriate tab. Also choose the Task or Resource option button, if applicable, to display the applicable custom items. For example, Figure 11.30 shows the Tables tab, with the custom tables I created earlier to hold my custom pick list and calculated fields.

Each tab in the Organizer dialog box contains two lists. The list on the left shows the views (or tables, filters, or whatever) that are saved in GLOBAL.MPT. The list on the right shows the elements that are saved in the current project file. To copy an item from the list on the left to the list on the right (that is, from GLOBAL.MPT to the current project file), click on the item name and then click on Copy>>.

To copy an item from the project file to GLOBAL.MPT, click on the item name and then click on <<Copy. (The arrows change direction depending on which side you choose to copy an item from.) If the file to which you're copying includes an item with the same name as the one you're copying, you'll be prompted to confirm that the copied file should overwrite the existing file.

Figure 11.30
The Organizer enables you to move custom items between files.

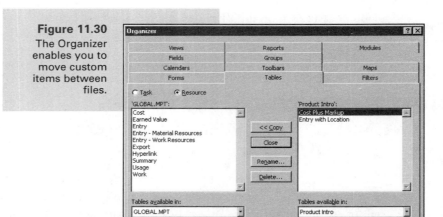

Use the Available In drop-down list (in the lower-left corner of any tab in the Organizer dialog box; the list name will specify the kind of item available) to control the file for which you're listing items on the left side of the tab. Similarly, use the Available In drop-down list (in the lower-right corner of the tab) to control the file for which you're listing items on the right side of the tab. If you want to copy a view or other item between two project files, rather than between a project file and GLOBAL.MPT, make sure that you change the Available In selection on the left to display the name of the second project file.

If you select an item from either list and then click on Rename, Project displays the Rename dialog box. Type a new name, and then click on OK. If you select an item from either list and then click on Delete, Project permanently deletes the item from the list for that file only, not from any other files that use the same item. Deleting an item from the GLOBAL.MPT file makes it inaccessible to all files, unless you previously copied the item to an individual schedule file. If you copied a custom item to multiple individual schedule files, remember that you need to remove it from each and every file to permanently delete it.

When you're finished working in the Organizer, click on the Close button, and click on Close again to exit the More dialog box, if applicable.

To save an item such as a view or table that you added to any project file, be sure to save the file. When you exit Project, the application automatically saves changes that have been made to GLOBAL.MPT.

Using the Rollup Views

Three other views—the Rollup views that affect how subtasks look when rolled up to summary tasks—warrant special mention because you need to perform a preliminary step before you use one of these views. The Rollup views are as follows:

- **Bar Rollup.** Rolls up subtasks to the summary task bar and displays the Task Name for each task.
- **Milestone Date Rollup.** Rolls up subtasks to the summary task bar, displays each subtask as a milestone, and displays the Task Name and start date.
- **Milestone Rollup.** Rolls up subtasks to the summary task bar, displays each subtask as a milestone, and displays the Task Name only.

These views can be more helpful than simply rolling up subtasks to a summary task bar, because they enable you to show more information on the rolled-up summary task. Thus they let you summarize your project but still have a clear picture of which tasks it contains.

Before you display one of the Rollup views in the current project file, you have to roll up subtasks and run the Rollup_Formatting macro, as follows:

1. In the Task Sheet of the Gantt Chart view, select the subtasks to roll up.
2. Click on the Task Information button on the Standard toolbar, click twice to check Roll Up Gantt Bar To Summary on the General tab, and then click on OK.
3. Repeat Steps 1 and 2 to roll up other groups of subtasks as needed. If you want to use the Rollup views for all summary tasks in your project, you'll need to use Steps 1 and 2 to roll up all subtasks for each summary task.
4. Choose Tools, Macro, Macros. The Macros dialog box appears.
5. Double-click on Rollup_Formatting in the Macro Name list. The Rollup Formatting dialog box appears (Figure 11.31).
6. Click to specify whether to display rolled-up tasks as Bars or Milestones, and then click on OK. The Task Sheet changes to display summary tasks only, and specially formatted (depending on your choice in this step) rolled-up Gantt bars appear in the Gantt chart at the right.

Figure 11.31
Specify whether
you want your
rolled-up tasks to
appear as Bars or
Milestones on the
Gantt chart using
this dialog box
from the
Rollup_Formatting
macro.

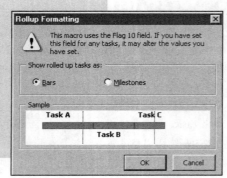

7. Click on the More Views button in the View Bar, and then choose the Bar Rollup, Milestone Date Rollup, or Milestone Rollup view, as needed. Figure 11.32 shows the Milestone Rollup view applied to a rolled-up summary task.

8. You can choose Gantt Chart view to display regular Gantt bars but return to one of the Rollup views as often as needed during the current work session.

Figure 11.32
The rolled-up
summary task at
right displays
milestones and
Task Names in
the Milestone
Rollup view.

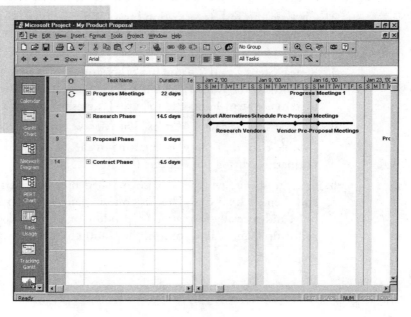

Using PERT Analysis

If you aren't confident that the timeline you're building for a project is accurate and you're not comfortable making an educated guess about the overall schedule, Project 98 offers special PERT analysis views to help do the job for you. You create your list of tasks and durations and enter resource information to evaluate whether the schedule can be completed in the time frame you estimate. Then you enter Optimistic (best case), Expected (most likely), and Pessimistic (worst case) durations that could occur for each task. Then you click on a toolbar button, and Project creates a weighted average of the Optimistic, Expected, and Pessimistic duration for each task, and changes the task Duration to that average. You can then display the estimate in Gantt Chart view. You can display the optimistic, expected, and best case dates you entered in the PA_Optimistic Gantt (Optimistic Gantt), PA_Expected Gantt (Expected Gantt), and PA_Pessimistic Gantt (Pessimistic Gantt) views, respectively. Here are the basic steps for making PERT Analysis calculations:

1. Display the PERT Analysis toolbar, which offers you the best access to all the PERT Analysis views and other tools. To display the toolbar, right-click on another toolbar and click on PERT Analysis.

Caution

You can't undo a weighted average calculation, so use the Save As command on the File menu to create a copy of your schedule file. Then perform the PERT Analysis calculation on the file copy, print the PERT Entry Sheet view showing the calculated results, and compare them to the original file.

2. (Optional) Click on the Set PERT Weights button on the PERT Analysis toolbar. This button displays the Set PERT Weights dialog box, which you use to tell Project whether the Optimistic, Expected, or Pessimistic dates you enter should be given the most consideration (the heaviest weighting) in calculations. The entries for these three weightings must add up to 6; by default, the Expected entry is 4, weighting it the heaviest. To weight each date equally, you would enter 2 in the text box beside it. Make your entries, and then click on OK.

3. Click on the PERT Entry Sheet button on the PERT Analysis toolbar to display the Task Sheet for entering the Optimistic, Expected, and Pessimistic Dur. (Duration) for each task. (To enter these settings for a

single task, select the task, click on the PERT Entry Form button on the PERT Analysis toolbar, enter the durations, and click on OK.)

4. Click on the Calculate PERT button on the PERT Analysis toolbar. The Duration column changes to display the calculated weighted averages.

5. To display the estimated (calculated durations), switch to the Gantt Chart view. Or click on either the Optimistic Gantt, Expected Gantt, or Pessimistic Gantt button on the PERT Analysis toolbar to see the Gantt Chart with the dates you entered for the desired scenario. (You can also choose these views from the More Views dialog box; each will have "PA_" in front of its name.)

12

Proofing and Printing a View

IN THIS CHAPTER

- Making sure you've spelled everything correctly
- Replacing entries
- Telling Project and Windows which printer you want to use, and what settings it should use
- Setting up the appearance of the printed pages
- Adjusting on which page information appears
- Getting a sneak preview of your printed document
- Printing your document

Unless you've developed telepathic capabilities or are connected to everyone involved with your project via network or e-mail, you're going to need some kind of method of sharing information. The most traditional method of sharing information is via printed hard copies. While "virtual" information sharing has its benefits, certain situations—such as meetings or bound proposals made for clients—call for printouts.

Like other Microsoft applications, Project 2000 provides you with a great deal of control over what you print and how it appears in the hard copy. This chapter focuses on the steps you need to take to prepare and print information from your schedule.

Checking the Project's Spelling

Although a program's spelling-check capabilities can't take the place of your basic ability to come up with what appear to be words in English, spelling checkers provide an essential backup for your brain.

To put your best, most professional foot forward, you should always—I repeat, *always*—spell-check your files in Project and any other business documents you create. Project's Spelling feature checks all the information in your schedule for correct spelling, starting from the first task in the Task Sheet and progressing through all your task information, no matter whether it's currently displayed. It even checks any information you entered as a Task Note or Resource Note. To spell-check a project file, follow these steps:

1. Make sure that the file you want to check is the open, active file.

2. Choose Tools, Spelling. Alternately, press F7 or click on the Spelling button on the Standard toolbar. The spelling check starts, and when the spelling checker encounters a word it doesn't recognize, it displays the Spelling dialog box (see Figure 12.1).

3. Look at the Not In Dictionary entry to see which word Project doesn't recognize; then use one of the following methods to adjust its spelling, if needed:

   ■ If the word isn't misspelled, click on Ignore to leave it intact, or Ignore All if you know that the word is used several times in the file. For example, if "Blalock" is in your client's company name and appears several times in the file, you want the Spelling feature to ignore all uses of "Blalock," meaning that for the rest of the spelling check, it assumes "Blalock" is spelled correctly.

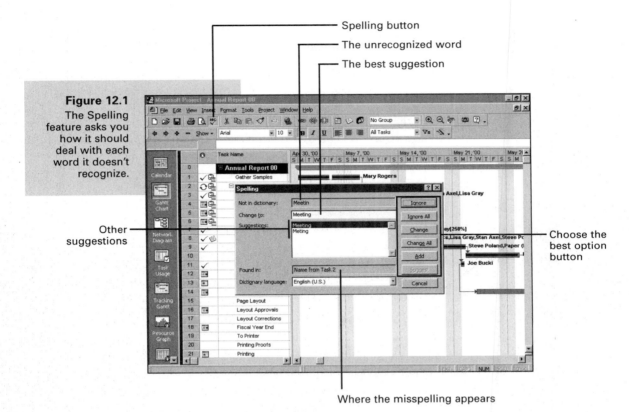

Figure 12.1
The Spelling feature asks you how it should deal with each word it doesn't recognize.

Spelling button

The unrecognized word

The best suggestion

Other suggestions

Choose the best option button

Where the misspelling appears

- If the word is wrong and the spelling in the Change To text box is correct, click on Change or Change All. Change corrects only the presently highlighted instance of the word, and Change All corrects it everywhere it appears in the Project file.

- If the word is wrong and the Change To spelling isn't correct either, you can edit the Change To text box entry, or click on another spelling in the Suggestions list to place that spelling in the Change To text box. (If you specified that suggestions shouldn't automatically appear on the Spelling tab of the Options dialog box, which is described in Chapter 25, "Creating and Using Macros," click on the Suggest button to display suggestions.) Then click either on Change or Change All.

4. After you tell Project how to adjust the unrecognized word, it displays the next unrecognized word so that you can adjust that one. Deal with each unrecognized word as explained in Step 3.

Note

If you edit the Change To entry (such as entering the client name "Blalock") and want Project to remember that spelling as a correct word for future files, click on the Add button to include the spelling in Project's dictionary.

5. When the spelling checker has reviewed the entire file, it displays a message informing you that the spell-check is finished (see Figure 12.2). Click on OK to close the dialog box.

Figure 12.2
Project informs you when it has checked the entire file.

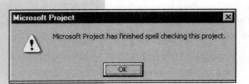

Using AutoCorrect for Entry Accuracy

To learn to type, you had to learn the pattern of the letters on the keyboard. If you learned a particular pattern incorrectly, chances are that you'll make the same typographical error (typo) over and over for the rest of your typing career—and you need a way to deal with the necessary repetitive fixes. Or, you might be a fine typist but would like a way to quickly enter certain words that you use often and are tricky to type. For example, you might not want to have to type "Blalock" each time it's needed in a file.

Project's AutoCorrect feature can help in either of these situations. In essence, you train Project to automatically replace your frequent typos (or abbreviations) with the correct (or full) terms you're trying to type. This ensures that certain terms are entered correctly in the first place, so you don't have to rely on the spelling checker to catch those errors. Use the following steps to create an AutoCorrect entry:

1. Choose Tools, AutoCorrect. The AutoCorrect dialog box appears (see Figure 12.3).

2. If you want Project to change the second letter in any word from uppercase to lowercase if you mistakenly type two capital letters, leave the Correct TWo INitial CApitals check box selected. Otherwise, clear this check box. You might want to clear it, for example, if you'll be typing a lot of state abbreviations.

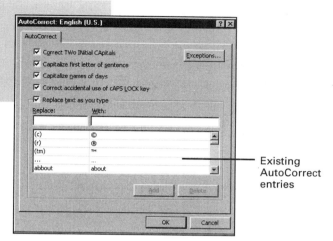

Figure 12.3
This is your chance to train Project to help you type more effectively.

Existing AutoCorrect entries

3. If you want an uppercase first letter in the first word of each entry, leave the Capitalize First Letter Of Sentence choice checked. Alternately, clear the check box to capitalize new sentences only when you specify. This option only works in fields that contain generic text entries, or in Task Names fields that contain task names with punctuation included; it doesn't work in any Notes fields.

Note

You can create exceptions that won't be corrected when you turn on the options described in Steps 2 and 3. Click on the Exceptions button in the AutoCorrect dialog box. To identify an instance when you don't want to capitalize the first word after a period (normally, this is after any abbreviation), type the abbreviation in the Don't Capitalize After text box on the First Letter tab, and then click on Add. If a specialized term begins with two capital letters, as in "CSi," click on the INitial CAps tab, type the term in the Don't Correct text box, and click on Add. Click on OK to finish creating your exceptions and return to the AutoCorrect dialog box.

4. Leave the Capitalize Names Of Days check box selected if you want Project to automatically capitalize day names when you type them.

5. If you have a habit of accidentally pressing the Caps Lock key when you're aiming for the nearby Shift or Tab key, leave the Correct Accidental Use Of cAPS LOCK Key check box selected to take care of the resulting capping errors. This feature applies in particular to Task Name entries and Resource Sheet entries.

6. For AutoCorrect to work, make sure that a check mark appears beside the Replace Text As You Type check box. If this option is not checked, Project will not make automatic replacements.

7. To create a new AutoCorrect entry, type the typo or abbreviation you want Project to catch and replace in the Replace text box. For example, you might type **bl** as the abbreviation you want to use for "Blalock." You can't include any spaces or punctuation in the Replace entry, but it can be up to 254 characters long.

Note

AutoCorrect doesn't make the correction until you type a full word and press the spacebar. So, you don't have to worry if the typo or abbreviation you enter as the Replace choice is the beginning of other words. For example, even though "bl" is the beginning of words like "black" and "blue," you can still use "bl" as an AutoCorrect abbreviation.

8. In the With text box, enter the correction you want AutoCorrect to make (for example, **Blalock**).

9. Click on Add to finish creating the AutoCorrect entry. Project adds this entry to the list of AutoCorrect entries, as shown in Figure 12.4.

10. Click on OK to close the AutoCorrect dialog box. New AutoCorrect entries take effect immediately.

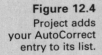

Figure 12.4
Project adds your AutoCorrect entry to its list.

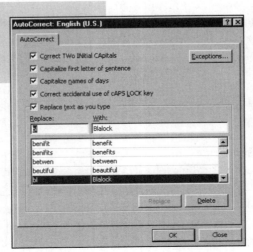

Replacing Entries

Other business changes might require that you make a correction to a term or entry that appears frequently in your project file. For example, a resource company may have changed names, or your company may have changed the accounting code used to track work by a particular department. In some cases you could run a spelling check to make the global correction, but doing so would also mean you'd have to review and work with other unrecognized words, making the process slower than needed. If you already added the term to replace to the Spelling feature's dictionary, however, running a spelling check won't work, because the Spelling dialog box will never stop on that term.

Instead, you can use the Replace feature in Project to find one or more occurrences of a particular entry in a field and replace those occurrences with a new entry that you specify. Follow these steps to replace information in a field:

1. Display either the Task Sheet or the Resource Sheet, depending on which one contains the information to find and replace. If you want the search to begin with a particular row, click on a cell in that row.

2. Choose Edit, Replace, or press Ctrl+H. The Replace dialog box appears.

3. Type the entry to search for in the Find What text box.

4. Type the new entry that you want to use as the replacement for each found entry in the Replace With text box.

5. Choose the field that holds the entries to find and replace from the Look In Field drop-down list. (Choose Name to search the Task Name field in the Task Sheet or Resource Name in the Resource Sheet, depending on which you displayed before opening the Replace dialog box.)

6. If you want to use an operator in the Find What entry, for example if you're searching for all numeric entries over a particular number (is greater than), choose the operator from the Test drop-down list.

Caution

I recommend using the Contains Exactly choice in the Test drop-down list as often as you can. For example, if you only use the Contains choice and are searching for an entry like "004," Project would stop on entries like "1004," "A004," or "10040," too, resulting in many more entries to sort through. Plus, you could inadvertently make an incorrect replacement.

7. Make a choice from the Search drop-down list to change the direction of the search. Project can search either Down or Up from the current row.

8. If you want each replacement to match the case (capitalization) of the entry in the Replace With text box and only want to replace entries matching the capitalization in the Find What text box, click to check the Match Case check box.

9. After you enter all the information to tell Project what entries to find and where to find them (see Figure 12.5 for an example), click on the Find Next button. Project highlights the first instance of the entry you told it to search for.

10. You can handle the highlighted entry in one of three ways:

   - Click on Find Next to skip the highlighted instance without changing it and highlight the next matching instance of the Find What entry.

   - Click on Replace to change the matching instance to the Replace With entry, and then highlight the next instance.

   - Click on Replace All to change all matching instances without pausing to ask you about them.

11. When Project finishes searching the field and making replacements, a message box appears to tell you the search is complete. Click on OK to close the message box.

12. Click on Close to close the Replace dialog box.

If you want to find an entry instead of replacing it, display the Find dialog box by choosing Edit, Find (Ctrl+F). The Find dialog box is nearly identical to the Replace dialog box. The Find dialog box lacks the Replace With text box (because you're not replacing anything) and the Replace All button. It does have a Replace button, which you can click to change the Find dialog box to the Replace dialog box. Otherwise, the Find dialog box offers the same options as the Replace dialog box, and you can use it just as described in the preceding steps for a replacement operation.

Figure 12.5

These choices find a particular Code field entry in the Resource Sheet, replacing each occurrence with a new code entry.

Replace		? X
Find what:	004	
Replace with:	A004	
Look in field:	Code	Test: contains exactly
Search:	Down	☐ Match case
	Replace	Replace All	Find Next	Close

Changing Printer Settings

If you're using Project in a small business or home office, you'll probably have only one printer attached to your computer system. If you work in a larger company, however, you might have access to multiple printers, for example, one in your office and one attached to your company network. In any environment, your computer also might have a built-in FAX/modem that you can "print" to, thereby faxing documents without making a hard copy; this is the same as having multiple printers.

If you have multiple printers attached to your system, you need a way to select the one you want to send your Project file to. In addition, each printer offers more than one set of capabilities. For example, your laser printer might be capable of printing at 600 dots per inch (dpi), but for everyday printing you might want to print at 300 dpi for faster printing. Similarly, many dot-matrix and inkjet printers offer a choice between letter quality and draft modes.

Before you set up your printout pages in Project, you should first select the printer you want to use and set the options you prefer. Select and set up the printer first, if needed, because different printer capabilities might affect the page setup options available in Project. Note that you don't have to set up a document or open any project file to print before setting up the printer. After you adjust printer settings, they remain in effect until you change them or exit Project.

If you're using an older dot-matrix or inkjet printer, any Project printouts that include graphical information might not appear as crisp and clean as you desire, and printing might be slow. In addition, depending on the printer, Project might present fewer options for altering the page setup, based on the printer's limitations. If you need to print many Gantt or Network Diagram charts, you should buy a laser printer, or even a color inkjet printer. (Or a plotter, if your organization has other purposes for it.)

Note

Remember, Project prints the view or report that currently appears onscreen, so make sure you adjust settings accordingly. Make sure you filter, sort, or group the Task or Resource Sheet before printing, if needed.

Figure 12.6
Part of the
purpose of the
Print dialog box
is to enable you
to choose and
set up a printer.

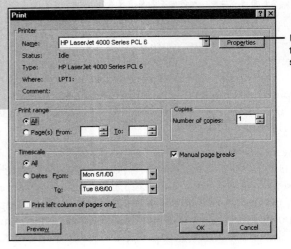

Use this drop-down list
to select a printer that's
set up on your system

To select and set up a printer, use the steps that follow. As there's quite a bit of variation between printers, and it's impossible to cover every option for every printer, this list covers only the most important options.

1. Choose File, Print. Alternately, press Ctrl+P. (*Don't* click on the Print button on the Standard toolbar, though. Doing so sends the current view to the specified printer, bypassing the Print dialog box.) The Print dialog box appears (see Figure 12.6).

2. Click on the drop-down list arrow to display the Name selections in the Printer area. The printers listed here are ones that have already been installed to work with Windows on your system or with a Windows NT or Windows 2000 network you're connected with. (To learn to set up a printer using the Windows Control Panel, see the Windows documentation or online help.) In this list, click on the name of the printer you want to print your Project files to.

3. After you select the correct printer, click on the Properties button beside it. If this is the first time you've worked with printer properties during the current Project work session, Project opens a dialog box alerting you that your printer settings will apply to all views you subsequently print—not just the currently displayed view.

4. Click on OK to continue. The Properties dialog box for the selected printer appears, as shown in Figure 12.7.

Figure 12.7
The Properties dialog box offers different options, depending on the capabilities of the selected printer.

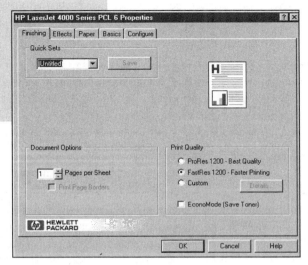

Note

In Windows, properties include information about a file, program, or piece of hardware, as well as the settings or options available for that file, program, or hardware.

5. Most printers allow you to control the following options, arranged on various tabs within the dialog box:

- **Paper size.** Use the list to display the list of sizes of paper your printer can handle. Click on the appropriate size to select it.

- **Orientation.** Select whether you want to print in a format where the paper's taller than it is wide (Portrait) or wider than it is tall (Landscape). To print the information upside-down in a landscape orientation, click to check the Rotated check box. Generally, a thumbnail picture in the preview or sample area shows you what effect your orientation selections will have on your document's printed layout.

- **Copies.** Change the Copies entry if you want Project to print more than one copy of each document (one is the default).

- **Restore Defaults.** This command button appears on each tab of the Properties dialog box. Clicking on it restores the tab's settings to the defaults for that printer.

- **Other.** Your printer may offer settings for printing multiple pages per sheet; choosing a resolution or toner-saving print quality; reducing, enlarging, or fitting a printout to a page; and more.

Tip

If you need information about one of the Properties settings for your printer, click on the question mark button near the right side of the Properties dialog box title bar, and then with the question mark pointer, click on the item you want information about.

6. After you specify all the property settings for your selected printer, click on OK to close the Properties dialog box and return to the Print dialog box.

7. At this point, you can click on the Close button to return to Project and alter the Page Setup for your project file, as described in the next section. Or you can use the Print dialog box to print your document, as described in the last section of this chapter, "Finishing the Print Job."

Controlling the Page Setup

In Project, the first step to determining what appears on your printout is to select a view. Project creates a printout of that view, so if you've displayed Gantt Chart view, the printout contains the columns at the left, and the Gantt bars on a schedule at the right. If you display only the Resource Sheet, Project prints the contents of the Resource Sheet. In a Task Sheet or Resource Sheet, you need to be sure that you display the correct table and filter the information, if needed, before printing. (See Chapter 11, "Working with the Different Project Views," to learn more about selecting and filtering a table.)

There are only a couple of limitations on what you can print. Project doesn't print any information or view pane that's a form.

In the selected view, you also need to specify formatting—such as adjusting the appearance of Gantt bars, changing the timescale, and changing column breaks (see the next section in this chapter)—to control how information appears in the final printout. The formatting changes you make appear both onscreen and in the printed document.

Note

Page Setup options are different from formatting changes, such as choosing a new font for text or adjusting how Gantt chart bars look. To learn more about formatting your project, see Chapter 16, "Other Formatting."

In contrast, the Page Setup options control only how the printed information appears. For example, you can adjust the header or footer that appears on each page of a printout, or specify how many pages you want the printout to occupy. To adjust the Page Setup options before printing, choose File, Page Setup to open the Page Setup dialog box for the selected view (see Figure 12.8).

The available options vary slightly depending on the selected view. The choices for each option that Project suggests by default also differ depending on the selected view (in Figure 12.8, for example, Project suggests printing the Gantt chart in the Landscape orientation). Finally, some of the settings you see in the Page Setup dialog box resemble the ones provided in the Properties dialog box for the printer. Remember that the printer Properties settings become the default for all Project files printed. Any Page Setup options you select for the current view take precedence over the Properties settings.

The remainder of this section describes the settings on each tab of the Page Setup dialog box. (Keep in mind that some of them might not be available in your selected view, in which case they'll be grayed out.) After you choose the settings you want from all tabs, click on the OK button to close the dialog box and have your changes take effect. (Or, using one of the other option buttons, you can preview your print job or jump directly to the Print dialog box to finish printing. Each of these operations is described later in this chapter.)

Figure 12.8
The Page Setup dialog box offers options specific to the selected view, which in this case is Gantt Chart view.

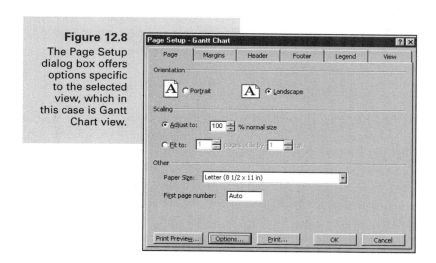

Page Tab Settings

Figure 12.8 shows the first tab in the Page Setup dialog box, the Page tab. In the Orientation area of the dialog box, specify whether you want the printout to appear in Portrait (tall) or Landscape (wide) format. The Scaling options enable you to scale the printed view or report to a particular size or page count. When the Adjust To option button is selected, you can enter a percentage that makes the printed image smaller (down to 10%) or larger (up to 500%) than its original size. I prefer, however, to use the Fit To option, which enables you to enter values telling Project how many pages wide and tall to make the printout. This is my preference because it's more error-proof; otherwise, you might have to print at a few different percentages to get a printed document that fits your needs. In most professional situations, I prefer to have a printout that's one page tall but as many pages as needed wide, because that format is easier for an audience to understand in a bound report. For a Task Sheet or Resource Sheet printout, on the other hand, you might prefer a result that's one page wide and multiple pages tall.

Under Other, you can use the Paper Size drop-down list to select a size, such as Legal, to use for the printout. The selected printer and its available paper sizes dictate the Paper Size choices in the Page Setup dialog box. Finally, you can enter a number in the First Page Number text box to specify the page number that Project starts with (if you specify page numbering in the header or footer) for the printout. For example, if you enter 4 and the printout requires four pages, Project numbers the pages 4, 5, 6, and 7. This is useful if you need to include the Project printout in a bound report that includes pages from other programs, such as a Word document. Adjusting the numbering for your Project printout enables you to seamlessly integrate its pages with the rest of the report.

Margins Tab Settings

The second tab in the Page Setup dialog box is the Margins tab. Click on the tab to display its options (see Figure 12.9). When you change the margin settings, you're changing the amount of white space that Project leaves around the information printed on a page. The Margins tab offers four text boxes—Top, Bottom, Left, and Right—where you can type the margin setting you want to use for your printout, in inches by default. To change one of the settings, double-click on its text box and type the new value or use the spinner buttons (the arrows at the right-hand side of the box).

By default, Project also prints a thin border around the information on every page of the printout. If you wish, you can change that setting in the Borders Around area of the Margins tab. If the selected view is the Network Diagram chart, you

Figure 12.9
Use this tab to control the margins (white space) that appear around the information in your printout.

Page Setup - Gantt Chart

| Page | Margins | Header | Footer | Legend | View |

Top: 0.5 in.

Left: 0.5 in.

Right: 0.5 in.

This sample shows how wide the specified margins will look

Bottom: 0.5 in.

Borders around
- ○ Every page
- ○ Outer pages
- ○ None

Print Preview... Options... Print... OK Cancel

can click to select the Outer Pages option button, which prints a border around only the first and last pages of the printout. For other views, you can click on the None option button to completely eliminate borders from the printout.

Note

Headers, footers, and legends print within any border included on the printout.

Header Tab Settings

Moving on, you can click on the Header tab in the Page Setup dialog box. A *header* appears at the top of a printout and provides information about the printout. A header can consist of any text you want to type in; for example, you might want to designate the printout as "In Progress" or something similar. Alternatively, you can build the header components using the tabs and buttons in the Alignment area of the Header tab.

Start by clicking on a tab in the Alignment area to select whether the entered header information will align to the left, center, or right. (Note that you can designate header information to appear simultaneously in two—or even all three—of these tabs.) To enter information simply by typing, click in the blank area below the tab and type the information you want; it appears in the Sample area as you type.

As indicated in Figure 12.10, you can use several of the buttons in the Alignment area to enter calculated fields of header information. For example, suppose that you want your header to include the printout date. Click within any information already entered for the header to specify where the date should be inserted, and then click on the button that inserts the printout date. A code that identifies where the printout date will be positioned appears in the header (see Figure 12.10).

Project enables you to automatically insert other kinds of information in the header—for example, the project Author or Project Start Date from the file Properties or Project Information dialog box settings—by using the General drop-down list at the bottom of the Alignment area. First, click to position the insertion point where you want the information inserted in the header. Open the General drop-down list to see the kinds of information you can insert; click on the name for the type of information you want to insert; then click on the Add button beside the drop-down list. Project inserts a code for that kind of

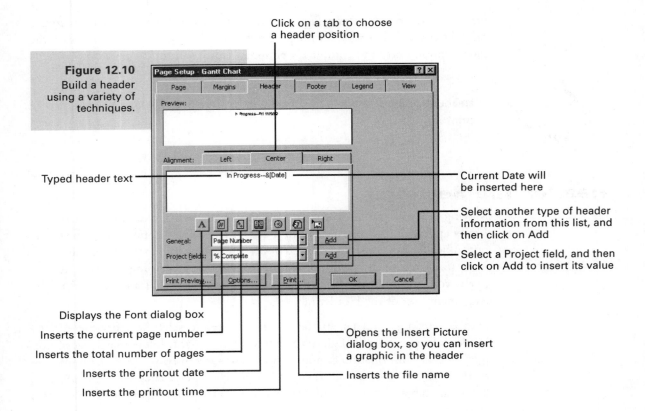

Figure 12.10
Build a header using a variety of techniques.

Click on a tab to choose a header position

Typed header text

Current Date will be inserted here

Select another type of header information from this list, and then click on Add

Select a Project field, and then click on Add to insert its value

Displays the Font dialog box

Inserts the current page number

Inserts the total number of pages

Inserts the printout date

Inserts the printout time

Opens the Insert Picture dialog box, so you can insert a graphic in the header

Inserts the file name

information in the header. The Project Fields drop-down list works in the same way and lists a number of calculated fields. Select the field you want from the drop-down list, and then click on the Add button beside it to insert the actual calculated value contained in that field into the header.

You can format the appearance of the text or inserted codes in any header area by dragging to highlight the information to format, and then clicking on the Formatting button in the Alignment area (this button is on the far left and has the letter "A" on it). Project then opens the Font dialog box, in which you can choose a new font, size, and so on for the selected text. Chapter 16, "Other Formatting," covers how to use the Font dialog box, which also appears when you format text in a Task Sheet or Resource Sheet. Suffice it to say here that you can make the changes you want, and then click on OK to return to the Page Setup dialog box.

If you want your company logo to appear on every page of a printout, insert the logo graphic in the header or footer.

Footer Tab Settings

Click on the next tab to move to the Footer options (see Figure 12.11). A footer resembles a header, but appears at the bottom of each printed page. You create a footer just as you would a header, so refer to the preceding information about creating a header to learn how to work with the Footer tab options.

Figure 12.11
The Footer options work just like the Header options.

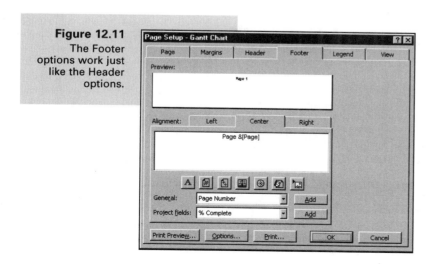

Legend Tab Settings

You can insert a legend explaining what the graphical chart symbols mean on your printouts. To specify whether or not a legend appears on your printout, click on the Legend tab in the Page Setup dialog box. The Legend tab options appear as shown in Figure 12.12.

Because a legend can include text, Project offers the kind of text formatting options available for creating headers and footers. Those settings work just like the ones on the Header and Footer tabs, so I won't explain them again here.

The Legend On area at the right side of the tab lets you control whether the legend appears on a given page. By default, Every Page is selected, meaning that the legend appears on every page of the printed hard copy. If you select the Legend Page option button, Project prints the legend on its own separate page, so that there is more room for the schedule's graphical information on the other printed pages. This is typically the best option for Gantt chart printouts; otherwise, the legend takes up about half of each page. The None option causes the printout to have no legend at all. You can control how wide the legend area is with the entry in the Width text box. If you need more room in the legend area—to include more detailed text in the legend, for example—double-click on the Width text box and type the new setting you want to use. Click on the Legend Labels button to open the Font dialog box, where you can choose the settings you want for formatting the text in the Legend. Chapter 16, "Other Formatting," covers how to use the Font dialog box.

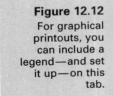

Figure 12.12
For graphical printouts, you can include a legend—and set it up—on this tab.

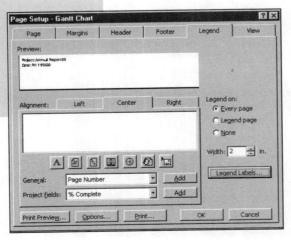

View Tab Settings

In the Page Setup dialog box, click on the final tab, called the View tab, to set a few final options specific to the selected view. Figure 12.13 shows how this tab looks for Gantt Chart view. Here's how to work with each of the listed options, when they're available:

- **Print All Sheet Columns.** When a view contains a chart with a timescale, Project prints only the columns in the accompanying Task Sheet or Resource Sheet that appear onscreen. If you drag the split bar so that only one sheet column is visible, then only that column prints. Click to select the Print All Sheet Columns check box if you want to print all the sheet columns, not just the presently displayed columns.

- **Print First . . . Columns On All Pages.** If you want to choose exactly how many columns in a Task Sheet or Resource Sheet to print, click to select this check box and then, in the accompanying text box, enter the number of columns to print. You can only use this option if you're printing a view that includes information charted on a timescale. This option doesn't always behave as you'd expect, however. If your printout is more than a page deep and more than a page wide, then all the far-left pages include the visible columns, not the number of columns you specify here. Thus, you ideally want to use this option only when you're sure that the printout will be one page deep but many pages wide. If you can't ensure that, then you'll have to drag the vertical split bar in the view to adjust the number of visible columns.

Figure 12.13
Fine-tune how your view prints by using the options on this tab.

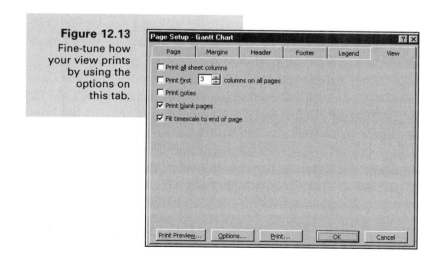

- **Print Notes.** When you click to select this option for the views where it's available, Project prints the notes you entered for a task or resource, depending on the view you are printing, on a separate page at the end of the printout.

- **Print Blank Pages.** For some of the views that contain charted information, you might end up with pages that don't actually contain any data. An example is the lower-left page of any Gantt chart printout that's more than one page deep and one page wide. If you want to save paper by not printing these blank pages, clear the check mark beside this option. However, if you plan to assemble the multiple pages of your printout into a large, single chart—perhaps by taping them together and hanging them on the wall of your office—leave this option selected.

- **Fit Timescale To End Of Page.** You saw earlier in this chapter that if your printer allows it, you can scale your printout by a certain percentage to control how small or large it prints. That's somewhat of an eyeball approach, and it doesn't ensure that your schedule fits neatly on the printed pages. You might end up, for example, with half a blank page at the end of your printout. If you want to ensure that the graphical portion of your printout (the timescale) takes advantage of all the available space on your pages, make sure that this check box is selected. Project then stretches the timescale (for example, by making each day take up slightly more space) to ensure that the graphical information fills the last printout page.

Controlling Page Breaks

You just learned that in any view that combines a Task Sheet or Resource Sheet with graphical or timescale information at the right side of the page, you must drag the vertical split bar to control how many columns of the sheet appear in the printout.

In addition, you might want to control which rows of task or resource information appear on each page of a printout. For example, you might know that you entered a milestone task in row 15 of your Task Sheet. You can control where the pages break in printouts of Gantt Chart view, Resource Usage view, and Task Sheets or Resource Sheets by inserting a manual page break. A manual page break tells Project to stop printing on the current page with a particular row and to begin the next page down with the information in the next row.

Tip

Manual page breaks don't affect how many pages wide your printout is. They only affect how many pages tall it is.

To add a manual page break, follow these steps:

1. Switch to the view you want to print.

2. In the Task Sheet or Resource Sheet, click to select a cell in the row that should be at the top of a new page. (You also can select the whole row by clicking its row number.) Project will insert the manual break above the selected row.

3. Choose Insert, Page Break. Project inserts a dotted line in the sheet to show you where the page break will occur (see Figure 12.14).

Your inserted page breaks do not work immediately, so if you go directly to the Print Preview (described in the next section), you won't see your inserted page breaks. You have to turn on a print option for the manual page breaks to take effect. To do so, choose File, Print to display the Print dialog box. Click to check the Manual Page Breaks check box. Then you can either click on the Preview button in the Print dialog box to display the Print Preview and see your manual page breaks or click on OK to send the print job to the printer.

Figure 12.14
A manual page break appears as a dotted line above the row you selected.

Inserted page break

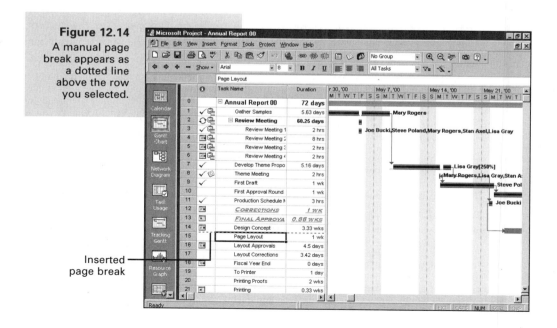

Caution

> Inserted page breaks can cause unexpected results in printed reports (see Chapter 14, "Creating and Printing a Report," for an in-depth look at reports). I recommend that you remove manual page breaks after you use them, unless you're sure that you won't be working with any reports.

To remove manual page breaks, either select the row just below the break by clicking on its row number, or click on the Select All button in the upper-left corner of the sheet. Choose Insert, Remove All Page Breaks.

Previewing the Printing

You've been diligent. You selected the proper view to print and designated which table columns should print and where you want page breaks to appear. You chose the correct printer and adjusted its properties, and double-checked all the options in the Page Setup dialog box. Despite all this, you still might not have a good idea how your printout will look.

You can waste a lot of paper by repeatedly printing your schedule and then making adjustments to ensure that the final version is exactly what you want. Or you can preview the print job onscreen, make any necessary adjustments, and only create a hard copy when it's right. To switch to the print preview for the current view of your schedule, click on the Print Preview button on the Standard toolbar. (It's the fifth button from the left and looks like a page with a magnifying glass over it.) Alternately, you can choose File, Print Preview. A preview version of your printout appears onscreen, as shown in Figure 12.15.

At first, Print Preview shows you the first page of your printout in a reduced view that provides a look at the overall page layout. You'll see whether the printout includes a legend (the one in Figure 12.15 does), how the margin spacing looks around the data, where the headers and footers appear, and more.

If the printout includes more than one page, you can use the left and right arrow keys to move forward and backward through the pages. The up and down arrows only activate if there are too many rows to fit on a single page. You can use the up and down arrows to view the extra rows, which will be on separate pages when you print the hard copy.

You might, however, want to zoom in to read particular details in the printout before printing; for example, you might want to check to see if a heading you

Arrows

Zoom in

Show one full page

Show multiple pages

Command buttons

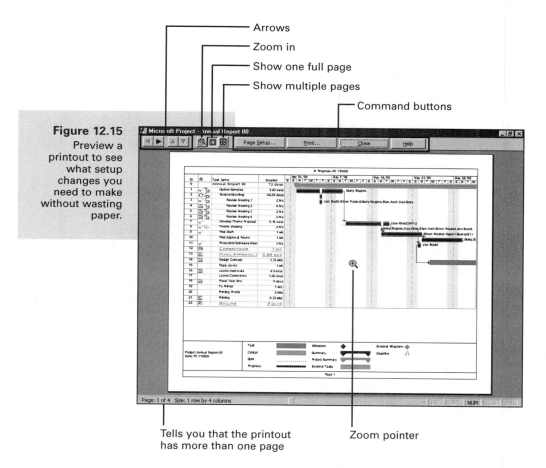

Tells you that the printout has more than one page

Zoom pointer

added looks the way you want it to. You can either click on the Zoom button at the top of the preview to zoom in on the upper-left corner of the page, or use the zoom pointer to zoom in on a specific area. After you've zoomed in, you can click on the button for displaying one full page (this button has a page on it) to return to the default view.

If the printout has more than one page and you want to view multiple pages, perhaps to see how the information is divided between pages, click on the button that looks like a stack of papers. Project displays multiple pages of the printout onscreen, as shown in Figure 12.16. Again, to return to the default view, click on the button for displaying one full page.

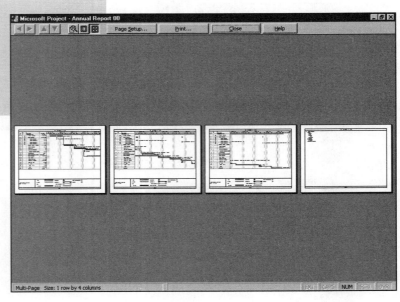

If the printout doesn't look the way you want it to, you need to make changes. Making most changes requires you to return to the normal schedule view, so click on the Close button to exit the print preview. In other cases, you can make your changes directly from the preview. For example, you may think that you've squeezed the printout into too few pages, making the information small and difficult to read. If you need to change a page setup option in such a case, click on the Page Setup button at the top of the preview to open the Page Setup dialog box. Make the needed changes, then click on OK to close the Page Setup dialog box. If the preview then meets with your approval, click on the Print button at the top of the Print Preview to go directly to the Print dialog box and complete the printout, as explained in the next section.

Finishing the Print Job

Figure 12.17 shows the Print dialog box, which you saw earlier in this chapter when you learned to select and set up a printer. To open the Print dialog box from any view but the Print Preview, choose File, Print (or press Ctrl+P). (Click on the Print button in the Print Preview view to display the Print dialog box.)

Print button

Print Preview button

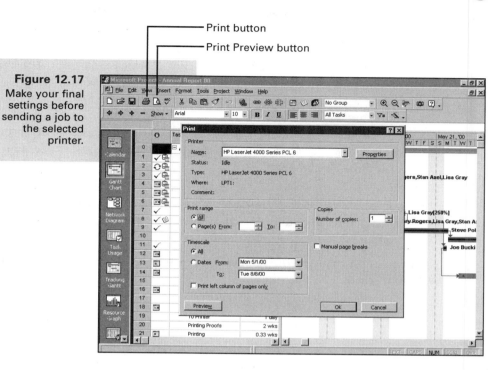

Figure 12.17
Make your final settings before sending a job to the selected printer.

If you want to print your schedule without going through the Print dialog box to specify final options, click on the Print button on the Standard toolbar. When you print using this method, Project automatically prints with the current printer settings and current Page Setup options.

The settings in the Print dialog box override any settings you made elsewhere, such as when you initially set up your printer. Here's a review of the final choices you can make from this dialog box before sending your schedule to the printer:

- In the Print Range area, leave the All option button selected to print all the pages in your schedule. Or, if your printout includes more than one page and you don't want to print the entire document, click on the Page(s) From radio button, and then enter the page number of the first page you want to print. In the To text box, enter the page number of the last page you want to print.

- To print more than one copy, change the entry in the Number Of Copies text box.

- You can use the Timescale options to control which tasks print. Leave the All option button selected to print all the tasks. To print only tasks starting within a particular range of dates, click on the Dates From option button and enter the starting date for the range in that text box. In the To text box, enter the ending date for the range. If you want only one page's worth of Timescale tasks to print, click to select the Print Left Column Of Pages Only check box.

- When the Manual Page Breaks check box is selected, the printout uses any manual page breaks you inserted. If you don't want to remove the page breaks you set up, but don't want Project to use them for this particular printout, clear the check box for this option.

After you finish changing the Print dialog box settings as needed, click on OK to send your schedule to the printer.

13

Working with Forms

IN THIS CHAPTER

- Understanding forms
- Creating a custom form

In Chapter 11, "Working with the Different Project Views," you learned how to change the view that Project uses to display and organize your schedule information onscreen. You learned that some views include (either alone or with other types of information) forms that are intended to make it easier to enter and edit information.

This chapter shows you how to work with forms on their own, rather than working with them as part of a view.

Understanding Forms

In the '70s, people had to communicate with programs run on large mainframe computers using punch cards. They would punch a pattern of holes on a card, and the computer would read (and presumably understand) the data from the card. For obvious reasons, this was one of many factors that discouraged people from working with computers—so that computing became a geeks-only affair.

Over time, many easier ways of communicating with programs have evolved. So far, you've seen that in Project you can enter information via spreadsheet-like tables or sheets, by dragging on a Gantt Chart or Network Diagram chart, via dialog boxes, and more. Forms are yet another method for entering data.

Forms resemble dialog boxes in that they include text boxes to let you enter and edit information and also look at other information such as calculated costs that you cannot edit. Although some views consist solely of a large form—or include a form in a lower pane—you can also display a form in its own floating dialog box (see Figure 13.1).

Project offers some forms for resource information (see Figure 13.2) and others for task information. Table 13.1 lists the predefined forms available in Project.

Table 13.1 Task Forms and Resource Forms in Project

Form Name	Description
Task Forms	
Cost Tracking	Displays cost information for the selected task, including baseline budget, current budget, and actual costs to the current date or status date based on work performed.
Earned Value	Displays earned value and cost variance information, such as the earned value schedule variance and cost variance (see Chapter 10 to learn more about costs); only lets you edit the task name and completion percentage.
Entry	Enables you to enter or edit basic information about the selected task, including its name, duration, start date, and finish date.
PERT Entry	When you're using PERTAnalysis, as described in Chapter 11, use this form to enter optimistic, expected, and pessimistic durations for the selected task.
Schedule Tracking	Shows the selected task's baseline and currently scheduled start and finish dates, and calculates the variance between the original and current dates.
Task Relationships	Displays and lets you edit the predecessors and successors linked to the selected task.
Tracking	Lets you enter actual start and finish dates, as well as completion information, for the selected task.
Work Tracking	Allows you to enter actual start and finish dates, as well as completion information, for the selected task.
Resource Forms	
Cost Tracking	Displays cost information for the resource selected in the Resource Sheet, including baseline cost, total cost (currently budgeted), and actual cost for work performed to date (or to the status date); none of these values can be edited.
Entry	Enables you to edit the basic information defining the resource, such as the resource's name, initials, and standard rate.
Summary	Summarizes the amount of work and budget for costs scheduled for the resource, including the amount of work assigned, Max Units, and cost and work variances.
Work Tracking	Displays the amount of work scheduled for a resource, the percentage completed, and variance in work completed to date or to the status date; these calculations can't be edited.

Figure 13.1
When you display a form independent of a view, it appears in its own dialog box.

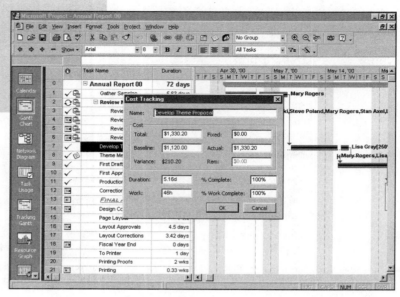

Figure 13.2
Here's an example of a form displaying resource information.

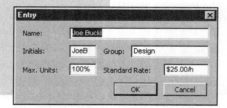

Selecting a Form

The process for selecting a form differs a bit from selecting some of the other types of view information, because there's no way to directly display a form via a menu or submenu choice. You have to use the Custom Forms dialog box, as described in the following steps:

1. From the Task Sheet or Resource Sheet, select the task or resource for which you want to display form information by clicking the Task Name or Resource Name cell in the appropriate row.

Note

> If you're working in a task view, you can't display resource forms, and vice versa. Thus it's critical to select a task or resource view to ensure that the correct form choices are available.

2. Choose Tools, Customize, Forms. The Customize Forms dialog box appears (see Figure 13.3).

3. In the Forms list, select the form you want by double-clicking on its name (or by clicking on the name once and then clicking on Apply). Project closes the Customize Forms dialog box and displays the form you selected onscreen.

4. If you need to edit any information in the form (assuming the form offers editable text boxes), double-click in each text box and then edit its contents.

5. Click on OK when you finish with the form.

Figure 13.3
Use this dialog box to select and manage forms.

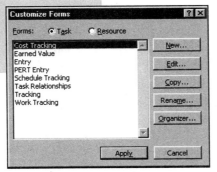

Creating a Custom Form

You might find that none of the custom forms in Project capture the information you want to show. For example, you might need a quick way to check actual task costs along with the resource name and group, in order to keep an eye on how much work by another department in your company you'll need to pay for. That is, you may want to track the costs that are coming from your project budget for work performed by resources from another group.

Project allows you to create your own custom forms, and to do so you don't need any programming experience. You simply need to be able to click and drag. You can add text to your form, or you can add information from any field in the Task Sheet or Resource Sheet. If a field contains a calculated value that you shouldn't edit, Project automatically formats the field so that it can't be edited on your form.

While there's a nearly infinite number of custom forms that you can create, the following steps and the example shown with them should give you a good start. Afterward, you can experiment on your own to discover the combinations of form information you'll find most useful.

ON THE

CD

I suggest reusing the *Annual Report Chapter 10* file if you need a file to practice with.

1. Choose Tools, Customize, Forms. The Customize Forms dialog box appears.

2. Click on either the Task or Resource option button at the top of the dialog box to indicate whether your form will display information from the Task Sheet or Resource Sheet. This is a critical step, because your choice here affects which fields you can add to your form.

3. Click on the New button. The Define Custom Form dialog box appears (see Figure 13.4).

4. Enter the form name in the Name text box. For example, if you're creating a form showing actual task cost, resource name, and resource group information, you might enter **Cost and Group**.

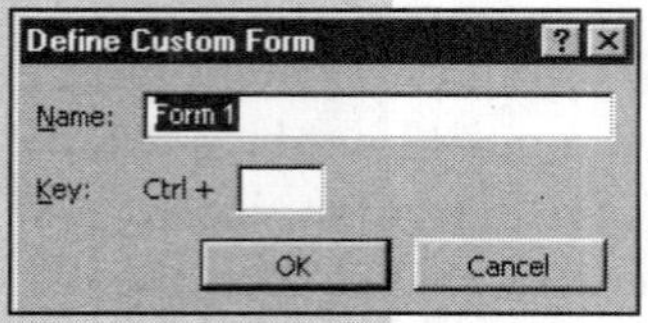

Figure 13.4
This dialog box enables you to begin defining your custom form.

Define Custom Form

Name: Form 1

Key: Ctrl +

OK   Cancel

5. If you want to be able to use a shortcut key combination to display the custom form, enter the second key for the combination in the Key text box. Project allows only letters here; you can't enter numbers, function keys, or special characters such as punctuation marks.

6. Click on OK to continue defining the form. Project displays the Custom Form Editor, with a new blank form background, as shown in Figure 13.5. Notice that the toolbar tools have been hidden, and that the available menus have changed to reflect that you're working with the Form Editor functions.

7. By default, a dotted outline appears around the border of the blank form dialog box to indicate that this box is selected. (If this boundary outline doesn't appear, you can display it by choosing Edit, Select Dialog.) If needed, you can change the size of the form by clicking and dragging the dotted line on any side of the dialog box, as shown in Figure 13.6.

8. Now it's time to begin adding elements to the form. Usually, you'll want to add a text label for each field you display. To add a text label, choose Item, Text. Project adds placeholder text to the form, surrounded by dotted boundary lines. Point to this text so that a four-headed arrow appears (see Figure 13.7), then drag it to a different location. You can adjust the size of the text by dragging one of its boundary lines.

Figure 13.5

Create custom forms with the Custom Form Editor shown here.

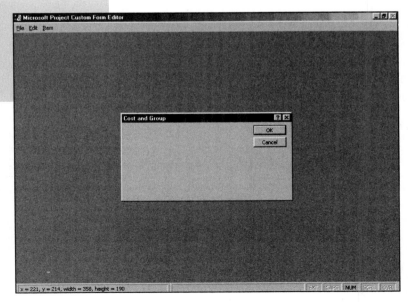

Figure 13.6
It's easy to resize the form by clicking and dragging its boundary lines.

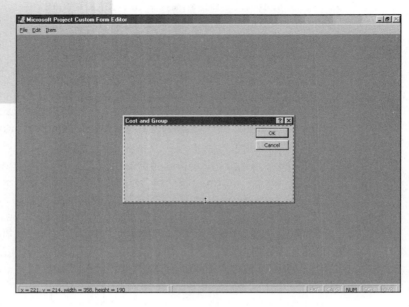

Figure 13.7
You can drag the text box placeholder into the position you prefer on the form.

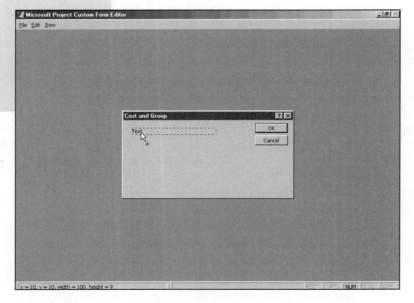

9. After you position and size the text placeholder, double-click on it on the form (or choose Edit, Information). The Item Information dialog box appears, as shown in Figure 13.8.

10. You shouldn't need to edit any of the top four text boxes, because you already defined the placeholder's size and position in Step 8. Simply double-click in the Text text box, and then type the text you want to appear in that area of the form—for example, I'll type **Task Name**. Click on OK to close the Item Information dialog box.

11. To add a field to the form, choose Item, Fields. Project opens the Item Information dialog box immediately, because you have to specify which field to display.

12. Click on the Field down arrow and then click on the name of the field you want to appear on the form. For example, I'll select Name to display the task name, as shown in Figure 13.9.

13. If you know that a field typically appears in an editable format on forms—as the Name field usually does—then click to check the Show As Static Text check box if you want Project not to enable editing of that field information in your form.

Figure 13.8
After you place an item on the form, you need to edit the information it displays.

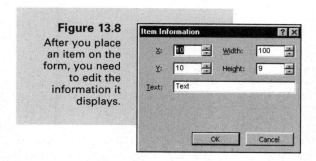

Figure 13.9
Tell Project what field information you want displayed on the form.

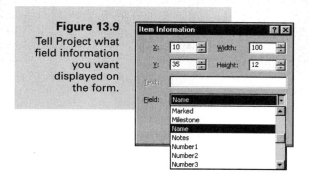

14. Click on OK. The field appears on the form, ready for you to resize and drag into place (see Figure 13.10).

To delete any item you added to a form, click on the item once so that a dotted selection line appears around it, and then press the Delete key.

15. Continue adding items to the form, using the same general process of making a choice from the Item menu, using the Item Information dialog box (if needed) to define what the item displays, resizing the item, and dragging it into position. For example, Figure 13.11 shows my completed form. I've used the Group Box selection on the Item menu to create the Stats box.

16. Choose File, Save to save your form with the name you provided in Step 4.

17. Choose File, Exit. Project closes the Form Editor and returns to the Customize Forms dialog box. Your new form appears there, as shown in Figure 13.12.

Figure 13.10
A field has just been added to the form.

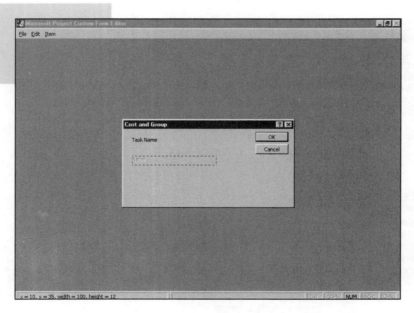

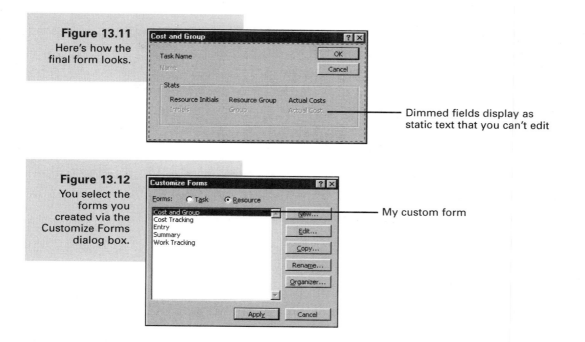

Figure 13.11
Here's how the final form looks.

Dimmed fields display as static text that you can't edit

Figure 13.12
You select the forms you created via the Customize Forms dialog box.

My custom form

18. At this point, if you displayed the appropriate sheet before creating the form, you can double-click on the form name to display it. (If you're at the wrong sheet view, you have to close the Customize Forms dialog box, switch to the appropriate sheet, redisplay the Customize Forms dialog box, and then select your form.) Figure 13.13 shows how my custom form appears when displayed.

It takes a little practice, but soon you can create a variety of useful forms. Pay attention to every detail if you want to achieve professional results. For example, make sure that your text boxes and field boxes align at both the left and right sides of the form whenever possible, and make sure that information looks centered when you intend it to. Also, make sure you're creating the right type of form. You can only display custom task forms in a task-oriented view like the Gantt Chart or Task Usage views. You can only display custom resource forms from a resource-oriented view like the Resource Sheet or Resource Usage view.

Custom forms that you create are saved only with the current project file, until you either copy them to Project's GLOBAL.MPT master file or delete them. To make a form available to all files or to delete a form, click on the Organizer button in the Customize Forms dialog box and use the Forms tab of the Organizer to make your changes. Chapter 11, "Working with the Different Project Views," discusses working with the Organizer.

Figure 13.13
A custom form that you create can look just as good as the forms that come with Project.

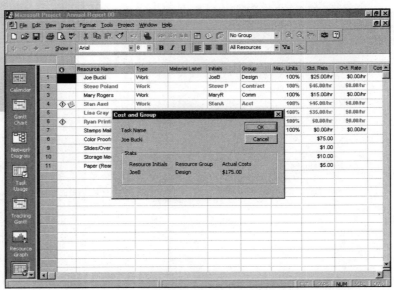

Creating a Toolbar Button or Menu Command to Display a Form

Note that each form only lets you display information about one task or resource at a time. Unlike forms used as part of a view, forms that you display on their own don't offer Previous and Next buttons to allow you to display information about other resources or tasks without closing the form. Because using the Tools menu to display a form over and over can become tedious and a shortcut key can be difficult to remember, you might want to create a toolbar button or menu command that displays this form.

Here are the steps for adding such a toolbar button or menu command (see Chapter 24, "Customizing Microsoft Project," for an in-depth look at creating menu commands and toolbar buttons):

1. Choose Tools, Customize, Toolbars, or right-click on any toolbar and then choose Customize.

2. Click on the Commands tab in the Customize dialog box.

3. Scroll down the Categories list on the tab; then click on All Forms in the list.

4. In the Commands list on the tab, click on the name of the form you want to create a button or command for; then drag the form name from the Customize dialog box onto the appropriate toolbar or menu.

Caution

Although you can change an existing toolbar button so that it displays a form rather than executing its currently assigned command, I don't recommend doing so, because it might prove very difficult (or impossible) to recall what the button's original command was if you ever want to reinstate it.

5. Right-click on the form name you just dragged onto the toolbar to display a shortcut menu with options for customizing the button or menu command (see Figure 13.14). Chapter 24 explains how to use the commands on this shortcut menu to control such features as the icon that appears on a button, the menu command name, and more. Refer to that chapter for details about using the shortcut menu.

I dragged this form
onto the toolbar

Figure 13.14
You can customize a toolbar button or menu command with this shortcut menu.

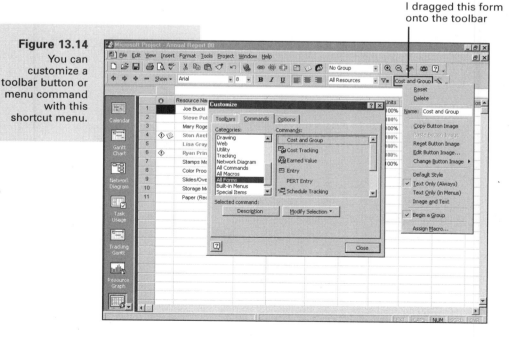

6. After you finish using the shortcut menu to make changes to the new button or command, click on Close to finish creating the button and close the Customize dialog box. Figure 13.15 shows an example form button.

Figure 13.15

I've added a custom form toolbar button near the right end of the Formatting toolbar; its ScreenTip is displayed.

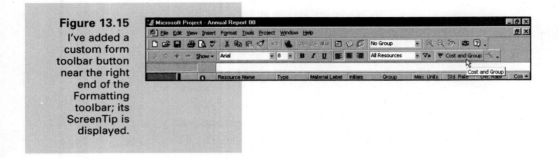

14

Creating and Printing a Report

IN THIS CHAPTER

- Learning what predesigned reports Project offers
- Selecting the correct report
- Fine-tuning and printing a report
- Designing a unique report

Software developers have placed a good deal of emphasis on offering more ways to work with the information you gather in a particular program. That's because the typical businessperson needs to share information with a variety of audiences, and each audience needs only a particular subset of the information. For a Project file, for example, you might need to prepare a weekly report of the current expenses for a project to give to your boss, a listing of upcoming tasks to give to the participants in a planning meeting, or a weekly to-do list for yourself to tickle your memory about issues you need to follow up on.

Project can generate these kinds of reports (and more) automatically. This chapter introduces you to reporting in Project.

Understanding the Report Types

The predefined reports offered in Project provide the most common types of summary information that you might need to provide to others within (and outside of) your organization. In Chapter 12, "Proofing and Printing a View," you learned how to select and filter different views for printing and to control the information appearing in your printout. Although that method of selecting and printing information works fine in many cases, it has a few drawbacks:

- It frequently requires several steps to display just the facts you want to see.
- You often can't capture totals for data in the format you prefer.
- There are some kinds of lists you just can't print from a view, such as a list of working days for the schedule.

Project's reports address these issues for you, providing a streamlined approach for selecting and printing information. In addition, using a report rather than printing a view yields a printout with an attractive layout that's suitable for distribution to readers whom you need to impress. Finally, the reports capture information in key columns; there's no need for the reader to wade through extraneous data in a report printout.

To create reports in Project, you work with the Reports dialog box. To open the Reports dialog box, start from any view. Choose View, Reports; the Reports dialog box appears (see Figure 14.1). This dialog box offers five icons (pictures) of different categories of reports: Overview, Current Activities, Costs, Assignments, and Workload. The sixth icon, Custom, enables you to create your own reports, as described later in this chapter, in the "Creating a Custom Report" section.

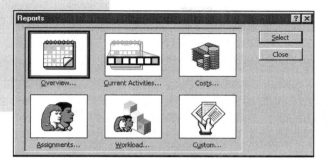

Figure 14.1
Use this dialog box to select from the report categories offered in Project.

To select a report category, click on the icon for the category and then click on Select (or simply double-click on the icon). Project displays a dialog box showing the different kinds of reports available in that category, including an icon for each report that shows a thumbnail view of what the report looks like. There's not room in this book to show you a printout of every report type, but the rest of this section introduces you to the reports in each category via the dialog box for that category. The reports that work best for you will depend on what information you're required to report to others, as well as how concerned you are about having frequent updates on specific information such as upcoming tasks or tasks that are under way. After you review the dialog boxes shown here for the various report categories, spend some time on your own experimenting to discover which reports you prefer to work with.

Clicking on Cancel from any dialog box listing specific reports closes that dialog box and returns you to the Reports dialog box.

Overview Reports

When you select the Overview Reports icon in the Reports dialog box, the Overview Reports dialog box appears (see Figure 14.2).

Current Activities Reports

The next category of reports, Current Activities, appears in the Current Activity Reports dialog box (see Figure 14.3), which appears after you select Current Activities in the Reports dialog box.

Reviews the numbers of tasks and resources, schedule by project and task, costs, and start and finish dates

Shows the tasks in the top outline level, including summary tasks and notes

Displays critical tasks, summary and successor tasks, and notes

Figure 14.2
Reports that provide project summaries at a glance.

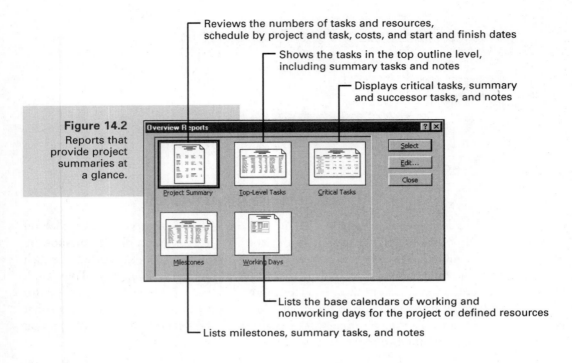

Lists the base calendars of working and nonworking days for the project or defined resources

Lists milestones, summary tasks, and notes

Lists tasks for which work hasn't started

Creates a list of upcoming tasks, along with needed resources and notes

Provides a month-by-month overview of tasks for which work has begun but has not been completed

Figure 14.3
Reports that provide project summaries at a glance.

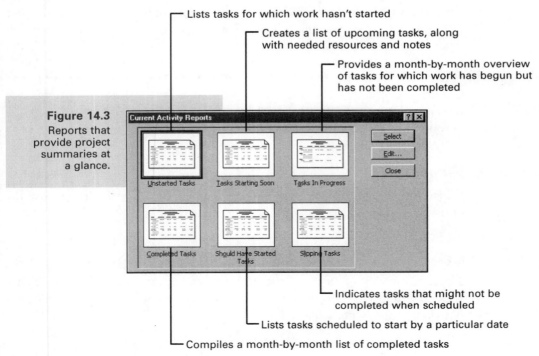

Indicates tasks that might not be completed when scheduled

Lists tasks scheduled to start by a particular date

Compiles a month-by-month list of completed tasks

Note

Two of the report types in the Current Activities category, **Tasks Starting Soon** and **Should Have Started Tasks,** require you to enter dates. Whenever Project prompts you to enter a date, type it using mm/dd/yy format, and then click on **OK** to continue.

Costs Reports

To take a look at the dollars and cents you're spending on your project, select the Costs category in the Reports dialog box to display the report types shown in Figure 14.4. It's likely that you'll get a lot of mileage from these report formats, as one of the key aspects of project management is monitoring the bottom line and adjusting planned expenditures as required. These reports not only compile the expenses you specify, but also total various expenses by column (category).

Assignments Reports

The Assignments selection in the Reports dialog box displays four report types (see Figure 14.5). Although you can print much of the same information by printing a Gantt chart, the reports summarize the information in a more

Compiles a week-by-week summary of costs for each task

Summarizes the total project budget, from the most expensive task to the least expensive

Lets you know which tasks might cost more than you've planned

Figure 14.4
These reports track and sum up costs.

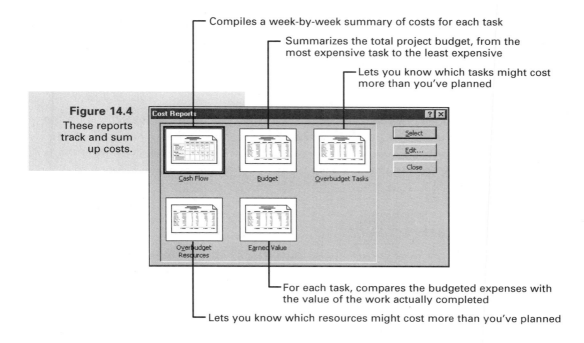

For each task, compares the budgeted expenses with the value of the work actually completed

Lets you know which resources might cost more than you've planned

Lists all task schedules

Lists tasks assigned to each resource, with scheduled work dates and hours

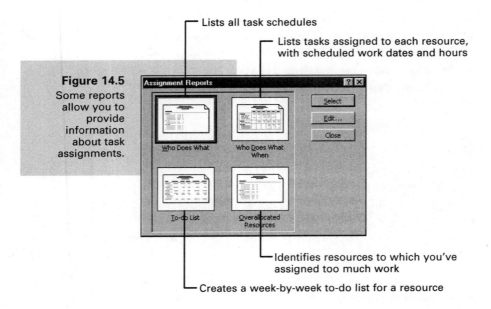

Figure 14.5
Some reports allow you to provide information about task assignments.

Identifies resources to which you've assigned too much work

Creates a week-by-week to-do list for a resource

accessible format that's suitable for presentation. For example, you can bind them as part of a project plan to be distributed at a meeting.

Two of these reports provide particularly valuable management tools. The To-Do List lets you prepare a list of all the scheduled tasks for a selected resource you select, when prompted, from the Using Resource dialog box. The Overallocated Resources report provides you with ammunition you might need to help you request more resources for a project—or for particular tasks—during a given time frame, by showing when currently available resources have too many assignments.

Note

Surprisingly, when you generate a To-Do List report, it doesn't display the name of the resource for whom that list applies! My suggestion for handling this is to use the Page Setup button from the Print Preview of the report to add the resource's name into the report header or footer.

Workload Reports

While the Assignments reports focus on enabling you to view work schedules by resource, the two reports available when you select Workload in the Reports dialog box enable you to examine the total workload scheduled during each week of the project. The schedule can be grouped by either Task Usage or Resource Usage (see Figure 14.6).

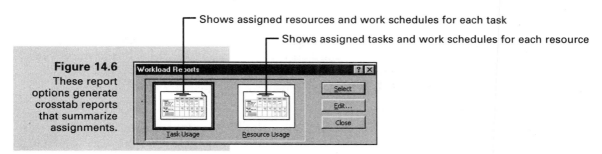

Shows assigned resources and work schedules for each task

Shows assigned tasks and work schedules for each resource

Figure 14.6
These report options generate crosstab reports that summarize assignments.

The Workload reports and some of the other reports you've seen are referred to as *crosstab* reports because they present information in rows and columns over intervals of time. At the intersection of each row and column is a cell with specific information about the resource or task listed in that row, on the date indicated by the selected column.

Selecting, Setting up, and Printing a Report

As noted at the beginning of this chapter, the report creation process begins with the Reports dialog box. After you select the report you want, Project compiles the report information and displays the report onscreen in Print Preview mode. When the report is onscreen, you can make modifications to its layout before printing it out. This section describes how you can tackle these tasks.

To select the report you want to work with and print out, open the project file for which you want to create the report, and then follow these steps:

1. Choose View, Reports. The Reports dialog box appears.

Caution

> **Be sure that you expand all subtasks in the Gantt Chart view before printing the report. If you don't expand the subtasks, the report won't include detail information.**

2. In the Reports dialog box, select the category of report you want by double-clicking on a category icon. Project displays the dialog box for the report category you selected.

3. Select the thumbnail icon for the type of report you want to use. Do so by double-clicking on the icon.

4. Some report types require you to specify a date or resource name, and prompt you to do so with a dialog box (see Figure 14.7). If a date is requested, enter it in mm/dd/yy format. If the dialog box prompts you to select a resource, do so using the drop-down list that's presented. After you specify either a date or a resource, click on OK to finish. (Some report formats prompt you for another date; if this happens, enter the date and click on OK again to finish.)

After you complete the preceding steps, Project compiles the report and presents it onscreen for viewing, fine-tuning, or printing.

You might encounter instances, however, when you have selected a report type that Project cannot compile, or have entered a date for which there's no data to report. For example, if you try to print a report about Slipping Tasks from the Current Activities category, and there are no tasks that are behind schedule on the date on which you try to print the report, Project displays the dialog box shown in Figure 14.8. Click on OK to close the message dialog box, and Project returns you to the Reports dialog box so that you can try again. Select a different report type, or try specifying a different date for the report you want.

Whenever you want to close the preview area where the report appears, click on the Close button near the top of the screen. Project returns to the Reports dialog box. Click on the Cancel button to close that dialog box and return to the active view for the project file.

Figure 14.7
Project may prompt you to specify a date or select a resource about which to report.

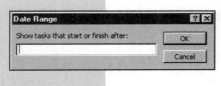

Figure 14.8
This message tells you there's no information to print for the report or date you specified.

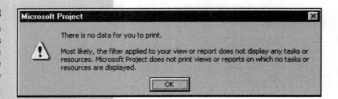

Navigating in the Report

The report you selected appears onscreen in a Print Preview view similar to the one you learned about in Chapter 12. This view offers a few special tools and icons that enable you to view different parts of the report, or to take a closer look at particular items in the report (see Figure 14.9).

Use the left and right arrow keys to move forward and backward through the pages in the report. The up and down arrows are enabled only if there are too many rows to appear in a single report page. You can use the up and down arrows to view the extra rows, which appear on separate pages if the report is printed.

By default, you'll see one page of the report, shown in a size that keeps the whole page visible in the preview. You might, however, want to zoom in to read particular details in the report before printing. You can click on the Zoom button at the top of the preview to zoom in on the upper-left corner of the report, or use the zoom pointer to zoom in on a specific cell. After you zoom in, click on the button for displaying one full page (the button has a page on it) to return to the default view.

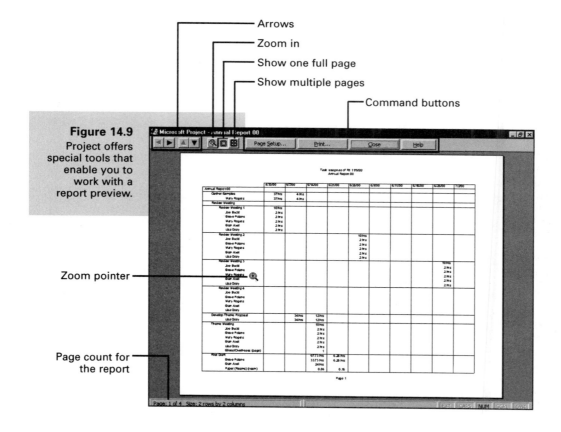

Figure 14.9
Project offers special tools that enable you to work with a report preview.

Arrows
Zoom in
Show one full page
Show multiple pages
Command buttons
Zoom pointer
Page count for the report

If the report has more than one page and you want to view multiple pages, perhaps to see how the information is divided between pages, click on the button that looks like a stack of papers. Project displays multiple pages of the report onscreen. Again, to return to the default view, click on the button for displaying one full page.

Obviously, you won't always want to print the reports you generate. Reports often are a fast way to check information such as the current budget total. You can generate the report, zoom in to check a detail or two, and then click on the Close button to exit the preview and the Cancel button to close the Reports dialog box.

Viewing Setup Options

As you learned in Chapter 12, "Proofing and Printing a View," you have control over numerous aspects of how a printout appears. For example, you can adjust margins to allow for more or less space around printed data, or you can specify whether a page number appears on every page. You adjust these options using the Page Setup dialog box, which you open from the Print Preview view by clicking on the Page Setup button at the top of the screen. The Page Setup dialog box for the report appears (see Figure 14.10).

Although the dialog box offers six tabs, two of them aren't available for many reports. These are the Legend and View tabs, which offer options that apply when you're printing certain charts and views. Additionally, other tabs may become disabled (grayed out) when you select a report type for which they don't apply. For example, you cannot adjust the header or footer for a Project Summary report.

Figure 14.10
This dialog box allows you to adjust how the final printout will look.

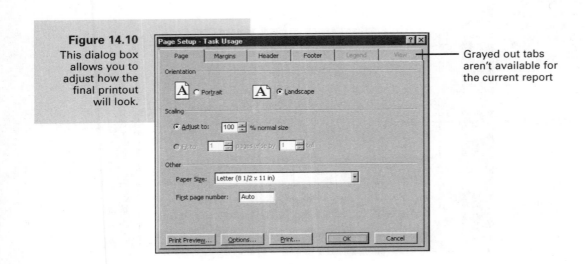

Grayed out tabs aren't available for the current report

As you learned in Chapter 12, to change a page setup option in the Page Setup dialog box, first click to select the tab that offers the option, then make your changes. Finally, click on OK to close the Page Setup dialog box (or click on Print to send the report to the printer). The four tabs of available Page Setup options for reports are as follows:

- **Page.** Enables you to specify whether the printout is wide (Landscape) or tall (Portrait); also lets you scale the printed information by entering a size percentage, choose another paper size, or specify the page number to use for the first page of the report printout.

- **Margins.** Allows you to enter a separate measurement for the margin for each of the four page edges, or to specify a printed border for report pages.

- **Header.** Enables you to edit the header that appears at the top of the report pages (see Figure 14.11), including what it contains (page number, company names, and so on) and whether it's centered or aligned left or right (see Chapter 12 for more information about creating printout headers and footers).

- **Footer.** Offers options similar to those found on the Header tab, but places the specified text at the bottom of each printed report page.

Printing

After you check the Page Setup dialog box to ensure that you chose the report you need and have made any changes you want, you're ready to print your report. To initiate the print process, click on the Print button found in either the Page Setup dialog box or the Print Preview screen. The Print dialog box appears.

Figure 14.11
You can specify the header for the report pages on the Header tab; the Footer tab is nearly identical.

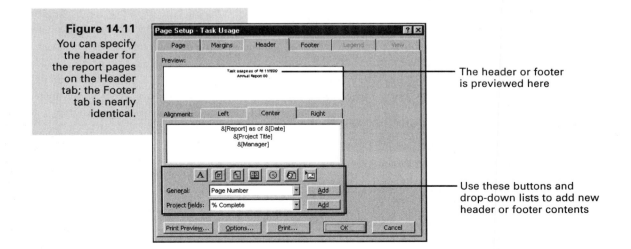

The header or footer is previewed here

Use these buttons and drop-down lists to add new header or footer contents

This dialog box is covered as part of Chapter 12's in-depth look at printing; however, a few options in the dialog box might be particularly attractive to you when you're printing reports. They are as follows:

- **Print Range.** By default, Project prints all pages in a report if the report has more than one page. You might, however, only want to print part of a report. To do so, click on the Page(s) From option button in the Print Range area, then enter the starting page in the From text box and the final page in the To text box. For example, enter 4 and 5 to print only pages 4 and 5 of the report.

- **Copies.** To print more than one copy at a time (such as 10 copies to distribute at a meeting), change the Number Of Copies text box by double-clicking on the current entry, and typing a new entry (such as 10).

- **Timescale.** Normally, unless a report by default asks you for a particular time frame, the report covers the full duration of the project schedule. If you want to print only the report pages that pertain to particular dates in the schedule, click to select the Dates From option button in the Timescale area. Then enter the starting date in the From box and the last date of the range you want to print in the To box.

After you specify the options you prefer in the Print dialog box, click on OK. Project sends the report to the printer and closes the print preview for the report. To close the Reports dialog box, which reappears onscreen after printing, click on Cancel.

Creating a Custom Report

The sixth category icon in the Reports dialog box, the Custom button, allows you to control various features of any available report, create a new report based on an already existing report, or start from scratch to build an entirely unique report to suit your needs. The report features you can change vary depending on the report you start working with. For some reports, such as the Project Summary report, you can only change the font and text formatting to adjust the report's appearance. For other reports, Project displays a dialog box enabling you to edit such elements of the report as its name, the time period it covers, the table it's based upon, filtering, and more.

To change, copy, or create a custom report, you work in the Custom Reports dialog box (see Figure 14.12). To open this dialog box, double-click on the Custom option in the Reports dialog box. The scrolling Reports list in this dialog box enables you to select a report to customize, if needed.

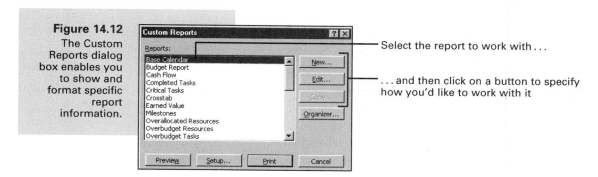

Figure 14.12

The Custom Reports dialog box enables you to show and format specific report information.

Select the report to work with . . .

. . . and then click on a button to specify how you'd like to work with it

From the Custom Reports dialog box, after you select a report in the Reports list, you can use the Preview button to display the selected report in Print Preview mode, the Setup button to go to the Page Setup dialog box for the report, or the Print button to go to the Print dialog box for the report. After selecting one of these buttons, you can work with the preview, setup, or printing options for the report just as described previously in this chapter. Click on Cancel to close the Custom Reports dialog box, and then click on Cancel to close the Reports dialog box.

Making Changes to an Existing Report

The fastest way to customize a report and arrive at both the report contents and formatting you need is to choose the report that most closely resembles what you want, and then make changes to it. To start this process, click on the name of the report to edit in the Reports list of the Custom Reports dialog box. Then click on the Edit button. Alternatively, you can click on the icon for a report in the dialog box for that report category, and then click on the Edit button (refer to Figures 14.2 through 14.6).

What happens next depends on the report you selected for editing. If you selected the Base Calendar or Project Summary report for editing, Project only allows you to change the fonts specified for the report, and therefore gives you the Report Text dialog box shown in Figure 14.13. Use the Item To Change drop-down list if you want the change to apply only to the Calendar Name or Detail information in the report; then use the Font, Font Style, and Size lists to select the text attributes you want. The sample area shows a preview of what your selections will look like when applied to text in the report. To underline the text, for example, select the Underline check box; to specify a color for text, use the Color drop-down list. After you've made the desired font selections, click on OK to implement your changes and return to the Custom Reports dialog box. From there, you can preview or print the edited report.

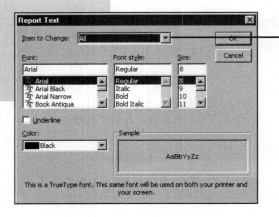

The Item To Change drop-down list

Caution

After you make changes to a report offered in your project file, the changes remain in effect until you specifically return the report to its original format. There's always a chance, however, that you might forget what the original format was. If you're planning to make major changes to a report, you're safer working from a copy of the original report, rather than working from the original.

For other reports you select from the Reports list, a different dialog box appears when you click on the Edit button. Depending on the selected report type, the dialog box that appears is named Task Report, Resource Report, or Crosstab Report. Each of these dialog boxes has three tabs, but the tab contents vary slightly, depending on the report category (as described next). After you specify the options you want in one of these dialog boxes, click on OK to implement your changes. From the Custom Reports dialog box, you then can preview, set up, or print the report.

Task Reports

A *task report* generally has the word "task" or "what" in its name in the Reports list of the Custom Reports dialog box. When you select one of these reports and then click on the Edit button, the Task Report dialog box appears (see Figure 14.14). The first tab of this dialog box, the Definition tab, enables you to work with the most basic information about the report, such as the report name. You might want to change the report name to reflect your changes, perhaps calling it "Weekly

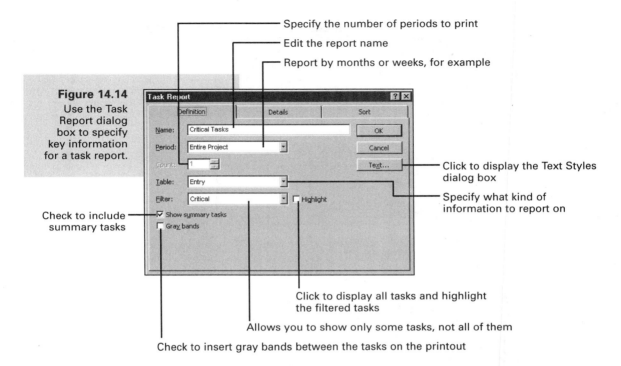

Figure 14.14
Use the Task Report dialog box to specify key information for a task report.

Specify the number of periods to print

Edit the report name

Report by months or weeks, for example

Click to display the Text Styles dialog box

Specify what kind of information to report on

Check to include summary tasks

Click to display all tasks and highlight the filtered tasks

Allows you to show only some tasks, not all of them

Check to insert gray bands between the tasks on the printout

Budget Report" instead of simply "Budget Report." This tab also allows you to control the time frame for which information is reported and to specify whether or not to apply a filter to display only some tasks in the project (Chapter 11, "Working with the Different Project Views," covers filtering in detail).

After you set the project definition options, click on the Details tab. The options on this tab (see Figure 14.15) control which details appear for the tasks you've chosen to display using the Definition tab.

Finally, click on the Sort tab to determine how to sort the tasks that appear in your report. Click to display the Sort By drop-down list (see Figure 14.16). Then choose the name of the field that contains the information by which you want to sort. Select Ascending or Descending to specify whether the information is sorted in A–Z (lowest-to-highest) order or Z–A (highest-to-lowest) order. For example, by default the Budget Report lists the most costly tasks first, but you might want to see the least expensive items first. To sort by other fields as well, use the additional drop-down lists provided on this tab. To specify that there's no field to sort by for one of the Then By drop-down lists in the Sort tab, select the blank line at the top of the drop-down list.

Figure 14.15
Here's where you specify which details appear in the report.

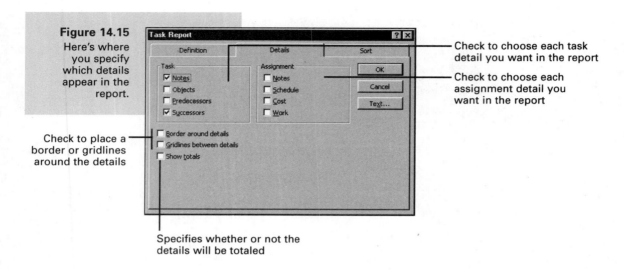

Check to choose each task detail you want in the report

Check to choose each assignment detail you want in the report

Check to place a border or gridlines around the details

Specifies whether or not the details will be totaled

Figure 14.16
The final touch in organizing your report is to sort it.

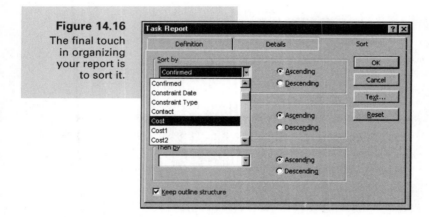

Resource Reports

A *resource report* provides information about resources, and generally includes the word "resource" or "who" in the report name. For example, the "Overallocated Resources" and "Who Does What" reports are both resource reports. When you select a resource report from the Reports list in the Custom Reports dialog box and then click on the Edit button, the Resource Report dialog box appears. This dialog box offers three tabs that look and work exactly like the tabs for the Task Report dialog box (refer to Figures 14.14 through 14.16).

Note

You can edit a resource report so that it shows resource cost rate tables, and then print that report. To do so, click on the Resource report in the Reports list of the Custom Reports dialog box, and then click on Edit. Click on the Details tab to select it; then click on the Cost check box to select it. Click on OK, and then click on the Preview button in the Custom Reports dialog box to display the edited report onscreen.

Crosstab Reports

A *crosstab report* is the last type of custom report you might want to customize. These reports summarize information in a grid of rows and columns and include reports such as Cash Flow. When you select a crosstab report from the Reports list in the Custom Reports dialog box and then click on the Edit button, the Crosstab Report dialog box appears (see Figure 14.17). You'll notice that the first tab here differs from that for the two previous report types. Use the Row drop-down list to specify whether the rows contain task or resource information. In the Column area, type an entry for how many units of time to display, and then (if needed) change the time unit type to something like Months using the drop-down list beside your entry. These choices determine how many columns appear in the crosstab (for example, eight weeks or two months). Then, in the drop-down list below your time selections, select what kind of information about the task or resource to display in each column below the date.

Specify what appears in each column

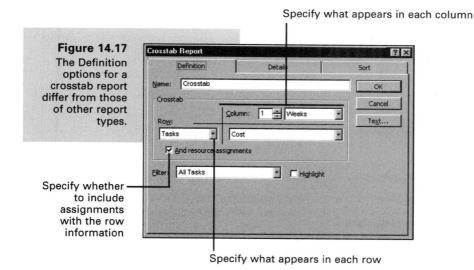

Figure 14.17
The Definition options for a crosstab report differ from those of other report types.

Specify whether to include assignments with the row information

Specify what appears in each row

The Details tab also offers a couple of unique choices for crosstab reports. On this tab, click to select the Show Zero Values check box if you want to have zeros displayed rather than blank cells. Make sure that the Repeat First Column On Every Page option is selected if you want to repeat the names of the listed tasks or resources on every report page for easier reference. Finally, use the Date Format drop-down list to control the appearance of any dates listed for your crosstab report.

The Sort tab for crosstab reports works just like the Sort tab for the Task Report dialog box (refer to Figure 14.16).

Creating a Report Based on an Existing Report

If you want to leave an existing report intact but create a new report based on it, follow these steps:

1. Open the Custom Reports dialog box.

2. In the Reports list, click to select the name of the report that you want to use as the basis for your custom report.

3. Click on the Copy button. Depending on the type of report you selected, the appropriate Report dialog box (such as the Task Report dialog box) appears.

4. In the Name text box of the Report dialog box, Project shows "Copy of" plus the name of the report you selected in Step 2. Be sure to edit this name to ensure that your custom report has a name you'll recognize. For example, you might edit it to read **Monthly Budget Report** if that's the kind of report you're creating.

5. Make any changes you desire to the various options in the three tabs of the Report dialog box, as well as any font changes using the Text button.

6. Click on OK. Your custom report appears, with the name you gave it, in the Reports list of the Custom Reports dialog box (see Figure 14.18).

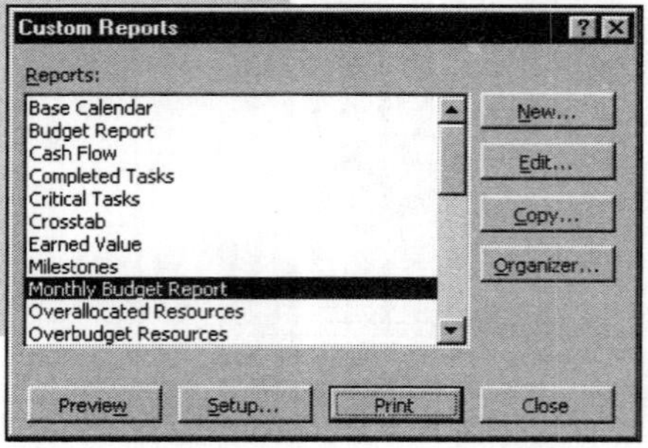

Figure 14.18
The highlighted report name is the custom report I've created based on the Budget Report.

Saving a Unique Report

If you ever want to define a new report completely from scratch, to avoid the possibility of making an unwanted change to one of your existing reports, you can do so by clicking on the New button in the Custom Reports dialog box. The Define New Report dialog box appears (see Figure 14.19).

In the Report Type list, select the type of report you want to create, and then click on OK. If you select Task, Resource, or Crosstab, Project displays the Task Report, Resource Report, or Crosstab Report dialog box, respectively. You work in any of these dialog boxes (refer to Figures 14.14 through 14.16) just as described earlier in this chapter when you learned how to edit different types of reports. Make sure to edit the report Name on the Definition tab (it starts out as "Report 1," "Report 2," or another sequentially numbered name) to make it more descriptive. Select any other options you want on the applicable tabs, and then click on OK. Your report appears in the Reports list of the Custom Reports dialog box.

If you select the Monthly Calendar choice from the Define New Report dialog box, Project displays the Monthly Calendar Report Definition dialog box, as shown in Figure 14.20. Most of the options in this dialog box work just like options you've seen on various tabs of the Report dialog boxes. Some options, however, are unique to calendar formats.

Note

Custom reports that you create are saved with the current project file until you either copy them to Project's GLOBAL.MPT master file, to another project file, or delete them. To make a report available to all files or to delete a report, click on the Organizer button in the Custom Reports dialog box, and then use the Reports tab to make your changes. Chapter 11, "Working with the Different Project Views," discusses working with the Organizer.

Figure 14.19
This dialog box enables you to build a report from scratch.

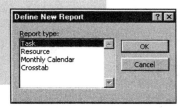

Figure 14.20
This dialog box
offers some
options
particular to
calendar reports.

For example, use the Calendar drop-down list to specify whether the calendar is based on one of the default schedule base calendars (Standard, Night Shift, or 24 Hours), a custom base calendar you have created, or the calendar for a particular resource. Use the Solid Bar Breaks and Show Tasks As options to specify whether or not to gray out nonworking days, and to control how the bars representing tasks appear on the report. Finally, use the Label Tasks With check boxes to specify whether each task is identified with its ID number, task Name, or task Duration (or any combination of these pieces of information). When you finish setting all these options, click on OK to close the Monthly Calendar Report Definition dialog box and add your new calendar report to the Reports list of the Custom Reports dialog box.

15

Working with Outlining

IN THIS CHAPTER

- Promoting and demoting tasks
- Controlling the outline display
- Using summary tasks
- Using WBS Codes

A t one time many artists and writers employed a method called *stream of consciousness*, which basically meant that the creator would sit down and just let the brushstrokes or words come out, leading where they would. The artist or writer made no effort to impose any type of structure on the output.

However most people, by nature, tend to prefer a more orderly approach to work—especially in the business world, where the most effective professionals excel at spelling out expectations and providing clear direction for what others need to do. To help you become more orderly as you build structure for your work, Project provides outlining capabilities. This chapter helps you learn how to create a work breakdown structure in online format.

What Outlining Does for You

Different project leaders have different styles. Some fancy themselves "big picture thinkers" and like to sketch out overall plans first; such a leader might even hand a project off to someone else charged with "figuring out the details." Other leaders treat project tasks as a puzzle, first laying out all the pieces, then grouping together pieces for the edge, the sky, the grass, and so on before proceeding to put the puzzle together. No matter which approach you prefer, you'll find that Project's outlining features can accommodate you as you build the *work breakdown structure* (the list of tasks, organized into groups related by activity, and numbered with traditional outline numbering—1, 1.1, 1.2, 2, 2.1, 2.2, 2.3, and so on).

If you like to build a schedule using a *top-down approach* where you identify and arrange major, general tasks before filling in the details, you can enter those major categories and then break them down into more specific action items. Conversely, if you like to simply do a brain dump and list every possible task (the *bottom-up approach*), you can later group your list into logical areas.

When you use outlining in Project, the major tasks within your Task Sheet are called *summary tasks*, because they summarize a series of actions in a given time frame. Each task that is part of the work required to complete a summary task is called a *subtask*. Project allows for thousands of outline levels (up to 65,000 if your system has enough resources to handle it), so keep in mind that you can have summary tasks within summary tasks.

Project uses special formatting to help you identify summary tasks and subtasks onscreen, as shown in Figure 15.1. Summary tasks usually appear in bold text in the Task Sheet, and use a special summary Gantt bar. By default, an outlining symbol appears beside each summary task. (You can turn these symbols off as

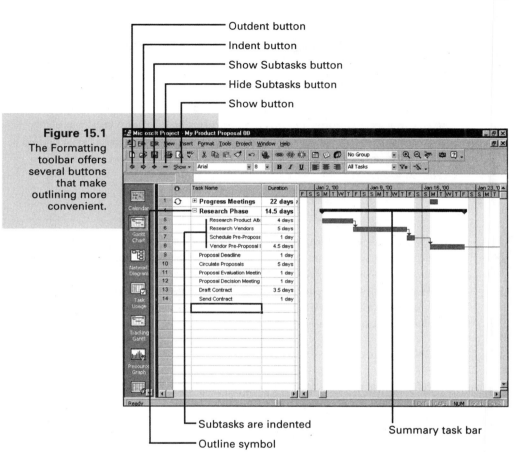

Figure 15.1
The Formatting toolbar offers several buttons that make outlining more convenient.

Outdent button

Indent button

Show Subtasks button

Hide Subtasks button

Show button

Subtasks are indented

Outline symbol

Summary task bar

described later in this chapter under "Hiding and Showing Outlining Symbols.") Subtasks are indented in the Task Name column of the Task Sheet; if a task is a summary task of a summary task, it's indented twice.

Summarizing work in this way not only gives you an idea of where major completion points in your project will occur, it can also help you make resource assignment decisions. For example, you may examine a particular summary task and its subtasks and decide to farm the whole mess out to a contractor who can provide multiple people to complete and add continuity to the summary task. Or you may see that the start and finish dates for two summary tasks are about the same and realize that those tasks are creating a "crunch period" in your schedule, during which you'll need extra resources—either additions to your team or authorized overtime hours for the existing team.

Note

Outlining isn't a difficult technique, but most users need to learn about basic task and resource entry before bothering with Project outlining. That's why I'm covering this technique so late in the book. Keep in mind that if you use the outlining techniques you'll learn about in this chapter with your existing schedule files, you'll need to double-check task links after you insert summary tasks. On the other hand, when you're building a new file from scratch, you may want to enter the summary tasks first, then insert and indent the subtasks to flesh out the outline (Work Breakdown Structure).

Caution

Microsoft Word 2000 and Excel 2000 also provide outlining features. However, those features don't mesh with the one in Project—if you copy outlined information from Word or Excel and paste it into Project, Project does not recognize the outline levels you assigned in Word or Excel. You still save the time and effort of retyping the information, but you'll have to reassign the outline levels.

You apply outlining in the Task Sheet for your schedule, and you can start from any view that includes the Task Sheet. The fastest way to work with outlining is to use the outlining tools on Project's Formatting toolbar. The Formatting toolbar appears onscreen by default, but if you need to display it, right-click on any toolbar and then choose Formatting. Refer to Figure 15.1 to identify the outlining tools.

Promoting and Demoting Tasks in the Outline

Whether you're using outlining for a list of existing tasks or using the outlining tools to organize a list of tasks that you're building, the process is generally the same. You select the Task Name cell (or the entire row) of the task for which you want to define an outline level, and then *outdent* (promote) it to a higher level or *indent* (demote) it to a lower level.

Since all tasks start on the top outline level by default, you begin outlining by demoting subtasks. Demoting a task automatically converts the task above it to a summary task. To demote a selected task by one level (to the next lower level), you can use one of these techniques:

- Click on the Indent button on the Formatting toolbar.
- Choose Project, Outline, Indent.
- Select the entire task by clicking on its row heading (row number). Then right-click on the row and choose Indent from the shortcut menu that appears.
- Point to the first letter of the task name until you see the double-arrow pointer, press and hold the mouse button, and drag to the right to move the task down a level. A vertical gray line appears to indicate the outline level to which the task is being demoted.

The demoted task is automatically formatted as a subtask, and the task above it is formatted as a summary task. Project prevents you from demoting a task if doing so would skip a level in the outline and result in some task ending up two outline levels below the task above it.

Tip

You can select multiple tasks that are on the same outline level and demote them simultaneously. To do so, drag across the row numbers to select the group of tasks; then click on the Indent button on the Formatting toolbar.

To promote a selected task, use one of the following methods:

- Click on the Outdent button on the Formatting toolbar.
- Choose Project, Outline, Outdent.
- If the task is a subtask and is not on the top level of the outline, select the entire task by clicking on its row heading (row number). Then right-click on the row and choose Outdent from the shortcut menu that appears.
- If the task is not on the top outline level, point to the first letter of the task name until you see the double-arrow pointer. Press and hold the mouse button, and drag to the left to move the task up a level, as shown in Figure 15.2. A vertical gray line appears to indicate the outline level to which the task is being promoted.

If a task is already at the top level of the outline, meaning that it does not appear indented in the Task Name column (keep in mind that there is some space to the left of task names by default), Project will not let you promote it. If the Planning

Figure 15.2
Point to the first letter of the task name until you see the double-arrow pointer, and then drag left to promote the task or right to demote it.

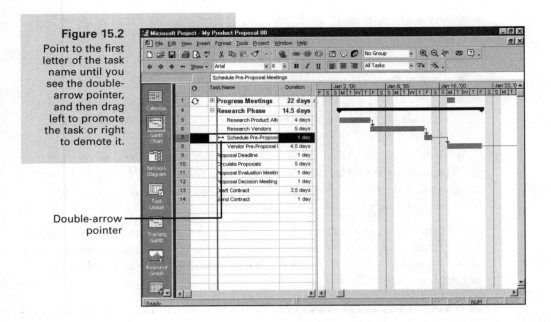

Double-arrow pointer

wizard is active when you attempt to promote such a task, the Planning Wizard dialog box appears onscreen to inform you that the task can't be promoted (see Figure 15.3). Simply click on OK to close the dialog box. Project returns you to your Task Sheet without making any changes. When you promote a task, the tasks listed below it that were previously on the same level become subtasks of the promoted task, and the promoted task is reformatted accordingly.

Note

> If you promote or demote a summary task, Project promotes or demotes its subtasks, as well.

Figure 15.3
If you try to promote a task that is already at the top level, the Planning wizard tells you that Project can't make the change.

Planning Wizard

The task(s) you selected cannot be outdented any further. They are already at the left edge of the outline, which is the highest outline level.

[OK]   [Help]

☐ Don't tell me about this again.

Inserting a Summary Task

If you're using a bottom-up approach to building your schedule, you may have a list of tasks, into which you want to insert summary tasks. It would be nice if Project simply allowed you to simultaneously demote all the tasks you typed in and then insert higher-level tasks, but it doesn't work that way. Instead, follow this multistep process:

1. Insert a blank row above the tasks you want to summarize. To do so, right-click on the row heading (row number) for the top task in the group you want to summarize; then click on New Task in the shortcut menu.

2. Enter the Task Name for the new task. You don't have to specify any other task details, even Duration. Project makes those entries for you when you define the subtasks for the summary task.

3. If the task above the newly inserted task is a summary task, Project typically treats the new task as a subtask, too, and indents the task automatically. To move it back up an outline level, select the new task, and then use the technique of your choice to promote it, such as clicking on the Outdent button on the Formatting toolbar.

4. Drag over the row headings for the tasks you want to convert to summary tasks (to select those rows). Then click on the Indent button on the Formatting toolbar. Alternately, you can choose Project, Outline, Indent, or right-click on the selected tasks and then click on Indent on the shortcut menu (see Figure 15.4). Figure 15.5 shows how the tasks in Figure 15.4 look when the indent operation is completed. A summary task bar has been added in the Gantt Chart for the newly designated summary task in row 9.

If you look closely at Figure 15.5, you can see that the subtasks above and below the inserted summary task are linked.

Inserting a summary task in this way did not disturb the existing links. However, if you promote a task that's linked to predecessor and successor tasks and then demote tasks below the newly promoted summary task, Project breaks the link between the summary task and its newly demoted subtasks. This might cause unwanted rescheduling in your project. To avoid such potential problems, apply outlining to your list of tasks before you establish links. Then, when you do link tasks, the best approach is to link only subtasks, not summary tasks. That's because summary tasks only summarize work; they don't represent the details in your schedule. The best way to capture how a schedule change in one task might affect other tasks is to create your links at that level of detail—the subtask level.

Figure 15.4
You can use the shortcut menu to demote (or promote) selected task rows.

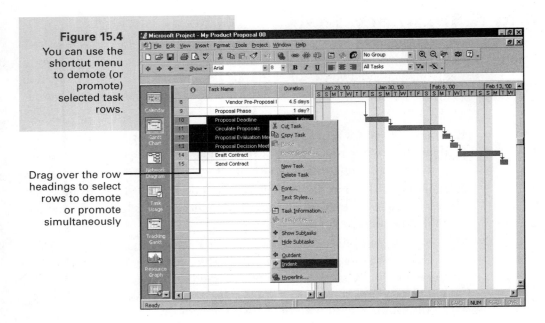

Drag over the row headings to select rows to demote or promote simultaneously

Figure 15.5
The newly inserted row is designated as a summary task.

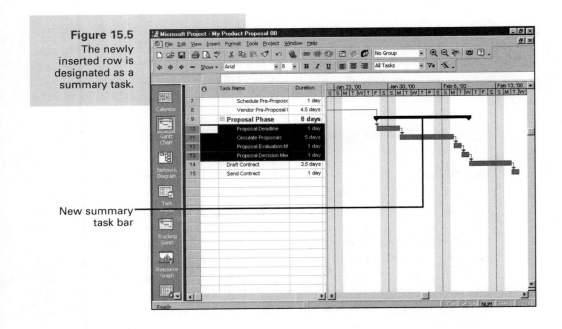

New summary task bar

Inserting Subtasks

To insert a subtask, you need to insert a new row for it in the Task Sheet. As you learned in the preceding section, when you insert a new row into a Task Sheet, the task in that row adopts the outline level of the task above it. Therefore, one of two situations might develop:

- If the task above the inserted row is at a summary level, you need to enter the Task Name and then demote the task in the newly inserted row. This will demote the subtasks, as well, so you'll need to select and promote them by one level to get them back where they belong.

- If the task above the inserted row is at the correct subtask level, just enter the Task Name. Notice that if you insert a new task row within a group of subtasks, Project does not demote the tasks in rows below the newly inserted row to a lower outline level. Instead, Project assumes that all tasks in the group should remain at the same level until you tell it otherwise.

Similarly, when you're entering brand new tasks into blank rows at the bottom of the Task Sheet, Project assumes that each newly entered task should adopt the outline level of the task above it. For example, if I type a new Task Name into row 17 of the Task Sheet shown in Figure 15.6, Project assumes it to be a subtask of the row 14 summary task, just like the subtasks in rows 15 and 16.

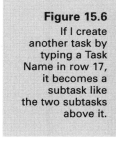

Figure 15.6
If I create another task by typing a Task Name in row 17, it becomes a subtask like the two subtasks above it.

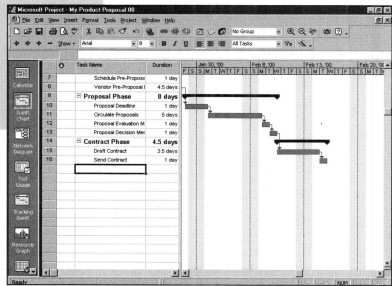

Adjusting Subtask Scheduling and Moving Subtasks

If you experiment at all with outlining, you might notice that the summary task duration and summary task bar on the Gantt Chart adjust to encompass both the earliest task start date for any subtask of the summary task and the latest task finish date for any subtask. For that reason, it's preferable to create your entire list of tasks, apply the outlining you prefer, and then add links and adjust the scheduling information as needed for all subtasks. If you enter dates for a task, convert it to a summary task, and then later demote it to a subtask, you lose the original duration information you entered for the task, anyway.

You can change the schedule for a subtask by using any of the methods for rescheduling tasks that were described in Chapter 5, "Fine-Tuning Tasks." The Duration, Start and Finish dates, and Gantt Chart summary bar for the summary task all adjust automatically to reflect the change. Figures 15.7 and 15.8 show an example of how increasing a subtask's duration changes the summary task.

Note

You can open the Task Information dialog box for a summary task. When this dialog box appears, it won't let you edit certain information such as the summary task Duration. Don't assume that all the information you can enter for the summary task also applies to all subtasks of the summary task; it doesn't.

No creative process is perfect, and you might find that you incorrectly positioned several tasks, including a summary task and its subtasks, in the outline. When this is the case, you can move the tasks as usual, by dragging task rows. To move a row, click on its row heading (row number). Point to a row border, and then press and hold the mouse button while you drag the row to its new location, dropping the row into place whenever the gray insertion bar reaches the location you want. There are, however, a couple of points to remember when dragging outlined tasks:

- **Subtasks travel with their summary task.** Therefore, if you drag a summary task to a new location in the task list, when you drop it into place, its subtasks appear below it.

- **Dragging tasks around can disturb links.** If you insert a group of subtasks linked by a series of Finish-to-Start links within tasks already linked by Finish-to-Start links, the results are unpredictable. This is yet another argument for nailing down your outline as much as possible before progressing too far with information about linking, scheduling, or resources.

Original summary task duration

Original subtask duration

Original summary task bar

Figure 15.7
The task 14 summary task totals the durations for tasks 15 and 16, which run consecutively in the schedule.

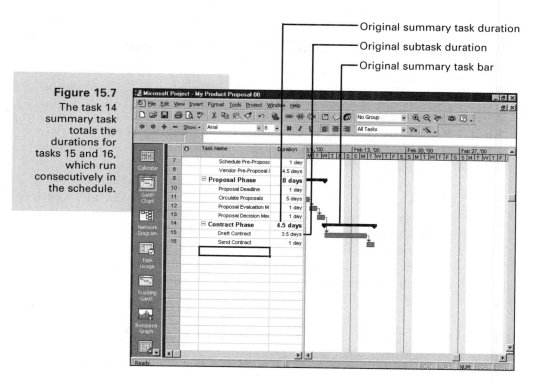

Figure 15.8
After I've increased the duration for the task 15 subtask, notice that the summary task duration has changed.

New summary task duration

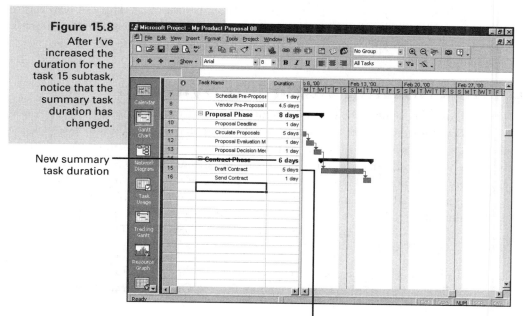

New subtask duration

Tip

Even though it may not be the best approach, you can link a summary task to other tasks by simply dragging between bars in the Gantt Chart. (Collapse all the subtasks first, to make creating the links easier.) The only restriction is that you cannot link a summary task to one of its own subtasks.

- **A moved task adopts the outline level of the task above it.** When you move a task, Project assumes that you want the task to be on the same outline level as the task above it in its new location. If you move a summary task (and thus its subtasks) to a location that demotes the summary task, click on the Outdent button on the Formatting toolbar to return the group of tasks to the proper outline level before proceeding. Project even demotes or promotes a moved task more than one level, if needed. For example, if you move a task to a Task Sheet row directly below a task that's two outline levels lower, Project demotes the moved task (and any subtasks that travel with it) two levels.

Controlling the Outline Display

As when you're outlining in a word processing application or spreadsheet program, one of the advantages of outlining in Project is that outlining enables Project to give you visual cues about how you structured your outline. This can help you to make intelligent decisions about scheduling changes and resource assignments. This section explains how you can work with the outlining display features.

Hiding and Showing Outlining Symbols

Outlining symbols help you differentiate summary tasks from subtasks. Any task that has subtasks below it is considered a summary task, and is indicated with an outlining symbol to the left of the Task Name. When the summary task has a plus (+) outlining symbol beside it, its subtasks are hidden. When the subtasks for a summary task are displayed, the summary task has a minus (–) outlining symbol beside it. If a task is at a summary task level (most often the top level of the outline) but has no subtasks, no outlining symbol appears beside it. By default, outlining symbols appear for summary tasks in the Task Sheet, at the left of the task names.

To hide outlining symbols, choose Project, Outline, Hide Outline Symbols. To redisplay the outlining symbols, choose Project, Outline, Show Outline Symbols.

You can add a Show/Hide Outline Symbols button to any toolbar for your convenience. Chapter 24 explains how to customize toolbars. The Show/Hide Outline Symbols button is found on the Commands tab of the Customize dialog box; click on Outline in the Categories list on the tab to display that button in the Commands list.

Note

In Chapter 5, "Fine-Tuning Tasks," you learned how to create a recurring task, which behaves somewhat like a summary task. When you display outline symbols, they appear on a recurring task (and each of its subtasks) just as they do on real summary and subtasks. However, the Gantt bars for a recurring task never look like the Gantt bar for a summary task created via outlining.

Specifying Which Outline Levels Appear

Summary tasks wouldn't provide much of a summary if you could never view them without their subtasks. Consequently, Project allows you to hide subtasks from view for your convenience. There are a couple of reasons why you might want to hide some or all subtasks in your schedule. First, you might want to print the schedule and have the printout only include summary tasks, not the details shown in subtasks. Second, if you have a lengthy list of tasks in your project, you might find it easier to move up and down through the Task Sheet if you hide subtasks until you need to view or work with the information for a particular subtask.

The fastest way to hide and display subtasks for a summary task is to use the summary task's outlining symbol. Click on the minus (–) outlining symbol beside a summary task to hide its subtasks or the plus (+) outlining symbol beside a summary task to redisplay its subtasks.

When you hide and redisplay subtasks using other commands, you do so for a single summary task by selecting that summary task first. Then, to hide subtasks, click on the Hide Subtasks button on the Formatting toolbar. Alternately, choose Project, Outline, Hide Subtasks. Figure 15.9 shows a Task Sheet with the subtasks for one summary task hidden. Notice that not only the subtask rows but also the corresponding Gantt bars are hidden, leaving only the summary task bar on the Gantt Chart.

To redisplay subtasks for selected summary tasks, click on the Show Subtasks button on the Formatting toolbar. Alternately, choose Project, Outline, Show Subtasks.

Click to redisplay subtasks

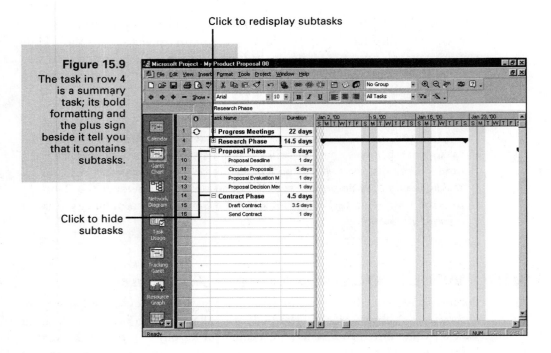

Figure 15.9
The task in row 4
is a summary
task; its bold
formatting and
the plus sign
beside it tell you
that it contains
subtasks.

Click to hide
subtasks

If you want to redisplay all subtasks without taking the time to select particular summary tasks, click on the Show button on the Formatting Toolbar and then click on All Subtasks, or choose Project, Outline, Show All Subtasks. Alternately, first select the whole Task Sheet by clicking the Select All button in the upper-left corner, or select the whole Task Name column by clicking that column heading. Then use the Show Subtasks or Hide Subtasks button on the Formatting toolbar as needed.

Tip

You can right-click on a summary task's row heading, and then choose Show Subtasks or Hide Subtasks from the shortcut menu as needed.

Project 2000 offers a new capability: displaying or hiding tasks down to a particular outline level. For example, you can show only the tasks on the first four outline levels. Tasks at all lower levels will be hidden. To take advantage of this feature, click on the Show button on the Formatting toolbar, and then choose the desired outline level from the menu that appears.

Finally, if you're working in the Task Usage or Resource Usage view, you can hide and redisplay the assignments for one or more selected tasks. To hide assignments, select the desired task, and then choose Project, Outline, Hide Assignments. You can also click on the minus (–) button beside the task to hide its assignments. To show assignments, select the desired task and choose Project, Outline, Show Assignments. Or click on the plus (+) button beside the task name. If you select the Task Name column by clicking on its column heading, the Project, Outline, Hide Assignments command hides all the assignments. You can then later select the entire column and choose Project, Outline, Show Assignments. However, you cannot select the Task Name column and then redisplay all assignments if you hid those assignments on a task-by-task basis; you can only redisplay all the tasks at once if you hid them all at once, a fact that becomes obvious if the Show Assignments choice isn't available on the Project, Outline submenu.

Rolling Up Subtasks

If you have a long list of subtasks within a summary task, you might lose track of how a particular task compares to the summary schedule. Or you might have a particular task near the middle of the summary task range that you want to highlight by having it appear on the summary bar as well as its usual location. To achieve this effect, you *roll up* the subtask to its summary task.

Click on the row heading to select the summary task to roll up, and then press and hold Ctrl while you click to select the row heading for the subtask to roll up; this selects both the summary task and its subtask. Then click on the Task Information button on the Standard toolbar to open the Task Information dialog box. On the General tab of this dialog box, click twice to place a check beside the Roll Up Gantt Bar To Summary choice; then click on OK. The subtask bar will then appear on the summary bar, as shown in Figure 15.10. To remove the effects of a rollup, select the summary task and subtask, reopen the Task Information dialog box, and clear the Roll Up Gantt Bar To Summary check box.

Do not select the Hide Task Bar check box in the General tab of the Task Information dialog box when you're rolling up tasks. If you do so, you won't be able to see the rolled-up task or any text that accompanies it.

If you want to roll up a summary task and several of its subtasks simultaneously, drag over the row numbers to select the rows. Open the Task Information dialog box, select the Roll Up Gantt Bar To Summary check box, and click on OK.

Figure 15.10

The subtask from row 6 has been rolled up onto the summary bar for the summary task in row 4.

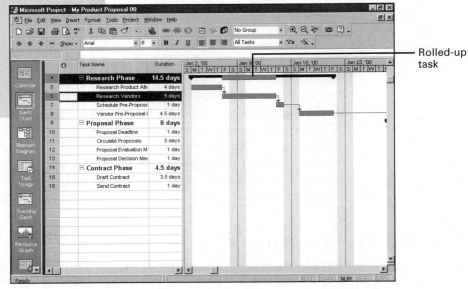

Rolled-up task

Tip

You can reformat the bars for summary tasks so that they display dates or have a different appearance that makes them stand out more when rolled up. For example, you can make the Gantt bar for a particular subtask red so that it stands out when rolled up. To learn how to reformat a Gantt bar, see Chapter 16, "Other Formatting."

Project 2000 enables you to display and remove the rollup bars for all the subtasks at once, which makes the job much easier if you have a lengthy project plan. Choose Format, Layout. The Layout dialog box, shown in Figure 15.11, appears. Click to check the Always Roll Up Gantt Bars choice to roll up the subtask bars for all the tasks in the project file, or clear the check box if you're turning this feature off. With Always Roll Up Gantt Bars checked, the Hide Rollup Bars When Summary Expanded check box becomes active. If you select this check box, Project displays the rollup bars on the summary task bar only when you've hidden (collapsed) the subtasks for the summary tasks. After you finish choosing your layout options, click on OK to close the dialog box.

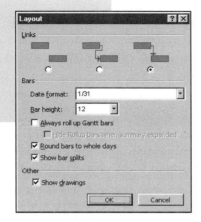

Figure 15.11
Check the Always Roll Up Gantt Bars check box to roll up all the subtask bars in the project file.

Using Summary Tasks to Reduce the Critical Path

As you learned in Chapter 8, "Optimizing the Schedule," the critical path for your schedule identifies tasks that can't slip without causing the overall project finish date to move. When you finish setting up all your schedule information, you might find that the schedule is longer than you want it to be. If that's the case, working with your summary tasks (perhaps hiding subtasks in the process) can help you to identify critical tasks. Here are a few ideas about how you can use summary task information to identify ways to condense the critical path:

- Look for ways to remove slack time between summary tasks.

- If none of your summary tasks overlap in timing, check to see if you can move up the schedules for subtasks under some later summary tasks, so that some summary groups run concurrently.

- Create a Gantt bar style for bars that indicate both summary and critical path information. See Chapter 16, "Other Formatting," for more details about bar styles.

Working with WBS and Outline Codes

Part of the work breakdown structure (WBS) includes a method of hierarchically numbering tasks in a traditional outline numbering format. By default, the WBS numbers (or WBS codes) are the same as the *outline numbers*.

In addition to enabling you to display and use WBS numbers in the Task Sheet, Project 2000 adds the capability for creating custom WBS numbers (a numbering scheme different from the default outline numbers) to match the needs of your organization. This last section of the chapter explores WBS codes.

Work Breakdown Structure Basics

When you use outlining, Project assigns the WBS numbers automatically, behind the scenes. As you move, promote, and demote tasks, Project updates the outline numbers and WBS numbers accordingly. Tasks at the top outline level are numbered sequentially. For example, the first 10 top-level outline tasks receive WBS numbers 1 through 10. Subtasks on the first level use the top-level number for their summary task plus a decimal value; for example, the first three subtasks of summary task 2 are numbered 2.1, 2.2, and 2.3. For the next outline level down, Project adds another decimal; for example, the first two subtasks under task 2.1 are numbered 2.1.1 and 2.1.2.

The WBS codes or outline numbers aren't the same as the task number. For example, let's say rows 1 through 5 hold a summary task and four subtasks—tasks 1 through 5. The WBS codes for those five tasks would be 1, 1.1, 1.2, 1.3, and 1.4, respectively.

Basically, WBS codes (and outline numbers) do a better job of identifying how your tasks fit into the overall project scheme than the simple task numbers do. And, as your project becomes lengthier, it's easier to refer to the tasks by WBS number rather than task name. For example, if your project has a few hundred tasks, Task Sheet and report printouts will be many pages long. If a question regarding "Task 5.10.7" comes up, it'll be easier to flip through the printout and find that task than by looking for its name, such as "Install fourth floor plumbing."

Displaying WBS Codes and Outline Numbers

You can add a field (column) to a Task Sheet table to display WBS numbers and outline numbers. Once you display the desired field, you can even sort by the

WBS numbers. The following steps explain how to create a custom table that includes both WBS and Outline Number fields:

1. From the default Gantt Chart view, Choose View, Table, More Tables. The More Tables dialog box appears.

2. Make sure Entry is selected in the list of tables, then click on the Copy button. The Table Definition dialog box opens.

3. Type a name for the new table in the Name text box. For example, type **WBS and Outline.**

4. In the Field Names column, click on the Indicators choice, then click on the Delete Row button. Also delete the Start, Finish, Predecessors, and Resource Names fields.

5. Click on the Name choice in the Field Names column, then click on the Insert Row button twice to insert two blank rows. A down arrow appears in the Field Name column for the first blank row.

6. Click on the down arrow to open the list, press the **W** key on your scroll bar to scroll down the list, then click on the WBS choice.

7. Press Enter to accept the entry and display the down arrow for the second new row.

8. Click on the down arrow to open the list, press the **O** key on your scroll bar to scroll down the list, scroll down further to display the Outline Number choice, then click on it.

9. Press Enter. At this point, your table definition settings should appear as shown in Figure 15.12.

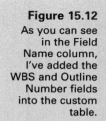

Figure 15.12
As you can see in the Field Name column, I've added the WBS and Outline Number fields into the custom table.

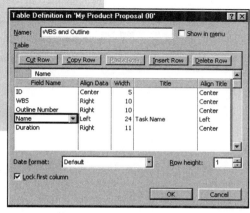

10. Click on OK to finish creating the custom table.
11. Make sure the new table, *WBS and Outline,* is selected in the list of tables, then click on Apply. Figure 15.13 illustrates how this custom table appears in the Gantt Chart view. As you can see, both fields display the same numbers by default, because the WBS codes are the same as the outline numbers unless you enter custom WBS codes.

You can also display WBS numbers along with the task name in the Task Sheet. To do so, choose Tools, Options. On the View tab of the Options dialog box, click to place a check beside the Show Outline Number option and click on OK. The assigned outline number appears to the left of each task name, as shown in Figure 15.14.

Note

If you copy the Task Name column into Word 2000 as unformatted text (see Chapter 20, "Using Project with Other Applications,") the WBS numbers are not copied with the Task Name entries, even if the WBS numbers were displayed in Project. If you need to include accurate WBS numbers in documents in other applications, create a custom table that includes the WBS column. Then make sure you also copy or export the WBS column information to Word or Excel.

Figure 15.13
The custom table displayed at the left side of the Gantt Chart view includes the WBS and Outline Number fields.

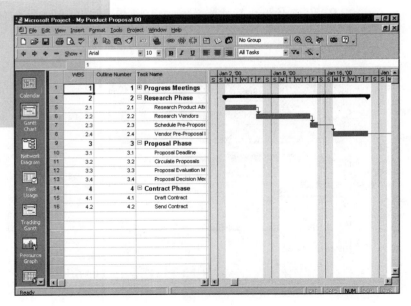

Figure 15.14
If you prefer, you can display each task's WBS number with the task name.

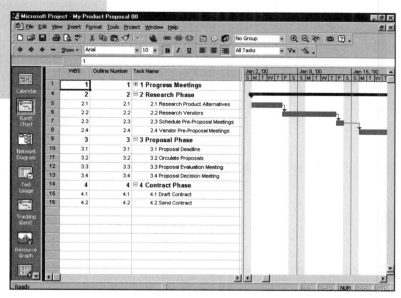

Creating Custom Codes

Your company might mandate a specific set of WBS numbers that you need to follow. You can assign custom WBS codes a task at a time. To do so, double-click on the task in the Task Sheet. In the Task Information dialog box, click on the Advanced tab. Double-click on the entry in the WBS Code text box and type the new entry you want, as shown in Figure 15.15. Click on OK when you finish editing the entry.

Figure 15.15
If your company requires specific WBS codes, you can change the ones Project creates in the WBS Code text box.

However, it would be tedious to type in a new code for each and every task in the Task Sheet—and you might make mistakes in incrementing the code numbers. Project 2000 now enables you to create a *mask* that assigns custom WBS codes for all the tasks in the Task Sheet. Follow these steps to create a custom WBS code mask in the current project file:

1. Choose Project, WBS, Define Code. The WBS Code Definition dialog box appears.

2. If you want your WBS codes to include a prefix that's specific to the project name or job number, type that code into the Project Code Prefix text box. You could also use your name, initials, or department number as a prefix.

Include a space or underscore character at the end of your Project Code Prefix entry if you need to set it off from the rest of the code.

3. Click in the first blank row in the Sequence column under Code Mask (Excluding Prefix). A down arrow appears beside the selected cell. Click on the down arrow, then click on the type of sequence to use for the top WBS code level. Here are your choices:

   - **Numbers (ordered)**. Inserts the specified number of Arabic numerals at that WBS code level.

   - **Uppercase Letters (ordered)**. Inserts the specified number of uppercase characters at that WBS code level.

   - **Lowercase Letters (ordered)**. Inserts the specified number of lowercase letters at that WBS code level.

   - **Characters (unordered)**. Inserts the specified number of asterisk characters at that WBS code level. If you choose Any from the Length column, this choice inserts three numerals, inserting sequential numbers at that WBS code level.

4. In the Length column for the first row, enter the number of characters Project should display for that WBS code level. For example, if you select Numbers (ordered) as the Sequence and then enter **2** as the Length, Project displays 11, 22, 33, and so on in the WBS code for that code level. You can also open the drop-down list for the Length cell and choose Any; this choice tells Project to use the required number of characters at that code level so it can display the proper letter or number (1, 112, 232, and so on).

5. Click on the Separator column for the first row. Open its drop-down list to click on the separator to use between the first level of the WBS code and the next level. Or you can type your own separator such as the ampersand (&).

6. Using subsequent blank rows, repeat Steps 3–5 to add as many levels as are required for your WBS code. If you've outlined your project tasks to six levels deep, then you need to create six WBS code outline levels. As you build your code levels, the Code Preview area shows how the WBS codes will look. Figure 15.16 shows the preview of my code, which has a prefix plus two code levels.

• •

To delete a code level row, click on its Sequence column entry, then press the Delete key.

• •

7. Leave the Generate WBS Code For New Task check box checked to ensure that Project will add the custom WBS codes for any new tasks you add into the project file.

8. Leave the Verify Uniqueness Of New WBS Codes check box checked to ensure that Project will prevent you from duplicating an existing code. (WBS codes you enter must match the pattern of the mask, however.)

9. Click on OK to finish defining the mask and display the new codes in the WBS column, as illustrated in Figure 15.17.

Figure 15.16
Use the blank rows in the Code Mask (Excluding Prefix) area to build the various levels of your WBS code.

WBS Code Definition in 'My Product Proposal 00'	? X

Code preview: `Dev 11.aaa`

Project Code Prefix: `Dev`

Code mask (excluding prefix):

Level	Sequence	Length	Separator
1	Numbers (ordered)	2	.
2	Lowercase Letters (ordered)	3	.

☑ Generate WBS code for new task
☑ Verify uniqueness of new WBS codes

Help		OK	Cancel

Figure 15.17
The WBS
column now
displays my
custom codes.

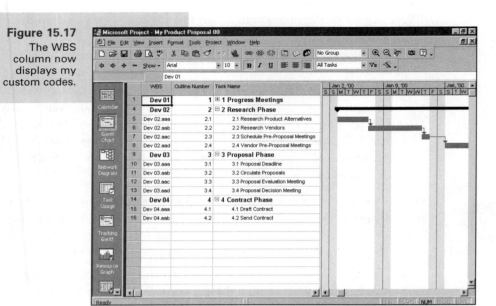

Figure 15.17
The WBS
column now
displays my
custom codes.

If you move tasks around or make other changes and Project fails to update the WBS codes, choose Project, WBS, Renumber to make sure your WBS codes are applied according to your custom mask. Leave Entire Project selected in the WBS Renumber dialog box; then click on OK to finish the renumbering.

16

Other Formatting

IN THIS CHAPTER

- Changing the appearance of selected text in a Task Sheet or Resource Sheet
- Working with a single chart bar or box
- Controlling progress lines and gridlines that appear on a chart
- Adjusting the appearance of a particular style of sheet text or a particular style of chart bar or box
- Controlling the display of details and choosing a layout for links
- Working with Project's drawing tools

When you're learning to use Project, the way that text and other elements look may be the furthest thing from your mind. At first, you worry about setting the schedules for your tasks, figuring out how different kinds of links work, determining how to allocate resources most effectively, and working out any kinks that unnecessarily extend your overall schedule.

After you set everything, however, you may begin to look at your schedule in a new light. You may become more interested in ensuring that your schedule is not only accurate but attractive, and also highlights key facts clearly. This chapter examines the tools that enable you to control the appearance of information in Project.

Tip

Consider leaving Project's original views intact and use the techniques described in this chapter to make changes to custom views that you create. That way, you'll be able to revert to the desired default view at any time.

Formatting Selected Sheet Text

Fonts are different types of lettering used for text. Within Project, you can select a different font—along with a particular font size, color, and so on—for any cell, row, or column that you select in a Task Sheet or Resource Sheet. The fonts you can choose depend on the fonts that you installed to work with Windows on your system. When you reformat selected text, the formatting changes (including the formatted text) appear both onscreen and in printouts.

Note

Font sizes are measured in *points*. Each point is 1/72 inch; 12 points equal 1/6 inch. Unfortunately, you can't make an exact prediction about how much space a font will take up based on its point size—the number refers to the height of the letters rather than their width, and some fonts are much denser than others. If the text isn't fitting the way you prefer, try a different font.

An easy way to apply formatting to selected text is to use the tools in the Formatting toolbar (see Figure 16.1). To display the Formatting toolbar if you've removed it from the screen, right-click on any toolbar, and then click on Formatting.

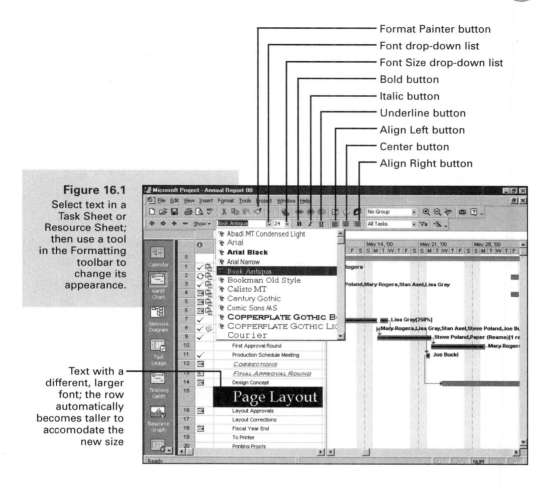

Format Painter button
Font drop-down list
Font Size drop-down list
Bold button
Italic button
Underline button
Align Left button
Center button
Align Right button

Figure 16.1
Select text in a Task Sheet or Resource Sheet; then use a tool in the Formatting toolbar to change its appearance.

Text with a different, larger font; the row automatically becomes taller to accomodate the new size

Note that the three alignment buttons—Align Left, Center, and Align Right—realign all cells in the sheet column, even if you have selected a single cell in the column. If you select a single row and then click on an alignment button, all columns in the sheet are realigned.

In addition to using the Formatting toolbar, you can format text by using the Font dialog box. Follow these steps:

1. Select the cell that contains the text that you want to format. Alternately, click on a column header to select an entire column, or click on a row header to select an entire row.

2. Choose Format, Font, or right-click and then click on Font in the shortcut menu. The Font dialog box appears (see Figure 16.2).

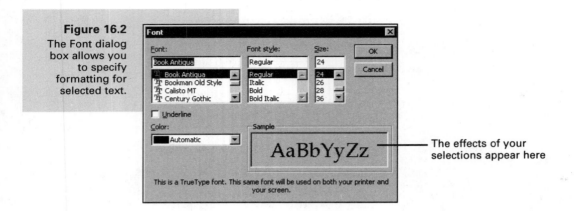

Figure 16.2
The Font dialog box allows you to specify formatting for selected text.

The effects of your selections appear here

3. Scroll the Font list and select the font you want to use.

4. If you want to format the text with an effect such as bold or italic, select the effect from the Font Style list.

5. Scroll the Size list and select the font size you want to use, or double-click on the Size text box and type the appropriate size.

6. If you want to apply an underline to the selected text, click on the Underline check box to check it.

7. If you want to format the selected text with a particular color (perhaps to call more attention to it onscreen or in color printouts), select the color from the Color drop-down list.

8. Click on OK to close the Font dialog box and apply your selections.

If you've added several formatting selections to some text and you'd like to use those same settings for other cells in the sheet, you can quickly copy all the formatting selections to other cells with the Format Painter button on the Standard toolbar. To do so, select the cell that holds the formatting to copy. Click on the Format Painter button, and then click on the cell to which you want to apply the formatting settings.

Formatting the Bar for a Selected Task

Just as you can use formatting selections to call attention to specific text in a Task Sheet or Resource Sheet, you can reformat the Gantt bars for selected tasks in your schedule. Suppose that you want to call attention to the Gantt bars for all the tasks that begin next week. You could make each of those bars yellow, so that they're brighter onscreen or in a printout. Alternately, you could include the text of a particular field of task information (such as the Actual Start date) in the Gantt Chart bar.

To reformat individual boxes in Network Diagram view, right-click the box; then choose Format, Box.

To adjust formatting options for one or more Gantt bars, follow these steps:

1. Click on the Task Name cell to select the task you want to reformat, or select row headers (or adjoining cells) to select multiple rows.

If you want to skip Step 1 and use the Format Bar dialog box to reformat a single Gantt bar, double-click on the Gantt bar itself. If you've marked the task as partially completed, be sure to double-click on the edge of the larger Gantt bar, not the smaller bar marking the completed work.

2. Choose Format, Bar. The Format Bar dialog box appears (see Figure 16.3).

3. Click on the Bar Shape tab, if needed, to display the Bar Shape options. This tab lets you specify the appearance of the selected Gantt bars, including overall thickness, color, and ending shapes or symbols.

4. To add a symbol to the left end of the selected bars, select it from the Shape drop-down list in the Start Shape area. (If you leave this option blank, the Start Shape will be invisible.) Then use the Type drop-down list to specify the ending fill pattern, such as Solid. Finally, to apply a color to the selected Start Shape, select that color from the Color drop-down list. Figure 16.4 shows some possible Start Shape selections.

Figure 16.3
The Format Bar dialog box contains numerous options for formatting selected Gantt bars.

This area previews your selections

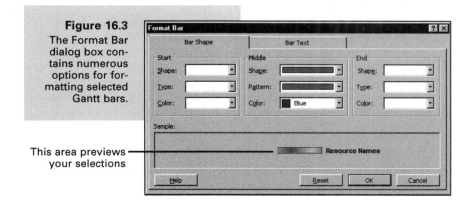

Figure 16.4
I've added a
start shape for
the selected
Gantt bar.

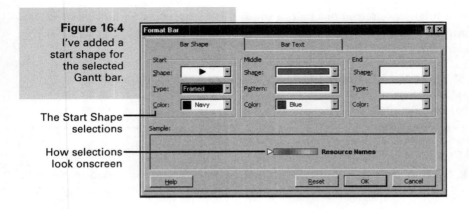

The Start Shape
selections

How selections
look onscreen

5. In the End Shape area of the dialog box, use the Shape, Type, and Color drop-down lists to specify and format a shape for the right end of the selected Gantt bars. These options are the same as the corresponding options in the Start Shape area.

Note

The Start Shape and End Shape settings do not have to match.

6. In the Middle Bar area, specify how the center of the selected bars will look. The Shape drop-down list enables you to specify how thick you want a bar to be and how you want to position it in relation to the start and end shapes—slightly up or down, or centered.

7. If the bar Shape that you specified is more than a thin line, use the Pattern drop-down list to adjust the relative density and hatching of the color used for the bar.

8. Select a Color for the bar. Figure 16.5 shows some selected bar shapes.

9. Click on the Bar Text tab to display the Bar Text options. You use this tab to specify how you want to display text in relation to the selected Gantt bars: Left, Right, Top, Bottom, or Inside. The tab offers a separate line for each of these options; you can enter text in any of them or a combination of them. (By default, resource names are displayed to the right of each bar.)

10. To add text to appear with a particular part of the bar, click on the cell beside the area name; then select the field of information to display with the Gantt bar from the drop-down list of fields (see Figure 16.6).

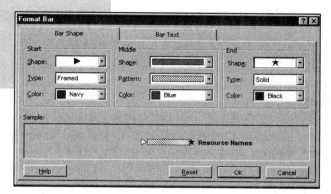

Figure 16.5
The final result of my bar color and shape adjustments.

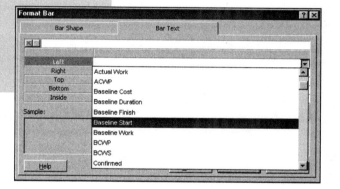

Figure 16.6
You can specify a field of text to appear at the left end of the Gantt bar.

Tip

If you want to remove text from a particular display area, highlight the existing field name, delete it, and then click on the Enter button that appears in the upper-left corner of the tab.

11. Use the technique described in Step 10 to edit any of the other text areas.

12. When you finish setting options in the Bar Shape and Bar Text tabs, click on OK to close the Format Bar dialog box. (Figure 16.7 shows a sample formatted bar.)

To return a Gantt bar to its default formatting, select the bar, open the Format Bar dialog box and click on the Reset button on either tab.

Figure 16.7
The Gantt bar for task 21 has new starting and ending markers, a patterned bar in the middle, and new labels.

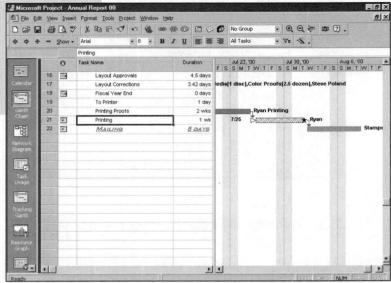

Formatting a Progress Line

Chapter 9, "Comparing Progress versus Your Baseline Plan," introduced the Project feature called *progress lines*. You add a progress line to a particular date on the Gantt chart to highlight in-progress tasks and provide a graphical representation of which tasks have not been completed by that date, or which are ahead of schedule. By default, the progress line for the current date or project status date, if you've displayed it, is red and has circular shapes at each point on the line. Progress lines for other dates are black and have no graphics. Because progress lines contribute to the appearance of your project screens, you'll want to be able to enhance them as needed for clarity and eye appeal. For example, you can change the pattern or color of a progress line.

Follow these steps to change the appearance of progress lines on your Gantt Chart:

1. Right-click on the Gantt Chart and click on Progress Lines. The Progress Lines dialog box appears.

2. Click on the Line Styles tab to display its options, as shown in Figure 16.8.

3. Click on one of the designs shown in the Progress Line Type area to change the overall shape of the progress lines. The choices here enable you

Figure 16.8
You can change the appearance of progress lines with the settings shown here; for example, you can choose a different color for progress lines.

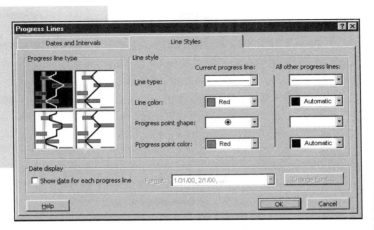

to specify whether the progress line points are sharp angles or blunted shapes. Also choose whether the progress line itself moves straight from point to point, or returns to travel along the progress line date.

4. The Line Style area offers four settings for the Current Progress Line or All Other Progress Lines (change the settings in the column that applies), some of which work like the similar settings you saw for formatting Gantt bars:

   - **Line Type**. Choose a dashed line style (or no line at all) for the actual line that travels between progress line points.
   - **Line Color**. Choose a color for the progress line.
   - **Progress Point Shape**. Choose a shape (or no shape) to appear at each progress line point.
   - **Progress Point Color**. Choose a color for the progress point shape you selected to make that shape stand out from its progress line or the Gantt bar to which it points.

5. If you want a date to appear at the top of each progress line to identify the progress date being charted, click to check the Show Date For Each Progress Line check box. Then you can open the Format drop-down list to select another date format for the displayed date, such as **Jan 31, '00**. Click on the Change Font button to open the Font dialog box and choose a different font for the displayed dates on the progress lines; this Font dialog box works as described earlier in this chapter.

6. Click on OK to apply your changes and change the display of the progress lines. Figure 16.9 shows some example progress lines that I've reformatted.

Dates added

Figure 16.9
Reformatting progress lines makes them more distinct and attractive.

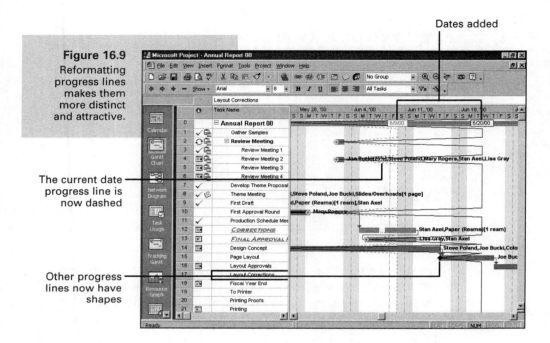

The current date progress line is now dashed

Other progress lines now have shapes

Working with Gridlines

Gridlines in Project, like gridlines in other applications that display graphical information, help your eye determine whether objects line up or where particular measurements occur. If you add gridlines to separate Gantt bars, you can easily tell which Gantt bars align with which Task Sheet rows. By default, the timescale in Gantt Chart view shows vertical gridlines that identify the major columns, which generally represent workweeks.

Some gridlines are horizontal, such as those that identify Gantt bar rows. Other gridlines are vertical. Generally, if the items for which you want to add gridlines appear in rows, the gridlines will be horizontal; if the items for which you want to add gridlines are organized in columns, the gridlines will be vertical.

Note

The lines that separate the rows and columns in Task Sheets and Resource Sheets are also considered to be gridlines and can be removed or reformatted. These gridlines are identified as the Sheet Rows and Sheet Columns options in the Line To Change list of the Gridlines dialog box.

When you change gridline settings, your changes apply to the entire schedule file; you can't change only the gridlines that correspond to selected tasks. To add gridlines to a graphical view in Project, follow these steps:

1. Choose Format, Gridlines, or right-click on the graphical area of the view (such as the Gantt Chart) and then click on Gridlines on the shortcut menu. The Gridlines dialog box appears (see Figure 16.10).

2. In the Line To Change list, select the item for which you want to add or edit a gridline. If the selected item already has some type of gridline applied, the specified formatting options for that gridline appear on the right side of the dialog box.

3. In the Normal area (the upper-right portion of the dialog box), specify the gridlines that you want for your Line To Change choices. Use the Type drop-down list to select the overall gridline appearance, such as dotted or dashed. Use the Color drop-down list to apply a color to the gridlines.

Note

If you want to remove displayed gridlines for the selected Line To Change item, select the Blank option at the top of the Type list. If you want gridlines to appear at intervals and not for every column or row, make sure that no line Type is selected.

4. In the At Interval area, you can specify the appearance of gridlines at a specified interval. If the normal gridlines are black, for example, you may want every fourth gridline to be red. Click on the 2, 3, 4, or Other option button (and edit the default Other value, if necessary) to specify which gridlines should use the alternative formatting. Then select the alternative gridline Type and Color.

5. Click on OK to close the dialog box and display your gridlines.

Figure 16.11 shows dotted gridlines used to separate Gantt rows. Every fifth gridline is a solid red line.

Figure 16.10
The Gridlines dialog box enables you to add gridlines to the Gantt Chart area of your view.

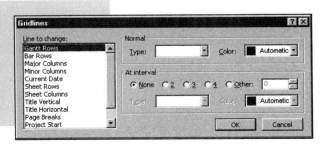

Figure 16.11
This Gantt Chart shows gridlines separating the Gantt bar lines.

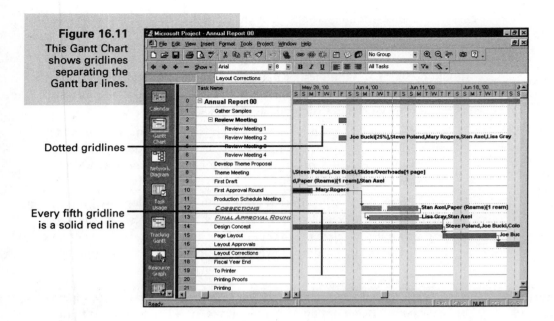

Dotted gridlines ———

Every fifth gridline is a solid red line ———

Formatting Text Styles

Based on the information you add to your schedule, Project classifies certain tasks based on their impact. The program marks all tasks on the critical path as being critical tasks, for example, and treats summary tasks differently from subtasks. Even though Project can track task categories easily, tracking might be a bit more difficult for you. To make the job easier, Project lets you apply special text formatting to any category of task or resource information in the Task Sheet or Resource Sheet. In Project, when you apply formatting to a particular category of information, you're defining a special text style. To work with a text style, follow these steps:

1. Display the view that includes the Task Sheet or Resource Sheet to which you want to apply the style.

2. Choose Format, Text Styles. Alternately, select a column, right-click on it, and then click on Text Styles on the shortcut menu. The Text Styles dialog box appears.

3. Select the category of information for which you want to adjust formatting from the Item To Change drop-down list (see Figure 16.12). If you want to change the font size of summary tasks, for example, select Summary Tasks here.

Figure 16.12
You select a style to change and then set its options.

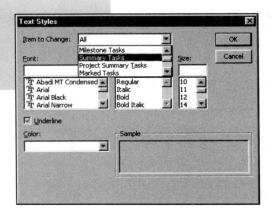

Note

The Item To Change list contains such items as column and row heads. The list is rather long, so check out everything that you can change.

4. Specify the text-formatting options for this category of information, just as you did for selected sheet text in the "Formatting Selected Sheet Text" section earlier in this chapter. The text-formatting options here work just like those you saw in Figure 16.2.

5. (Optional) If you want to set the formatting for other categories of information, repeat Steps 3 and 4.

6. Click on OK to close the Text Styles dialog box and apply the styles. All text in that category displays your formatting changes. (Figure 16.13 shows an increased font size for summary tasks.)

Adjusting the Bar or Box Styles for Charts

Just as Project applies a particular style of text to different categories of tasks or resources, it applies a particular style of formatting to the corresponding charted information. The adjustments that you can make in charted information depend on the selected view in Project. The formatting options are different for Calendar view bars, Gantt Chart view bars, Network Diagram view boxes, and Resource

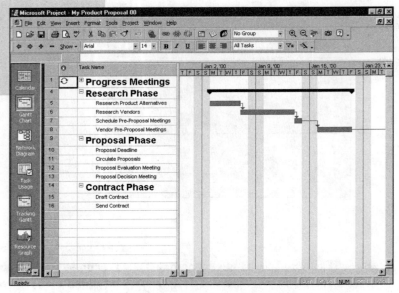

Graph bars. The following sections provide an overview of the most important options for each type of display.

The formatting options that are available for bars and boxes vary, depending on whether the graphical information appears in a combination view or in a single pane. The options also might change based on the type of information displayed.

For all views but Calendar view, you can open a dialog box that contains the appropriate bar- or box-formatting options by double-clicking on the chart area. For all charts, you can right-click on the chart area and then click on Bar Styles or Box Styles on the shortcut menu. If you prefer to use menu commands, choose Format, Bar Styles (for Calendar, Gantt Chart, or Resource Graph view) or Box Styles (for Network Diagram view). After you make changes in the appropriate dialog boxes, click on OK to close the dialog box and apply your selections to the appropriate bars and boxes.

Style Options in Gantt Chart View

Figure 16.14 shows the Bar Styles dialog box that appears in Gantt Chart view. To adjust a bar style, edit the column entries and Text and Bars tab settings. To add a new bar style, scroll down the list, enter the information for the style in each column, and then specify the Text and Bars tab options. To delete a style, select it in the Name list and then click on the Cut Row button near the top of the dialog box.

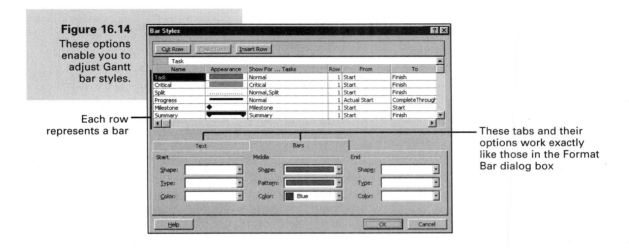

Figure 16.14
These options enable you to adjust Gantt bar styles.

Each row represents a bar

These tabs and their options work exactly like those in the Format Bar dialog box

Figure 16.15 shows an example of the formatting possibilities for the summary task bars. Not all the style columns are self-explanatory, so the following list reviews them:

- The Name column displays the name you enter for the style.
- The Appearance column displays the style's settings, which you specify by using the Text and Bars tabs at the bottom of the dialog box.

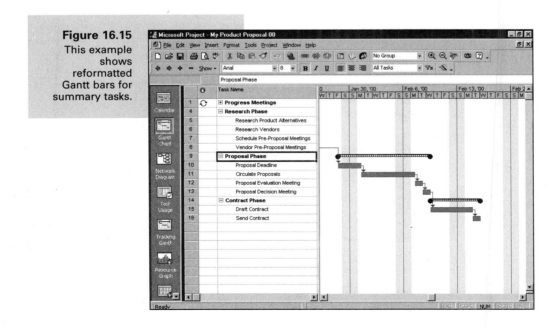

Figure 16.15
This example shows reformatted Gantt bars for summary tasks.

- The Show For . . . Tasks column specifies which fields or types of tasks the bars represent. Use the drop-down list to select a field. (You could, for example, create a bar style that applies to tasks Not Started Yet.) If you want to add multiple fields, type a comma in the text box after the last listed field and then select an additional field from the drop-down list.

- If you want to display multiple bars for each task (as in Tracking Gantt view), enter a value other than 1 in the Row column for a style. If you create a new style for tasks Not Started Yet, for example, you might enter 2, so that the Not Started Yet bar appears below the task's default bar.

- The From and To columns can also display fields. The fields that you select determine the length of the Gantt bars for the style. For the Not Started Yet bars, for example, you might want to specify Baseline Start in the From column and Start (for the currently scheduled starting date) in the To column. Those options draw a bar that leads up to the default bar for the task. Use the drop-down list at the far right of the text box to make your entries for these columns. However, for milestones, the From and To columns should show the same time period; for example, From *Start* To *Start*.

Style Options in Calendar View

If you displayed the Bar Styles dialog box in Calendar view, select a Task type from the list in the upper-left corner; then choose the various Bar shape options (which work just like those for Gantt Charts). This dialog box offers a few options that are unique to Calendar view (see Figure 16.16):

- Use the Split Pattern drop-down list to specify whether you want a dashed, dotted, solid, or no line to appear between the bar segments for split tasks.

Figure 16.16
Change the bar styles for Calendar view by using these options.

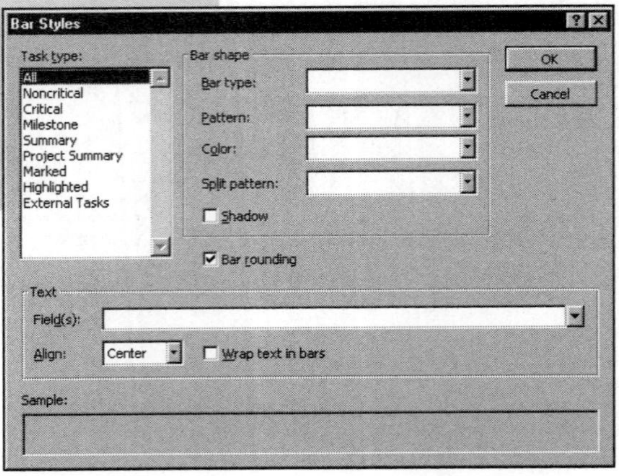

- If you choose the Shadow option, Project displays a drop shadow below bars of that style to provide a 3-D appearance.

- The Bar Rounding option makes bars of that style appear in full-day increments, even when an actual task's duration is less than a full day.

- The Field(s) box enables you to specify what field information is used to label bars of the selected style. You can select fields from the drop-down list at the far right of the box. Again, you can separate multiple fields in the text box with commas.

- The Align options enable you to specify where in the bars the specified text should appear.

- The Wrap Text In Bars option allows the specified text to occupy more than one line, if necessary.

Style Options in Resource Graph View

Figure 16.17 shows the Bar Styles dialog box for Resource Graph view.

The options available in this dialog box vary radically, depending on whether this graph appears by itself or in the lower pane of a combination view. The Filtered Resources options apply only to filtered resources when the Resource Graph appears by itself onscreen or is in the top pane of a split window; otherwise, the settings apply to all resources. The Resource options apply to the displayed resource.

Another factor that affects the options in this dialog box is which details you have chosen to display (see the "Working with Details" section later in this chapter). If you have chosen to display cost information in the graph, for example, the Bar Styles dialog box looks like Figure 16.18.

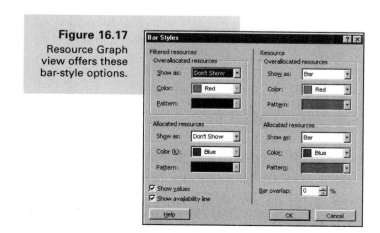

Figure 16.17
Resource Graph view offers these bar-style options.

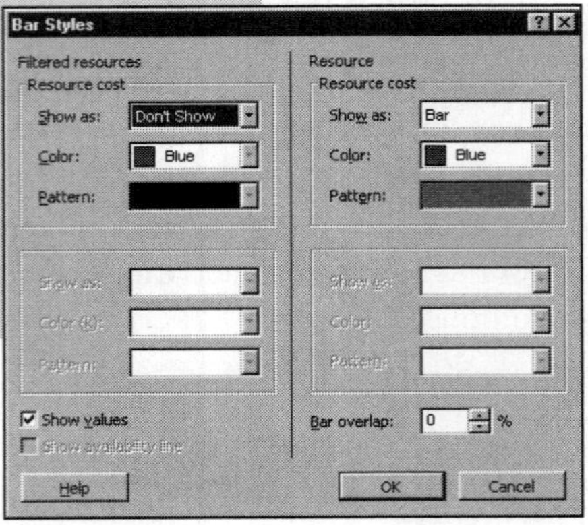

Figure 16.18
The Resource Graph bar-style options have changed because cost information now appears in the graph.

No matter which kinds of information you can format, the options are similar:

- Use any Show As drop-down list to specify whether the information appears as a bar, line, area, or other type of chart indicator.

- Select a color for the graphed information from the corresponding Color drop-down list.

- Select a pattern from the corresponding Pattern drop-down list.

- The Show Values option displays the values for the charted information at the bottom of the graph.

- The Show Availability Line option displays an indicator that shows whether the resource has any available working time. (This option is available when you're charting work information, as opposed to cost information.)

- If you want to display more than one type of bar for each time period in the graph, you can specify a Bar Overlap % option to allow the charted bars to overlap slightly, so that more information fits into less horizontal space. Figure 16.19 shows bars with a 25 percent overlap. The legend at the left side of the display shows what each style of charted information means.

Style Options in Network Diagram View

In Network Diagram view, you adjust box styles (instead of bar styles) by using the Box Styles dialog box shown in Figure 16.20.

This dialog box contains the following options:

- Choose the type of task box for which you want to make formatting changes from the Style Settings For list.

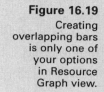

Figure 16.19
Creating overlapping bars is only one of your options in Resource Graph view.

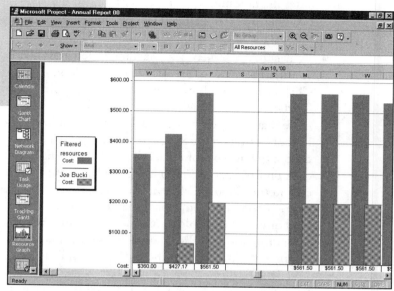

Figure 16.20
Full Network Diagram view enables you to control the appearance of the boxes.

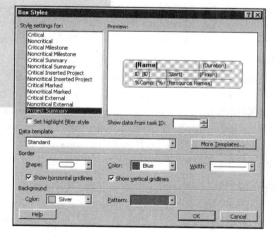

- Check the Set Highlight Filter Style check box and then choose a color from the Color drop-down list in the Background area to specify a background color to use for the box when you apply a filter that affects the specified type of task.

- Enter a task ID into the Show Data From Task ID text box to display the data for the specified task in the Preview area of the dialog box. For example, if you chose Critical in the Style Settings For list, you'd want to enter the task number for a critical task in the Show Data From Task ID text box to ensure that you can see how your changes will affect a task of the specified type.

- By default, each Network Diagram node box is divided into seven cells. If you want to show other information, click on the More Templates button. Click on the New button in the Data Templates dialog box. Type a name for the new template in the Template Name text box. If you want to show more than three rows and columns of cells in each node, click on the Cell Layout button and use the settings in the Cell Layout dialog box to choose the number of cells, cell widths, and merging for blank cells; then click on OK. Back in the Data Template Definition dialog box, use the cells in the Choose Cell(s) area to define what field data to display. Click on each cell, and then choose the desired field from its drop-down list. At the bottom of the dialog box, use the Font button to choose font formatting for the cells. Change the Horizontal Alignment and Vertical Alignment settings using those drop-down lists, if needed. Use the Limit Cell Text To drop-down list to specify whether each cell can hold multiple lines of text. Check Show Label In Cell if you want the field name to appear. Finally, if you've added fields that hold date information, choose a date format from the Date Format drop-down list. Click on OK to finish creating the new data template, then click on Close to close the Data Templates dialog box. Back in the Box Styles dialog box, open the Data Template drop-down list and choose the name of your new template.

- Use the Border options to set up the box outline. Select the style of box (for a particular type of task) from the Shape drop-down list; then select a Color and Width for the box outline using the drop-down lists of those names. Clear the Show Horizontal Gridlines and Show Vertical Gridlines check boxes to remove the gridlines that separate the cells in the node box, if desired.

- Under Background, use the Color and Pattern drop-down lists to specify the fill for the box.

After you specify all the Box Styles settings for one type of Network Diagram node, you can choose another type of box from the Style Settings For list, and then choose its settings. After you finish making all the box formatting adjustments you want, click on OK to close the Box Styles dialog box and apply your changes.

Working with Details

In the "Graphing Individual Resource Work and Costs" section in Chapter 10, you learned that you can right-click on the graph area on the right side of

Resource Graph view to open a shortcut menu, from which you select the information you want to view. You can select Percent Allocation, for example, to display a daily percentage of how much of the workday a resource will spend on a given task.

Similarly, you learned in Chapter 11 that you can right-click on any form that's part of a combination view to open a shortcut menu that enables you to specify which information the form displays. In the lower pane of Task Entry view, for example, you can right-click on the form and then click on Predecessors & Successors on the shortcut menu. The form then displays information about all predecessor and successor tasks for the selected task.

The equivalent of these shortcut menus is the Details submenu of the Format menu (see Figure 16.21). This submenu becomes available only when you select a pane that can morph to display different information. The submenu options vary depending on the nature of the selected pane. Simply select the type of information you want to display in the selected pane—the submenu closes, and the display changes accordingly.

Choosing a Layout

The layout features control how graphed bars appear in relation to one another in Calendar, Gantt Chart, and Network Diagram views. The layout options for

Figure 16.21
The Details submenu becomes available when you're in a pane that can display various types of information.

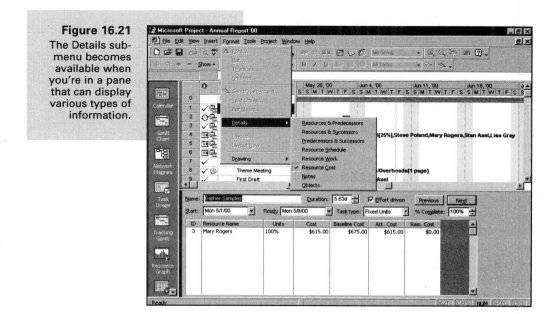

bar and box styles vary, depending on the selected view. To display the layout options for one of these views, choose Format, Layout, or right-click on a blank space of the chart area and then click on Layout on the shortcut menu.

Layout Options in Calendar View

The layout options for Calendar view are simple, as Figure 16.22 shows. If you want each week to show more task information, select the Attempt To Fit As Many Tasks As Possible option. To ensure that bars for split tasks are divided into segments, make sure the Show Bar Splits check box is checked. Select the Automatic Layout option to tell Project to adjust the calendar to accommodate inserted and moved tasks.

Note

As you might surmise from the presence of the Automatic Layout option in the Layout dialog box, by default Calendar view doesn't update automatically when you move or reschedule tasks in Gantt Chart view; neither does Network Diagram view. If you need to update Calendar view or Network Diagram view to reflect the current schedule and task relationships, choose Format, Layout Now, or turn on the Automatic Layout option in the Layout dialog box.

Figure 16.22
The layout options are limited in Calendar view.

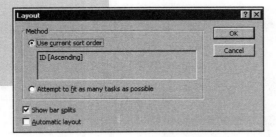

Layout Options in Gantt Chart View

Figure 16.23 shows the Layout dialog box for Gantt Chart view.

This dialog box contains the following options:

- Select the Links option to specify how (and whether) you want task-link lines to appear.
- The options in the Date Format for Bars drop-down list enable you to control the display of any date information that accompanies Gantt bars.

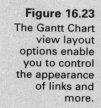

Figure 16.23
The Gantt Chart view layout options enable you to control the appearance of links and more.

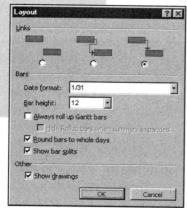

- The Bar Height option enables you to make all bars (and their rows) larger or smaller.

- As described in Chapter 15, you can check the Always Roll Up Gantt Bars option to display rollup bars for individual subtasks on the corresponding summary task bar. Also check Hide Rollup Bars When Summary Expanded if you want to hide the rollup bars when the subtasks for the summary task are expanded (displayed) rather than collapsed.

- The Round Bars To Whole Days option tells Project to format each bar as a full day—even for, say, a three-hour task.

- To ensure that bars for split tasks are divided into segments, make sure the Show Bar Splits check box is checked.

- If you added a drawing to the Gantt chart area, make sure that the Show Drawings check box is selected, so that the drawing appears. To hide the drawing temporarily (for printing, for example), clear this check box.

Layout Options in Network Diagram View

Figure 16.24 shows the Layout dialog box for Network Diagram view.

This dialog box contains the following options:

- Under Layout Mode, leave Automatically Position All Boxes selected to tell Project that boxes cannot be dragged on the chart. Check Allow Manual Box Positioning if you want to be able to drag boxes into the position you desire on the chart.

- Under Box Layout, use the Arrangement drop-down list to specify how Project arranges the node boxes. For example, you can choose Centered

Figure 16.24
These layout options are available for Network Diagram view.

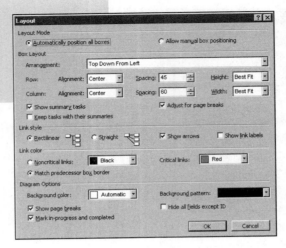

From Top rather than Top Down From Left, the default. Then, use the Row and Column Alignment, Spacing, and Height/Width choices to adjust how the boxes align within the specified arrangement. Clear the Show Summary Tasks check box if you want to hide the node boxes for summary tasks. If you leave summary tasks enabled, however, you may want to check the Keep Tasks With Their Summaries check box to keep summary tasks and subtasks together on the diagram. Make sure that the Adjust For Page Breaks option is selected. Later, when you choose Format, Layout Now, Project moves task boxes that appear on a page break to one page or the next, so that the box doesn't split in the printout.

■ As you can for a Gantt Chart, you can use the Link Style and Link Color choices to specify how links appear on a Network Diagram chart. Choose whether the links should be Rectilinear or Straight. Check the Show Arrows and Show Link Labels options to indicate if those features should appear with the links. You can use the drop-down lists to specify a color for Noncritical Links and Critical Links. Or leave Match Predecessor Box Order selected instead to have each link use the formatting of its predecessor link.

■ The settings under Diagram Options enable you to set up the overall chapter appearance. You can choose a Background Color and Background Pattern. Leave Show Page Breaks checked to display dotted lines in the view, so that you'll know which boxes will print together on a page. The Mark In-Progress And Completed check box determines whether lines marking percent complete appear in task node boxes. If you want to simplify the layout, you can check Hide All Fields Except ID, which changes all the node boxes so they display only the task ID number (task number).

Creating a Drawing in Project

In Chapter 17, "Copying and Moving Project Information," you learn how to insert a drawing from another application into your Gantt Chart as an object. Although Project is by no means a drawing application, it includes some basic drawing tools that you can use to add simple graphics to your Gantt Chart. You might want to display a box with some text to call attention to a particular task, for example. If you have a great deal of time, you can be creative, layering numerous drawn objects for a nice effect. By default, the drawn objects that you add appear onscreen and in any printout of a view that contains your Gantt Chart.

The drawing tools in Project work like those in Word, Excel, and many other Microsoft applications. An exhaustive discussion of drawing is beyond the scope of this book, but this section shows you how to draw objects, select and format them, and position them in relation to the correct date or task in the Gantt Chart. Follow these steps:

1. In Gantt Chart view, scroll the chart to the blank area where you want to create the drawing.

2. Display the Drawing toolbar. To do so, choose Insert, Drawing, or right-click on any toolbar onscreen, and then click on Draw.

3. The seven buttons at the center of the Drawing toolbar—Line, Arrow, Rectangle, Oval, Arc, Polygon, and Text Box—enable you to create those objects. To use each of these buttons, just select the tool, and then click and drag. (There are two exceptions: To use the Polygon button, you have to click for each point and double-click to finish; to use the Text Box button, you have to type text.) When you finish drawing the object, release the mouse button (the object appears with black selection handles around it). Figure 16.25 shows an example of using the Oval tool.

4. Double-click on the object you just drew; the Format Drawing dialog box appears (see Figure 16.26). Alternately, click on the object to select it (if it's not already selected), and then choose Format, Drawing, Properties.

5. Choose the Line and Fill options that you want to use. The Preview area shows the result of your choices.

6. Click on the Size & Position tab, which contains the following options:

   - **Size.** You probably don't need to worry about these options (near the bottom of the dialog box), because you defined the size when you created the object.

Figure 16.25
Click on a drawing button, and then drag to create a shape.

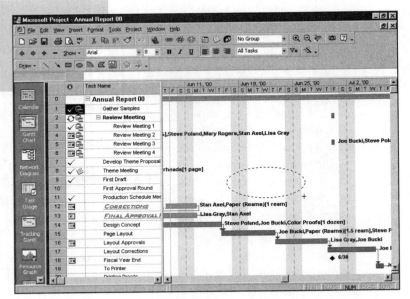

Figure 16.26
Format an object with this dialog box.

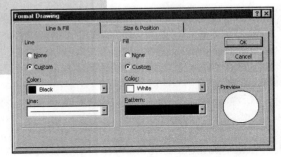

- **Position.** These options enable you to attach the drawing to a particular date (the Attach To Timescale option button) or task (the Attach To Task option button) in the Gantt Chart.

  By default, Attach To Timescale is selected, with the Date and Vertical entries reflecting the way that you positioned the object when you created it.

  The Attach To Task option attaches the drawn object (from its upper-right corner) to the Gantt bar for the specified task in the list. Enter the ID number for the Gantt bar to which you want to attach the graphic in the ID text box. Click on an Attachment Point option button to specify whether the upper-right corner of the graphic should be positioned relative to the left or right end of the Gantt bar. Adjust the Horizontal and Vertical entries to control how close the upper-right corner of the graphic is to the specified end of the Gantt bar.

Note

I find using the Horizontal and Vertical entries counterintuitive. Entering higher values moves the graphic down and to the right of the Gantt bar. To move the graphic above or to the left of the Gantt bar, you need to enter negative values. For example, if you attach a graphic to the right end of the Gantt bar, you might need to enter –1.00 as the Vertical setting to position the graphic above the selected Gantt bar.

7. When you finish selecting options, click on OK to close the Format Drawing dialog box.

8. Create another object, if you want. Figure 16.27 shows a newly created text box.

9. Double-click on the new object to set its formatting options. If you're adding a text box over an oval and you want the text to look like part of the oval, choose None for both the Line and Fill Color options (on the Line & Fill tab) in the Format Drawing dialog box. Close the dialog box.

Figure 16.27
This is a second new object.

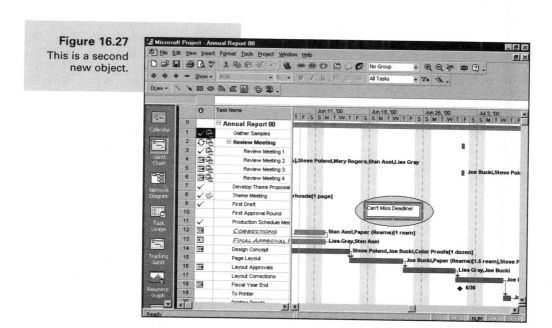

10. You have to use a special method to format the text in a drawn text box. Click on the box to select it (you click to select any drawn object), and then drag over the text within the box to select (highlight) it. Next, choose Format, Font; finally, use the Font dialog box to specify the formatting you want. Close the dialog box. Figure 16.28 shows the resulting text box.

11. Save the file to save your drawing on the Gantt Chart. If you close the Project file without saving it, you lose your drawing.

The objects you draw appear in invisible layers, with the object drawn most recently appearing on the top layer. You can use the Bring To Front or Send To Back choices in the Draw menu on the Drawing toolbar to send the selected object to the top or bottom layer, respectively. If you want to move the selected drawing object up or back by a single layer, use the Move Forward or Move Backward commands.

Figure 16.28
A text box superimposed over another object can be an attention-getting reminder.

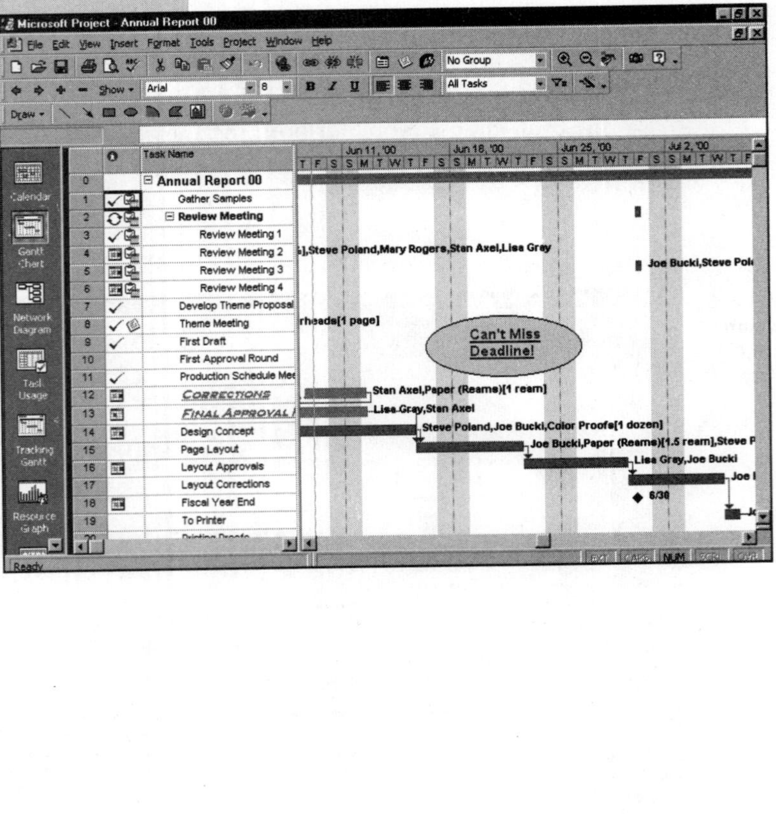

Part V
Handling Multiple Projects

17

Copying and Moving Project Information

IN THIS CHAPTER

- Copying data between projects
- Moving data between projects
- Understanding how copying and moving affects task links

There's no shame in using shortcuts; in fact, smart businesspeople seek them out and use them as tools for repeating successes. If you wrote a new-sales-call follow-up letter that enabled you to close a sale, you'd be silly to write a new follow-up letter after the next call. Instead, you'd reuse as much as you could of the letter that had already worked for you.

When you have invested a good deal of time entering information about resources and certain kinds of tasks in Project, and when you find that information to be valuable, you may want to reuse it. If different projects that you manage have similar tasks or use some of the same resources, you can save time by copying or moving information between those projects.

Copying Information between Projects

When you copy or move information in Windows applications, Windows places the information in the Clipboard—a holding area in your computer's memory. (For a copy, it leaves the original information intact; for a move, it deletes the original.) When data is in the Clipboard, you can paste it into a new location or into several locations. The file or location from which you copy or move information is called the *source,* and the place where you paste the information is called the *destination.*

The following sections show you how to copy information between two Project files. The steps that you take vary a bit, depending on whether you're copying all the information about a particular task or resource or only part of the information.

Note

You can copy and move information within a Project file as well. Simply select the information, cut or copy it, select another location for it in the Task Sheet or Resource Sheet, and then paste it into place.

Copying Task and Resource Information between Projects

When you select and copy an entire task row (or multiple rows), the entire set of information related to that task from the current table—the task name, resources assigned to that task, the duration, the start time, and so on for the Entry table of the Task Sheet, for example—is copied. If you select two or more linked tasks and paste them into another project, the link information that connects the tasks is copied, too.

You can also copy resource information to other projects. Copying resource rows picks up all the fields defined in the current table of your Resource Sheet. If you frequently copy the same resource information to new projects, choose Tools, Resources, Share Resources to create a common set of resources that are available to multiple projects. To learn more about shared resources, see Chapter 19, "Consolidating Projects."

To copy tasks or resources between projects, follow these steps:

1. Open the files for the two projects in question, select the same view in each project window (Gantt Chart view, for example), select the same Task Sheet or Resource Sheet table in each view, and arrange the project windows so a portion of each window is visible. You can choose Window, Arrange All to tile the project windows automatically. Alternately, you can press Ctrl+F6 to toggle between the active files.

2. Select the entire task or resource row to copy by clicking on the row number. To select multiple consecutive rows, hold down the Shift key and click on each row heading. To select multiple nonconsecutive rows, hold down the Ctrl key and click on each row heading.

3. Open the Edit menu and click on Copy (Task) or Copy (Resource). Alternately, do any of the following: right-click on the selection and then click on Copy (Task) or Copy (Resource) in the shortcut menu; press Ctrl+C; or click on the Copy button on the Standard toolbar. (The command name reflects the type of information that you selected—task or resource.)

4. If you're copying the information to another Project file, click on a portion of the destination window (such as the title bar) to tell Project that you want to copy information to that file. Then select the first cell of the row in which you want to place the copied information. No need to create a new row—Project does not paste the information over the contents of the current row. It instead inserts a new row for each copied task.

5. Choose Edit, Paste. Alternately, do any of the following: right-click on the row to paste to, and then click on Paste in the shortcut menu; press Ctrl+V; or click on the Paste button on the Standard toolbar. The task or resource information is pasted into the selected row, and the existing information is pushed down as needed.

You can also use Project's drag-and-drop feature to copy task or resource rows between project windows. Follow these steps:

1. Open the project files and arrange the windows so that the source and destination rows are visible.

2. Select the rows to copy by clicking on the appropriate task or resource row numbers.

3. Position the mouse pointer on the border of the selected area. The pointer changes to an arrow.

4. Drag the selected information to the first cell of the destination row. As you drag, the pointer changes to an arrow and a plus sign, indicating that the copy operation is in progress.

5. Release the mouse button to drop the copied information in the new location.

Figure 17.1 shows the drag-and-drop operation in progress.

Figure 17.1
You can use the drag-and-drop feature to copy Task Sheet or Resource Sheet rows to other project files.

This pointer appears when you drag to copy information

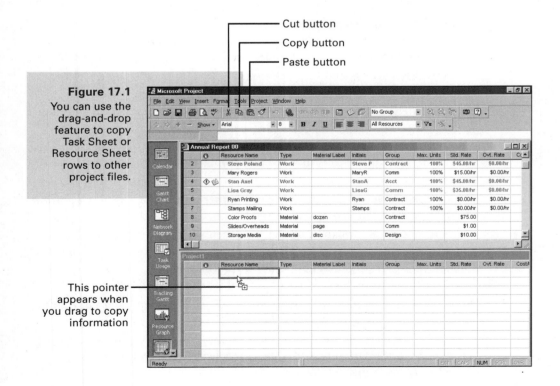

Note

When you drag and drop to copy information, Project also inserts a new row for the pasted information.

Copying Cell and Column Information between Projects

In some cases, you want to copy selected information about tasks or resources from one Task Sheet or Resource Sheet to another. You can copy a list of task names only, for example, or you can copy the hourly and overtime rates for one resource to the corresponding cells for another resource.

When you copy information from cells, all the other original information for the task or resource is left behind; only a copy of the cell contents is placed in the destination project. When you copy partial task or resource information to another project, the default values for Duration and Start Date (tasks), Accrue At and Baseline (resource), and so on are assigned to the task. You can edit those settings as necessary.

Caution

Keep the field (column) format types in mind when you copy information between Task Sheets or Resource Sheets. Typically, you should copy only between fields of the same type—from a Task Name field to a Task Name field, for example. Otherwise, you might get unexpected results. In some cases, if you try to paste an entry into a cell that needs a different kind of data (if you're trying to paste a name into a cell that contains an hourly rate, for example), Project displays a warning, as shown in Figure 17.2. Also, Project does not allow you to paste information into any calculated field.

To copy cell information between projects, follow these steps:

1. Open the two projects between which you want to copy information, select the same view in each project window, and arrange the project windows so that a portion of each is visible.

Figure 17.2
You'll see a message if a copy operation could create unwanted results.

I tried to copy this name . . .

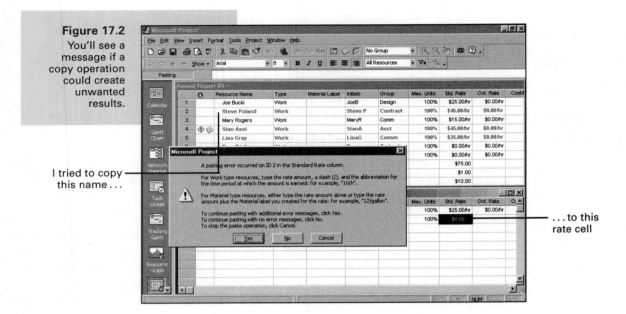

. . . to this rate cell

2. Select one or more cells to be copied. To select multiple consecutive cells (a range or block of cells), select the upper-left cell of the range, and then hold down the Shift key and click on the lower-right corner of the range (see Figure 17.3). To select multiple nonconsecutive cells, hold down the Ctrl key and click on each cell that you want to copy.

Click on this cell . . .

Figure 17.3
You can select a range of cells.

. . . then hold down the Shift key and click on this cell

3. Choose Edit, Copy (Cell). Alternately, right-click on your selection and click on Copy (Cell) in the shortcut menu, press Ctrl+C, or click on the Copy button on the Standard toolbar. (The command name reflects the type of information that you selected—in this case, a cell.)

4. If you're copying the information to another Project file, click on a portion of the destination window (such as the title bar) to tell Project that you want to copy information to that file; then select the first cell of the row in which you want to place the copied information.

Caution

When you paste a copied cell range (selection), the information you paste replaces any information in the destination location. Make sure you select blank cells to prevent overwriting project information that you need.

5. Choose Edit, Paste. Alternately, do any of the following: right-click on the selection you're pasting to, and then click on Paste in the shortcut menu; press Ctrl+V; or click on the Paste button on the Standard toolbar. The cell information is pasted in the selected area.

As you would expect, you can use the drag-and-drop feature to copy cell information between projects. Select the cells that you want to copy, point to the selection border so that you see the arrow pointer, drag the information to the destination, and release the mouse button to drop the information in place.

You can also copy and paste entire columns of information from one project to another. Suppose that you are creating a new project that has all the same tasks as an existing project, but the associated Duration, Start, and Finish entries—and the resources—are different.

To copy the Task Name entries from the existing project to the new one, click on the column heading (Task Name, in this case) to select the entire column. Then do any of the following: choose Edit, Copy (Cell); press Ctrl+C; or click on the Copy button on the Standard toolbar. In the window for the new project file, click on the Task Name column heading. Then do any of the following: choose Edit, Paste; press Ctrl+V; or click on the Paste button on the Standard toolbar. The entire list of task names is pasted into the new project.

Tip

If you often work with multiple projects at the same time, you can save the open projects and window positions as one unit. Save each of the open projects individually, and then choose File, Save Workspace. Give the workspace a meaningful name and click on OK to save it. The next time you open the workspace file, the project windows open in the place where you last left them. Chapter 3, "Working with Files and Help," covers saving a workspace in more detail.

Finally, you can make entering information in a single column easier by filling—an operation that's similar to copying. Start by selecting the cell that contains the information you want to copy to other cells that are lower in the list. Next, hold down the Shift key and click on the bottom cell of the group of cells that you want to fill, or hold down the Ctrl key and click on other noncontiguous cells lower in the column. Then choose Edit, Fill Down (or press Ctrl+D). Project fills all the selected cells with the information that appears in the first cell that you selected.

Moving Information between Projects

In addition to copying, you can move information between Task Sheets or Resource Sheets in open Project files. Moving information is almost identical to copying, except that you cut the information from the source file, leaving the selected row, column, or cells empty, rather than leaving the information in place, as you do when you copy. Then you paste the information where you want it.

As in copying, the moved information replaces existing information unless you're moving an entire row, in which case the moved information is inserted between existing rows. Finally, moving an entire row of information carries all the task or resource information for that row, except for linking information.

Tip

To ensure that the information you're moving doesn't overwrite existing entries in your destination Task Sheet or Resource Sheet, open the Insert menu and click on New Task or New Resource before you perform the move. Project inserts a new row in the location of the currently selected cell and moves existing rows down in the sheet.

The possibilities for moving information are almost endless. You may want to move information if you have more than one project under way and decide to move a resource from one project to another. In such a case, you need to move the contents of the row that contains that resource from the Resource Sheet of the first project file to the Resource Sheet of the second project file.

To move information between two Task Sheets or Resource Sheets, follow these steps:

1. Open the files for the two projects in question, select the same view in each project window (Gantt Chart view, for example), choose the same table for the Task Sheet or Resource Sheet in each file, and arrange the project windows so that a portion of each is visible. You can choose Window, Arrange All to tile the project windows automatically.

2. Select the task or resource row, column, or cells that you want to move.

3. Open the Edit menu and click on Cut (Task) or Cut (Resource). Alternatively, do one of the following: right-click on the selection and then click on Cut (Task) or Cut (Resource) in the shortcut menu; press Ctrl+X; or click on the Cut button on the Standard toolbar. (The command name reflects the type of information that you selected—task or resource.) Cutting removes the information from its original location and places the information in the Windows Clipboard.

Caution

Information stays in the Clipboard only while your computer is on. If you shut off the computer, or if it loses power for some reason, the Clipboard empties. Also, if you cut or copy anything else to the Clipboard, the new information wipes out the existing Clipboard contents. Therefore, make sure that you paste information as quickly as possible after cutting it.

4. If you're moving the information to another Project file, click on a portion of the destination window (such as its title bar) to tell Project that you want to move information to that file. Then select the first cell of the row in which you want to place the moved information.

5. Choose Edit, Paste. Alternately, do any of the following: right-click on the selection you're pasting to, and then click on Paste in the shortcut menu; press Ctrl+V; or click on the Paste button on the Standard toolbar. The task or resource information is pasted into the area.

To use the drag-and-drop feature to move information between projects, you use a process that's similar to copying. First, select the information that you want to move. Next, point to the selection border so that you see the arrow pointer, hold down the Ctrl key, and drag the information to the destination. Release the mouse button to drop the information in place, and then release the Ctrl key.

Affecting Links When You Copy and Move Information

Many of the tasks in the Project files that you create are part of a series of tasks linked via Finish-to-Start (FS) links. The tasks are strung together like beads on a string. If one of the beads cracks and falls off, the remaining beads slide together to fill the gap.

When you copy or move a group of linked tasks from one project file to another, the links stay intact within the group. If you move or copy a single task, link information doesn't travel with the task.

By default, when you move a task that's linked via FS links to a series of other tasks within a Project file, Project adjusts the linking information so that the linked tasks still flow continuously. If you move the linked task to a location that's higher or lower in the Task Sheet list, the links update to reflect all new task predecessors and successors.

In Figure 17.4, for example, the tasks in rows 1 and 4 are linked via an FS link, as are the tasks in rows 2 and 3. If you drag the task from row 1 to a location between tasks 2 and 3, the links rearrange, as shown in Figure 17.5. If the linking change will create a scheduling problem, the Planning wizard warns you (by default), as shown in Figure 17.6.

Figure 17.4
These two pairs of tasks are linked via Finish-to-Start (FS) links.

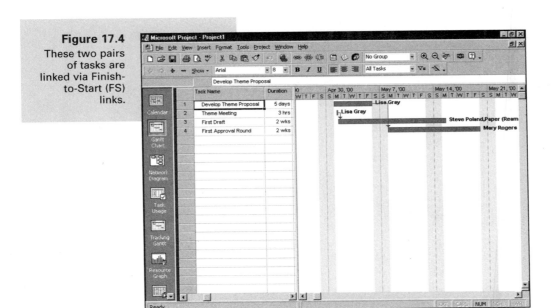

Figure 17.5
Moving the task that was originally in row 1 changed the links.

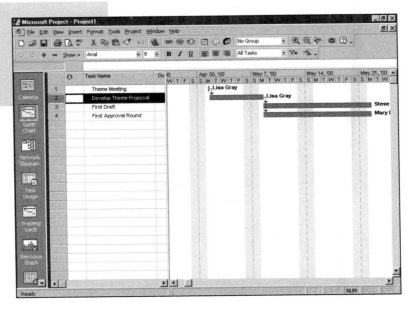

Figure 17.6
The Planning wizard warns you if moving or copying tasks will cause a linking problem.

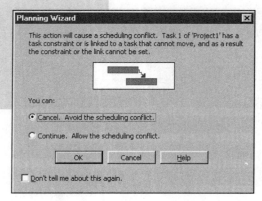

Pasting a copied task within a series of linked tasks can also disturb the linking relationships. If you want to be able to move tasks that are linked by FS relationships without changing the links, choose Tools, Options to open the Options dialog box. Click on the Schedule tab, clear the Autolink Inserted Or Moved Tasks check box, and click on OK. Otherwise, you can avoid messing up links simply by not moving or pasting tasks within a series of linked tasks, or by moving only tasks that aren't connected to a predecessor or successor via an FS relationship.

18

Working with Templates

Clothing makers a couple of centurieswago had to have strong powers of visualization. Unless they had an old garment to take apart and copy the pieces from, they had to envision how each piece of fabric should be shaped to come together into a garment.

Then some genius determined that you could make a prototype for a garment out of cheap muslin, and the muslin pieces could be copied as a paper pattern to use when cutting fabric for duplicates of the garment. The pattern does the grunt work, freeing the user to focus on improvements and fine-tuning, and that's exactly what a template file does for you in Microsoft Project 2000. In this chapter, you'll learn how to put a template to use.

Why Templates Can Save Time

When you save a file in Project 2000, it's saved by default as a regular project file, and it includes all the task and resource information you entered. When you open the file, it opens the one and only copy of that file, and when you save the file, it saves changes to that file.

In this scenario, it's not necessarily convenient to reuse all the information stored in your Project file. If you have a similar project and want to save the trouble of reentering all the information, you'll have to do some careful saving (and saving as) to reuse the information you want without overwriting the original file.

A better way to make your basic task and resource information available for reuse is to save that information as a template file. The template file is like a pattern of project tasks and resources that you can use as many times as you want. Using a template saves you the trouble of entering similar task and resource information over and over.

The template file sets up your basic task and resource information for you. Then you can edit it to fine-tune it for the unique requirements of your current project. Before I launch into describing the templates Project provides and how to work with them, here are a few situations where you might want to create a template:

- You have a project such as a newsletter or publication that recurs on a regular basis.
- You have a schedule file into which you've entered a tremendous amount of task or resource information, and you think you might have other similar projects.

- You want to create an example file of how numerous links work so that you don't have to create the links again.

- Members of your company's sales force need a basic tool for plotting out schedules for customers, and you want to provide a schedule blueprint with typical task durations.

- You're training others to manage a particular type of project in your company, and you want to provide a framework to help them with planning and to ensure that they don't miss any steps.

Using a Template

When you install the typical Project features, the Setup process copies a number of predesigned templates to your system. Although you can create your own templates (as you'll learn later in this chapter), and the process for using one of your own templates is the same as the process for using a template provided with Project, it's worth reviewing the templates that come with Project in the hopes that some will be useful to you. Table 18.1 lists the templates that ship with Project 2000.

You can use one of Project's templates to create a "practice" file that you can use to learn to work with Project features. That way, you only risk messing up sample information, not vital schedule information that you spent your own time entering.

The previous version of Project (Project 98) offered several more templates. These were found in the folder C:\Program Files\Microsoft Office\Templates\Microsoft Project by default (on a standalone system using Windows 95 or 98). If you didn't delete your old version of Project and installed Project 2000 to a new folder, you may be able to access the old template files. Project 2000 stores its files in a different folder, which I'll discuss later in this chapter.

Project and Windows identify template files with an MPT file name extension (which normally is hidden) instead of the MPP extension used for normal Project schedule files. Because the template files are identified differently "behind the scenes," opening a template file is slightly different from opening a regular Project file.

To open a template file that came with Project, follow these steps:

1. Choose File, New. The New dialog box appears.

Table 18.1 Templates Installed with Project 2000

Template	Description
Commercial Construction	Offers a detailed plan for designing and building a commercial space such as an office building, including all phases of preparation and construction.
Engineering	Holds a plan for the engineering design phase of a new product.
Infrastructure Deployment	Plans for implementation of a major infrastructure (technology or plan change) for a facility.
Microsoft Project 2000 Deployment	Provides a plan for rolling out Project 2000 in your organization.
MSF Application Development	Details a Microsoft standard plan for software product development.
New Business	Helps you organize and move through the tasks for launching a brand new business.
New Product	Provides a blueprint for launching and marketing a new product offered by your company.
Office 2000 Deployment	Presents a plan for rolling out Office 2000 in your organization.
Project Office	Gives a plan for setting up a project management office.
Residential Construction	Maps out the steps for building a single-family residence.
Software Development	Maps out the process of developing and launching new software, including feature set planning, programming, testing, manufacturing, market planning, advertising and public relations, developing relationships with vendors and customers, and the product release announcement; this plan could potentially be adapted for other products.
Windows 2000 Deployment	Presents a plan for rolling out Windows 2000 in your organization.

2. Click on the Project Templates tab. Icons for the templates appear on the tab, as shown in Figure 18.1. These templates are stored in the C:\Program Files\Microsoft Office\Templates\1033 folder by default on a Windows 98 system. (The templates appear in a different folder on Windows NT systems.) As you'll learn later, you'll store user templates you create in another location. This cuts down on the possibility that you might accidentally delete one of Project's templates.

3. Click on the icon for the template to use. If available, a preview of the template appears in the Preview area at the right side of the dialog box.

Figure 18.1

You can use the Project Templates tab in the New dialog box to open templates offered in Project.

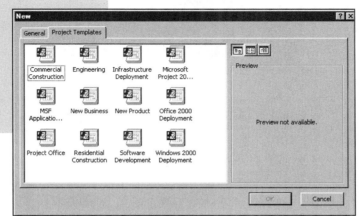

4. Click on OK to open the template. At this point, Project might open the Project Information dialog box to prompt you to enter a start date. Fill in the Project Information dialog box as needed, and then click on OK.

5. Before you make any changes, I recommend immediately saving the template as a Project file. By default, when you try to save a template file, Project assumes you want to save a copy of the template file as a regular Project file. To start the save, choose File, Save (or press Ctrl+S). Alternately, click on the Save button on the Standard toolbar. The Save As dialog box appears.

6. In the Save As dialog box, navigate to the drive and folder in which you want to save the file using the Save In list. (To avoid confusion, you shouldn't save the file in the default templates folder.)

7. In the File Name text box (see Figure 18.2), edit the suggested file name to save the file with a name that's different from the template name—one that's more descriptive of your project. For example, you might include the name of the product you're marketing in the file name for your copy of the New Product template, as in **Big Stick Product Plan**.

8. Click on Save to finish saving your file. The Planning wizard, if enabled, asks whether you want to save the file with a baseline (see Figure 18.3).

9. I recommend saving the plan without a baseline, because you haven't yet entered your real schedule information. Click to select the Save '(Current File)' Without A Baseline option button, if needed; then click on OK.

Save to a folder other than
the default templates folder

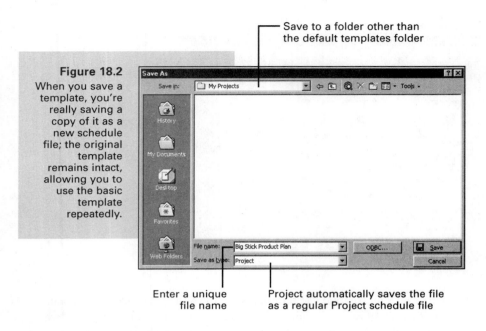

Figure 18.2

When you save a template, you're really saving a copy of it as a new schedule file; the original template remains intact, allowing you to use the basic template repeatedly.

Enter a unique
file name

Project automatically saves the file
as a regular Project schedule file

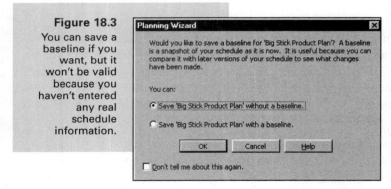

Figure 18.3

You can save a baseline if you want, but it won't be valid because you haven't entered any real schedule information.

After you open the template you want and save a copy of it as a regular file, you can begin editing it to include your actual schedule information. The types of edits you need to make and the available bells and whistles vary depending on the contents of the template. For example, the Windows 2000 Deployment template (Figure 18.4) provides a suggested list of tasks and a suggested duration for each task. Therefore all you need to do is to enter correct start dates for tasks in the Task Sheet and assign resources. In the Event Planning template, the text and Gantt bars are already attractively formatted and color-coded (the top summary

Figure 18.4

Project's Windows 2000 Deployment template offers a road map for implementing Windows 2000 in your organization.

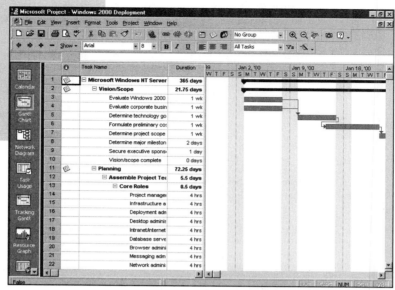

task is in red) to make them easy to tell apart. Other templates might include special tables and views you can apply, or other kinds of formatting. Simply make the edits and formatting changes you want, saving and printing when needed. After you save your copy of the template, it behaves as other Project files do.

Creating a Template

Because a template works like a pattern, it can consist of just a few pieces or as many pieces as are needed to create the final product. Thus a Project planning template can include numerous pattern pieces (types of information) that anyone opening the template can use. Any template you create can include these kinds of information and tools, among others:

- Lists of tasks in the Task Sheet, including suggested durations and links.
- Lists of resources in the Resource Sheet; for example, if a particular project always requires a resource, such as a shipping company that charges a per use and hourly rate, include information about that resource (especially its costs) with the template.

- Text formatting applied in the Task Sheet or Resource Sheet, including formatting applied to individual cells as well as Text Style changes for categories of information.

- Formatting applied to chart elements, such as Gantt bars.

- Custom views, tables, reports, and filters that you created and stored with the file using the Organizer. (See "Dealing with the Organizer to Work with Views, Macros, Tables, and More" in Chapter 11 to learn how to use the Organizer to save special elements with a file rather than in the default Project template, GLOBAL.MPT.)

- Macros and custom toolbars or toolbar buttons (see Chapter 25 for more information about macros) that you saved with the file or added to the file using the Organizer.

To build your own template, start by opening a new file and creating all the elements you want the template to include, such as the types of elements just listed. If you want to use a project file you previously created as a template, open that file. For example, if you created a My Product Proposal schedule that worked well for you, such as the one shown in Figure 18.5, you can save it as a template.

Figure 18.5
This project schedule file worked well, so I'll save it as a template to reuse it.

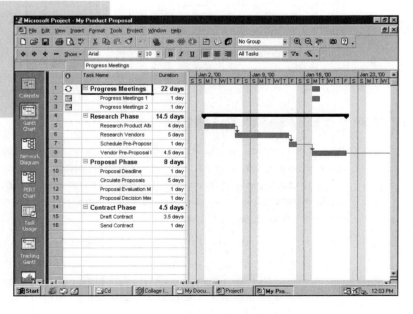

ON THE

CD

I've included the *My Product Proposal Chapter 18* file on the CD-ROM if you want to use it to try saving a template.

Note

Make sure that you include as much file Properties information and as many **Task Notes** and **Resource Notes** with your template file as possible. This information will remind you and other users how to use the template and will help you recall what particular entries mean.

Next, follow these steps to save your creation as a template:

1. Use the Organizer to ensure that you save all custom elements, such as views, reports, macros, and toolbars to the file that you want to save as a template (see "Dealing with the Organizer to Work with Views, Macros, Tables, and More" in Chapter 11). If you don't do so, those elements won't be available in your template.

2. Choose File, Properties. The project file's Properties dialog box appears.

3. Click on the Summary tab, if needed. Then click to check the Save Preview Picture check box. This option saves a thumbnail picture of the file, so that you'll be able to see that preview of the template before you select and use it. Click on OK.

4. Choose File, Save As. The Save As dialog box appears.

5. Open the Save As Type drop-down list; then click on Template. Project automatically changes to the C:\Windows\Application Data\Microsoft\ Templates folder in the Save In drop-down list. When you save your templates in that default folder, they will appear on the General tab of the New dialog box, making it easier for you to access and use your custom templates.

6. Edit the File Name entry to make it easy to see that the file is a template, as shown in Figure 18.6.

7. Click on the Save button. The Save As Template dialog box appears, asking whether you want to exclude certain information from the

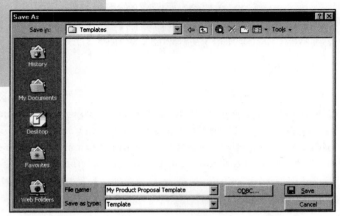

template file. This is a new feature in Project 2000 that lets you have greater control (with less work) over the contents of the template file.

8. I recommend that you save the template without a baseline so as not to interfere with baseline calculations for schedule files based on the template. I also recommend that you exclude actual values you may have entered in the file that you're saving as a template. So click to check both the Baseline Values and Actual Values check boxes, as shown in Figure 18.7. If you also want to exclude resource rate information from the Resource Sheet and fixed cost information you entered, click the appropriate check boxes.

9. Click on Save. The title bar for the file changes to indicate that the currently opened file is a template file.

10. Choose File, Close. This removes the template file from the screen. At any time, you can reopen the template file and save a copy of it as described in the next section to begin working with the copy.

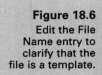

Sometimes you might want to make changes to one of your custom template files, or one that came with Project. Say, for example, that you have a template file in which you included resource information, and you discover that the standard hourly rates and overtime rates for several of the resources have increased. You can open the template file, edit the template, and resave it as a template file. Here are the steps:

1. Choose File, Open.

2. Open the Files Of Type drop-down list in the Open dialog box, and then choose Templates.

3. Use the Look In list to navigate to the folder that holds the template. If you saved it in the default folder, that will be C:\Windows\Application Data\Microsoft\Templates.

4. Double-click on the name of the template file to open it.

5. Make any changes you want to make in the template.

6. Choose File, Save As.

7. In the Save As dialog box, select Template from the Save As Type drop-down list. Leave all other settings intact to ensure that your changes are saved within the same template file.

8. Click on Save. A dialog box asks whether you want to replace the existing file.

9. Click on OK. The Save As Template dialog box appears.

10. Choose the settings you want in that dialog box, then click on Save.

11. Choose File, Close to close the template file.

Opening a Template You Created

If you saved a template that you created in the default folder, you'll have no trouble finding and using it. Project displays user-created templates stored in the default folder on the General tab of the New dialog box. Use the following steps to access and use a custom template:

1. Choose File, New. The New dialog box opens. Your custom templates appear on the General tab of the New dialog box, along with the Blank Project icon, which you can select to open a blank project file.

2. Click on the icon for the custom template you want to open. If you saved a preview of the template, it appears at the right side of the dialog box in the Preview area, as shown in Figure 18.8.

Figure 18.8
The General tab in the New dialog box lists templates you created and saved in the default templates folder.

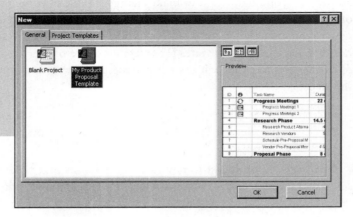

3. Click on OK to open the template. At this point, Project might display the Project Information dialog box to prompt you to enter a start date. Fill in the Project Information dialog box as needed, and then click on OK.

4. Immediately save the project file, giving it a new name if needed. You're ready to go with your template!

Note

If you saved your template to a folder other than the default folder for templates, you have to use the File, Open command to find and use it. In the Open dialog box, choose Templates from the Files Of Type drop-down list, use the Look In list to navigate to the appropriate folder, and then double-click on the desired template file.

19

Consolidating Projects

IN THIS CHAPTER

- Consolidating projects
- Using and adjusting the consolidated information
- Linking individual tasks between projects
- Sharing resources between projects that aren't consolidated

After you become a Microsoft Project guru (I know you will with this book in hand), you'll use the program to manage more forms of work than you could have imagined.

You may have two, three, or more project plans running simultaneously. In such a situation, the challenge for you as the project leader is to understand and prioritize work between projects, as well as to understand and prioritize work between tasks in a project.

This chapter shows you how to better manage all of the work on your plate by consolidating information from multiple project files.

When to Combine Projects

If you need a single printout of the tasks from two projects, you can print them out separately, trim the excess, tape the two together, and make a photocopy so that you have a single, solid document. This solution, however, is inelegant and forces you to do the dirty work rather than having your computer do it.

Project offers a workaround for situations like this; it's called *consolidating* projects. When you consolidate two or more schedule files, Project places all the information from each of the selected files (sometimes called *subprojects* or *source projects*) into a single consolidated file (sometimes called the *master project*). Then you can change the view, print, and otherwise work with the combined information. You can consolidate up to a thousand different project schedules (assuming your system has the horsepower to do so) in a single consolidated file, but that's really not practical. Once you consolidate a few dozen files or so, you can see real degradation in system performance, and the likelihood of file corruption is increased.

Here are just a few situations in which you might want to consolidate projects into a single file:

- You're managing multiple projects and you want a list of in-progress tasks to jog your memory about things on which you need to follow up. You consolidate the tasks and then filter the Task Sheet so that it lists only the in-progress tasks.

- You want to display a list of all the tasks in your projects that will start in the near future. You can print them before a meeting with your boss, so the two of you can discuss shifting priorities and identify some tasks to reschedule.

- You want to print a list of all the resources you're using for all projects.

- You have two projects using the same resources, and you want to see if there are any resource overallocations. You can consolidate the files and switch to Resource Usage view to find overallocations.

Combining Projects

Consolidating schedule files places all of the information from the specified individual files into a consolidated file. The "live" information the consolidated file contains helps you see multiple projects in perspective. When you save it, you can assign it a unique name of your choosing. Alternately, you can insert other schedule files into the current file to consolidate them; the current file then becomes the consolidated file. The rest of this section explains the details of creating and working with a consolidated file.

Consolidation Methods

Consolidated files can work in two different ways. The consolidated file can exist independently of the files from which its information came, or it can remain linked to the original source files. The first situation is fine if you want to work with the consolidated file on a one-time basis only. If, however, you want to reuse the consolidated file over a period of days, weeks, or longer, the schedules for the individual original project files might change, making the consolidated file obsolete—unless you link it to the original files when you create it.

Using the first method described next, you can create consolidated files with or without links. The second method is faster and can only be used when you want to consolidate project files with links.

Inserting a Project to Consolidate Files

The primary method for consolidating files in Project 2000 is to insert a schedule file into a row in an existing project file, which then becomes a consolidated or master project file. Each inserted source project or subproject file is linked to a single Task Sheet line in the master project. At first, you don't see all the tasks for the inserted subproject; instead, you see a single summary task and Gantt bar summarizing the inserted project. By default, the start date entered in the inserted subproject file is the same date it uses in the master project file; when the files are linked, you can change the start date in either file to update it for both. The duration of the full schedule for the inserted subproject file becomes the duration for the subproject summary task entry in the master project Task Sheet. So, if all the tasks listed in the subproject will take 95 days to complete, the master project shows 95d as the duration entry for the subproject task, and you can't edit that entry.

Note

> At times you'll need to readjust the start date for a subproject. See the "Controlling Dates in Consolidated Projects" section later in this chapter for more details.

You have to create the source or subproject files before adding them to the consolidated project file. You can't insert a file that doesn't exist, after all. You don't, however, have to initially create the tasks within the subproject file. You can simply open and save the file with the name you want, and then close and add it to the consolidated master project. You can reopen the subproject file at any time to enter its tasks. This approach works best in many cases, because it ensures that you don't have to go back and manually update a subproject start date.

To insert a project (source project or subproject) within an existing project file (which becomes the consolidated or master project), follow these steps:

1. Create and save the subproject files.

2. Create or open the file where you want to insert other files. This file will become the consolidated or master project file.

3. Click on the Task Name cell for a blank Task Sheet row in which you want to insert another project. Or click on a cell in the row above where you want to insert the project. (Actually, you're specifying the row where the summary task representing the inserted task will appear).

Note

> You can insert a project at any outline level and later demote or promote it by demoting or promoting the summary task that represents it.

4. Choose Insert, Project. The Insert Project dialog box appears, as shown in Figure 19.1.

5. If needed, use the Look In drop-down list to navigate to the drive and folder holding the file to insert.

6. Click on the file you want to insert. If you want to insert more than one file stored in the same drive and folder, you can click on the first file; then press and hold Ctrl and click on additional files to select them.

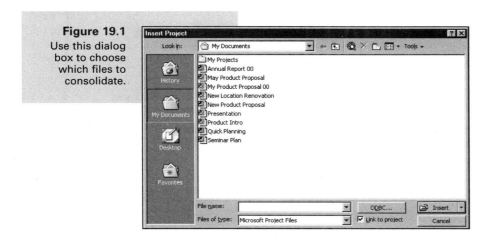

Figure 19.1
Use this dialog box to choose which files to consolidate.

7. By default, the inserted subproject file is linked to the consolidated (master project) file, so the Link To Project check box will be checked. If you do not want the files to be linked (meaning changes you make in one of the files will not appear in the other), clear the Link To Project check box.

8. Click on Insert. The inserted (subproject) task appears in the file, as shown in Figure 19.2.

Figure 19.2
This is how a consolidated file appears; two source projects (or subprojects) have been inserted into this project.

Indicator for an inserted project

Summary Gantt bar for inserted project

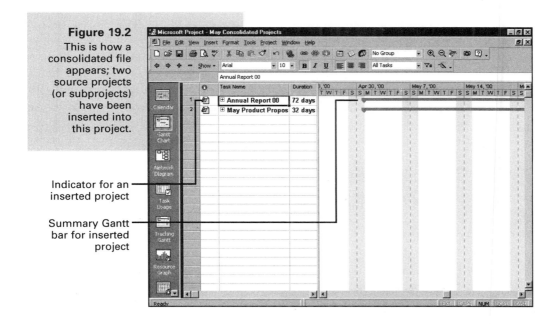

Tip

To insert a project file as read-only (preventing you from making any changes to the original subproject file from the consolidated file), click on the drop-down list arrow beside the Insert button and then click on the Insert Read-Only choice in the submenu that appears.

Note

If the inserted file name doesn't show up as it should or you want to use another way to identify the inserted file in the consolidated file, double-click on the task for the inserted file and change the Name entry on the General tab of the Inserted Project Information dialog box.

9. Save the master project file to save the links to subprojects.

You can use the preceding steps to link other subprojects to the master project file.

Combining Multiple Projects in a New Window

There is a somewhat faster way to create a consolidated file, but as usual with such matters, you have to give up a little flexibility to save time. To use this method, begin by opening each of the files you want to consolidate. Make any changes you want to the files and save them. Choose Window, New Window. The New Window dialog box appears. In the Projects list, click on the name of the first file to consolidate. Press and hold down the Ctrl key; then click on additional files to select them (see Figure 19.3). Click on OK, and Project compiles the consolidated file onscreen into a brand new file. (By default, the consolidated file is linked to the original subproject or source files. In addition, the resource pools for the individual files are not consolidated.) You can then save and work with the

Figure 19.3
This is a quicker but less flexible method to select files for consolidation.

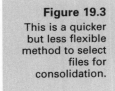

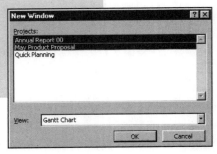

consolidated file. The source files remain separate and intact on disk. So, with this method, you're creating a brand new file rather than altering an existing one.

Working with Resource Pools (Sharing Resources)

Another name for the list of resources you create in the Resource Sheet for a particular project is the *resource pool*. If you consolidate projects and then display the Resource Sheet, you may notice that Project lists the resources from each subproject file in the Resource Sheet. As shown in Figure 19.4, the row numbers start over where the resource list for each inserted subproject starts.

When multiple files use the same resource, the Resource Sheet lists that resource multiple times. This might lead you to believe that the views and reports will automatically add up the work assigned to one resource from each of the subprojects. Unfortunately, that's not how it works. For your consolidated project file to total the work, you must *share* the resource pool in the individual files *before* consolidating the files. For example, let's say a file named "Mayland Building Construction" holds your entire list of resources. You want to consolidate that file with another one named "Jenkins Building Construction," which uses roughly the same resources. In this case, you need to open both files, go to the "Jenkins Building Construction" file to make it the active one, share the resources from the "Mayland Building Construction" file, save both, and then consolidate them into a third file. Then that third file will "collate" and total the assignments for the shared resources in all the views, so you'll be able to see how the work adds up. (If you share resources after you consolidate in the consolidated file, the reports will typically add up all the resource work, but the views won't.)

You already know that when you're working with individual (unconsolidated) files, each list of resources is saved along with the project file where you created

Figure 19.4
The Resource Sheet in the master project file by default lists the resources from the subproject files.

	�", id	Resource Name	Type	Material Label	Initials	Group	Max. Units	Std. Rate	Ovt. Rate	Cos
1		Joe Bucki	Work		JoeB	Design	100%	$25.00/hr	$0.00/hr	
2		Steve Poland	Work		Steve P	Contract	100%	$45.00/hr	$0.00/hr	
3		Mary Rogers	Work		MaryR	Comm	100%	$15.00/hr	$0.00/hr	
4	◇ 🖼	Stan Axel	Work		StanA	Acct	100%	$45.00/hr	$0.00/hr	
5		Lisa Gray	Work		LisaG	Comm	100%	$35.00/hr	$0.00/hr	
6		Ryan Printing	Work		Ryan	Contract	100%	$0.00/hr	$0.00/hr	
7		Stamps Mailing	Work		Stamps	Contract	100%	$0.00/hr	$0.00/hr	
8		Color Proofs	Material	dozen		Contract		$75.00		
9		Slides/Overheads	Material	page		Comm		$1.00		
10		Storage Media	Material	disc		Design		$10.00		
11		Paper (Reams)	Material	ream		Design		$5.00		
1	◇	Joe Bucki	Work		JoeB	Design	100%	$25.00/hr	$0.00/hr	
2	◇	Steve Poland	Work		Steve P	Contract	100%	$45.00/hr	$0.00/hr	
3	◇	Mary Rogers	Work		MaryR	Comm	100%	$15.00/hr	$0.00/hr	

it. Any Project file can access the resource pool that's saved with another file through resource sharing. When you start a new project file and want to use the entries in the Resource Sheet saved with another file rather than typing in a whole new list of resources, you can do so by sharing resources.

Following are the steps for sharing resources. You use the same steps whether you're working with a consolidated file or separate files:

1. Open the file in which you've already created and saved the resource information that you want to reuse. This is an important initial step because only those files that are open and using their own resources will appear in the Use Resources From drop-down list in the Share Resources dialog box.

2. Open or create the file that will share the existing resource information, if you're working with individual files.

3. Choose Tools, Resources, Share Resources. The Share Resources dialog box appears.

4. Click on the Use Resources option button, then use the From drop-down list to select the file containing the resources you want to share (see Figure 19.5).

Note

You'll want to use the file that holds the most resources possible to make all the resources available for reporting purposes. For example, say one of your files holds 12 resources and the other holds 3, all of which also appear in the list of 12 resources in the other file. Obviously, you'll want to choose the file that holds all 12 resources.

5. In the On Conflict With Calendar Or Resource Information area, select Pool Takes Precedence (meaning that Project will make changes to the resource list in individual files based on changes to the pool file) or Sharer Takes Precedence (meaning that Project will make changes to the file

Figure 19.5
Select the file containing the resource pool you want to reuse.

Share Resources

Resources for 'May Consolidated Projects'
- ○ Use own resources
- ● Use resources

From: [   ]
    Annual Report 00
    May Product Proposal

On conflict with
- ● Pool takes precedence
- ○ Sharer takes precedence

[Help] [OK] [Cancel]

holding the resource pool based on changes to the individual file sharing the pool).

6. Click on OK to finish sharing the resources. The resource pool from the file you specified is now used for the current file. Save the current file to save the resource sharing information.

7. Consolidate the files sharing the resources.

When you save and close a file that uses the resource information from another file, Project keeps track of the fact that the two files are linked. When you reopen the file containing the link to resource information, Project must open the other file. It displays the Open Resource Pool Information dialog box asking if you want to open the resource pool or not. Make your choice and click on OK. If you've made changes to the Resource Sheet in the file you're sharing information from and specified that the resource pool should open, those changes appear in the file that shares the information.

Conversely, if you reopen the file where you originally entered the resources, the Open Resource Pool dialog box presents a few options (Figure 19.6). You can open the resource pool as read-only, open the resource file normally so that you can make changes to it (although if you choose this option and your files reside on a network, other users won't be able to change the resource pool), or open the file with the resource pool and any other files using the resource pool in a new master project file.

Note

If one of the files in a consolidated file holds the resource pool for all the consolidated files, you'll see both the options for opening a file that uses shared resources and for opening a file that holds the resource pool.

Figure 19.6

When you open the project file that holds your resource pool, you have to specify whether or not you want to be able to make changes to it.

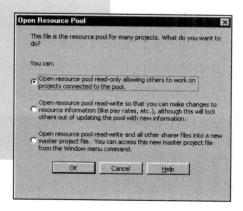

You can make changes, such as updating rates for the resource information, in the file that holds the resource pool, and then simply open the other files that also use that resource pool to update the resource information for those files, too. However, if the resource pool file is stored on a network and others can make changes to it, and you have left a file using that resource pool open for several hours, your resource information may not be up to date.

You can refresh the resource information (to get the latest information) without closing and reopening your file. Instead, choose Tools, Resources, Refresh Resource Pool. Conversely, if you make changes in any file that uses the resource pool on the network and want the pool to be updated with those changes, choose Tools, Resources, Update Resource Pool.

If you open a file that uses resource information from another file, you can edit the resource link information. To do so, reopen the Share Resources dialog box by choosing Tools, Resources, Share Resources. In the Share Resources dialog box, make the changes you prefer (such as selecting another file to use resources from, or opting not to use resources from another file at all), and then click on OK. Project closes the dialog box, and your resource sharing changes take effect. Make sure that you save the current file to save these changes.

In practical terms, this means that you can create a project file that's strictly for listing resources. For example, if you use the same resources over and over, you can create a single file, named Resources, where you store every resource you use for every project. You then can specify that every other schedule file you create uses the resources stored in the Resources file. Up to 999 files can share the same resource pool in Project 2000. Be aware, though, that this strategy may lead to a huge resource pool file if everyone in your organization is using the same pool file stored on a shared network drive. Even on a fast network, a huge resource pool file can slow down the performance of the individual files sharing the resources from the pool.

Working with Your Consolidated Information

When you're working with the consolidated file, you can do everything that you can do in an individual Project file. You can change any entries you want, or change the view. For example, choose View, Resource Sheet or click on the Resource Sheet icon in the View Bar to view the Resource Sheet for a consolidated project file. If you are sharing the resource pools for the consolidated files, any resource overallocations are highlighted in bold red text. Also, if you have shared resources before consolidating the files, you can choose View, Resource Graph or click on the Resource Graph icon in the View Bar. When you display a resource that's assigned to more than one project, the overallocated hours for that resource are graphed (see Figure 19.7).

Figure 19.7
Here's the Resource Graph for a consolidated file with shared resources.

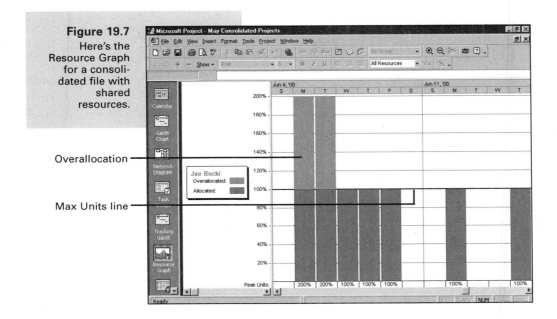

Overallocation

Max Units line

Note

If you open a consolidated file where resources have been shared between the subproject files and don't see any resources in the Resource Sheet, you need to open the file that holds the resource pool.

Another thing to note is that when you're working with the information in a consolidated file, the name for each of the subproject or source project files you inserted appears as a numbered summary task row in the Task Sheet of any view that includes the Task Sheet (such as Gantt Chart view). When you consolidate multiple files into a new window, these rows are treated by Project as summary tasks at the highest level of the outline (see Chapter 15, "Working with Outlining," to learn more about outlining). The top-level tasks from the source files appear as subtasks of the source files. All tasks that were subtasks within the original project files are hidden, and all individual project tasks holding subtasks appear in bold (see Figure 19.8). However, if you consolidated the file by inserting a file, the summary task for the inserted file appears at the same outline level as the task below which it was inserted.

If you click on the Task Name column and then click on the Hide Subtasks button on the Formatting toolbar, the Task Sheet displays only the names of the consolidated files (see Figure 19.9).

Information from the next
source file starts here

Figure 19.8
Project provides
cues to help you
identify which
tasks came from
which subpro-
jects (source
files) and which
tasks include
subtasks.

This bold task was
a top-level task in
the source file and
includes subtasks

Figure 19.9
This file
consolidates two
other files.

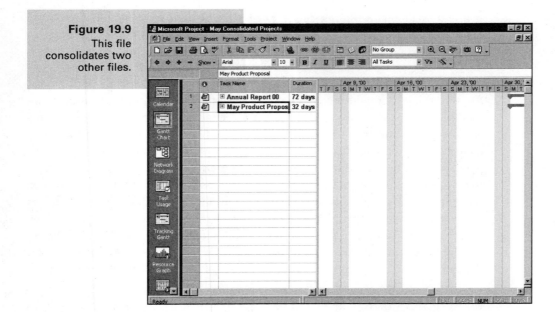

By now, you get the idea. The consolidated file behaves much like other project files in terms of how you can change its contents.

Note

> This sounds odd, but you have to display all subtasks for a report you run to include information from the subtasks. For example, if you have a recurring meeting task set up, you need to expand all its subtasks before you generate the report to ensure that information gets included in the report.

Opening Subprojects

Even though the subproject files and consolidated (master project) file remain as separate entities on disk, by design they share information so that they always reflect the same dates. For example, if you reschedule several tasks in a subproject to make the total subproject duration longer, you'll want the new duration to be reflected in the master project file. It helps to understand how this automatic updating occurs; it takes place through opening files.

To update subproject and consolidated project information, open each subproject file as usual, update its contents, and save it. Then you open the consolidated (master project) file, which is automatically updated with the latest information you added into each subproject file. Make sure that you then save the consolidated file to save its changes, too. When you save or close a consolidated file in which the individual files share resource pools, you might be prompted to save the resource pool as a separate file. Follow the prompts to do so, to streamline the file relationships.

Working with Subprojects

In most cases, working with an inserted subproject is identical to working with other summary tasks and subtasks. You can expand and collapse the inserted task's subtasks, and you can update information such as actual start dates and work completed for any subtask. However, you'll need to use some unique steps when you're working with the inserted subproject's summary task, covered in this section.

Changing Subproject (Inserted Project) Information

When you double-click on the summary task for an inserted subproject, or click on the task and then click on the Task Information button on the Standard toolbar, the Inserted Project Information dialog box appears. In most respects, this dialog box resembles the Task Information dialog box. It offers the same five tabs, which in most cases have identical options:

- **General.** The General tab appears in Figure 19.10. You can use it to change the inserted project's summary task Name and Priority, or to control the display of the summary tasks Gantt bar and any rolled-up subtask bars.

- **Predecessors.** Use this tab to link the inserted project's summary task to another task in the consolidated file. For example, if two inserted projects need to finish by the same date, you could create a Finish-to-Finish relationship between their summary tasks. The settings on this tab work just like those for a regular task.

- **Resources.** Use this tab to assign resources to the summary task for the inserted subtask. You might want to do this in an instance where you make a resource responsible (a supervisor) for all aspects of the inserted project. Again, the settings on this tab work just like those for a regular task.

- **Advanced.** This tab (Figure 19.11) differs most significantly from the corresponding tab in the Task Information dialog box for a regular task. In the Source Project area of the dialog box, you can specify whether the inserted subproject is linked to the consolidated project (Link To Project), and if so, whether the link is read-only. The name of the inserted file appears in the text box in the Source Project area. To insert another subproject file instead in the same location in the Task Sheet, click on the

Figure 19.10

Some options on the General tab of the Inserted Project Information dialog box are dimmed, meaning you can't edit them.

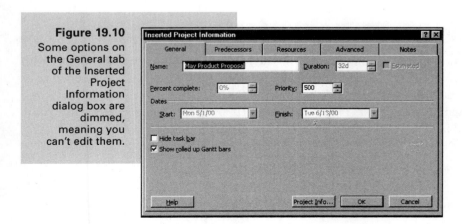

Figure 19.11
Use this tab to control which project file is inserted and how it's inserted.

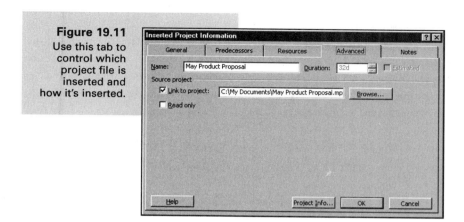

Browse button to reopen the Inserted Project dialog box and then choose a different file to insert.

■ **Notes.** Use this tab to insert, format, and edit a note for the inserted task's summary task. Use the same techniques on this tab that you would use on the Notes tab for an individual task.

The bottom of each tab in the Inserted Project Information dialog box displays a Project Info button. Click on that button to open a Project Information dialog box similar to the one shown in Figure 19.12. You can use this dialog box to change such key features as the Start Date for the inserted project or the Calendar it uses. Its options work just like those for the regular Project Information dialog box, which you can use in the open subproject. If you want to change the same information for the inserted subproject without opening the subproject file, open the Project Information dialog box by clicking on the Project Info button in the Inserted Project Information dialog box.

Figure 19.12
Use this dialog box to change overall schedule information for the inserted project.

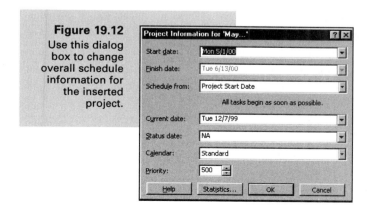

Deleting a Subproject

If you want to delete the source project or subproject, right-click on its row number, and then click on Delete Task. If the Planning Wizard is enabled, a dialog box appears (Figure 19.13) asking you to confirm the deletion. To finish the deletion, leave the first option button selected and click on OK. If you made changes to any of the inserted project's information in the consolidated project file, you'll also be prompted to specify whether or not to save those changes to the subproject file before the subproject is removed from the consolidated project. Click on Yes to do so, or No to remove the inserted subproject without saving changes.

Figure 19.13

The Planning Wizard asks you to verify whether to delete the inserted project's summary task.

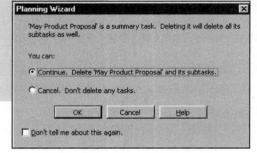

Controlling Dates in Consolidated Projects

Sometimes you'll need to make manual adjustments to ensure that the schedules in your subproject files and master project file are in sync.

For example, an inserted subproject file might include old schedule information, so you might need to adjust its start date to match the master project's start date. This would happen, for example, if you created the subproject file on April 7 (so that its original project start date was April 7), but then waited until April 8 to create the master project file and accepted that date as the master project's start date. You'd then need to change the inserted project's start date to April 8 to make sure its schedule falls within the consolidated master project schedule. Simply updating the inserted project's start date doesn't fully work because the schedules for individual subtasks of the inserted project's summary task don't generally update correctly. To update a subproject file so that its start date reflects the start date you entered in the master project and so that the work for all its subtasks is correctly rescheduled, use these steps:

Note

> **Keep in mind that the following steps also reschedule the start date and scheduled work in the individual subproject (source project) file if the files are linked. Changes you make in the subproject file appear in the consolidated file, and vice versa, for linked files.**

1. Open the master project file.
2. In the Task Sheet, display the summary tasks for the inserted subproject. (Click on the plus sign beside the inserted project's summary task, or click on the summary task and click on the Show Subtasks button on the Formatting toolbar.)
3. Drag over the row headers for the inserted project's summary task and all the displayed subtasks to select all the task rows.
4. Choose Tools, Tracking, Update Project. The Update Project dialog box appears.
5. Click to select the Reschedule Uncompleted Work To Start After option button (Figure 19.14). Click on the drop-down arrow for the date text box shown beside that option button; then use the calendar that appears to select the new start date (which should be the start date for the consolidated master project or a later date).
6. Click on the Selected Tasks option button to ensure you don't inadvertently reschedule tasks that aren't subtasks of the inserted project.
7. Click on OK. If automatic recalculation is on, you've properly established links, and tasks don't use constraints that prevent them from moving; Project reschedules the inserted subproject to start on the adjusted dates. The subtasks are rescheduled accordingly, with each subtask's duration, link, constraint, and other settings controlling exactly how it's rescheduled. If the inserted subproject and its subtasks don't move automatically, press F9 to recalculate the schedule.

Although links stay intact, you should review the moved tasks to ensure that they still make sense in light of the newly scheduled dates. For example, if a task is rescheduled during a period when a resource is on vacation, the task duration might have been greatly increased, so you might want to move the task manually or select another resource for it.

In some cases, task constraints will interfere with your ability to move out one or more tasks. For example, if a task has a Must Start On, Must Finish On, Finish No Later Than, or Start No Later Than constraint entered in the Constrain Task area of the Advanced tab in the Task Information dialog box, and the associated

Figure 19.14

To synchronize uncompleted work in the inserted subproject with the start date for the consolidated master project, use this dialog box.

Select inserted project and subtasks

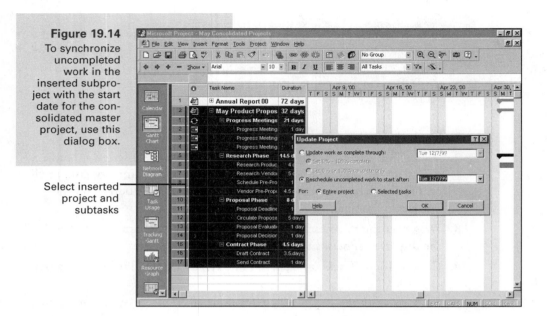

constraint date is earlier than the date to which you want to reschedule the task, Project warns you that there's a scheduling conflict when you try to move the task. Click on OK to continue; then remove the task's constraint or select another constraint type, such as As Soon As Possible, As Late As Possible, Start No Earlier Than, or Finish No Earlier Than. (Remember that you can open the Task Information dialog box simply by double-clicking on the task.)

Another problem occurs if you try to move out a single linked task rather than all of the tasks. If you move a task and the link creates a scheduling conflict, you can remove the conflict by clicking on the Task Name for the successor task, and then clicking on the Unlink Tasks button on the Standard toolbar.

Note

If the subproject contains work already marked as completed, and the start date for that work precedes the start date you specified for the master project file, you can remove the conflict by removing the work specified as completed. To do so, choose Tools, Tracking, Update Tasks. Edit the % Complete entry to be 0; then click on OK. Or, if the work really has started for the task, move the start date for the subproject entry in the master project to an earlier date, and also change the start date for the master project (choose Project, Project Information to open the proper dialog box) so that it begins earlier.

Linking Tasks between Projects

Another reason to consolidate files is to create a Finish-to-Start link between two tasks in different (separate) project files. Such a link lets you ensure that the tasks happen in the proper order even if they're in different project files. For example, you may have an external resource scheduled to handle both tasks, and you might want to link them to have a clear picture of what the impact is on both projects if the resource begins to run behind. Follow these steps to create a link:

1. Open the consolidated file.

2. In the task list, click on the Task Name cell for the earlier task, which will be the predecessor task for the link.

3. Press and hold the Ctrl key, and click on the Task Name cell for the second task to link, which will be the successor task.

4. Click on the Link Tasks button on the Standard toolbar. Project links the tasks. Project adjusts the schedule for the successor task and any tasks linked to it as needed to honor the new link. Figure 19.15 shows such a link.

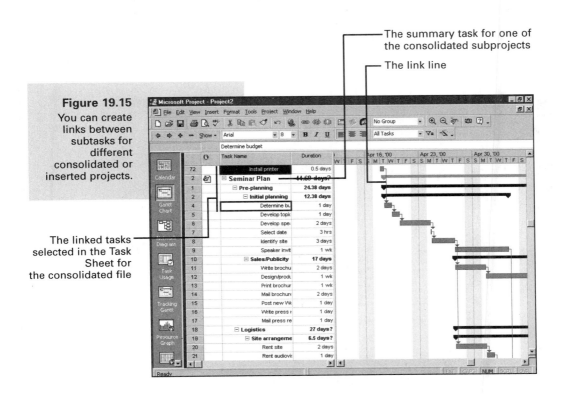

Figure 19.15
You can create links between subtasks for different consolidated or inserted projects.

The linked tasks selected in the Task Sheet for the consolidated file

The summary task for one of the consolidated subprojects

The link line

If you then open one of the subproject (source) files, you'll see that a special task has been inserted to identify the external *predecessor* or *successor* task. For example, Figure 19.16 shows the external predecessor task for one of the consolidated files linked in Figure 19.15. Note that the external task's name is dimmed, meaning that you can't edit it. Its Gantt bar is gray as well because you can't move or otherwise reschedule the task. When you open the subproject file that holds the successor linked task, the task row displays a special Predecessor field entry that points to the full path and file name for the file holding the predecessor task, followed by a backslash and the task ID number. If you want to link tasks between two files without first consolidating them, simply open the file that holds the successor task you want to link and make an entry in the Predecessor column for that task. That entry should give the full path and file name, followed by a backslash and the ID number, for the predecessor entry, as in **C:\My Documents\ Work\Budget.mpp\14**.

If you want to break the link between tasks in different files, you can clear the Predecessor field entry in the file that holds the successor task. Or you can redisplay the consolidated file if you saved it. Click on a cell in the successor task row, and then click on the Unlink Tasks button on the Standard toolbar.

External predecessor task name

Predecessor entry

Figure 19.16
Project inserts a special task to let you know when individual tasks are linked between projects.

Successor task in the subproject file

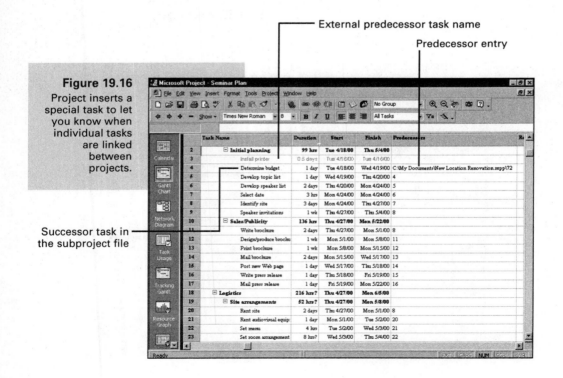

PART VI
Sharing and Publishing Project Information

Using Project with Other Applications

IN THIS CHAPTER

- Enhancing a project's Gantt Chart views with graphics from other applications

- Copying Gantt charts and other Project images into other applications

- Using OLE objects to create dynamic links between applications

- Understanding data maps

- Importing and exporting Project data

No one software program can handle all your business functions, though different applications can work with similar information.

You may need to use features from one application to accent your work in Microsoft Project 2000. Or you may have to share information with a colleague who doesn't use Project. This chapter covers features that let you share tools and data between Project and other applications.

Using Text and Graphics from Another Application

As a companion to the Microsoft Office suite of applications, Project was designed with information sharing in mind. All Office applications (and many other Windows applications) are built to enable you to share information between applications easily. You can create information in one application and then copy that information and use it in another application.

Suppose that your boss types a list of key operations for a project in a word processing program—say, Microsoft Word. The list is about three pages long. If you're not a skilled typist, typing such a list could take you an hour or more. If you have Word installed on your computer, however, and if your boss e-mails you a copy of the file that contains the list, you can get the job done in minutes by copying the list from the Word file to a file in Project.

Every time you retype information the potential exists to make errors. When information has already been spelling-checked or proofed for errors, always copy it rather than retype it.

Following are just a few other examples of text and graphics from other applications that you can copy and paste into Project:

- You can convert a to-do list created in Word to a list of tasks in Project.
- You can use a list of committee members assigned to a project as the foundation of a Resource Sheet list.
- You can paste the names of people in your department from a spreadsheet to a Resource Sheet.

- You can include graphic images such as company logos in a Gantt chart to make the printouts more attractive and informative.

- You can paste electronic images of product designs or chart images of product information in the Objects box of the Task Form for particular tasks.

- If you have scanned in photos of colleagues or of equipment to be used to complete a task, you can add those images to the Objects box for the resources in the Resource form.

The procedures for copying text and graphics are different, so the following sections cover the procedures separately.

Note

When you paste information into blank rows in a Task Sheet or Resource Sheet, Project automatically creates new tasks or resource entries in those rows and adds the default settings for fields (columns) into which you do not paste information. If you paste a to-do list in the Task Name column of a Task Sheet, for example, Project adds a default duration of 1d (one day) for each task and sets the defaults for remaining columns.

Using Lists from Other Applications

You can copy information from any application that supports OLE (see "Working with OLE Objects," later in this chapter) and enables you to create lists—this includes most Windows-based word processing and spreadsheet programs—and then paste that information into a Project file. When you paste, you're restricted to pasting the information into a Task Sheet or Resource Sheet. Therefore, you can paste information into any view that shows the Task Sheet or Resource Sheet, or into any table that's a variation on those sheets.

Keep in mind that if you're copying cells from a spreadsheet program (such as Excel), Project tries to paste to an area that's similar in shape—say, three columns wide by two rows deep. Also, no matter what kind of application you're pasting from, Project won't allow you to paste a type of information that's inappropriate for the destination. You can't paste text information into a cell that calls for an hourly rate, for example. In most cases, you probably will simply paste a one-column list into the Task Name or Resource Name column of the Task Sheet or Resource Sheet.

To copy text information from an application and paste it into Project, follow these steps:

1. Open the document that contains the text that you want to copy to Project.

Caution

> Text information that you paste replaces any information that's in the selected destination cells. Be sure to select only a blank area of the Task Sheet or Resource Sheet if you don't want to wipe out any existing information.

2. Select the text; then choose Edit, Copy (or click on the Copy button, if available). Figure 20.1 shows an example.

3. Open or switch to the Project application. You can press Alt+Tab or click on the Project button on the Taskbar to switch to Project. If Project isn't open, use the Windows Start menu to start Project.

4. Select or open the Project file into which you want to paste the copied information.

The Copy button

Figure 20.1
You can copy information from a word processing program.

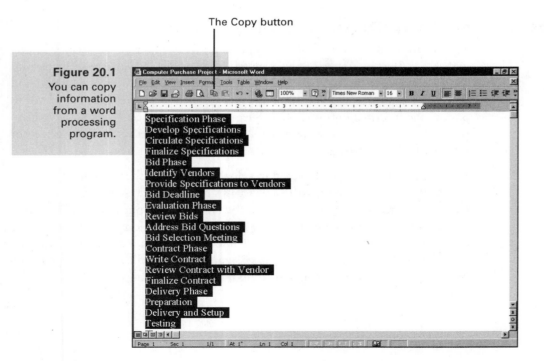

5. Select the view that you want to use, such as Gantt Chart or Resource Sheet.

6. Select the upper-left corner of the range of cells into which you want to paste the information. To paste a list of tasks, for example, you could click on the top cell of the Task Name column.

7. Choose Edit, Paste. Alternately, do any of the following: right-click on the selection to paste to, and then click on Paste on the shortcut menu; press Ctrl+V; or click on the Paste button on the Standard toolbar. The text is pasted into the selected cells.

Caution

When you copy and paste specially formatted text from another application into Project, you will lose the special formatting. For example, if you copy an outline from Word and paste it into Project, you end up with simple text that lacks the outline formatting.

Figure 20.2 shows the text copied from Figure 20.1 pasted into the Task Sheet.

Figure 20.2
The word processing list is now a list of tasks.

Project has assigned the default duration

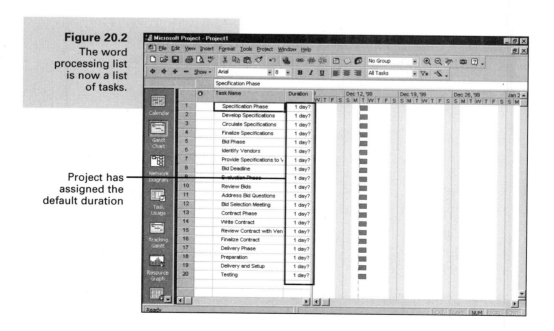

Using Graphics to Enhance Your Project

You can copy graphics—such as electronic images of company logos, products, and charts—created in other applications into Microsoft Project graphic areas. These graphics can range from purely decorative (an image that you use to jazz up a Gantt chart) to purely informational (a graphic of a resource that enables widely separated team members to recognize one another). Although Project offers drawing capabilities, you may want to use a graphic that already exists in another application or that may need to be created with tools that Project doesn't offer (as with scanned images). For these reasons, Project enables you to use graphics copied from other applications.

You can copy a graphic to any view that shows a Gantt chart, such as Gantt Chart view (see Figure 20.3). When you paste a graphic into a Gantt chart, Project enables you to format the graphic just as you would format a drawing that you created in Project. (For more information on formatting, refer to Chapter 16, "Other Formatting.") You can also paste a copied graphic into the Objects box of the Task Form or Resource Form, or into any view that offers one of these forms. The Task Form, for example, appears as the bottom pane of Task Entry view.

To display the Task Form or Resource Form, choose View, More Views to open the More Views dialog box; then double-click on Task Form or Resource Form in the Views list. To display the Objects box for the form, right-click on the form and

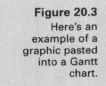

Figure 20.3

Here's an example of a graphic pasted into a Gantt chart.

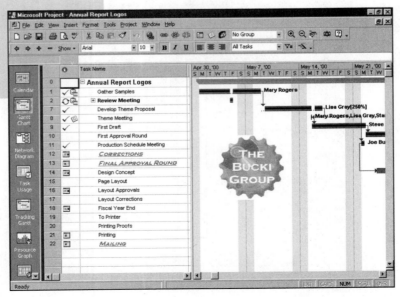

Figure 20.4
Here's an
example of a
graphic pasted
into the Task
Form.

Objects box

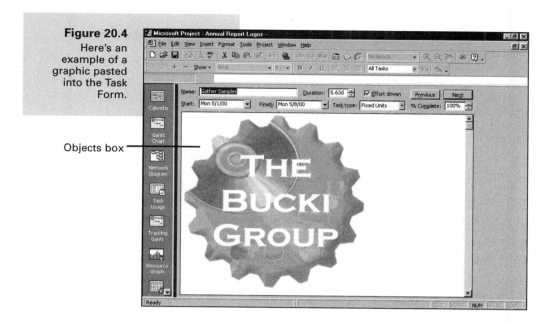

then click on Objects on the shortcut menu. The Objects box is the big blank area at the bottom of the form. Figure 20.4 shows a graphic pasted into the Task Form.

To copy a graphic image from another application, follow these steps:

1. Start the application that contains the graphic object that you want to copy to Project. (All Windows users have at least one graphics program, called Paint, for working with graphic images.)
2. Open the file for the graphic image, or create the new image.
3. Select the image (or any portion of the image) that you want to use in Project, using the program's selection method. (Many programs offer a Select All command on the Edit menu to enable you to quickly select the full image.) Figure 20.5 shows a graphic selected in Microsoft PhotoDraw, which is part of the Premium Edition of the Microsoft Office 2000 suite.

Note

Graphics files can be rather large. If you'll be sharing your Project files with other people via e-mail or floppy disks, adding numerous graphics to your project files can make transfer more time-consuming and difficult. Under such circumstances, you should use graphics files sparingly.

4. Choose Edit, Copy to copy the graphic to the Clipboard.

5. If this object is the only one that you need to copy, exit the application.

6. Open or switch to the Project application. (You can press Alt+Tab or click on the Project button on the Taskbar to switch to Project if it's open.)

7. Select or open the Project file into which you want to paste the copied information.

8. Select the view that you want to use, such as Gantt Chart view, or display either the Task Form or Resource Form to paste the information into the Objects box on the form.

9. In a Gantt chart, scroll to the section of the view where you want the graphic to appear. In a Task Form or Resource Form, click in the Objects box.

10. Choose Edit, Paste. Alternately, right-click on the selection to paste to, and then click on Paste on the shortcut menu (or press Ctrl+V). The graphic object is placed in the upper-left corner of the Gantt chart area or Objects box.

If you don't like the location of the graphic in the Gantt bar chart area, you can drag the object to the exact position you want. Move the mouse pointer over the object. A four-headed arrow appears on the selection pointer, indicating that you can drag the object to a new location. Click outside the object when you finish moving it to deselect it. In an Objects box, however, you can't move an object after it's been placed.

Using Project Information in Other Applications

You can copy almost all the information and views in Project to other applications. Copying information into Project saves time and reduces errors; copying information from Project and using it elsewhere does the same thing. Following are a few examples of how you can use Project information in other applications:

- You can copy Gantt chart timelines as *pictures* (graphics that can't be edited) and paste them into a weekly status report in Word.
- You can copy resource cost tables, showing how much time various people have spent on the project, and paste that information into a spreadsheet.
- You can paste a list of tasks from Project into a project update memo for company executives.
- If you added the field for e-mail addresses to your Resource Sheet, you can copy resource names and addresses into a note for distribution to all team members.

Project enables you to copy information as straight text, as an object (for more information on objects, see "Working with OLE Objects," later in this chapter), or as a picture. Information that appears in the timescale area on the right side of a view, such as the chart portion of Gantt Chart view or the schedule portion of Resource Usage view, can be copied only as a picture or an object, not as text. In addition, the table information that appears to the left of the charted information is always copied as well. You can't copy a picture of a few Gantt chart bars without copying a picture of the accompanying task information.

Copying Project Information as Text

When you paste to most programs, such as a spreadsheet program like Excel or a word processing program like Word, Project assumes (by default) that you're pasting the information as text. The pasted cell entries will appear in spreadsheet cells or as entries separated by simple tab characters in a word processor.

If you select the task or resource row before copying, the entire set of task or resource fields is copied and pasted at the destination. If you want to copy only some fields (columns) from the Task Sheet or Resource Sheet, select the individual cells that you want to copy and paste.

Note

> **The text in Calendar and Network Diagram views cannot be copied to other applications. These views can be copied only as pictures or Microsoft Project objects.**

To copy information from Project as text, follow these steps:

1. Select the Project view that contains the text that you want to copy to another application.

2. In the Task Sheet or Resource Sheet, select the task or resource row or the individual cells that you want to copy. (To select noncontiguous groups of cells, drag over the first group, press and hold the Ctrl key, drag over additional groups of cells, then release the Ctrl key.)

3. Open the Edit menu and click on Copy (Task), Copy (Resource), or Copy (Cell). Alternately, right-click on the selection, and then click on the appropriate command on the shortcut menu (or simply press Ctrl+C). The command name on the Edit or shortcut menu reflects the type of information you selected: task, resource, or cell. The text is copied to the Windows Clipboard.

4. Exit Project, if this is the only copy operation you need to perform.

5. Open or switch to the destination document.

6. Select the area in which you want the Project text to appear. In a spreadsheet application, select the upper-left cell of the range of cells in which you want to paste the text. In a word processing application, position the insertion point where you want to paste the text.

7. Choose Edit, Paste—or click on the application's Paste button if one is offered. The text appears in the document as unformatted text.

Figure 20.6 shows some resource information pasted into Excel.

If a simple paste operation using the Paste button on the Standard toolbar pastes as Microsoft Project Graphic objects (not as text) in an application, you must use the Paste Special command on the Edit menu. In the Paste Special dialog box that appears, click on the Text or Unicode Text option in the As list, and then click on OK to finish pasting as text.

Pasting a Picture of Project Information

Pasting a picture of Project information enables you to insert that image into the destination application as a graphic. This method can be a good way to go if you won't need to edit the information in the destination application, if you don't

Figure 20.6
Resource
information
pasted into Excel
appears where
you specify.

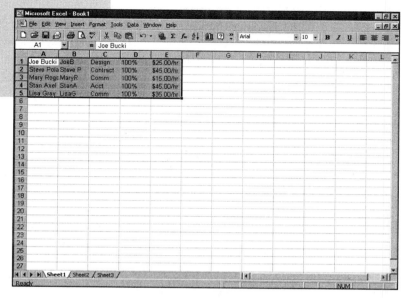

Figure 20.6
Resource
information
pasted into Excel
appears where
you specify.

want to reformat any text after pasting, and if you want to include Gantt bars, Network Diagram charts, or timescale information in the destination application.

To copy Project information as a picture of the information, rather than text that can be edited, follow these steps:

1. Select the Project view that contains the information that you want to copy.

Note

When you copy and paste Project information as a picture-formatted object (a noneditable graphic), only the portion of the current view that corresponds with the selected Task Sheet or Resource Sheet information is copied. Whether you are in Calendar view, Gantt Chart view, or any of the Resource views, be sure to scroll to the appropriate section of the view and select the right rows in the table before using Copy. (The same applies to Cut operations as well.)

2. Select the task row, resource row, or Network Diagram chart area that you want to copy. In a view like the Gantt Chart view, if you've selected whole task rows, you should also adjust the vertical split bar between the Task Sheet and the Gantt area at right so that the Task Sheet displays only the columns that you want to appear in the linked object.

3. Click on the Copy Picture button on the Standard toolbar. The Copy Picture dialog box appears (see Figure 20.7).

4. If you want to copy only the information in the same size as the current screen view, leave For Screen selected. If you want to copy a larger view, select For Printer. If you want to create a .GIF graphic file of the image (perhaps to include it in a Web document), select the To GIF Image File option button. The path and suggested name for the graphic file appear in the accompanying text box; if you want to change either, use the Browse button.

5. If you've copied from some views like the Gantt Chart view, the Copy and Timescale options near the bottom of the dialog box are enabled. In the Copy area, you can select Rows On Screen to copy all the information currently displayed, or keep Selected Rows as the choice if you selected specific rows of information to copy in Step 2. Similarly, you can copy the Timescale portion of the view As Shown On Screen. Or you can choose a specific period of the timescale to include. To do so, click on the From option button; then use its drop-down calendar and the To drop-down calendar to specify the time period for which you want to show timescale information.

6. Click on OK to copy the Project view to the Windows Clipboard (or create the GIF file, in which case you don't have to perform further steps).

The Copy Picture button

Figure 20.7
The Copy Picture dialog box enables you to specify the picture format, and more.

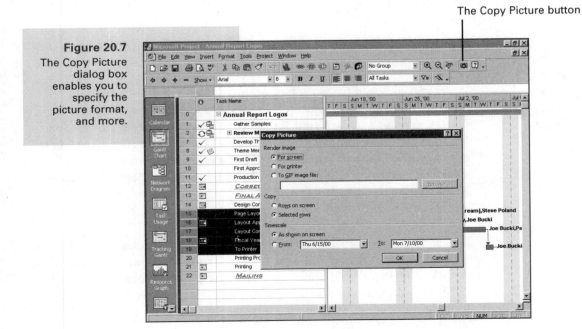

7. Switch to (or open) the document into which you want to paste the picture.

8. Place the insertion point where you want the picture to appear.

9. Choose Edit, Paste. Alternately, press Ctrl+V or click on the Paste button on the Standard toolbar. The Project picture appears in the document.

Figure 20.8 shows a Gantt Chart view selection copied to a Word page.

Working with OLE Objects

Object linking and embedding (OLE) allows applications to share information dynamically. Basically, the information is created with the source application or its tools; then that information is displayed in the container application. If the information in the container application is linked to the original information in the source application, you can make changes in the source document and those changes will show up in the linked information in the destination document.

Embedding enables you to edit an object that was created in another application. You can edit a chart created in Excel and embedded in a Word document by using the menus, commands, and other features of Excel from within Word. You don't have to exit Word, start Excel, edit the object, cut the object, and paste it back into your Word document.

Figure 20.8
Gantt chart information can be copied into a Word document.

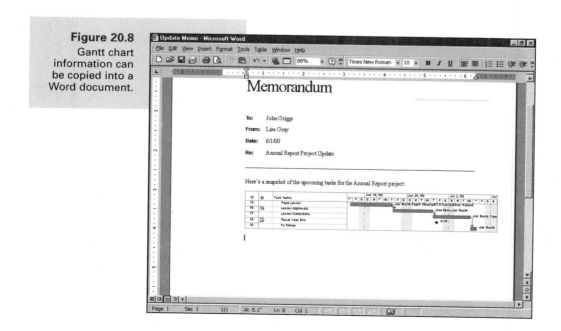

The following sections cover the basic procedures for creating linked and embedded objects based on Project data. Keep in mind that you can also do the reverse—link and embed information from other applications in Project files.

Creating a Linked Object

When you link information from a view, the linked object looks like a picture in the container document. Thus the linked object can include Gantt bars and timescale information.

To link information from Project to a document in a container application, follow these steps:

1. Select the information that you want to place in another document. The information can be from a Task Sheet, a Resource Sheet, or even a Network Diagram chart. In a view like the Gantt Chart view, if you've selected whole task rows, you also should adjust the vertical split bar between the Task Sheet and the Gantt chart area at right so that the Task Sheet displays only the columns that you want to appear in the linked object.

2. Choose Edit, Copy. Or, right-click on the selection and then click on Copy on the shortcut menu. Project copies the information to the Windows Clipboard.

3. Open or switch to the document into which you want to paste the linked Project object.

4. Position the insertion point where you want the linked object to appear.

5. Choose Edit, Paste Special. The Paste Special dialog box appears (see Figure 20.9).

6. Click on the Paste Link option.

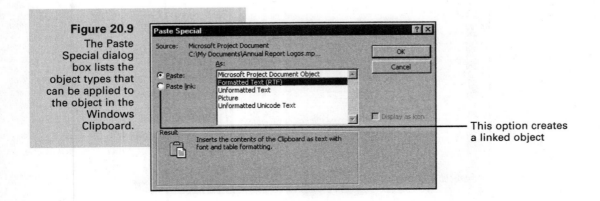

This option creates a linked object

7. In the As list box, select Microsoft Project Document Object. You can also select the Picture object type in the As list box if you want to paste the object as a bitmap graphic. The bitmap object will still be linked to the Project document.

Note

> Working with the Paste options for a particular application may take some experimentation. Excel's options, for example, include weird-looking items called BIFF, BIFF3, and BIFF4. These options represent different kinds of Excel text and will paste the copied information into a group of cells, for example.

8. Click on OK. The Project information appears in the destination document, as shown in Figure 20.10.

Managing a Link's Update Setting

By design, a linked object is updated each time the object's source document is changed or updated. By using the Links command, you can specify when the changes in the source document are reflected in the linked object. You have two choices of link-update timing. You can update the linked object automatically

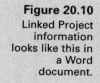

Figure 20.10
Linked Project information looks like this in a Word document.

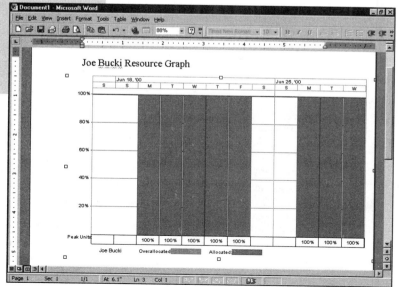

each time the source document changes, or you can update the object manually by making menu and dialog box choices. To select a link's update setting, follow these steps:

1. Open the document that contains the linked OLE object.

2. Click on the linked object to select it.

3. Choose Edit, Links. The Links dialog box appears, displaying a list of linked objects in the document. The dialog box lists the link name and the path name of the source document, and indicates whether the link is set to update automatically or manually. Also, the name of the object that you selected in Step 2 is highlighted.

4. Click to select the Manual option button at the bottom of the dialog box.

5. Update the link by clicking on the Update Now button. The object is updated with any changes that have taken place in the object's source document.

6. Click on OK. The Links dialog box closes, and the link is set for manual updating.

With the link set for manual updating, you must open the Links dialog box and click on the Update Now button to update the object with the latest changes in the source document. In some cases, depending on the application and document holding the linked information, you can right-click on the linked object, and then click on Update Link on the shortcut menu.

Using Other Linking Options

The Links dialog box contains a few other buttons that allow you to manage the links to objects in your documents:

■ **Open Source.** This button opens the source document of the currently selected link. With the source document open, you can make changes in the source object, investigate surrounding information, or just refresh your memory as to the name and location of the source file.

You can open any OLE object's source application without displaying the Links dialog box. To do so, double-click on the linked object.

■ **Change Source.** This button opens the Change Source dialog box, which enables you to select a new file as the source document for the linked object.

- **Break Link.** This button removes the link to the selected object. If you click on this button, a dialog box appears, asking whether you are sure that you want to break the link to the selected object. If you are sure, click on OK; otherwise, click on Cancel. After you break a link, you must perform a cut-and-paste operation to reestablish the linked object.

Creating Embedded Objects

The process of creating an embedded Project object is similar to the process of creating a linked object, but the connection between the source document and the destination document is different. The information in the embedded object does not depend on the source document; that is, you can make changes in the embedded object that don't show up in the source document.

Note

> Unlike the process with a linked object, when you embed an object, Project copies all the tasks or resources in the selected Task Sheet or Resource Sheet. This means that after you choose Edit, Paste Special to place the embedded information in the container document, you can click on the object and then drag the black resizing handles to control how much of the information appears.

To create an embedded Project object, follow these steps:

1. Select the view that you want to use to create the embedded object. If the view includes a Task Sheet or Resource Sheet, click on any cell in the sheet, and drag the vertical split bar to control which sheet columns appear (the same ones will appear in the embedded object).

2. Choose Edit, Copy. Alternately, do any of the following: right-click on the selection and then click on Copy on the shortcut menu; press Ctrl+C; or click on the Copy button on the Standard toolbar.

3. Open or switch to the destination document.

4. Position the insertion point where you want the embedded object to appear.

5. Choose Edit, Paste Special. The Paste Special dialog box appears (refer to Figure 20.9), listing the available paste options. The default Paste Special options are set up to create an embedded object. That is, the Paste option should be selected, not the Paste Link option.

6. Click on the object type Microsoft Project Document Object in the As list. Notice that the Result area of the dialog box indicates that the selected settings enable you to use Microsoft Project to edit the object.

7. Click on OK to paste the object. The object appears at the insertion point location.

Note

> **You cannot create an embedded object from an image that you copied by using the Copy Picture button on the Standard toolbar. The Copy Picture button creates a bitmap image of the selected area; it does not maintain the information that is necessary for embedding.**

Editing an embedded object is a simple, straightforward process and one in which the primary advantage of embedding comes into play, because you do not have to recall the name and location of the source document that created the object. You simply double-click on the object and the source application (Project) tools appear, enabling you to edit the object.

When you finish making changes in the object, click outside the object. The source application tools close, and you return to the container document and application. (In some applications, you may have to choose File, Exit to close the source application.)

You can also embed or link an object in the Notes tab of either the Task Information or Resource Information dialog box. For example, the following steps show how to embed a resource's picture along with other resource notes:

1. Display the Resource Sheet for the project file.

2. Double-click on the name of the resource in the Resource Name column to open the Resource Information dialog box.

3. Click on the Notes tab to display it.

4. Enter any notes as needed in the Notes text box at the bottom of the tab, and then position the insertion point at the location where you'd like the inserted picture to appear.

5. Click on the Insert Object button, which is the far right button at the top of the Notes text box. The Insert Object dialog box opens.

6. Click on the Create From File option button to select it.

7. Click on the Browse button to open the Browse dialog box.

8. Use the Drives and Directories lists to navigate to the drive and folder that holds the picture file to insert.

Figure 20.11
Embed or link a
picture or other
object in the
Resource
Information or
Task Information
dialog box.

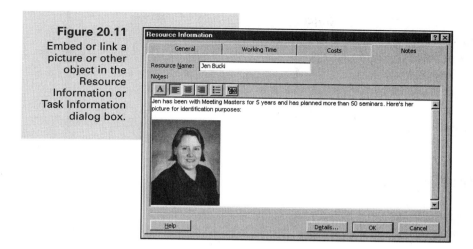

9. When the picture file name appears in the list of files at the left, click on the picture file's name in the list, and then click on the OK button to return to the Insert Object dialog box.

10. If you want to link the inserted picture to the original picture file, click to check the Link check box.

11. Click on OK to finish inserting the picture. Figure 20.11 shows the inserted picture in the Resource Information dialog box.

12. Click on OK to save your changes and close the Resource Information dialog box.

Importing Other Project-Management Files

Project enables you to work with information stored in a variety of file formats. If you need to bring in information from an application that saves information in tabular format (such as a spreadsheet or database program), you can import that information rather than copy it. Table 20.1 lists some of the file formats that Project can accept.

The data that you import needs to be properly formatted for Project to recognize it. For example, the first row in an Excel workbook file should contain field names that identify the data in the column (field). If you have any questions about how the type of data you want to import needs to be set up in its source application, export some test data from Project into that format (including choosing the

Table 20.1 The Most Common File Types That Project Can Read

Application	File Format
Microsoft Project	MPP, MPX, MPT
Microsoft Project Database	MPD
Microsoft Excel	XLS
Microsoft Access (as well as FoxPro and dBase III and IV, which share the same format)	DBF
Plain Text (ASCII)	TXT
Comma-separated values	CSV

corresponding export map, if needed). Then open the exported file in its source application to see how Project set the file up, named fields, and so on. Exporting is covered later in this chapter.

Tip

If your software (especially other project planning software) isn't listed in Table 20.1, see whether the program enables you to use its File, Save As command to save files in one of the listed formats.

The procedure for importing a file is similar to the procedure for opening a file that you learned in Chapter 3, "Working with Files and Help." Follow these steps:

1. Choose File, Open; press Ctrl+O; or click on the Open button on the Standard toolbar. The Open dialog box appears.

2. In the Look In drop-down list, select the drive where the file that you want to import is stored.

3. Double-click on a folder to display the contents of that folder. (You may need to double-click on subfolder icons to find the name of the file that you want to open.)

4. In the Files Of Type drop-down list (see Figure 20.12), select the format for the file that you want to import.

5. When the file that you want to open appears in the list, double-click on its name, or click on it and then click on Open to load the file into Project. A dialog box appears. Figure 20.13 shows examples of this dialog box.

497

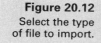

Figure 20.12
Select the type
of file to import.

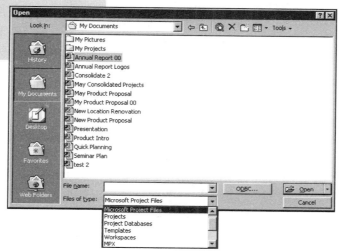

Figure 20.13
The dialog box
for importing
information has
a different name
and provides
different options
depending on
the type of file
you're trying
to import.

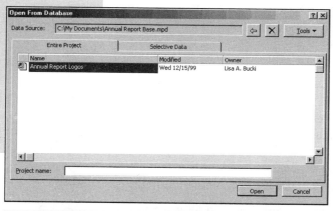

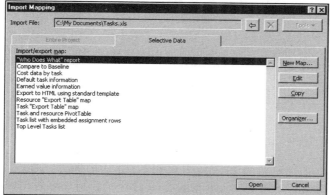

6. The type of file you chose to import in Step 4 determines which of the tabs is active in the importing dialog box:

- For database formats such as Microsoft Project Database, the Entire Project tab is enabled. If the imported file has information for more than one project, select the correct project to open from the Name list. Enter the name for the new project file to create from the imported data in the Project Name text box.

- For importing files in other formats, the Selective Data tab is enabled. The Import/Export Map list displays "maps" that specify which fields of information to import. For example, the Default Task Information choice imports ID, Task_Name, Duration, Start_Date, Finish_Date, Predecessors, and Resource_Names fields. Click on the map to use the list. (For more on maps, see the next section, "Understanding Data Maps.")

7. Click on Open to finish the import operation.

If necessary, Project adds default information for columns that are not filled in by the imported information, such as the Duration column. Conversely, it warns you if the data being imported doesn't work for a particular field, and skips the import for that data.

Understanding Data Maps

When you're importing or exporting data, you may not want to include all the fields of information from the original file. In such a case, you can use a data map in Project to tell it which fields to import or export, and the location for the imported or exported fields. If you refer to the bottom image in Figure 20.13, you can see that Project comes with multiple data maps.

However, you may need to create your own data map. For example, you want to export information from the Name (Resource Name) field on the Resource Sheet to a column named Full Name in a new Excel workbook. To accomplish a change like this (that is, to *map* the data to a new field), you need to create your own data map. To do so, click on the New Map button on the Selective Data tab of the dialog box for importing or exporting data. The Define Import/Export Map dialog box appears.

Enter a name for the data map you're creating in the Import/Export Map Name text box. Then, in the Data To Import/Export area of the Options tab, check an option to specify whether you want to import or export information pertaining to Tasks, Resources, or Assignments (see Figure 20.14). This activates the appropriate tab to the right—Task Mapping, Resource Mapping, or Assignment Mapping—so you

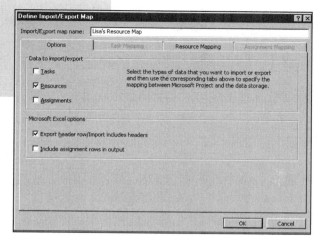

Figure 20.14
Start your map
by naming it and
identifying what
type of data to
import or export.

can map the fields. Be sure to leave the Export Header Row/Import Includes Header check box checked if you want to add a header row including the field names to the exported data, or if the data being imported has a header row identifying the field names in the source file.

Click on the appropriate tab to begin the mapping process. The process differs slightly depending on the import or export application, but the options on the selected tab should be fairly straightforward. If you need to name a destination worksheet or apply an import or export filter, do so. Then, using the grid in the middle of the dialog box, identify how applicable fields from Project should match up with each field of data being exported or imported. For example, in Figure 20.15, I selected the Name field from the drop-down list of Project field names on the first row, then entered the field name to use in a new Excel worksheet created by the export operation in the To column on the same row.

When you finish mapping the fields, click on OK in the Define Import/Export Map dialog box to return to the dialog box for the import or export operation. Make sure your map is selected in the Import/Export Map list on the Selective Data tab, and then click on Save to finish the import or export operation using your map.

Tip

Project stores new maps you save in GLOBAL.MPT, so you need to use the Organizer to move a map into any new file that you intend to send to someone else or move to another computer. Refer to "Dealing with the Organizer to Work with Views, Macros, Tables, and More" in Chapter 11 to learn more about working with the Organizer.

Figure 20.15
A preview shows how the mapped fields will look in the exported data.

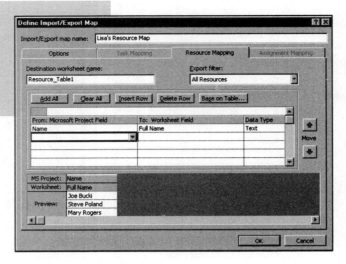

Exporting Project Files

The flip side of importing is exporting. When you export information from a Project file, you save it in a format that another application can use. The formats to which you can export are generally the same as the import formats listed in Table 20.1 earlier in this chapter, with two exceptions. You can also export project information as an Excel PivotTable (a dynamic table that you can reorganize by dragging categories on a grid) or a Web Page (HTML) file.

The next few subsections walk you through a few specific exporting examples, so you can get a feel for how the exporting choices work. Because importing resembles exporting, these examples will also help you learn to import information. Where needed, the examples explain how to create a data map to complete the export operation.

ON THE
CD

Use the file *Annual Report Chapter 20* from the book's CD-ROM to practice exporting data if you don't have your own project file to use. Then use the exported data files to practice importing information.

Example: Exporting to an Excel Worksheet

You can export task, assignment, or resource information to a worksheet in a new Excel workbook file. In this example, follow the steps to export resource information to a workbook file:

1. With the file holding the information to export open in Project, choose File, Save As. The Save As dialog box appears.

2. Navigate to the drive and folder where you want to save the file, using the Save In drop-down list and the folders that appear below it. (Double-click on a folder icon to open that folder so you can store the file there.)

3. In the File Name text box, type the name you want to give the file.

4. Open the Save As Type drop-down list, then choose Microsoft Excel Workbook in the list.

5. Click on the Save button. The Export Mapping dialog box appears.

6. Click on the New Map button on the Selective Data tab. The Define Import/Export Map dialog box appears.

7. Enter a name for the map in the Import/Export Map Name text box at the top of the dialog box. For example, you could enter **Resource Name and Group.**

8. Click to check the Resources check box under Data To Import/Export, and leave the Export Header Row/Import Includes Headers option checked as well. (Of course, you would click on Tasks or Assignments to export that type of information, instead.)

9. Click on the Resource Mapping tab to display its options. (Or use the applicable tab for the type of data you chose to export in Step 8.)

10. Enter a new name for the exported worksheet tab in the Destination Worksheet Name text box, if desired. For example, you could enter **Name and Group.**

11. If you want to filter the exported information to export only information that matches the filter, select the filter to use from the Export Filter drop-down list.

12. Using the rows near the center of the dialog box, choose the fields to export and specify the names to use for the exported fields (columns) in the worksheet. For example, Figure 20.16 shows some export fields I've specified. In the From column, I clicked on each of the first two cells, and then used the drop-down list arrow that appeared to display the list of fields and select the fields I wanted. Then I edited the suggested field names for the exported data in the To column.

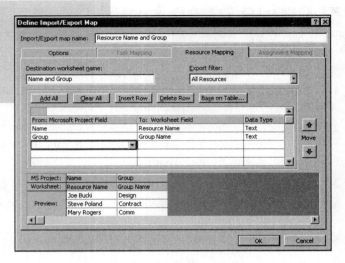

13. Click on OK to finish creating the map. Make sure it's selected in the Import/Export Map list of the Selective Data tab of the Export Mapping dialog box.

14. Click on Save. Project exports the file, saving it with the name you specified in Step 3.

15. Open Excel and open your exported file. Figure 20.17 shows how the map settings shown in Figure 20.16 result in two columns of exported data.

You can export *timescaled data* (that is, data from one or more selected fields broken out by day, week, month, or other time unit) from Project to Excel, and even graph the data during the export operation. However, you need to load an add-in to get the job done, and this isn't a well-documented process in Project. To start, choose Tools, Customize, Toolbars. Click on the Commands tab in the Customize dialog box. Click on the Tools choice in the Categories list, then drag the COM Add-Ins choice from the Commands list and drop it onto any toolbar. Click on the Close button to close the Customize dialog box. Then click on the new COM Add-Ins button that you added to a toolbar. In the COM Add-Ins dialog box that appears, click on the Add button. Use the Add Add-In dialog box that appears to navigate to the \Program Files\Microsoft Office\Office Folder. In the list of files that appears, click on the Anlyzts.dll file, then click on OK. Make sure the Analyze Timescaled Data in Excel add-in is checked in the Add-Ins Available list, then click on OK to close the COM Add-Ins dialog box. Next, right-click on any toolbar and click on the Analysis choice to display the Analysis toolbar. Click on the Analyze Timescaled Data In Excel button on that toolbar to start a wizard that leads you

Figure 20.17
In this case, the data map exported two columns of data. From here, I could format or sort the data. If I exported fields with numeric information, I could perform calculations on that information.

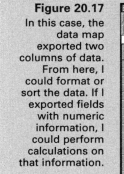

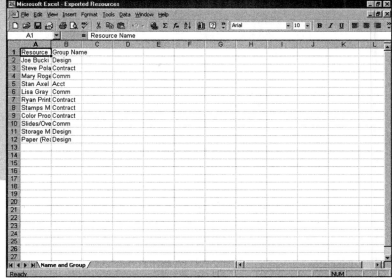

through the process of choosing the fields, the timescale periods, and whether or not to graph the timescaled data in Excel.

Example: Exporting an Excel PivotTable

Project offers a data map that enables you to export information to an Excel *PivotTable*—a special table you can use to analyze your project information. While I'm not going to cover how to use a PivotTable (consult an Excel how-to book to learn more about that topic), the following steps demonstrate how to export information into a PivotTable that enables you to view cost information by resource:

1. With the file holding the information to export open in Project, choose File, Save As. The Save As dialog box appears.

2. Navigate to the drive and folder where you want to save the file, using the Save In drop-down list and the folders that appear below it. (Double-click on a folder icon to open that folder so you can store the file there.)

3. In the File Name text box, type the name you want to give the file.

4. Open the Save As Type drop-down list, and then choose Microsoft Excel PivotTable in the list.

5. Click on the Save button. The Export Mapping dialog box appears.

Figure 20.18
Several quick
steps in Project
lead to a
powerful Excel
PivotTable.

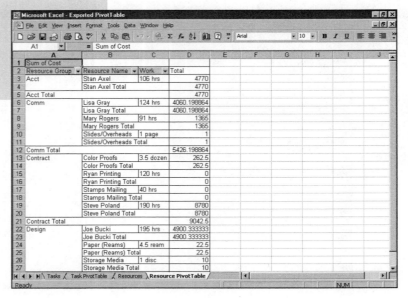

6. Click on the Task And Resource PivotTable choice in the Import/Export Map list on the Selective Data tab.

7. Click on Save. Project exports the file, saving it with the name you specified in Step 3.

8. Open Excel and open your exported PivotTable file. As Figure 20.18 illustrates, the exported file holds four worksheet tabs. Two of them—Task PivotTable and Resource PivotTable—hold predefined PivotTables that you can use to manipulate data and control how you want to view information about work and costs.

Example: Exporting to Access

When you export information from Project to Access, you have the choice of exporting all the Project data or using a map to select which data elements to export. I'll caution you right away that if you export the entire project file, the export operation breaks the information out into numerous database tables, each of which contains numerous fields of calculated coded information that won't be meaningful to you at first glance. This would make it extremely difficult to find and use the information you need, so I recommend using or creating a map, as in the following example:

Note

Access doesn't do a good job of displaying some types of Project data, such as calculated duration information. So you may need to experiment with the data maps you create and the formatting in the Access table to get the export operation to work as you wish.

1. With the file holding the information to export open in Project, choose File, Save As. The Save As dialog box appears.

2. Navigate to the drive and folder where you want to save the file, using the Save In drop-down list and the folders that appear below it. (Double-click on a folder icon to open that folder so you can store the file there.)

3. In the File Name text box, type the name you want to give the file.

4. Open the Save As Type drop-down list, and then choose Microsoft Access Databases in the list.

5. Click on the Save button. The Export Mapping dialog box appears.

Tip

If you're saving to some database formats, you can append additional tables to an existing database file. To do so, navigate to and select the file in the Save dialog box, so that its name appears in the File Name text box. Select the file type from the Save As Type drop-down list. After you click on Save, a dialog box appears to warn you that you've chosen an existing file. Click on the Append button, and then enter a unique name for the project table in the Name To Give The Project In The Database text box.

6. Click on the Selective Data tab, and then click on the New Map button. The Define Import/Export Map dialog box appears.

7. Enter a name for the map in the Import/Export Map Name text box at the top of the dialog box. For example, you could enter **Task Name, Start Date, and Cost**.

8. Click to check the Tasks check box under Data To Import/Export. (Of course, you would click on Resources or Assignments to export that type of information, instead.)

9. Click on the Task Mapping tab to display its options. (Or use the applicable tab for the type of data you chose to export in Step 8.)

10. Enter a new name for the exported database table in the Destination Database Table Name text box, if desired. For example, you could enter **NameCostGroup**.

11. If you want to filter the exported information to export only information that matches the filter, select the filter to use from the Export Filter drop-down list.

12. Using the rows near the center of the dialog box, choose the fields to export and specify the names to use for the exported fields (columns) in the worksheet. For example, I chose to export the Name, Start, and Cost fields, and entered **Task_Name, Start_Date,** and **Cost** (respectively) as the names for the fields in the exported table.

• •

In earlier software, you always had to use an underscore to separate the words in the name of an exported table, worksheet, or field names. Project still suggests using the underscore in many instances, but you can use a space instead if you're exporting to Excel. In Access, however, you do need to use the underscore rather than a space in the names for exported fields.

• •

13. Click on OK to finish creating the map. Make sure it's selected in the Import/Export Map list of the Selective Data tab of the Export Mapping dialog box.

14. Click on Save. Project exports the file, saving it with the name you specified in Step 3.

15. Open Access, open your exported file, and open the table that the export map created for you. As you can see in Figure 20.19, my table data would look more attractive if I adjusted the formatting for the Start_Date and Cost fields.

Sharing Project Data with ODBC Databases

Project can also share information with database programs that are ODBC-compliant, meaning that those databases can communicate in a particular way. For this feature to work, ODBC drivers need to be installed on your system using the ODBC Data Sources (32bit) icon in Windows Control Panel. (Describing how to do this is beyond the scope of this book; chances are that if your company requires you to work with its central databases, your company's computer support staff will already have set up this capability for you. The installation process for some versions of the Microsoft Office 2000 suite also set up some of the ODBC drivers by default.) The installation of those drivers means that you can save

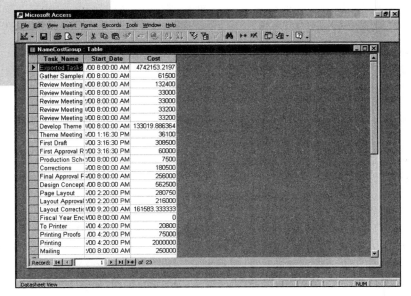

Figure 20.19
I've exported data from Project into an Access table.

Project data in a database from any other ODBC-compliant database application that your system is set up to save to, or use information from those databases in Project.

To work with ODBC database information, you click on the ODBC button in the Save As or Open dialog box, depending on whether you want to export data to an ODBC database or open it from one. You also might want to display the Workgroup toolbar by right-clicking on any toolbar, and then selecting Workgroup. This toolbar offers the Save To Database As and Open From Database buttons, which are equivalent to the ODBC button in the Save As and Open dialog boxes, respectively.

Note

Only text or numerical information from the project, such as task names, start and finish dates, resource names, and resource assignments, is stored in the database. No formatting or graphical information is stored.

Saving Project data to an ODBC database requires two general operations. First, you have to create the *data source* if it doesn't already exist. The data source tells Project which ODBC driver to use to create and work with the database. Next, you save the Project data as a database in the data source. Use the following steps to accomplish both operations:

1. Create and save your schedule information in Project.

2. Choose File, Save As. In the Save As dialog box, click on the ODBC button. Rather than displaying the Save As dialog box, you can click on the Save To Database button on the Workgroup toolbar.

3. In the Select Data Source dialog box that appears, type a name for the data source file in the DSN Name text box (Figure 20.20), and then click on New.

4. In the Create New Data Source dialog box that appears, select the database driver you want in the list of drivers (the list will vary depending on what drivers have been installed on your system); then click on Next.

5. Type a name for the data source in the text box of the next Create New Data Source dialog box. (This assigns a name to the data source you're creating to hold the database file; use the same name you entered in the DSN Name text box.) Then click on Next.

6. Review your choices in the final Create New Data Source dialog box that appears, and then click on Finish.

7. In the ODBC . . . Setup dialog box that appears, click on the Create button to open the New Database dialog box, as shown in Figure 20.21.

8. Type a name for the database file in the Database Name text box. If necessary, use the Directories and Drives lists to specify a different location for saving the database file, and then choose a save Format. Click on OK.

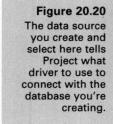

Figure 20.20
The data source you create and select here tells Project what driver to use to connect with the database you're creating.

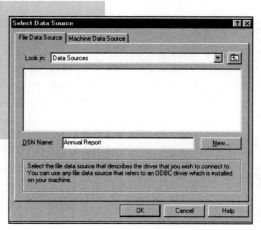

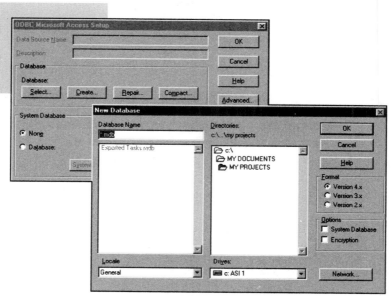

Figure 20.21
At this point, specify a name for the database file itself.

9. When a message box informs you that the database file has been created, click on OK again.

10. Click on OK again to exit the ODBC... Setup dialog box.

11. In the Select Data Source dialog box, click on the name of the data source you just created from the Look In list, and then click on OK.

12. The Save To Database dialog box appears, with the Entire Project tab selected. Type a name to use for the project information in the Project Name text box; then click on Save.

Note

Some ODBC drivers are for spreadsheets such as Excel. If you use one of these drivers, the Selective Data tab will be selected instead. Use it as described in earlier examples to map the imported or exported data.

13. The Planning Wizard dialog box may appear to ask you whether or not to save the information with a baseline. Click on the option you want, and then click on OK. Project saves the database.

After information from a schedule has been saved as an ODBC-compliant database, you need to open it from the database file to use it again in Project. Follow these steps to retrieve the information from the file:

1. Choose File, Open, or click on the Open button on Project's Standard toolbar. In the Open dialog box, click on the ODBC button. Alternately, click on the Open From Database button on the Workgroup toolbar.

2. In the Look In list of the Select Data Source dialog box, click on the name of the data source you created when you saved the file. Click on OK.

3. In the Import Format dialog box, click on the title you assigned to the project data (in Step 12 of the preceding set of steps) in the list on the Entire Project tab.

4. Click on Open. Project opens the information from the database file.

21

Communicating with the Team

L ike most other business-oriented applications, Project 2000 has evolved to
allow you to work with information online. These new features enable you
to connect quickly to information you need, or to make schedule information
easily available to your colleagues and contacts.

In addition, Project 2000 offers paperless, automated project management alternatives through its workgroup message-handling capabilities. Workgroup messaging works in conjunction with e-mail in Windows to allow you to
automatically send assignment and update information to—and receive status
reports from—resources that you communicate with via e-mail.

This chapter walks you through using Project's workgroup messaging features.

Preparing to Communicate with a Workgroup

The workgroup for a project includes all the resources you've entered in the
Resource Sheet. You can use workgroup features in Project to send automatic
messages to the workgroup via e-mail. (See Chapter 23, "Creating and Managing
a Web Workgroup," to learn to use messaging features via a Web workgroup.)
This capability is called *workgroup messaging* or *team messaging*.

Setting up for E-Mail Messaging

You first need to select e-mail as the default workgroup communication method
for the current project file.

Note

The e-mail system used with workgroup e-mail features must be 32-bit,
MAPI-compliant. Depending on whether you have Windows 95 or 98,
Windows NT, Windows 2000 Professional, or Microsoft Office 2000
installed—and depending on the standards for your company—you'll
have a different e-mail program. Project 2000's *Workgroup Message
Handler* (the behind-the-scenes software that formats team messages and
routes them between Project and the e-mail program) supports Microsoft
Exchange, Microsoft Mail (for Windows NT only; not for Windows 95 or
98), Lotus cc:Mail 7.0 for Windows and Windows NT, Lotus Notes 4.5a for
Windows and Windows NT, and Outlook. The figures in this book show
examples only from Microsoft Outlook 2000.

Follow these steps to set up the current project file for communicating with the workgroup via e-mail:

1. Choose Tools, Options. The Options dialog box appears. Click on the Workgroup tab, if necessary.

2. Near the top of the dialog box, click to open the Default Workgroup Messages For (Current File) drop-down list. Then click on Email (see Figure 21.1). This tells Project that you'll be communicating with resources via e-mail rather than a workgroup Web server.

3. If you want the e-mail choice to apply to all of your schedule files, click on the top Set As Default button. Otherwise, your changes apply only to the currently opened file.

4. Click on OK.

Specifying Resource E-Mail Addresses

Just as you have to address paper mail or regular e-mail, you need to tell Project what each resource's e-mail address is to ensure that Project properly addresses the messages you send. You also need to verify whether the resource is set up to use e-mail messaging, to ensure that Project sends the message correctly.

To tell Project what a resource's e-mail address is and what message method the resource uses, follow these steps:

1. Switch to the Resource Sheet view (choose View, Resource Sheet, or click on the Resource Sheet icon in the View Bar).

Figure 21.1
Choose Email to send workgroup (team) messages via e-mail.

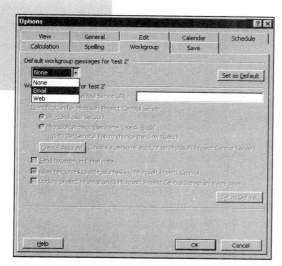

2. Double-click on the Resource Name for the resource for which you want to specify the e-mail address.

3. Click on the General tab of the Resource Information dialog box, if needed, to display its options.

4. Enter the e-mail address in the Email text box. Figure 21.2 shows an example. Or, if you've entered information about the contact into your Address Book, you can type the resource's name exactly as it appears in the Address Book rather than the e-mail address. To check the resource's name or e-mail address in your Address Book (for Microsoft Exchange, Windows Messaging, or Outlook), click on the Details button. The Check Names dialog box appears. The Summary tab shows the exact name or e-mail address to use. Click on OK, and then enter the name or e-mail address into the Email text box.

Note

The messaging options are disabled for material resources. So if you need to send messages to a person regarding material resource assignments, you'll need to enter that person as a resource with a 0% Max. Units setting and specify the resource's e-mail address. Then assign that resource to tasks along with the needed material resource—but make sure you assign another work resource or remove effort-driven scheduling from the task. Otherwise, assigning the resource with 0% units will reduce the calculated task duration.

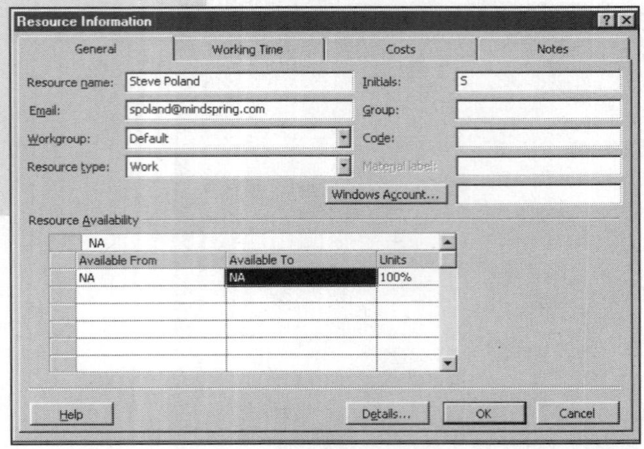

Figure 21.2

Enter the resource's e-mail address in the Resource Information dialog box.

Resource Information	? X

5. By default, the Workgroup drop-down list is set to Default. You don't have to change this choice if you've already set up the current project file for e-mail messaging, as described in the prior set of steps. However, if you set up the file for Web messaging as described in Chapter 23, but the resource you selected in Step 2 only communicates via e-mail, then open the Workgroup drop-down list and click on Email to ensure that you can send workgroup messages via e-mail to the selected resource.

• •

To disable e-mail workgroup messaging for a resource, choose None from the Workgroup drop-down list on the General tab of the Resource Information dialog box.

• •

6. Click on OK to finish creating the address and setting the messaging method to use.

7. Repeat Steps 2–6 if you want to specify an e-mail address and messaging method for additional resources.

Installing the Workgroup Message Handler

When you install Project 2000, the setup process by default also installs the Workgroup Message Handler, which enables Project to format messages and communicate with your e-mail program. If the recipients of your workgroup messages don't have the full Project 2000 program installed, at the very least each recipient must install the Workgroup Message Handler. There are three different ways to install the Workgroup Message Handler:

- If your resources (message recipients) have access to a Project 2000 program CD-ROM, they can insert the CD-ROM in their CD-ROM drive and then click on the Install Microsoft Project Workgroup Message Handler button in the Microsoft Project 2000 Setup window that appears.

- If the resources are connected to your company's network, you can copy the \Wgsetup\ folder (and all of its contents), on the CD-ROM to a shared network drive. Then users can run the Wgsetup.exe file from the shared folder to install the Workgroup Message Handler.

- If the resources are at another location and can't access your network or a Project 2000 CD-ROM, you can create Workgroup Message Handler install disks and ship them to resources as needed. This process requires two floppy disks. Copy the Extract.exe, Prj2k_1.cab, Setup.ini, Wgsetup.exe, Wgsetup.inf, Wgsetup.lst, and Wgsetup.stf files from the \Wgsetup\ folder on the Project CD-ROM to Disk 1. Copy only

Prj2k_2.cab to Disk 2. Then a resource can run the Wgsetup.exe file from Disk 1 to start the setup process, which will prompt the resource to insert Disk 2 when needed.

Sharing Information with the Workgroup

After you've set up your project file and your resources to use team messaging, you can in most cases use the commands on the Workgroup submenu of the Tools menu to send different types of messages to the workgroup members. This section covers how to use those features, as well as how to send and route files.

E-Mailing or Routing a Project File

There may be instances, such as when the project schedule is finalized or when you receive a request from a superior to review the schedule, when you might want to send your entire project file as an attachment to an e-mail message. Of course, doing so assumes that the recipient of the message also has Microsoft Project installed and will be able to open and review the file. It also assumes that the file is a reasonable size (some e-mail programs limit file attachments to 2MB or so) and that the recipient's system can access a shared resource pool, if required.

The WorkGroup toolbar offers buttons for sending files and other workgroup messages. To display this toolbar, point to any toolbar onscreen, right-click, and then click on WorkGroup.

When you send a file, it's sent to your e-mail program's Outbox. You then have to launch your e-mail program and send the message from there, as described later in this chapter in the section, "Finishing the Send."

To send a project file as an attachment to an e-mail message, use these steps:

1. Open the file you want to send, make any last-minute changes you want, then save the file.
2. Choose File, Send To, Mail Recipient (As Attachment); or click on the Send To Mail Recipient (As Attachment) button on the WorkGroup toolbar. If Exchange or Windows Messaging prompts you to specify a Profile, select a different one from the drop-down list, if needed, and click on OK to continue. The e-mail message window appears with the project file already inserted as a file attachment, as shown in Figure 21.3.

Send To Mail Recipient
(As Attachment) button

Send To Routing Recipient button

Use the To button to address the message

Figure 21.3
Your e-mail
program
automatically
helps you create
the message in
which to send
your file. This
message
window is from
Outlook 2000.

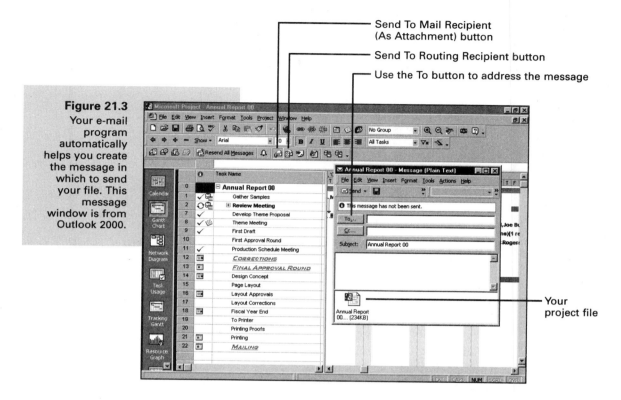

Your
project file

3. If the resource's e-mail address isn't in your Address Book, you can type the address in the text box beside the To button. Otherwise, click on the To button to display the Select Names or Address Book dialog box, depending on the e-mail system you're using. Click on a name in the list at the left; then click on To to add the name to the list of Message recipients. Add other names as needed, then click on OK.

4. If you want to include text—perhaps to describe what the file contains or to ask the recipient a specific question—click in the message area above the file icon, and then type your message (see Figure 21.4).

5. Choose File, Send. Alternately, click on the Send button at the left end of the message window toolbar. The message with the file attachment is sent to your e-mail Outbox. When you later open your e-mail program and send and receive messages, the message will be mailed to the recipient.

You can route a message including a file to a number of users and have a copy automatically come back to you when the last recipient closes the file after working with it. You can send the message to all recipients at once, or set it up so that it goes to the first recipient, who then must forward it to the next recipient, and so on.

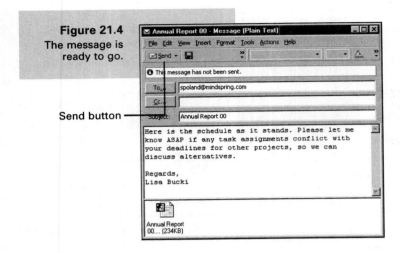

Figure 21.4
The message is ready to go.

Send button

To route a file, choose File, Send To, Routing Recipient, or click on the Send To Routing Recipient button on the WorkGroup toolbar. The Routing Slip dialog box appears. Click on the Address button to open the Address Book dialog box. Click on a name from the list at the left; then click on To to add this name to the list of recipients at the right. Add all the names you want, and then click on OK to close the dialog box and return to the Routing Slip dialog box.

The Routing Slip dialog box shows the routing order (see Figure 21.5). If needed, click on a name in the To list and click on one of the Move arrows to change the

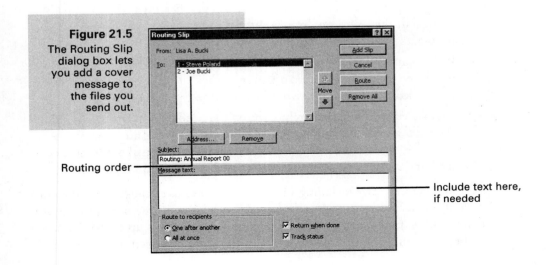

Figure 21.5
The Routing Slip dialog box lets you add a cover message to the files you send out.

Routing order

Include text here, if needed

selected name's position in the list. Click in the Message Text area and enter whatever message you want to appear. In the Route To Recipients area, tell your e-mail system and Project messaging whether you want the message to be routed to the listed recipients One After Another or All At Once. Make sure that there's a check mark beside the Return When Done option if you want to automatically receive a copy of the routed file back after the last recipient in the list works with the file and closes it. The Track Status feature, when checked (and when you're routing the file from one recipient to the next), generates a notification message to you when each recipient on the list forwards the file to the next recipient. Click on Route after you specify all the settings you want; this sends the routed file to your e-mail Outbox. You can then launch your e-mail program and send and receive messages to forward the routed message.

Sending Assignments, Updates, and Status Requests

The TeamAssign, TeamUpdate, and TeamStatus commands on the Workgroup submenu of the Tools menu all work in concert with your e-mail program to let you share task information with the resources assigned to particular tasks. These Workgroup commands take advantage of the Workgroup Message Handler that comes with Project. Selecting any of these commands generates a special message in the workgroup messaging format, which is then sent to your e-mail Outbox as an attachment to a regular e-mail message.

The workgroup message lists the resources you're sending the message to and key data about each of the tasks you selected to send or request information about. It includes suggested message text, so you don't even have to type instructions if you don't want to. It lists information such as the task name, start and finish dates, number of work hours, and percentage of work complete. It also offers a comments column for each task. The recipients of each workgroup message can make changes to the task information and then automatically return the message to you via their e-mail Outbox.

Each of these commands has a particular purpose, so I'll review each of them in turn:

- **TeamAssign.** This type of message asks a resource to verify acceptance of an assignment, as well as the schedule you've set for it, as shown in Figure 21.6.

- **TeamUpdate.** A message of this type (see Figure 21.7) allows you to report changing task information, such as a revised start or finish date. For this to work, you have to have already sent information about tasks and incorporated resource replies into these tasks (as you'll learn to do later in this chapter). Otherwise, Project tells you that there are no tasks in the schedule to update.

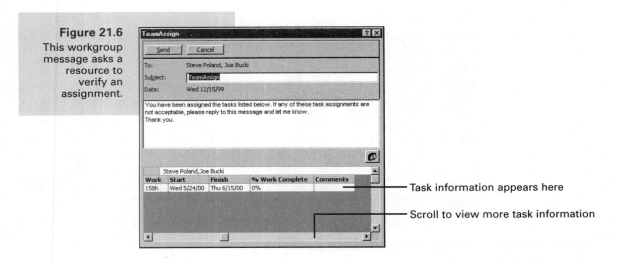

Figure 21.6
This workgroup message asks a resource to verify an assignment.

Task information appears here

Scroll to view more task information

Figure 21.7
Workgroup messaging makes it easy to communicate an update to a team member.

■ **TeamStatus.** This type of message queries the recipient to tell you how work is progressing on a task (see Figure 21.8).

The steps for sending each type of workgroup message are similar and are as follows:

1. Update information in the schedule in Gantt Chart view and save your file. (Messaging features don't work in other views, such as the Resource Sheet.) If you don't save now, you'll be prompted to save later.

2. If you want to send a workgroup message about a particular task or group of tasks, click to select a single task; then hold down Ctrl while clicking on any additional tasks you want to select.

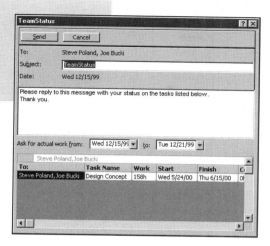

Figure 21.8
You can ask resources to report to you about progress on tasks.

3. Choose Tools, Workgroup to display a submenu, and click on TeamAssign, TeamUpdate, or TeamStatus. Alternately, click on the TeamAssign, TeamUpdate, or TeamStatus button on the WorkGroup toolbar.

Note

Depending on which e-mail system you're using or whether or not you're presently logged onto your e-mail program, you might or might not be prompted to specify a profile when you send messages of any type. Make the appropriate selection, if prompted, and then click on OK to continue.

4. The Workgroup Mail dialog box appears (see Figure 21.9). Click to specify whether to send the message regarding All Tasks or the Selected Task, and then click on OK.

5. The workgroup message appears onscreen. Edit any of the information you want, such as the Subject or text of the message; then click on the Send button at the top of the message window. The message is sent to your e-mail Outbox or the Web TeamInbox. You'll learn shortly what to do with it from there.

Figure 21.9
Specify whether you want to send a message for all tasks.

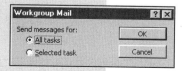

The Check Names dialog box may appear if Project needs to verify the e-mail address for any of your message recipients when you send a file or send one of the team message types described later. Click on the resource's name in the list of matches and then click on OK. If necessary, use the New Contact button, enter the resource's contact information in the Properties dialog box, then click on OK twice to finish the new Address Book entry and use it as the contact's e-mail address for workgroup messages.

Sending Notes to the Team

Project can automatically set up an e-mail message for you, building the recipient list based on options you specify and enabling you to select whether the attached file should hold your entire schedule file or just a graphic picture (.BMP file) of any tasks you selected in the Task Sheet. This kind of note can be sent to e-mail addresses that you specify.

To send an automatically formatted message like this, follow these steps:

1. Update information in the schedule in Gantt Chart view and save your file.

2. If you want to send a message about a particular task or group of tasks, you need to select the task or tasks. Click to select a single task; then hold down Ctrl while clicking any additional tasks you want to select (you may be limited to 10 or so).

3. Choose Tools, Workgroup, Send Schedule Note. The Send Schedule Note dialog box appears, as shown in Figure 21.10.

4. In the Address Message To area, specify the recipients for the message and whether the list should include the Resources and Contacts from the Entire Project or Selected Tasks.

Figure 21.10
Specify who will receive a Schedule Note and what attachment it will contain.

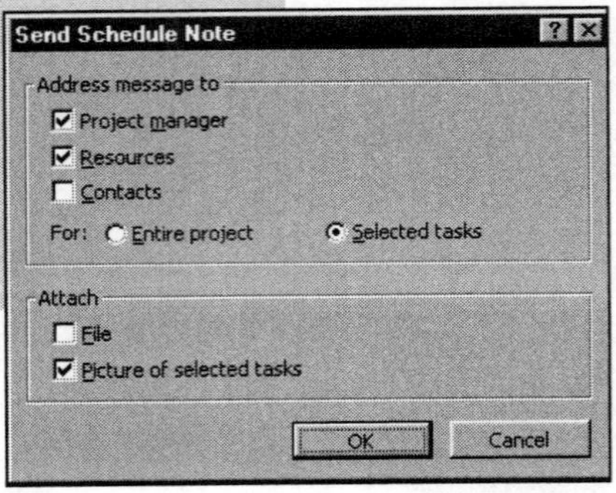

5. In the Attach area of the dialog box, specify whether the attachment message should be the entire File or just a Picture Of Selected Tasks.

6. Click on OK. If any of the selected recipients lacks an e-mail address on file, you're prompted to specify the needed address as described earlier in this chapter. (You may be prompted to choose a profile; do so, and then continue.) Then the message appears onscreen, as shown in Figure 21.11.

You can delete the attached file from the message if you want. Your addressing information remains intact. To delete the attachment, click on its icon, and then press the Delete key.

7. Type a Subject for the message; then click in the message area above the attached file and type the note you want to send.

8. Choose File, Send. Alternately, click on the Send button at the left end of the message window toolbar. The message with the file attachment is sent to your e-mail Outbox, from which you can later send it.

Finishing the Send

All the workgroup messages you've learned to create so far in this chapter were sent from Project to your Outbox folder within your e-mail program. This makes sense, because Project and the Workgroup Message Handler aren't e-mail programs; they simply prepare your information to be sent via e-mail.

Now you need to send your messages from the Outbox to the intended recipients. To send workgroup messages from an e-mail program, you use whatever method

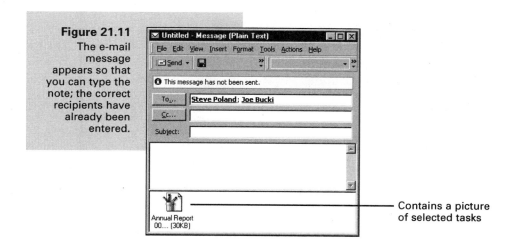

Figure 21.11
The e-mail message appears so that you can type the note; the correct recipients have already been entered.

Contains a picture of selected tasks

you normally would use to send messages from the Outbox. For example, to send messages from Outlook 2000, follow these steps:

1. Go to your Windows desktop and double-click on the Microsoft Outlook icon to start Microsoft Outlook 2000. Alternately, click on the Start button on the Taskbar, point to Programs, and click on Microsoft Outlook. Outlook loads and appears onscreen, with your Inbox folder open.

2. (Optional) Click on the Outbox folder icon to open it and show outgoing messages (see Figure 21.12).

3. Click on the Send/Receive button on the toolbar.

4. Outlook connects to your mail system (an Internet Service Provider, for example, or your company's e-mail server) and delivers the messages, keeping you informed onscreen as the messages are delivered. It also checks for incoming e-mail messages and places them in your Inbox.

If you need to take any steps to retrieve regular messages from your e-mail system to get those messages to appear in your Inbox, then you'll need to do the same for workgroup messages. For example, if you need to click on a Connect button to dial your Internet connection, you'll be prompted to do so.

Responding to Assignments and Updates

When you're on the receiving end of workgroup messages, they appear in your e-mail Inbox folder along with the rest of your incoming e-mail messages. To read a workgroup message, double-click on it. If you have received a project file as a message attachment, a routed file, or information sent as a schedule note, the message simply opens like a normal e-mail message. If you're opening a TeamAssign, TeamUpdate,

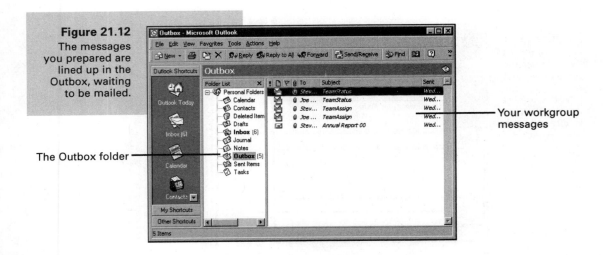

Figure 21.12
The messages you prepared are lined up in the Outbox, waiting to be mailed.

The Outbox folder

Your workgroup messages

or TeamStatus message, Project's messaging features launch and open the message, which appears in a special message dialog box onscreen (see Figure 21.13).

Click on the Reply button to prepare your response to the message. The window automatically adjusts to enable you to reply, and RE: appears beside the window title and in the beginning of the Subject text. An insertion point appears in the Message area; type your overall reply there. In your reply, enter work completed on a particular day for the Report Period being shown, in one of the blank cells. To make an entry, click in the cell, then type your entry and press Enter. Figure 21.14 shows some example entries. If you're responding to a TeamAssign message,

Figure 21.13
Here's an example of how a workgroup message—a TeamStatus request—looks to its recipient.

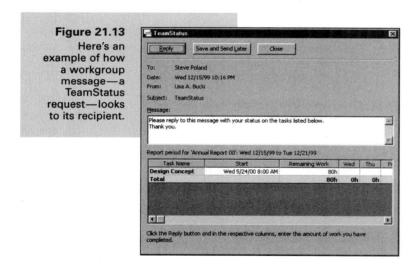

Figure 21.14
Here's a response to the status request from Figure 21.13.

Type your overall response

Report period

Enter completed work in these cells

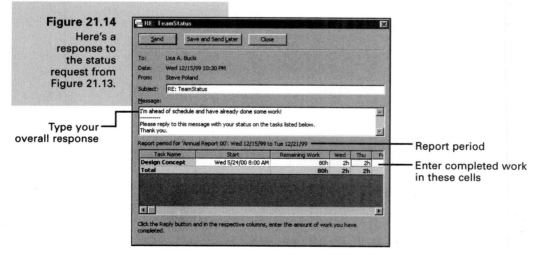

you can double-click on the Accept? cell entry to toggle between Yes and No; doing so informs the project manager whether or not you accept the assignment. (This is crucial so that the project manager doesn't accidentally accept your assignment; if you select No, Project does not finalize the assignment.) Click on the Send button to send the reply to your e-mail Outbox. From the Outbox, send the reply to the project manager using the steps outlined in the preceding section.

If you're a project manager, your resources will send replies to your assignment and status requests. Such responses appear in your e-mail Inbox, and you can double-click on each one to open it. For example, the response shown in Figure 21.14, after being sent to the project manager, resembles Figure 21.15 when the project manager opens it.

If the resource's response isn't satisfactory, click on the Reply button to send a follow-up message. If the resource simply confirmed the existing schedule, you can click on the Close button to close the message, and click on No if you're asked whether to update the Project file. If the response suggests some schedule changes or reports completed work and you want to enter these changes into your project file, click on the Update Project button. If Project isn't open, it starts and the file opens for updating. The schedule changes are made to the appropriate task in the schedule, and the status update message closes. Save your project file to keep these changes.

Figure 21.15
This status update has been received from a resource.

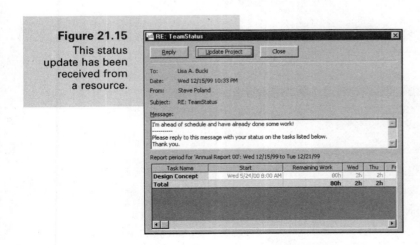

How Project Interacts with Outlook 2000

When you accept an assignment or assignment change via a TeamAssign or TeamUpdate message in Outlook, Outlook automatically adds that assignment into your Outlook Tasks list. As shown in Figure 21.16, when you click on the Tasks icon in the Outlook Bar at the left (which is analogous to the View Bar in Project) or the Folder List, the Tasks list appears and includes any new assignments that you accepted via a team message.

So, if you are the project manager, you'll need to send TeamAssign messages to yourself for your assignments in the project. You need to reply to the message to accept the assignment. Then open the response message (open it in your Outbox if it doesn't send it back to you automatically—you don't have to *send* the message, you just have to complete the process steps) and click on the Update Project button to accept the assignment response and add it into the Project file. You can then delete the message from your Outbox (or Inbox if the message was sent automatically).

Caution

What I've just described is presently the only way to add your own assignments into your Outlook Tasks list. While you can copy and paste or drag and drop a task from Project to the Tasks list, the task information doesn't fill in completely in Outlook.

Figure 21.16
Assignments you accept via team messages appear in your Outlook Tasks list.

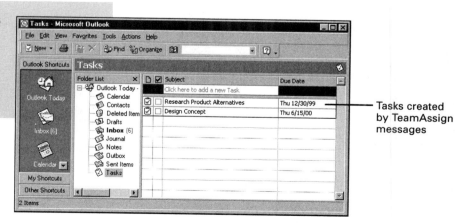

Tasks created by TeamAssign messages

You might use Outlook 2000 to remind you of your tasks in the Task list. You can also use it to remind you before a task is set to begin, so you can either begin the task (if you're assigned to it) or check in with resources. In the Task Sheet, select the tasks for which you want reminders by dragging over the row headers. Choose Tools, Workgroup, Set Reminder. In the Set Reminder dialog box that appears, use the settings to tell Outlook when to display the reminder (they're self-explanatory); the default is 15 minutes before the start of the task. Click on OK to finish setting the reminder. However, this method of setting the reminder only works if you're the project manager or have access to the project schedule file.

To set a reminder on your own, double-click on the task in your Outlook Tasks list. The task window opens. To turn on the reminder, click to check the Reminder check box (see Figure 21.17). You can then use the accompanying drop-down lists to specify the reminder date and time, and use the button with the speaker on it to choose a reminder sound. When you finish, click on the Save and Close button to set the reminder and return to your Outlook Tasks list.

Note

If you're the project manager and you use the Outlook Journal feature to track your work on various types of Office files, you can turn on the tracking for Project files, too. To do so, choose Tools, Options in Outlook. On the Preferences tab of the Options dialog box, click on the Journal options button. In the Also Record Files From list, click to check Microsoft Project. Then click on OK twice to accept your choice and close the two dialog boxes.

Figure 21.17
Check the Reminder check box to have Outlook display a reminder about a task that's been added to your Tasks list.

22

Using Project with the Web

IN THIS CHAPTER

- Browsing the Web
- Adding hyperlinks into a Project file
- Saving Project information in Web format
- Formatting your Web information

With tens of millions of users worldwide, the *Internet* (a global network of connected networks) has become one of the most important communication tools in the business world. Different *sites* (individual server computers) on the Internet organize and handle information on what seems like every subject that anyone could imagine. This chapter explains how to use Project 2000's basic features for working with the Web. (The next chapter explains how to use Web workgroup features to manage project progress.)

The Web coverage in this chapter assumes that your system is set up to connect to the Internet and that you have a Web browser program (which enables you to display Web pages) installed and configured to launch when needed.

Embedding a Hyperlink

In Project, hyperlinks can not only point to Web pages but also to files stored elsewhere on your computer or in a shared folder on a network server. You can embed a hyperlink along with a task row or resource row in the Task Sheet or Resource Sheet of any view. Then you can click on the hyperlink indicator in the Indicators column to launch your browser and display the Web page the link points to. Selecting a hyperlink that points to a file opens that file—and its application, if needed.

As an example, if an external resource has a Web site that you want to view to find updated product pricing information, you could add a hyperlink for that resource's Web site to the resource's entry on the Resource Sheet. Or you may want to consult the file for another project that's on your company network before you update a particular task, so you could create a hyperlink to that file.

To create a hyperlink to a path on your hard disk, use the full path and file name to identify the file, as in **C:\My Documents\NewProduct.mpp**. You can use the same format if a file is stored on a *mapped network drive;* basically, a mapped drive is a particular storage area on the network that has a particular drive letter assigned, usually H. For other networks, you may instead need to enter the *UNC (Universal Naming Convention)* address to point to the file on the network server. Enter the UNC address in the format **\\Server\Share\Path\FileName.ext**, where *Server* is the name of the network server computer and *Share* is the name of a shared area or partition that network users can access. If you've worked at all with files on your company's network, you probably have experience with which method to use to name and access network files, and should use the same method for creating hyperlinks.

To insert a hyperlink, follow these steps:

1. Display the view with the Task or Resource Sheet holding the task or resource for which you want to add a hyperlink, then click on the desired task or resource to select it.

2. Choose Insert, Hyperlink, press Ctrl+K, or click on the Insert Hyperlink button on the Standard toolbar. The Insert Hyperlink dialog box appears.

3. In the Text To Display text box, enter a short name to display for the hyperlink. This entry appears onscreen instead of the full path or URL when you point to the hyperlink indicator.

4. In the Type The File Or Web Page Name text box, enter the Web page or file address. If you're creating a link to a file on your hard disk, you can click on the File or Web Page button under Browse For to open a dialog box for selecting that file or Web page. Or, you can click on one of the buttons under Or Select From List, and then click on a file or URL in the list that appears to select the specified file or URL. Figure 22.1 shows an example network link address entered in the Type The File Or Web Page Name text box.

Insert Hyperlink button

Figure 22.1
Use this dialog box to create a hyperlink.

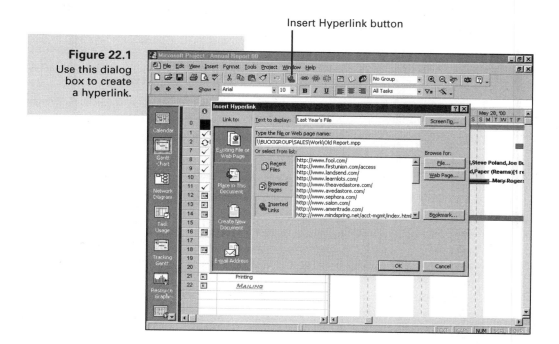

Tip

You can also use the ScreenTip button to increase the amount of information that appears when you point to the hyperlink indicator. After you click on the button, enter text in the ScreenTip Text text box, and then click on OK.

5. If the file you're opening uses easily referenced labels like cell addresses (spreadsheets), bookmarks (word processors), or task ID numbers (Project file), click on the Bookmark button to open the Select Place In Document dialog box. Use its choices, which change depending on the type of file or page to which you linked, and then click on OK.

6. Click on OK to finish creating the hyperlink. An indicator for the hyperlink appears in the Indicators column.

Your hyperlink is now complete. To see the short text or address/URL and the ScreenTip (if any) for the hyperlink, move the mouse pointer over the hyperlink indicator, as shown in Figure 22.2.

To display the Web page or document that the link points to, click on the hyperlink indicator. Project launches the source application for the specified file and connects to the Internet, if needed, then displays the specified file or page. If you open another Project file, the Web toolbar also appears in Project. See the next section to learn how to use that toolbar.

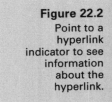

Figure 22.2
Point to a hyperlink indicator to see information about the hyperlink.

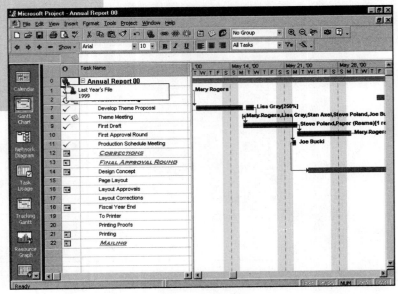

If you need to change the location for the hyperlinked page or file, or want to remove the hyperlink, you can display the Edit Hyperlink dialog box, which has options nearly identical to those in the Insert Hyperlink dialog box shown in Figure 22.1. To change or remove a hyperlink, click on a cell in the row for the task or resource that holds the hyperlink. Click on the Insert Hyperlink button on the Standard toolbar. In the Edit Hyperlink dialog box, change the text box entries as needed. Or, to remove the link, click on the Remove Link button. Click on OK to close the dialog box.

Using the Web Toolbar to Surf

When you click on a hyperlink to open a linked Project or Office document, the Web toolbar appears near the top of the screen, just under the Formatting toolbar. You can also display the Web toolbar at any time by right-clicking on another toolbar and then clicking on Web. Figure 22.3 shows the Web toolbar.

The Web toolbar offers buttons you can click on to display particular Web pages or hyperlinked files. Many of the buttons on this toolbar work just like buttons in your Web browser. For example, the Back and Forward buttons move backward and forward through pages and files you displayed during the current project work session. Click on the Stop Current Jump button to stop loading a hyperlinked file, or click on the Refresh Current Page button to update the Project files that are currently open.

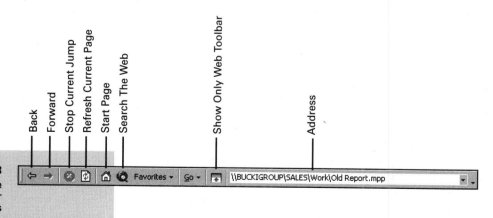

Figure 22.3
You can also use the Web toolbar to display files and Web pages.

The Start Page button launches your Web browser and displays the start page or home page (the first Web page your browser has been set up to display). The Search The Web button also displays your browser and a page with tools and links for searching the Web for a particular topic. Clicking on the Favorites button opens a drop-down list naming the pages you've added to the Favorites list in your Web browser; click on a page name to launch your browser and jump to the page. The Go menu offers commands that correspond to some of the buttons already described, as well as Set Start Page and Set Search Page for changing the Web page that either of those Web toolbar buttons display. Click on the Show Only Web Toolbar button to hide or display other on-screen toolbars.

Finally, you can enter a Web address or file path and name in the Address text box, and then press Enter to display the linked page (or the linked file) in your Web browser. To jump back to a previously displayed page, click on the down arrow beside the Address text box, and then click on the name of the link to follow.

Saving Project Information as a Web Page

The section called "Exporting Project Files" in Chapter 20 noted that one of the formats you can select for exporting data is the Web Page (HTML) format. You can use the File, Save As command and choose Web Page from the Save As Type drop-down list in the File Save dialog box, and then continue exporting the file as described in Chapter 20.

In addition, the File menu includes the Save As Web Page command. Choosing that command displays the Save As dialog box with the Web Page choice already selected, as shown in Figure 22.4. Project suggests the name of the original schedule file as the File Name. You can edit that name or the location to which the file will be saved. Click on Save to continue the export process. The Export Mapping dialog box appears. In the Import/Export Map list on the Selective Data tab, click on a map to specify which fields of information from the Project file will appear in the Web document. Or, you can create your own map as described in the "Understanding Data Maps" section of Chapter 20. After choosing or selecting a map, click on Save to save the document as the HTML Web page, with the .html file name extension.

After you create the Web page, you can use it in two ways. First, you can copy it to the Web (http://) server folder (on your company's Internet or intranet Web

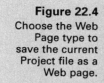

Figure 22.4
Choose the Web Page type to save the current Project file as a Web page.

site), where other users can access it. If your Web site is on an ISP or configured in certain ways, you may need to use a program such as CuteFTP to transfer the file. You can then build hyperlinks in other documents (Web and otherwise) to display the Web page from the folder where you posted it. If you have trouble with this, consult your company's network administrator or Webmaster to learn how to post your pages.

Alternately, you can e-mail the Web page (HTML file) or provide it on disk to anyone who uses it. Any recipient with a relatively recent Web browser version will be able to open the file from an e-mail message or from disk. After saving or copying the page file to a folder on the hard disk, the recipient can navigate to the folder using My Computer or Windows Explorer, and then double-click on the file to launch the Web browser and display the file. (You can use this technique to view the file from your hard disk, as well.) Figure 22.5 shows an example of information from a project schedule file exported as a Web document and displayed in the Internet Explorer 5.0 Web browser.

Note

If you have a program that lets you open HTML documents, you can use it to edit the exported Project Web page, adding graphics or changing fonts. For example, you can open any HTML (or HTM) file in Microsoft Word 2000 and use Word to improve its look and layout.

Figure 22.5
Project data
saved as a Web
page includes
title information
and a table
of fields.

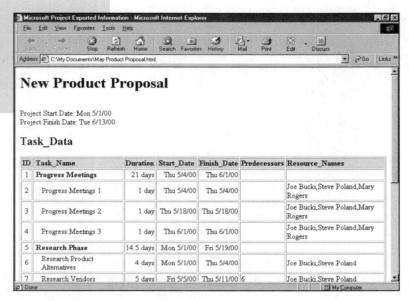

Specifying a Web Template
for a Web Page

The Web page shown in Figure 22.5 looks pretty generic. Luckily, Project does offer a few options that enable you to improve the Web page's appearance. To create a Web page with a custom look, you create a custom map that includes a Web page template to assign a colorful appearance for your data. You can also add in a graphic like a logo. Use the steps that follow to spice up a Web page generated from your schedule file:

1. Open the schedule file in Project, make any last-minute changes to the file, and then save the file.

2. Choose File, Save As Web Page. Project displays the Save As dialog box with the Web Page choice already selected (refer to Figure 22.4).

3. Edit the suggested name in the File Name text box, if needed. You can also change the location to which the file will be saved using the Save In list.

4. Click on Save to continue the export process. The Export Mapping dialog box appears.

5. In the Import/Export Map list on the Selective Data tab, click on the map the offers the fields of information you want to appear in the Web document. You're going to make a copy of this map and modify the copy by specifying a template in addition to the selected fields. (If you want to create a brand new map, you can do so by clicking on New, specifying what data to export, and then continuing to Step 7.)

6. Click on the Copy button. The Define Import/Export Map dialog box opens.

7. Edit the name in the Import/Export Map Name text box to specify a name for your new map.

8. Click to check the Base Export On HTML Template check box in the HTML Options area of the Options tab in the Define Import/Export Map dialog box. The Browse button beside the check box becomes active. Click on it to open the Browse dialog box. Use it to browse to the templates folder for Project (\Program Files\MicrosoftOffice\Templates \1033); select the template to use, and then click on OK to apply the template.

9. If you want to add an image file, click to check the Include Image File In HTML Page check box. Click on the activated Browse button beside it, use the Browse dialog box to select an image file (it must be a .GIF, .JPG, or .PNG image), and then click on OK. At this point, your choices might

Figure 22.6

In this instance, I'm including both an HTML template and a graphic with the data map.

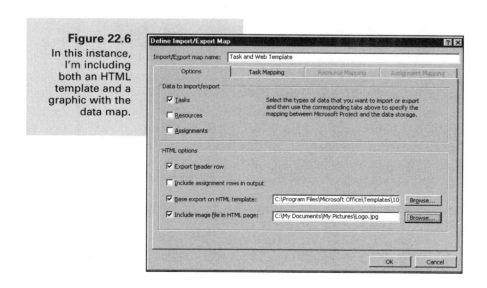

look like Figure 22.6.

10. Click on OK to finish defining your new map. Make sure the map is selected in the Import/Export Map list on the Selective Data tab of the Export Mapping dialog box.

11. Click on Save to save the document as the HTML Web page, with the .html file name extension.

12. Open the new Web page in your browser. It will look something like Figure 22.7.

Figure 22.7
Here's the fancy version of my Web page.

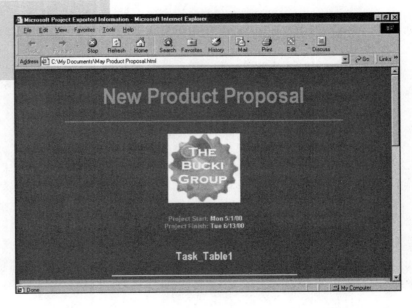

23

Creating and Managing a Web Workgroup

IN THIS CHAPTER

- Setting up and administering Project Central with Microsoft Project 2000

- Sending and receiving assignments and task status messages

- Using Project Central to create and manage status reports

- Using Project Central to view projects or portfolios of projects

As you have seen in earlier chapters, building a project schedule just initiates the process of managing your project. Because the schedule is a living document and because plans never go precisely as expected, most of the work involved after the schedule is in place involves tracking the schedule and communicating any changes in the current plan. Sharing plan updates with a large group of people, or with people who are spread across large or different organizations, can be very difficult.

Happily, Project 2000 has a new companion tool that facilitates the schedule management and communication processes. *Project Central* enables you to publish your project data onto an intranet or the Internet and allows participants in your project to modify and update their project activities through their Web browser. Project Central greatly expands on the features present in the Web Inbox that shipped with Project 98.

This chapter outlines the project management processes to which you can apply Project Central and shares some things you will want to consider before you start to use the tool. The chapter also explains how to use various key functions and features of Project Central. Project Central offers so much functionality that it alone could be the subject of a book, but you can learn about the most important features here.

When Project Central Becomes Useful

Although you can use Project Central in all phases of project planning and tracking, it's most effective after you've set up your project plan. It does give resources the ability to add tasks and to delegate responsibility, but you will most likely want to work in Project 2000 to build the basic structure of your schedule and to assign resources to activities. Project Central has most value in the tracking and managing phase of your project, as it is designed to allow resources to directly enter actual progress on scheduled activities and to make minor corrections to the plan as it progresses. Giving resources the ability (and the responsibility) to update the schedule with their actual work ensures that your schedule will be up to date and credible. Project Central also has powerful features in sharing project information.

Note

Making the resources who are doing the work responsible for posting their own progress on the work enhances the impact of using the schedule as a management tool. First, if resources are responsible for reporting on the schedule, they will be looking at the schedule and will have a better understanding of what work they are expected to do. Second, by getting data directly from the resources, you may find differences between what is actually happening and the story that gets filtered up to the management level. This adds to the credibility of the schedule. And last, it saves you the work of determining progress on the many activities in your project, potentially allowing you to build more detail into your plan.

Project Central has more stringent system requirements than Project 2000. Project Central requires a Web server connected to the network on which you are going to share project data. This network can be an internal intranet or a connection to the Internet. Microsoft recommends that this be a Windows NT 4.0 Server (with Service Pack 4 or later), or Windows 2000 Advanced Server or Professional running Internet Information Server 4.0 or later for best performance. Windows NT 4.0 (workstation) can be used if you install Option Pack 4 (available as a download from Microsoft), which contains Internet Information Server. You will be limited to 10 connections here, but that may be suitable for a small group. Microsoft Windows 2000 can also be used with Internet Information Server 5.0, which comes with Windows 2000. Setup of the tool is fairly simple using the Installation wizard provided.

The Project Central application actually consists of two parts—a database that stores the Project Central data, and a Web-based application that enables you to administer and interact with the data in the database. The Web-based application retrieves, formats, and presents the data in combination with the user's Web browser.

The database that ships with Project Central is Microsoft's MSDE, which gets installed automatically during the setup process. Scripts for allowing Project to use either SQL Server 7.0 or Oracle 8 databases (if you have them available) are provided.

Caution

> **Making your project accessible across the Web will help your team access information remotely. On the downside, it may also enable others to access the information remotely. If your project is sensitive, you will need to be careful that the files on your network are accessible only to your team. If you set up Project Central on a corporate network, be sure to check with your network administrator on how to configure your installation of Project Central so that it is secure. If you are doing it yourself, don't rely solely on the user authentication present in Project Central to secure your Web site. Make sure you understand the security settings for your Web server, and make sure they are properly set. If you are running Project Central within an intranet with no external connections, then you should have relatively few security worries.**

From here, the text goes back and forth between covering how to configure Project Central and Project 2000. The text follows the process you will take to get Project Central set up and get your schedule data out there for the first time, so please bear with the switching back and forth.

Installing Project Central

When you insert the Project 2000 CD in your CD-ROM drive, the Setup program launches automatically. Click on the Install Microsoft Project Central Server button to start the Project Central setup process. The Project Central setup takes care of creating and naming the directory where the Web files will be stored. It creates the database for the data to be stored, the connection between the webserver and the database, and the virtual directory on the Web server at the root level (by default it's http://<your-webserver-name>/ProjectCentral), so you really don't need to specify anything during setup. Project setup really is a one-click process.

Logging In to Project Central for the First Time

Once you have the application installed and available over the Web, you are ready to start using Project Central. The first thing that you want to do when you log in to the tool is to set a password for the administrator and set up the initial settings for Project Central.

To start, open your browser and enter the location (URL) of Project Central. Check with your Web administrator for this URL if you did not set it up yourself.

Once you have reached the site, a login screen will appear. Select Administrator. You will be directed to the Administration Overview page, which shows the many administration options. At this time you should see a warning that no password has been set for the administrator. Click on Yes in the warning message box and enter a password for the administrator. You will want to remember and protect this password. Anyone who logs in as Administrator can delete data, shut down the Web site, or change user accounts and passwords—either by accident or intentionally. It is possible for you to change the password at any time by going to the Security – Account Creation page. After you enter the password, the warning message box closes, returning you to the Administration Overview page.

As an administrator you have access to the Administration Overview page (Figure 23.1), which offers numerous options to help you administer the Web site. If the page doesn't appear when you log in, you can get there by choosing the Admin tab, choosing Admin from the Actions menu on the home page, or by selecting the Administration section of the home page.

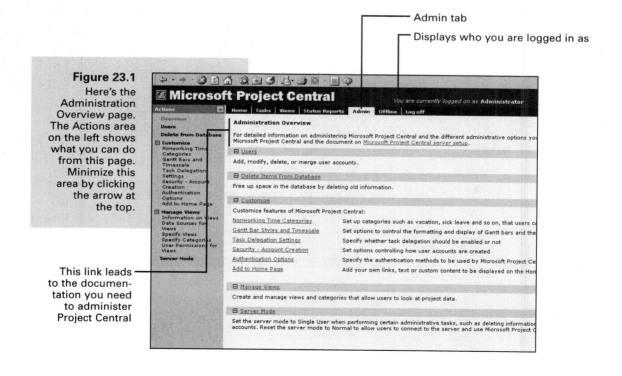

Figure 23.1
Here's the Administration Overview page. The Actions area on the left shows what you can do from this page. Minimize this area by clicking the arrow at the top.

This link leads to the documentation you need to administer Project Central

Admin tab

Displays who you are logged in as

The actions you are most likely to use in this mode are working with user accounts, setting security, and deleting items from the database as it gets larger. The default settings for most of the other features work well for most situations. If you need more information about them, the Microsoft Project Central Server Setup document gives you the details; the link to that document appears in the top of the page, just above the Users section.

You can create, modify, and delete user accounts using the Users settings. To get there, click on Users in the Administration Overview page or in the Actions bar at the left. The Users page (Figure 23.2) presents a list of users with the properties for each one. You will not see any names other than Administrator until you have actually posted a project schedule to Project Central.

Because you can create user accounts by sending assignments to the resources in your project schedule, you won't need to create each user's account from this page. You will use this page primarily for modifying and deleting accounts.

The Users page itself explains most of the information you need for adding, modifying, and deleting resources. One setting to consider adjusting is the role of the user. There are three roles available, as shown in Figure 23.3—Administrator, Manager, and Resource. An administrator has power over security, configuration, user accounts, and general Project Central server maintenance. A manager is

Figure 23.2
You can add and delete users on this page.

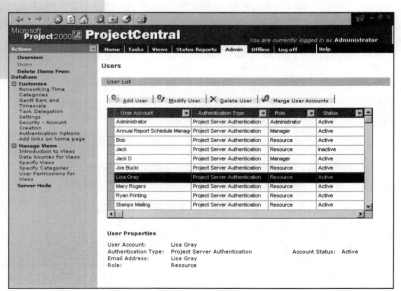

Figure 23.3
Use the Role drop-down list to change the role setting for the selected user.

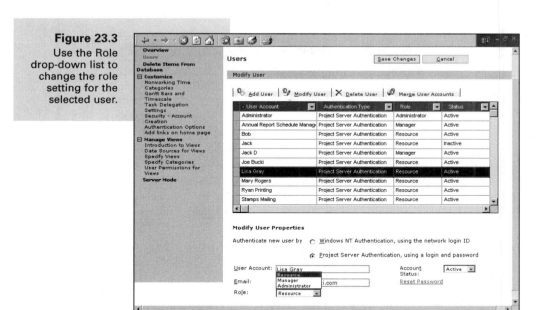

associated with a project and is the one who is managing the schedule (this is you, typically). A resource is one of the people working on the team.

Security consists of selecting an Authentication mode and setting permissions for Account Creation. Authentication controls how the users are recognized, and Project Central offers three options. The first is Windows NT Authentication, which will log valid users on automatically if they are on a Windows NT network. The second is Project Central server authentication, in which users are logged on using a login ID and password stored on the Project Central server. The last option is mixed, which allows both types of authentication. (Click on the Server Mode link on the Administration Overview page or in the Actions list and follow the instructions for setting the server mode to single user before you change authentication options.)

If you are going to allow only Windows NT authentication you should create an account for the person who will be administering the server and assign that user the Administrator role before you switch the Authentication mode.

Deleting items from the database is another action you may want to take after your project has been active for quite a while. To do this you need to set the server mode to single user and then choose Delete Items From Database from the Actions list on the left side of the Project Central screen. This leads to the Delete Items From Database page (Figure 23.4). You can delete Tasks, Messages, Status

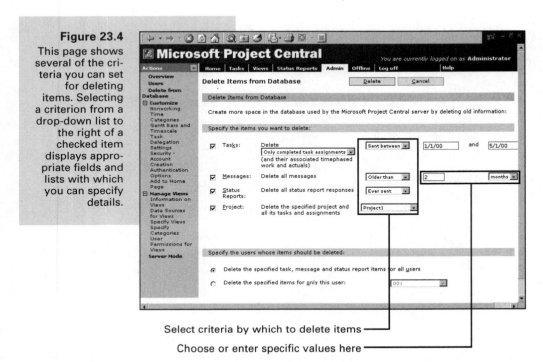

Select criteria by which to delete items ⎯

Choose or enter specific values here ⎯

Reports, or entire projects according to criteria you set. You also can delete items for specific users, useful if someone has left the project.

Reviewing Configuration Considerations

Once you have logged in as Administrator you have several options in setting up the site. Before you dive into those options you will need to answer several questions about how best to use Project Central in your organization. You also need to prepare your file in Project 2000 so that the updates are done correctly. These questions fall into several basic categories:

- What information do I want to get and give?
- How often do I want it?
- With whom do I want to communicate?
- How much autonomy do I want resources to have?

Before addressing how to set up and customize your file in Project 2000 to meet your particular needs, let's return to Project 2000 for a moment and see how to set it up to connect with Project Central.

The first step in configuring Project 2000 to connect with Project Central is to choose the identity that will be used by the person or people who are going to manage the project schedule. If more than one person will manage the schedule, or if you are just planning to have someone else fill in while you go on vacation, select an identity that can be shared. Messages sent to resources are sent by (addressed from) a particular user. When the user responds to the messages, the response returns to the same sender. If you send out the request under your user name, only you can see and use the response. If another person tries to update the file the following week using a different user name, that person would not be able to receive the update messages.

The best idea here is to create a generic user for the project ("Project X Schedule Manager," for example) and use that user name when sending requests and updating the project. You can create this generic user name simply by choosing Tools, Options in Project 2000. Click on the General tab, then enter the name into the User Name text box, as shown in Figure 23.5. (Leave the Options dialog box open for the moment.)

Once you have decided on a user name, the next step is to configure the workgroup. Click on the Workgroup tab in the Options dialog box. Open the Default Workgroup Messages For (File) drop-down list and click on the Web choice, shown in Figure 23.6. (Focus now on settings for the Web; setting e-mail options is covered later in the chapter.)

You will also want to create a *personal account* for the schedule manager on Project Central server. Project Central recognizes this account user as the manager of the

Figure 23.5

Set a generic user name for the schedule manager in the Options dialog box.

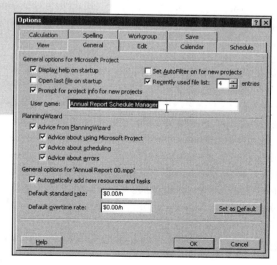

Figure 23.6
Setting the
default
configuration
for using Project
Central.

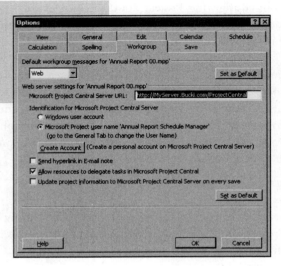

schedule, the one who has the ability to set rules for automatically handling updates and may also need to receive and approve many of the changes that team members make to the schedule. If you specified a generic user name as discussed earlier, be sure to select the Microsoft Project User Name (Name) option button. Then create the account by clicking on the Create Account button on the Workgroup tab of the Options dialog box. Project 2000 will confirm that the account has been created successfully by bringing up the message box shown in Figure 23.7. Click on OK to close the message box.

If you get an error message when you try to create the personal account (also see Figure 23.7), the first place to look would be at the URL you have entered in the Project Central URL text box on the Workgroup tab of the Options dialog box. If that is correct, check to see that the Project Central server is running and is in server mode rather than single user mode.

Tip

Using the Create Account button is a good way to check that your connection with the server is properly set up and is running at any later time. If the connection is active when you click on the Create Account button, you'll see a message that there is already an account by that name. If the server or connection aren't active, an error message will let you know that you have a problem. Sending a task assignment is an alternative way to test the server connection, but this technique creates a message on the server that you may need to remove later.

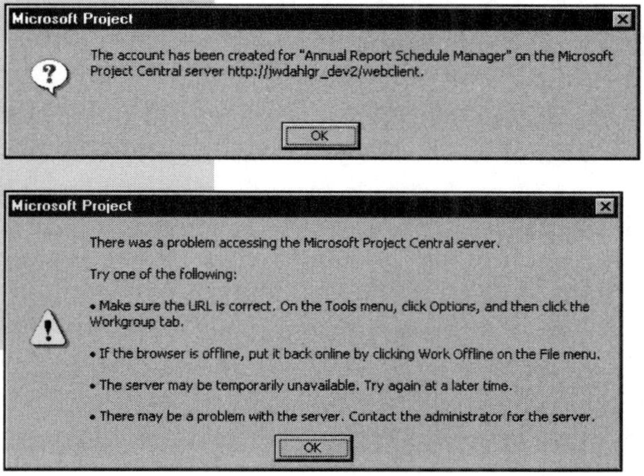

Figure 23.7

The top message box verifies that you've created a personal account for the project manager. The bottom message box appears if there's an error during account setup.

You may want to set other options on the Workgroup tab of the Options dialog box. For example, check Send Hyperlink In E-mail Note to tell Project to send a reminder to the team members when Project Central has new information they need to respond to; the e-mail message includes a hyperlink the message recipient can click on to connect to the Project Central Web site. Check this option if some of the team members will not be involved in the project every week, and will therefore need a reminder to give an update. The e-mail address information comes from the Email address field in the Resource Information dialog box for the resource entry.

You might try checking Allow Resources To Delegate Tasks In Microsoft Project Central if you're working with an experienced team. (I'll cover how delegation works later in this chapter.) For teams using Project Central for the first time, it may be a good idea to introduce this feature after they have gotten used to the basic functionality.

The last Workgroup tab option to consider is the Update Project Information To Project Central Microsoft Server On Every Save check box. If you are anticipating doing a lot of work on the schedule and running different what-if scenarios, leave this box unchecked. Also leave this option unchecked if you have the AutoSave function turned on. There is no need to update the server with the many incremental changes you would be making in these cases.

With the options completed you are ready to move on to determining what information you are going to send out to your team, so click on OK to close the Options dialog box and accept your changes. To control the information flow, you need to understand what information Project Central is capable of gathering and distributing.

Considering Activity Information

Project 2000 can send the information from almost all of its fields to Project Central for your team to see and update. This includes Start, Finish, Deadline, Actual Work, Remaining Work, Overtime, and Cost, as well as all the custom date, text, and number fields. Users can update most of these fields through Project Central except for those that are calculated (slack would be an example of a calculated field).

The first question you need to answer before you choose which fields to work with in Project Central is how you are measuring progress. Project Central enables your team to update tasks either by entering the actual hours and remaining hours on activities (with this information perhaps captured via timesheets or other means) or by entering an assignment completion percentage. If your schedule is resource-driven and you want to gather and understand the total amount of effort that has gone into the work, then actual hours would be preferred. For activities in which actual hours might not be known (hours of work by an outside vendor, for example) or are not important, then a completion percentage value might be better. (See Chapter 6, "Managing Resources," for a more complete discussion of effort-driven or resource-driven scheduling.)

You may also want the resources to enter some additional data or comments about the assignments that have been posted to Project Central, or you might want to take advantage of the new deadline feature and use the deadline field to communicate this information to your team. Once you have determined what it is you are going to post, you are ready to set up your project file for those activities.

Choosing Which Project Fields to Export to Project Central

To display the settings that control the fields to be exported from Project to Project Central, choose Tools, Customize, Workgroup. The Customize Workgroup dialog box appears (Figure 23.8).

The lists at the top part of the dialog box enable you to control which fields Project exports to Project Central. By default, Project exports Task Name, Work, Start, Finish, Completed and Remaining Work, and Comments. You can add to this list by selecting additional fields in the Available Fields list at the left and clicking on the arrow button to move them to the Fields In Workgroup Messages list at the right. The double arrow button >> moves the entire list of Available Fields. Double-clicking on an item will move it from one list to another.

Directly below the Fields In Workgroup Messages list box, you can see two check boxes: Include In TeamStatus Message and Let Resource Change Field. You must

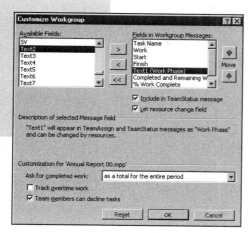

Figure 23.8
The Customize Workgroup dialog box controls all of the information Project will be sending to Project Central.

click on each field in the Fields In Workgroup Messages list, and then specify whether either or both of the check box settings apply to the selected field. When Include In TeamStatus Message is turned off (unchecked), the field is not shown in TeamStatus messages, but is included in TeamAssign messages. Exporting the field but not showing it in the status message may seem odd; the value of this is in keeping the TeamStatus messages simple and still allowing resources to view a wide variety of information in the assignment window. You will want to leave this box checked for any fields that you will be expecting resources to update or that are useful in giving context that will help identify the assignment.

The Let Resource Change Field check box indicates whether the resource can change the contents of the selected field. Of the default fields, the resource can change Start, Completed and Remaining Work, and Comments by default. If you click on one of these fields in the Fields In Workgroup Messages list, you can see that the Let Resource Change Field check box is checked but grayed out. This indicates that you have no choice about changing that setting for these fields.

Several of the available fields do not offer the option to enable the resource to change the field. This applies to calculated fields, which hold information derived from schedule calculations rather than user input. The fields that do allow resource input are Contact, Deadline, Marked, all user-defined Cost fields, Date, Duration, Start and Finish fields, all Flag fields, Number, Outline Code, and Text fields. Be careful as you choose which fields to show your resources so that the display in Project Central does not become too cluttered.

In the center of the Customize Workgroup dialog box, Project shows you how the currently selected field in the Fields In Workgroup Messages list will be displayed and what options you have chosen. You will notice that any customized names for the fields will be used when the activity is sent out. If you have customized the Text1 field to use the title "Work Phase," then the field will show up as "Work Phase" in Project Central.

The bottom of the Customize Workgroup dialog box offers three more settings. The first, Ask For Completed Work, controls how the users will report the work they have done. Two of the choices in this drop-down list—Broken Down By Day and Broken Down By Week—are self-explanatory. The remaining drop-down list choice, As A Total For The Entire Period, asks the resource to enter work for the reporting period you have set. Here you will have to make a decision about how much detail you are going to require from the resources. If you choose Broken Down By Day, your schedule file will become larger due to the additional number of work records it must hold; this is probably not a limitation for most projects. If you don't need daily totals, then choosing As A Total For The Entire Period will probably be best, because that setting enables you to specify the range of dates for which you are requesting data.

Check the Track Overtime Work to enable the resources to enter overtime work separately from their regular work in Project Central. With this option unchecked, Project Central and Project record all work as regular work. Lastly, checking the Team Members Can Decline Tasks check box gives your resources the ability to decline the tasks you have assigned them. If they do so, you will receive a message stating that the task has been declined, along with any comments the resource has included.

If you need to return to the default settings for the Customize Workgroup dialog box at any time, click on the Reset button. Otherwise, click on OK to close the dialog box and apply your changes. Once you have set these options, they will stay the same from week to week unless you make further changes. The Customize Workgroup dialog box settings apply only to the current project file, so if you have multiple project files, you will need to open the dialog box for each of them and choose the desired settings, or incorporate the files into a master project file set up with the appropriate Customize Workgroup settings. The Organizer does not allow you to transfer these settings from file to file.

You are now one step away from sending your schedule data to Project Central.

Selecting Tasks to Export

You have two choices when it comes to exporting tasks to Project Central. The first is to export all tasks. The second is to export selected tasks. One of the best ways to select a group of tasks to export is to create a filter that shows only the tasks you are interested in, then select those tasks by clicking in the Select All box at the upper-left corner of the Task Sheet. (See "Creating a Table or Filter" in Chapter 11 to learn more about custom filters.) For a large project, it is good practice to create a filter that displays only the tasks you expect your team to work on in the near term. You don't want to clutter the Project Central display with tasks that aren't expected to begin for months or years. It's a good idea to make the range broad enough that if resources start an assignment ahead of schedule, that assignment is included in Project Central; this way, the resources can post work to it.

Project does not export tasks without resources, so you will want to make sure that you have assigned resources to any task for which you are expecting updates. Tasks with multiple resources assigned will be displayed to all of the resources. When the first resource reports actual work on a task, Project Central reports an Actual Start date for the task.

Also don't forget to consider how you plan to account for overhead. Most resources working on projects also spend time on things such as organizational meetings, writing reports, travel time, training, and other activities that are not part of the project plan but require time from team members. If you are going to correctly forecast the availability of resources, you will want to capture how much time has been spent on these activities. One way to do this is to create a special "Overhead" task, then assign each team member to it. This can be one long task in the project that is not directly linked to any of the other activities, so its schedule doesn't affect the overall schedule. Another way is to simply assume a percentage maximum availability that is less than 100%. The third option is to ignore overhead and assume that this work will be spread evenly across all the project activities.

If one element of overhead is particularly large or important, then you could create ongoing or recurring tasks for it, as well.

Determining the Frequency of Updates

With Project 2000 and Project Central you can assign tasks, request status reports, or update project members as often as you want, and in some projects a daily update is important. However, in most cases there is a trade-off between the value of daily information and the time that you and the resources in your project will take to enter and make sense of this data. On the other hand, asking someone to enter how many hours they spent on a task three weeks ago Friday may be a bit unreasonable. Choosing a weekly update frequency is a good compromise.

Many organizations set this "posting" period well in advance of any weekly update meetings, allowing time to identify problems with the schedule and verify them with the responsible parties before the meeting. This approach is more efficient than confronting people with schedule issues for the first time at the meeting itself, which often results in discussions about posting problems or bad schedule data, instead of suggestions for solving the problem.

Taking the time to walk your team through the schedule process and clearly communicating what is expected of them is an important part of making the schedule run smoothly. If some members of your team are not posting their progress, a false picture may be presented when the project schedule is updated. Presenting the schedule process to them and making sure they have a clear set of instructions—a "cheat sheet" for the posting operation—will make the first few update cycles go well and will increase your team's confidence in the process. Setting the option that automatically sends an e-mail message with the hyperlink to Project Central will also help to remind them.

Sending an Update

After determining and communicating the process you are going to follow, you are finally ready to send out activity assignments and status requests to your team for the tasks you selected in the Task Sheet. These assignments and requests will show up as messages when your team members log in to Project Central. This part is easy.

The commands for sending out messages to Project Central appear on the Tools, Workgroup submenu (shown in Figure 23.9). Note that these are the same commands you use to send team messages if you're communicating via e-mail only.

Note

> Your Web server must be up and running to accept the messages you send. If it is not, you will get an error message stating that the action could not be completed and to contact the administrator. If you are sure the Web server is running, recheck the Project Central URL that you entered in the Workgroup tab of Project's Options dialog box to make sure it is correct. By default it is http://<your-webserver-name>/ProjectCentral.

The submenu offers three commands which send messages to resources on the project, and one command that the manager uses to work with Project Central. TeamAssign sends an assignment to selected resources. TeamStatus requests status from the resources and TeamUpdate sends an update containing changes to

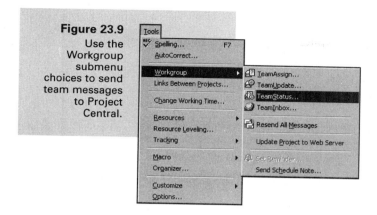

Figure 23.9

Use the Workgroup submenu choices to send team messages to Project Central.

assignments to resources. TeamInbox is what the manager would select to log into Project Central and update the project with responses from the team.

The TeamAssign command sends a message to each resource who lists the tasks they have been assigned and all the other data fields you have decided to send along. Sending a TeamAssign message at the beginning of the project clearly communicates all the tasks you expect the resource to handle for the project. As you saw in setting up the fields to be included in the messages to Project Central, you can have fields exported in a TeamAssign message that are not sent in a regular TeamStatus message. The idea is that the TeamAssign message sets up a master list of tasks and the TeamStatus message requests status on some or all of those tasks. If you have chosen to allow resources to decline tasks, then you may get some responses back that some tasks have been declined. If resources can't decline tasks, then no response is required.

The TeamUpdate command is used to let resources know that something has changed in the project plan. The update is specific to the assignments that have been affected by the change. Examples of such changes are delays in the starting date of an activity, or the deletion or re-sequencing of an activity.

The TeamStatus command sends a request for updates about work completed on the selected tasks. You can send TeamStatus requests even if you didn't send an earlier TeamAssign message about the selected tasks. TeamStatus messages create a task list for the team member to update in Project Central. As discussed earlier, a TeamStatus request will most likely not include all of the tasks in the project, but should be limited to the tasks that are expected to be worked on in the near term.

A TeamStatus request also differs in that it has a clearly defined period associated with it. You set this in the dialog box that appears (Figure 23.10) after you have chosen Tools, Workgroup, TeamStatus.

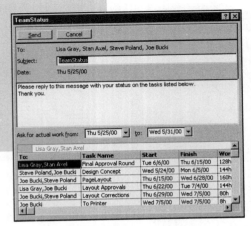

Figure 23.10
The TeamStatus dialog box allows you to determine the period for the request, as well as the subject and text for the message.

The key activities associated with this box are setting the status period. Fill in the From and To text boxes beside Ask For Actual Work—the dates you request determine the period. By default, the period is a week, but you can enter any period that you like. You will also want to provide a Subject for the message—doing so will help you and your team to distinguish messages later. If you don't provide a Subject, Project 2000 will just label the message "TeamStatus."

You also can include a message to the TeamStatus message recipients. The text box below the Date allows you to include such additional information if you like; do so when you have some special instructions or information to convey. If the Subject line itself is self-explanatory, you can even leave this field blank.

The final activity you can perform here is to review which tasks you're sending, and to whom you are sending them. Using the scroll bar on the right side of the list of tasks at the bottom of the TeamStatus message window, you can scroll down the list, which is organized by task. Notice here that the To column may show several resources for the same task. When you send the message, the individual assignments will be broken out to the individual resources. When you have large numbers of resources to which to send, you might want to consider constructing some groups of resources and sending out status requests to each group separately. This will make scrolling through the assignments in this box easier.

Once you have checked the message you are sending, click on the Send button, and you're finished. You can tell the tasks on which you have requested status by the small icon that shows up in the Indicators column (Figure 23.11), or by looking at the contents of the Team Status Pending field. A response to a TeamStatus request is required from Team members, so this icon will remain until the response is received and the project is updated.

Figure 23.11

The icon that looks like an envelope with a question mark indicates that you have sent a request for the status of this item to the resource assigned to it.

	❶	Task Name
0		⊟ **Annual Report 00**
1		Gather Samples
2		⊞ **Review Meeting**
7		Develop Theme Proposal
8		Theme Meeting

Note

If you want to remove the status indicators, you can use one of two methods. The simple way is to log in as that user (have the Project Central administrator reset the password for you, if necessary) and reply to the message. The administrator could also merge the old account with another one. That way, all of the previous user's tasks can be assigned to a new person.

Working with Project Central

Whereas the administrator generally controls the behavior of the Project Central application, the manager controls the way Project Central works to help manage the team. This includes setting rules for accepting and processing messages and setting format and period for the status reports for the team. The team members—the individual resources—work with Project Central to help keep the overall schedule up to date and make sure everyone is informed of progress. This section will first take a look at what Project Central does for the team member and then show you how to manage that information.

Viewing Messages as a Team Member

To log on, team members need to enter the URL for the Project Central Web site into their browser and go to the site. The URL by default is http://<your-webserver-name>/ProjectCentral. This is the same URL you use when you are sending messages.

When team members reach the site, they will see a login screen where they can select their name from a list of users and enter their password. Like the administrator, the team members have no password until one has been set up. If you are working over an intranet and have used valid usernames to identify your resources, then they will automatically be logged in and will see their home page, as in Figure 23.12.

When team members log in, they have various options. The main thing they will want to do is to look at their new messages and respond to them. They can do this by clicking on Messages in the Actions list at the left side of the screen, or by following the link to the Microsoft Project Central Inbox. Each team member will see his or her own messages, not those of the rest of the team.

Users will find messages here from the manager or perhaps other team members, as shown in Figure 23.13. The initial message they will receive is the TeamAssign message sent out at the beginning of the project. Double-clicking on the message will open it, so it looks like the example in Figure 23.14.

The TeamAssign message shows the team member what tasks have been assigned. If the manager has set the option for allowing resources to decline tasks, then the resource can choose to decline selected tasks by using the Accept? column in the list of tasks in the TeamAssign message, and clicking on the Reply button to respond to the manager via Project Central. After replying, the tasks become items in the team member's task list.

A TeamStatus request (Figure 23.15) asks the team member for status on the tasks to which they have been assigned. Clicking on a TeamStatus message in Project Central opens the message in the Timesheet view, as in the example shown in Figure 23.16.

Figure 23.12
Here's a user's home page, which enables the user to review messages, tasks, and more.

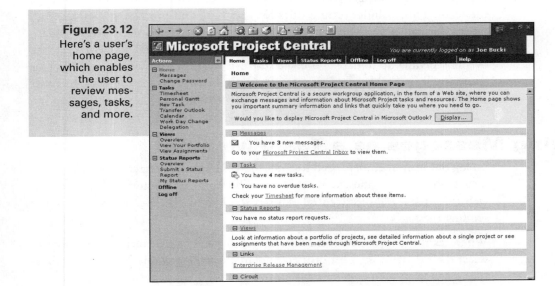

Figure 23.13
The users see messages in their own inbox.

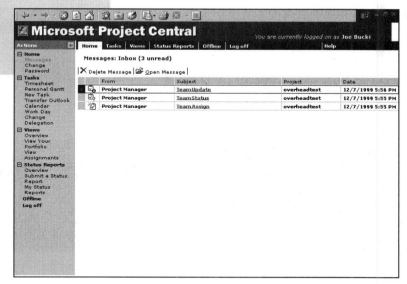

Figure 23.14
Here's how a TeamAssign message looks when the resource views it in Project Central.

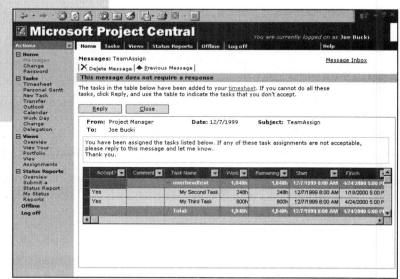

Figure 23.15
Here's how a
TeamStatus
request looks in
Project Central.

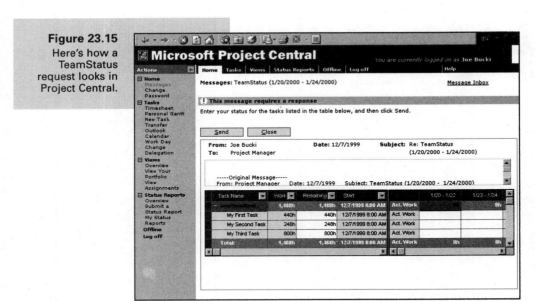

The user can adjust the timescale
to see shorter or longer periods

Figure 23.16
The Timesheet
view shows
tasks and allows
resources to fill
in hours worked.
The user has the
option of saving,
sending,
delegating, or
adding a task to
the list.

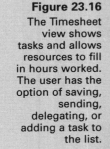

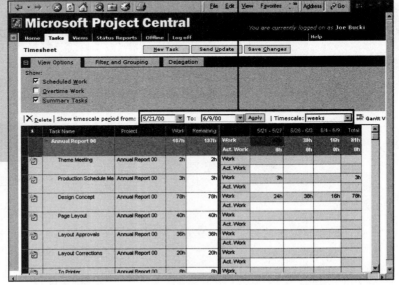

The team member then fills in the amount of work done on the tasks in the Act. Work (for actual work) row at the right for the requested period, and then clicks on the Send Update button to send the information back to the manager via Project Central. Project Central automatically reduces remaining work for the applicable tasks in the Project file by the amount of actual work entered by the user (resource).

Note

Automatically reducing remaining work by the amount of actual work entered is fine when the work on the activity was correctly estimated. However, it's common for tasks to take longer than expected. In that case, before sending the update back to the manager, the team member should *increase* the entry in the Remaining column of the Timesheet view to account for the new estimate of effort required for the task.

Team members can make updates to the Timesheet view and choose to save the changes rather than sending the reply right away if they plan to make more changes later. For example, users could enter actual work at the end of each day, save, and then send their updates to the manager at the end of the week.

Tip

Sending out the status request at the beginning of the time period rather than when status is due will give the team members a fresh list of activities to be working on. Limiting the status request to the most critical activities can focus the team members' attention on those tasks.

Team members can also view the TeamStatus request as a Gantt chart (Figure 23.17) that shows what work is planned for the period they have selected. This gives the team members a way to view their own personal schedules without having access to the master schedule file.

Team members may also see a TeamUpdate (Figure 23.18) or a delegation message in the inbox. A delegation message would come from another member of the project who has delegated responsibility for a task. You can reply to either of these types of messages to deny the request; otherwise no response is required.

The final type of messages are those that were returned by the manager. Some of these may be returned automatically by the rules the manager has set, others may be personally returned by the manager. The team member will have to make changes to the response (which will be self-explanatory onscreen) and send it back to the manager.

Figure 23.17
Project Central can display a Gantt Chart view of a team member's ongoing activities.

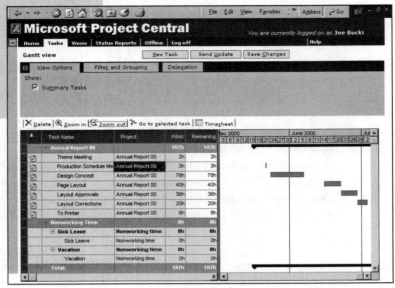

Figure 23.18
TeamUpdate messages don't require a response unless you disagree with the change.

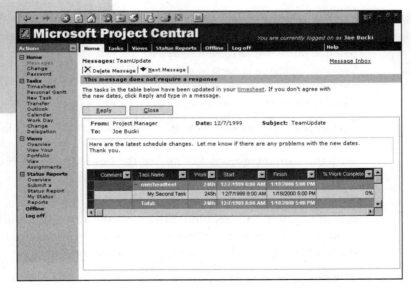

Accepting Responses into the Project Plan

To update your project or respond to messages that your team members have sent, open your project file and from the Tools, Workgroup menu choose TeamInbox. This will display the Project Central web site. If you are using Windows NT Authentication you will automatically go to your home page when you log in. If you are using Microsoft Project Central server authentication, select your name from the drop-down menu and enter your password. On your home page, under the Messages section, you should see the number of new messages you have received. Clicking on the "Messages" header or the link to Microsoft Project Central Inbox will bring you to your inbox. All the responses to the requests that you have made via Project Central return to your inbox here. The process you follow to update the project is fairly simple. Open the message or response and click on the Update button; doing so will bring you back to your project file and update the schedule with the information contained in the response from the team member. If the update causes a change to other tasks in the file that other resources are working on, Project will send out a TeamUpdate to the affected resources. Clicking on the Reply button sends the response back to the team member if you don't accept it or if you need him or her to make any changes. Clicking on the Close button closes the message for you to deal with later.

Setting Response Rules

One way to make your life as a manager easier is to set some rules for handling the responses you get from your team. Project Central lets you create rules to tell it to automatically perform actions (accepting, deleting, rejecting) on messages based on the content, message sender, or both.

By default, the manager of the team is the one who sent the message to the team from within Project 2000. The Project Central administrator can add or change the manager for a project through the user administration functions discussed earlier.

You access the rules settings from the home page, which shows up when you log in as a manager. Click on the Rules link in the Actions list along the left side of the screen. This displays the first Rules wizard page (Figure 23.19), which shows which rules you have and will allow you to run rules or create and modify rules.

Figure 23.19

The Rules wizard
enables you to
create and
modify rules and
run them on
specific projects.

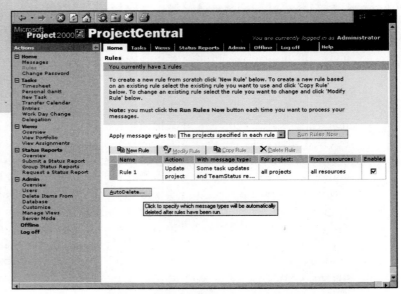

Rules do not run automatically—every time you want to apply a rule you must run it.
A good practice would be to run the rules when you are ready to start processing
updates.

To create a rule, click on the New Rule button just above the list of rules. A Rules
wizard starts, displaying a page (Figure 23.20) that asks which types of messages
you want to accept automatically. The choices are more restrictive the further
down the list you go, from All Of The Below Message Types to setting specific criteria that messages must meet. The first option, Accept All, minimizes the work
that you need to do, but will potentially allow unchecked information into your
schedule and allow your team members to delegate and add tasks without bringing those new assignments to your attention. Choosing this option would be
appropriate for a team that is experienced and capable of working independently.

The next choice for types of messages to accept is All New Task Requests. This
covers all messages from team members where they have decided to add a task to
the schedule. Allowing team members to add a task can make keeping the schedule up to date easier, but most of the time you will probably want to review those
tasks before you accept them. Once these changes are in the project file, you will
also want to make sure you set any constraints, predecessors, or successors for the

Figure 23.20
Step 1 of the Rules wizard allows you to set criteria for automatically accepting different types of messages.

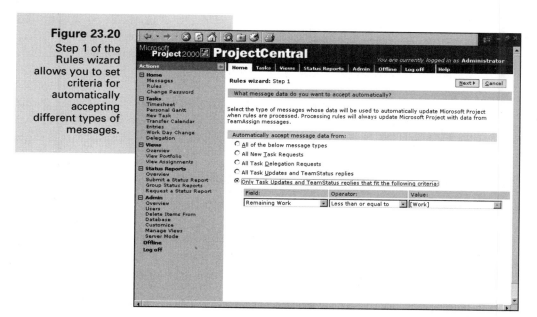

added tasks. Project Central only enables team members to select which summary task or project the new task becomes a part of.

The next choice, All Task Delegation Requests, tells Project Central to accept all task delegation messages. You can turn off this ability in the Administration/Customize/Task Delegation page. Managers should probably be aware of delegation going on in the project, but if you really don't want to be informed of this, then set the rule to automatically accept delegations.

The next choice, All Task Updates And TeamStatus Replies, tells Project Central to accept all task update and status requests. This is a useful rule when you have many requests and updates to process. As you will see in the next step of the wizard, you can customize this rule to apply to some or all of your team members.

The final choice, Only Task Updates And TeamStatus Replies That Fit The Following Criteria, enables you to add specific criteria for accepting task updates and status request responses. With this setting you can set criteria that ensure that the changes posted are within an appropriate range or whatever else you would like to check. This gives you the ability to screen out responses that may have errors in them before you incorporate them into your schedule. You still have the option of accepting these responses, but running the rule will not automatically update your schedule with them.

After you make your choices in the first wizard screen, click on the Next button in its upper-right corner. The second step in the Rules wizard enables you to select which project to which you want to apply the rules. Select the project in the left window and click on the arrow to move it to the right. If you have a rule that you think will be consistent across many projects, there is an option to make it applicable to all future projects. Once again, it is a good idea to check to see that the rule is working well on one project before you apply it to all. You can always modify it later. Click on Next after you make your choices on the second Rules wizard page.

The final step in the Rules wizard is to select to whom the rule applies and what the rule will be named (Figure 23.21). Click on the top option button, All Current And Future Resources Registered In The Web Client Database, if you want the rule to apply to all resources.

Click on the Only The Resources Specified Below option button if you want to limit the rule to messages from certain resources. (Also check Including All Future Resources, if desired.) Then, to select the applicable resources, click on each resource in the Available Resources list on the left and use the Add arrow to move the selected resource to the Auto-Accept Message Data From These Resources list on the right. Selecting a large number of resources is probably best done by moving all the resources to the right and then removing the exceptions.

Figure 23.21
Step 3 of the Rules wizard enables you to determine which resources the rule applies to. This is also the step where you set or change the name of the rule.

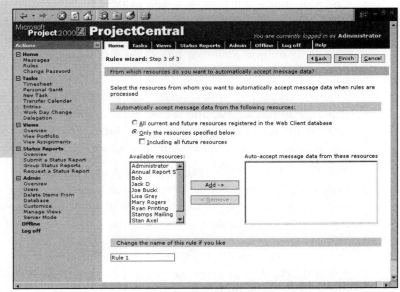

Tip   If you are allowing your team members to create new users to which to delegate tasks, you might want to leave the Including All Future Resources check box unselected. That way, messages about new resources will show up in your inbox and you will be aware of their existence. Then you can make sure that the new resources respond properly.

Enter the name of the rule in the Change The Name Of This Rule If You Like text box at the bottom of the last wizard screen. It is a good idea to set a descriptive name and include the project with which it is associated if you have many project-specific rules.

Status Reports

Status reports are another feature within Project Central. They allow a team manager to request and combine status reports from team members. These status reports can include schedule data from Project 2000, but are primarily text-based and don't interact directly with Project 2000. A manager requests a status report by choosing the Status Report tab along the top or by selecting Request A Status Report from the Actions list at the left. A wizard starts, enabling you to create a status report form. After defining the report sections and setting a frequency (daily, weekly, monthly) for the report, you can send the form to the team.

Team members will see the request under the Status Reports section on their home page and can open the request by clicking on it. An example form appears in Figure 23.22.

After inputting the status information, the team member can save the report by clicking on the Save button. A team member can save as often as needed, and then send the response to the manager at the end of the week by clicking on Send. Managers see the link to the report in the Status Reports section of their home page.

Figure 23.22
Here's a sample status report form, ready to be filled out by a team member.

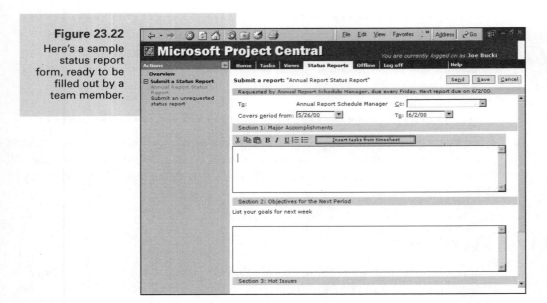

Views

Microsoft Project Central includes a number of predefined views that enable you to display project information for a single project or a portfolio of projects. A view is composed of a set of fields and filters that allows you to focus on certain areas of your projects. You can create and define your own views to see a collection of projects, to see details of an individual project, or to look at Microsoft Project Central assignment information.

Before you can start using views, you must have them set up by the administrator by going to the Administration Overview page and then following the links to Manage Views. In the documentation, Microsoft states that there are several specific procedures necessary to set up views. You should review the documentation prior to starting to define views, as the scope of this book doesn't offer room to cover the view features in detail.

PART VII
Working with Advanced Features

24

Customizing Microsoft Project

IN THIS CHAPTER

- Making adjustments to menus
- Hiding and displaying toolbars, and working with toolbar tools
- Working with the Options dialog box

Throughout this book, I've noted numerous situations in which you need to tweak how Project 2000 reacts to your commands, or even how you communicate with Project to give it commands. This chapter provides an overview of all the customization options available to you in Project, and explains how to make Project look and work the way you want it to.

Creating a Custom Menu

Early on, many computer programs deserved the reputation of being difficult to learn. Each program used its own terms for particular operations (such as opening a file, which was also called "getting," "retrieving"). Moreover, each program had different menus that grouped commands differently. From one program to the next, you never knew exactly how to navigate. Software publishers have come a long way toward standardizing terms and menus so that what you learn in one program applies in another, but they've also left in plenty of flexibility for controlling the way menus look and work.

In fact, in Project and many other applications, you can create custom drop-down menus and custom menu commands to suit your needs and working style. The menus you create or modify can execute standard program commands, macros that come with the programs, or macros that you create. To work with menus in Project, choose Tools, Customize, Toolbars. Or, right-click on the menu bar, and then click on Customize. The Customize dialog box (see Figure 24.1) appears, displaying the list of menu bars and toolbars available in Project. (In Project 2000, you use similar steps to create menu bars and toolbars.) Each menu bar offers a list of menus, which in turn list commands. To display a different menu onscreen, click to check its check box in the Toolbars list of the Toolbars tab in the dialog box, and then click on Close to close the dialog box. If you no longer want a particular menu to appear onscreen, click to clear the check box beside its name before closing the dialog box.

• •

To display a menu bar you've created, right-click on any onscreen menu bar or toolbar to open a shortcut menu, and then click on the name of the menu you want to display.

• •

You can also use the Customize dialog box to add a new command to a menu, to add a new menu to a menu bar, or to create an entirely new menu bar. For example, to create a new menu bar, click on the New button on the Toolbars tab in the Customize dialog box. The New Toolbar dialog box appears. Type a name for the

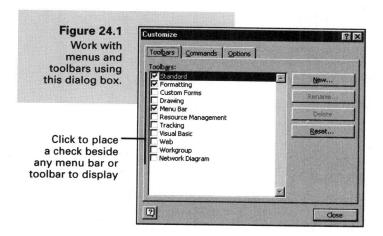

Figure 24.1
Work with menus and toolbars using this dialog box.

Click to place a check beside any menu bar or toolbar to display

menu in the Toolbar Name text box, preferably a name that distinguishes the new bar as a menu bar rather than a toolbar. Click on OK, and the new menu bar appears onscreen as a small, blank floating toolbar.

Next, you want to create the first menu on the menu bar. Click on the Commands tab in the Customize dialog box. Scroll down the Categories list; then click on New Menu in the list. A New Menu choice appears in the Commands list at the right side of the dialog box. Drag the New Menu choice from the dialog box onto the new menu bar. A New Menu placeholder appears on the menu bar. Right-click on the placeholder or click on it and then click on the Modify Selection button in the Customize dialog box. Then, in the Name text box, type a menu name, such as **Favo&rites** (see Figure 24.2). Press Enter. Project knows that you intend the entry to be a menu name, and automatically places a drop-down arrow beside it. The ampersand (&) before the "r" is how you tell Project to format that letter as a selection letter; your custom menu will be called Favorites, and pressing Alt+R will open it when you are finished.

For obvious reasons, you can't use the same selection letter for two menu names on the same menu bar, or for two commands on the same menu. You also should be careful not to duplicate selection letters in menu names if you plan to display more than one menu at a time.

Tip

You can also add a menu to any toolbar that's displayed onscreen by dragging the New Menu placeholder onto the toolbar rather than onto a menu bar.

Right-click on the new menu

Figure 24.2
You can create a
completely new
menu on a
menu bar.

Drag this
placeholder onto
the menu bar

Enter the
menu name

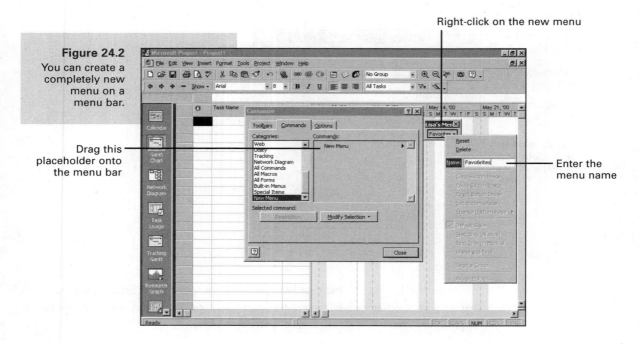

On the Commands tab of the Customize dialog box, scroll through the Categories list and click on the category that holds the first command or macro you want to add to the menu. If you're not sure what category to choose, click on the All Commands or All Macros choice. Then scroll down the Commands list until you see the command you want to add to the menu. Drag the command from the Commands list to the new menu name on the menu bar; when the blank menu opens below the menu name, drag the command onto the menu and release the mouse button. The command appears on the menu, which remains open. If you want to rename the command or change its selection letter, right-click on the command or click on it and click on the Modify Selection button in the Customize dialog box. Edit the Name text box entry, and then press Enter. To add each additional command to the menu, simply click on the Categories choice you want and drag a command from the Commands list to the position on the menu where you want it to appear. Then drop it into place as shown in Figure 24.3.

Note

You have to leave the Customize dialog box open to make all your menu changes. Otherwise, the techniques described in this section won't work. If you need to reopen the Customize dialog box, choose Tools, Customize, Toolbars.

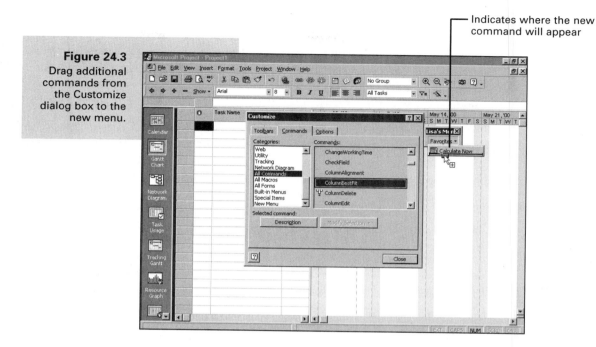

Figure 24.3
Drag additional
commands from
the Customize
dialog box to the
new menu.

If you want to create a command to display a submenu, select New Menu in the Categories list of the Commands tab of the Customize dialog box, and then drag the New Menu choice onto a menu. Name the submenu just as you would name a menu. Then select command categories from the Categories list and drag commands from the Commands list onto the submenu you added to the menu.

You might want to be able to group commands on your menu for easier access. You can do so by inserting a separator line. Open the new menu, and then click on the command above which you want the separator line to appear. Click on the Modify Selection button in the Customize dialog box or right-click on the selected command. To insert the separator line, Choose the Begin A Group choice in the menu that appears. To remove the separator, reopen the shortcut menu for the selected command and click on the Begin A Group choice to toggle it off.

Continue using the techniques just described to add additional commands to your menu. Anytime you want to start a new menu on the menu bar, click on the New Menu choice in the Categories list, and then drag the New Menu placeholder from the Commands list to the desired position on the menu bar. If you make a mistake and add an unwanted menu bar or command, simply drag the menu or command off the menu bar where it resides and onto the Project work area, and then release the mouse button. Alternately, you can drag a menu name to change its position on a menu bar, or drag a command to move it up or down in a menu. For example, if you're right-handed, you may want to move the File menu on the default menu bar to the right to make it easier to work with. When you finish making your menu bar changes, click on Close to close the Customize dialog box. Then you can drag the new menu bar to the position you desire onscreen. If you drag it to the top of the screen, you can drop it above an existing toolbar or menu bar to "dock" it in a horizontal position.

Although starting from scratch when creating a menu is fine, you may be better off adding a copy of an existing menu to your menu bar and modifying it to suit your needs. Click on the Built-In Menus choice in the Categories list of the Commands tab in the Customize dialog box. Then drag the name of the menu that most approximates your needs from the Commands list to the appropriate position on a menu bar or menu. Finally, make changes to the menu and commands as needed.

If you make changes to the Standard menu bar and later want to undo the changes, display the Customize dialog box, click on Menu Bar in the Toolbars list of the Toolbars tab, and click on the Reset button.

Note

Your custom menu bars and toolbars are stored by default with the GLOBAL.MPT file where Project settings are stored. If you want to e-mail a schedule file and have it offer the custom menu bar or toolbar, you need to copy the custom menu bar or toolbar—as well as any macro modules holding macros for commands or toolbar buttons—to that particular file. Use the Organizer command on the Tools menu to display the Organizer, which enables you to copy the custom feature. See Chapter 11, "Working with the Different Project Views," to learn more about the Organizer.

Working with Toolbars

Toolbars are as easy to customize as menu bars, and most users find toolbars easier to use. You've seen numerous instances elsewhere in this book where displaying different toolbars or working with particular toolbar buttons can help you get the most out of certain Project features. This section shares more information about how you can work with Project's toolbars.

Displaying and Hiding Toolbars

Every toolbar is accessible via the other toolbars. You can right-click on any toolbar to display a shortcut menu. Then click on the name of another toolbar you want to display or click on the name of a toolbar that's already onscreen that you want to hide. Similarly, you can click to open the View menu and point to the Toolbars choice to display a submenu listing toolbars and menu bars; in the submenu, you just click on the toolbar you want to hide or display.

An alternative method of choosing which toolbars appear onscreen and which don't, as well as accessing other commands for working with toolbars, is to choose Tools, Customize, Toolbars. The Customize dialog box appears (refer to Figure 24.1). To open the Customize dialog box using the mouse, right-click on any toolbar; then choose Customize.

Click on the check box beside any toolbar you want to display in the Toolbars list of the Toolbars tab. If you want to hide a toolbar that's onscreen, simply click on its check box in the Toolbars list to remove the check mark. Click on the Close button to close the Customize dialog box and finish making your choices.

Customizing the Buttons on a Toolbar

You can make any changes that you want to the contents of a toolbar. The process for doing so is very similar to creating and editing a menu, which you learned about earlier in the chapter. You can remove buttons, add buttons, or edit the function of any button. To add and remove buttons on a toolbar, use the following steps:

1. Open the toolbar that you want to edit onscreen.
2. Choose Tools, Customize, Toolbars. Alternately, you can right-click on any toolbar, and then choose Customize. The Customize dialog box appears.
3. To add a button to one of the displayed toolbars, click on the Commands tab to display it. Click on one of the Categories list choices to display the available buttons and commands in that category. Then drag a button or command from the Commands list onto the toolbar in the position you want, as shown in Figure 24.4. Release the mouse button to drop the new toolbar button into position.

Note

To add a toolbar button or menu command for a macro you created, select All Macros from the Categories list box of the Commands tab in the Customize dialog box. Then drag the macro from the Commands list to a menu bar or toolbar.

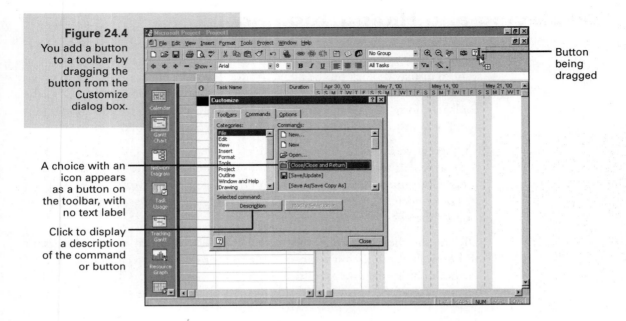

Figure 24.4
You add a button to a toolbar by dragging the button from the Customize dialog box.

Button being dragged

A choice with an icon appears as a button on the toolbar, with no text label

Click to display a description of the command or button

Note

The Commands list of the Commands tab in the Customize dialog box clues you in as to whether a command you add to a toolbar will appear as a picture button only or a text command only. A choice that has an icon will appear as a picture button when you drag it onto a toolbar. If a choice lacks an icon, the command name will appear on the added toolbar button.

4. To move an existing toolbar button to a new position on the same toolbar, which you must do while the Customize dialog box is open, just drag the button and release the mouse button to drop it into the new location.

5. To remove a button from a toolbar while the Customize dialog box is open, drag the button off of the toolbar and release the mouse button. (Make sure that you don't accidentally drop it on another toolbar.)

6. When you finish dragging buttons onto, off of, and around on toolbars, click on Close to close the Customize dialog box.

The buttons available in the Customize dialog box are, for the most part, buttons that already exist on a Project toolbar or menu. If you want to place a custom button image on a toolbar button, display the toolbar and the Customize dialog box. Right-click on the toolbar button you want to change. Then point to Change Button Image to display a palette of available button images, as shown in Figure 24.5. Click on the image you want to apply to the button. (You can also use this technique to add an image to a menu command.)

If you can't find a button that's exactly what you need, click on a button that's close in appearance. Then right-click on the toolbar button with the image you want to edit and click on Edit Button Image in the shortcut menu that appears. The Button Editor appears onscreen, as shown in Figure 24.6. Click on a color or Erase in the Colors area; then click on a square (called a pixel) on the Picture to change that pixel to the selected color. Click on OK when you finish making

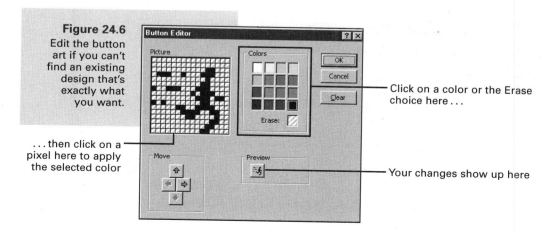

Figure 24.5
Click on a new image in this palette of choices to apply it to the current toolbar button.

Figure 24.6
Edit the button art if you can't find an existing design that's exactly what you want.

Click on a color or the Erase choice here . . .

. . . then click on a pixel here to apply the selected color

Your changes show up here

changes. The edited image appears on the toolbar button only (it's not available on the palette for other buttons).

You can change the command or macro assigned to a button or its status bar description using the Customize Tool dialog box. (This technique applies to menu commands, too.) With the Customize dialog box open onscreen, click on the toolbar button (or menu command); then click on Modify Selection on the Commands tab or right-click on the toolbar button. In the menu that appears, click on Assign Macro. The Customize Tool dialog box appears. To change the existing command, macro, or custom form assigned to the button (or menu command), open the drop-down list for the Command text box. Scroll through the list, and click on the selection you want to assign to the button. (Forms and macros are listed under "f" and "m" respectively; for example, a custom form might be listed as *Form "Summary"* and a macro as *Macro "Adjust_Dates."*)

Click on the Name text box and type or edit the button name, which will pop up as a screentip to describe the button whenever you point to the button with the mouse. Then click on the Description text box and type a description for the button, which will be used to explain the button in the status bar whenever you point to it. Figure 24.7 shows some sample entries. Click on OK to finish editing the toolbar button, and then adjust other buttons or close the Customize dialog box.

If you want to get to the Customize Tool dialog box to make changes to any button on any toolbar without opening the Customize dialog box, press and hold the Ctrl key, and then click on the button. Make any adjustments you want in the Customize Tool dialog box, using the same techniques just described for creating a custom button; then click on OK.

Figure 24.7
Here are example entries for a button in the Customize dialog box.

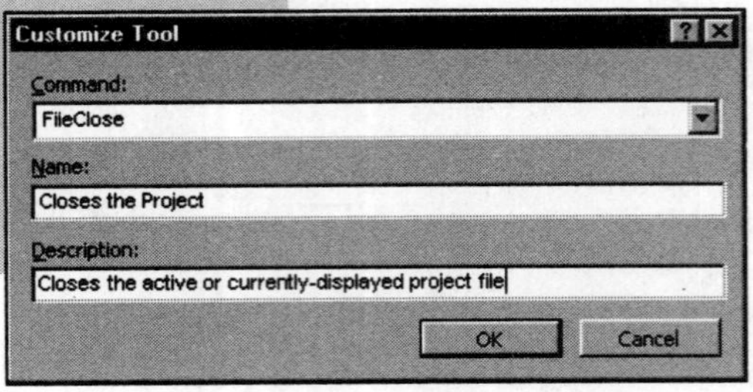

Creating a Custom Toolbar

You can create a brand new toolbar or one that's based on an existing toolbar. To do so, right-click on a toolbar, and then choose Customize. Alternately, choose Tools, Customize, Toolbars. The Customize dialog box appears. On the Toolbars tab in the dialog box, click on the New button, type a Toolbar Name in the New Toolbar dialog box, and click on OK. This displays a new blank toolbar onscreen.

After the new toolbar appears, click on the Commands tab in the Customize dialog box to add or remove toolbar buttons, as described earlier. You can also right-click on any individual button on the toolbar to display a menu of commands for modifying that button.

Deleting a Custom Toolbar or Menu Bar

Project does not let you delete any menu bar or toolbar that comes with the program. You can, however, delete the custom menu bars or toolbars you create. To delete a custom menu bar or toolbar, right-click on any menu bar or toolbar onscreen, and then choose Customize to open the Customize dialog box. In the Toolbars list of the Toolbars tab, click to select the name of the custom menu bar or toolbar you want to delete. Click on the Delete button. Project asks you to confirm that you want to delete the menu bar or toolbar. (You're warned because you can't undo the deletion.) Click on OK to do so; then click on Close to close the Customize dialog box.

Customizing Workgroup Message Fields

Chapter 21, "Communicating with the Team," explains how to send specialized messages called workgroup messages from Project to make resource assignments, send task updates, and request status reports from resources. In each of these messages, Project lists certain fields for each task you're communicating about, such as Task Name or Remaining Work Hours. You can customize the fields that appear for tasks listed in these messages by using the following steps:

1. Choose Tools, Customize, Workgroup. The Customize Workgroup dialog box appears, as shown in Figure 24.8.
2. To add a new field, scroll through the Available Fields list at the top left and click on the name of the field you'd like to insert the new field. Click

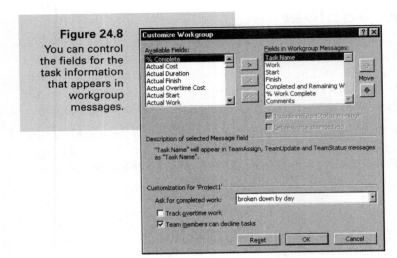

Figure 24.8

You can control the fields for the task information that appears in workgroup messages.

on the add (>) button. The field moves to the Fields In Workgroup Messages list at the top right.

3. Click on the newly added field name in the Fields In Workgroup Messages list, then use the Move arrow buttons to move the field to the desired position in the list (see Figure 24.9).

4. With the appropriate field still selected in the Fields In Workgroup Messages list, clear the check mark for the Include In TeamStatus Message option only if you want to restrict the inclusion of the new field to TeamAssign and TeamUpdate messages. If the Let Resource Change Field

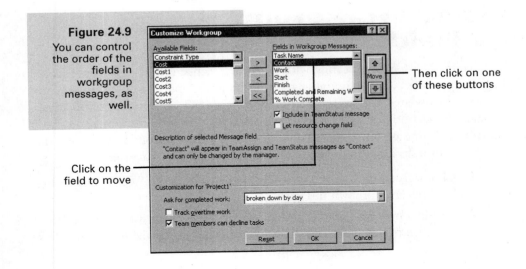

Figure 24.9

You can control the order of the fields in workgroup messages, as well.

Click on the field to move

Then click on one of these buttons

option is available, check it or clear it to specify whether you want resources to be able to change the field when replying to you.

5. To remove one of the fields from the Fields In Workgroup Messages list, click on the field, and then click on the remove (<) button.

6. If you'll be sending TeamStatus messages to the resources assigned to some tasks in your project, make a choice from the Ask For Completed Work drop-down list. Your choice here adds a field telling each resource how quickly you expect to receive a status report via e-mail in response to your TeamStatus message.

7. Click to check the Track Overtime Work check box if you want your TeamStatus messages to include a field prompting recipients to respond to your TeamStatus message with e-mail reporting actual overtime hours worked.

8. If you want to include a field enabling recipients to decline tasks (via e-mail) you assign via TeamAssign messages, click to check the Team Members Can Decline Tasks check box.

9. If at any point you're not satisfied with the Fields list or the other changes you made, click on the Reset button.

10. When you finish specifying the custom fields for your workgroup messages, click on OK.

Setting Project Options

As with most other application programs today, Project offers dozens of options that you can set to control how the program looks and behaves. To set options for the Project program, choose Tools, Options. The Options dialog box has nine tabs, each of which relates to a particular functional area of Project. The upcoming sections describe each of the tabs and its choices. Click on a tab to display its options; then make the changes you want on that tab. When you finish specifying your choices for all the tabs in the Options dialog box, click on OK to close the dialog box and put your changes into effect.

View Options

The first tab in the Options dialog box, the View tab (see Figure 24.10), specifies how Project looks onscreen when you run it. Here are the choices you have there:

■ **Default View.** Choose a view from this drop-down list to specify the view Project uses for the current schedule when you start the program.

Figure 24.10
Project offers options for controlling its onscreen appearance.

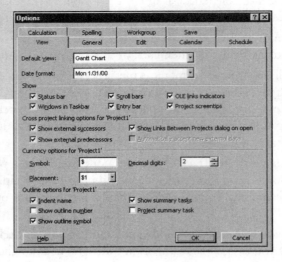

- **Date Format.** Your selection from this drop-down list specifies how dates appear in the Task Sheet for any column holding date information.

- **Show.** In the Show area, you specify which of the following window features of Project should appear—Status Bar, Scroll Bars, OLE Links Indicators, Windows In Taskbar, Entry Bar, and Project Screentips. Click to place a check mark beside each feature that you want to appear.

- **Cross Project Linking Options For (Current File).** If you linked tasks between files or consolidated projects (see Chapters 17 and 19), use these options to control whether and how the links appear. Click to check the Show External Successors or the Show External Predecessors check boxes (or both) if you want tasks linked to other projects to appear in the current project file; clear these check boxes to hide the linked tasks. Click to check the Show Links Between Projects Dialog On Open check box if you want Project to prompt you about whether or not to update links when you open a file that contains linked tasks. When that check box is cleared, you can click to check the Automatically Accept New External Data check box to have project update the tasks without displaying a dialog box. Alternately, clear both check boxes to simply open the file without updating the linked tasks.

- **Currency Options For (Current File).** In the Symbol text box, specify the currency symbol, if any, that should appear to the left of columns containing cost information. The Placement drop-down list lets you control how the specified currency symbol appears in relation to the currency value. In the Decimal Digits text box, enter how many decimal places should appear after whole numbers in currency values. For example, enter **0** to see whole currency values only.

- **Outline Options For (Current File).** When the Indent Name check box is selected, any tasks you indent move to the right in the Task Name column. When the Show Outline Number check box is selected, Project displays an outline number that you can't edit beside each task in the Task Name column of the Task Sheet. You can use the Show Outline Symbol check box to turn on or off the display of the outlining + (summary task) and − (subtask) symbols. If you clear the check mark beside the Show Summary Tasks option, summary tasks won't appear in the Task Sheet, so you won't be able to use outlining features. The Project Summary Task option inserts a summary task for the whole project file, as described in Chapter 4.

General Options

Click on the General tab to display the options shown in Figure 24.11. Here's what you can do with each of these options:

- **Display Help On Startup.** Leave this option checked if you want to see the Microsoft Project Help window when you start Project.
- **Open Last File On Startup.** Click to place a check mark beside this option to tell Project to automatically reopen the last schedule file you worked in when you restart Project.

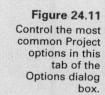

Figure 24.11
Control the most common Project options in this tab of the Options dialog box.

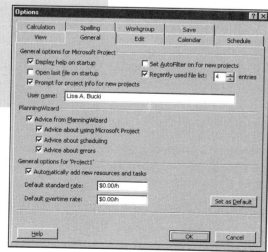

- **Prompt For Project Info For New Projects.** Click to place a check mark beside this option to have Project ask you for Project schedule information when you create a new project.

- **Set AutoFilter On For New Projects.** When checked, this option automatically turns on the AutoFilter feature in all new project files. As you learned in Chapter 11, AutoFilter arrows appear on Task Sheet and Resource Sheet column headings, providing a speedy way for you to display only entries with similar information in a particular field.

- **Recently Used File List.** Enable this check box to specify that the names for files you worked with recently appear at the bottom of Project's File menu. Use the spinner buttons beside the Entries text box to tell Project how many file names should appear on the File menu; clicking one of those file names on the menu quickly opens the file.

- **User Name.** Type your name in this text box.

- **PlanningWizard.** When no check mark appears beside the Advice From PlanningWizard option, no Planning wizard choices are available. You can click to place check marks to determine whether you want Project to display Advice About Using Microsoft Project; Advice About Scheduling (asks whether you want to create links where they're possible, and so on); or Advice About Errors (informs you when your changes will create a scheduling conflict or other problem).

- **General Options For (Current File).** A check mark beside the Automatically Add New Resources And Tasks option means that any name you type when making assignments becomes a row entry in the Resource Sheet; otherwise, Project prompts you for resource information. If Automatically Add New Resources And Tasks is selected, you can specify a Default Standard Rate and Default Overtime Rate in the text boxes below the check box.

- **Set As Default.** If you want to make the changes on this tab the defaults for Project, click on this button.

Edit Options

The Edit tab enables you to specify which editing features you want to use in Project. Click on this tab to display it, as shown in Figure 24.12.

When a check mark appears in the box beside any of the options here, that option is available; otherwise, you can't use the specified editing technique. The first option, Allow Cell Drag And Drop, controls whether you can drag to move information in the Task Sheet or Resource Sheet. Move Selection After Enter means that the cell selector moves down to the next row when you press Enter

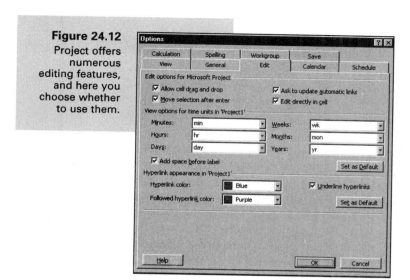

Figure 24.12
Project offers numerous editing features, and here you choose whether to use them.

after making an entry in the Task Sheet or Resource Sheet. Ask To Update Automatic Links means that Project prompts you about links if you update a file that's linked to task or resource information in another file. Edit Directly In Cell lets you make changes in a Task Sheet or Resource Sheet cell rather than having to click on a cell and then click in the Entry bar to make needed changes.

The options under View Options For Time Units In (Current File) allow you to choose how time measurements are displayed in the Task Sheet and Resource Sheet. You can use the six drop-down lists to control how the labels (abbreviations) for minutes, hours, days, weeks, months, and years appear. In addition, click to check the Add Space Before Label check box to insert a space between the number and label for any time value in the Task or Resource Sheet. Click on the Set As Default button to make your time label setting changes the defaults for Project.

If you use hyperlink fields in your project plan, use the options under Hyperlink Appearance In (Current File) to control the link colors. Choose colors from the Hyperlink Color and Followed Hyperlink Color palettes. Leave Underline Hyperlinks checked if you want Project to format hyperlinks with underlining, as well. Click on the Set As Default button to make your hyperlink settings the default for all Project files.

Calendar Options

The Calendar tab of the Options dialog box (see Figure 24.13) enables you to specify the default base calendar for the current schedule file. Use the top two

Figure 24.13
Use the Calendar tab to establish the default calendar for the current schedule file.

Options

| Calculation | Spelling | Workgroup | Save |
| View | General | Edit | Calendar | Schedule |

Calendar options for 'Project1'

Week starts on: Sunday

Fiscal year starts in: January

☐ Use starting year for FY numbering

Default start time: 8:00 AM

Default end time: 5:00 PM

Hours per day: 8.00

Hours per week: 40.00

Days per month: 20

Set as Default

Help   OK   Cancel

drop-down lists to specify the start of each work week and fiscal year in your calendar for the current schedule file. Depending on which month you select from the Fiscal Year Starts In drop-down list, the Use Starting Year For FY Numbering check box becomes enabled. Use that check box to tell Project which year to use to label your company fiscal years. Click on the check box to label the fiscal year according to the starting year (calling it fiscal '01 if the fiscal year spans 2000 and 2001). Clear the check box to label the fiscal year according to the ending year (calling it fiscal '00 if the fiscal year spans 2000 and 2001).

The remaining choices affect only the current file; they work as follows:

- **Default Start Time.** The time you enter here is the time of day Project uses for new tasks you add to the Task Sheet, unless you specify otherwise.

- **Default End Time.** Sets the time of day when Project cuts off work on tasks for the day, unless you specify otherwise for a particular task or its assigned resource.

- **Hours Per Day.** When you enter durations in terms of days, this entry determines how many working hours each day contains.

- **Hours Per Week.** As with the preceding option, the number of hours you enter here is reflected in the schedule. If you enter **35**, each work week contains 35 hours by default.

- **Days Per Month.** Use this setting to control the number of workdays per month that Project assumes when you assign durations in terms of months. For example, if you change this setting to 22, each one-month task you create would be scheduled for 22 days of work.

- **Set As Default.** Click on this button to make your changes in this tab the default settings used by Project.

Schedule Options

The default scheduling options, displayed by clicking on the Schedule tab of the Options dialog box (see Figure 24.14), control how Project responds when you enter information in the Task Sheet. The first option is Show Scheduling Messages. When this option is checked, Project warns you if you make a mistake that will cause a scheduling error. This tab offers numerous key settings for the current file, as well:

- **Show Scheduling Messages.** Project can't prevent you from making certain errors when you enter date information in the Task Sheet, but when you check this box, it can warn you when an entry will create an error.

- **Show Assignment Units As A.** Choose an option from this drop-down list to specify whether Assignment Units appear as a Percentage or Decimal value. To display Assignment Units for individual assignments, you must display the Task Usage view and then add the Assignment Units field to the Task Sheet. (See Chapter 11 to learn more about displaying different views, and Chapter 4 to learn how to add a column or field to the Task Sheet in a view.)

- **New Tasks Start On.** Choose whether the default start date Project enters for new tasks is the project start date or the current date.

- **Duration Is Entered In.** Your choice here specifies the time units (minutes, hours, days, weeks) that Project assigns to Duration column entries if you don't specify a unit.

- **Work Is Entered In.** Your choice here specifies the time units (minutes, hours, days, weeks) that Project assigns to Work column entries if you don't specify a unit.

- **Default Task Type.** Your choice from this drop-down list specifies whether tasks in the active project have a Fixed Duration, Fixed Units, or Fixed Work. Fixing one of these choices means that its value remains constant, even if you change the other two values. For example, if you select Fixed Duration here and then double the work allowed for a task, Project cuts the units value in half to ensure the duration stays the same. Any change you make in the Task Type choice of the Task Information dialog box for a particular task takes precedence over the Default Task Type choice on the Schedule tab.

Figure 24.14
This tab enables
you to specify
how Project
handles
scheduling
choices.

Note

> The *duration* is the time between the start and finish dates that you
> enter. *Units* represent the total number of resources assigned to the
> task—two resources full-time for example. *Work* stands for the number
> of person-hours required to complete the task.

- **New Tasks Are Effort Driven.** This check box controls whether or not
  adding resources to a task or removing them from a task affects the task
  duration by default. Check this option if you want task durations to
  adjust when you add or remove resources.

- **Autolink Inserted Or Moved Tasks.** If you insert or move tasks within a
  series of tasks linked by Finish-to-Start (FS) relationships and this option
  is checked, Project links the inserted tasks within the group of linked
  tasks. If you reschedule tasks, Project automatically asks whether you want
  to create links where they're possible.

- **Split In-Progress Tasks.** When this option is checked and you
  automatically reschedule uncompleted work, uncompleted work on in-
  progress tasks is rescheduled, in addition to work scheduled for tasks that
  haven't yet begun.

- **Tasks Will Always Honor Their Constraint Dates.** This check box
  controls the behavior of tasks with negative total slack (that is, tasks that
  cannot slip or move out without delaying the entire project's finish date).
  When this option is checked, tasks will honor their constraints and not

move to correct the negative slack situation. If you prefer that tasks move according to their links to help compensate for negative slack, clear this check box.

- **Show That Tasks Have Estimated Durations.** Leave this option checked if you want Project to display a question mark in the Duration field for tasks where you've specified an estimated duration only. Having this visual cue allows you to judge where you may need to check with resources to verify the duration you've plugged in, for example.

- **New Tasks Have Estimated Durations.** Leave this option checked if you want Project to assume that all new tasks you add have an estimated duration, again reminding you that you may need to revisit the duration and adjust it later.

- **Set As Default.** Click on this button if you want your choices on the Schedule tab to apply to all new project files you create.

Calculation Options

Calculation options (Figure 24.15) indicate whether Project automatically updates all calculated values (such as actual cost figures that equal actual hours worked multiplied by hourly rates). In the Calculation Options area of this tab, specify whether calculation should be Automatic or Manual. Calculate All Open Projects tells Project to recalculate all open files each time it recalculates; if you do so and you have large consolidated or linked files open, recalculation may be slow. In such a case, you may want to choose the Calculate The Active Project option

Figure 24.15
Set calculation options here to control when and how Project calculates certain fields based on your entries elsewhere.

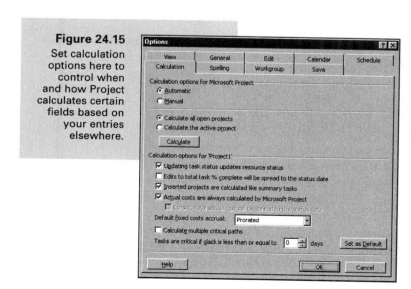

instead to recalculate only the current file. If calculation is set to Manual, you can display this tab and click on the Calculate button to recalculate all values in all open projects.

The following settings in the Calculation Options For (Current File) area of the dialog box apply to the currently open schedule file:

- **Updating Task Status Updates Resource Status.** Select this check box if you want information you enter into task views to be reflected in calculated fields in resource views. For example, if you enter an actual task completion amount, it's reflected in terms of actual hours worked and costs for a particular resource.

- **Edits To Total Task % Complete Will Be Spread To The Status Date.** Check this option if you want your % Complete entries to spread to the next status date set for the schedule or the finish date for the task. For example, if you enable this check box and your project has a status date of 4/14/00 and the finish date for a task is 4/28/00, marking the task as 100% complete marks it complete only through 4/14/00.

- **Inserted Projects Are Calculated Like Summary Tasks.** When you consolidate project files, this options tells Project to recalculate schedules when you insert and link subproject files.

- **Actual Costs Are Always Calculated By Microsoft Project.** Check this option to have Project calculate actual costs for each task until it is marked as 100% complete, at which point you can then enter a differing actual cost value. This ensures that you won't enter an actual cost value prematurely; however, if you already entered an actual cost, don't turn on this check box unless you want to reenter that information.

- **Edits To Total Actual Cost Will Be Spread To The Status Date.** When the preceding check box is cleared, this check box becomes active. Clicking on it then specifies that actual cost information you enter for a task applies only through the status date of the file, not through the task finish date.

- **Default Fixed Costs Accrual.** Your choice from this drop-down list tells Project when and how to add cost information for new tasks with fixed costs into the actual costs calculated for the task and project. For example, if you want to assume the task's fixed cost is spent as soon as the task begins, as with a nonrefundable retainer fee you pay in advance, click on Start. If you won't pay a resource at all until a task is finished and you inspect and accept the work, click on End. If you agreed to pay the resource a partial fee even if the resource doesn't complete its work or are paying a monthly fixed fee for the resource's work, you can choose Prorated.

- **Calculate Multiple Critical Paths.** If you have a few different groups of linked tasks that span your project duration rather than a single string of linked tasks, you can enable this check box to have Project calculate multiple critical paths. The effect is that more tasks will be marked as critical, so you'll be able to identify all the tasks that could potentially delay the project finish date if they slip out.

- **Tasks Are Critical If Slack Is Less Than Or Equal To.** Enter a value here to control how many tasks are considered critical tasks (are part of the critical path). Higher values mean that fewer tasks are marked as critical.

- **Set As Default.** Click on this button if you want your choices on the Calculation tab to apply to all new project files you create.

Spelling Options

By default, the spelling checker in Project reviews most task and resource text information. Using the options on the Spelling tab (see Figure 24.16), you can speed up the spelling checker by selecting which information it checks; you can also specify other options related to the spelling checker.

To tell the spelling checker not to review information in a particular task or resource field, click to select the field in the Fields To Check list. Then click on the drop-down list arrow in the right column and click on No.

The next options on the Spelling tab are the Ignore Words In UPPERCASE check box and the Ignore Words With Numbers check box. When these options

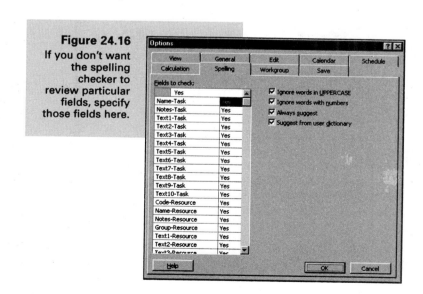

Figure 24.16

If you don't want the spelling checker to review particular fields, specify those fields here.

are checked, the spelling checker does not check the spelling for words typed entirely in uppercase (such as **IN**) or words including numbers (such as **Qtr1**), respectively. Always Suggest, when checked, means that the spelling checker displays a list of suggested corrections for any unrecognized word it finds. Suggest From User Dictionary, when checked, means that the spelling checker includes corrections from your user dictionary with the suggestion list.

Workgroup Options

Click on the Workgroup tab to display options for controlling how some online features work by default (Figure 24.17). Chapters 21 through 23 discuss how to work with online features in more depth.

The options in the Workgroup Messages Transport For (Current Project) area of the tab enables you to specify defaults for workgroup messages you send, such as TeamAssign messages. You can set the following options for those messages:

- **Default Workgroup Messages For (Current File).** Your choice from this drop-down list controls how Project attempts to send e-mail messages. The Email choice sends messages to the Outbox of your e-mail program, so you can then launch the e-mail program and send the messages. The Web choice sends the messages to a Web server on the Internet or your internal company intranet. You can also choose to send each message in both ways.

Figure 24.17
Control how some online features work and look with these options.

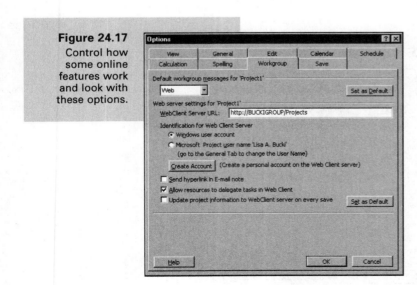

- **Microsoft Project Central Server URL (Current File).** If you're using a Web server to communicate with team members and chose Web or Email And Web as your choice for the preceding option, enter the URL for the Web server in this text box. For example, if you've set up a Web site on your computer and connected it to your company's network, your URL might be something like this: http://BUCKIGROUP/Projects. Note that you have to choose Web from the Default Workgroup Messages For (Current File) drop-down list and then enter the URL here to enable the remaining options on this tab.

- **Identification For Web Client Server.** Use the options here to choose whether to log on to the Web Client server as a generic Windows user or under a specific user name. Click on the Create Account button to tell Project to create a new account for your user name if you choose the Microsoft Project User Name (Current User) choice. (You must be connected to the Web Client server for this to work.)

- **Send Hyperlink In E-mail Note.** Check this option to provide better notification when you send a message to the Web server for the workgroup. This "teaser" message contains a hyperlink to the Web server, so the recipient can double-click on it to look for the message.

- **Allow Resources To Delegate Tasks In Web Client.** Leave this option button checked to allow resources to use automated features in the Web Client to reassign work to other resources.

- **Update Project Information To WebClient Server On Every Save.** Leave this option button clicked to ensure that your changes are saved to the WebClient server every time you save the project file. Enabling this choice ensures your information will be up to date on the server, but it will slow you down a bit as you work.

Finally, if you're comfortable with your choices on the Workgroup tab and want those choices to apply no matter which file is open, click on the Set As Default button.

Save Options

Project 2000 offers a new tab of Save options (Figure 24.18) to allow you to have more control over how, when, and where project file information is saved. Here's the lowdown on how these options work:

- **Save Microsoft Project Files As.** Use this drop-down list to specify that you want Project to save files by default in an alternate file format, such as Microsoft Access Databases (*.mdb).

Figure 24.18
New save
options appear
in Project 2000.

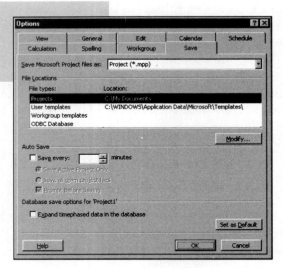

- **File Locations.** Click on a choice under File Types, then click on the Modify button to change the default drive and folder in which Project stores the specified type of file. After you navigate to the proper location using the Look In list in the Modify Location dialog box, click on OK.

- **Auto Save.** Like its Microsoft Office siblings, Project can now save your files automatically as you work, ensuring that you won't lose all your work if your system crashes or restarts unexpectedly. To enable Auto Save, check the Save Every check box, and then adjust the setting in the Minutes text box to control how often the Auto Saves occur. If you want to Auto Save all open files, click on Save All Open Project Files to select that option rather than Save Active Project Only. I also recommend that you clear the check beside Prompt Before Saving, just to save yourself the trouble of having to verify every save.

- **Expand Timephased Data In The Database.** If you use the very first option to save your files as a Project or Access database, check this option to ensure that the database contains all the time-based details—how work occurs and costs accrue on a day-by-day basis. Otherwise, the resulting database includes totals only.

- **Set As Default.** As on the other tabs, click on this button to make your settings the default for all files.

25

Creating and Using Macros

IN THIS CHAPTER

- Adjusting macro security levels
- Recording and playing back macros
- Changing macro information, such as the shortcut key
- Making changes in or removing macros
- Finding more help about VBA
- Creating your own command or button for a macro
- Looking at a few last ideas about macros

Every company's needs and projects are unique. Even seasoned temporary workers need a bit of on-site training to conform to the specific processes of a new client company.

While company A might want temps to organize files and information by project name, company B might want the information to be ordered by job number. Although such differences seem trivial, misunderstanding the requirement or making filing mistakes can create hours of work down the line for someone else who is searching for particular files.

Like a temporary worker, Project can conform to your unique needs in building schedules. Project does this by enabling you to create macros, which are mini-programs that you create to perform certain tasks.

Setting the Macro Security Level

Even if you don't create your own macros, you may be using Project files from other sources that contain custom macros. If you've heard about Word macro viruses, then you know that macro viruses can cause you to lose data or can completely corrupt a file. While I haven't yet read about or encountered any macro viruses affecting Project, the possibility of Project macro viruses certainly exists.

As a result, Microsoft has added macro virus protection in Project 2000. The virus protection warnings depend on the VBA project developer acquiring a *digital certificate* and signing the VBA project with the certificate. (Organizations such as VeriSign and Microsoft issue certificates as a means of tracking macro, Web, and programmed content; these organizations can help track down the source of particular content based on the information stored in the certificate.) When you open a Project file that includes a digitally signed VBA project or macros, or try to run macros from other sources, Project asks whether you want to add the macro developer to your list of *trusted sources*. If you do so, Project copies the digital certificate for that source to your system.

Tip

A *VBA project* or *VB project* stores extensive macro code in a Microsoft Project file. You have to create a VB project programmatically; in other words, you don't create a VB project when you simply record a macro. However, the security settings do apply to individually recorded macros, too.

Once the digital certificates for trusted sources are on your system, you can choose Tools, Macro, Security to open Project's Security dialog box (Figure 25.1). Use the options on the Security Level tab to control whether or not macros run or you see warnings.

The Low choice enables all macro projects and macros and displays no warnings. If you select Medium, Project displays a warning when you open a file with a project that's not signed or not on your list of trusted sources, or try to run a macro that's unsigned or from an unknown source. You can choose whether to enable the macros and whether to add the source to your list of trusted sources. If you select High, Project doesn't open unsigned macros at all, and doesn't give you the option of using them. If the macro or macro project comes from a trusted source, it's automatically enabled. If the macros are signed with an unrecognized certificate, you can choose whether or not to enable the macros and whether or not to add the source to the list of trusted sources.

To remove a source from your list of trusted sources, click on the Trusted Sources tab in the Security dialog box, click on the source you want to remove, and then click on the Remove button.

Click on OK to close the Security dialog box after you finish making your security choices. Then save and close all your files, exit Project, and restart Project for the new settings to take effect.

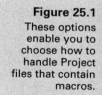

Figure 25.1

These options enable you to choose how to handle Project files that contain macros.

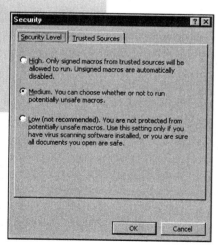

Creating Macros

Macros store a series of commands or steps as a single entity, so that you can execute the entire series via the single step of selecting the macro. In earlier computer applications, macros had to be created manually via scripting, which was a "user-friendly" euphemism for programming. Thus most people didn't use macros, because they were too difficult to create.

Today's applications, including Project, enable you to record macros. You don't have to be a whiz to create a macro. All you need to know is how to start the macro recorder and how to execute the commands that you want to save as a macro. Unless you specify otherwise, a recorded and saved macro becomes available to all the files that you work with in Project.

Note

> The macros you record in Project are built behind the scenes with Visual Basic for Applications (VBA) commands, a macro programming language used in all Microsoft Office applications. Each macro is stored in a VBA Macro module, which is like a single sheet that can hold multiple macros. By default, the modules and macros are saved with the GLOBAL.MPT file, a file that saves your default information for Project. You can use VBA programming to develop more powerful macros; however, programming with VBA is beyond the scope of this book.

You should record macros to automate a task in these two basic situations:

- **When the task is lengthy and requires many steps.** Creating a macro to store such a process helps other users work with the file, particularly if the file is stored on a network. If several users need to create and print a particular report, for example, you can create a macro for that purpose rather than try to teach each person all the steps that are involved.

- **When the task is repetitive.** Even though formatting the text in a cell as red takes only a few steps, you might regularly need to format cells in red; if so, you'll save time with a macro that does the job for you.

Project enables you to record and work with macros by means of commands in the Tools menu or tools in the Visual Basic toolbar (see Figure 25.2). To display that toolbar, right-click on any toolbar, and then click on Visual Basic.

To record a macro, follow these steps:

1. Take whatever preparatory steps are necessary to bring you to the point at which you want to begin recording the macro. If you want to record a

Run Macro button
Record Macro button
Visual Basic Editor button

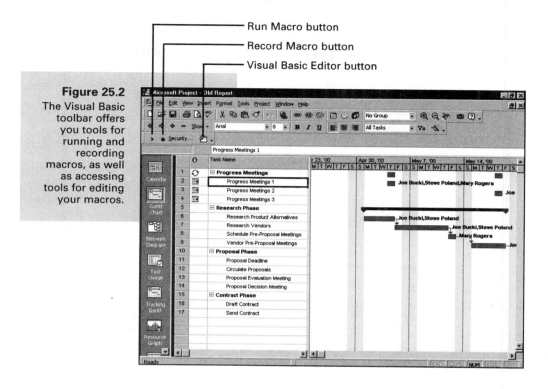

Figure 25.2
The Visual Basic
toolbar offers
you tools for
running and
recording
macros, as well
as accessing
tools for editing
your macros.

macro that formats a selected cell's text in green, for example, go ahead
and select a cell in the Task Sheet.

2. Choose Tools, Macro, Record New Macro, or click on the Record Macro
button on the Visual Basic toolbar. The Record Macro dialog box appears,
as shown in Figure 25.3.

Figure 25.3
Assign a name
and settings for
your macro after
you start the
recording
process.

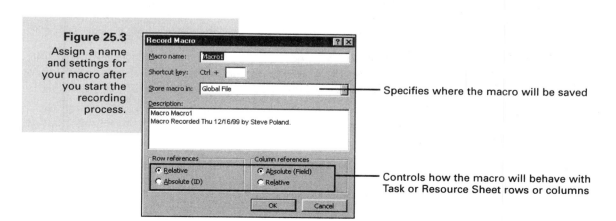

Specifies where the macro will be saved

Controls how the macro will behave with
Task or Resource Sheet rows or columns

3. In the Macro Name text box, enter a unique name for the macro. The name can include an underscore character but can't include spaces or punctuation. Green_Text, for example, is an acceptable name.

4. If you want to be able to run the macro by pressing a shortcut key, click in the Shortcut Key text box and enter the second keystroke for the combination in the Ctrl+ text box. You can enter any A–Z keyboard character. You can't use numbers, punctuation marks, or function keys.

Note

Avoid specifying a shortcut key that's already assigned to a command in Project, such as Ctrl+X (the Cut command). If you attempt to specify such a key, Project later asks you to choose another shortcut key (see Step 9).

5. If you want the macro to be stored only with the currently open file (not recommended, because you might need to use the macro in future files), click to open the Store Macro In drop-down list. Then click on the This Project choice. If you leave Global File selected instead, Project stores the macro in GLOBAL.MPT, the file that stores macros, forms, settings, and other default and custom information you specify for Project.

Note

You need to select the This Project option if you'll be saving the open project file as a template file and want the macro to be part of that file.

6. If you want, edit or add more detail to the Description of the macro.

7. The options in the Row References area control the way the macro interprets row selections in the Task and Resource Sheets, and the way it handles those selections during playback. Select one of the following options:

   ■ **Relative** means that during playback, the macro selects rows based on the location of the selected cell. Suppose that you selected three rows or cells in three rows (such as rows 1–3) when you recorded the macro, and that before you played back the macro, you selected a cell in row 4. The macro selects rows 4–6, or the specified cells in those rows, during playback.

- **Absolute (ID)** means that during playback, the macro always selects the same rows (by row number) that were selected when the macro was recorded.

8. The options in the Column References area control the way the macro interprets column selections in a Task Sheet or Resource Sheet, and the way it handles those selections during playback. Select one of the following options:

   - **Absolute (Field)** means that during playback, the macro always selects the same field (by field or column name) that was selected when the macro was recorded.

   - **Relative** means that the macro selects columns based on the location of the selected cell. Suppose that you selected two columns or cells in two columns (such as the Start and Finish columns of the Task Sheet) when you recorded the macro, and that before you played back the macro, you selected a cell in the Predecessors column. The macro selects the Predecessors and Resources columns (or the specified cells in those rows) of the Task Sheet during playback.

9. After you make all your selections, click on OK to begin recording the macro. If you specified a shortcut key that's already assigned (back in Step 4), at this point Project displays a warning (see Figure 25.4). Click on OK, specify another shortcut key, and click on OK in the Record Macro dialog box to continue.

10. Perform the steps that you want to record in your macro.

11. When you finish performing all the steps, stop the macro recording by clicking on the Stop Recorder button on the Visual Basic toolbar, or by choosing Tools, Macro, Stop Recorder.

Figure 25.4
Project warns you when the shortcut key you specified isn't available.

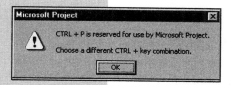

● ●

If you're creating a macro and want to select only the range of cells in the Task Sheet or Resource Sheet that currently contains entries, select the cell in the upper-left corner of the range. Then press Ctrl+Shift+End. This method is better than selecting the entire sheet. This method is also the one to use when you might end up running the macro on different sheets or filtered lists of differing lengths, because it ensures that the macro highlights all the rows that contain entries, not just the number of rows that was correct during macro recording.

● ●

Running a Macro

After you create a macro, it's immediately available for use. Running a macro is sometimes referred to as *playing back* the macro. To play back any macro, follow these steps:

1. Perform whatever preparatory tasks you need to complete before running the macro. If your macro applies green formatting to text in Task Sheet or Resource Sheet cells, for example, select the rows, columns, or cells to which you want to apply the formatting.

2. Use one of the following methods to execute the macro, depending on how you set up the macro when you created it:

   - Press the shortcut key combination that you created for the macro.

   - Click on the Run Macro button on the Visual Basic toolbar, or choose Tools, Macro, Macros. The Macros dialog box appears. If you want the Macro Name list to display only macros contained in a particular file (which narrows the display and may make the macro you want easier to find), click to open the Macros In drop-down list. Then click on the name of the file you want. Select the name of the macro in the Macro Name list (see Figure 25.5). Then click on the Run button.

Changing Macro Options

The information and options that you specify when you create and store a macro aren't carved in stone. If you initially don't assign a shortcut key to the macro, for example, you can go back and add one. If you want to change the description for a macro, you can do that, too.

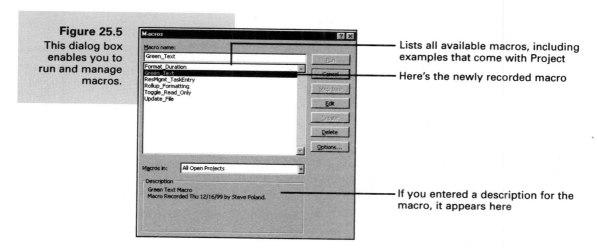

Figure 25.5
This dialog box enables you to run and manage macros.

Lists all available macros, including examples that come with Project

Here's the newly recorded macro

If you entered a description for the macro, it appears here

To adjust the options for a macro, follow these steps:

1. Choose Tools, Macro, Macros. Or click on the Run Macro button on the Visual Basic toolbar. The Macros dialog box appears.

2. In the Macro Name list, select the name of the macro for which you want to change the options. If you don't see the macro you want, click to open the Macros In drop-down list, click on the name of the file that holds the macro, and then select the macro when it appears on the Macro Name list.

3. Click on the Options button. The Macro Options dialog box appears, as shown in Figure 25.6.

4. Edit the Description and Shortcut Key options as needed, by using the techniques described earlier in the steps for creating macros.

5. Click on OK to close the Macro Options dialog box.

6. Click on Close to close the Macros dialog box and activate your new macro options.

Figure 25.6
Use this dialog box to adjust the macro description or shortcut key.

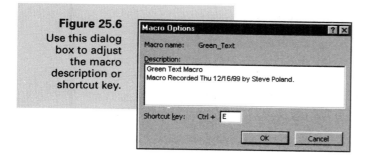

Editing Macros

Unless you have time to learn VBA programming, you probably don't want to bother with editing macros, especially if they are fairly simple. In such cases, the fastest way to make changes in a macro is to delete it (as described in the following section) and re-record it. In other cases, however, making a change or two in a macro is much speedier than creating it again from scratch.

This section explains the basics of macro editing so that you can experiment if you are so inclined. Macros and their VBA coding are stored in modules, which are like pages in the Project GLOBAL.MPT file. Each module can store numerous VBA macros. You use the Visual Basic Editor to open a macro and display it (within its module) for editing. In the module, you edit the commands just as you would edit text. When you save your changes and exit the Visual Basic Editor, Project returns you to Gantt Chart view (or whichever view you prefer to work in) and your changes to the macro take effect.

Note

Even if you are experienced in editing VBA code, there's always the chance of introducing an error that really fouls up the macro. As a precaution, print the original macro code before you make any changes, so that you have a record of what the macro's contents were when the macro worked. To print Project macros, simply click on the Print icon on the Standard toolbar when the macro is displayed in the Code (Module) window of the Visual Basic Editor.

Project and the Visual Basic Editor can provide help about using specific VBA commands in Project, but this help isn't installed by default. Therefore, before you begin editing macros, install Visual Basic Help. Use these steps to do so:

1. Click on the Visual Basic Editor button on the Visual Basic toolbar to display the Visual Basic Editor.
2. Choose Help, Microsoft Visual Basic Help. The Office Assistant appears.
3. In the Office Assistant's yellow thought bubble, click on the option button for installing Visual Basic Help.
4. Insert your Project 2000 CD into your CD-ROM drive if prompted, and then click on OK. After the update finishes, you can start using the Office Assistant in the Visual Basic Editor and in Project to get Visual Basic Help.

After Visual Basic Help is installed, you can use online Help within Project to learn more about the overall process of VBA programming with Project, and use online Help within the Visual Basic Editor to learn more about specific VBA commands, syntax, and more.

After you make Help available and review key topics, you'll definitely be ready to try basic macro editing. Suppose that you created a macro that enters a new task—named "Staff Meeting"—in the Task Sheet and assigns the task a duration of **2h** (two hours). You can use the macro to plug in the Staff Meeting task at any point in any project. Later, you decide that you no longer want to have staff meetings; you just want to prepare and distribute staff reports. Accordingly, you want the macro to specify the task name as "Staff Report." To make this change, follow these steps:

1. Choose Tools, Macro, Macros. Or click on the Run Macro button on the Visual Basic toolbar. The Macros dialog box appears.

2. In the Macro Name list, select the macro that you want to edit—Staff_Meeting, for this example. If you don't see the macro you want to edit, click to open the Macros In drop-down list, click on the name of the file that holds the macro, and then select the macro when it appears on the Macro Name list.

3. Click on the Edit button to display the Visual Basic Editor, with the module for the macro displayed in its Code window. The Code window for the Staff_Meeting macro appears in Figure 25.7.

4. Make your changes in the macro's contents, using the same editing techniques that you would use in a typical word processing program such as WordPad or Word 2000. For this example, because you want to change the task name, first look for the line that defines the Name column (TaskField) and then look for the value assigned there, which is what you want to change. You can double-click on the word *Meeting* to select it, as shown in Figure 25.8, being careful not to select the quotation marks. Then simply type **Report** to replace the selection.

5. When you finish making your changes, open the Visual Basic Editor File menu and click on the Save (File Name), to ensure your macro changes are saved. To close the Visual Basic Editor and return to Project, click to open the File menu again, and then click on Close And Return To Microsoft Project.

6. Test the macro to make sure that your changes work correctly.

Figure 25.7
The macro looks like specially aligned text in the module.

Project Explorer window

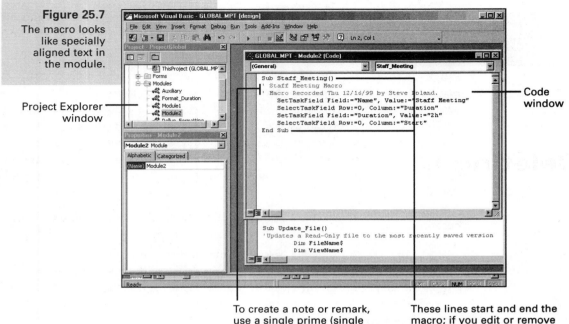

Code window

To create a note or remark, use a single prime (single quote) at the beginning of the statement

These lines start and end the macro; if you edit or remove them, the macro won't run

When text is highlighted, simply begin typing to replace it

Figure 25.8
To modify macro contents, use the editing techniques that you would use in a word processing program.

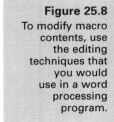

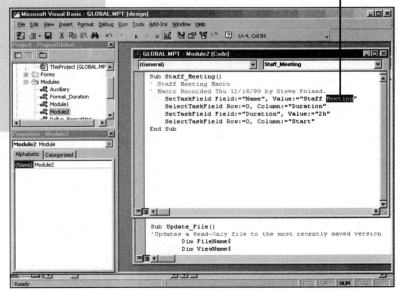

Project comes with several macros, which provide a good illustration of how to structure VBA code. These macros are excellent learning tools for would-be macro gurus. If you want to see how one of these macros is written, select it in the Macro Name list in the Macros dialog box, and then click on Edit. Alternately, if the Microsoft Visual Basic window is already open, double-click on a macro in the Project Explorer window to display the macro's contents in a code window.

Deleting Macros

When you no longer need a macro, you can simply delete it from the Macro Name list in the Macros dialog box. If you use many macros, it's good practice to occasionally review and delete the macros you no longer need, just to keep your macro modules and GLOBAL.MPT file slim and trim.

To delete a macro, follow these steps:

1. Choose Tools, Macro, Macros. Or click on the Run Macro button on the Visual Basic toolbar. The Macros dialog box appears.

2. In the Macro Name list, select the macro you want to delete. If you don't see the macro you want to delete, click to open the Macros In drop-down list, click on the name of the file that holds the macro, and then select the macro when it appears on the Macro Name list.

3. Click on the Delete button. Project asks you to verify that you want to remove the macro (see Figure 25.9).

4. Click on Yes to delete the macro.

5. Click on Close to close the Macros dialog box.

Figure 25.9
Verify that you want to delete the selected macro.

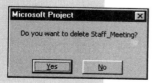

Creating a Menu Command or Toolbar Button for a Macro

Although you can create shortcut keys for the macros you create, remembering shortcut keys can be as difficult as remembering the exact names of macros.

In Chapter 24, "Customizing Microsoft Project," you learned the general steps for editing Project's menus and toolbars. You can use that knowledge to edit any Project menu bar, adding a menu that lists all of your macros. This procedure not only provides quick access to your macros but also provides more room for listing macros than the Tools menu does. In addition, you can add a command for an individual macro to any menu, or add a button for any macro to a toolbar.

Adding a Menu Listing All Macros

If you want to be able to run any macro simply by selecting its name from a menu, you can add a special menu listing all the macros available in the GLOBAL.MPT file in Project. You can add this menu to Project's default menu bar, or to any toolbar. To create a menu for your macros, follow these steps:

1. If you want to add the macro menu to a toolbar, display that toolbar.

2. Choose Tools, Customize, Toolbars. Alternately, right-click on any on-screen menu bar or toolbar and click on Customize. The Customize dialog box appears.

3. Click on the Commands tab to display its options.

4. Add a brand new menu for the macros to the menu bar or toolbar where you want the macros menu to appear, as described in Chapter 24, "Customizing Microsoft Project." Briefly, scroll down the Categories list and click on the New Menu choice. Drag the New Menu placeholder from the Commands list to the menu bar or toolbar that will hold the menu, and then drop the placeholder into the appropriate location, as shown in Figure 25.10.

5. To rename the placeholder for the new menu, right-click on it, edit the contents of the Name text box in the menu that appears, and then press Enter. Remember, if you want the menu name to have an underlined selection letter, insert an ampersand (&) before that letter in the menu name.

6. In the Categories list of the Commands tab in the Customize dialog box, click on the Special Items choice.

7. In the Commands list, scroll down to display the [Macros] choice, and then drag that choice onto the new menu, as shown in Figure 25.11. Release the mouse button to drop it onto the menu.

Drag the New Menu placeholder from here . . .

. . . and drop it into place on a menu or toolbar

Figure 25.10
You can create a new menu that lists all available macros.

Select to display the new menu placeholder

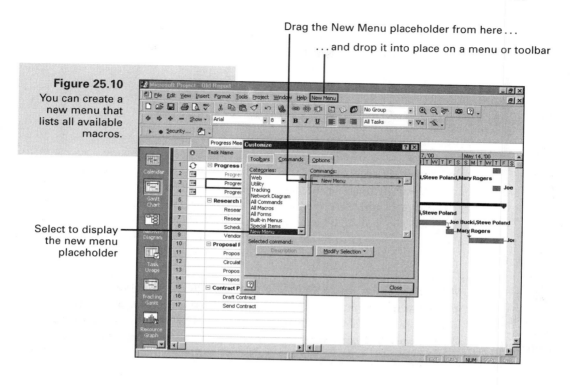

. . . over the menu name, and down onto the menu

Figure 25.11
Drag the [Macros] choice onto the new menu to place a list of macros on that menu.

Drag from here . . .

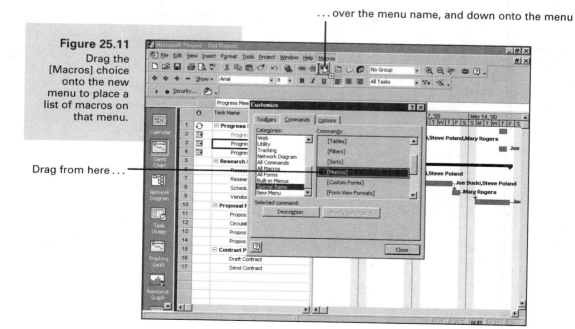

8. Click on Close to close the Customize dialog box.

When you open the new menu later, it lists available macros, as shown in Figure 25.12.

Adding a Macro Command or Button

Although adding a menu for macros as just described gives you easy access to all your macros, it can be cumbersome if you created dozens of macros. Such a menu is slow to appear onscreen, and you still have to take the time to scan through the menu to find the macro you need. For the ultimate in easy access to the macros that you create, add a custom menu command or toolbar button for the macro to any menu or toolbar. Then you can execute your macro simply by selecting its name from a more streamlined menu or by clicking its toolbar button.

Caution

Although you can assign a macro to an existing toolbar button, thereby replacing the command that was originally assigned to that button, this procedure is not recommended. It would be difficult to recall what the button's original command was, should you want to reinstate it.

Figure 25.12
You now have a menu listing all the macros.

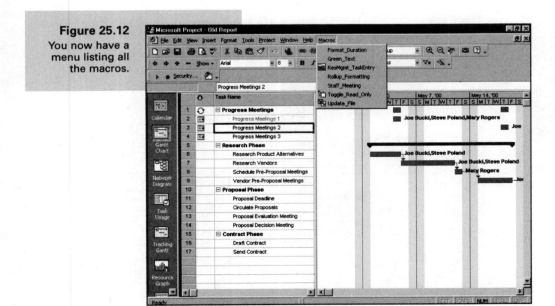

To create a menu command or toolbar button for a macro, follow these steps:

1. As you learned in Chapter 24, start by displaying the menu bar or toolbar that you want to hold the command or button.
2. Display the Customize dialog box. To do so, choose Tools, Customize, Toolbars. Alternately, right-click on any toolbar or menu bar and click on Customize.
3. Click on the Commands tab to display its options.
4. Scroll down the Categories list and click on the All Macros choice. The Commands list then lists all the macros available in Project.
5. Scroll down the Commands list until you see the macro for which you want to create a menu command or toolbar button.
6. Drag the macro from the Commands list to the menu or toolbar that you want to work with; then drop the macro into the appropriate location. Note that if you drag the macro over a menu and drop it into place on the menu, it becomes a menu command. If you drop the macro directly onto a toolbar, it becomes a toolbar button. See Figure 25.13 for an example of each.

Figure 25.13
Drag the macro from the Customize dialog box onto a menu or toolbar.

Choose this option to list macros in the Commands list

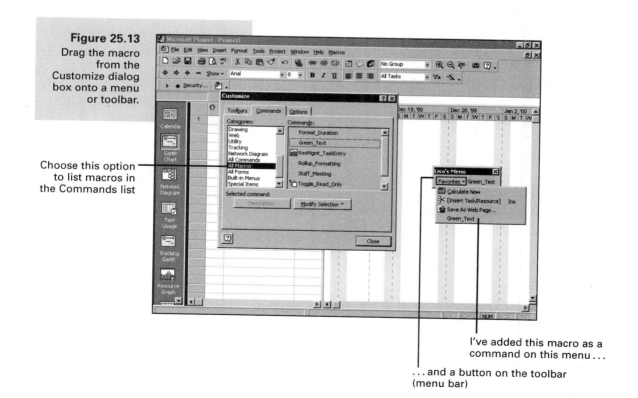

I've added this macro as a command on this menu . . .

. . . and a button on the toolbar (menu bar)

7. Click on the Close button to close the Customize dialog box and finish your menu and toolbar edits.

Adjusting the Macro Command or Button

After you add your menu command or toolbar button for a macro, you might want to fine-tune it a bit. For example, you might want to display an icon rather than the macro name on a toolbar button, or change the wording of the macro command on the menu.

Chapter 24 covers how to make changes to a command or button in more detail, but review these steps for a refresher.

1. Display the menu bar or toolbar that holds the command or button you want to edit.

2. Choose Tools, Customize, Toolbars. Alternately, right-click on any toolbar or menu bar and click on Customize. The Customize dialog box appears.

3. Right-click on the menu command or toolbar button to edit. A shortcut menu of commands appears, as shown in Figure 25.14.

Figure 25.14
Use the commands here to edit a custom menu command or toolbar button.

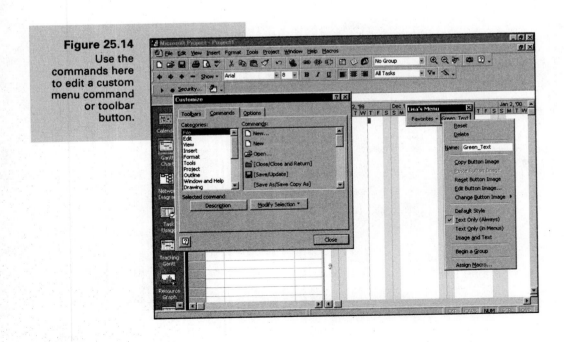

4. To make changes to a menu command (or text that you want to appear on the toolbar button), edit the Name text box contents and press Enter.

5. If you're working with a toolbar button and want it to display an icon only, right-click on the button and then click on the Default Style option in the shortcut menu to toggle that choice on. (The default for buttons is to show only an icon.) Then right-click on the blank button to return to the shortcut menu, point to the Change Button Image choice, and click on an icon in the pop-up palette that appears. Figure 25.15 shows the toolbar button for the Green_Text macro, changed to display only an icon.

6. If you're working with a menu command or toolbar button and want it to display text and an icon, right-click on the command or button. Then click on the Image And Text option in the shortcut menu to toggle that choice on. Then right-click on the menu command or toolbar button to return to the shortcut menu. Edit the contents of the Name text box. (Do not press Enter.) Point to the Change Button Image choice and click on an icon in the pop-up palette that appears.

7. Click on Close to close the Customize dialog box and finish making your changes.

Green_Text macro
toolbar button

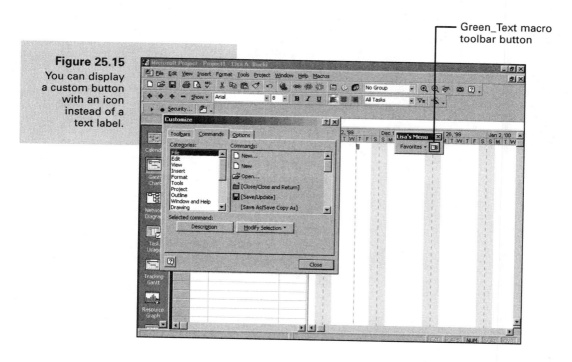

Figure 25.15
You can display a custom button with an icon instead of a text label.

A Few More Macro Ideas

This chapter—the final one in the book—has shown you how to create macros to make your work in Project faster and more efficient. Here are a few other ideas about how to use macros to get the most out of Microsoft Project:

- Create a macro that inserts a new task—with a particular name and duration—that you want to use more than once. Assign a shortcut key to run the macro and add the task.

- Create a macro to format summary commands in a way that calls even more attention to them. The macro can apply a particular font, color, or emphasis (such as italic). Add a button for the macro to the Formatting toolbar.

- Create a macro that inserts your company logo where you specify (such as in a Gantt chart), so that the logo appears on printouts you send to clients.

- Record macros that change the active view or display a particular Task Sheet table. Create a shortcut key or button for each macro.

- If you supervise a team of people and use Project to manage multiple tasks, create a macro that assigns each person (as a resource) to the currently selected task. Then you can assign a task to a particular worker with a single shortcut key, reducing the time that you spend making assignments.

- If you regularly need to print a particular form or report, create a macro that automates the process, and assign the macro to a toolbar button.

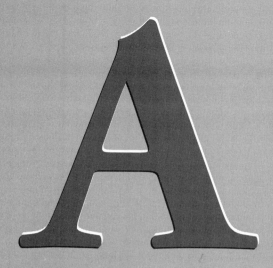

Other Online Resources

IN THIS APPENDIX

- Learning the tools to use
- Creating a presentation

Online resources for Microsoft Project help aren't quite as plentiful as the resources for other major Microsoft applications, particularly those in the Office Suite. And the resources about project management are likewise limited. Still, there are online resources you can consult when you need an answer to a technical question (and don't want to be on hold with a technical support line), want to find a Microsoft Project or project management consultant, or would like to check into add-on products available for Microsoft products.

Here are the key online resources that I've consulted in using Microsoft Project:

Note

These links were all correct as of the date when I wrote this appendix. As the Web continues to evolve rapidly, you may find changes that apply in this list. If you do, please be sure to make a note of it here in the book.

- **http://www.pmi.org**. The Web site for the Project Management Institute (PMI) includes links to copious educational and certification materials, books about project management, and some links to Project consulting companies.

- **http://www.microsoft.com/office/project/default.htm**. This is the main Microsoft Web page for the Microsoft Project product. Consult it from time to time to get news, order product updates and patches, and get hints about using Project. (Note that this page is different from the page you see when you choose Help, Office On The Web in Project.) The page also includes a link that you can click on to subscribe to an e-mail newsletter about Project called the Microsoft Project Report, so Microsoft will deliver the latest news and updates directly to your e-mail address. In addition, the newsletter provides information about downloadable files to enhance your use of Project, as well as news of local seminars and tips for using the product.

- **officeupdate.microsoft.com/articles/projassociates.htm**. This page lists Project and project management consulting companies, as well as links to user groups and training resources. If your organization needs a custom Project solution, visit this page.

- **microsoft.public.project newsgroup**. You can visit this public Internet newsgroup to post your questions about using Microsoft Project and to view questions posed by other users. This group is staffed by a number of Microsoft Valued Professionals (MVPs), many of whom work with top Project software and consulting companies, and boasts a very active group of key users who respond quickly to questions. When I've posted questions here, I've typically been able to return in a couple of hours to see multiple responses to my question. The microsoft.public.vc.project_mgt newsgroup is a similar group that focuses on project management as a discipline, as opposed to the Project software.

- **http://www.mpug.org**. This is the Web site for the Microsoft Project User's Group (MPUG). If you join MPUG (for a modest individual, corporate, or student rate), you'll receive newsletters, invitations to members-only regional and national professional meetings and breakout discussions, and access to both a private Web site and a private newsgroup for MPUG members.

- **http://www.zdnet.com/downloads**. Go to this site, enter Microsoft Project in the Search For text box, and then click on the Go button to find downloadable Project add-ins. If you go to http://www.zdnet.com and just search for "Microsoft Project," the results will include a much more expansive list of downloads, articles, and reviews.

B

What's On the CD?

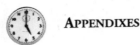

The CD that accompanies this book contains shareware and author-supplied programs that will help you use the book more effectively.

Running the CD

To make the CD more user friendly—and so that it takes up less of your disk space—no installation is required. This means that the only files transferred to your hard disk are those you choose to copy or install.

Caution

> **This CD has been designed to run under Windows 95/98 and Windows NT4. Neither the CD itself nor the programs on the CD will run under earlier versions of Windows.**

Windows 95/98/NT4

As there is no install routine, running the CD in Windows 95/98/NT4 is a breeze, especially if you have autorun enabled. Simply insert the CD in the CD-ROM drive, close the tray, and wait for the CD to load.

If you have disabled autorun, place the CD in the CD-ROM drive and follow these steps:

1. From the Start menu, select Run.
2. Type **D:\CDInstaller.exe** (where D:\ is the CD-ROM drive).
3. Select OK.

The Prima License

The first window you will see is the Prima License Agreement. Take a moment to read the agreement, and click the "I Agree" button to accept the license and proceed to the user interface. If you do not agree with the license, click the "I Decline" button to close the user interface and end the session.

The Prima User Interface

Prima's user interface is designed to make viewing and using the CD contents quick and easy. The opening screen contains a two-panel window with three buttons across the bottom. The left panel contains the structure of the programs on the disc. The right panel displays a description page for the selected entry in the left panel. The three buttons across the bottom of the user interface make it possible to install programs, view the contents of the disc using Windows Explorer, and view the contents of a help file for the selected entry. Buttons that are grayed out, or dimmed, are unavailable. For example, if the Help button is grayed out, it means that no Help file is available.

Resizing and Closing the User Interface

As with any window, you can resize the user interface. To do so, position the mouse over any edge or corner, hold down the left mouse button, and drag the edge or corner to a new position.

To close and exit the user interface, either double-click on the small button in the upper left corner of the window, or click on the exit button (marked with a small "x") in the upper right corner of the window.

Using the Left Panel

The left panel of the Prima user interface works very much like Windows Explorer. To view the description of an entry in the left panel, simply click on the entry. For example, to view the general information about Prima Publishing, Inc., click on the Prima Publishing Presents entry.

Some items have subitems nested below them; these "parent" items have a small plus (+) sign next to them. To view the nested subitems, simply click on the plus sign. When you do, the list expands and the subitems are listed below the parent item. In addition, the plus (+) sign becomes a minus (–) sign. To hide the subitems, click on the minus sign to collapse the listing.

Note

You can control the positon of the line between the left and right panels. To change the position of the dividing line, move the mouse over the line, hold down the left mouse button (the mouse becomes a two-headed arrow), and drag the line to a new position.

Using the Right Panel

The right panel displays a page that describes the entry you chose in the left panel. In addition to a general description, the page may include the following information:

- **World Wide Web Site**. Many program providers have a Web site. If one is available, the description page provides the Web address. To navigate to the Web site using your browser, simply click on the Web address (you must be connected to the Internet). Alternately, you can copy the Web address to the clipboard, and paste it into the URL line at the top of your browser window.

- **Email Address**. Many program providers are available via e-mail. If available, the description page provides the email address. To use the e-mail address, click on it to open your email program. Alternately, copy the address to the clipboard, and paste it into the address line of your e-mail program.

- **Readme, License, and other text files**. Many programs have additional information available in files with such names as Readme, License, Order, and so on. If such files exist, you can view the contents of the file in the right panel by clicking on the indicated hyperlink (such as the word "here" displayed in blue). When you are done viewing the text file, you can return to the description page by clicking again on the entry in the left panel.

Command Buttons

The command buttons that help you use the CD are as follows:

- **Install**. Use this button to install a program onto your hard drive.

- **Explore**. Use this button to view the contents of the CD using the Windows Explorer.

- **Help**. Click on this button to display the contents of the Help file provided with the program.

- **Read File**. The Install button turns into the Read File button when you make a selection that has an Adobe Acrobat file attached. Clicking on the Read File button launches Adobe Acrobat Reader and opens the selected file. You must have previously installed Adobe Acrobat Reader, either on your own or from the disc included with the book.

Pop-Up Menu Options

The pop-up menu options on the CD are as follows:

- **Install**. If the selected title contains an install routine, choosing this option begins the installation process.
- **Explore**. Selecting this option allows you to view the folder containing the program files using Windows Explorer.
- **View Help**. Use this menu item to display the contents of the Help file provided with the program.

The Software

The software included with this publication is provided for your evaluation. If you try this software and find it useful, you must register the software as discussed in its documentation. Prima Publishing has not paid the registration fee for any shareware included on the disc.

Following are brief descriptions of the shareware and evaluation software you'll find on the CD:

- **PERT Chart Expert**. This Microsoft Project add-on product allows you to create presentation-quality PERT charts directly from your Microsoft Project plans. Loaded with features to configure and print many different styles of PERT chart diagrams, PERT Chart Expert contains extensive PERT charting capabilities unlike those found in Microsoft Project's PERT chart.
- **Project Commander**. Project Commander combines Microsoft Project's powerful project management engine with a comprehensive and easy-to-use set of functions that make planning, tracking, analyzing, and reporting a snap. With Project Commander you will quickly become a Microsoft Project power user, quickly developing successful project plans.
- **Project KickStart**. Project KickStart is a project planning software for managers, executives, consultants, and incidental project planners. The software guides you through an eight-step process for creating a thought-out project strategy by considering the goals and objectives of the project, anticipating obstacles or risks to be encountered in performing the work, and identifying people involved in the effort. Project KickStart includes a Gantt chart for quick scheduling and eight presentation-ready reports. Once the project plan is developed, you can click on Project KickStart's "hot-link" icon and export data into Microsoft Project for budgeting, scheduling, and tracking.

- **Project Reporter**. Project Reporter is an innovative tool that automatically generates Web-based project status reports, using files created with Microsoft Project or other compatible project management software. Project Reporter makes it easy and cost-effective to share project information with team members and project stakeholders, in an accessible format and without requiring special-purpose software.

- **TeamWork**. TeamWork provides all of the benefits of process management while working directly within Microsoft Project. Start by building a customized work plan template in Microsoft Project, then incorporate and automate your organization's methodologies as you link tasks to all of the intellectual assets required to perform the task—detailed methodology steps, Microsoft Word or other document templates, multimedia files such as PowerPoint presentations, hot links to Internet URLs, Excel spreadsheets, Access databases, faxes and email communications.

- **WBS Chart**. This Microsoft Project add-on product allows you to plan and display your projects using a tree-style diagram known as a Work Breakdown Structure (WBS) Chart. WBS Charts display the structure of a project, showing how the project is broken down into summary and detail levels. Plan new projects using an intuitive "top-down" approach or display existing Microsoft Project plans in an easy-to-understand diagram.

- **WebSked - The Web Scheduler**. WebSked produces schedules that are easily accessible, informative, and which reduce the need for reams and reams of paper. WebSked creates hypertext-style linked Web pages based on the hierarchical structure of Microsoft Project schedules.

Glossary

actual information. As work on the project progresses, you enter actual start dates, finish dates, costs, and work completed, which Project can compare to your original plan and its calculated data.

assignment. The intersection between a task and a resource. When you add a resource to a task, you create an assignment for the resource. Each task can hold multiple assignments (resources assigned to it), and each resource can have multiple assignments (multiple tasks on which it will be working or for which it will be used). View assignments in the Task Usage or Resource Usage views.

base calendar. The overriding calendar you specify for a project in the Project Information dialog box (24 Hours, Night Shift, and so on). Use the Tools, Change Working Time command to create custom calendars. You can assign a particular calendar to a task or a resource, too.

baseline. The "snapshot" you save of your original project plan in the areas of timing, costs, and work. You can later use Project to compare actual project progress to the baseline.

consolidated project. See *master project*.

constraint. A scheduling limitation you assign to a task to indicate whether or not Project can move the task based on task links and scheduling changes. For example, if you set a Must Start On constraint, Project cannot move the task start date either earlier or later.

cost. The charge for using a resource. For most work resources, you specify an hourly Std. Rate (standard rate) and Ovt. Rate (overtime rate). For material resources, you specify a particular cost per material label, such as $100/dozen.

cost table. In the Resource Information dialog box, a type of table you use to enter varying rates and rate changes to apply for a resource over time.

critical path. A series of tasks, typically linked, that are most important (from a mathematical perspective) in the project schedule. These tasks must finish on time for the whole project to finish on time.

critical task. A task on the critical path.

current date. The date, either as pulled from the computer's system clock or specified in the Project Information dialog box, that Project uses by default for numerous progress calculations. See also *status date*.

current date line. A line on the Gantt chart that indicates the current date.

data map. When you import and export Project data, you use or create a data map to identify which Project fields correspond to which fields in the imported or exported file.

duration. The span of time between the start date and end date for a particular task. See also *work*.

earned value. As time passes and you mark work as completed in Project and enter actual costs, Project calculates and compares various earned values. These tell you how much work was scheduled to be completed by the current date or a status date and how much that work was scheduled to cost, versus the actual data you've entered.

effort-driven scheduling. The default scheduling method in Project, whereby it adjusts task duration based on the amount of resource work (the number of work resources) you assign to the task.

elapsed time. A method whereby Project schedules a task over consecutive hours, days, or weeks, rather than adjusting the task schedule per the base calendar for the project file.

fill. In the Task Sheet and Resource Sheet, you can drag the fill handle at the lower-right corner of the selected cell to copy that cell's entry up or down the column.

filter. Limiting the entries displayed in the Task Sheet or Resource Sheet, so the sheet lists only entries matching one or more criteria you specify.

fixed cost. A resource-independent cost you specify for a task, such as a lump sum fee. Enter fixed costs in the Cost table of the Task Sheet.

free slack. If you need to reschedule a task to a later date, the free slack measurement tells you how much time is available to delay the task (by how many days) without delaying the task's first successor task. If you delay the task by more than the free slack measure, you will delay the successor task, too. See also *total slack*.

Gantt chart. A chart that represents each task as a bar on a linear horizontal calendar, with links between tasks indicated.

Gantt Chart view. The default view in Project, which consists of the Task Sheet at the left and the Gantt chart at the right.

global file. The GLOBAL.MPT file, which holds certain Project file defaults as well as custom items you create such as calendars, tables, and macros.

HTML. The acronym for HyperText Markup Language. You save information in HTML format so it can be displayed via Web browser software, either from a local drive or over the Internet.

hyperlink. Code that ties information in one file to information in other files, particularly HTML files.

indicators. Symbols that give you information about a particular task or resource, appearing in a column at the far left of the Task Sheet and the Resource Sheet.

lag time. A delay between two linked tasks. That is, time between when the predecessor task ends and the successor task begins.

lead time. An overlap in time between two linked tasks. For example, the successor task might be scheduled to begin when the predecessor task reaches 75 percent complete.

leveling. A feature in Project whereby it looks for ways to fix the scheduling for overallocated (overbooked) resources. With leveling, Project might split or delay tasks until a resource becomes available.

link. A relationship or dependency between two tasks. You establish links so that Project can accurately calculate the project schedule.

macro. A set of steps you save in Project so that it can complete a repetitive task for you.

master project. When you consolidate multiple projects into a single file, the master project file holds the inserted file.

material label. The quantities (reams of paper, sets of proofs, or whatever) used to measure the amount of material purchased and consumed for a task.

material resource. A resource that represents a quantity of a consumable used during the project.

milestone. A task with a duration of 0 that marks an important point in the schedule.

node. In the Network Diagram (formerly PERT chart view), a box representing a task.

overallocation. Overbooking a resource on a particular date.

per use cost. A cost that accrues each time you assign a resource to a task.

Planning wizard. A form of help in Project, the Planning Wizard dialog box appears to warn you when a change might affect the scheduling, a task link, and so on.

predecessor task. A task that is linked to a subsequent or later task called a predecessor task. Often, the completion of the predecessor task affects the scheduling of the successor task.

Project Central. The Web server for Web-based messaging in Project.

project information. Base-level data about your project file, such as the start date for the project and the base calendar it will follow. Choose Project, Project Information to view and change project information.

Project Summary Task. A task you display (numbered 0) to graphically sum up the project schedule.

recurring task. A task that repeats over specified intervals, such as a monthly staff meeting. Setting a series of meetings as a recurring task is faster than entering individual meeting tasks in Project.

report. A document Project can generate for you from its data to present the desired statistics. For example, you can display and print a report of upcoming tasks or create reports about various project costs.

resource. See *material resource* and *work resource*.

resource calendar. Calendar changes you make for a resource, if that resource's schedule varies from the base calendar you've assigned for the project or to a task. For example, if a resource has vacation scheduled or works a flextime schedule, you should edit the resource's calendar accordingly for accurate scheduling.

resource leveling. See *leveling*.

resource pool. When you reuse the resources from one project file in another project file, the resources become a resource pool. You must share the resources in the resource pool when you consolidate projects.

Resource Sheet. The default tabular view in which you enter resource information.

resource-driven scheduling. See *effort-driven scheduling*.

slippage. The amount of time by which a task is running late, according to the difference between your baseline plan and actual data.

Standard calendar. The default base calendar used in Project, representing a five-day, 40-hour workweek with each day's schedule spanning from 8 A.M. to noon and then 1 P.M. to 5 P.M.

status date. A date as of which you want Project to calculate project progress (if different from the current date). You enter a status date in the Project Information dialog box.

subproject. A project file inserted into a master (consolidated) project file.

subtask. When you outline a project, a subtask appears below a summary task (task at the next higher outline level).

successor task. A task linked to an earlier task called a predecessor task.

summary task. When you outline a project, a summary task holds subtasks.

table. A group of specific columns (fields) that you can display in either the Task Sheet or the Resource Sheet to enter different data or display particular data. For example, the default table for the Task Sheet is the Entry table, but you can display the Cost table instead to enter and review cost information.

task. A discrete item that must be accomplished in a project.

task calendar. If the calendar for a task varies from the project base calendar you've assigned, you can specify a different calendar for the task in the Task Information dialog box. For example, if a particular task will be handled on a 24 Hours schedule rather than the Standard calendar, you can assign the 24 Hours calendar to the task.

Task Sheet. The sheet where you enter and view task information. By default, the Task Sheet appears at the left side of the Gantt Chart view.

team messaging. Project feature that allows a project manager to send assignments and request updates via a compatible e-mail system.

template. A file that holds basic project information, which you can then use as a starter for other project files you create.

total slack. As you reschedule tasks, the total slack measurement tells you how much time is available to delay a particular task (by how many days) without affecting the overall project schedule. If you delay the task by more than the total slack measure, you will delay the project finish date. See also *free slack*.

units. The amount of time per workday (as a percentage) that a work resource is available to work on assigned tasks. For example, if a resource can only devote half days to your project, use 50% as the Max. Units entry on the Resource Sheet. If an external resource will actually devote two persons to each task, specify 200% for that resource's Max. Units.

variance. The difference between the actual and baseline timing, costs, or work.

View Bar. The group of icons at the left side of the Project screen that you can use to display different views.

Web workgroup. Project feature that allows a project manager to set up a Web site to communicate about the project.

work. Generally, the number of person hours applied to a task or assignment.

Work Breakdown Structure (WBS). A coding system roughly analogous to outline numbering. You use or create WBS numbering to number tasks in the way that your company requires.

work resource. A resource that contributes hours of work for completing the project.

working hours. According to the project, resource, or task calendar, the time periods during the workday when work actually occurs.

Index

License Agreement/Notice of Limited Warranty

By opening the sealed disk container in this book, you agree to the following terms and conditions. If, upon reading the following license agreement and notice of limited warranty, you cannot agree to the terms and conditions set forth, return the unused book with unopened disk to the place where you purchased it for a refund.

License:

The enclosed software is copyrighted by the copyright holder(s) indicated on the software disk. You are licensed to copy the software onto a single computer for use by a single concurrent user and to a backup disk. You may not reproduce, make copies, or distribute copies or rent or lease the software in whole or in part, except with written permission of the copyright holder(s). You may transfer the enclosed disk only together with this license, and only if you destroy all other copies of the software and the transferee agrees to the terms of the license. You may not decompile, reverse assemble, or reverse engineer the software.

Notice of Limited Warranty:

The enclosed disk is warranted by Prima Publishing to be free of physical defects in materials and workmanship for a period of sixty (60) days from end user's purchase of the book/disk combination. During the sixty-day term of the limited warranty, Prima will provide a replacement disk upon the return of a defective disk.

Limited Liability:

THE SOLE REMEDY FOR BREACH OF THIS LIMITED WARRANTY SHALL CONSIST ENTIRELY OF REPLACEMENT OF THE DEFECTIVE DISK. IN NO EVENT SHALL PRIMA OR THE AUTHORS BE LIABLE FOR ANY OTHER DAMAGES, INCLUDING LOSS OR CORRUPTION OF DATA, CHANGES IN THE FUNCTIONAL CHARACTERISTICS OF THE HARDWARE OR OPERATING SYSTEM, DELETERIOUS INTERACTION WITH OTHER SOFTWARE, OR ANY OTHER SPECIAL, INCIDENTAL, OR CONSEQUENTIAL DAMAGES THAT MAY ARISE, EVEN IF PRIMA AND/OR THE AUTHOR HAVE PREVIOUSLY BEEN NOTIFIED THAT THE POSSIBILITY OF SUCH DAMAGES EXISTS.

Disclaimer of Warranties:

PRIMA AND THE AUTHORS SPECIFICALLY DISCLAIM ANY AND ALL OTHER WARRANTIES, EITHER EXPRESS OR IMPLIED, INCLUDING WARRANTIES OF MERCHANTABILITY, SUITABILITY TO A PARTICULAR TASK OR PURPOSE, OR FREEDOM FROM ERRORS. SOME STATES DO NOT ALLOW FOR EXCLUSION OF IMPLIED WARRANTIES OR LIMITATION OF INCIDENTAL OR CONSEQUENTIAL DAMAGES, SO THESE LIMITATIONS MAY NOT APPLY TO YOU.

Other:

This Agreement is governed by the laws of the State of California without regard to choice of law principles. The United Convention of Contracts for the International Sale of Goods is specifically disclaimed. This Agreement constitutes the entire agreement between you and Prima Publishing regarding use of the software.